EDWARD SCHILLEBEECKX: A THEOLOGIAN IN HIS HISTORY

Volume I: A Catholic Theology of Culture (1914–1965)

Erik Borgman
Translated by John Bowden

continuum
LONDON • NEW YORK

Continuum

The Tower Building, 11 York Road, London SE1 7NX

370 Lexington Avenue, New York, NY 10017-6503

Translated from the Dutch
Edward Schillebeeckx: een theoloog in zijn geschiedenis.
Deel I: Een katholieke cultuurtheologie (1914–1965),
published 1999 by Uitgeverij H. Nelissen B.V.Baarn.

© Uitgeverij H. Nelissen B.V.Baarn
and Provincialaat Dominicanen, Nijmegen 1999

Translation copyright © John Bowden 2003

First published in English by Continuum 2003

British Library Cataloguing in Publication Data
A catalogue record for this is available from the British Library

ISBN 0-8264-6194-8

Typeset by YHT Ltd, London
Printed and bound in Great Britain by Bookcraft (Bath) Ltd,
Midsomer Norton, Bath

Contents

Form of quotations, list of abbreviations and abbreviated references   vi

Introduction   1
Edward Schillebeeckx the theologian   1
Biography as contextual historiography   6
Approach and plan   10
Acknowledgements   14

Chapter 1   Youth and Training up to 1944   17
The bombardment of modern times   17
  Birth in 1914   18
  Youth in the midst of tensions in society and the church   24
  Not a Jesuit but a Dominican   29
Study with the Dominicans   37
  Studying philosophy in Ghent   38
  Studying theology in Louvain   51
Inauguration as an independent theologian   61

Chapter 2   Working out the Project of a Theology of Culture in the 1940s 68
After the war   68
  'Theology of culture' in the midst of cultural reorientation   69
  'Catholic cultural life'   79
Christian humanism as 'humble humanism'   87
  Humanism   88
  'Supernatural exclusivism'   93
  'Spiritual life'   99
The situation in France as a mirror   103
  The example of Congar and Chenu   103

CONTENTS

Evaluation of the French situation   111
Dominican religious life   117

**Chapter 3   The View of the Church as a Form of the Theology of
Culture in the 1950s**   122
Between cultural challenge and church pressure   122
    The encyclical *Humani generis* and its consequences   126
    The church in the centre   132
The laity central   139
    The mission of the Catholic laity   142
    Lay people in Flanders and the Netherlands   147
    Bishop, priest, layman: different functions within the church   154
    Being a Christian in the world   159
Life orientated on God   165
    Belief in a history   166
    Life redeemed by hope and love   171
Mary as the image of the believer   179
    Immaculate conception   180
    A model of Christian life   184

Chapter 4   The Louvain Theological Synthesis   191
A synthesis   191
    Systematic theologizing on the basis of Thomas Aquinas   192
    The aura of the mysteries of faith   197
'The sacramental economy of salvation'   199
    The mystery theologies of Odo Casel and Edward Schillebeeckx   201
    The sacraments as human and divine reality   207
    Man's outreach to God and God's descent to man   211
The theology of the Louvain courses   216
    Thinking about the God who is manifest in salvation history   217
    Concepts of faith and the reality of faith   224
    Theological reflection on faith as living culture   227
    The mystery of Christ: a synthesis of nature and supernature   233
    The primordial sacrament of the *Deus humanissmus*   238
    Both on the way to God and united with God   241
    Heaven, hell and purgatory   244
    Creation theology as theology of culture   252
    '*Deus salutaris est creator*'   254
    Creation as a basis for culture   259
    Creation and grace   265
Marriage as a saving mystery   269
    The Catholic discussion of marriage and sexuality   270
    Marriage as a human reality elevated to become a sacrament   276

CONTENTS

Chapter 5   A Dutch Council Theologian   283
  Breakthrough of changes   283
    Schillebeeckx's move to Nijmegen   285
    An innovative contribution   289
  The preparation for the Council   294
    The announcement   294
    The figure of John XXIII   299
    Reactions to the plan for the Council   303
  The Dutch contribution to the preparation   307
    Episcopal collegiality and the faith of the believers   309
    'The Bishops of the Netherlands on the Council' 316
  The Council as a breakthrough   320
    The breakthrough of a renewing theology   321
    Concern for doing the Christian truth   329
    Theology of the eucharist   337
  The result of the Council   345
    Verve and conflict over giving form to the church   346
    Keeping the spirit of the Council alive   351
    A renewed start to the project of the theology of culture   355

Postscript   Notes on the Theological Yield   366
  Theology as a historical enterprise   368
  Human history as theological terrain   373
  Biography as theological autobiography   379

Notes   382

Index   466

Form of quotations, list of abbreviations and abbreviated references

In order to facilitate reading, the spelling and punctuation in all quotations have been adapted to current rules except when this would deprive the reader of information. Obvious mistakes have been quietly corrected. Of course this does not apply to titles and names.

To prevent the footnotes being longer and this book even thicker, for the texts of Schillebeeckx reference has been made simply to the place where they are most easily accessible. This is often in reprints in later collections of articles. In that case the title of the original is given, even if this is different from the title of the reprinted text, and the year of the original appearance is put in brackets. Readers who are interested in the original texts can then easily track these down by the chronological or alphabetical list in the *Bibliography of Edward Schillebeeckx OP*, compiled by T. Schoof and J. van de Westelaken, Baarn 1997.

Also to save space, regular use is made in the notes of abbreviations and abbreviated references. The significance of most of them is generally known or is self-evident. The significance of the rest is explained here.

Abbreviations of works of Edward Schillebeeckx:

Christ	see *Gerechtigheid*
Christ the Sacrament	see *Christus sacrament*
Christologie	*Christologie*, lecture notes, Louvain 1953–54, I/II (unpublished)

Christusontmoeting

De Christusontmoeting als sacrament van de Godsontmoeting: Theologische begrijpelijkheid van het heilsfeit der sacramenten, Antwerp and Bilthoven 1958

Christus sacrament
(Christ the Sacrament)

Christus sacrament van de Godsontmoeting, Bilthoven 1959; ET *Christ the Sacrament,* London and New York 1963

Concilie I/II

Het tweede Vaticaans concilie I/II, Tielt and The Hague 1964/1966 (partly translated as *Vatican II: The Struggle of Minds,* Dublin 1964, and *Vatican II: The Real Achievement,* London and Melbourne 1967)

Eschatologie

De eschatologie, Louvain lecture notes (n.d., unpublished)

Eucharist

see *Tegenwoordigheid*

Geloofsverstaan
(Understanding)

Geloofsverstaan: Interpretatie en kritiek, Theologische peilingen 5, Bloemendaal 1972; ET *The Understanding of Faith,* London 1974

Gerechtigheid (Christ)

Gerechtigheid en liefde: Genade en bevrijding, Bloemendaal 1977; ET *Christ,* London and New York 1980

God and Man

see *God en mens*

God en mens
(God and Man)

God en mens, Theologische peilingen 2, Bilthoven 1965; ET *God and Man,* London 1969

Heilseconomie

De sacramentele heilseconomie: Theologische bezinning op S. Thomas' sacramentenleer in het licht van de traditie en van de hedendaagse sacramentsproblematiek, I, Antwerp and Bilthoven 1952

Huwelijk (Marriage)

Het huwelijk, aardse werkelijkheid en heilsmysterie, I, Bilthoven 1963; ET *Marriage: Human Reality and Saving Mystery* (two volumes), London 1965

Inleiding	*Inleiding tot de theologie*, lecture notes, Louvain 1951–2 (unpublished)
Jezus (Jesus)	*Jezus, het verhaal van een levende*, Bloemendaal 1974; ET *Jesus*, London and New York 1979
Maria I	*Maria, Christus' mooiste wonderschepping: Religieuze grondljjnen van het Maria-mysterie*, Antwerp 1954
Maria II (Mary)	*Maria, moeder van de verlossing: Religieuze grondlijnen van het Maria-mysterie*, Haarlem 1955; ET *Mary, Mother of the Redemption*, London 1964
Marriage	see *Huwelijk*
Mary	see *Maria II*
Mission	see *Zending*
Openbaring (Revelation)	*Openbaring en theologie*, Theologische peilingen 1, Bilthoven 1964; ET *Revelation and Theology* I, London and New York 1967; II, New York 1968 (= *The Concept of Truth and Theological Renewal*, London and Sydney 1968)
Revelation	see *Openbaring*
'Sacramentaire structuur'	'De sacramentaire structuur van de openbaring', *Kultuurleven* 19, 1952, 785–802
Schepping	*Theologische bezinning op het scheppingsgeloof*, lecture notes, Louvain 1956–57 (unpublished)
'Situatie'	'Christelijke situatie', *Kultuurleven* 12, 1945, 82–95; 229–42; 585–611
Tegenwoordigheid (Eucharist)	*Christus' tegenwoordigheid in de eucharistie,* Bilthoven 1967; ET *The Eucharist*, London 1968

Testament	*Theologisch testament: Notarieel nog niet verleden*, Baarn 1994
'Theologie' ('Theology')	'Theologie', in *Theologisch woordenboek* 3, 1958. 4485–542, reprinted in *Openbaring*, 71–121; ET 'What is Theology?', in *Revelation* I, 93–183
Wereld (World)	*Wereld en kerk*, Theologische peilingen 3, Bilthoven 1966; ET *World and Church*, London 1971
World	see *Wereld*
Zending (Mission)	*De zending van de kerk,* Theologische peilingen 4, Bilthoven 1968; ET *The Mission of the Church*, London 1973

Other abbreviations:

AAS	*Acta Apostolicae Sedis*
Alfrink, *Vragen*	B. Alfrink, *Vragen aan de kerk: Toespraken van kardinaal Alfrink in de jaren van het concilie*, Utrecht and Baarn 1967
Arch.	Archive of Schillebeeckx's personal texts as listed by the Catholic Documentation Centre
Bilanz	*Bilanz der Theologie im 20. Jahrhundert: Perspektiven, Strömungen, Motive in der christlichen und nichtchristlichen Welt*, ed. H. Vorgrimler and R. Vander Gucht, Freiburg, Basel and Vienna 1969
Bibliography	*Bibliography 1936–1996 of Edward Schillebeeckx OP*, compiled by T. Schoof and J. van de Westelaken, Baarn 1997
Borgman, 'Cultuurtheologie'	E. Borgman, 'Van cultuurtheologie naar theologie als onderdeel van de cultuur: De toekomst van het theologisch project van Edward Schillebeeckx', *TvT* 34, 1994, 335–60

Borgman, 'Identiteit'

id., 'Identiteit, solidariteit, theologie', *Wending* 43, 1988, 3–13

Borgman, 'Universiteit'

id., 'Theologie tussen universiteit en emancipatie', *TvT* 26, 1986, 240–58

Borgman, *Sporen*

id., *Sporen van de bevrijdende God: Universitaire theologie in aansluiting op Latijnsamerikaanse bevrijdingstheologie, zwarte theologie en feministische theologie*, Kampen 1990

Chenu, *Parole* I/II

M.-D. Chenu, *La parole de Dieu, I: La foi dans l'intelligence; II. L'évangile dans le temps*, Paris 1964

Conc.

Concilium. International Journal of Theology, 1965ff.

Denzinger

Enchiridion symbolorum, definitionum et declarationum de rebus fidei et morum, ed. H. Denzinger and A. Schönmetzer (the numbering follows the thirty-sixth edition or later)

De Petter, *Begrip*

D. M. De Petter, *Begrip en werkelijkheid. Aan de overzijde van het conceptualisme*, Hilversum and Antwerp 1964

Jacobs, *Andere kerk*

J. Y. H. A. Jacobs, *Met het oog op een andere kerk: Katholiek Nederland en de voorbereiding van het Tweede Vaticaans Oecumenisch Concilie 1959–1962*, Baarn 1986

Leprieur, *Rome*

F. Leprieur, *Quand Rome condamne: Dominicains et prêtres-ouvriers*, Paris 1989

Maltha and Thuys, *Dogmatiek*

A. H. Maltha and R. W. Thuys, *Katholieke dogmatiek*, Roermond and Maaseik 1951

Oosterhuis and Hoogeveen *God nieuw (God New)*

H. Oosterhuis and P. Hoogeveen, *God is ieder ogenblik nieuw: Gesprekken met Edward*

Schillebeeckx, Baarn 1982; ET *God is New Each Moment*, Edinburgh 1983

Puchinger, *Toekomst*

G. Puchinger, *Toekomst van het Christendom*, Delft 1974

Schoof, 'Aandrang'
('25 Years')

T. Schoof, '"… een bijna koortsachtige aandrang …"': Schillebeeckx 25 jaar theoloog in Nijmegen', in *Meedenken met Edward Schillebeeckx*, ed. H. Häring et al., Baarn 1983, 11–39; ET 'E. Schillebeeckx: 25 Years in Nijmegen', *Theology Digest* 37, 1990, 313–32; 38, 1991, 31–44

Schoof, *Aggiornamento*
(*Breakthrough*)

id., *Aggiornamento: De doorbraak van een nieuwe katholieke theologie*, Baarn 1968; ET *Breakthrough: Beginnings of the New Catholic Theology*, Dublin 1970 (US edition *A Survey of Catholic Theology, 1800–1970*, Paramus, NJ, etc. 1970)

Struycker Boudier,
Wijsgerig leven, I-VII

C. E. M. Struycker Boudier, *Wijsgerig leven in Nederland en Belgie 1880–1980, II: De dominicanen*, Nijmegen and Baarn *1986; III. In Godsnaam: De augustijnen, carmelieten en minderbroeders*, Nijmegen and Baarn n.d.; V. *De filosofie van Leuven*, Louvain and Baarn 1989; *VII. Op zoek naar zijn en zin*, Nijmegen and Baarn 1992

TGL

Tijdschrift voor Geestelijk Leven, Louvain 1945ff.

TvP/TvF

Tijdschrift voor Philosophie/Filosofie, Louvain 1939ff.

TvT

Tijdschrift voor Theologie, Nijmegen and Louvain 1961

Understanding

see *Geloofsverstaan*

Van den Hoogen, *Chenu*

A. J. M. van den Hoogen, *Pastorale teologie: Ontwikkeling en struktuur van de teologie van M.-D. Chenu*, Alblasserdam 1983

Van Schaik, *Alfrink*   T. A. H. van Schaik, *Alfrink: een biografie*, Amsterdam 1997

Introduction

The theologian 'in ... historical research really has to do with the thing itself, the mystery of salvation'

It happened when I was in the top class at secondary school, half-way through the 1970s. The school was a Catholic secondary school, but almost all my classmates had quite thoroughly distanced themselves from the religion into which the vast majority of them had been baptized. Some had done so in the wake of their parents, others in emphatic rebellion against them. On a rainy day during a camping holiday, some of my class played a game rather like Twenty Questions: one person thought of a well-known figure and the rest had to discover his or her name by asking questions. As an up and coming theological student I had chosen Edward Schillebeeckx, but in retrospect it is striking that my secularized friends quite quickly guessed his name. And when his name was guessed, no one needed to ask who he was.

EDWARD SCHILLEBEECKX THE THEOLOGIAN

In the 1960s and 1970s Schillebeeckx was beyond doubt the best-known theologian in the Netherlands, certainly among Catholics. During the period when Dutch Catholicism with its go-ahead concern for reform was of great interest to committed Christians and outsiders at home and abroad, he was an important leader of opinion.[1] He was regarded as the theological voice of progressive Dutch Catholicism, and when in 1968 it became clear that the highest Vatican authorities had started an investigation into his orthodoxy, a great many Dutch Catholics felt that this was also an attack on them. I was in the top class of junior school then, and the teacher talked about the

1

case with us. And when in the second half of the 1970s Schillebeeckx again came under fire from Rome, the indignation was perhaps even greater.[2] On closer inspection all this is quite striking. For first, Schillebeeckx is a true scholar, and initially there seems little in his theological work that would appeal to the general public. And secondly, by origin he is not a Dutchman at all.

Edward Cornelis Florent Alfons Schillebeeckx was born in Antwerp on 12 November 1914. He spent his youth in Flemish Kortenberg, studied philosophy and theology with the Flemish Dominicans, and immediately after the Second World War became a lecturer at their theological seminary in Louvain. Theologically he was orientated above all on France and to a lesser degree on Germany. Only at the beginning of 1958 did he come to the Netherlands, to become professor in dogmatics and the history of theology at the theological faculty of what was still then called the Roman Catholic University of Nijmegen.

However, just over a year after Schillebeeckx's arrival in Nijmegen Pope John XXIII announced a general assembly of the church which again had to bring the Catholic Church 'up to date', so that it could once more become a light to the peoples in an alliance with both the joy and the hope and the grief and the anguish of contemporary men and women. During the preparation, at the sessions themselves and in the period immediately after the Second Vatican Council (1962–5), Schillebeeckx advised and assisted the Dutch bishops. In this period he became *the* theological spokesman of the Dutch standpoint both for Dutch Catholics and for the international press. He came to be regarded as one of the important Catholic theologians concerned for renewal, who to a significant degree influenced the course of the Council, in the eyes of many people even in a decisive way, and who wanted to bring the church, faith and theology into a more direct relationship with contemporary culture. With his colleagues Yves Congar from France, Karl Rahner from Germany and Hans Küng from Switzerland, in 1965 he was involved in the start of the international theological journal *Concilium*, which sought to radiate and keep alive the open spirit of the Council, orientated on freedom within the church and worldwide dialogue.

1974 saw the appearance of Schillebeeckx's great study *Jesus*, in which he investigated what could be discovered historically about the figure of Jesus of Nazareth and tried to portray him for men and women today as a credible embodiment of 'salvation from God'. The way in which the book combined technical exegesis and discussions of systematic theology definitively established Schillebeeckx's name as one of the great Catholic theologians of this period. His approach to the figure of Jesus and his apparent detachment from church dogma, which spoke of Jesus Christ as one person in two natures, as both God and man, were controversial. But Schillebeeckx's view of Jesus Christ and the Bible, and of the place of the church in the midst of the world, not forgetting the ministry within this church, decisively influenced the opinions of many people. These were not only professional theological colleagues, but also pastors and 'ordinary' Catholic faithful who, at any rate in the Netherlands and in Flanders, bought his books in strikingly large numbers and often made considerable efforts to work through them. These books evidently offered them the possibility of becoming informed about recent theological developments in a way which supported the development of their own faith.

Schillebeeckx's work was appreciated not only by the grass-roots faithful in the church and by his professional theological colleagues but also by key cultural figures: not only was he awarded a large number of honorary doctorates, but in 1982 he received the Erasmus Prize for European culture.[3]

For 25 years Schillebeeckx was professor of dogmatics and the history of theology at the theological faculty of the Catholic University in Nijmegen, from 1958 until his retirement in 1983.[4] When I began to study theology in Nijmegen in the second half of the 1970s, his influence there was very strong. It was to be a long time before I discovered how strong, and before I realized that the broad and open theological discussions that were carried on there were special, and also somewhat controversial. At other places it proved not at all to be taken for granted that systematic theology was to be done in a secularized university climate, without theologians having to worry about whether their discipline was up to existing in such a climate. However, in my experience this attitude in particular offered the possibility of developing a way of doing theology which was committed and in a certain sense 'confessing', but not confessional. It proved that theology need not be what quite a few outsiders imagine it to be and what it all too often deteriorates into: it could be something other than a presentation of the church's confession of faith, thought through and systematic, but in fact presented quite uncritically. It is not that in Schillebeeckx's view the church's confession of faith is unimportant; far from it. But his starting point is that faith is just as alive in the consciousness of present-day men and women, and that the confession of faith yields up its meaning only when it is confronted with that consciousness. Schillebeeckx did not form any school in the strict sense in the Dutch-speaking world, as for example Karl Rahner did in Germany. But by being introduced and initiated into a theology which was strongly marked by his influence, I became convinced that theology, in the midst of contemporary culture and involved in the cultural discussions which were being carried on in a number of places, could be a critical science, with its own contribution to make and its own focus. I pledged my heart to such a form of theology and I am glad to be able to try to contribute towards its future.[5]

In 1961, at the founding of *Tijdschrift voor Theologie*, for which he devised the formula, that of a journal which was scholarly and theological in form but in content alluded to current developments, Schillebeeckx expressed the hope that 'by its down-to-earth but at the same time clear-sighted theological scholarship it [would] really make faith a constructive element in our human society'.[6] The vocabulary is dated and the solemnity inimitable, but the commitment expressed here is as timely now as it ever was. Theology does not revolve around preserving intact a presupposed treasury of faith and analysing it conceptually, whether this treasury is located in the biblical writings, church tradition or the intimations of our deepest feelings. Religion and theology are ultimately concerned to disclose reality in the footsteps of the biblical writings and the post-biblical traditions, so that reality shows itself to be the space and time of the God of salvation; and precisely because of the presence of this God, the world shows itself to be a place that can be lived in.[7]

Because Schillebeeckx's theology embodies in an impressive way this conviction, which is far from being self-evident, it is still important. At least, that is the conviction in which this book has been written.

But this book would not have come into being had I not been commissioned by the Dutch Dominicans in 1989 to study Schillebeeckx's theology and its developments in relation to its context. My work was meant to result in a kind of intellectual biography in which the changes that are perceptible in his published work were connected with the contemporary changes in the social, cultural, theological and ecclesiastical landscape. Granted, Schillebeeckx was not a member of the Dutch province of Dominicans and formally has always remained Flemish, but at the start of my investigation into his development he had been a Dominican in the Netherlands for around 30 years. His Dutch brothers thought that he deserved a study which placed him in the context of his history. In this way a new perspective on his ultimate significance for the church and theology could emerge.[8]

That was the central idea. But within it the intended study – the book which you are reading – tries to fulfil several purposes at the same time. First of all the intention was that it should provide a good deal of material in a relatively handy way. An important part of Schillebeeckx's comprehensive *oeuvre* came into being in a social, cultural, religious and ecclesiastical climate radically different from that of today, and the traces of this history can still be found in his most recent writings. That is unavoidable, because every theology always also reflects the history of the theologian, even if its significance is far wider; however, it makes access for present-day readers difficult. Especially those who did not consciously experience the period of the Second Vatican Council (1962–5) and the Pastoral Council of the Dutch Church Province (1966–70) – in other words those born after 1955 – find it difficult to see the commitment in Schillebeeckx's texts, at the heart of his work, the pivot on which everything hinges. That is even more true for foreigners who are interested in him. Schillebeeckx himself, the University of Nijmegen and those who have been occupied professionally with his work are still regularly visited by people who are usually researching into part of his theology or studying his thoughts and ideas on a particular theme. It proves very difficult for them to get an adequate view of the history of society, culture, church and theology, especially in Flanders and the Netherlands, so that they have a good idea of the background to some of his views, and thus of their scope and significance. In order to clarify this, I go in detail into the relationship between Schillebeeckx's writing and politics and culture, the social, ecclesiastical and theological circumstances in which they came about, and the influence of these circumstances.

The text became so long that it had to be divided into two volumes: the present volume covers roughly half of Schillebeeckx's life, the period from his birth in 1914 to the conclusion of the Second Vatican Council in 1965. A second volume will start with the new beginning that the period of the Council marked for him as a theologian. In the first chapter of that book I shall investigate the enthusiasm after the Council and the new problems which, from around 1963, increasingly demanded Schillebeeckx's attention.

But those who commissioned this book did not just want a historical study. The aim was not to put Schillebeeckx, even while still alive, into the mausoleum of important figures who nevertheless definitively belong to the past. The ultimate aim was to further the influence of his theology today. This does not conflict with a primarily historical approach to his work. In fact it is precisely by studying Schillebeeckx's position in the midst of the context in which he was entangled that one gains sight of his theological distinctiveness, if only because one's attention is focused on the whole of his *oeuvre*. For a wider public Schillebeeckx's name is above all bound up with what happened in the Catholic Church in and around the Council, and with the skirmishes afterwards. Those who buy and read his books – they still sell in quantities which are strikingly large for academic studies – usually seem to be attracted by his pastoral concern and intellectual boldness, the open and unprejudiced way in which he approaches the church tradition. In their experience such qualities cannot be taken for granted within the Catholic Church, and Schillebeeckx's faithful readers feel closely associated with his commitment to a humane and democratic church.[9] Now zeal for reforms in the church and theology is indeed a not unimportant aspect of Schillebeeckx's theology, but it is not the central aspect. The centre of Schillebeeckx's theological commitment is somewhere else.

I was born in the second half of the 1950s and thus already belong to a generation for which an interest in religion and theology did not naturally issue in a commitment to reforms within the church. That is even more the

case for those born in the 1960s and 1970s. I am convinced that Schillebeeckx's work is of potentially great importance particularly for people who
do not find theology interesting primarily because of its significance within
the church, but see it as reflection on a standpoint within contemporary
culture, in dialogue and confrontation with the Christian tradition. But that
importance can be seen only if Schillebeeckx sheds his image of being above
all a theologian of the Council and a leader of the Catholic reform of the
1960s.

BIOGRAPHY AS CONTEXTUAL HISTORIOGRAPHY

The core of Schillebeeckx's *oeuvre* is his view of the relationship between
God and the world, his basic conviction that knowledge of God is possible
through human experience in and of the world.[10] This leads him to a religious and theological view of human culture which he developed to an
important degree in the period covered by this book. That is why I devote so
much attention here to the 'Flemish Schillebeeckx', whose work so far has
been little studied. A theology along the lines of the approach which he
developed in his Flemish period still makes possible meaningful and interesting reflections on reality, culture and human life, out of an interest in
what brings salvation and redemption, and along these lines it can show the
relevance of the Christian tradition. Theology which starts from the still
dominant idea that it should explain what is handed down to us from the
past is certainly easier to grasp than a theology which wants to speak of
reality as a whole, focusing on the God of salvation as the tradition speaks
of this God. At first sight such theology also offers more certainty, but it
achieves this by denying the complexity of human history and negating the
obscurity of the human situation. In his theological project Schillebeeckx is
ultimately engaged in finding the God of salvation in the midst of the
complexity in which human beings lead their lives, in a world that it is
impossible to comprehend completely.

So I am concerned here with Schillebeeckx's theological project as a
whole. In that case he does not appear primarily as someone who has
adopted a number of standpoints that were more or less striking in the
climate of the church and theology of his time, although of course this will
be indicated on occasion. Rather, the aim is that in this book he should be
depicted as someone who above all *does theology*, and in doing it, and in
constant conversation with the tradition and with the present situation of
culture and philosophy, the church and theology, develops a view of reality
as a whole, and of religion, church and the individual as part of it. In this
study I shall use one of Schillebeeckx's own terms, 'theology of culture', to
denote his overall project and theological approach.[11] As will become clear,

until 1965 a theological view of culture stood at the centre of his writings, a conception of how far and in what way the activity of human beings in creating culture ultimately has a religious significance. Here he understood 'culture' in the same broad sense as the Second Vatican Council did later; the Council was to describe culture as the different ways of using things, of working and self-expression, of practising religion and of behaviour, of establishing laws and juridical institutions, of developing science and the arts.[12]

Since in this conception 'culture' denotes the way in which human beings deal with the world in order to find a place to live in it, a home, 'theology of culture' can refer to a theological view of reality as a whole and to human life and action in its midst, which is ultimately religious. In that case, theology, with the help of the Christian tradition, is a matter of sounding out human experience in all its aspects. This book makes it clear that Schillebeeckx's ideas in the 1940s, 1950s and the first half of the 1960s on God and Jesus Christ, on the church and the sacraments, on the priesthood and on faith, hope and love, formed part of a project of a theology of culture in this sense. Whereas many of his specific standpoints are no longer adequate in the present situation, in my view the project of a theology of culture of which they form a part still has a future.[13]

In order to give some idea of Schillebeeckx's theological project, I shall map his theological development. This book has indeed become an intellectual biography as was intended, and has been written with the notion that insight into the biography of a theologian helps us to understand her or his theology.[14] But it is not a biography in the most usual sense of the word. The starting point of a biography is usually that the life studied forms a unity and has its own logic, that the facts of this life do not follow one another fortuitously but are related to one another. The logic and connection are then usually sought in the personality of the man or woman studied. However, I definitely do not aim to bring out the 'personality' of Edward Schillebeeckx, nor do I make any attempt to depict his 'soul'. I do not look for his 'theological character', his 'theological genius'. In short, I am not concerned to discover some innermost core of his theological approach, which would increasingly unfold during his development and would be the hidden source of his texts.

Certainly Schillebeeckx is a man of faith and hence an inspired theologian. Especially those who have heard him speak have often been moved – and still are moved – by the impact of the solemnity with which he exercises his profession, the urgency with which he engages in discussions and the conviction with which he puts forward his insights. Various students to whom he lectured before the Council saw that what was special about him

7

was that he could show that theology is about questions which also affect us existentially: that was quite exceptional in this period. Not only was his great theological expertise notable, but above all the way in which he could combine this expertise with passion. I, too, admire Schillebeeckx's theological achievements. I still find the breadth of his knowledge and the depth of his insights always very impressive, and I am also personally grateful for what I have learned from him – and, thanks to him, from others. But I am convinced that the importance of his work does not lie in the personal style of thinking to which his texts bear witness. What is interesting is the manner of working that they embody, their approach, the way in which they ask theological questions and answer them. In other words, I have not set out to portray a unique person in his inimitable profundity. My concern is to clarify a theological approach, a way of depicting the tradition of faith and theology which illuminates human existence and human culture. The point is that in principle it can be followed by others – and in the broad sense also deserves to be followed by others.

So this book is about the biography of Schillebeeckx, but not about his personality in so far as it lies behind the texts that he has written. I do not understand his theological *oeuvre* here as an *expression* of a theological view which is, as it were, hidden in the depths of his soul, but as its *form*. The theological texts and the approach which is evident in them are the form taken by his view, which is characterized both by faith and theoretical thought. They are the form in which this view makes contact with others and invites people to adopt a similar approach. That is why in this book all the emphasis is on Schillebeeckx's theological texts. They are analysed, the shifts in them are determined and explained, the fractures are interpreted, and the continuity which perhaps lies behind them is traced. And all this is done in the hope that the theological approach to which they bear witness will prove to be inspiring.

So here biography is understood as a description of the history of a thinker in the context which surrounds and permeates him or her, and at the same time as a description of the surrounding history in the light of the history of this one thinker. People form themselves and are formed in and through their interaction with their environment, by acting, speaking and writing – and in the case of Schillebeeckx by writing theology – in relation to the context. So it is not enough, to quote a phrase of the historians Jan and Annie Romein, to put Schillebeeckx 'in the framework of his time'. The Romeins rightly say that such a metaphor gives a wrong picture of the relationship between people and the time in which they live.

There is indeed a connection between framework and description, but this is external. In reality here we have an intrinsic connection. The 'great man' also shapes the cultural matrix of his time. In our view the criterion of a 'great man' as the creator of 'eternal values' is not in dispute. Indeed, in so far, thinking historically, one can speak of eternal values, we would even venture the paradox that the genius is more in a position to do this, since he has penetrated more deeply into his time as it has penetrated more deeply into him.[15]

Nowadays this language may seem somewhat bombastic. But here I am adopting the view expressed in it that people of stature are interwoven with their own time and context, and suggesting that they show their greatness precisely in the way in which they deal with their context, not in their independence from it.[16]

In their still magisterial book, quoted above, at the end of the 1930s Jan and Anni Romein described Dutch history between 1325 and 1927 in 36 portraits. They did not so much intend to depict special personalities or characteristic *oeuvres*; rather, through these portraits they wanted to give a kaleidoscopic picture of 'the history of Dutch civilization' in order to discover what the 'typical Dutch contribution' was to what in an untroubled way they still saw as European civilization.[17] In the 1950s – and of course this will come out in much more detail later in this book – Schillebeeckx wrote in a comparable way about the history of theology. In his view, studying the history of theology was about regaining the distinctive perspective of a theologian as the author of a writing or the distinctive standpoint of those who composed a church document. These texts must then be seen ultimately as the embodiment of a view of God and the divine revelation. A view of the Christian tradition as a whole could come about only through the kaleidoscopic picture of separate views which were bound to a specific place and time. According to Schillebeeckx, it was precisely in their particularity that theological views pointed beyond their particularity and in their own way opened up a view of what he described as 'the thing itself, the mystery of salvation'.[18] I am treading in his footsteps when I go on to see his work as a historical form of dealing with the mystery of God and salvation, which is the central issue in the history of theology.

According to Schillebeeckx, precisely such an approach to the history of faith and theology was an indispensable contribution to current theologizing. He stated emphatically that what he denoted by the classical term 'positive theology' did not consist in the collection of more or less curious facts. The study of the history of theology was a thoroughly theological discipline, inseparable from systematic theology, which in this period he still called 'speculative theology'.

For although positive theology makes use of purely historical methods, in this historical investigation it is concerned with the thing itself: a better understanding of the mystery of salvation in which holy scripture, patristics, high scholasticism and all subsequent periods of the church were interested. Everywhere and in all times the mystery of salvation betrays something of its inner, integral content ... Among other things it is the task of positive theology to discover the thematic differences which are also expressed in these views, so that speculative theology can arrive at an integral synthesis in which all these facets of faith are properly illuminated.[19]

APPROACH AND PLAN

In line with this view, here by means of 'purely historical methods' I want to contribute to a better view of 'the thing itself' in theology. In the end I regard this historical study of the theologian Edward Schillebeeckx in his history as a theological book. The postscript investigates the specifically theological elements of that. Here I shall simply spell out in three points the approach that I have adopted.

First, as I have said, this intellectual biography sets out to map the relationship between history from 1914 to midway through the 1960s, especially the history of the Catholic Church and theology in this period, and the history of Edward Schillebeeckx as a theologian within this history, as part of it. His personality comes into view only indirectly and in passing; I have paid no specific attention to his psychology and inner life and therefore have cited above all public sources about him: books, articles, and also lecture notes and, later, published interviews with him. In other words, I have used texts which were intended as a public expression of his theologizing. My main concern is with the Schillebeeckx who emerges here, and only incidentally shall I refer to texts from the private sphere – letters, notes for personal use – or make use of information from personal conversation.

I have also deliberately refrained from interviewing Schillebeeckx at length about his development and working out his background on the basis of what he remembers. That would certainly have saved a good deal of time, but it would almost inevitably have meant that I was following Schillebeeckx's interpretation of his own history today. And that is not what I wanted. On the basis of facts which are in principle verifiable I have tried to write a reliable history of Schillebeeckx as a public figure, as the author of a very great many pages of text which he will leave to us. Typically, he has never put the slightest obstacle in my way; he has allowed me to make use of his personal archive and at my request has been ready to comment on texts. He certainly noted that my picture of his theology partly differed from his own, but thought that only natural and generously did no more than note the fact.

Secondly, here I examine the context of Schillebeeckx's theological *oeuvre* in the broad sense. Because of my interest in his theological project, my concern is not to explain his standpoint in detail in terms of specific influences on him. I have not tried to discover whose influence was precisely responsible for what. As he once wrote to me, on the occasion of an earlier version of part of this book which I had sent to him, 'the question of "influence" by whom' always remains problematical. 'Usually there are plenty of influences', and one can rarely speak of just one dominant influence.[20] This book sets out above all to reconstruct the climate in which Schillebeeckx's views must be set and, within that, the way in which the development of his project can be understood. I shall try to discover what the questions and the fears were, in what terms particular groups and individuals produced them and what answers and solutions were circulating. Now and then this book may look like a history of Catholic theology from after the Second World War, focused on the contributions to it by one theologian; however, its aim of course always remains that of giving a good picture of Schillebeeckx's place in the midst of this history.

In such a reconstruction, after the event it proves difficult to avoid giving the impression that some connections are more compelling and some influences more direct than they seemed to be at the time. But of course all the theologians, philosophers and other writers who have a voice in this book, together with the nameless people for whom they thought, spoke and wrote, created the climate in which Schillebeeckx could develop into the theologian which he was ultimately to become. When, for example, around the middle of the century I note a certain change in his theology, from a Christian orientation on culture to attention to the church as really being the living form of the theology of culture that he was still seeking in the 1940s, I may give the impression that this shift was caused by the appearance of the encyclical *Humani generis* in 1950. However, that is not the point. The point is rather that it is connected with a development in the church climate of which *Humani generis* was an expression, and in which at the same time the document played an important role.

Thirdly, I should indicate the specific plan of this book. In principle it is chronological, except that now and then the chronology is interrupted to achieve a systematic clarity of presentation. Chapter 1 covers the period of Schillebeeckx's youth, from his birth at the beginning of the First World War up to and including his first official lecture as a theological teacher at the end of the Second World War. It is about the situation of Flemish Catholicism during the inter-war period and the way in which Schillebeeckx came into contact with it. It describes the influences which he underwent during his studies and the way in which he assimilated these influences. Chapter 2 is generally concerned with the second half of the 1940s. Schillebeeckx is placed among those who were seeking reorientation in all kinds of social spheres after the war, in Catholic circles and outside them, and his first attempts to arrive at a theology of culture are analysed, as is the view of spirituality which for him is associated with them. I describe how his short stay in France in 1945 was of abiding influence on his development. He came into contact with the worker-priest movement and the theologians associated with it, who in concrete links with the great cultural questions of their time realized forms of faith and theology which he envisaged in his project of a theology of culture. The chapter ends with Schillebeeckx's view of Dominican spirituality, which he put into practice and to which he wanted to introduce his Flemish students. Chapter 3 then concentrates on the 1950s, up to the moment that Schillebeeckx went to the Netherlands. In this period the conflict with Catholics concerned for renewal and the hierarchical leadership of the church was growing. The encyclical *Humani generis* attacked the theologians, and the worker-priest experiment was ended by orders from above. I describe how in this period Schillebeeckx concentrated theologically more on the church, and in fact put it forward as the living form of the cultural theology which he sought. Here it will also become clear how he devoted a good deal of attention to the position of the laity in the church, and how in this way he remained true to his commitment to a church which realizes itself in the midst of, and in responsibility to, the world and its culture. At the end, the chapter shows how Schillebeeckx's publications on Mary halfway through the 1950s – on the occasion of the solemn pronouncement of the dogma of Mary's bodily assumption in 1954 – express the same double attitude towards the church.

Chapter 4 to some degree breaks the chronological order. It presents the comprehensive theological view of the Louvain Schillebeeckx as expressed in his more specialist theological work: inevitably, this chapter is the most technical in the book. It gives an extended analysis of his 1952 book on 'The Sacramental Economy of Salvation' (*De sacramentele heilseconomie*, never translated into English), the lectures which he gave to his Dominican students in Louvain and his book *Marriage: Human Reality and Saving Mystery*. Granted, this 'dogmatics of marriage' appeared only after Schillebeeckx had already been in the Netherlands for a number of years and had its direct occasion in the Dutch situation at the end of the 1950s and the beginning of the 1960s. The approach used, though, is still very much that of the Louvain years, although the study also already heralds the reorientation that Schillebeeckx's theology would undergo after the Second Vatican Council. Finally, the Council is central to Chapter 5. It describes Schillebeeckx's arrival in Nijmegen on the eve of the announcement of the Council, and the significance that this had in the Dutch situation of the time. However, the emphasis is on Schillebeeckx's activities in connection with the Council, his work for the Dutch bishops in the period of preparation and during the sessions, his role as commentator in the press, and the way in which he developed into a national and international personality. At the same time the chapter depicts the rapid change in climate within the Catholic Church during the time of the Council and the way in which this raised new questions for faith and theology. In 1965, Schillebeeckx's orientation on the world and its cultural humanization also entered a qualitatively new phase as a result of his involvement in the Council. In the second half of the 1960s he was to look in an almost feverish way for new theological approaches adequate to the modern, secularized situation.

Thus I try to put the work of Edward Schillebeeckx in its specific context, its own history. At any rate for readers today, the writings which are discussed here also bear unmistakable traces of the time and the developments in the midst of which they came into being. Much of Schillebeeckx's work arose in reaction to outside impulses. This is true to some degree of every thinker, but to a greater extent than many others, in his theological life Schillebeeckx in fact carries on one ongoing conversation, on the one hand with authors whom he has read and on the other with readers for whom he thinks that he is writing or the public that he is addressing. His articles and books are the account of this conversation. However, the language and concepts which he uses in his texts are the language and concepts of the conversation as it is being carried on at the moment that he is writing. Often people think that theology is a static business and assume that it undergoes little change. Yet there is little that confronts a reader so much with the changes in theology in most recent decades as the reading of theological texts of 50, 40 or even only 30 years ago. The terminology customary until well into the 1960s can still be understood with some effort, but it is not always easy to see what connotations the key words had and what existential importance people attached to the discussions and the standpoints adopted in them.

It cannot be the aim of this study to do away with this distance. The Schillebeeckx of the 1940s, 1950s and 1960s will never become simply a contemporary of present-day readers. But I do try to explain why particular theological questions were thought important, and why, and in what sense, particular positions were controversial. In this indirect manner and by adopting this roundabout approach I presuppose that the Schillebeeckx of before and during the Second Vatican Council can again become the reader's conversation partner. In this way this 'young' Schillebeeckx can at any rate again become my conversation partner as a writer. Schillebeeckx is still doing theology and the results are still being published with a degree of regularity. This book also sets out to contribute to a better understanding of his later texts, and therefore remarks can be found scattered through the text about how ideas which emerged in his early work come through in his later writings. But at the same time I think that his earlier ideas as these are expressed in this part of his intellectual biography have become dated as a result of the later developments, though they have not been superseded in a

13

deeper sense. As is often the case, on closer inspection the legacy of this 'testator' proves to be greater than it first seemed.

Sometimes I allude to the current importance of a discussion or approach that is being examined, but that only happens in a quite incidental way. As author, I ask readers to be ready to some degree to immerse themselves in Schillebeeckx's project as a whole and the way in which it develops. I try to persuade them to take part in it by describing it in context. I am convinced that then the insight will gradually grow that Schillebeeckx's problems are still also ours in the broader sense, despite all the changes in the context. Especially by emphasizing that his theology is a 'theology of culture', I think that I can bring to light the continuity between our situation and his.

In the postscript I try to spell out what this means for contemporary theological thought.

ACKNOWLEDGEMENTS

It remains for me to express some words of thanks.

This book would never have come into being without Anton van Harskamp and Ted Schoof. It is thanks to them that the Dutch Dominicans commissioned me to investigate 'the theology of Schillebeeckx in its context'; in this way they not only ensured that I could remain a professional theologian at a moment when this was by no means a matter of course because of complications in church politics, but they also forced me to immerse myself in a new way in the only theologian of whom I would be willing to call myself a 'pupil' in the full sense. In almost all the current discussions in which I am theologically involved – on liturgy and church, politics and ethics, God and Jesus Christ, the theological foundation of theology and spirituality – the standpoints which Schillebeeckx has developed are still well worth considering. During the writing of this book I have discovered that without even realizing it I often follow in his footsteps, a discovery which has again clarified my own position. Moreover, Ted Schoof and Anton van Harskamp have always been closely involved in the project and have supported me in all kinds of ways, Ted almost day by day. Contact with him prevented me from feeling too lonely, but he also made the progress of this project his responsibility. Without hesitation he put his great knowledge of the history of theology in general and of Schillebeeckx's development in particular at my disposal, but did not hinder me from going my own way. I still find it almost incredible that in the last phase he was even ready to relieve me of much time-consuming work in the final redaction of this book

I am also much indebted to the Dutch Dominicans. In the end it is thanks to them that I could remain a theologian even after 1989. The fact that they saw many affinities between my theological approach and the central values of the Dominican tradition, and did not simply commission me as a researcher into Schillebeeckx's theology but also appointed me 'their' theologian, helped me, too, increasingly to begin to feel a Dominican theologian. The executive committee under the leadership of the Provincial, Piet Sturik, which appointed me made it clear that I might take a broad view of my task and encouraged me to adopt a standpoint 'along the lines of Schillebeeckx' in current theological discussion. The two committees under the leadership of Provincial David van Ooijen, which came next, above all tried to ensure that I had sufficient time for historical research into Schillebeeckx's theology, so that this book really could be published. Both forms of involvement in my work have been important.

I am also grateful to the steering committee which read and commented on the texts as I wrote them. In addition to, once again, Anton van Harskamp and Ted Schoof, this was made up of Bertrand J. De Clercq, Karel Dobbelaere, Jan Jacobs, Nico Schreurs, Ambroos-Remi Van de Walle and Ad Willems. Dobbelaere had to resign his membership of the committee soon after the beginning of the research because of pressure of work, and Van de Walle died in 1993. Finally, I want to thank Edward Schillebeeckx once more for his combination of restraint and accessibility.

The first things can only be said last, and the most important things often cannot be said at all. Fortunately that is usually not necessary anyway. It hardly needs saying that I could not have written this book had I not regularly been invited to write or speak about theology, had there not been listeners and readers who wanted to take note of my thoughts and enter into conversation with me, so that I remained confident that theology still has something to say in the midst of present-day culture. I hope that it is also self-evident that I could not have continued to work had I not regularly encountered kindred souls in my colleagues at the Dominican Study Centre for Theology and Society, in my friends in the Dutch Dominican movement, in the Study Commission of the Eighth of May Movement, in the liturgical team of celebrants and preachers in St Dominic's Church in Amsterdam, and in all the other places where I am able to engage in theological discussions with others.

What really should be said, though, is how much I owe to Anya, to Kyra and to Michal, all the more so because this is something that I myself do not always recognize sufficiently. However, it cannot be expressed in words and of necessity I limit myself to this acknowledgement. In the way which comes closest to me they embody the culture in the midst of which and with an eye to which I do my theology. Sometimes the responsibilities of my work as a theologian is in tension with building up and maintaining everyday relationships and daily life, and sometimes the two things really get in each other's way. Without being a hypocrite I cannot promise to improve, but I emphatically express my gratitude here to my 'three women', both for their constant tolerance of my work and for the indignation about it which regularly flares up.

Chapter 1

Youth and Training up to 1944

'All the same, there is no disguising the fact that I was born under a heavy bombardment'

THE BOMBARDMENT OF MODERN TIMES

In the second half of the 1920s, every week a boy wrote a letter from his boarding school in Flemish Turnhout to his 'dear parents' and his brothers and sisters in Kortenberg. In almost every letter he spoke with reverence about his father who 'has to work so hard' to make it possible for him and his brothers to study. He regularly wrote about the competition to be first, i.e. best in the class, in the various subjects. Years later Edward Schillebeeckx was to be a famous Catholic theologian, renowned for his capacity to work and the speed with which he grasped the essence of a text. As a boy he said that the motto of his family was *Credo, pugno* – 'I believe, I fight' – , a slogan which was popular in the circles of the Young Catholic Workers, and on 10 March 1933, at the age of 18, he wrote to his father that he was convinced that he had to give himself 'utterly and completely' to 'the salvation of souls' because of all the 'misery' that he saw around him:

> Isn't there a crisis of faith, a crisis of authority and a crisis of morals? Isn't there a financial crisis with all its bankruptcies, failures and bank moratoria? It seems to me that these are simply the result of a crisis of faith, authority and morality and of the mistrust and despair among the nations, which are nevertheless all children of one and the same Father, our Dear Lord and God.[1]

Thirty-five years later he was to become known for his commitment to a church which had a respect for people and their quest for salvation, and ten years after that he would publish a very extensive theological study entitled (in Dutch) *Gerechtigheid en liefde: Genade en bevrijding* (Righteousness and Love, Grace and Liberation: the English and German translations were to be entitled *Christ*). When he was 12 or 13, out of a romantic desire to make 'our Dear Lord and God' better known, he drew above his letters ships and bicycles 'for mission', and from a note which he himself added much later it proves that he was mocked for this by his brother. When he was 57 he gave an introduction to the political option for Christians over which many of those who stood personally and theologically close to him shook their heads because it so clearly lacked any practical sense.[2]

In short, there is much to be said for Schillebeeckx's lamentation during a interview:

> I have discovered that interviews usually begin with the theological training of a rising theologian and not the years preceding it: yet I think that they are very important ... the years of childhood count in someone's training and experience.[3]

This study does begin right at the beginning. This chapter is about the youth, upbringing and education of Edward Schillebeeckx. But the interest is not psychological. This chapter does not aim to reconstruct feelings and experiences. In this sense I shall heed Schillebeeckx's own reservations about the explicit reporting of anecdotes from a person's life in connection with his theology, however much one also wants to take into account the 'auto-biographical breeding ground' of any theologizing.[4] The subject of this chapter is not the inner life of the child Edward and the explanation that this perhaps offers of his later development. I am concerned with the history of the development of Schillebeeckx the theologian. I shall try to discover in what way birth and origin, upbringing and education gave him a place in church and culture and how he came into contact with the spiritual life and theology. How during the years of his youth and education did he learn religious and theological outlooks, what view did he develop of the modernity which from the First World War increasingly came to determine the situation in the world, in Europe and in Belgium?

Birth in 1914

Edward Cornelis Florent Alfons Schillebeeckx was born at the beginning of what for a long time was called 'the Great War', the First World War. Later he would still clearly remember the field kitchens of the German soldiers behind his home in Kortenberg. To be more precise, Edward's birth took place one hundred days after Belgium was invaded by German troops on 4 August 1914 and five days before the fourth German army would be given orders to reinforce the positions they had conquered so far and, for the moment, to leave a small part of Belgium unoccupied.[5]

The circumstances in which Edward Schillebeeckx came into the world were marked in a quite concrete way by military action. He himself has given different versions of the story of his birth, but his sister Greta has reconstructed the precise circumstances from her father's archive.[6] Constant Johannes Maria Schillebeeckx and his wife, Johanna Petronella Calis, had come with their five children to live in Kortenberg in 1913. When war broke out, mother and the children went to Geel in Kempen, where Constant and his wife had both been born and where their parents still lived, supposing that they would be safer there. Constant remained in Kortenberg to commute every day from there to Brussels, where he worked in the Ministry of Finance, until because of the war this was moved to Antwerp. Then he too went to live in Geel. When Antwerp was besieged by the Germans, however, he could no longer return to Geel in the evening and stayed in the house of a brother who had meanwhile fled to England. There he lived until the relief of Antwerp at the beginning of October. With a great many others he fled to the Netherlands, first to Roosendaal and later, after being united with his wife and children whom he had brought to Luyksgestel, to Valkenswaard and Vlissingen. There he investigated the possibilities of crossing over to England, but was told that he should not attempt this for the moment. However, a boat was shortly to sail for Antwerp and the family resolved to take it, because the baby was expected very soon. In Antwerp the family lived in the house of Constant's brother, 'uncle Laurent', who had gone to England, and remained there until the beginning of February 1915. Then they returned to Kortenberg. Edward was born in Antwerp on 12 November 1914, the sixth child of the family.

In his own stories about his birth Schillebeeckx always emphasized that he was supposedly born during a bombardment of Antwerp. Although on occasion his father explicitly denied this, Edward remained convinced of it. The story of his birth while the bombs were falling evidently had a deep symbolic, almost mythical, truth for him: 'All the same, there is no disguising the fact that I was born under a heavy bombardment.'[7] This expression in fact has something of a birth legend about it. Although it is not true in the literal sense, it makes an essential statement about Schillebeeckx's life.

For good reasons it has been suggested that the First World War marks the real beginning of the twentieth century, with its turbulent and violent history that changed everything. It was a century which was ever more rapidly to come under the influence of science and technology, with its violent conflicts fuelled by great ideologies like nationalism, liberalism, socialism, Fascism and National Socialism. After 1914, what Karl Marx and Friedrich Engels had predicted 70 years before had really taken place:

All fixed, fast-frozen relations, with their train of ancient and venerable prejudices and opinions, are swept away, all new-formed ones become antiquated before they can ossify. All that is solid melts into air, all that is holy is profaned ...[8]

That is indeed like a bombardment, with very profound consequences for society and especially for the church and theology. For the whole of his adult life Edward Schillebeeckx was most emphatically to be a theologian in the midst of this bombardment, and in the years in which he grew up and was educated he had to try to find his place in the midst of the bombardment under which he was born.

But of course the First World War was not an absolute beginning to the modernization of north-west Europe. In the second half of the nineteenth century increasing industrialization resulted in ever greater groups of the population beginning to become part of an ever more tightly organized and strongly institutionalized society, through their labour force, through the wages that they received and through their life in the rapidly growing cities. As a consequence of this there was an increased need for education, and the press, film and radio, which were then developing rapidly, became more and more important. Through these media the members of society gained a picture of rapidly changing modernity. They had a view of the world around them and the time in which they lived which was not available to their ancestors.

It was partly the consequences of this process that came to light in all their intensity as a result of the 1914–18 war. But the tendency towards increased scale and national integration was also considerably reinforced by it. Expressions of national identity were offered from above to justify the military mobilization, and they were disseminated with the help of the new mass media. Moreover, the mass active involvement of young men from every corner of the countries involved in the war created a real sense of community. Perhaps for the first time in history it became possible for people from the lower classes to feel not only inhabitants of a particular district, city or region, but really part of a nation and members of a people.

Initially, the European peoples went to war quite eagerly and optimistically, but that soon changed. The horrors of this first war in which modern technology played a central role came to light especially in the deprivations in the trenches and the mass deaths of ordinary soldiers from the lower classes. This led to a common opposition to the rulers and a great receptivity to ideologies orientated on social change. Immediately after the war, in 1918 and 1919, impulses towards revolution developed in various places in Europe. In Belgium all this assumed a specific form, since social oppositions there coincided to an important degree with the opposition between the French- and the Flemish-speaking population. Flemish soldiers had served under French-speaking officers on the so-called Yzer front. The story of Flemish young men needlessly killed because they did not understand orders given in French was a powerful propaganda weapon in the hands of the Flemish movement. After 1918 the Flemish opposition to the predominance of France and the French speakers increased and spread.[9]

Throughout Europe the First World War in fact represented the definitive end to clearly ordered nineteenth-century society and the breakthrough of a culture in which mobility and change were central. Desire for change and belief in the possibility of substantial social progress began to form part of the feelings of large groups of the population. Certainly opposition also developed to the mass culture which was coming into being and the materialistic attitude which in the perception of many critics of culture went with it. But they too shared the presupposition that culture could be changed and that the future could to a large degree be made. However, in contrast to what they saw being announced, they looked to a future which was stable and based on what they regarded as 'natural' values. Especially Catholics in this period between the two world wars were to prove to have a great affinity to this position.[10]

More than most others, Schillebeeckx made the commitment to become a theologian precisely in these new circumstances, which were economically, politically and culturally unstable and therefore also unstable in religious terms. He explored the possibilities and limits of theology in them. I am convinced that his abiding significance lies in the way in which he was and still is a theologian in the changing and in many respects chaotic world which came into being after 1918, even more than in what he wrote about specific theological topics – about the doctrine of creation and marriage, about liturgy and sacraments, about the church and its ministries, about Jesus of Nazareth confessed as the Christ. All this will be discussed at greater length in this study. Just as the modern novel not only tells a story but also has the telling of stories itself as a theme, just as in modern poetry the poetics is itself an important subject, and modern graphic arts do not simply depict but at the same time reflect on looking at images and creating them, so too modern theology can exist only by constantly giving itself new form. It needs constantly to invent and construct itself in that bombardment of its structures and their foundation which is a regular feature of modernity. This was precisely what Schillebeeckx did as far as he could; of course he did it in a way that was bound up with the specific circumstances of the time in which he lived, but I am convinced that the project itself can be a model for doing theology now and in the future.

In 1936, when he was a student with the Dominicans, Schillebeeckx in fact wrote his first real article. It was printed in *Biekorf* (Beehive), the stencilled journal of and for Flemish Dominican students. In it he already made some observations which shed a little light on what believing and doing theology mean in the unstable situation of modernity. The real subject of his argument was the meaning for the development of the student of the so-called 'humaniora', the traditional secondary-school teaching orientated above all on instruction in the classical languages. But here he developed a number of ideas about what it means for young men living in the present to be confronted with venerable words and texts from the past, with a tradition. It is striking that in his view the real worth of this form of instruction was not that it brought the student into contact with the culture of antiquity, as was suggested by many champions of the classic humaniora. The contact was usually too superficial and too fragmentary for that. In his view, the important thing about being taught Greek and Roman language and culture was the often dry and laborious translation of texts which were difficult to fathom.

He was not simply concerned with the content of the tradition but with the translation of it, the process of translation itself. Here he distinguished three aspects:

First, the material understanding of the Greek or Latin text ...; then, by means of the material understanding, grasping what the writer actually thought; in other words one has to think oneself into the thoughts, the state of mind, of the writer ...; then follows putting that entering-into-the-thought of the author into one's own mother tongue.[11]

It was important actively to appropriate the classical tradition, and that called for a spirit which allowed itself to be formed actively and which formed itself actively: 'Translation is in the first place the initiative of the translating mind' (11). According to Schillebeeckx, for all their attention to the classical tradition, the humaniora were concerned in depth with training and shaping a mind which took this initiative and provided form; without that the tradition remained incomprehensible. Schillebeeckx would devote the whole of his theological life to the formation of a faith which is active in this sense, a faith which appropriates the tradition and which recognizes the significance of what it finds there in the contemporary situation.

For Schillebeeckx, the view that he developed about what is really the most important thing in the humaniora meant criticism of the form that it was given and the way in which it actually functioned. Later, as a theologian, he would again repeatedly undertake such a correction of the existing situation on the basis of what he saw as its most important features. And the failings that he noted in the classical humaniora were to a large degree analogous to what he was to find lacking in the way of doing theology that was offered him. Thus he accused classics teaching of skating over the surface and forms of the classical texts and paying too little attention to what was said in them. In theology Schillebeeckx was to devote a great deal

22

of attention to discovering the deeper content and meaning of the tradition, because he was discontented with traditional formulae. And it is amazing to see how in his twenties he already objected to the one-sided orientation in the teaching of the humaniora on translating classical texts and complained about the neglect of the language and culture into which they had to be translated. In the course of his life theology was increasingly to become a way of thinking 'in search of the living God', in the midst of one's own culture and one's own situation.

Finally, it was significant that in 1936 Schillebeeckx thought that teaching the classical languages gave pupils too little spiritual orientation (14–21). After 1945 his theological quest would be to a large degree focused on what could offer direction in and for human culture, but for a long time he thought that this orientation could not come from human culture itself; that would change only at the end of the 1950s. In 1936 he thought it a great problem that the 'humaniora' were only what their name indicated: a study of human things. He thought:

The humaniora must teach us to take a first step towards later intellectual life. But if things simply stop there, they are extremely uneven. At the same time the humaniora must also take a first step towards the Higher; they must arouse enthusiasm for all that is good and holy, and incite college students to be attentive to the Truth: they must make them 'love' truth, teach them to work seriously, aiming at something Higher (21).

In his view, humaniora which therefore did not remain 'at the purely human level' would deserve another more exalted name. For Schillebeeckx, from the first phase of his thought, faith and theology, church and world, nature and supernature, God and man already belonged together, in the service of true humanity. But he did evidently still see them to a certain degree as rivals.

Yet, as early as 1936, there were the beginnings of an attempt to overcome this dualism. He thought it necessary, in 'taking a first step towards the Higher', for the teaching in the secondary education of pupils to be open to explicitly Christian cultural material, but that was not enough. He argued that the Christian faith did not need to be taught in the usual way as a collection of soulless truths, but as a living force with an intellectual attractiveness (cf. 20). In other words, he was concerned with faith, not as submission to a system which itself claims to represent the truth, but as a living movement of the spirit which allows itself to be formed actively by the tradition, and then actively gives form to this tradition in its own present. Faith is not just a correction of culture but also a form of culture.

Youth in the midst of tensions in society and the church

At first sight, the unsettling, revolutionary and secularizing tendencies of modernity which definitively broke through with the First World War in Western Europe have little to do with the thoroughly Catholic family into which Edward Schillebeeckx was born. His later description of his home as 'extremely Christian and churchy' does not exactly conjure up an image of dynamics and conflict.

But all kinds of innocent details indicate that family life was very closely bound up with the ongoing dispute over what form life should take that was characteristic of modern times: during the first half of the twentieth century the Catholic Church wanted to play a major role in determining this form, at any price. Thus the simple fact that the Schillebeeckx family was ultimately to number fourteen indicated the stubborn church opposition to so-called neo-Malthusianism and any form of birth control. In this climate, having a large number of children was itself an expression of loyalty to the church and a sign of the Catholic opposition to what was seen as the modern addiction to enjoyment and ease which undermined faith and morality.[12]

Moreover, Schillebeeckx qualified the description of his home as 'extremely Christian' by adding the words 'though somewhat anti-clerical'.[13] Here he was putting his earliest history in a thoroughly turbulent context. The addition conjures up the great tensions in the church, but ultimately also in society, which were hidden behind the apparent stability of Flemish Catholicism. For ultimately, as so often in Belgium, the term 'anti-clerical' also evoked the tension between Flemings and Walloons. In Flanders, where Schillebeeckx grew up, the church hierarchy was closely associated with the French-speaking ruling class. Under the leadership of Archbishop and later Cardinal Désiré Mercier, the leadership of the Belgian episcopate was largely intent on preserving national and Catholic unity. The bishops regarded all the initiatives for change and for giving the Flemish language a place of its own as threats to this double unity. When during the First World War the call to improve the position of Flanders, the Flemings and Flemish grew ever louder, 'Mechelen' (the seat of the Belgian archbishop) with 'Le Havre' (the seat of the Belgian government in exile) were of the opinion that the restoration of Belgian sovereignty after the war was a top priority. In 1925 the episcopate still emphatically prohibited priests from becoming involved in the Flemish movement, whereas the lower clergy had long been an important pillar of it. In 1927 the diocese of Ghent even forbade all its Catholics to take part in Flemish activism.[14]

Constant Schillebeeckx worked as an accountant at the Ministry of Finance, so he belonged to the growing army of officials needed for the efficient functioning of the Belgian state and economy, which were being modernized. The culture at home was soundly middle class. According to

24

Schillebeeckx's later testimony, his mother forfeited a career as a singer by getting married. They lived in what he would later describe as a 'nice big house' and later as 'an enormously big house'. Petronella Calis had maids for both day and night and a nanny. There was a gramophone, and the Schillebeeckx children played with the children 'of the doctor and the minister of state'. At the age of 11 Edward went to a boarding school run by the Jesuits, which in Flanders too was regarded as the right kind of educational institution for the future Catholic middle class. Nevertheless, according to his son, 'the chartered accountant Schillebeeckx was ... considerably less well off than appearances might suggest', and his father had to work 'day and night'. Constant Schillebeeckx sometimes found it very difficult to pay the fees of the five children, who were all at the boarding school at the same time.[15]

Now for a long time, for Flemings, climbing the social ladder and being incorporated into the government apparatus meant submission to French-speaking culture. In the light of this it is striking that Edward was brought up to be fully Dutch-speaking. 'As a boy of eleven ... I spoke exclusively Dutch' he was to say later.

Like every Fleming, from the moment that he could speak Schillebeeckx became part of a social and cultural conflict which raged vigorously in Belgium after the First World War. He would experience it directly, for although the position of the Flemish was slowly improving after the war, for a long time French still remained the language of the official culture. When Edward Schillebeeckx left home in 1926 and went to the Jesuit college in Turnhout, which was likewise in Flanders – the province of Antwerp – teaching there was still almost completely in French. This harshly confronted him with his origins:

> It was terrible. I didn't know a word of French, and from one day to the next I had to listen to the language and speak it; all the notices were also given out in French.[16]

Because he clearly excelled at junior school, Schillebeeckx went to the Jesuit college really a year too young, at the age of 11. However, in Turnhout 'after a few weeks' he had 'to begin two years lower', and because of his lack of knowledge of French in fact had to 'redo the higher classes of the junior school'. This affected him a great deal. Like many others who had to fight against the handicaps of their origin in order to attain their position in society and culture, this event gave him, as he was to say later,

> the sense that I simply have to study hard. This passion for working hard began with this 'move' and it has never stopped. It has remained with me all my life: having to work hard is really second nature.[17]

However, the work ethic evidently fitted in well with what he was used to at home, with the picture that he had of 'father who was always working ... Father *couldn't* do *nothing* for a minute; he *had* to be busy.'[18]At all events, the result was that from then on at college he was always around the top of the class, and anyone who sees the notes that he made during his studies at secondary school and later will still be impressed by his capacity for work.

Moreover, the way in which the college confronted Schillebeeckx with the dominant position of the French made him define his political and ideological position for the first time. At school, according to his later testimony, he was an ardent nationalist Fleming. Indeed the sign of Catholic Flemish militancy, AVV – VVK (All for Flanders, Flanders for Christ), written in the form of a cross, appears on the notebooks from his boarding-school days. Later, in 1937, he would write an article for the Dominican student paper *Biekorf* in which he sympathized with the campaign for the constitutional unity of the Netherlands and Flanders, the so-called 'Dutch order', because this would be a fertile breeding-ground for a rich flourishing of the supernatural. In another article he was to fight for Dutch as a language of culture and for active efforts to achieve a 'Dutch expression of consciousness and the conscious'.[19]

Now dedication to the Flemish cause was not completely out of order at school. Whereas pressure from above forced the diocesan clergy to show great restraint in the social sphere, the religious clergy were very active in this area. Jesuits and also Dominicans played a prominent role in the Flemish movement. In this sense the designation 'anti-clerical' used of his home perhaps also denotes a position within the church. At all events, Schillebeeckx was to recall teachers from his time at school who committed themselves to the Flemish cause and opened the eyes of their pupils to philosophical questions and social, political and economic problems, also in a very specific way. Thus he told how with a socially-committed Father De Wit he gave lessons in religion to the young people from the poor neighbourhood of Turnhout who made the beds in college and served the pupils at table, and created a magazine for them.[20] Thus during his time at the Jesuit college Schillebeeckx developed a marked interest in social problems which was constantly to remain in his later work.

That the family from which Edward Schillebeeckx came was 'extremely Christian' was expressed specifically in their daily attendance at mass in the parish church in Kortenberg. From the age of 6 or 7 Edward served at mass. So they formed part of the wider structure of the Catholic Church, which, confronted with the bombardment of modernization, was also profoundly changing even between the world wars.

As the industrialization and modernization in Belgium continued, the leadership of the Catholic Church noted that it was losing its grip on cultural developments.[21] A whole set of new functions and professions was coming into being, which were needed to keep the ever more complicated society and its growing bureaucracy going. The organizational structure of the church and its culture of faith, which was strongly orientated on traditional rural society, was alien to the life of these new officials.[22] This gave pastors the feeling that a world was in the making in which they and their church would no longer play a role, from which they were excluded. The contemporary streets, the trams, the factories and workshops, the houses, the cafés and the assembly rooms, the songs and the books of modern culture, breathed a spirit which they could only understand as anti-religious. As a result, an increasingly intense debate developed over how the church had to react to modern society and how it needed to organize the Catholic influence on society which was thought necessary.[23]

This debate was being carried on all over the world. The real confrontation between the Catholic Church and modern society began in the first half of the nineteenth century with a thorough restructuring of the church. In order to safeguard its independence from the great changes in bourgeois society and the nation states, which were growing in power and influence, Roman church lawyers adopted in a new way the mediaeval idea that the church was a perfect, self-sufficient society, a *societas perfecta*. In this it differed from other social groups which were part of a greater whole, and so it had a right to complete independence from the state. Halfway through the century, Pope Pius IX (1846–78) adopted this argument and it was laid down in official church documents.[24] The intention of this operation was beyond doubt to protect the church against modern influences, but in order to achieve this, the hierarchy restructured the church as a modern counter-society. The church was organized on the model of the centralized nation state, with the pope at its head as an enlightened absolute ruler. In support of the fight against modernity which they believed to be necessary, from the second half of the nineteenth century church leaders emphasized the need for internal discipline and concentrated on organizing effective control of the everyday life of the faithful. In this connection all kinds of specific devotions and religious practices were propagated, in order to bind the people more closely to the church. These included daily churchgoing and – later, under Pius X (1903–14) – also daily communion.[25]

With the pontificate of Leo XIII (1878–1903) there was an important change in the confrontation of the Catholic Church with modernity. Leo's fundamental attitude to modern society continued to resemble that of his predecessors; according to him, too, modern society was in fact a 'counter-church', against which the Catholic Church needed to defend itself as a 'counter-society'.[26] Leo XIII attributed all that was bad – his first encyclical *Inscrutabili,* in a colourful summary, refers to the civil strife, the wars, the contempt for the laws of morality and justice and the insatiable craving for things perishable – to 'the setting aside of the holy and venerable authority of the Church'. He therefore commanded Catholics to defend and maintain 'the Church of Christ and the honour of the Apostolic See'.[27] But he was no longer content for the church just to defend itself; he wanted it to take the offensive against modern culture. In his view the church had to engage in conflict with the modern world in the various areas of modern culture itself, *in* the democratic political order, *in* the workers' movement, *in* science, *in* art and philosophy.[28] Leo XIII gave Catholics the explicit task of showing in all these spheres that the church had the solution to the urgent modern social problems that others were seeking. And that in fact meant a far-reaching shift in the church's attitude. The church no longer regarded modernity as a threat and opposed it, even if in fact it had the help of an organizational structure which was itself modern. What according to Leo XIII the church had to strive for in fact had the features of an alternative form of modernity: a harmonious, Catholic form. Leo XIII developed his own view of the outlines of such a Catholic modernity in the social doctrine of his famous encyclical *Rerum novarum*.

Leo gave the Catholic attitude towards what in Catholic circles was called 'the world' two aims, which could not easily be reconciled. Internally, everything was focused on maintaining unity and discipline, while externally an effort was made to achieve a Catholic presence in all the different spheres of life, a presence which was at first seen as being realized primarily by the clergy, but later also by the laity. Thus there was a clash between closedness and openness, antipathy and seeking contact with one another.[29] Champions of each attitude regularly clashed with those who thought that the other side of the Catholic attitude to modernity needed to be emphasized; each could always refer to official church documents for their case.

In the period before 1914 Belgian Catholicism was in fact dominated by the conservatives. They put strong emphasis on the independence of church government and were intent on maintaining and reinforcing unity and internal discipline. The Catholic restraint towards the Flemish movement fitted in with this attitude. Over against this stood those who called themselves 'Christian Democrats' and who emphasized the need to protect people against the evil consequences of modernity, especially the social distress that it caused. They wanted to challenge this with a Catholic view. The attitude of the Catholic intellectuals within the Flemish movement followed these lines. The conservatives thought that the Christian Democrats were stimulating the modern materialistic spirit of greed and ambition, and were ensuring that this, too, gained influence within the church, while the Christian Democrats accused the conservatives of leaving the people to their own devices and being concerned only with maintaining their own privileges.[30]

After the First World War the influence of the Christian Democrats in the Belgian church rapidly increased, although for some time the episcopate still maintained the conservative line. In particular, the fact that the introduction of the single universal vote for men[31] in 1919 led to the loss of the Catholic majority in the Belgian parliament for the first time since 1884 convinced wide circles that opposition to modern developments was not enough. The important thing was to guide them, to bring about a different modernity from the one that threatened to come into being.

Schillebeeckx was to grow up intellectually in a climate of open confrontation with modern developments, with the aim of influencing these in a Catholic direction. His first theological publications were also to be along these lines.

Not a Jesuit but a Dominican

In Turnhout the Belgian Jesuits had two schools side by side: one for boys who intended to become Jesuits and one for others. Louis, the oldest son of Constant Schillebeeckx and Petronella Calis, had been trained at the former institution before he became a Jesuit and was sent to India; with a number of his other brothers Edward went to the latter. After the summer vacation of 1926, at the age of 11, he was sent to college. According to his later memories he became particularly clear about the kind of Catholic that he did *not* want to be: he did *not* want to oppose the modern world. He went in search of another attitude, which he found among the Dominicans.

However, there are different interlocking levels in Schillebeeckx's memories of his schooldays. First of all, he evidently did not flourish in the boarding-school atmosphere. Later in interviews he made it abundantly clear that in the eight years that he spent at college – training lasted six years, plus the two preparatory years that he had to go through – he was not particularly happy:

> A boarding school and a minor seminary cannot be a substitute for father and mother. From your tenth or eleventh year you lack the warmth of the nest. I myself missed it a lot. I was extraordinarily happy when the holidays came and I could go home again, three times a year.[32]

For him the climate at the college contrasted too sharply with the situation at home and the relative freedom which the Schillebeeckx children had there; so for him boarding school was 'a kind of banishment into an alien world'.[33] He will not have been the only one. In one of his letters home he showed quite dramatically how the boys longed for news from home:

> We usually get letters here at mid-day, during dinner ... Father Prefect then has a whole packet of letters and distributes them to the boys, and

then you sit there open-eyed, to swallow up the letters, and then if you see that there's a letter for you, that's so nice.[34]

The fact that several Schillebeeckx children were at the college in Turnhout did not relieve the solitude, since, according to Schillebeeckx, 'pupils from different classes ... could not exchange words with one another. "A principle is a principle," said the Jesuit fathers.'[35]

This criticism of 'a principle is a principle', which he regarded as typical of the Jesuits, takes us to a second level. Schillebeeckx began to associate the oppressive rigidity of the boarding school regime directly with the spirituality of the Jesuits and later mentioned 'a principle is a principle' as an important reason for not seeking his future in this order. In connection with this he related how Father De Wit, the very person who had prompted him to do something for the 'servants' of the college, saw him talking with another boy during study time, when this was forbidden.

I claimed that it was quite reasonable to talk because the other boy was 'stuck'. But De Wit said: 'It is not allowed on principle.' 'The principle doesn't mean anything to me,' I retorted. 'That boy needed me.' Later, De Wit said to me: 'You were right. But principles take precedence.' I didn't like that at all ...[36]

In the religious atmosphere of the Jesuit college, based on rules, dogged dedication and a fighting spirit, Schillebeeckx evidently found 'no real inspiration but a rigid framework'.[37] It stood in too sharp a contrast with the intimate religion which he associated with his home. One of his earliest memories is a remark by his father who was explaining the figures in the crib to him: 'You see all those human figures there – and there is God, that baby is God.'[38] It is the feeling of the nearness of an awe-inspiring mystery, a feeling that was repeated whenever as a server at mass he saw the priest elevate the host, which always played an important role in his religion. According to the later ordering of his experiences, as a result he felt related to the 'priority of grace and "letting God be God"', which in his view were at the core of the spirituality of the Dominican order.[39] This is the third level of his reminiscences of the Jesuit college: his explanation of his later choice of the Dominicans. He felt that they had a much more open attitude to human nature and contemporary culture than the Jesuits. Of course this became clear only slowly. Schillebeeckx himself remarks that when he was about 15, in other words around 1929 or 1930, he was quite convinced that he wanted to become a Jesuit. He had become interested in Hinduism and Buddhism and like his brother wanted to go to India to study these religions.

He had arrived at this interest in Hinduism and Buddhism by reading the autobiography of the Jesuit William Wallace (1864–1922), *From Evangelical to Catholic by Way of the East*. This book, which his brother Louis had recommended him to read, told the story of an Anglican missionary with a very evangelical orientation who went to India from Ireland and through making close contact there with Hinduism, and becoming convinced of its religious authenticity, ultimately became a Catholic. Immediately after his conversion to Catholicism, in India Wallace had entered the Belgian province of the Jesuits, who had a mission to what was then Bengal, and served the last part of his novitiate at Drongen near Ghent. This relationship with his brothers in the Belgian order will be the reason why his biography, which was originally written in English, was translated into French and Dutch so soon after its appearance.[40]

From Evangelical to Catholic was a striking book. Wallace told how he departed from the custom of English missionaries and rented an Indian house in order to live among the Indians, not primarily to give them religious instruction but so as to be instructed by them in their thought and their culture. This approach started from what has now almost become a cliché, but at that time was an idea that was only slowly gaining ground, that the Christian faith would become attractive to Indians only if it proved possible to Christianize Indian thought, just as the church fathers had Christianized Greek thought.[41] This certainly appealed to Schillebeeckx's interest in society and culture. Wallace's book made it clear that such an interest did not clash with a commitment to Christian faith: quite the opposite. The central discovery which eventually led to Wallace's conversion was that *sanatana dharma*, the 'eternal religion', which he had learned to see after long study and observation as the religious heart of the collection of rites and customs which Westerners had baptized as 'Hinduism', 'is a natural "tutor to Christ"'. Conversely, Catholic faith was 'the fulfilment and perfection' of this religion.[42]

Wallace's view of Hinduism much resembled the way in which Schillebeeckx among the Dominicans was later to learn to look at modern Western culture: as the expression of a desire for God which, however, is at an impasse from which only Catholic Christianity can redeem it. Wallace saw in Hinduism on the one hand an authentic desire for God, a desire to die to the world in favour of 'being-alone-with-God', which in his view was also central to Christianity. On the other hand, in his view Hinduism fell short as a religion because people did not create the right means for fulfilling this longing. The consequence was that in his eyes 'despair ... [was] unavoidable for the millions of India', a despair which according to Wallace led them to seek refuge in magic and idolatry and which finally led to the opposite of authentic religion: to 'enjoyment of the world and forgetfulness of God'. In his eyes the solution to this aporia was offered by Catholicism, in which dying to the world and rising to God was a matter not of one's own efforts but of fellowship with Jesus Christ. This is the necessary way to take and it invites all to enter into fellowship with him through the church.[43]

The harmony between the social interest of Indian life, the intellectual interest of the Indian religions and the superiority of the Christian faith which automatically comes to light in this process, all of which were suggested by Wallace, made Schillebeeckx long to go to India too, to study Hinduism and Buddhism and to compare them with Christianity. Just as Wallace wrote in his later years that he had almost given up preaching in favour of 'the study of Hindu thought and Hindu spirituality', so Schillebeeckx recalled that he did not so much have the intention of 'playing the missionary'. His main concern was 'the confrontation between Christianity, Hinduism and Buddhism'.[44] He remembered above all being struck by the 'parallels between the Trinity in Christian teaching and similar features, such as the Trimurti with Brahma, Vishnu and Shiva in Hinduism'.[45]

During the penultimate year, the classes of the Jesuit college in Turnhout went on retreat. In the academic year 1932/3 it was the turn of Schillebeeckx's class. The aim was that the boys themselves, led by a Jesuit father and in the manner that Ignatius Loyola describes in his *Spiritual Exercises*, should consider the question of the choice that they should make for their future life. However, Schillebeeckx would later recall the retreat as 'angling', 'fishing for vocations' to the Jesuit life, 'indoctrination in the garb of objectivity'. This put his back up. According to a later interpretation it made him realize that his desire to enter the Society of Jesus was more about going to India than about becoming a Jesuit.[46] Probably it is more accurate to say that he increasingly began to doubt whether the ideal of a missionary and intellectual life in public which was on offer and as he had found it in Wallace's *From Evangelical to Catholic* was in fact compatible with Jesuit spirituality, which he identified to a large degree with the strict rules of boarding school life: 'I thought, "Before you get a chance to live, they spoil your life."'[47]

Whether or not it happened as a result of the retreat we can no longer discover, but in the academic year 1932/3 Schillebeeckx was strongly preoccupied with the growing conviction that he had to give himself 'wholly and utterly to the salvation of souls'. 'Even before Christmas that ideal began to take possession of me like a passion,' he wrote to his father on 10 March 1933. He wanted to make a direct contribution and

here I was stupid about everything. People here often accuse me of being too extreme and idealistic in everything. I wore myself out, above all in the evening when I was thinking about this in my bed. In the morning when I got up I felt shattered: a severe headache. I studied and swotted, so

32

as to achieve that ideal later in the best way. I acknowledge it now, it was somewhat excessive. There wasn't enough calm in my soul.

Evidently he had written about this to his brother in India, but his father had caught sight of the letter and urged him to be calm. Edward promised that he would stop wearing himself out, would be calm, 'study often but in moderation, play and pray, as you advise me', though he added that it would cause him 'a great, great deal of difficulty, since I'm so impetuous'.

We cannot now discover what took place in Schillebeeckx's soul in the first half of 1933. It is certain that it was completely clear to him that he had a 'vocation' and wanted to dedicate himself to the salvation of souls. The secular priesthood did not attract him, probably also because as a diocesan priest he would have no opportunity to be involved in the social questions in which he had become interested at the Jesuit college.[48] As he himself says, he then began systematically to read the accounts of the lives of the founders of the great monastic orders: Ignatius of Loyola, Dominic, Francis of Assisi and Benedict of Nursia. On the basis of this comparative investigation he ultimately opted for the Dominicans. On 14 May 1933 he wrote a letter to the prior of the Dominican convent at Ghent, where the novitiate for the Flemish Dominicans was based.[49] The book by Humbert Clérissac (1864–1914) on the spirit of St Dominic played a central role in this move to the Dominicans.[50] For apart from a single chance meeting, Schillebeeckx had never had any contact with the Dominicans. Clérissac's book gave him the idea that Dominic had inspiration and little feeling for rules, a combination which specially attracted him after experiencing what he felt to be precisely the opposite for years at boarding school: many rules and little inspiration.

Much later he formulated the attraction of the Dominican spirit for himself like this:

> [The] constant allusion by St Dominic, in faith, to concrete historical circumstances, out of an intellectual reflection on the faith which so characterizes the theological inspiration of St Dominic, was most attractive to me.[51]

Now in this remark beyond doubt he projected back the combination of 'the two poles which I rediscover everywhere in my theology: the world of God – the religious world – and the worldly situation of the human world' on to the founder of the order to which he belonged and on to the book that lies at the origin of his own association with it. But Schillebeeckx's interpretation of the spirit of Dominic is very much along the lines of Clérissac's book. Clérissac himself had become a Dominican after reading the life of St Dominic by Dominique Lacordaire (1802–61).[52] All his life Lacordaire sought a place for Christian faith in the radically changed circumstances after the French Revolution. He vigorously opposed the nostalgia of French Catholics for the *ancien régime* and wanted to start from the separation of church and state. In his view, in this situation it was not primarily the structures or specific church customs that were important but the inspiration that a radical Christian life could provide for post-revolutionary culture. Hence he committed himself to the restoration and reform of the religious life. He found inspiration for this in the biography of Dominic who, at the beginning of the thirteenth century, deliberately dissociating himself from established church structures, went around preaching in poverty and precisely by so doing could successfully proclaim the Christian message. In 1836 Lacordaire joined the Dominicans in Rome, and in 1840 he succeeded in re-establishing the order on French soil after religious orders had been forbidden there since 1790.

Clérissac did not write a biography of Dominic, but made an attempt to present the Dominican spirit as he saw it, along the lines of Lacordaire. In his view, an unconditional dedication to the supernatural truth was fundamental to Dominican spirituality. However, he did not regard this truth as dry intellectual knowledge. The central image in his book is that of the Catholic empire established by Benedictine monks as colonists in Europe, which subsequently had to be permeated with the vital spirit of 'love' (*caritas*) and 'truth' (*veritas*); Francis and his order embodied the first aspect of this spirit, Dominic and his order the second.[53] According to Clérissac, in order to continue to embody this spirit of *veritas* in the changed circumstances of modern times, a form of study was needed which put people in a position to see every branch of scholarship as a contribution to the knowledge of the natural and revealed truth and to catch a glimpse in it of what Clérissac calls, in a paraphrase of the Gospel of John, the light which lightens every man and has come in this world.[54] There is a clear affinity between this theological view of scholarship, focused on God and the divine presence in the world, on the one hand, and on the other the breadth of Schillebeeckx's later conception of theology and his propensity to enter into conversation with other disciplines.

However, according to Clérissac, just as necessary as study is the religious experience which as it were forms its soul, the personal, serene and complete grasping of the exaltation of God as the ultimate object of all faith and knowledge.[55] According to Clérissac, life in the Dominican spirit is life in this presence, and this conviction leads him to make a remark which the 18-year-old Edward Schillebeeckx evidently took to heart, given his later way of working: 'When we study, teach or preach, let our heart and our wills follow the impulse of our mind towards God.'[56] A clear line runs from Clérissac's view of the Dominican spirit to Schillebeeckx's constant emphasis on the need to do theology from experience with a view to clarifying that experience, 'in search of the living God'.[57]

34

As I have said, on 14 May Schillebeeckx wrote a letter to the novitiate of the Dominicans, and on 16 May Father Mannes Matthijs, prior of the Dominican convent in Ghent, replied with a letter inviting him to come to visit them, 'for there are things which one must investigate or see at close hand to have a right view of them'.[58] Some weeks later Matthijs, evidently at Schillebeeckx's request, was to approach his father to ask him to approve this visit.[59] What was more important in connection with Schillebeeckx's future, however, was that in his answer, as Schillebeeckx was later to remember, Matthijs enclosed a reproduction of a fresco in which Dominic was embracing Francis. This made a great impression:

> It radiated warmth. Friendships were not allowed in the Jesuit houses and anything that was even remotely connected with emotion was squashed at once. But suddenly a Dominican I didn't even know sent me a picture depicting human warmth.[60]

Having first been interested in the Dominican order for intellectual reasons, Schillebeeckx was now touched at a place where he was vulnerable. At college he had had the feeling of being starved of human warmth. Whereas – rightly or wrongly – he thought that the Jesuits stood in the way of the unfolding of life, Matthijs emphatically assured him of his desire to make him happy. All this confirmed him in his choice of the Dominicans, as did later visits to the convents in Ghent and in Louvain: 'I feel happy here,' he wrote to his father during his first visit to Ghent, and he reported straight away that he wanted to become a Dominican: 'to pray, to study and to do penance, and so to help one's fellow human being'.[61]

Schillebeeckx entered the Dominican order on 20 September 1934 in Ghent. When he entered the order, the Dominican Henricus Suso (1295–1366) became his patron. The name of the author on most of the publications from his Flemish period is Henricus, sometimes Henricus Maria Schillebeeckx. Suso was a disciple of Eckhart, but more than the latter emphasized the surrender of one's own will and one's own mind to God, and abandonment as the other side of the sweet vision of God's wisdom in the form of the crucified Jesus. During the first period of Schillebeeckx's theological development the motif of sacrifice would play a prominent role in his work, perhaps also as a consequence of reading Suso's work.

He remembers liking the novitiate. Although he had little contact with the outside world – 'we hear nothing about what's going on with Hitler or Mussolini', he wrote to his parents on 15 November 1934 – he found a bit of the freedom which he knew from home. Outside the compulsory initiation into the religious life, to his satisfaction he was allowed a good deal of free time which he used to read 'the great mystics': Ruysbroeck, Teresa of Avila, Catherine of Siena, John of the Cross, Tauler, Eckhart 'and my Dominican patron, Henricus Seuse, Suso'.[62] Although in retrospect Schillebeeckx suggested that it was an independent initiative and a personal characteristic, he was standing in a Dominican tradition when in order to be initiated into an independent and adult spiritual life he turned to the mystics. Whereas especially in the eighteenth century mysticism was increasingly seen as a miraculous, direct contact with the divine, granted only in very exceptional circumstances to very special people, a turning point came at the end of the nineteenth century. In 1885 the French Dominican André-Marie Meynard, in his 'Treatise on the Inner Life', presented mysticism not as something miraculous but as the supreme expression of the virtues directed towards God which the Holy Spirit gave to all believers: faith, hope and love. In the period between the two world wars, another French Dominican, Réginald Garrigou-Lagrange (1877–1964), described mysticism along these lines as a further flourishing of a consistently Christian life of faith, but one that was in principle normal.[63] A Dominican school in the interpretation of mysticism developed in his footsteps. The picture of the mystic as an advanced believer made it logical to read mystical texts to intensify and deepen the life of faith, as Schillebeeckx did at the time of his novitiate. Throughout his further career, moreover, he was to continue to be interested in the mystics.

In contrast to his time with the Jesuits at boarding school, among the Dominicans Schillebeeckx clearly felt at home. But the novitiate was not an unqualified delight. Thus he later recalled the parting from his parents as emotional and difficult. They felt that their child was distancing himself from them, and to a great degree indeed he was: at that time a religious could maintain contact with their family only by letters. Moreover, he remembers that his novice master was a cool, distant man. 'None of us liked him.'[64]

He would, though, remember in the first instance being deeply impressed by the monastic night prayer, from 3 a.m. to 4 a.m., while people outside were sleeping. However, when he wrote home about this, he got back a sobering letter from his father, which in retrospect he regarded as '*the* most uplifting experience of [his] novitiate'. At this time Petronella Calis and Constant Schillebeeckx had just had their fourteenth child and his father wrote to him, according to Edward's later paraphrase:

> My boy, mother and I get up three or four times a night to calm a crying baby, and that is less romantic than your nocturnal worship. Remember it: religion is not a state of feeling but an attitude of service.[65]

This is more than an interpretation of his father's letter in the light of his later theological views, although beyond doubt it is also that. His father's letter has not been preserved, but in Schillebeeckx's reaction as it has been handed down, it appears that his father had in fact accused him of a 'romantic longing to give himself wholly'. And in fact he confessed that before he entered the religious life that he had seen it as doing 'one great deed'; though he said that by now he knew that it was a matter of 'tackling little things which stand in the way of human nature' and which thus must teach him to be a good religious; during these years (the letter is dated 11 October 1934) he still thought of the religious life strongly in terms of dying to the world and a misdirected human nature which was shut in on itself. With the emphasis that he put in his later theologizing on the practical experience of faith in God, and with the opposition that he indicated to religious ideas and feelings isolated from reality, Schillebeeckx at all events seems to have developed along the lines of his father's religious attitude.

However much he was impressed by choral prayer in the middle of the night combined with the 'Dominican fasts which began with the elevation of the cross on 14 September and went on to the following Easter', Schillebeeckx found life as a novice difficult. In retrospect he related that in the choir he regularly fainted and eventually had to go to bed with serious anaemia. Be this as it may, he later interpreted the fact that this did not lead to his expulsion from the house but to a dispensation from night prayer and fasting as confirmation of the idea that among the Dominicans human wellbeing was rated higher than the rules. As Schillebeeckx remembers it, the then provincial of the Belgian province made the terse remark: 'Better a living ass than a dead lion.' When he himself later took on the responsibility of training young Dominicans, Schillebeeckx tried to continue this line:

I thought that religious life had to be a happy life: make you whole, not destroy you physically. Later as *spiritualis* of the student brothers I often asked them whether they felt happy and also physically well with us in the house. If that was not the case, I consistently (of course after many difficult conversations) sent them home again.[66]

STUDY WITH THE DOMINICANS

The novitiate aimed at introducing young men to life within the Dominican order. A year after his entry, on 21 September 1935, Schillebeeckx made his profession and began his training for the priesthood. At this time this training consisted of three years' study of philosophy and four years' study of theology. In the meantime the students were also trained further as Dominicans; the so-called *magister* (master) of the students was responsible for this training. Schillebeeckx studied philosophy in Ghent, in the same house in which the novitiate was also based. The master of the students and professor in philosophy there was Dominicus De Petter, who was to have a great influence on Schillebeeckx's development.

Studying philosophy in Ghent

When Schillebeeckx began his study, everything within Catholic philosophy was shifting. That was directly connected with its key position in Leo XIII's offensive against the modern world. In Leo's view modern society was governed by a collection of pernicious convictions. In particular he attacked the liberal idea of freedom: in his view the great importance that the modern world attached to freedom ultimately led to 'the rejection of the holy and venerable authority of the Church' which 'in God's name rules mankind, upholding and defending all lawful authority'. Leo set over against the emphasis on freedom the need for submission to an absolute authority, specifically that of 'the Church of Christ and ... the Apostolic See'.[67] But if this call was to be credible, a comprehensive system of thought was necessary which gave expression to the church's claims in the modern world. This system of thought needed to offer an alternative to liberalism and socialism, which in different ways gave freedom a central place, and to be capable of holding the church together as a *societas perfecta*. Leo found such a system in the work of the mediaeval theologian Thomas Aquinas. In 1870 his encyclical *Aeterni patris* declared that in Thomas's work reason and faith, philosophy and theology, were brought together in a synthesis which was a model for Catholics. Catholic thinkers had to take his system as a starting point and oppose all kinds of false systems of thought which were the cause of disasters – war, social unrest – that affected modern culture in so clearly visible a way.[68]

The interpretation of the work of Thomas Aquinas which was dominant within Catholic thought roughly between 1850 and 1950 reflected the project formulated by Leo XIII. Its starting point was that Catholics in the different social spheres had to fight on behalf of the power of the church, because only the church could save modern society, which had broken loose of all norms and ties. To support this position he appealed to Thomas's starting point that grace did not destroy nature, but perfected it. In ecclesiastical Thomism, 'nature' here stood for the world as it is in itself, for human beings with their particular needs and desires, and for society and culture as they try to make provision for these needs and desires. 'Grace' stood for what according to the church's conviction God had revealed about this world in the Bible and the Catholic tradition, for the sanctifying effect of the church on individual human life and for the corrective influence of the church on modern society and culture. With the help of Thomas's slogan, ecclesiastical Thomism succeeded in combining two thoughts here. Human reason and human culture had to be developed as much as possible – grace does not destroy nature – but this development needed to be subjected to the faith of the church – grace perfects nature – and more specifically to the power and influence of the church hierarchy.[69]

When after the First World War the dynamizing power of modernity came to light with renewed vigour, there were all kinds of attempts to reformulate Leo XIII's programme so that it was adequate for the changed circumstances. With renewed intensity there was a discussion of the church's attitude to contemporary culture – I shall be returning to this at length – and in theology and especially also philosophy there were different attempts to interpret the work of Thomas Aquinas in a way which left room for a real conversation and real confrontation between church faith on the one hand and the modern world, human nature and contemporary philosophy based on human reason on the other. As a student of philosophy, Schillebeeckx came almost directly into contact with these attempts. He would join in them with all his heart. One example of the climate of thought that he entered was the work of that Mannes Matthijs (1892–1972) who as prior of the Ghent convent had invited him for a visit in 1933. Matthijs also taught philosophy to the Dominicans, but as he was nominated professor at the Dominican university in Rome, the Angelicum, in 1935, Schillebeeckx would not have any lessons from him.[70] Nevertheless, Schillebeeckx later spoke with great affection of 'the man through whose loving philosophical influence I had finally become a Dominican'.[71]

Schillebeeckx interpreted the picture of Francis and Dominic embracing which Matthijs had sent to him as a sign that human friendship was not opposed to relations with God, but that this natural human affection had an organic place in striving for an encounter with God. This accurately conveyed Matthijs' conviction. His thought was governed by the idea that the human soul was by nature Christian because it was created in the image and likeness of God. Christian faith was the explicit answer to the revelation of this same God. Therefore in Matthijs' eyes Christian faith had to be on the same wavelength as the natural desire in human beings; the natural, created order and the supernatural order were at the deepest level in harmony with one another. According to Matthijs, reason in its reflection on created human existence ultimately had the same focus as faith: with reason a person presumed and with faith believed that human nature was capable of ever greater perfection. God has revealed himself 'in order to lead man to his final supernatural destiny', although this destiny lies 'far above the demand of purely created nature, however much it is also in harmony with it'.[72]

In the 1930s, however, this was no longer truly innovative, but in Dominican circles rather the current exposition of Thomas's view of the relationship between 'nature' and 'supernature'. Indeed, at his death Matthijs was especially praised as a good specialist, as 'a great expert in the teaching of Thomas, which he could analyse very perceptively'. However, it was characteristic of the climate in which Schillebeeckx was brought up that Matthijs had a predilection for 'the philosophical approach to theological problems', as was said in his obituary.[73] Specifically, this meant that he clung to an independent way of thinking faith through with the help of human reason and in confrontation with contemporary human culture. He had no affinity with theology as a discipline, which at this time was usually limited to handing down and expounding traditional doctrine and demonstrating that it was in accordance with the official statements of the hierarchy.

Dominicus – 'Domien' – De Petter (1905–71) was the man who in this climate actually taught Schillebeeckx philosophy and in this way had a deep influence on his later theology. De Petter brought Schillebeeckx into direct contact with the tradition of the specifically Catholic philosophy which resulted from the impulse that Leo XIII had given to it. Matthijs had received his philosophical training at the major seminary of the dioceses of Luik and Hasselt at St-Truiden.[74] As a would-be teacher in philosophy De Petter was deliberately sent by his Dominican superiors to the Higher Institute of Philosophy at Louvain.

Various initiatives were developed at the instigation of Leo XIII with the aim of developing a Catholic philosophy which was really in a position to formulate an answer to the questions raised by modern times and modern thought. One of them was the establishment at Louvain of the 'Institut Supérieur de Philosophie' in 1889, associated with the Catholic university there, but independent of it. The spiritual father of the institute was Désiré Mercier (1851–1926), who was later to become Archbishop of Belgium. In the 1920s and 1930s lectures were also increasingly given in Dutch at the originally completely French-speaking institute; as a result of this it also became quite influential in Flanders.[75] Mercier himself had already given the philosophy of the Institut Supérieur a clear colouring of its own. Although Mercier, too, following the line of Leo XIII, regarded the synthesis of 'Aristotle and St Thomas' as the abiding norm for all philosophy, he emphasized strongly that philosophy was *seeking* truth and therefore presupposed freedom of thought. This meant that philosophy at Louvain did not preach a rigid doctrine, legitimated by the church hierarchy, but developed into a true intellectual confrontation of Catholic thought with modernity.

Louvain epistemology is especially important in connection with Schillebeeckx's philosophical development. For Mercier, the basis of all human knowing was the givenness of experience. People experienced reality, and this was subsequently reshaped, through analysis and synthesis, description, comparison and induction, from a diffuse and disordered whole into synthetic knowledge of the truth. In this view the specific disciplines were focused, by means of a well-considered methodology, on a specific and limited area of experience; metaphysics penetrated to the last causes and gave an account by bringing together what it discovered to form a comprehensive synthesis.[76] Following Mercier's line, De Petter also firmly emphasized that experience is the starting point of all knowledge, a view which Schillebeeckx was to adopt. Moreover, De Petter took into account the views of his immediate teachers on the experiential basis of metaphysics. Léon Noël (1878–1953) posited that in the experiential knowledge of entities being is immediately present in an intuition, as the object of metaphysical thinking.[77] Along the same lines, Nicolas Balthasar (1882–1959) defended the view that being is experienced intuitively along with the entity.[78]

As a philosopher De Petter was not interested in a rigid construction of thought, nor did he want any system. He supported a philosophy which 'is born in a living contact of the reflective spirit with reality itself, as this may then really be accessible in its own time'. And that implied that he did not want to do philosophy as a form of neo-Thomism. As a Catholic thinker he wanted to philosophize in connection with his own culture. Born into a French-speaking family, De Petter powerfully championed equal rights for Flemish, and a distinctive Flemish contribution to philosophical life.[79] He was convinced that 'the revival of Dutch culture in Flanders had reached the level of philosophical thought' and therefore along with a number of other Dominican ex-students at the Higher Institute in 1939 founded *Tijdschrift voor Philosophie*, intended as a broad Dutch-language forum for the practice of philosophy.[80] The journal set out to give direction; emphatically not, however, by

> imposing a narrow and closed standpoint, but by assimilating in a broad constructive spirit all valuable elements both of tradition and of modern philosophical life, and in this way helping to build up an enriched philosophical synthesis.[81]

As I have said, De Petter was a professional philosopher. He was not at all afraid of technical discussions. The central starting point in his philosophy was the conviction that knowledge did not just presuppose a known object and a knowing subject. In his view this was wrongly the starting point not only of modern epistemology in the tradition of René Descartes, Francis Bacon, David Hume and Immanuel Kant, but still also of the phenomenology of Edmund Husserl. According to De Petter, Husserl's philosophical renewal was of great importance, and he derived a great deal from Husserl's philosophy, but in his eyes Husserl did not go far enough. According to De Petter, knowledge of an object presupposed just as much an implicit grasp of the whole of the reality of which object and subject together made up a part. With Noël and Balthasar he turned against the notion that the thought of entities is brought into being through the abstract concepts of metaphysics, a notion which had a large following in ecclesiastical Thomism. In this view, which De Petter labelled 'conceptualistic', it was the metaphysical concepts which brought reality together into a totality. In fact this meant that the

41

concepts which had been developed in the Thomistic tradition, and thus this tradition itself, are seen as the guarantor of the correct view of reality. The consequence that this had for church politics was that the abandonment of Thomistic concepts was seen as a departure from Catholic thought. In De Petter's view, metaphysical concepts explicated an experience implicitly present in the knowledge of reality, which made it possible to ask whether the traditional Thomistic concepts expressed this experience adequately. According to him, philosophical reflection on the fact that I know something brought to light the fact that the knower and the known, subject and object, form part of a whole that binds them together. Shortly after Schillebeeckx had studied with him, De Petter was to launch in public the notion of an 'implicit intuition of totality', a contact with the whole of reality as this is present in the knowledge of each part of it.[82]

De Petter's philosophy was to become the starting-point for Schillebeeckx's specific theological approach: as Schillebeeckx himself was to say later, he 'really laid the philosophical basis of my later theological thinking'.[83] Whereas the conceptualistic approach of neoscholasticism in principle made philosophy and theology a collection of the correct doctrinal statements that unified human experience, which was chaotic without them, for De Petter philosophizing in terms of 'implicit intuition' connected Catholic thought directly with human experience. As will become clear later, Schillebeeckx was to combine the totality of being which is also experienced in the implicit intuition more explicitly than De Petter with God as spoken of in Christian faith. This produced specific complications, but also new possibilities.

During the time that Schillebeeckx was studying in Ghent, as well as teaching philosophy De Petter was also *magister* of the students of philosophy and responsible for their further spiritual training. In retrospect Schillebeeckx was to say that De Petter was 'very strict' in this function, but he also depicted him as an amiable man who regarded the rules of monastic life as secondary, a necessary means of getting to the heart of it, communion with God:

> ... from him I also ... gained the sense of the absolute priority of grace over all human efforts, and that produced ... calm, despite all his strictness; that avoided coercion. From De Petter I learned – I experienced with him – that God is to be trusted.[84]

But De Petter's main influence on Schillebeeckx was intellectual. De Petter was the specific reason why Schillebeeckx – like other student priests of his generation and also of the generation after him – was initially more interested in philosophy than in theology. In philosophy a reasonable degree of freedom prevailed within Catholic thought. Moreover, philosophy in

Ghent, also under the influence of De Petter, was open and focused on human beings and society. By contrast, theology was usually a lifeless analysis of church doctrine, subject to rigid rules. Or, as Schillebeeckx himself was to put it later: 'theology was at that time mainly a matter of juggling with concepts'.[85] Against this conceptualism he was to test the possibilities that De Petter's idea of an 'implicit intuition' offered. Thus he succeeded in allowing the dynamic which Catholic philosophy was able to develop to influence theology in its confrontation with modernity, and he could make it clear that theology was about real, existentially important, questions.

He published his first philosophical article as early as 1936, in the Dominican student journal *Biekorf*. With good reason this creative use of the approaches of De Petter, who was a militant supporter of the use of Flemish, had as a title a quotation from Guido Gezelle (1830–99), who was regarded as *the* poet by the Flemish movement: 'When the soul listens . . .'.[86] In the first instance Schillebeeckx quoted only the first two lines of this poem, and even then not in full: 'When the soul listens, it speaks a language.' After this, the poem has 'that lives', and by omitting these words Schillebeeckx distanced himself from the romantically coloured nature mysticism which is expressed in the poem. Unlike Gezelle, in this article he saw the soul first of all as the comprehending, rational aspect of being human, in full agreement with the Aristotelian–Thomistic tradition. However, it is striking that the more emotional aspect did play a major role, but in direct connection with thought. Indeed, in the end the article seems meant as a commentary on the whole poem:

When the soul listens
it speaks a language that lives,
the gentlest whisper
also has a language and sign:
the rustling of the trees
chatting quickly together,
the burbling of the streams
clapping loudly and happily,
wind and wave and clouds,
paths of God's holy foot,
speak and interpret
the deeply delved Word so sweet . . .
when the soul listens.[87]

Schillebeeckx's article also introduced a dogmatic reference to God's Word as the divine origin of creation.

It is a good illustration of the possibilities offered by De Petter's philosophy that Schillebeeckx could connect this emotional, mystical poem with

Aristotle, the 'rigid, surly, uncompromising, steely thinker' who was known in scholasticism as 'the Philosopher' and as such played such a central role in Catholic thought. His abstract thought about God as thinking which thinks itself and as an unrestricted act of contemplation had been taken over in Catholic philosophy. Schillebeeckx thought that in Aristotle he had found an intuition of reality which supported these thoughts and gave them ultimate significance, an intuition which resembled that of Gezelle's listening soul. This intuition ensured that Aristotle's thought was ultimately 'coloured by life, by higher life' (6). It seems to be the true joy of discovery – 'something just struck me that I want to develop' – that made Schillebeeckx quote Aristotle's definition of *theoria*, contemplation, calling it the 'delight and the best' of human existence. In the quotation that Schillebeeckx had come across, Aristotle goes on to argue that if God – as contemplation *per se* – is always in this good state in which human beings are only now and then, it is admirable, and if he is in a better state, that is even more admirable: and indeed God is in this better state. In this passage Schillebeeckx thought that he had grasped Aristotle as 'truly emotional, in the deepest life of his soul', and in order to express that, he paraphrased Aristotle's argument as follows:

> Contemplation ... is of the best, the noblest, that there is: the supreme pleasure. We have that happiness only now and then, just once in a while. That's all. That God always possesses this happiness is truly striking. And there is more: that He has this to a still higher (infinite) degree, how sublime that is! It is impossible to understand something so entrancing ... and yet true.[88]

First of all, it was important for Schillebeeckx that Aristotle as the thinker *par excellence* could be caught up in the same ecstasy as the poet, that the truth discovered by reason could be as emotional as the poetic view. It proved that metaphysics could lead to admiration, and was capable of making the philosopher 'stand in ecstasy before the transcendent deity' (4f.). According to him, Aristotle made it clear that thought could be as emotional as poetry, and as religious. If Gezelle's view can be called poetical and mystic, then the view that Schillebeeckx developed in 'When the soul listens ...', in dialogue with Aristotle, is rational and mystical. His concern was to develop this rational, mystical view.

In his view, reason, philosophy, lived by contact with being in things, which ultimately was the presence of the divine. With the obvious pleasure of the budding lecturer he explained here how according to Aristotle knowing was not knowing about material things in themselves but knowing about their ideas. These ideas did not rest in themselves and for Aristotle were therefore incomplete. But precisely in their incompleteness they pointed to an idea that *was* complete, in other words an idea which not only knew other ideas but also produced them in thought. According to Aris-

44

totle, this idea which thought itself, which produced all ideas and brought them to unity, was God. Schillebeeckx concluded from this that for Aristotle reality points in its depths to God, in other words 'not the reality that we only see' but 'the same reality into which we have insight'. He read in Aristotle that the human being was an image of God and through reality was to be seen as a pointer to God. On the one hand the human being was a broken image, for, as Aristotle already said, whereas God always contemplated himself, human beings contemplated God only now and then. Nevertheless, by contemplating God, in reality human beings participated in God's self-contemplation, and according to Schillebeeckx this fact, together with having knowledge of it and knowing that in this way one was being taken up and finding oneself in God's life, was the deepest and ultimate ground of the ecstasy which Aristotle expressed when he talked about God as contemplation *par excellence* (5f.). In his view this was at the same time the basis of the joy of the believing thinker.

Anyone who knew the idea, the presence of the divine or – in the terms which Gezelle in his poem had borrowed from the beginning of the Gospel of John and which Schillebeeckx took over – of the 'deeply delved Word' in things, knew God (20f.). And according to Schillebeeckx that was ultimately the same God who created heaven and earth and all things. 'Each thing interprets a notion of God,' he said, following mediaeval scholasticism, 'and when the soul listens, this idea is grasped in everything'; then the word that expresses this thought is heard in things (14). Here was religious experience in the sense in which Clérissac had used this word in his book about the spirit of Dominic: grasping the exalted nature of God as the ultimate object of all knowledge. Now the notion that natural, philosophical thought could in this way lead to knowledge of God was not without problems in Catholic thought. It undermined the conviction that the church tradition was the only trustworthy access to God. At the end of 'When the soul listens ... ', in the classical manner Schillebeeckx still tried to maintain the difference between the philosophical and the theological approach to God: whereas Aristotle as a philosopher on the basis of intellectual life did not evade the conclusion *that* God is, as a theologian Thomas Aquinas was to disclose on the basis of the life of faith *who* God is (23). But according to Schillebeeckx's reading of Aristotle, precisely this distinction was difficult to maintain. In 'When the soul listens ... ' he described philosophy as reflection on an intuitive lived contact with reality and with the divine in it.

In the course of his development he was to begin to see theology increasingly as a deeper fulfilment, a special form of philosophy in this sense, a further focus of its way of thinking and the content of its thought.[89]

However, for the moment Schillebeeckx was presenting himself as a philosopher. In 1937 and 1938 an article by him in two parts appeared in *Biekorf* on the philosophers who were thought to represent the prehistory of their discipline, the so-called pre-Socratics. Against the background of the dominant picture of philosophy in ecclesiastical Thomism it is striking that in their undisciplined text, lacking clear, let alone technical and abstract, terminology, he saw the expression of authentic philosophizing. Because he had learned from De Petter that what is determinative for philosophy is not a systematizing terminology but the living contact with being in things, in his eyes the pre-Socratics were philosophers indeed.[90]

More important for Schillebeeckx's development is the article published in *Biekorf* two years after 'When the soul listens ... ' under the title 'Consciousness of being and rationality'. It is an attempt to elaborate the notion that philosophical knowledge is based on an intuition of being which is implied in living contact with reality. The article is in fact a technical philosophical essay, which according to Schillebeeckx's later testimony was written at the request of De Petter, who had asked him 'to find out the best ways of transcending conceptuality', a question which deeply interested him.[91] It is probably more accurate to say that Schillebeeckx here showed how much he had made De Petter's approach his own. 'Consciousness of being and rationality' is dated November 1938, and some months later, at the beginning of 1939, the article in which De Petter summed up his epistemology appeared under the title 'Implicit intuition'.[92] Completely in line with De Petter, in 'Consciousness of being and rationality' Schillebeeckx was concerned above all with the contact between thought and living reality, and criticized the dominant scholasticism for its 'conceptualism'. Here, according to Schillebeeckx, it a priori joined up with 'all that is good in present-day philosophy', which was interested in concrete reality, and touched on it in contradiction with 'our mind', which calls us 'to the concrete' (170). Schillebeeckx wanted to link up with what he saw as a central discovery of contemporary existentialist philosophy:

The present-day philosophical reflections which are bound up with life have rightly branded rationalism a living lie. The tame Enlightenment ideal of equilibrium, self-confident citizenship, has just had a rude awakening. Reality cannot be formulated. People have again gained a sense of mystery – including natural mystery. For our life is permeated with mystery. People now 'believe' in mysteries. And in all human knowledge there is doubtless a grain of irrationality, a crumb of 'faith', a touch of risk, a bit of verve (110).[93]

According to 'Consciousness of being and rationality', all knowledge presupposed a living, evident intuition of the total of reality, albeit confused and implicit.

The whole thing amounts to the fact that the content of our consciousness makes no sense, cannot be explained in such a way that we do not put at the beginning of it – as something that always remains – an intuition, an experience which comprehends the original whole, which expresses all those perfections in the rational content, synthesizes them in itself in an inexpressible way (125).

In knowledge human beings stand over against an entity which shows itself to be independent, gives itself to be known and can be known. Here the subject experiences itself on the one hand as an entity which stands over against the known entity, and on the other as an entity which is united with this entity in knowledge. That can be the case only because there is something in which both participate, and this is being: therefore every experience contains what in 'Consciousness of being and rationality' is called an 'intuitivity of being'. His conclusion is that 'the basic experience of a human being is thus the experience of his being-implied in being' (127), in which it is taken up with everything and everyone. Being is experienced along with all experiences and integrates them; it is the condition of their possibility and their background:

> Because in [the] experience of being the intellectual, the volitional and even the emotive grow together into one intellectual act – intellectual experience – I would dare to call the experience of being a feeling of being, in the supra-rational sense of the word (and thus not in the infra-rational sense of a purely subjective emotion, 'feeling'). It is a presence, and that is perhaps the best expression for those who understand the fullness of the word (137).

In Schillebeeckx's view the concepts of philosophy and the sciences simply explained this presence, but as abstractions from the concrete experience of being in things, so that they were necessarily inadequate. Because any expression was inadequate, progress was possible in knowledge, a growth in adequacy, something that in his view was in fact inconceivable within conceptualism.

The whole of the second part of 'Consciousness of being and rationality' was devoted to the relative but real value of conceptual knowledge, rational knowledge in the narrower sense. Although Schillebeeckx says explicitly that investigation of this was the real purpose of his article, the emphasis in fact lay on the statement that all knowledge is in depth an orientation on being, and thus ultimately on God: 'Knowledge is implicitly seeking contact with God; where this – implicit – contact with God is not, there is no knowledge' (148).[94] Thus in a technical philosophical argument he spelt out the basic conviction that also already emerged in 'When the soul listens . . . ' The basic conviction that knowledge of God was implied in, and lay at the basis of, the

47

knowledge of reality as experienced concretely was to give his later theology its imposing breadth. It was to make it possible for him to strive for what, in 1945, he was to call a 'theology of culture', a theology which regards human culture as the place where the human desire for God is to be found.

In 1938 Schillebeeckx's study of philosophy was complete as far as the curriculum was concerned, and so he began on his four-year study of theology. However, this happened in unusual circumstances. Like all student ministers in Belgium, he had to do military service, and in 1938–9 he sat for a year 'in the military camp of Leopoldsburg', where he tells us that the Belgian religious officers – priests, pastors and rabbis – at that time received their military training together. There in particular he got to know members of other orders and congregations, for, as he wrote home in a letter, they were 'totally segregated from the camp proper, so that there is not the least danger to morality in general or in particular!' To this he added that there was only one Protestant among them. However, military service above all gave him the possibility of continuing to study undisturbed. According to his later testimony, through the intermediary of an army chaplain with whom he became friends he was exempt from all military duties, 'except for the compulsory lessons on caring for the sick'. He had a 'separate room', and although he was formally a student of theology he remarks that he immersed himself especially in the philosophy of Edmund Husserl (1859–1938), Martin Heidegger (1889–1976) and Maurice Merleau-Ponty (1908–61).[95] All three had influenced De Petter, and like him had called attention to being, totality, meaning as these were also experienced with the experience of concrete things and in human existence. Husserl especially was an important inspiration for De Petter's epistemology, although De Petter wanted to correct the shortcomings in his thought. Heidegger paid more attention than De Petter to the historicity of the experience of being, and his influence can be detected in the statement, formulated at the beginning of a 1939 article by Schillebeeckx, that the nature of each age is to be characterized by its relation to God.[96] That in the same article Schillebeeckx spoke less about the implicit intuition of being and the divine, and directed his attention to the longing of the finite human being for God, perhaps indicates that he tried from a Catholic perspective to take into account the contribution of the atheist Merleau-Ponty and his reflections on human finitude.

This article appeared in *Biekorf* in 1939 under the title 'Person and grace', and as Schillebeeckx later remembered it marked the conclusion of his study of philosophy.[97] It was formally philosophical, but in content it in fact moved on the borderline between philosophy and theology. Moreover, in a certain sense it is a summary of the insights that he developed during his study of philosophy and makes clear how at the beginning of his study of theology he thought that this discipline should be practised. And he could connect this directly with the contemporary sense of life. On the basis of current philosophical and literary work, in 'Person and Grace' Schillebeeckx described his own time as a time full of nostalgia, of dissatisfaction with what is and a desire for something qualitatively different. And he interpreted this aspect of the spirit of modern times as the expression of what in scholasticism was called the *desiderium naturale*, in other words the desire for the knowledge of God that according to Thomas Aquinas is part of human nature (65).[98] The precise characteristics of this yearning had already long been a point of discussion and polemic in Catholic theology, but there was a general tendency to locate it in the quite abstract intellectual insight that natural, created reality is finite and thus not self-sufficient. Therefore it would be in conflict with the human desire for knowledge just to keep to this view, and it was 'natural', on the basis of the insight into these failings of 'natural' reality, to move on to the affirmation of the existence of God.[99] By contrast, Schillebeeckx located the *desiderium naturale* – and this was quite surprising – in the experience, implicit and confused but no less real, of a lived desire for the true, the good and the divine.[100] In line with his earlier articles he saw this desire as 'positive consciousness of being of the Supernatural', of God's real gracious presence (92).

Schillebeeckx seems to have been well aware that here he was on dangerous ground. Right at the beginning of his article he urged those who saw it to read it 'wholly and utterly or not at all'. According to the division of labour current in Catholic thought, philosophy needed to show that God existed and that human beings and the world therefore needed knowledge of God. Along the lines of Leo XIII's programme, however, it had to become clear that modern culture lacked this knowledge and that only faith, theology and ultimately the hierarchical church possessed it. Now Schillebeeckx certainly denied – with ecclesiastical Thomism and completely along the lines of Thomas Aquinas – that human beings were in a position really to know God by virtue of their nature. But in 'Person and Grace', with the help of the concepts derived from De Petter, he explained that human beings could know their own nature, which in this context meant their own concrete historical existence in the midst of modern culture, as a *desire* for God, a 'tendency towards something transcendent' (79). Certainly some knowledge of God was implied here, albeit knowledge of God as 'a Presence, the emphatic content of which we are not aware', but at any rate a Presence in contemporary existence (90).

What is at first sight the rather technical argument of 'Person and Grace' had far-reaching consequences. Schillebeeckx assured his readers that he did not want to say that the *need* for God's gracious care for human beings was to be derived from the human question of God. To fail to do justice to God's freedom in such a way was regarded as a fundamental heresy, and according to Schillebeeckx, too, along with the overwhelming majority of the tradition, it was God himself who 'out of free, totally free, not-necessitated initiative gives himself'. God's gracious concern for human beings must be accepted because 'God ... bears witness that he reveals himself'. But in the Catholic thought of the time this last conviction usually implied that the obligation to accept Catholic doctrine was based on the divine origin that was claimed for it. Faith ultimately meant surrender to God, but according to the Catholic teaching of this time it corresponded with submission to the Catholic Church, to what it said about God and what it presented in God's name as true and good. This obligation was based on the fact that God was the source of the church's message. Catholic apologetics did not try to make the content of doctrine acceptable, but was concerned to 'prove' that the church had the authority to make statements with a reference to God's revelation.

It was this course of things that Schillebeeckx directly opposed. In his view, Christian faith was credible only if it became clear that 'our life, our nature' called for the 'acceptance of faith' (96f.). He made it clear that God and the divine needed to be 'desirable' for human nature, which according to Christian faith was created by the same God. What is presented as the divine offer of grace needed to make sense for this nature, in other words for the human being living in contemporary culture. Elsewhere, Schillebeeckx presented human nature as 'advent', as preparation for the coming of God. At its simplest, and virtually without technical jargon, in his view this amounted to the fact that 'God is happiness' and that human beings are created by God as a 'craving for happiness'; craving and fulfilment therefore needed to connect with each other.[101]

As published in *Biekorf* in the year 1939–40, 'Person and grace' was evidently meant to be the first part of a larger whole. The article ended with 'to be continued', but the sequel never appeared. This would often happen in Schillebeeckx's career: for him the announcement of a sequel to a text was evidently also a way of expressing the feeling that he had not yet studied all the facets of a problem. In a wider sense, much of what he was to write in subsequent years can be seen as a sequel to 'Person and Grace'. This article focused on letting go of the strict difference between human nature, which is what philosophy was said to be about, and supernature, about which only theology could make statements. For Schillebeeckx, the reality in which human beings live was always already characterized by God's saving presence, was always already – as he put it – 'theandric': in other words a divine–human order of salvation. Philosophically, that is, without referring back explicitly to the Christian tradition, there was much to be said for speaking of being human in terms of desire and craving, but only in the light of faith was it possible to develop a truly adequate view of human existence.

This implied that comprehensive talk about human reality needed to be theological, not in the sense of expounding truths of faith presented by the church, but as talking about 'the full ontological reality of the *homo deificus*, of our being children of God', which embraced all that was natural and human. This reality was there for all human beings, but the Christian faith spelt it out and brought it to consciousness. According to Schillebeeckx, it was therefore 'a moral and scholarly obligation ... for the theologian', as an orientation for 'our neurotic age' which has lost contact with God, to develop a 'renewed scholarly insight' into this reality (67–72: 84).

As a student, but above all as a lecturer in theology, he was to be concerned with developing an insight into the divine reality which was significant for people living in modern culture. However, it did not prove so simple to gain access to theology as it was taught and practised in the 1930s and 1940s from the questioning which he had developed during his study of philosophy.

Studying theology in Louvain

At the beginning of August 1939 Schillebeeckx was discharged from military service. Six weeks later, however, he was mobilized again because of the threat of German invasion. Although on 1 November 1939 he told his parents that he was happy 'to be able to stand among our ordinary soldiers, to talk with them and hear their suffering', he was later to recall the period of mobilization above all as 'endless boredom'. Following the capitulation in May 1940, after a number of peregrinations he arrived at a boarding school run by Dominican sisters in Boulogne. For the first time he was really confronted with the war, and an impression written for *Biekorf* is clearly under the impact of the confused and confusing natural forces which surface in people in extreme circumstances.[102] He succeeded in getting back from there to the convent in Louvain, where, after his arrival in June 1940, he was able to continue his education virtually undisturbed for the rest of the war, and all the disruptions that it caused.

He now began actually to do theology courses, though he had already been a theology student for two years. He did not like them, and later he was to say that he had 'no good memories' of his theological training. 'In contrast to the progressive philosophical studies in Ghent, Dominican theology in Louvain was at that time more traditional and old-fashioned.'[103] Later, however, he was to have positive memories of Jules Perquy (1870–1946) from his time of study in Louvain.[104] Perquy was an important figure in the Christian workers' movement and up to 1943 was director of both the Flemish Centrale Hogeschool voor Christelijke Arbeiders and the Walloon École Centrale Supérieur pour Oeuvres Chrétiennes (Central High School

51

for Christian Workers). He was thus responsible for the training of generations of social workers. Perquy was also a leading intellectual and a much sought-after speaker on the social teaching of the church within the Christian Democrat movement in the broad sense. As I have said, this was being strengthened among the Belgian Catholics in this period.[105]

Moreover, Perquy had begun as an assistant to Schillebeeckx's fellow Dominican Ceslaus Rutten (1885–1922), one of the founders of the Catholic workers' movement in Belgium, who at the beginning of the century went to work among the miners in the Walloon Borinage as a worker-priest *avant la lettre*, in order to learn 'the mentality and the heart' of those to whom he devoted himself. When the theological faculty of the Paris province of the Dominicans was forced to move to Kain in the Borinage in 1903 as a result of the anti-clerical legislation in France, a relationship developed with Rutten. Thus in a sense he presided over the birth of the interest shown by Le Saulchoir, the Dominican house established near Paris – in Etiolles – in the period after the Second World War in the attempts of those who were in fact called worker-priests to make contact with the daily life, the experiences and the desires of people engaged in modern working-class life.[106] When in the period immediately after the war Schillebeeckx rounded off his studies at Le Saulchoir, the commitment to this movement, especially shown by Marie-Dominique Chenu, made a great impression on him. When he was responsible for the training of Dominican theological students in Louvain later he would also try to put them in contact with it.

From the time of his theological studies in Louvain he was also to have good memories of Raymond-Marie Martin (1878–1949). Originally a moral theologian, Martin had turned into a great and internationally recognized specialist in the history of mediaeval philosophy and theology. For Schillebeeckx it was the effect above all of his often extremely detailed philological work that the theology of Thomas Aquinas, whose *Summa theologiae* was central to Dominican theological teaching in Louvain – and of course everywhere else – was put in its theological context.[107] In this way Thomas's work, usually seen within the Catholic thought of this time as a timeless and unchangeable doctrinal system, lost its inapproachability. When Schillebeeckx later studied in Paris, he would feel that the historicizing of his view of the work of Thomas was being continued. The effect of this was that when he himself began to teach theology, he took great trouble to give Thomas's synthetic work, which for him too was in the first instance the central point of reference, a place in the ongoing history of theology, before and afterwards.

According to Schillebeeckx's own testimony, however, it was again De Petter who ensured that he developed a real interest in theology as a discipline. In 1938 De Petter was put in charge of study in the Belgian Dominican province. According to Schillebeeckx's later reconstruction, after some time De Petter noted that Schillebeeckx had in fact continued to study philosophy for two years on his own initiative, and that theology, especially that of Thomas's *Summa*, was of little attraction to him. So De Petter stimulated him to begin reading the work of the Tübingen theologian Karl Adam (1876–1966).[108] Adam was one of the few Catholic theologians who did not base themselves on the scholastic apparatus of concepts. He was concerned to show that faith was a living reality for living human beings, rooted in a concrete culture and popular spirit. Humanity has its roots and goal in life in God; therefore in Karl Adam's eyes, to concentrate on life was a way to God.[109] For Schillebeeckx, reading Adam's *oeuvre* did not lead to the conviction that a technical, specialist theology was meaningless, or that the analytic reasoning of scholastic theology had to be supplemented with another theology concerned with proclamation which addressed contemporary men and women in their desire for salvation. He was later explicitly to reject this last argument, which was to be defended quite often in the 1930s and 1940s. Once he was a trained specialist theologian, Schillebeeckx always maintained that well-trained theological thinking was necessary for an authentic living faith and that conversely even the most technical theology is, or at least should be, ultimately a theology *of salvation*. Adam showed him concretely that it was indeed possible, reflecting on the human experience of existence in the midst of culture, to come to speak of God.[110] In further confrontation with Adam's thought, however, the conviction was to grow in him that here it was important to maintain particular Thomistic principles. In his view Adam had wrongly neglected these principles.

The presence in his milieu of Thomistic thinkers who were anything but other-worldly encouraged him in the long run to see that the work of Thomas Aquinas, despite the appearance of abstractness and elevation above history, was just as much a reflection on the experience of existence in faith as Adam's work was. The work of his French fellow-Dominican Antonin-Gilbert Sertillanges (1863–1948), which was unmistakably Thomistic and at the same time could link up with the modern sense of life, was very influential in the Dominican sphere. And among the Flemish Dominicans, Joannes Dominici Maes (1892–1945), De Petter's predecessor as master of the students and regent of studies, was regarded as 'a persuasive guide who radiated a spirit of renewal'; he was aware of the need for an intensive conversation between faith and 'the philosophies of the time, in that broad yet principled spirit ... which once constituted the living greatness of St Thomas Aquinas'.[111]

However, as he remembers it, Schillebeeckx truly gained access to Thomas's work only through the study by the French Jesuit Pierre Rousselot (1879–1915), *L'intellectualisme de Saint Thomas*, dating from 1908. This made it clear – in broad outline in accordance with the philosophical tradition with which he had come into contact through De Petter – that Thomas's whole *oeuvre* was held together by the conviction that the intellect is at depth a feeling for the real, and as a feeling for the real is a feeling for the divine.[112] The apparently abstract arguments of Thomas's *Summa* were ultimately attempts to express the divine presence in reality as this becomes visible in the light of faith. Once Schillebeeckx saw this, and thus redis-covered in the *Summa theologiae* of Thomas Aquinas the conviction which had matured during his study of philosophy, it was clear to him that something authentic was at stake in theology, and it therefore became possible for him to 'study theology in a really personal way'.[113] The basis for his later theological work was laid.

However, in 1942, towards the end of his study of theology, there was a crisis in Schillebeeckx's development. Looking back 30 years later, he was to recall that his basic theological choice was in two ways the focus of a conflict. First, the Roman authorities turned against the work of his teacher De Petter and ensured that he was dismissed by his superior as regent of studies. The specific reason was that his philosophy of the 'implicit intuition' was thought to relativize the traditional, scholastic doctrine too much and implied too great an openness in contact with contemporary philosophy.[114] 'Precisely what at that time I experienced as "the truth" was disowned by Rome', and that was hard in the circumstances which at that time domi-nated in the Catholic world. Not only did Schillebeeckx ask himself whether as a pupil of De Petter he had a future in theology, but the intervention was a question of conscience: 'I wondered: are we wrong?'[115]

The same question must have plagued him when, secondly, in that same year he saw the unpublished text of a speech which Karl Adam, whom he so admired, had given in 1939 about the National Socialist world-view and its attitude to church and Christianity.[116] By reading *Die geistliche Lage des Deutschen Katholizismus* ('The Spiritual Situation of German Catholicism'), evidently for the first time, Schillebeeckx came into contact with Adam's partially positive attitude towards Nazism, and of course in the midst of the war that came as a shock. However, by then Adam's attitude had been clear for almost ten years. Adam had spoken out about Nazism three times in the period of the Third Reich.[117] The tone was already set in the year in which Hitler seized power. In 1933, in an article entitled 'Deutsches Volkstum und katholisches Christentum' ('German Peoplehood and Catholic Christ-ianity'), Adam complained about the growing social oppositions, the party strife and class hatred, along with the enlightened pressure towards auto-nomy and the anaemia and sterility of scholarship and art in the Weimar Republic. This led him to call for a new social and cultural programme which could solve these problems, to call for

54

a living man who has access to the hidden roots, to the secret sources of life of the people and thus can arouse it, in other words a man in whom the whole essence of the Volk, its fear and hope, its anger and pride, its exalted sense and its heroism, have become flesh and blood, in whom the people recognizes and experiences the best in itself.

And, Adam thought in 1933, such a man has come:

> Adolf Hitler. From the south, from the Catholic south he came, but we did not know him. However, the hour came when we saw and recognized him. Now he stands before us as the one whom the voices of our poets and wise men have called, as the liberator of the German genius who removed the blindfold from our eyes and through all the political, economic, social and confessional veils again made us see and love the essential: our unity given in the blood, our German self, the *homo Germanicus*.[118]

On 21 January 1934 Adam again called in a lecture to more than ten thousand people for a 'positive and clear "yes"' to 'the deepest and authentic nature' of the National Socialist movement, to the 'moral forces which we cannot but call Christian energies'.[119] This time Adam turned explicitly to those within National Socialism who were in search of a pagan religion. He stated: 'However much we unreservedly endorse these forces [of Nazism], we can endorse them only in their bond with Christ, see and endorse them only as Christian forces.' Partly as a result of a misunderstanding, this statement brought him into sharp conflict with the National Socialist Party, but that did not mean that his position had fundamentally changed by comparison with 1933.[120]

The text of the speech which Schillebeeckx saw in 1942 was also along these lines, though in 'The Spiritual Situation of German Catholicism' Adam did not go explicitly into the relationship between Catholicism and National Socialism. In 1939 he thought that a world-view was 'an essentially political matter' and therefore 'not something for theology'. Nevertheless, he thought that the promotion of the German national spirit, the manifestation of the German approach in the doctrine, discipline and culture of Catholicism, was what the situation called for. In the speech Adam emphatically endorsed the 'German' virtues which were brought to the fore in the National Socialist movement, such as 'a fresh initiative and daring, tenacious perseverance and a creative drive, a sense of community and the readiness to devote oneself to it, in general the cultivation of a stern, resolute masculinity'. And he explicitly opposed an ethic which 'in the name of Christianity puts the emphasis on passive and feminine virtues'.[121]

Because of his enthusiasm for Adam, as Schillebeeckx later remembered it his reading of this speech was 'indeed a moment of crisis' for him.[122] He was confronted with the problematical aspects of openness to contemporary human experience. It is typical of him that he did not cope with this shock by fiercely attacking Adam or quietly turning away from him. Instead, he wrote for *Biekorf* a quite technical article of around 200 duplicated pages entitled 'Nature and Supernature'. Its tone is surprisingly restrained. Schillebeeckx seemed ready to forgive Adam much, with a reference to the 'heat of the conflict of war', and emphatically said that his criticism in no sense tarnished his respect for Adam 'as one of the best theologians alive today'.[123] He also left a very great deal out of account. For example, he did not investigate the social causes of Adam's statement of his standpoint or the question whether it was not also caused by a certain affinity between the Catholic and Nazi criticism of modern culture, nor did he discuss its political effects. Schillebeeckx concentrated exclusively on what he evidently regarded as the main problem of Adam's theological approach. And in his view that problem was one of method.

Schillebeeckx saw that Adam's positive attitude to National Socialism did not arise from a fortuitous lack of a capacity for judgement. Adam's view of 'life' and the way in which he brought faith and theology into contact with it led him near to the National Socialist world-view.[124] 'Life' was the central category in Adam's theology. Time and again he emphasized that there is no contradiction between true, completely human life and Christian faith, and that it is therefore possible to think about faith, to do theology from life and by reflecting on life. This basic conviction and the 'warm modern rhetoric' in which it resulted in this 'master of presentation' had particularly attracted Schillebeeckx to Adam's work.[125] But now he suddenly read: 'What constantly supports our being Christians is our German nature', with all the connotations that the phrase 'German nature' had during the period of National Socialist domination. Adam made a direct connection between this statement and the classical scholastic adage that God's grace presupposes human nature; does not destroy it but fulfils it and perfects it. In the first half of the twentieth century this adage had helped different Catholic thinkers to break through the strict division between nature and supernature, between philosophy and theology, between human thought and the truths of faith dominated by the hierarchical church, a breakthrough at which Schillebeeckx himself also aimed. But in Adam's 1939 speech he all of a sudden saw quite clearly that the view that supernature is 'gracious participation in the divine life' by 'the whole man' could lead to dubious conclusions.[126]

In the *Biekorf* article 'Nature and supernature', Schillebeeckx tried to demonstrate that the cause of this lay in a theological error. In his view, the way in which Adam connected nature and supernature with each other was wrong, as was the concept that he had of grace as the perfection of nature. The statement that grace did not destroy nature but fulfilled and perfected it was correct but also incomplete (26). He thought that there was a failure to say that to look at nature by faith, in other words by contact with super-nature, meant that the centre of this reality is moved elsewhere, outside what can be seen and experienced directly. It was not that supernature needed to be understood from nature, but vice versa: life, human nature and culture had to be understood from the new centre. According to Schillebeeckx, in theological terms the consequence was that

> nature ... [becomes] a secondary value: for if God gives himself as the purpose of human nature, [all] cultural values pale. All attractive earthly values, even ethical and religious values, pale and are relativized (27).

For 'nature is there ... only on behalf of supernature' and 'supernature is the condition for the existence of nature'. From a theological perspective, according to Schillebeeckx it was more accurate to say that nature fulfils grace than the other way round. In his view, anyone who endorsed 'nature' – human existence and the way in which this is understood in human culture, as it was in itself, ultimately put it in an 'unreal world order' and acted as though it was not taken up into a supernatural whole.

This was a somewhat roundabout means of rejecting the unqualified way in which Adam took up existing concepts of human reality. In Schille-beeckx's view it was impossible to speak of God and the supernatural directly and simply in categories like 'the soul of the people, homeland, personal vocation, individual character'. Certainly he too thought that the aspects of reality denoted by these categories were 'receptive to grace'; the supernatural was present in the midst of the world and near to it, and reverence for it was the expression of the necessary 'reverence for God's presence', but in this they did not remain unchanged. They became 'pro-portionate to the supernatural determination of our life'.[127] In fact this meant, for example, that faith and church on the one hand had to assume a human and thus also a national 'form and colouring' and that 'we Flemings ... thus have to ensure that we give a Dutch colouring and form to the Catholica that transcend the Low Countries' – here a militant Catholic supporter of the use of the Flemish language was speaking – but at the same time the importance of the national had to be radically relativized.[128] He thought that Adam acted as if the natural reality was enclosed in itself and self-sufficient, but in his view exactly that was the effect of original sin, an expression of turning away from God, a deification of that which is not God, and which thus assumes demonic proportions (47). At a more critical level, Schillebeeckx opposed Adam's adoption of the cult of masculinity and heroes by National Socialism, which he thought to be particularly German. He called this 'the apotheosis of the natural talent with the consequent completely graceless failure to recognize any inferiority', and argued that what was a characteristic of the 'Christian hero' could very well go with 'natural lack of gift' (130). In a variety of ways Schillebeeckx criticized Adam for the 'extreme one-sidedness' of his presupposition that 'there is a unity without tension, e.g. between Christianity and German nationalism' (201).

The conclusion that he drew from the need that he noted to correct 'nature' by 'supernature' was to prove far-reaching. He did not yet seem to sense this directly in 'Nature and Supernature', since in this article he spoke, apparently casually, of 'the Christian philosopher, the theologian' (60) and of the need to lay the foundation 'for a future theology of culture' (9). These words indicated that he could not accept the division of work which still applied in Catholic thought and that he was in fact developing a complete new task for theology. The impossibility of maintaining the strict division between nature and supernature and thus between philosophy and theology, specifically with a view to the necessary confrontation with modernity, had become clear to him in the course of his philosophical studies. The reading of the work of Rousselot and Adam had confirmed him in this. The shock of Adam's association with National Socialist thought did not lead him to retrace his steps, but convinced him that a true view of reality, a view which corresponded to the relationship between nature and supernature established by God, could only begin from theology. Whereas at the end of his philosophical training he could still write that human nature as analysed by the autonomous philosopher, restlessly searching, suggests the supernatural,[129] his wrestling with Adam's position brought him to a sharpened insight that only 'the Christian philosopher, the theologian' could understand man's quest for meaning and truth, his 'metaphysical unrest', as that which in his eyes was ultimately also real, namely a 'natural desire for the living God' (60).[130]

This meant that according to Schillebeeckx, theology could not just continue to stand alongside philosophy, as in fact it usually did at this time, and in an autonomous way expound 'the doctrine of faith' with no message for human reason, human culture and human experience. Conversely, it meant that theology also cannot just continue to build on philosophy and a philosophically developed grasp of reality and human existence, providing it with extra legitimation. In fact Schillebeeckx conjured up a vision of a new synthesis of theology and philosophy, in which the orientation of human nature on God is directed towards this nature, in personal life and culture itself, and conversely the orientation of supernature on the fulfilment of human desire is exposed in what the Catholic tradition had to say about this supernature. He expressed this as follows:

> Grace perfects nature in two ways, in a transcendent and in an immanent way; because it makes the human being more than human and at the same time more human, more profoundly human (196).

58

In his view a theology of culture was necessary to work out this last, to demonstrate how grace changed human life from within.[131] The quest for a theology of culture in this sense was from that moment to determine the main line of his theological development, even if he was constantly to keep using other terms.

This quest took divergent forms. For example, immediately after he wrote 'Nature and Supernature', it took the form of what at first sight was a technical exegetical study. Looking back later, Schillebeeckx said that during the closing phase of his theological studies he turned to exegesis out of a 'dissatisfaction with "speculative theology"',[132] but that is a misleading statement. Not only was it a selective aversion, as is evident from what was after all a highly technical and speculative article prompted by Adam, which according to the dating was completed on 14 September 1942. Over and above this, while the final theological essay which he completed less than two months later – according to the dating, on 11 November 1942 – may have rounded things off with an exegetical topic, its interest is clearly in systematic theology.[133]

It seems probable that he worked alternately on 'Nature and Supernature' and this essay on 'The sinful prehistory of Christianity according to St Paul'. The two texts can be read together as a kind of diptych. Whereas in the first Schillebeeckx argued for a theology of culture, in the second he tried to discover Paul's view of human culture. Whereas in 'Nature and supernature' he saw it as his task to uncover 'the implicit longing for the blessed vision' in order to make it clear that human beings are 'by nature, intrinsically, though passively, capable of receiving grace',[134] according to 'The sinful prehistory of Christianity' Paul showed that the failure of 'the economy of the law among the Jews and the economy of wisdom among the Gentiles' was 'a last cry for help from the redeemer'. Or as he also put it, in a formulation which was a combination of the theological jargon of the time and the vocabulary of the apostle: in the letters of Paul 'the *sarx*-economy of the tyrant Sin and Death ... is described so that by contrast "the economy of the Christian pneuma of life" (Rom. 8.2) proves all the more glorious'.[135]

For those who read his final essay now, it is striking how unhistorical Schillebeeckx still was in his discussion of Paul's texts, certainly for someone who was later to make a name for his historical approach to theology and the biblical writings. For example, he did not prove to be interested in any way in the question whether Paul really was the author of the letters attributed to him by the tradition, and now and then based his interpretation of Paul's theology without scruples on a text put on his lips by the author of the Acts of the Apostles. In his reading of Paul, too, Schillebeeckx wanted to be historical but – to keep to his own terminology – 'salvation-historical'. In other words, he did not read the texts as a collection of statements about the supernatural reality but as testimonies to God's history with human beings, testimonies which sought to take the present-day reader up into the dynamic of this history. Here, moreover, he reflected the state of affairs in Catholic theology, which in this period had only just begun to open itself up to the scholarly investigation of the Bible.[136] It was still to be some time before the historical-critical exegesis of the Bible which had already been practised for about a century in Protestant circles would really penetrate the Catholic circle in all its facets.

'The sinful prehistory of Christianity' was in fact an attempt to indicate the sphere within which Paul's view of human existence was played out. The essay also borrowed the term *sarx* from Paul. According to Schillebeeckx, *sarx*, 'flesh', stood primarily for human weakness, lowliness and smallness, but because according to the apostle these were in fact among the consequences of the sovereignty of sin, *sarx* also becomes a designation of the fact that human beings have succumbed to evil. 'Sin', the 'flesh' fallen to sin, and redemption from sin were at this time understood almost exclusively within theology and piety in individualistic terms. In an individual effort believers have to distance themselves from their sinful inclinations, and more specifically from their bodily desires. Against this background it is striking how much in 'The sinful prehistory of Christianity' Schillebeeckx depicts sin as an all-embracing *atmosphere*. According to him, Paul speaks of a 'pre-Christian, human world stage' on which an 'intrigue' is played out (1). In his view, the people of the twentieth century, too, were still on this world stage, and therefore in principle they could learn from Paul how to deal with their situation in a Christian way. This notion takes up an idea current at this time in a wider circle among social Catholics orientated on a Christian inspiration for modern culture. As 'apostle of the Gentiles' Paul was in an excellent position to help people find a dynamic relationship with the contemporary 'new paganism' which was arising.[137] It was obvious that there was not much interest here in the historical context of Paul's letters, but the focus was on the view of culture which was expressed in them.

In 1942, Schillebeeckx thought that, with Paul, he had to start from the fact that sin, the flesh and death ultimately made up one structural whole (96). Here he was giving a biblical foundation to a conclusion which he reached in 'Nature and supernature' and which there above all had the function of distancing itself from Adam's attempt to make Christian faith unproblematically attach itself to existing culture: 'However attractive the natural values may be in themselves, the acceptance of supernature at the same time requires the renunciation of nature.' [138] However, this statement also indicates that despite everything the theology of the young Schillebeeckx still remained stamped by a certain degree of dualism. At the decisive moment he set human reality and modern culture, as intrinsically bound up with evil, over against God's gracious, self-revealing, saving goodness as guarded by the church. He was still to return many times to the relationship between nature and supernature, between human nature and faith received from God, before he had left this dualism behind him.

INAUGURATION AS AN INDEPENDENT THEOLOGIAN

However, Schillebeeckx already took the way towards conquering this opposition between human and divine activity, between dedication to natural values and acceptance of supernature, with a text which at the same time marked the end of his student days and the programmatic beginning of his work as a theological lecturer. On 26 September 1943 Schillebeeckx, then 28, gave his *lectio inauguralis* on receiving the office of lector in the Dominican house of studies in Louvain. In this lecture, entitled 'Towards a Theology of Life?', he in fact continued his discussion with Karl Adam, but at the same time succeeded in taking it a step further than in 'Nature and Supernature'.[139]

In 'Towards a Theology of Life?' Schillebeeckx put himself between two fronts. He did not defend a middle position, but dissociated himself from a basic conviction which in his view both the theological positions that he rejected had in common. One front was marked by the so-called 'theology of proclamation' or 'kerygmatic theology'. This theological trend turned against what was understood by many as the sterile play with concepts in the dominant scholasticism and its inability really to come to grips with the living questions and problems of contemporary believers. After 1850, Catholic thinkers regularly and persistently complained about this, and this complaint was ultimately an expression of dissatisfaction with the completely negative attitude towards modern culture of the official Catholic Church and its theology. The church presented itself as a stronghold of security in the midst of threatening modern chaos, as an impregnable bulwark of the truth. Yet the theology, presented as eternal and unchanging, which kept this bulwark in place scarcely had any relationship to what preoccupied Catholics – and especially Catholic laity – in their lives. Time and again, however, when an attempt was made to reform theology in order to bring it into a more direct connection with this life, after a while it was blocked by the official church. In the late 1930s kerygmatic theology was yet another attempt to break through the alien nature of theological scholasticism, an attempt which began especially from a number of theologians on the Jesuit faculty in Innsbruck.[140]

In 1936, Joseph Andreas Jungmann argued for a theology in which the revelation of God is made visible as a value of life, a theology which to achieve this adopted itself in its presentation to the figurative language of the good news – the so-called 'kerygma' – as this was proclaimed as living and life-giving reality in the New Testament and among the church fathers.[141] Made wise by what had happened in the past to theologians with leanings towards reform, the champions of the theology of proclamation emphatically stressed the legitimacy and necessity of a doctrinal scholastic theology. But, as Hugo Rahner remarked, quoting an aphorism of John Henry Newman, just as we must not regard the chemist as a cook, so we cannot act as if simplified school theology is preaching. According to Rahner the issue was to transform traditional theological knowledge in such a way that it became usable for preaching, in the basic conviction that theology was not just scholarship but also a message of salvation.[142] Schillebeeckx felt attracted by this effort and was himself also concerned to make theology visible as reflection on real salvation. However, he thought that the champions of a kerygmatic theology had made too great a distinction here between faith and life on the one hand and scholarship and reflection on the other.[143]

According to Schillebeeckx, the danger of such a division emerged in a book which in his inaugural lecture he called 'controversial' and 'notorious', but now is almost forgotten: *Die Gnosis des Christentums* (The Gnosis of Christianity), by Georg Koepgen. This book marked the other front on which Schillebeeckx fought. Koepgen did not want to make connections with life but defended the need for a radical break between everyday, natural existence characterized by modern objectivity and eloquence, and faith and thus also theology. With a rigorism that recalls early dialectical theology, Koepgen opposed 'the harmony of God and world, nature and grace, derived from Greek thinking', a standpoint which appealed to Schillebeeckx's opposition to the way in which both spheres were all too unproblematically harmonized by Karl Adam. But Koepgen went much further and stated that 'the holy cannot be contained in our everyday forms of thought, whether with the logical or with the dialectical'. He said that doing theology is a matter for saints:

> Universities and scholars have certainly done a lot for theological scholarship, but the creative impulse for theological thinking always came from men who fulfilled the ideal of a heroic form of life.[144]

For Koepgen, life as a saint meant a break with life in the 'natural' world of modernity. In his view such a break, but in the intellectual sense, was necessary in order to think theologically. For him, theology was not about a controllable logic, but about the capacity to forge life symbolically into a unity, to combine the different levels with one another and to see the unity of the biblical tradition. Everything was defined by the 'myth', the 'gnosis' living in faith and liturgy from which reality is seen and experienced by believers. Theology needs to be nothing other than working out and grounding this 'myth', spelling out this 'gnosis'. But this spelling out was not

62

a defence, and in his view in principle always proved insufficient to convince outsiders.

Now Schillebeeckx's confrontation with Koepgen's book is striking in the light of later developments. The book can be seen as a radicalization and a focusing of an idea in the history of Catholic theology which comes from Johann Adam Möhler (1796–1838), namely that Catholic faith is an organically connected whole in which all concrete details are the expression of the communal and all-determining 'principle'.[145] This idea ultimately leads to the conviction that communion with the Catholic Church and Catholic doctrine as this has taken concrete form under the leadership of the hierarchy is a necessary presupposition for authentic theologizing, and thus cannot be put at risk during this theologizing. The theologians of the international journal *Communio*, including Joseph Ratzinger, later to become prefect of the Congregation for the Doctrine of Faith, were to gather around this conviction more than 30 years after the appearance of Koepgen's *Die Gnosis des Christentums*. The action taken by the Congregation, under Ratzinger's leadership, against theologians critical of the church, in 1990 resulting in the Instruction on the Ecclesial Vocation of the Theologian, *Donum veritatis*, is ultimately an expression of this conviction. The *Communio* theologians presented their journal from the beginning emphatically as an alternative to the other international journal, *Concilium*, which had appeared in the meantime. *Concilium* always regarded itself as the defender of free discussion and open confrontation with the spirit of the time which was expressed during the Second Vatican Council. From the beginning Schillebeeckx was intensively involved with the Second Vatican Council, with *Concilium* and with this journal's aim of open discussion.

In 1943 he noted in Koepgen above all the explicit expression of an effort which in his view was omnipresent in contemporary reflection on the faith. Koepgen aimed at striving to

detach from the life of faith and the theology that grows out of it what people call the conceptual, the rational and the systematic: with the aim of transposing this life of faith and reflection on it to a Gnostic, a-logical or non-conceptual way of thinking. In this, faith and theology would indeed be removed from the difficult questions that they cannot escape at the level of the conceptual moment.[146]

In his eyes the same anti-intellectualism also governed kerygmatic theology, and he vigorously opposed this anti-intellectualism.

In his criticism of both the kerygmatic theologians and Koepgen, Schillebeeckx began from a well-defined reading of the work of Thomas Aquinas. Along the lines of the outcome of his confrontation with Adam, as he himself says, he did not defend 'Thomistic theology as it could exist here or there', but wanted to begin 'from the purified Thomistic principles as such'.[147] His argument amounted to the fact that it was in the spirit of Thomas to say – quite differently from what was suggested by kerygmatic theology – that precisely *because* theology was concerned with the living faith of human beings, it had to be technical and scholarly and that – in contrast to what Koepgen thought – it showed its orientation on God precisely in the way in which it was dispersed and fragmented.

Over against the orientation of kerygmatic theology on the existential aspect of faith, Schillebeeckx set the description of faith as *assensio cum cogitatione* along the lines of Thomas. Here he understood *assensio* as agreement with what is believed, but in his view this assent is coupled with – *cum cogitatione* – a 'concomitant research into and quest for insight in the content of faith'. In other words, according to Thomas faith was not just submission, but in its very structure was also always orientated on intellectual insight and transparency (4–6).[148] Therefore, Schillebeeckx went on to argue, in Thomas intellectual reflection and scholarly theology were not in conflict with nearness and attachment to the faith.

Theology wants to do what faith does spontaneously and pre-scientifically, namely to reflect on faith ... in a scientific, i.e. 'deliberately reflexive, methodically guided and systematically ordered way'. It is simply a deliberately reflective appropriation of Christian faith (6).

Schillebeeckx pointed out that in Thomas's view theology was a *scientia subalternata*, in other words a science which did not maintain its own basic principles but received these from elsewhere. In his interpretation – and in line with what he had said earlier about the abiding dependence of philosophy on human experience – this meant that theology was permanently dependent on the knowledge of God and of the salvation that human beings find in God. These are two things 'in which the theologian takes part only through his life of faith'. In his view theology could therefore really be orientated on its own object only by remaining bound up with living faith. Although he did not spell this out, here at the same time he indicated that the dominant scholastic theology which exclusively occupied itself with the statements defined by the magisterium as 'truths of faith', did not meet the demand for a scholarly theology as seen by Thomas Aquinas, the one who by its own account was *the* philosophical and theological authority.

Thus Thomistic theology which respects its inner structure ... cannot and will not be alien to faith or life and will never explain away the facts of faith; it is centripetal to the facts of faith and not centrifugal, seeking a centre and not fleeing a centre.

Schillebeeckx quoted Thomas in summary: 'The whole of theology is orientated on feeding faith', '*tota theologia ordinatur ad fidem nutriendam*' (6–8).[149]

Schillebeeckx did not just assert that what the kerygmatic theologians wanted for part of theology, attachment to the living faith, must be the starting point for any theological thinking. In general this conviction was clearly gaining ground among Catholic theologians, and Schillebeeckx took part in this development. He went his own way. However, it was very important for him that faith was not just an existential experience, as the kerygmatic theologians emphasized, or an unconditional submission to the absolute mystery, as it was for Koepgen. Faith was also a form of real, albeit diffuse, knowledge of God. Schillebeeckx thought that he read in Thomas Aquinas that theology was ultimately about spelling out and deepening this knowledge by scholarly reflection. According to Schillebeeckx, theology on Thomistic principles sought to

> reflect on the faith in concepts which are more adequate than the non-philosophical, spontaneous and vulgar concepts ... so that its insights are really a deeper penetration into faith itself and thus aim to be more completely adequate, and so that it stands closer to faith than the theology of proclamation, which rather rejects all technical conceptuality and thus conceptuality which tends towards adequacy (8f.).

Thus theology is a service to faith and is the nourishment of faith, but is so precisely by doing its intellectual work in a strict sense; it is a technical science.

For Schillebeeckx this meant that the theologian in his scholarly activity must work in two directions at the same time. Here he indicated his own programme and in fact also to a large degree his own future approach. On the one hand, in his view the theologian must try to discover the content and significance of faith 'with all the critical apparatus which that requires, in and through the documents, in and through concrete facts in the past and present of the church' – and, moreover, he added 'guided by the magisterium of the church'. Here in his own way he took up the intention of kerygmatic theology by attaching himself to living faith in past and present. But in his view this was not yet an exhaustive description of the task of theology. On the other side the theologian had equally to be orientated on a speculative penetration of these facts. Their context and – this was particularly important for him – the particular way in which they point to God needed to become clearer. He thus took over something of Koepgen's intention in order to clarify the distinctive context of theological facts. But whereas Koepgen called doing theology a matter for saints, Schillebeeckx put all the emphasis on the sober humanity of theology as a profession. He did not see speculative theologizing as the unfolding of a gnosis which was ultimately inexpressible, far less as arising on the basis of statements by the church authorities. On the basis of former attempts to bring philosophy and theology, faith and human thought closer together, in 1943 he arrived at the view that the theological speculations about God emerged from the natural desire of the human mind for insight into the world, its structure and origin, and into the connection between all that is. This was in principle the same desire that expressed itself in other disciplines in other ways (9–11).[150]

One consequence of the reflections in 'Towards a Theology of Life?' was not particularly shocking at first sight, but proved far reaching. Schillebeeckx could see theology as an intellectual activity comparable with other forms of scholarship. In his view the adage that grace perfects nature could be translated at the intellectual level into the statement that faith perfects and strengthens the mind, *fides perfecit et roborat intellectum*. Therefore he could see theology as a sober and human science, which nevertheless could support and deepen the spontaneous insight into life precisely by taking great pains over the difficulties of technical and scientific work.

As I have indicated, for him this meant on the one hand that it was necessary to adopt a certain distance from life:

> Theological work as such is not a pious elevation of the soul but a science; in other words, it is technical. It is and must be that: with all the hard and nerve-racking nature of a painstaking analysis, of fair and serious thought, often against the dynamism of its own effort, and of an almost anxious use of methodological precision. Now to a certain degree there is necessarily a certain tension between every science and life, because science requires a certain distance, a distancing from life.[151]

But on the other hand and at the same time that meant taking up life. Thought is part of life and an expression of it: with a striking boldness, in 'Towards a Theology of Life?', Schillebeeckx stated that theology is always bound up with the 'historical milieu of the spirit in which the theologian lives'. He saw in the work of Thomas Aquinas – and this is remarkable at a time in which people still usually read this work as a supra-temporal fixed system – a 'recasting' of the mediaeval problems of faith. He thought that precisely by taking up contemporary questions of faith, Thomas could serve as an example for twentieth-century theologians. If theology was the link between faith and the mind, the mind was concerned with 'the cultural level and the sphere of interest in which this mind finds itself here and now'. Granted, in his view the theologizing mind was 'universally human and objective', but was so always in the contemporary form 'with all its question-marks and problems in life' and not as 'a neutral mind which passes over all contemporary problems' (18f.).

For those who know about Schillebeeckx's later development, it is difficult not to read here an announcement of his later attention to the social, political and cultural context of theology. At all events, his view of the way in which theology is conditioned by life and times betrayed the influence of the French Dominican Marie-Dominique Chenu, who even before the Second World War was making striking attempts to connect Thomas's works with the spiritual climate of the time in which they were written. Chenu, too, saw Thomas as a theologian who could still be a model, precisely because of the way in which he was bound up with his time.[152] In 1945, a year after the liberation of Belgium, Schillebeeckx was to go to Paris to continue his studies, among others with Chenu. As he himself says, this '(sometimes rather sloppy but) great visionary' had a major influence on him, not only in his reading of Thomas's work but also in his involvement in the present situation.[153] The way in which he developed as a Dominican student in Ghent and Louvain, with the support of many and under the strong influence of De Petter, but also to a striking degree by his own efforts, had laid a good basis for a fruitful encounter.

Chapter 2

Working out the Project of a Theology of Culture in the 1940s

'The one who has been given grace sees and loves everything with the eye and the heart of God, his Friend'

AFTER THE WAR

If the First World War can be seen as a bombardment of the bulwarks of European civilization which had hitherto seemed unshakable, within the same image the emergence of the Nazi regime and the Second World War can be seen as the conflagration which was the result of that bombardment. Clearly under the impact of the burning of books by Jewish and 'un-German authors' which the Nazis organized in Germany immediately after their seizure of power, the German-Jewish author Elias Canetti expressed this view as early as 1935 in his apocalyptic novel *Auto-da-fé*. In it, the main character, Peter Kien, esconces himself in his well-ordered library to protect himself from the constant threat of the chaos of the outside world. However, when the base desires of ordinary people succeed in penetrating this stronghold in the person of his housekeeper, he sees no way out other than to burn his library and to perish along with his books.[1]

And after the war, in 1946, the writer Walter Mehring reconstructed on paper the library of his father, who had twice had to flee before the advance of National Socialism, losing his library in the process. He did so, not out of nostalgia for the culture rudely destroyed by Hitler, but in an attempt to write the autobiography of a culture and to understand how it had produced the terrors in which it had itself perished. He inexorably showed its bankruptcy.[2] Such a sharp insight into the break which Nazism represented in the history of Europe was exceptional in the period immediately after the Second World War. Especially the discussion of the implications of the annihilation of six million Jews really got going only in the second half of the 1960s. Nevertheless, there was a widely shared spontaneous feeling that the war had shown that the Western tradition and its values was not tailored to the contemporary situation and that the culture needed to change fundamentally.

'Theology of culture' in the midst of cultural reorientation

In 1938, in his novel *Nausea*, the French philosopher Jean-Paul Sartre had urgently described the experience of 'alienation' and not being at home in the world, the feeling of being thrown alone into the world with an insatiable desire for meaning and community.[3] In the form of a fictitious diary Sartre described the experience that all the well-tried ways of ordering the world and making it a home – from fixed customs and an organized life, though memory of the past, to studying history and the intellectual tradition – had lost their influence. What remained was simply naked existence itself. Only from the deliberate acceptance of this in all its absurdity could a feeling of reconciliation now and then shine out. During the war Sartre worked out this view in *Being and Nothingness*, a very technical book which is virtually inaccessible to non-specialists, and one which was hardly noted when it appeared.[4] However, Sartre also developed his view in plays like *The Flies* (*Les mouches*, 1943), *Closed Doors* (*Huis clos*, 1945) and *The Devil and the Good God* (*Le diable et le bon Dieu*, 1951), and in the film scenario *The Die is Cast* (*Les jeux sont faits,* 1947). They communicated a view of life in which the world remained alien, meaningless and absurd for human beings and threatened hell for them in the other. Nowhere can it be inferred what has to be done.

Especially the idea that existence in principle has no basis and is arbitrary, and therefore that being human is a nonsensical task, was recognized by many people after the war as an adequate expression of the way that they felt about life. Existentialism in this sense was immensely popular, above all among people who had grown up during or shortly after the war. In the different countries which had been affected by the war, in the 1940s and the beginning of the 1950s a number of literary publications appeared which showed how out-of-date pre-war cultural, ethical and religious values were, and in which humanity was sought in the acceptance of standing with empty hands.[5]

In 1950 the young Flemish Catholic poet H. Van Herreweghen wrote: 'People may find it regrettable, but existentialism is the *doctrine* – or the

69

faith – which most crudely but most faithfully formulates the *sense of life* at this time.'[6] Van Herreweghen's remark was made at the end of a vigorous debate immediately after the war about the state of affairs in Flemish literature and in the broader sense in Flemish culture. This debate had begun in August 1945 with an article by the writer Gerard Walschap in the journal *Dietsche Warande & Belfort*, in which he expressed his disappointment about what the younger authors were producing after the war. Walschap, who was a public figure – he had also written a notorious book in 1945 in which he had given a public account of his departure from the Catholic faith – had already asked even before the war, 'Where are the young?' In August 1945 he wrote that he had expected that the 'respect for freedom' practised during the occupation, 'the sense of worth and right which had grown up in the dark defiance, would have become the substance of a rebellious youth which would affirm itself with great power'. After the war, however, nothing of this seemed to emerge. He thought that the voices that he heard were 'without passion', 'trite', 'purely literary'. He argued for a literary renewal which was not primarily formal but 'is the burning testimony of human beings'. 'Our Flemish literature must remain open and become more open, to full life, with wide views over Europe and the world.'[7]

Walschap's voice was part of a larger chorus. Immediately after the war, countless new and small literary journals appeared in Flanders which presented themselves as the mouthpieces of 'the young men' and sought to give them an opportunity to present their voice in public. Often these journals spoke emphatically about what they saw as the state and the future of literature or culture; after its appearance, everyone was in explicit or implicit debate with Walschap's article. His feeling that the literary harvest of the post-war generation of writers did not radiate the passion which had characterized the work of young writers after the First World War was widely shared. Here, however, it was immediately noted that this was connected with the very experiences of the war. The war was said to have made the younger generation sceptical and antipathetic to the abuse of slogans and ideals. 'No, we are not idealists. We've had too many lessons in that,'[8] was the attitude against which Walschap protested.

Walschap's call for more literary and cultural verve was taken up to some degree in the Catholic milieu. Here the call was usually regarded as an incitement to strive for a new Christian culture on the basis of a Catholic sense of community, which was to make possible a 'more vigorous and greater, deeper and more intense life'. According to the Flemish Catholic youth, 'a self-confident intellectual élite' had to arise from the 'smoking ruins of modern European pseudo-culture'. 'We are striving for a neo-humanism of which the humanity ennobled by God's grace forms the centre.' 'Purification, the glad acceptance of life and moderate romanticism, these are the components of the most recent poetry' which they had in view.[9] All this was meant to offer a credible alternative to existentialist nihilism.

It was in this situation that in 1945 for the first time Edward Schillebeeckx addressed a wider public as a theologian. He directly grappled with existentialism as an expression of feelings about life, with the desire for spiritual orientation, shattered idealism and the will to accept life which was expressed by the texts of the young Catholics. It was striking that as a theologian he did not feel compelled to define his position *over against* the expressions of the spirit of the time and to comment on and judge this from outside, from the standpoint of the church or the Christian tradition. For him the cultural confusion was the contemporary Christian situation of which he formed part and about which he could speak only from within. Under this very title, 'The Christian Situation', he then looked outwards from within the spirit of the time for openings for the Christian faith, and conversely at the same time subjected this tradition of faith to a revision in the light of contemporary questions. Down to the terminology, which seems high-flown and sometimes even over-solemn to the present-day reader, he expressed his solidarity with the sometimes frenzied quest of others of his generation. In his eyes that quest made clear the urgency of questions about views of life.

'The spirit of the time is irresistible!' Schillebeeckx wrote, and made his influence also felt among Catholics. In his view, above all 'our youth' were sensitive to existentialism as an expression of the contemporary sense of life. Then he seemed after all to adopt the position of the outsider who judges the world from a quasi-divine standpoint. Moreover, he put himself in the tradition of the Catholic criticism of culture from after the French Revolution and said that the dominant thought and feelings were governed by the 'self-glorification of modern man'. For him, too, this meant that a fundamental correction of this culture in the light of a Christian Catholic spirit was necessary. Nevertheless, the rise of existentialism meant that in principle a new situation had developed:

> However, this self-glorification of modern man is not a rock-steady risk-free self-confidence from the period which intoxicated itself with rationalistic regularity. Rather, it is the glory of the heroic pessimism which ... wells up from the feelings of our time: the immanent solution lies in the heroic acceptance of our fearful finitude.[10]

Schillebeeckx associated existentialism with a fundamental ambiguity which he perceived in the contemporary sense of life, an ambiguity which he also found in the literary journals of the young Catholics. On the one hand he thought that, just as before the war, the young 'are looking for fresh air, for a task, for bold creative actions'. He described their programme with a

71

good deal of empathy: 'We trumpet noble and good humanity, the acceptance of life, enthusiasm for culture and daring achievement, supported by a fresh, living, conquering Christian faith' (84). But at the same time the war had made it clear that there was another side to the coin:

> And a fleck of shadow falls on the sunny mood of life. The facts blackly surround it; a very stormy shore is littered with the wrecks of a noble and good humanity which, with the violence of its sense of life and its loss of achievement, with its bond with the people, its commitment and its daring achievement, smashed on a rock and suffered shipwreck, along with all that it had brought with it (85).

Writing at a time when Belgium had already been liberated but the war was not yet over, in his reflections on 'The Christian Situation' Schillebeeckx again took up the confrontation with Karl Adam which he had begun earlier. He explicitly recalled the 'daring German theologians' who during the war had tried to make 'a kind of synthesis between the Catholic and the National Socialist world-view'. In the same breath he referred to 'experts in France and elsewhere' who during the war had opposed the German occupation or had been in prisoner-of-war camps, and who 'more than once raised their voice, "*Au nom du ciel, sauvons la terre*", let us save the earth in the name of heaven' (93). He identified himself to a large degree with their efforts and their commitment. For Schillebeeckx in the period immediately after the war, the question that they raised about the relationship between orientation on heaven and commitment to the earth was the central theological question. It was not any 'transient fashionable problem that comes and goes', although the 'programmatic bond with life and the people' which had come into being among Catholics, especially among their intellectual élite, hastened the posing of this problem. But that did not alter its fundamental theological importance. Precisely because the question of the religious significance of the commitment to a human culture inescapably raised itself, in his eyes 'the objectivity, I mean the actual givenness of the problem', was evident. 'Life itself forces the problems on us; the present situation is problematical.' He was convinced that life and theology in 1945 faced new questions which could not be settled with the old answers: it did not involve any 'academic question the solution of which one already has up one's sleeve and which one can produce with brio at the psychological moment' (92).

The situation brought Schillebeeckx back to the notion which in his student days had led to involvement with Karl Adam's project: that a contemporary faith and a contemporary theology need not be alien to life and culture, but had to accept unreservedly 'earthly life in all its goodness and all its beauty'.[11] At the same time, in his view it was equally necessary not to forget the shadow sides of human existence and the ascetic line in

Christianity which was concentrated on sacrifice and cross. He had begun to see the theoretical need for this during his discussion with Adam's thought, but existentialism, which was at the same time self-assured and realistically tragic, made it clear that a similar two-sidedness lurked in Christianity. Catholic faith as he saw it made him experience as it were the two sides of the spirit of the time in an intensified way:

> In turn we are drawn to two poles: the evidence – and I really mean evidence – of the value of harmony: all that is by nature beautiful, noble, fine, in short all that is authentically human can blossom fully in the life of grace, but on the other hand the Christian evidence that it must be possible to give up all those human values for the sake of the life of grace; hence [the] need for radical self-denial (91).

For Schillebeeckx in 1945 the question implied by these two obvious features of Christian faith, that of the relationship between 'earth' and 'heaven', between the naturally human and Christian life, was not a subordinate question or one of technical theological interest. What was at stake for him was to fathom 'human beings', 'human existence'. In his eyes the clarification of human existence was a central theological task.

At the end of his analysis in the first of the three articles about 'The Christian Situation', which was published in 1945, Schillebeeckx reiterated a statement that he had already made in 1942 in 'Nature and Supernature': in order to understand the human and Christian situation properly it was necessary to work zealously on a 'hitherto new treatise in our theology, namely a theology of culture which must be incorporated into the treatise on creation' (93).[12]

From the point of view of the history of theology, the way in which the term 'theology of culture' crops up in Schillebeeckx is surprising. The term is usually associated particularly with the Protestant theologian Paul Tillich (1886–1965). As early as 1919 Tillich developed some basic outlines of a theology of culture. In the broad sense there is certainly an affinity between what Schillebeeckx envisaged and Tillich's desire to bring theology out of its cultural isolation by entrusting to it the task of uncovering our unconditional concern in culture, bringing to light the religious content which breaks through the limiting cultural forms. In a later phase of his development Schillebeeckx was to occupy himself at length with Tillich's theology, though not directly with his theology of culture. But in the 1940s – like most European theologians – he was not familiar with the work of Tillich, who had migrated to America in 1933, nor had he been initiated into the theological discussion on culture which had already been carried on in German Protestantism since the Enlightenment and in which Tillich took up a position.[13]

What Schillebeeckx envisaged in 1945 by 'a theology of culture' was still closest to what Gustave Thils (1909), first lecturer at the Mechelen seminary and later professor of theology at the University of Louvain, had branded 'theology of earthly reality' or 'theology of history'. Thils argued that commitment to earthly values and earthly hope were an integral part of Christian faith, and that it was the task of Christians to realize in the contemporary world something of the harmony and splendour which are characteristic of the universe in its infinite glory.[14] His project was also closely akin to that of the Louvain philosopher Albert Dondeyne (1901–85), who in the same issue of the journal in which Schillebeeckx's first article appeared wrote that religious and earthly mysticism had to be kept together and that neither of them was possible without the other.[15]

However, all these approaches emerged from a broad reassessment of the relationship between Catholic faith and culture in the wider sense, which had begun in the period between the wars. In Germany the articles of the philosopher Peter Wust (1884–1940) on 'The Return of German Catholicism from Exile' had proved to be a catalyst in the origin of a movement which by spiritual influence again wanted to give Catholicism a normative significance in Western spiritual life.[16] Karl Adam formed part of this movement, as did the very popular and influential Romano Guardini (1885–1968), who was trained as a professional theologian and philosopher, but as professor of the Catholic view of life in Berlin, Tübingen and Munich entered into dialogue with German, viz. European, culture in its full breadth. Also important for Schillebeeckx was the influence of the French 'renouveau catholique', a movement of Catholic intellectuals of different origins who were concerned to influence contemporary culture in a Catholic spirit. As well as literary works by authors like Georges Bernanos (1888–1948) and François Mauriac (1885–1970), the work of the philosopher Jacques Maritain (1882–1973) on 'art and scholasticism', 'the primacy of the spiritual' and 'integral' – i.e. Christian – 'humanism' was particularly influential.[17]

In his quest for a theology of culture Schillebeeckx was not concerned with a doctrinal view of contemporary culture or a programme of cultural reform in the Catholic sense. He was concerned with a really theological view of reality. He summed up what he envisaged here in criticisms of Dondeyne's work, though he admired it a great deal. He thought that in the end Dondeyne did not make it sufficiently clear

> how the orientation on the Absolute is 'present' precisely in the world itself (in the openness of human existence towards the world), so that precisely in order to be itself, what is within the world betrays a tendency to transcend itself and for that reason *cannot* be content in or with itself.[18]

According to Schillebeeckx, an orientation on the Absolute was present in the human orientation on the world, in the efforts to realize a culture in the midst of and in dialogue with the world. So in his quest for a theology of culture he had begun to point to this orientation and qualify its content.

Throughout Europe in the first years after the war there was a period of reflection on the situation and on the future, on the relationship between the different ideological currents and their contributions to culture. On the one hand this was a consequence of the shock of the war and the collapse of European civilization which had become visible in it, but on the other hand it was also caused by the accelerated modernization in the post-war period, not least as a consequence of the impulse given to the economy and industry by the American Marshall Plan. The result was a boost to the attempts to make a Catholic contribution to culture in the broad sense, socially and ecclesiastically, at the expense of currents which wanted to maintain a closed Catholic sub-culture. In the first instance it seemed that the discussion about the desired orientation of Catholic thought could take place in relative freedom. However, time and again measures were taken against theologians and philosophers who in the eyes of Rome did not distance themselves sufficiently from modernity and its thought-world and gave too little evidence of belief in the immutability of Catholic doctrine. Gradually it became increasingly clear that the hierarchical church did not want any fundamental changes and was continuing to hold tightly to the need for a fundamental gulf between the church and the modern world. This standpoint seemed to be definitively sealed by the encyclical *Humani generis*, which appeared in 1950. This situation was really to change only when, in 1958, Pope John XXIII unexpectedly announced the Second Vatican Council. At that moment, especially the Catholic intellectual élite again got the feeling that open confrontation with the world was possible after all. Bishops and other pastors too were convinced of the importance of such a confrontation, and the Catholic Church began to prepare itself for an assembly of the church in which there would be a thorough discussion of the delicate points which had come to light during the previous period.[19]

In Belgium, the situation immediately after the war seemed in principle favourable to a fundamental reflection on the present and the future. Whereas the surrounding countries had to concentrate exclusively on the material restoration and rebuilding of the economy, Belgium was relatively well off. Of course, Belgium, too, had been stripped by the occupying forces, and during the occupation there had been a shortage of decent food and a lack of fuel. But the retreat of the German troops in 1944 had been so rapid that they had had no opportunity to destroy vital industrial installations. Although this industrial equipment was antiquated, production could therefore be resumed as soon as the necessary raw material became available. Moreover, because of the delivery of raw material from the Belgian Congo to the Allies during the war, Great Britain and the United States had a substantial debt to Belgium which was repaid after the war. The foreign exchange capital was once again substantially increased after 1944 when Antwerp began to function as a transit port for the provisioning of allied troops in Northern Europe and the services provided were paid for in dollars. Thus, Belgium was not only in a position to buy sufficient food, but at the same time could get hold of the necessary raw materials. As a result the economy quickly got moving again. In the years immediately after the war the country was an exception in Europe because of its prosperity and economic activity, and as early as 1948 it had again achieved the 1939 level of productivity and prosperity.[20]

As in other countries, already during the war there were more or less secret reflections on the desired political and social relations in Belgium, both in resistance circles and among those who had fled the country at the beginning of the occupation. Some socialists and Catholics – especially from the French-speaking part of Belgium – began to break through the old ideological opposition and to organize themselves into a broad people's party which was to commit itself to greater social justice. However, when the Flemish socialists re-founded the Belgian Workers Party as the Belgian Socialist Party and in June 1945 organized a 'victory congress', and when in August of the same year the old Catholic Party had re-founded itself as the Christian People's Party/Parti Social Chrétien (CVP), it was already quite clear that no really far-reaching breakthrough would come about. As an expression of the efforts of the French-speaking Catholics to break out of the pre-war political conditions, in June 1945 the Union Démocratique Belge was also founded, but in February 1946 this party got no more than 2 per cent of the votes. This disappointing result, which in fact finished it off, was due not least to the Belgian episcopate, which before the elections had spoken out against the UDB and forbidden Catholics to vote for the party. Thus, at all events, the bishops maintained their pre-war view. For them, the political unity of Catholics came first and they wanted to be able to control a strong centre party which committed itself to the Catholic inspiration in society and which could ward off the anti-clerical attacks on the church and its social position.[21]

So after the war Belgium remained a denominationally segregated country, according to the wishes of the majority of, at any rate, the Catholic élite. Nevertheless, the parties changed their attitudes and appeals quite fundamentally, and this had important consequences for public discussion. For example, in the first post-war socialist declaration of principles the emphasis was not so much on the defence of the interests of the working class as on the spiritual and moral verve of the party, on its commitment to justice and its militant humanism. On Catholic ground, the establishment of the CVP meant the definitive victory of the current in Catholic politics orientated on the Christian Democrats and an increase in the influence of the politically minded on the confessional groups as a whole. Although in practice it was by no means always implemented consistently, the programme of the CVP emphatically dissociated itself from the idea that it was the secular arm of the church and derived its right to exist from the defence of Catholic interests. The CVP shaped itself as a party with a programme. It began from the unity of Belgium, and within this emphasized the cultural independence of the linguistic communities, aiming at a social peace on the basis of justice and consultation between social partners. According to its activists, in content this was a practical expression of the social teaching of the church; however, the aim was not to implement this Catholic doctrine but to make a contribution to modern, secular culture. In its so-called Christmas programme in 1945, the CVP wrote that it wanted to

> build on the human values which form the foundations of our Western civilization. Historically they were brought to us by Christianity, but today they are the common possession of both believers and unbelievers.[22]

Schillebeeckx's efforts towards a theology of culture fitted well into this open climate.

However, the climate proved unstable. During the 1940s a situation developed which led to a return to the very standpoints that people had wanted to abandon immediately after the war. In Belgium, coming to terms with the German occupation was politically a highly complicated process in which the traditional oppositions between Catholics and anti-clericals and between Flemings and Walloons again became sharper. The way in which political and economic collaboration with the Germans was prosecuted and punished during the period of so-called repression and 'epuration' (purging) provoked so much controversy that even today in Belgium a balanced judgement on it seems impossible. It is certain that the Flemings had the feeling that the opposition were abusing the repression in order to get at the Flemish movement as a whole, and that Catholics regarded the repression as being to an important degree a cloak for a reckoning with the predominantly left-wing and French-speaking opposition to Catholic Flanders. By contrast, from the left-wing and Walloon side people saw this very reaction as characteristic of the Catholic–Flemish refusal to take seriously the political and moral questions relating to the war and the occupation, because they aimed at a restoration of the old balance of power.[23]

Anti-clericals and Walloons had the feeling that this verdict was confirmed by the attitude of Catholics and Flemings at the time of the so-called monarchy question. The decision of Leopold III in 1940 not to flee to France and later to London with the Pierlot cabinet but to allow himself to be taken prisoner-of-war by the Germans along with his officers – the king was supreme commander of the Belgian army – was already controversial

77

when it was made. The king's readiness to negotiate with the Germans – and ultimately, in November 1940, with Hitler himself – together with his abiding reservations about the Belgian government in exile meant that Leopold had very little credit among those who had opposed the occupying force in principle. However, he became thoroughly controversial as a result of the document found at the liberation in which he gave his view of what needed to be done in Belgium after the war. There was no word of appreciation for the efforts of the Allies and the internal resistance. Leopold demanded that the Pierlot government should apologize for its criticism of him in May 1940 and proposed an authoritarian reform of the state which would put him at the centre of power. When Leopold was liberated from his prisoner-of-war camp in Austria in May 1945, the question whether he could return to the Belgian throne was thus acute.

From the beginning the Catholics were partisan in this question, because in June 1940, after the king's meeting with Hitler, Archbishop Joseph Ernst Cardinal Van Roey had strongly opposed the politics of the Pierlot government in a pastoral letter and had identified Leopold's cause with the salvation of the fatherland. Generally speaking, even after the war the attitude of the episcopate and of the whole Catholic élite towards the king was positive.[24] The CVP constituted itself as a defender of Leopold III and made itself the spokesman of the king's personal desire that the people should express their views in a referendum on his position. The further details of the political complications are not relevant here.[25] But what is important is that the way in which the question of the monarchy ultimately developed considerably strengthened the position of the CVP in Belgian politics, and at the same time increased the oppositions between the Catholics and the other political currents. A referendum did indeed take place on the question of the monarchy on 12 March 1950. A majority of 68 per cent of the electors supported Leopold's return to the throne: in predominantly Catholic Flanders 72 per cent voted for the king; in the more socialist and anti-clerical Wallonia this was only 42 per cent. Perplexity over the question whether this small majority was sufficient to restore Leopold to his dignity led to the calling of new elections on 4 June, which the CVP won overwhelmingly. This made a homogeneous Catholic cabinet possible, and on its proposal, on 19 July the Chamber and the Senate, meeting in joint session, ended the regency of Prince Charles after a very fierce debate. However, the socialists were able to mobilize such a mass protest that the government, afraid of a confrontation between 100,000 demonstrators and the state police, felt compelled in the night of 31 July/1 August to persuade the king to hand over authority to his son. When Leopold abdicated from the throne on 16 July 1951 and on 11 August was succeeded by Boudewijn, who at that time was still a minor, there was little left of the spirit of renewal and breakthrough.

No direct traces can be found in Schillebeeckx's work of the controversies over repression and epuration, or of the question of the monarchy. Rather, his texts moved at the level of the general orientation of the culture, the relationship between religion and responsibility for the world, commitment to earthly values and giving form to history. Or they were about questions relating to the concrete life of the Catholic Church. But his writings do clearly express the desire for a credible orientation of life in a time of uncertainty and shattered trust. Here the change both in the situation of Catholic theology and in the cultural and political climate in Belgium around 1950 did leave traces in his work. In this chapter the main focus is on Schillebeeckx's texts from the second half of the 1940s; in the next chapter the emphasis will be on his writings from the period 1950–7. At the beginning of 1958 he was to move to the Netherlands. However, throughout the period when he was a lecturer to the Dominican theological students in Flanders a clear line can be drawn through his theological development.

In 1950 the Flemish poet Van Herreweghen, with his view that existentialism formulated the post-war sense of life 'most roughly but most truthfully', described the contemporary poetry for which he stood as 'stylized disorder', as 'modern unrest in a classical measure', evidently meaning that the two were connected and that the existentialist spirit of the age could adequately be expressed in classical forms.[26] One could say that from 1944 Schillebeeckx tried to contain within the forms of classical Catholic theology this spirit of the time, which he also interpreted as the Christian situation, in all its disorder and unrest. In the 1940s he did so with striking boldness; in the 1950s he was more circumspect, but deep down he always remained convinced of the possibility of the enterprise. The Catholic tradition was rich enough to include the contemporary sense of life in its fullness and to give it an authentic Christian form.

'Catholic cultural life'

In the first five years after the war, Schillebeeckx in fact to an important degree formulated the starting points of his later thought. Although he never used the term again later, his whole work can be characterized as 'a theology of culture', in two ways. He not only tried to develop a theological *view* of culture but did so in a theology which was aware that it formed *part* of culture, although both this view and this awareness were to undergo far-reaching changes during his development. IIis first theological articles appeared in the post-war years in two journals which saw themselves as a platform for the Catholic contribution to Flemish culture: the journal

Kultuurleven (Cultural Life) and *Tijdschrift voor Geestelijk Leven* (Journal for Spirituality).

Kultuurleven was founded by Flemish Dominicans in 1930 as *Thomistisch Tijdschrift voor Katholiek Kultuurleven* (Thomistic Journal for Catholic Cultural Life). The designation 'Thomistic' first of all referred to the programmatic offensive carried on by Leo XIII, based on Thomist theology and aimed at a Catholic penetration of modern society. In the first issue the editors proclaimed in unmistakable words that they were working in the conviction that 'the modern world can be saved from the general trend towards materialism and brought back to an authentic cultural life only by the triumph of the Catholic view of life'. 'Under the kingship of Christ', the journal wanted to contribute to 'a noble human existence in this world, the herald and preparation for perfect life in God'.[27] 'Under the kingship of Christ': in 1925 Pope Pius X (1922–39) had instituted the feast of Christ the King as a weapon in the fight against what was then called 'laicism': the attempts to challenge or at any rate to force back the rule of the church over all spheres of life and the striving for human autonomy. In the encyclical *Quas primas* he showed that the purpose of this was that 'believers generally should begin to understand that they have to wage a bold and persevering fight under Christ's banner'.[28] From the beginning of his pontificate Pius XI strove to intensify the Catholic effort in culture. He was convinced that after the First World War 'true peace' had not yet returned. On the contrary, he wrote in 1922 shortly after his coronation, in the encyclical *Ubi arcano Dei*, that the war had markedly brought about the decline of Christian practices. He saw a restoration of Christian thought in the individual, in the family and society as the only remedy for this.

Pius XI then designated as 'Catholic Action' the fight which was needed and in which he emphatically wanted Catholic laity also to be engaged under the watchful leadership of the hierarchy.[29] Here he took up a term which Pius X had coined as early as 1905, but intensified Pius's programme, which was aimed at 'restoring all things in Christ', and moreover gave it a new direction. With its emphatic dedication to 'the kingship of Christ', the *Thomistisch Tijdschrift voor Katholiek Kultuurleven* was presenting itself in 1930 as a supporter of this programme in the broad sense.

Pius X had used the term 'Catholic Action' for the first time in 1905, in the encyclical *Il fermo proposito*, but then still in a very general sense as an indication of divergent Catholic initiatives in the social sphere. It was a collective term for Catholic attempts to contribute to the solution of what was then called 'the social question'. Pius X spoke positively of 'all these works, sustained and promoted chiefly by lay Catholics, and whose form varies according to the needs of each country'.[30] In the encyclical, the laity are emphatically encouraged not only to practise the virtues, but also to 'use every means in seeking to restore Jesus Christ to the family, the school and society'. Here they had above all to 'take to heart the interests of the people, especially those of the working and agricultural classes, not only by inculcating in the hearts of everybody a true religious spirit ... but also by endeavouring to dry their tears, to alleviate their sufferings and to improve their economic situation'.[31] These are striking words, but they were written for a church-political purpose. In his encyclical, Pius X was opposing groups in Italy which were in favour of a more autonomous Catholic social movement, free from the direct influence of the hierarchy. In his view one could by no means consider 'works which are primarily designed for the restoration and promotion of true Christian civilization and which constitute Catholic action in the above-mentioned sense' to be 'independent of the counsel and direction of the ecclesiastical authority', far less in conflict with this authority.[32] In *Ubi arcano Dei*, and in the explanatory letters about it at the end of the 1920s, including one to the Belgian cardinal Van Roey, Pius XI reinforced this line of opposition to the great autonomy of the laity. The pope made Catholic Action a proper name and clearly stated that it denoted the participation of the laity in the mission of the hierarchy, understood as a supplement to existing pastoral care and with the aim of restoring all things in Christ. He pressed the bishops to set up an organization embedded in the church structures which was adequate for a Catholic Action in this sense.[33]

Under the leadership of Van Roey people in Belgium in fact went over to it in the 1920s. This led to a complicated dispute between divergent parties. Catholic Action, as Van Roey tried to set it up on the urging of the pope, thought strongly in terms of the church and aimed to influence society indirectly through the renewed animation of Catholics. The General Christian Workers Alliance (ACW), the Catholic professional movement, was particularly opposed to this; it wanted to combine religious education directly with concrete social and political action. The Catholic 'trade unions', in the wake of the social teaching of Leo XIII's *Rerum novarum*, had come into being as a Catholic answer to the concrete social need. This need was interpreted in religious terms as being both an expression and cause of the spiritual decline of the time. In the circles of the ACW people thought that social and political commitment to the improvement of the fortunes of workers and education in Catholic doctrine were on the same wavelength. Given this view, trade-union members regarded Catholic Action as it took form under the stimulus of the hierarchy as a rival, an attempt especially to withdraw training from the responsibility of the laity and put it in the hands of the hierarchy. Here it was not just a question of who had a say; given the attitude of the Belgian episcopate, if the hierarchy had a greater say, in all probability that would mean that Catholic social teaching would be used to reinforce unity among Catholics and would be presented as a stimulus to co-operation between different classes and social trends. In trade-union circles, *Rerum novarum* was read primarily as a call to work for the improvement of the position of the workers.[34]

In a sense, the attempts to bring Catholic activities in the social sphere under the umbrella of Catholic Action were in fact along the same lines as the ongoing efforts of the Belgian episcopate to preserve Catholic unity at all costs, and they bore witness to the tendency to regard the defence of the church and its teaching as the main goal of Catholic social organizations. But the dispute between Catholic Action and the ACW can also be seen as an intensive debate on the way in which religion could play a role in contemporary culture and could contribute to the resolution of social questions. For Catholic Action too, as in fact it came into being, was, in substance, to an important degree backed by a concern to improve the social position of the workers. This was seen as a consequence of a Catholic view of human beings and society. The Flemish priest Joseph Cardijn (1882–1967), who was also to be the great animator and *the* central symbol of Catholic Action, embodied this commitment. In 1921 Cardijn had founded the Christian People's Party for industrial and agricultural workers in opposition to the conservative Catholic Party; in fact it was a direct forerunner of the CVP of 1945.[35] Because he saw in Catholic Action as propagated by Pius X and Pius XI a possibility for a true improvement for the workers, in 1925 Cardijn founded the Young Catholic Workers (KAJ), of which almost immediately he became the national chaplain – 'provost' – nominated by the bishops. This organization was quickly to spread all over the world and was recognized up to the highest circles in the church as the model of an adequate form of Catholic Action. As a reward for his efforts, in 1965 Cardijn was created a cardinal by Pope Paul VI. Cardijn's view to a large degree determined what Catholic Action was about.[36]

Cardijn was convinced that religion was 'the only lever which can permanently raise up the working class', and for him moral and religious elevation was therefore more important than the improvement of material circumstances. This was not for want of being moved by the lot of the workers, but Cardijn was convinced that they could achieve their rights only in a totally different social culture and that therefore work needed to be done on the culture. The Young Catholic Workers, Cardijn wrote in 1935, were concerned to achieve 'a true Christian ordering of society'; their efforts were directed towards 'a new youth for a new world order under the kingship of Christ'. He saw this building of a new world order as the real task of the workers in the 'organized and able-bodied lay apostolate under the hierarchy of the church', i.e. in Catholic Action. In order to be good builders, young workers had to be equipped, by faith in the social teaching of the church and 'under the leadership of the provosts and better educated lay people', ultimately to come to see, judge and act about this themselves in their own situation. Along these lines, Cardijn was concerned more than anything else with the social and religious autonomy of the workers.[37]

The ambiguity of Cardijn's attitude is to a large degree the ambiguity of the open view of Catholicism with which the post-war *Kultuurleven* also worked. We shall also see this ambiguity in Schillebeeckx. On the one hand, in Cardijn there were clear traces of paternalism; for example, the view of the KAJ on how one judged and treated people was to an important degree determined by the hierarchy or its delegates and what they saw as the interest of the church. On the other hand it meant that the famous three-some 'see, judge, act' was clearly impossible for Catholic Action on the basis of obedience to the hierarchy and existing church teaching alone. There could be Catholic influence on social developments only if there were Catholics who had come of age who had sufficient insight to develop in the midst of society the new world order which had been begun. That gave the Catholic laity, who stood in the midst of society, an important and in-dependent role in the mission of the church in the service of this new world. By its broad presentation of information about contemporary develop-ments, church teaching and philosophical and theological views, *Kultuur-leven* sought to support this mission, and under the kingship of Christ to contribute to 'a noble human existence in this world, the herald and pre-paration for the perfect life in God'.

In May 1940 the journal *Kultuurleven* – evidently the original title was quickly felt to be too cumbersome; the designation *Thomistisch Tijdschrift* had already disappeared in the early years – ceased to appear. When it came out again after the war, its aims were also reformulated and sharpened. In the programmatic text in the first issue of 1945, the chief editor Jan-Hendrik Walgrave stated that given the great social problems which people faced in the post-war period, traditional Catholic thought had to change profoundly. 'There is ... no philosophical world-view which holds the great Catholic world together ideologically.'[38] And in his view it was precisely here that there was a great need. *Kultuurleven* had to be

> a combative organ of active, synthetic prompting of the spirit, to restore the foundation and the unity of culture. We therefore want our journal to be not so much the reflection of the many kinds of achievements in every domain of spiritual work as an instrument of our active efforts to build up the one, healthy culture permeated with meaning.[39]

The ultimate aim was a reorientation of the whole of culture. *Kultuurleven* aimed at the 'self-examination and self-criticism of culture' in all its breadth, and therefore the articles covered virtually all the sub-areas of culture and society. However, this self-examination and self-criticism had to be done on the basis of the 'forgotten centre' of culture: 'the meaning of life'.[40]And there was no doubt whatsoever that this meaning was to be found in the Catholic faith.

The man who expounded this programme, Jan Walgrave (1911–86), had joined the Dominicans in Ghent some years before Edward Schillebeeckx, where he was given the religious name Henricus.[41]After his philosophical and theological training, in 1943 he gained his doctorate at the Catholic University in Louvain with a study on the work of the English cardinal and theologian John Henry Newman (1801–90). He was to be occupied with Newman all his life; reverence for Newman and identification with him drove Walgrave increasingly to call himself Jan-Hendrik, thus combining both his baptismal and religious names. Walgrave was above all attracted by what Newman wrote about the gradual growth of the insight that human beings always already lived within the power of attraction of the 'kindly light', which was what God ultimately is. This light led people all the more faithfully, the more faithfully that they followed its sign. Walgrave pointed out that Newman's view was in fact a modern variant of the idea that as creatures, human beings have a share in God, precisely in their desire for him.[42] This so-called doctrine of participation, which in particular can also be found in Thomas Aquinas, also played a major role in Schillebeeckx's work from this period, and the two Dominicans were in many respects close to each other.[43] In 1943 both Schillebeeckx and Walgrave were lecturers at the Dominican house of studies. Schillebeeckx was to become a professor at the Higher Institute for Religious Studies at the Catholic University of Louvain in 1956, and Walgrave in 1957.

Among the Dominicans Walgrave was a lecturer in – as it was called at this time – 'theodicy and fundamental theology'. Here 'theodicy' did not have the more limited meaning, developed by G. W. von Leibniz, of the problem how God's goodness can be reconciled with the existence of evil in the world. In scholastic terminology since midway through the nineteenth century the word had come to designate all the results and problems relating to the philosophical knowledge of God. Thus Walgrave's work was on the borderline between philosophy and theology, and his task explicitly included reflection on the relationship between them. Along the lines of the climate of thought among Flemish Dominicans, his starting point, like Schillebeeckx's, was that human existence is characterized by a natural openness to and orientation on God which is to be fulfilled in Christian faith. Walgrave tried to find the synthesis between Christian tradition and human openness not only theoretically, as a theologian and metaphysician,[44] but also in more direct dialogue with contemporary culture. Not only did he, as its chief editor, guide the attempts of *Kultuurleven* to bridge the gap between a thoroughly unworldly faith and an unbelieving world, but for years an article appeared in every issue under the pseudonym 'Humanus', in which Walgrave consistently expounded what in his eyes a Christian humanism could be and what he thought that a Catholic view of human beings and culture would look like.[45]

Under the leadership of Walgrave, after the war the programme of *Kultuurleven* was orientated more emphatically than before, not on the defence of the social position of the church in the light of modernity, but in giving form to another, Catholic, modernity. Walgrave and the people around him were concerned to permeate modern culture with a Catholic spirit.[46] He was convinced that the church, and especially the clergy, had not to become too involved with 'political, social and educational concerns and services', but to focus on building up a deliberate world-view, giving culture 'a principle of synthesis' and 'a form of self-criticism'.[47] The post-war rebuilding of society had not to concentrate on a rapid solution of its burning problems but on an internal purging and deepening of life by developing a synthetic Catholic world-view. In 1945, it was evident to Walgrave that culture needed such a world-view, for anyone who looked around in 'our modern world' would be struck by a 'scenario of great disorder'. Therefore, in his view, 'almost everywhere' there was a sense that order was needed and unbelievers had 'broad sympathy' for the Catholic Church as the 'only power which could bring about the spiritual restoration of culture'.[48]

The programme of *Kultuurleven* was characterized by the same ambiguity as that of Catholic Action as formulated by Cardijn, or for example also as the ambiguity of the renewal of Catholic philosophy as this emanated from the Higher Institute for Philosophy in Louvain. On the one hand connections were made with one of the central presuppositions of the Catholic offensive against modernity for which Leo XIII had laid the basis: the crisis and the violence of modern culture and the perplexity of modern men and women were attributed to the cutting of the bond with Catholicism by modern thought in the name of human autonomy. On the other hand, the circles of *Kultuurleven* began from the conviction that the synthetic Catholic world-view which could bring about the necessary spiritual restoration could not be presented to modern men and women as an abstract, true system. They would not abandon the idea that the Catholic faith contained in itself the solution to all the problems of modernity for which others were searching so diligently, but this idea was given another content. The synthesis which already existed most deeply in Catholic doctrine had 'also to be recaptured from present-day ideas and circumstances'; according to Walgrave's orientating article in 1945, a far-reaching investigation into the 'whole situation of the modern spirit' was needed, but the outcome of this investigation was already fixed. Later he was to say that the so-called Christian humanism that he propagated in *Kultuurleven* in the post-war period aimed

at a renewed unity of life of Christian religion and earthly culture and ...
[tried] to demonstrate theologically that distinctive human cultural
activity had to be taken up unsullied and undiminished in the concrete,
personal and social structure of Christian life.[49]

In his articles on a cultural theology which appeared in *Kultuurleven* in 1945,
Schillebeeckx investigated what it would mean for theology if 'distinctively
human cultural activity had to be taken up unsullied and undiminished in
the concrete, personal and social structure of Christian life'.

Much later, during the period of polarization within the Catholic Church
after the Second Vatican Council, Schillebeeckx and Walgrave were to be in
two different church-political camps. From its founding, Schillebeeckx was
involved in the international theological journal *Concilium*, which wanted to
maintain the conciliar openness of the church and make it more fruitful.
Walgrave became a member of the Dutch editorial board of the international Catholic journal *Communio*, set up as its counterpart. And whereas
Schillebeeckx's theology was looked on with mistrust during the 1960 and
1970s from the official church side, in 1974 Walgrave became a member of
the International Theological Commission established by the Vatican, which
had to adopt semi-official standpoints on tricky theological themes; however, here he found himself in the company of prominent Council and
Concilium theologians like Yves Congar and Karl Rahner. Yet from its
foundation in 1960 until 1976, when he had to retire on reaching the age of
65, Walgrave was also a member of the editorial board of *Tijdschrift voor
Theologie*, set up by Schillebeeckx, and he contributed to the special issue of
this journal on the position of the theologian which appeared on the
occasion of Schillebeeckx's sixtieth birthday.[50] Nevertheless, perhaps from
the beginning a not unimportant difference of emphasis can be noted in the
work of the two Dominicans. In 1952 Schillebeeckx devoted a discussion to
a collection of Walgrave's 'Humanus' articles. In it he made clear that
however much he recognized himself in Walgrave's view of culture and
associated himself with him in his work, he also had a serious matter of
principle to put to his fellow Dominican. In the theological jargon customary at the time Schillebeeckx wrote that he had the impression that for
Walgrave 'the natural values within the Christian system of life have only
instrumental value in respect of the life of grace'. And he asked himself
whether a concern for a culture which was healthy for human beings was not
an essential part of the Christian faith for its own sake. This implied a far-
reaching question on a practical level. The question was how far the work of
ordinary Catholic laity in the world, in their activities in service to others
and to human culture, was an independent and essential contribution to the
mission of the church. From a religious perspective, was what they did really
important – and Schillebeeckx was convinced of that – or was it important

simply in so far as it made possible or facilitated the proclamation of the supernatural truth of faith by the hierarchical church?[51]

CHRISTIAN HUMANISM AS 'HUMBLE HUMANISM'

Despite its ambiguities, the programme of *Kultuurleven* offered Schillebeeckx the context for going further in his quest for the 'fundamental principles of a theology of culture' on which he had begun at the end of his student days. He could go outside the closed world of theological students within a religious order of which he was later to say in an interview: 'My theological training, which took place during the war, did not have any connection whatever with what was actually happening. We lived as if the war was not going on.'[52] But evidently this did not stand in the way of contact with the spirit of the time. In the articles on 'The Christian Situation' with which after the war he entered the public forum in *Kultuurleven*, remarkably Schillebeeckx stuck closely to what he had written as a student in *Biekorf*. Some passages were taken over almost word for word from the *Biekorf* article 'Nature and Supernature', on his confrontation with Karl Adam. *Kultuurleven* brought to light how far his theological work was bound up with the wider debate on the future of culture and its place within Christianity, as this took place in Belgium after the Second World War.

The history of the spiritual climate in Europe after the Second World War is remarkable. In retrospect, what is so striking in the two decades after this large-scale devastation, after unprecedented catastrophes which are indicated by simple place names like Auschwitz and Hiroshima, is that there appeared to be a heyday of hope. Rarely was the confidence that a new world could be built up with the aid of science and technology so great as in the post-war period. A clear witness to this optimism can still be seen in Belgium, namely the Atomium in Brussels, the Belgian pavilion for the World Exposition of 1958, which takes the form of a crystal of ice magnified 150 billion times. At the opening of 'Expo 58', the Belgian king Boudewijn remarked:

> The aim of this world exposition is the creation of an atmosphere of collaboration and peace. We must now choose between the arms race, as a result of which the new scientific developments are threatening to turn against humanity, and closer collaboration. Only along this last way can a true peace come about. We hope that when they have returned home, the many foreign visitors may bear witness that a new humanism is arising, which can expand only through peace and collaboration, but which can conquer the world.[53]

The optimism which resounds in these words seems characteristic of the spirit of the age, until halfway through the 1960s, when a change came about.

But this optimistic mood grew only gradually. As the economic reconstruction of Europe succeeded and prosperity reached unprecedented heights, the modern eddies of change were increasingly experienced as irresistible progress. But it seems that people also above all wanted to believe in progress. In 1994 the Spanish writer Jorge Semprun described his own inability to confront his recollections of Buchenwald concentration camp. After the war the first priority was to survive: 'The hideous dead here, my comrades, [did] not need any explanation. They needed us to live, simply to live with all one's strength in the recollection of death.'[54] I am not concerned here to present Semprun as an interpreter of the spirit of the post-war age; rather, the spiritual climate after 1945 seems to an important degree to have been governed by the feeling that life first had to be rebuilt, collectively and personally, in order to gain new confidence in life by doing precisely this.[55] Hence the nagging undercurrent of uncertainty, which expressed itself in the key position of existentialism in the philosophical and cultural landscape, already indicated. The fear of meaninglessness, the void and arbitrariness could not be suppressed.

Humanism

Confronting this existentialism, in the post-war years Schillebeeckx tried to sketch a picture of the human situation from a Christian perspective. At this time the key word was 'humanism', human experience orientated on full human life, on humanity, and in his articles for *Kultuurleven* Schillebeeckx reflected on the theological basis for a Christian humanism. In doing so he did not spare his readers. It was characteristic of his approach from the beginning that as a theologian he could not limit his attention to the phenomena that immediately came to light, even in articles which in principle were intended for a wider public. He complained unreservedly in 'The Christian Situation' about the superficiality and

> pragmatism of those who in their rash ventures on the surface never plumb the depths that support them; who are content in their daring to pit their strength against the waves in the storm and feel no need in a basic treatment of fundamental questions first to descend into the depths from which the storm has arisen.

However, he likewise wanted to dissociate himself from the notion that he was wanting to make a plea on behalf of those who constantly hide themselves in the deep and never surface; who on any contact with the surface shoot into the depths like shy fish, safely hidden there from being burnt by current problems, to go on weaving undisturbed the insubstantial net of their own profound contemplations.[56]

At the heart of his articles on 'The Christian Situation' there was a systematic exposition of what in fact a speculative theological anthropology was. In Schillebeeckx's eyes this established the basic principles of what he saw as a theology of culture.

The starting point was the classic Thomist conviction that as creatures human beings are supported by God and are orientated on God. In his student days Schillebeeckx had rediscovered the importance of the starting point that, as he now wrote, man was 'of God'. In his eyes human beings came from God above all in the dynamic of their development, in the orientation of their desire and will; from this Schillebeeckx concluded that for these human beings, 'maintaining their personality, their "self-love", is directly and spontaneously love of God'. As far as he was concerned, this also applied when this love of God did not come to light as such. Again in the imagery of depth and surface, he put it like this:

Our weak eye sees only what floats on the surface of the deep sea: the ship, not the depth and the buoyancy of the waters on which it floats. Thus, too, only the humanistic contribution [of human activity] is evident to the eye, whereas the tendency of God which bears [the human being] towards the harbour of self-fulfilment remains invisible (231).

In his view, that human beings were always already bound up with God took the form of the quest for fulfilment in God. The theological anthropology that Schillebeeckx sketched out was not that of the static-scholastic 'thinking animal' with an intellectual immaterial soul, which is in a position to grasp abstract, eternal truths. Along the lines of his teacher De Petter, with modern philosophy his starting point, was that the human being, 'to use a saying of Heidegger's, is "a being of possibility"'.[57] And in this sense Schillebeeckx then went on to interpret the traces which Aristotle's teleology had left in the thought of Thomas Aquinas – the notion that every being is characterized by orientation on a specific goal. In Schillebeeckx's own words, God planted

humanity ... not from the start as a tree bearing fruit; rather he cast a seed, a precious grain laid down in the furrow. In its own inner life-force, swelling under the rays of God's sun and the watchful care of the great Gardener, it has to develop into a full-grown form. Thus man is created as a growing value, as a power which constantly receives from God's creative hand, but also swells and ferments from within.

The consequence of this was that in his view to be human was to develop and grow, and had no significance 'other than in the function of complete incarnation, in the function of steadily ripening into a noble and good humanity experienced integrally'. However, in his view this noble and good humanity could not completely 'blossom in the individual', and 'therefore is the fair consummation of all that being human means ... a communal task'. His conclusion was: 'the human being as nature is directed towards the human being as culture; here we understand culture in the broadest possible sense as the blossoming of all the virtualities that there are in man' (230).[58] Thus he made clear both the need for a theology of culture as a sub-division of the theology of creation and its possibility.

What was possible was a theology of culture as reflection on the human being who, as a created being, orientated on interpersonal fellowship, was in this orientation pointed to God. Such a theology of culture was necessary because in his view this orientation on God did not come to light in contemporary culture. Just like the Christian Democrat movement in post-war politics, just like Walgrave and the other *Kultuurleven* people, Schillebeeckx was looking for a Christian alternative to actual developments in modern times. In 1945 he interpreted directly in theological terms the lack of attention to the orientation on God which had also been created by God. He saw it as an expression of original sin, the destruction in principle of the relationship between human beings and God which had been dominant since Adam had turned away from God and had disobeyed God's commandment in paradise. In Catholic doctrine, original sin was traditionally understood as the situation in which human nature has turned away from God and is focused on evil.[59] Schillebeeckx emphasized this first aspect: through original sin human nature is bent back on itself, shut up in itself. The orientation on God is cut off. Nature remained 'a divine jewel, a force of life which strives for complete unfolding and fulfilment', but through original sin this life force is 'not paralysed, but purposeless'. For him, 'not paralysed, but purposeless' meant that intrinsically nothing changed in the human orientation on God. But the consequences of original sin were far-reaching, for people began to develop 'a view of life within the world'. 'It is here that the curse of original sin lies: we have lost God and found ourselves', as a result of which human nature remains behind as 'a precious pearl, but one which has been thrown away' (236f.).

Thus, according to Schillebeeckx, human culture had become meaningless without a link to supernature, to divine grace, and involvement with Christianity and the church. But in his view, along the lines indicated above, the specific effect of grace, Christianity and the church was that God broke through the self-imprisonment of human beings. Grace restored human beings as creatures and brought them to a new completeness:

> Human nature is not just presupposed and raised above itself by grace to become a child of God ... In addition, at the same time it is ennobled as nature: through grace the human being also becomes more than human, divine-human ... The human person [finds] in Christianity a transcendent consummation of his personality and can ... at the same time, through the higher supernatural consummation, raise his own natural consummation to an apotheosis (241).[60]

In his discussion with Karl Adam, Schillebeeckx had already said that grace made human beings both more-than-human and more human, endowing them with a noble and good humanity.[61] Now he worked out what this meant rather more closely. According to him, 'noble and good human nature' entered the 'divine order of life' and through this was 'steeped and permeated with a supernatural dedication' to become a sanctuary for the divine life (242). This implied that for the believer, working on the humanization of culture was in itself and at its deepest a religious activity:

> For the physician, trust in his healing practices does not lie at the periphery of his Catholic, spiritual life, just as for a mother, too, the spiritual life largely consists in bringing up her children in the love of God (597).

Because the orientation on God permeated the whole of human culture, even though it often proved invisible, the church had no need to subject the world through its hierarchy and fill the life of lay believers from outside with an orientation on God. The important thing was for believers to learn to listen to the world in the right way and thus find possible ways of breaking open from within the situation in which it was closed off from God and closed in on itself. 'Starting from a deeper experience of faith, the Catholic lay community must take in hand the activity of culture and give it direction' is what Schillebeeckx actually says, and as we shall see, he would later work out this view more closely in what is called a 'lay spirituality'. But immediately after making his statement in 'The Christian Situation' about influencing culture through the action of lay people, he seems to take fright and goes on to retract it: 'However, this takes time, and meanwhile the church *as such* must not give up its earthly positions of power, so that its freedom of movement is not paralysed' (609). This addition, though, seems to say more about what he thought he could allow himself than about his view of the relationship between church and culture.

In the 1940s and 1950s, existentialism presented itself as the true humanism, the authentic acceptance of the human condition. Similarly, with the help of his theological anthropology, Schillebeeckx tried to demonstrate that being truly, authentically human was ultimately a matter of being Christian. To be Christian was to take upon oneself being human as an orientation on God, and in this sense, in his view it was the duty of every human being to be Christian. 'What a sunflower ... does by virtue of its natural drive, the human being must do in freedom: just as it seeks the sun, so he must seek the Father of creation,' he wrote; human beings were 'morally obliged to do what they must do out of free will'. At the same time, in his view being Christian, being Catholic, was based on a well-considered decision, like the existentialist choice to accept as a task the human situation of thrownness and radical finitude. According to him there was

> no reason for the Catholic to envy those who boast of their attitude as the result of a royally free, daring decision. His attitude to life, too, has the character of a venture and stems from his free, irreplaceable decision (588f.).

But in Schillebeeckx's eyes the substance of this decision differed fundamentally from the existentialist decision heroically to endure the human situation. Although he emphasized strongly how much the stress on the need for 'trust in life' and 'more faith in the goodness of life' was a risk and a heroic virtue, particularly in the situation of 'post-war uncertainty and disillusionment', for him Christian faith was about abandoning the idea that the meaning of life depended on one's own efforts. It turned on the 'reversal' of tragic human existence 'into a glad, bold and free trust in God' (596). What was impossible for existentialism was, in his view, one of the possibilities for Catholicism: despite everything, to know that one was most deeply at home in the world.

According to Schillebeeckx, the Christian was at home by being at home with – '*in*' – God. 'The one who has been given grace', he wrote – and at this time in his view that naturally coincided with the baptized and confessing Catholic – 'looks on everything from the standpoint of God who has become his friend. He sees and loves everything with the eye and heart of God, his Friend.' It was just like a human friendship, in which someone

> is enriched in heart and soul with the heart and soul of his friend, so that their thinking and feeling, their striving and longing, and all the stirring of their two souls, flow together in one and the same rhythm of life. And now he sees and loves human beings and things much better and much more. Now he also sees and loves in them what his friend sees and loves in them, and why his spirit and heart were closed when he stood alone.

According to Schillebeeckx, the analogy to this notion of friendship, which was ultimately derived from Aristotle, was

> the supernatural gift of grace ... in the literal sense a loving spiritual embrace of God and human beings, true friendship. And as in this inner

friendship God is the one who is completely superior, the man sees and loves all the rest – culture, nation, people or whatever – only in so far as it interests the Friend and as he sees it and loves it (589f.).[62]

And he concluded that believers may still only 'will, value, love these things "in" God's will, "in" Gods evaluation, "in" God's love, and thus, as and in so far as they are willed, evaluated and loved by God' (591). For him the gaze of the believer must ultimately coincide with God's gaze. He calls this position 'supernatural exclusivism': only God's view counts.

'Supernatural exclusivism'

In 1945 Schillebeeckx ultimately worked out his theological view of human effort and human culture under the label of 'supernatural exclusivism'.[63] As he understood this term, it implied on the one hand that Catholics might appropriate the modern efforts towards human autonomy without reservations. In his view, such an effort was even a task for them, a religious commandment, for since human beings as creatures are orientated on God, to realize humanity as fully as possible is to realize the bond with God by which faith lives. But at the same time the term indicated Schillebeeckx's rejection of existing modern culture and the direction in which this was developing. So from a Christian point of view detachment from culture was necessary. Detachment and at the same time nearness: for the believer – I have already quoted this in the present chapter – in the first instance this created quite a confused situation:

> In turn we are drawn to two poles: the evidence – and I really mean evidence – of the value of harmony: all that is by nature beautiful, noble, fine, in short all that is authentically human can blossom fully in the life of grace, but on the other hand the Christian evidence that it must be possible to give up all those human values for the sake of the life of grace; hence [the] need for radical self-denial (91).

The quotation goes on:

> In being tossed to and fro like this it becomes difficult to say 'sacrificial value' and 'harmony value' in the same breath: and it is there after all that the question lies (91).

He called the solution to this 'question' 'supernatural exclusivism'.

Schillebeeckx's 'solution' was remarkably technical and abstract. He wrote:

> Although from an ontological perspective the cultural goods in the presence of the life of grace are of course values of harmony, they are at

the same time, seen in terms of the economy of salvation, of course sacrificial values (603).

'Of course' here is not a synonym for 'as a matter of course', but has the typical Flemish meaning of 'by nature'. In God's order of creation – 'ontologically' – for Schillebeeckx dedication to human culture and dedication to God were not in conflict with each other; on the contrary, the whole creation is orientated on God. But according to the theological notion of the great saving acts of God – 'the economy of salvation' – people after the fall lived in a perverse, twisted world in which human culture had turned against its natural orientation. In this situation the Christian bond with God – 'the life of grace' – implied the abandonment of the tie with the prevalent culture. A short time later Schillebeeckx developed this thought further and located the cause of the actual situation in the fundamental ambiguity of the relationship between God and his creatures. In his view, God's gracious involvement with human beings called for an ultimately absolute priority to be given to their orientation on God. But this implied a tremendous possibility for conflict, for human beings could also reject this priority and turn exclusively to the creatures.[64] Completely along the lines of what he had already written about this in his student days, he stated that this possibility had become a reality with original sin and that this situation was expressed in human culture as it was. Existing – viz. modern – culture is directed only towards the creation and creatures and therefore is always already in competition with God, cultural life with the life of grace. In this situation earthly values can become authentic values once more only if they are first sacrificed in their existing form and taken up again 'in Christ' or 'in God' and made new. For the Schillebeeckx of the 1950s the death and resurrection of Jesus Christ are the central symbol of his sacrifice of everything in favour of a life with God. Then in Christ, by grace, the cultural task of humanization which is offered has to be purged and taken up again with renewed perseverance.[65]

Here there were unmistakable echoes of a long tradition. Setting oneself apart from the world, dissociating oneself from it by means of asceticism, has been a central element of Christian faith since the New Testament. To a certain degree any plausible interpretation of Christianity must be able to give a place to this fact. For Schillebeeckx, this was all the more the case since as a religious he stood in a tradition which had cultivated precisely this ascetic side of Christianity, forsaking everything for God's sake.[66] Moreover, the fundamental conflict between Christian faith and the modern world was strongly emphasized in particular in the Catholic conflict with modernity, above all also with a reference to the ascetic line in the Christian tradition. So it was almost inevitable that this constant Catholic effort to keep a distance from the dominant expressions of culture would leave traces in Schillebeeckx's work.

But this was not all. His confrontation with Karl Adam made it clear that for Schillebeeckx there really were two *evidences* in the relationship with culture. The 'evidence of the value of harmony', the conviction that 'all that is by nature beautiful, noble, fine, in short all that is authentically human ... [could] blossom fully in the life of grace' really stood alongside the equally great 'evidence of the value of sacrifice' and the 'need for radical self-denial'. He had fundamental objections to the emphasis on human effort and strength which dominated modern culture. This in fact gave his approach to human beings and culture a colouring of its own, which contrasted with other attempts to reconcile the Catholic tradition with modern culture, in particular the influential attempt for which the starting point was laid down by the French Catholic philosopher Jacques Maritain.

Although Maritain was originally a Protestant intellectual who grew up under the influence of philosophical rationalism at the Sorbonne around the turn of the century, he became one of the most important representatives of the so-called *'renouveau catholique'* in France. For him, too, personally, Catholic doctrine, and especially Thomist philosophy, was a way out of the problems and aporias which modern culture created. He also expressed this in his work, and evidently with success. His friend the philosopher Nikolai Berdyaev, who was of Russian origin, said that he was 'the first to have introduced Thomism into culture', and a number of important cultural figures – for example, the writer Jean Cocteau and the composer Igor Stravinsky – converted to Catholicism under his influence.[67] His work was of great importance for the changes in Catholic thinking on the relationship between faith and culture which would ultimately find expression in the Vatican II constitution *Gaudium et spes*. The starting point of this document was to be the same as that of Schillebeeckx's theology of culture, namely that 'it is one of the properties of the human person that he can achieve true and full humanity only by means of culture, that is, through the cultivation of the goods and values of nature. Whenever, therefore, it is a matter of human life, nature and culture are intimately linked together.' And it was to state that the fact that Christians 'in their pilgrimage to the heavenly city are to seek and relish the things that are above' makes it not less but more important that they should work 'with all men ... towards the establishment of a world that is more human'.[68] Thus religion appeared as part of the inspiration for human cultural activity.

Maritain also had considerable influence in the Dutch-language area in the period between the world wars. His most important works quickly became available in translation and were much read by those who strove for Catholic renewal and an open but combative attitude towards modern society.[69] The Catholic cultural journal *De Gemeenschap*, which appeared in the Netherlands from 1925 to 1941 – the subtitle, 'Monthly for Catholic Reconstruction', made it clear how much the 'Catholic youth' who produced this journal were also striving for a 'Catholic renewal' in the Netherlands – based themselves on Maritain's philosophy of culture. In the first issue, immediately after the introduction there was an article by Maritain in which he stated: 'To discover a really living religious art, the whole of modern art must be put on a higher plane, spiritualized and changed on the basis of God.' This is also a good summary of Maritain's view of culture in the broad sense: Catholics must not isolate themselves from modern culture but inspire it from within with 'the spiritual life of the saints'.[70] Now that more and more of the structures which had guaranteed Christian influence on culture were falling away, it was important to Maritain that Catholics, on the basis of a strong spirituality, should in their own persons reshape contemporary culture, which had succumbed to indifference to supernature and real community, in a Christian sense. Over against the prevalent humanism which in his eyes was only semi-humanism because it cut off human beings and culture from God and community, Maritain set what he called an 'integral humanism' that needed to be a 'theocentric humanism'. In order to propagate humanism, in his view a strongly militant Catholic élite was needed, a 'new Christianity'.

Like the people of *Kultuurleven* and like the young Schillebeeckx, Maritain put all the emphasis on the orientation of creation on God. And like them he was concerned to see a Christian culture in which the creature is restored to honour in God.[71] Nevertheless, Schillebeeckx emphatically opposed Maritain at one quite decisive point. He evidently thought that Maritain put too much trust in autonomous human powers and the human ability to build a Christian culture. Certainly Maritain spoke of 'the way of the cross' which was necessary to realize this culture, and the insight of modern man that culture cannot build 'a throne on earth in accord with all the dues of God's majesty' but can only create the earthly conditions for a life on which 'the sovereign love may be able to come down'.[72] However, after his clash with Karl Adam on this point, for Schillebeeckx this was no longer radical enough. He quoted Thomas Aquinas to the effect that 'the goodness of grace which is given to an individual is greater than the goodness of the whole of creation'. And for him the expression 'supernatural exclusivism' meant a fundamental criticism of Maritain's efforts towards a Christian culture. 'This is a reversal of our "integral humanism"' is his commentary on the quotation from Thomas, clearly with the aim of rejecting Maritain's position.[73]

Maritain argued for an unconditional commitment to a human culture based on 'brotherly love'. That called for an 'ongoing effort'. Because of this difficulty and effort, which, however, at the same time was convinced of victory, he spoke of a 'heroic humanism'.[74] According to Maritain, Christians were the heroes of a new, Christian culture of society.[75]According to Schillebeeckx, however, they had to have abiding reservations about *any* culture. From his perspective there could not be a Christian culture in the strict sense. He wrote that in this world 'connection between nature and supernature remains an unfinished symphony, a harmony in becoming that can fall apart at any moment'.[76] In his view the 'Christian humanist will always have to experience, in a real sense and in fact, inner detachment from society by reason of the absolute greater value of the gift of salvation in humility: he knows that terrestrial humanism is an unfinished symphony with unavoidable (relative) fiascos'.[77] Of course it was very important for Christians to try to permeate their cultural activities with the Christian faith, but Schillebeeckx continued to emphasize that the result of this would always be ambivalent. Therefore he argued not for a heroic but for a 'humble humanism', a humanism which not only made the sacrifices necessary for building up culture, but also maintained an inner distance from the culture which it built up itself. This was indeed a Christian cultural activity based on a theology of culture, but precisely because of that it was not an attempt once again to create a Christian society.

Schillebeeckx was driven by different motives in his limited polemic with Maritain. First of all, of course, he was driven by the desire to guarantee the necessary distance between the transcendent God and the people who were working on culture in God's name. Secondly, he was convinced that human beings were not exclusively strong, but at decisive moments also weak, and that in their weakness too they were supported by God: this conviction played a central role in his views of Christian faith. For him, in Maritain there was too much emphasis on human strength. Thirdly, he evidently also thought it very important to state that cultural dedication to human salvation was important in its own right, also and precisely in the quite limited specific meaning that it had. In his eyes human action became significant only because it formed part of a comprehensive cultural project of a 'new Christianity', far less so when it took on meaning by forming part of a Catholic supernatural project led by the hierarchy. He felt that its religious or supernatural meaning lay in dedication to the world itself, and he evidently saw that ultimately this starting point was not sufficiently respected by Maritain. And perhaps, finally, as in his little confrontation with Walgrave, it was clear to him that his view of things made it more plausible 'finally ... to put "the world" in the hands of the Catholic lay community', and in so doing to give this complete autonomy, that is, without due supervision from those who by virtue of their office had to guard church teaching.[78]

What Schillebeeckx in 1945 called 'supernatural exclusivism' and later also termed 'supernatural absolutism' was an attempt to break with the idea that faith and theology are about an independent world detached from the world of human culture and human experience and at the same time to maintain the idea that faith also calls for conversion and that glory is due to God alone.[79] As will emerge further, the quest for a theological position which made this possible was a long process. Schillebeeckx did not always succeed in doing justice to the two starting points. But he hardly exaggerated when much later he wrote that in the 1940s and 1950s he constantly fought 'tooth and nail' against any thinking in terms of 'two worlds'.[80]

Supernatural exclusivism was to prove very productive. It gave Schillebeeckx the possibility of entering into dialogue with culture very broadly from the perspective of the Catholic faith. Here it would become increasingly clear to him that theology is a systematic reflection on a particular view of human existence, and thus also human culture, and in what sense it has this character, ultimately remaining implicit, but nevertheless expressing itself in words and concepts. In the light of this notion he was to change theology fundamentally from within. In 'The Christian Situation' Schillebeeckx wrote that he hoped 'elsewhere' to investigate the theology of culture that he sought on a 'technical level'.[81] As is evident from the notes that he made, the elaboration of a theology of culture had in fact intensively occupied him for a long time in his further studies. When he went to France after the liberation to complete his studies there, his plan was to do a doctorate on this subject.[82] Nothing was to come of that for practical reasons. Nevertheless, he did take some important steps in seeking the 'basic principles of a theology of culture'. The technical theological results of his efforts would ultimately find their way into the enormous number of stencilled lecture notes which formed the basis of his teaching activity in Louvain: I shall return to this material at length in Chapter 4. Then the approach which he called 'supernatural exclusivism' gave him the possibility of occupying himself further with cultural questions and discussions, as will become evident in this and the next chapter.

But his real concern was a 'supernatural exclusivism'. The actual culture in which people had to live was in his view 'in the present-day state of original sin' a culture the propagated values of which were in conflict with the Catholic faith and which posed a threat to it. Catholics needed to dissociate themselves from it, among other ways through the classic ascetic practices of fasting and abstinence, which at this time were still very much part of the Catholic subculture. Schillebeeckx did not hesitate to point to the example of 'Abraham who at God's command reached for the knife to slay his own blood', to kill his own child: the greatest sacrifice conceivable, made for no other reason than that God calls for it and God must be loved above all.[83] This is also a remnant of an ascetic ideal of poverty which sees nearness to God and detachment from the world as two sides of the same coin; traces of this can often be found in Schillebeeckx's work up to the

1960s. But he was always concerned with the pedagogical effect of asceticism, not with asceticism itself. Any specific practice was ultimately at the service of the human orientation on God in which 'we find ourselves at our finest and most glorious. "Whoever loses his life will gain it." Humanism is thus the other side of the surplus of supernatural exclusivism', indeed it is already 'paradise, i.e. the attractive harmony between integral noble and good humanity and the life of grace for which we long so much . . . promised for the hereafter'.[84]

'Spiritual life'

Schillebeeckx was convinced that the effort to give a Catholic form to modernity in the sense of a humble humanism on the basis of supernatural exclusivism was not just a matter of the Catholic view of life in general. It was ultimately a matter of

> the attitude of this or that Catholic person. The solution must thus be given in individual and concrete, not general and abstract terms; indeed it differs from person to person. How the intrinsic connection between human existence and the life of grace must be made in individual and concrete terms is in fact fundamentally a question of personal taste and sense refined by grace . . .[85]

Culture had not to be taken into the service of a supernatural goal from outside. The important thing was for it to be permeated at every level by a Christian spirit. And that could happen only through Christians with a cultivated spiritual life. With precisely this in view, the circle of Flemish Dominicans immediately after the war took the initiative to set up *Tijdschrift voor Geestelijk Leven* ('Journal of the Life of the Spirit'), later referred to as *TGL*. Schillebeeckx was closely involved in this initiative right from the start.

In an interview on the fiftieth anniversary of the founding of the journal he said that the idea came from his fellow Dominican Stefan Axters (1901–77).[86] Axters was a specialist in the palaeography and manuscript tradition of the works of Thomas Aquinas, but as well as that above all in the history of mysticism in the Low Countries. Halfway through the 1940s he published an extensive anthology of Dutch mystical literature, in the conviction that this was among the greatest treasures of the culture. In the Dominican spirit he saw mysticism as an experience of the divine urged on by the innate and natural human hunger for God. In his view 'the mystical literature of the Netherlands' was 'one attempt to capture the inexpressible in the humble garb of the Dutch language'.[87] The programme of *Tijdschrift voor Geestelijk*

Leven was in this spirit; programmatically its declared aim was to support 'all noble souls who with perseverance and constancy want to become detached from themselves and from all that would hinder the complete breakthrough of God in them'.[88] Probably because of this attention to the experience of God and the associated conviction that the life of faith was bound up with one's own culture, Axters sought contact with the young Schillebeeckx, who was thought to be very promising, and whose ideas as a dogmatic theologian were also markedly in this direction.

However, in retrospect Schillebeeckx recalled that he still felt that he was too young. He advised Axters to ask the advice of 'older fathers' for *TGL*, and so Bavo Van Hulse (1908–50) came to be involved in the initiative. He was a valued broadcaster, preacher and journalist in the sphere of – as Schillebeeckx was to write on his premature death – 'the spiritual life ... and theology put into practice'. From the beginning of 1946, as chief editor Van Hulse was in practice in charge of the journal. He proved to be very skilful at this and made *TGL* grow 'into a universally valued leading organ in the sphere of the spiritual life'.[89] After Van Hulse died in 1950, Schillebeeckx took over as chief editor and remained in this position until 1963. However, from the beginning his influence on the journal seems to have been very great, as is evident from language in editorials which is typical of him. Thus it was said that *Tijdschrift voor Geestelijk Leven* seeks to 'attach the thread spun by theological scholarship to life and to draw out its value'.[90] Schillebeeckx also to a considerable degree determined the image of the journal and contributed more articles than any other author. After he had become spiritual guide to the Dominican theological students in 1947, responsible for the further development of their spirituality, he published in *TGL* many versions of the weekly lectures that he gave to them.

With his students Schillebeeckx experimented with a more open form of religious life, more orientated on the world. By his own estimate, the growing practical orientation on the world outside the convent only slowly began to influence the way in which spirituality was written about in the journal. For however emphatically the explicit intention even from the beginning was to combine theology and spirituality with life, according to Schillebeeckx's later assessment, when the journal was founded it was still above all an abstract principle. 'We still took no account of the real context in which people live.'[91]

Tijdschrift voor Geestelijk Leven formed a kind of pair with *Kultuurleven*. The two journals agreed in their overall view of the state of culture and the intended Catholic reaction to it. In the 'To our readers' of the first issue of *TGL* the editors stated that 'our time ... unmistakably bears an explicit character of crisis'. The resolution of this crisis was not sought in a direct intervention by the church, but there was a desire to 'honour the autonomy of natural structures'. The need was acutely seen 'for *immanent* solutions to the tragic questions of today' and so, it was thought, it was important for people themselves to change 'by a deliberate return to the eternal, supernatural values'.[92] But where *Kultuurleven* – as an 'instrument of our active striving to rebuild the coherent healthy culture permeated with meaning' – wanted to be a mirror of 'the intellectual work in all the great spheres of culture', *TGL* saw it as its task to work on 'an ever growing inner experience of [the] divine life in us'. According to the editors a 'serious deepening of the spiritual life' needed to be the goal 'of the possible rebuilding of the shaken world'. *TGL* gave itself the aim of the spiritual formation of the Catholic élite: *TGL* was addressed 'to the priest, the religious and the lay person, not specifically in so far as they have the *care* of souls in one way or another but in so far as they themselves have a *soul* which is called to holiness'. Along this way the journal wanted to exercise indirect, but in its own conviction absolutely essential, influence on 'the apostolate in its broader and in its broadest sense', in other words on the shaping of culture in a Catholic spirit.[93]

In his first article in *TGL*, stating the perspective of the theological programme of the journal, Schillebeeckx explained what in his view it meant to combine theology with life. Here he did not begin from practice but gave a theoretical definition of what 'spirituality' really had to mean in a theological sense. Of course here he took up approaches which he had developed earlier, in discussion with Karl Adam and with 'kerygmatic theology'. The starting point was the image, which had become familiar in the meantime, of human beings as creatures for whose life an orientation on God was essential but at the same time by no means obvious. That was also indicated in the title of the article: 'A creaturely sense as the foundation for our spiritual life'. According to Schillebeeckx, Christian spirituality was a matter of living by a correct concept of God as that was developed in patient theological reflection:

> Religion or spiritual life, when pure in its orientation, is the correct concept of God put into practice: it involves making the objective relations between God and human beings apply in disposition and activity.[94]

Schillebeeckx's further thoughts about spirituality were primarily theological and doctrinal. Central for him was a statement from Catholic doctrine which, following scholasticism and the First Vatican Council, was fundamental, but at first sight somewhat speculative: God does not create because he is lacking in something – God is himself perfect – but out of overflowing love and goodness. Taken by itself, this statement made clear above all the distance between God and creation. God needed nothing and no one, was himself sufficient, and so the world, and therefore also human activity in the world, could not add anything to his glory or take anything from it. That is how this statement in fact functioned in the Constitution on Faith of the First Vatican Council, *Dei Filius*, and the constitution used the statement to make it clear that from the creation it is impossible to gain knowledge of God as he is in himself. According to Vatican I, *that* God is can be deduced from creation, but to know *what* this God is on whom everything is dependent and who determines being, order and morality, people need the church.[95] However, for Schillebeeckx the statement took quite a different turn. He put the emphasis primarily on the altruism of God's act of creation, the orientation on the other as other: 'It was not to increase his own happiness that God spoke his word of creation, but to reveal his own glory through the many good things that he communicates to creatures.' For Schillebeeckx, though, this loving orientation on the other was not the main thing: he was above all interested in what he saw as the content of God's creative action out of overflowing love: 'There is only one motive in creation: not God's love for his creatures, but God's love for himself.' And from this, in his view, there followed the orientation of creation, and thus of human beings, on God. For Schillebeeckx it was

> unavoidable that man is orientated on God through what he is. Doctrine tells us that he is created for God's glory. In other words, the inner sense and direction of human existence is God.[96]

Here he worked out what he said in 'The Christian Situation' about human culture in a view of man, taking up the insight that he had had in his student days in confrontation with Aristotle. For him the paradox of Christian anthropology was that precisely in their independence human beings are completely dependent on God, and that therefore modern human autonomy is not in principle in conflict with the orientation on God. On the contrary, according to Schillebeeckx the dependence on God made independent human striving for the good possible in the first place and was its abiding basis. 'It is of me, but it does not come from me, except through God's power, and precisely through this it becomes "mine".'[97]

Despite their apparent abstraction, these philosophical and theological reflections had far-reaching consequences for Schillebeeckx's view of spirituality. Spiritual life was not a separate sphere with its own customs, but in principle was a life in the world, a way of dealing with God as God could be encountered in dealing with the world, in other words with human culture. In his own words:

> Spiritual life is nothing but being still, listening and obeying, doing loyally, before and afterwards, what God whispers to us through the circumstances of life, from hour to hour: nothing but, given the circumstances of every moment of life, listening honestly to our upright conscience.[98]

Or to put it in yet another way, spiritual life as Schillebeeckx saw it was the existential dimension of the theology of culture that he stood for. It was the theology of culture in the form of a lived, individual faith.

Negatively, this also meant that in his view the spiritual life did not primarily consist in all kinds of devotional practices or the concrete exercise of detachment from the world. In his view *Tijdschrift voor Geestelijk Leven* had first of all to focus on spirituality in the sense of cultivating attention to God's manifestation in dealing with the world. His first contributions were primarily focused on this. At the same time he struggled to show that according to their deepest intention the traditional ascetical practices and customs also needed to be understood in this sense. In some reflections on the eucharist and confession, on praying the rosary, on asceticism and obedience for religious, on dying as submission to God's will and very extensively on Mary, which were closely connected with pastoral questions, he tried to show that 'the rousing call of God's love for mutual love, for religion and prayer' was not an attack 'on our human nature, at which every chivalrous person must rise up in defence as against an alien slavery, in order to be able to remain true to himself'.[99]

THE SITUATION IN FRANCE AS A MIRROR

Schillebeeckx had declared that his intention and that of a number of fellow Dominicans in *Tijdschrift voor Geestelijk Leven* to make a connection between theology and life was still 'an abstract principle' immediately after the war. As far as his own theology is concerned, it seems more accurate to say that it was open to a direct contact with life and in a sense called for such a contact from within, but did not arise out of that contact.

However, at an early stage he had already come in contact with a 'Christian situation' in which both spheres were bound together in a quite concrete way. He had to wait two years, but after the summer of 1945 it happened: he was sent to Paris to continue his studies.

The example of Congar and Chenu

In Le Saulchoir, the house of studies of the Parisian province of the Dominicans in Étiolles, he met his brother Dominicans Yves (Marie-Joseph) Congar (1904–95) and Marie-Dominique Chenu (1895–1990). A long time later, when Congar died, Schillebeeckx said that he had admired him for his erudition, but had also found him closed, withdrawn and impatient. Looking back, he said that Congar's lectures had been 'a cold shower' for him: 'When lecturing, Congar seemed distant, tired, dull.'[100] He remembered his contact with Chenu quite differently: 'a natural talent with a delight in life' and a 'dynamic theologian'.[101] Indeed: at a time when space for intellectual adventure in Catholic thought was at best to be found in philosophy, and theology was seen as tied up by official church doctrine, Chenu more than anyone else within the Catholic world emphasized that in principle the theologian was free, theoretically, but above all also in practice. With verve he insisted on the theological freedom of allowing oneself to be addressed by

> the word of God in the midst of the world, where the spirit is still present even now and also in human thought (theological thought), both indivi- dually and collectively, continues and consummates the system of Christ's incarnation.[102]

According to Chenu, the fact that God has become man in Jesus Christ meant that from then on God and the world could be had exclusively in mutual connection.

Schillebeeckx always emphasized his affinity to Chenu. There was in fact a great deal of agreement between the Christian way of dealing with culture as his articles on 'The Christian Situation' showed him to understand this and the attitude towards culture and society for which Chenu argued in a then very well-known article which he had written in 1937, 'Dimensions nouvelles de la chrétienté'. Schillebeeckx's title can even be seen as an attempt to provide an adequate Dutch equivalent to the almost untranslatable word *chrétienté*.[103] The picture of the theological work of Thomas Aquinas as it emerged from the early work of Schillebeeckx also had a great affinity to that of Chenu and was also dependent on him. As a theologian Chenu was primarily a specialist in the history of mediaeval theology and was one of the first to have given Thomas's work a historical interpretation in the 1920s. With great erudition he put him on the one hand in the concrete circum- stances of his time and on the other in the more comprehensive living church tradition before and after him. In this way he broke through the image of Thomas as the unique and holy genius who had constructed the system of Catholic thought that once and for all brought faith and reason into the correct relationship to each other – the central claim of ecclesiastical Tho- mism. In the portrait that Chenu painted of him with much accuracy, Thomas was described as a theologian who tried to express the faith for his own time on the basis of the contemporary situation. By doing this, according to Chenu he performed the task which as a theologian *par excellence* he had to do. In this sense, for him Thomas Aquinas was a model theologian precisely as a thinker bound to mediaeval conditions.[104] Thus Schillebeeckx will already have known that to a considerable degree Chenu was a kindred spirit before he met him in Paris in 1945. At the meeting he was impressed above all by the way in which from his view of theology

Chenu engaged concretely with critical initiatives, movements and (church) groups.[105]

Chenu supremely embodied the powerful, living and open confrontation between Christian faith and contemporary culture which was everywhere regarded as typical of French Catholicism even during the inter-war period, but to a heightened degree immediately after the war.[106] For a long time the French church had been weak and Catholics had barely played a role in French public life, also as a result of the militant 'laicism' which was dominant in political and government circles, namely the effort to make the public sphere completely free of religious influences and keep it so. But already before the First World War a Catholic revival had begun not only in terms of organization but also intellectually and spiritually. It was to establish itself more strongly after 1918. During the inter-war period laicism lost much of its power of conviction, and Catholics increasingly got the chance of again occupying key positions in state and society. After the condemnation by Pius XI in 1926 of the 'Action Française' of Charles Maurras (1868–1952), a strong nationalist movement which stood for the restoration of the monarchy and which regarded the Catholic Church as a necessary foundation for this, French Catholicism began to turn completely towards the spiritual permeation of contemporary society. The programme for this orientation was given in 1927 by Jacques Maritain in his book on 'The Primacy of the Spiritual'. No longer did French Catholics dream of a restored mediaeval Christianity in which the church was the all-embracing and all-determining factor; moreover, they no longer orientated themselves especially on the defence of the church and its freedom over against the modern state and modern society, which were constantly pressing on further. They no longer tried to evade the bombardment of modernity or to withstand it in a well-built bunker. They directed attention to the apostolate in the midst of society and culture in order to influence society and politics through spirituality.

The Dominicans were very much involved in this growing orientation on presence in the midst of contemporary culture. Here they showed themselves loyal to the spirit of Henri-Dominique Lacordaire, who in 1843 had refounded the order in France and saw Dominican life as a response to the situation of faith and the church after the laicization and democratization which had proved successful with the French Revolution. On the basis of this he had become actively involved with the religious and political questions of his own time.[107] Here, moreover, the French Dominicans were a source of inspiration for their Flemish brothers. To an important degree *Kultuurleven* was modelled on *La vie intellectuelle*, founded in 1928 by Marie-Vincent Bernadot (1883–1941).[108] And the fact that in 1945 in Flanders a *Tijdschrift voor Geestelijk Leven* had been founded which was thought to form a pair with *Kultuurleven* was probably connected with the fact that *La vie spirituelle*, associated with *La vie intellectuelle*, was likewise founded by Bernadot.[109]

In addition to these two journals, Bernadot had also founded the journal *Sept*, the first issue of which appeared on 3 March 1934. As a distant echo of the journal *Ère nouvelle* founded by Lacordaire, *Sept* set itself the aim of following political and social events in the turbulent time that France was experiencing at that moment. However, on 27 August 1937 *Sept* had to cease publication on the intervention of Rome. This was an offshoot of the unrest that the left-wing popular-front government of Leo Blum, which came to power in 1936, caused in Catholic circles. As a response to the political and social turbulence and the unrest among the French workers, Blum carried on a programme of social reform in a coalition government with parties which had a markedly anti-clerical tradition; however, his government was to survive only until June of the following year. *Sept* was punished for having given the impression of being not unsympathetic to the Blum government.[110] The history of *Sept*, in other words the conflict that arose over the bold standpoint of the journal and the need to abolish it because of pressure from the church authorities, was to prove a prime example of the different later initiatives towards the renewal of church life in France.

Schillebeeckx's stay in Paris in 1945 ushered in a new phase in his religious and theological confrontation with modernity. Initially he had a tendency to follow a synthetic Catholic view on culture along the same lines as Walgrave. In France he now met people who did not want to maintain their Catholic identity by standing above the parties and remaining apart from the real social turbulence, but wanted to discover it in the midst of all this. In confrontation with them Schillebeeckx redefined his position.

In the period which extended from midway through the 1920s to midway through the 1950s, French Dominicans took many initiatives which bore witness in an evocative way to the new missionary spirit which seemed to have come from the French church. The Dominican faculty of Le Saulchoir and the Parisian Dominican house of Saint-Jacques were thus in fact renewing a tradition which had begun at the beginning of the century with Ceslaus Rutten, and trying to make connections with the world of the workers alienated from the churches. Chenu, who during part of this period was responsible for studies at Le Saulchoir and whose voice was also very influential afterwards, played an important role here.[111]

Thus, the Dominicans stood in a broader stream. In 1927 a book had appeared by Pierre Lhande on 'Christ in the Suburbs'; this emphasized how much a Christian in working-class districts was confronted with the absence of faith and awareness of God.[112] In the years which followed, a long series of further publications appeared, all of which in one way or another showed how little church and faith had penetrated the world in which 'ordinary' French people lived. Thus the idea grew that a new kind of mission was necessary, particularly in France, which after all had always been regarded as 'the oldest daughter of the church'. To an increasing degree connections were sought with the approach which Josef Cardijn had developed and which was directed towards a militant Catholic presence in the different social spheres. Attempts were made to equip believers to formulate and to embody a Christian perspective effectively in the midst of the culture and in the concrete situations with which they were confronted. In 1937 a report on the de-Christianization of the countryside was a direct occasion for the start of the first projects of what soon afterwards was to be called the 'Mission de France': a coherent and programmatic attempt to penetrate to the specific situation in which French people were living by means of new forms of priestly presence, new forms of Catholic lay organization and the training needed for this. In this way it was hoped to win people back to the church. The driving force behind this 'Mission de France' was Emmanuel Cardinal Suhard (1874–1949); in 1937 he was still Archbishop of Reims, but from 1940 he was Archbishop of Paris.[113]

In this last function, in 1943 he was presented with a memorandum about the situation of the church among the workers of Paris written by two chaplains of the Christian youth movement inspired by Cardijn, the Jeunesse Ouvrière Chrétienne (JOC). According to tradition, the memorandum by Henri Godin and Yvan Daniel gave Suhard a sleepless night and when soon afterwards it was published as a book, it went off like a bomb. The title, provided with a question mark as a precaution, began to act as an outcry, a cry of distress and a summons to the conversion of the whole French church: France, a land of mission, *La France, pays de mission?*[114] This inspired Suhard to increased missionary activity and renewed verve in attempts to bridge the gap between the church and the working-class world. He established the so-called 'Mission de Paris', and within the framework of this a group of priests went to work in the factories, in his view giving adequate form to their pastorate in the world of the workers: as worker-priests they were to attract a good deal of attention in the subsequent period.[115] But just as important was the fact that quite generally the conviction grew that the French church as a whole was in a 'state of mission'. In other words, people abandoned the idea that there was a comprehensive Christian society, a 'Christianity' in this sense, and saw that the church still had to penetrate modern life with all its questions and problems.

The French Dominicans played a central role in this discovery. It was Congar who, in 1937, aptly christened this new view of faith the 'mystique of incarnation' and made it clear that only a faith that could find God in ordinary everyday life could discover the real significance of Christianity for the world, and of the church as a place where the gospel is proclaimed in the midst of the world.[116] And Chenu played a key role in much that happened at this period. He sat like a spider in a web of groups, circles and initiatives. For example, he was involved in the presentation of Godin's and Daniel's memorandum, at the start of the 'Mission de Paris', and at the origin of the worker-priest movement. Moreover, he played an important role in the reformulation of the theological implications of the new view of the mission of the church.[117]

In terms of church politics, the situation in France which Schillebeeckx found in 1945 was extremely tense. Formally he was sent by his superiors to the Dominican theological faculty of Le Saulchoir in Étiolles. However, according to his later testimony his activities as a student there were limited to attending the five compulsory lectures, and from Tuesday to Friday he lived in the Dominican convent of Saint-Jacques in Paris, from where he went to lectures at the Sorbonne, given, among others, by Chenu.[118] For along with Schillebeeckx's teacher De Petter, in 1942 Chenu had been condemned by Rome; he had had to resign his post as head of studies in Le Saulchoir and was moved to Saint-Jacques. To evade the church prohibition to teach, at the invitation of the École des Hautes Études, a prestigious state institution, he had been appointed professor of mediaeval history. In retrospect Chenu himself called his forced move from Étiolles to Paris a gift of God – 'une grâce de Seigneur' – because his stay in the city brought him even more intensively into contact with the activities which arose from the new missionary sense in the French church. He developed an interpretation of faith and theology in which the practical building up of society and culture had a central place.[119] Of course this was completely contrary to the intentions of Rome. In 1954 he was again condemned on the basis of an article in which against this theological background he defended the worker-priest experiment, an experiment that had been stopped that year through intervention from Rome. As we shall see, according to the Roman authorities the essential importance of the bond of the priest with the church as an institution was far too little heeded in the work of the worker-priests. The same applied to Chenu's article.[120]

Moreover, Chenu's condemnation in 1942 had a comparable background. On the basis of a lecture which he had given a year earlier, in 1937 Chenu published on his own initiative and in a limited edition a book with the title Une école de théologie: Le Saulchoir. In it he made an attempt to describe and to provide a basis for the way of doing theology which was practised under his leadership at Le Saulchoir, but he did so by giving a fundamentally different view of theology from that of neo-scholasticism, which was regarded as the only correct way. Chenu took up central thoughts of one of his predecessors as regent of studies at Le Saulchoir, Ambroise Gardeil

(1859–1931). Gardeil saw God's revelation, on which everything turned in the church and theology and on which everything was dependent, as a given synthetic, comprehensive view of reality with God at the centre, which was initially grasped intuitively by the believer. According to him, faith was a matter of participating through one's experience in this view and inwardly recognizing its truth.[121] The conclusions which Gardeil drew from this for theology were as yet extremely restrained and formal. However, Chenu concluded that theology needed to take shape as reflection on faith along Gardeil's lines, and thus not as a further explication of church doctrine. According to Chenu, every time and every milieu had its own existential relationship to God, and this existential relationship, this spirituality, found its intellectual expression in a theology. Therefore, over the course of church history there had been many divergent theologies, and these were also legitimate in their distinctiveness. Nor did Chenu hesitate to speak emphatically about the 'relativism' and 'relativity' of any theological system, including dogmatic formulations: he even called the Thomistic philosophy sanctioned by the church, and the theology based on it, 'relative'.[122] If theology wanted to be worthy of its name and really to speak of God, it needed to be the expression of a living faith, a lived-out view of reality. Theology was a spirituality which had found the right rational instruments for expressing and illuminating its religious experience.[123] By presenting it in this way Chenu thought that he had restored its due dignity: from reflection on abstractions, theology became reflection on a concrete element in human history, a history that Chenu was convinced had been taken up by God into a plan of salvation which according to biblical ideas developed in time, in a salvation history.[124]

Roman circles, however, saw this view – and the way of doing theology which corresponded to it – as an unprecedented relativization of official church doctrine, of ecclesiastical Thomism, and with it of the anti-modern form of the church which was guaranteed by both of these. In 1943 the encyclical *Mystici corporis* would expound systematically and authoritatively the image of the church, and in 1950 the encyclical *Humani generis* the doctrine which in the Roman view could alone lay claim to the predicate 'Catholic'. The promulgation of these documents in fact condemned a current in the French church and in French theology which was designated *'nouvelle théologie'* in the broad sense. The same antipathy to forms of faith and theology which aimed at open confrontation with modernity also led in 1943 to a complicated conflict between the pope and the Dominican order: *Une école de théologie* was put on the Index and Chenu lost his function in the order as regent of studies of the Paris province and thus his responsibility for the course of affairs at Le Saulchoir.[125]

It was somehow appropriate that here he shared the fate of Schillebeeckx's teacher Domien De Petter, with all the arbitrariness of this kind of

Roman intervention. At all events the view of theology which Schillebeeckx had developed with the help of De Petter's theory of implicit intuition was at a number of points clearly related to the view that Chenu developed on the basis of Gardeil's thinking. Schillebeeckx will especially have recognized himself in Chenu's view that theology is an expression of a lived-out, synthetic view of reality. He had arrived at a comparable conviction in his student days and in 1952, on the basis of a detailed analysis of the work of Thomas Aquinas, he was to state that all philosophical and theological statements about God are inadequate, but derive their significance from the degree to which they are supported 'by a real and positive knowledge of God which ... remains unexpressed but ... forms the matrix of the elements of concepts in our knowledge of God'.[126] When he became a professor in Nijmegen and in his inaugural lecture summed up the results of his Louvain period, along these lines he said that theology was thought 'in search of the living God'. He spoke of 'the world of nature and of history in which the *religious* man lives' as a 'phrase in his dialogue with God'; everything 'takes on a much more profound dimension through this personal living relationship with God'.[127] The direct influence of Chenu on Schillebeeckx which is most clearly traceable lies in this concern for history. In the footsteps of Chenu he attached great importance to the knowledge of the history of theology as an indispensable background and source for contemporary theological reflection. The result of this was that in all his major studies he would pay attention to the presentation and analysis of the facts of the history of theology. As he himself was to say in retrospect almost 50 years later:

> Later in my own lectures I tried to clarify all [the major theological themes] from the Old Testament to the twentieth century in the process of [their] historical development – which was really impossible. But I was convinced that faith, history and reflection on faith had to be studied in close connection with one another.[128]

This concrete approach was very much along the lines of his antipathy to what, in 1949, he called 'butterfly dilettantism'.[129]

As the author of theological texts Schillebeeckx was closer to Congar than to Chenu, who trusted markedly in his bravura and *esprit*. Although only around ten years younger, Congar was to a large degree Chenu's pupil, a pupil who worked out his master's principles more consistently than he did. Out of the same involvement with the French church which was renewing itself, and out of an equally great desire for a living theology, Congar wrote theological studies which bore witness to an extensive knowledge of the history of theology. These were studies in which so-called 'positive theology', i.e. the investigation of reflection on faith from the past, formed an integral part of theological reflection generally; and 1946 saw the appearance of a very long lexicon article by him on the nature, method and context of theology. In it he not only stated that the intellectual penetration of what was handed down in the Bible and from all periods of the tradition was a central theological task, but devoted extensive attention to the history of the concept of theology, very much in line with this view.[130] Chenu was to say of this article that it was a faithful working out of the theological approach of Gardeil, which amounted to saying, his own.[131]

Despite the disappointment that he recalled in personal encounters and at lectures, something of what Schillebeeckx was later to write about the Louvain philosopher Albert Dondeyne probably applied to Congar's work as he saw it. Having stated with clear distaste that there was often much heated talk about the problems of the church, in contemporary fashionable words and slogans 'until one felt inclined to ask these friends to stop their wild chatter', Schillebeeckx went on to say that Dondeyne's work – and as I have remarked, in his eyes the same thing applied to that of Congar – was inspired by the emotion which drove others to wild statements. It also proved, according to Schillebeeckx, that:

> the way others ramble on at the same time points to the seriousness and the reality of a living problem, which, precisely in order to deny the blessed self-confidence with which yet others deny the same problems or remain stuck in older formulas, gives rise to bitter reactions. By contrast [his] inner emotion ... manifests itself in ... calm argumentative serenity ... Sober analyses time and again bring us to solutions of which one must say: indeed, obvious ...

Congar's work did something of the same sort. It did not sparkle, like some of Chenu's texts, but as a reader one got the feeling that all the emotion was transformed into studious power and erudition. The same is true of Schillebeeckx's own writings from this period.[132]

Evaluation of the French situation

Despite the growing tensions with the Roman authorities, the movement in the French church which strove for an open confrontation with the modern world was at its most powerful immediately after the war. Numerically, the group of Catholics who were conservative in a religious and political sense remained great, but their reputation had been seriously damaged by their massive support for the Vichy regime of Marshal Pétain, who had collaborated with Nazi Germany. Therefore during the 1940s, in France and far outside it, at all events the general picture arose that the French church with great verve – in his influential Lenten letter of 1947 Cardinal Suhard spoke of a 'springtime of the church'[133] – was seeking a new Christian existence which broke with the old Catholic triumphalism. 'Anyone who has not experienced the years 1946–47 in French Catholicism has missed one of the most attractive moments in the life of the church,' Congar was to write in retrospect, and in an interview Chenu spoke respectively of 'a period which carried us along'.[134]

So Schillebeeckx did not miss this period. Everything suggests that his stay in Paris in 1945 made a great impression on him. He spoke later of 'a tremendous year', 'full of new perspectives'.[135] It was in line with his orientation on the theology of culture that he wrote an article for *Kultuurleven* in which he informed readers about the different spiritual currents in post-war France.[136] Characteristically, he nowhere gave any hint of doubts about his capacity to have a good view of the situation and to describe it adequately. Without noticeable hesitation he trod in the footsteps of the Jesuit Jean Daniélou, nine years older than him and born in France, whom he knew from lectures, and who in 1945 wrote an influential sketch of 'intellectual life in France'.[137] Following the line of his theology of culture, Schillebeeckx concentrated especially on the relationship between religion and culture in France. However, rather than offering an analysis of the French situation, the article offered a definition of his position over against the 'mystique of incarnation' of the progressive Christians with whom Chenu and Congar were associated, their way of giving form to the Christian presence in the midst of culture.

Schillebeeckx's attitude ultimately remained ambivalent. On the one hand he took a stand against the existentialism of Sartre and Merleau-Ponty because in his view, while they gauged well the unrest and fear in the human heart, they made these issue in an explicit atheism, a blindness to the attractive sides of human life. In his view this led to 'an apotheosis of "disgust" as such'. Over against this he set the philosophers whose lectures he attended and who worked along the lines of Henri Bergson's (1859–1941) philosophy of life, like Louis Lavelle (1882–1951) and René Le Senne (1882–1954); these tried to reconcile existentialism and metaphysics. In their strictly academic and speculative philosophy they were doing what he thought necessary. They

> accept that the character of fear is essentially bound up with the human condition as the driving force of finite and free beings, but they detest the cult of fear and confirm the orientation on the absolute which makes us overcome fear, not in a cynical acceptance of the unavoidably brutal but through the hopeful prospect of an attractive future which also depends on our free will. Here this draws on the source of an all-embracing Presence of a personal being, God.

He identified strongly with this quest for an all-embracing Christian philosophy; he even did not hesitate to say that it was thanks to them that 'the spiritual and intellectual values' were 'still French traditional material' (12–14).[138]

At the same time, as he saw it, what *Kultuurleven* meant for Flanders was to an important degree being realized in France. There was a broad-based and powerful Christian humanism which engaged with society and its problems. He told his Flemish readers that it took the concrete form of attempts 'to integrate the self-awareness of the masses of the workers ... into the Catholic view of life' (17). He proved to have adopted to an important degree the perspective of the worker-priests and of his teacher Chenu: 'the pressure of the working-class mass towards emancipation' seemed to him 'at the moment to be the most decisive event in French culture' (149).[139] In France he saw a tendency towards 'humanistic, Christian "socialism", one of inspiration but different in a more concrete effect', and in principle he seemed to affirm this tendency (18). He dryly stated that the 'Catholic will for social and political reform to a large extent [ran] parallel to the Communist will for reform' (19). But here, by virtue of his background, he put the emphasis in a different way from Chenu and his followers. Along the lines of the project of an all-embracing Catholic world-view as an orientation for culture in the midst of the ongoing rise of modern chaos, which Walgrave had formulated in the 'Orientation' for the first post-war issue of *Kultuurleven*, Schillebeeckx continued to emphasize the antithesis between Catholicism and other streams of thought. He emphasized that existentialism and Marxism based themselves on a positive atheism and anti-theism, and that they were therefore an expression of the tendency of human beings to refuse to be open to God because of original sin. And they in particular strongly influenced popular culture in France.

In other words, whereas Chenu and his followers really seemed to have taken leave of the idea that the spirit of modernity was apostasy from the Catholic tradition, Schillebeeckx now and then expressed the feeling that the contemporary streets, the trams, the factories and shops, the homes, the cafés and the assembly rooms, the songs and the books breathed an anti-religious spirit. He wrote:

> In the metro and the train one often sees shopworkers and semi-intellectuals gobbling up *Les Mouches* or *Huis clos* [existentialist novels by Jean-Paul Sartre], and to all appearances existentialism is the centre of interest in the salons of Paris. It is clear that a foul-smelling 'taste for the perverse' which is blowing in all its greyness and roughness from the Sartrean *'condition humaine'* contributes quite a lot to such a lightning success (13).

For example, he also referred emphatically to the anti-religious propaganda of the Communist party, which was very influential in working-class circles, as a result of which 'in broad layers of the people' it was said to have become an 'accepted dogma that religion is against the working class' (15). That was why in his view the rise of social Catholicism was so important: over against a culture which had succumbed to anti-religion, it represented a Christian humanism orientated on permeating every aspect of modern life. According to Schillebeeckx, almost everything depended on the question whether this would succeed:

> Is France on the edge of an abyss into which tomorrow French culture will fall, or is this painful unrest rather 'the vertigo of a great time which is coming'? The future will make this clear (26).[140]

In this sketch of the current situation, with its strikingly apocalyptic tone, he made clear to his readers that in his eyes France was 'really mission territory' and that involvement in this mission was of the utmost importance (21).

Later, too, Schillebeeckx was to continue to follow the developments around the worker-priests in France, even when as time went on these became increasingly turbulent. Incidentally he provided them with marginal notes. In 1949 he spoke about the developments surrounding the Union des Chrétiens Progressistes (UCP), a group of Christians established in 1947 which stood for close collaboration with the Communist Party. During the first decade after the Second World War the Cold War was at its height and relations between the Catholic Church and the Communist movement reached a nadir with the arrest and condemnation of the primate of Hungary by the Communist regime. Cardinal József Mindszenty was arrested on 27 December 1948, and after what was generally regarded as a show trial was condemned for high treason on 8 February 1949. In his imprisonment he became a powerful symbol of the impossibility of reconciling Catholicism and Communism. In this situation, the question whether co-operation between Communists and Catholics was possible – a question which in the period immediately after the war was topical in France and was being intensively discussed – was of course a highly loaded one. It made the UCP very controversial from the beginning.

In this climate, the leadership of the Catholic Church constantly spoke out all the more emphatically against any form of collaboration with Communists. On 31 January 1949 a leader of the Italian Catholic Action, Franco Rodano, was condemned because of his plea for such collaboration, and in June of the same year a decree appeared from the Holy Office in which subscription to Communist theory and structural collaboration with Communists was forbidden on pain of excommunication.[141] In this situation, and on the occasion of the discussion which had already arisen around the UCP, Cardinal Suhard felt obliged to make a statement, which was issued on 13 March 1949. In it he said that on the one hand the greatest problem of the time was 'that people continue to practise social injustice' and he encouraged Catholics 'with all their might and with the help of their Christian faith to collaborate in establishing a just order'. At the same time he warned against the dangers brought by collaboration with the Communist party. He urged Catholics 'to work out their views and to engage in their actions without identifying themselves with a thought and action the fundamental principles of which contradict their own at so many points'; in other words, distancing themselves completely from the Communist party.[142]

Given the importance that Schillebeeckx attached to an integral Christian view of culture, it was obvious that for him the question of a possible collaboration between Catholics and Communists was 'a tricky problem'. In the article about the relationship between culture and religion in the France of 1946 he did not yet speak clearly about the legitimacy of this; he only indicated the opposed positions that were being adopted. Some French intellectuals, he said, wanted a close collaboration with Communists 'on the basis of the common ideal', social and political reform in favour of the workers. By contrast, others were markedly aware that the Marxist insight into the exploitation of the workers 'in fact still always goes with an ideology which is unacceptable to Christians' and assumed an anti-Communist attitude (19). In 1949 he returned to this. Immediately after the appearance of Suhard's letter he wrote an article which adopted the standpoint of the statement and gave it further theological support. The article was published in *Kultuurleven* under the title 'Forms of Tomorrow'.[143] However, while Schillebeeckx was working on this article, the document by the Holy Office mentioned above appeared, and he felt compelled to go into it. Following a well-known Catholic strategy which often proved successful, he tried as far as possible to limit the scope of this text, in favour of the more moderate statement by Suhard. Thus he pointed out that the decree was first of all directed against particular groups of Christians in Eastern Europe who were said to support Communist teaching and not against those who 'attack Communist theory but are favourably inclined to Communism in the sphere of social reforms', as in his eyes the French progressives were. Moreover, he emphatically expressed the thought to which evidently some people had subscribed, that 'to condemn Communism ... [was] to speak in favour of capitalist and liberal principles in the social and economic sphere'. He emphatically pointed out that these too had been condemned by the church on various occasions in the recent past (36–8).

According to Schillebeeckx, the correct Catholic attitude was in principle contained in the UCP slogan: progressives, because first of all Christians, *'progressistes parce que premièrement chrétiens'*. In the language of his project on the theology of culture, but wholly along the lines of Suhard's argument, he stated that striving 'for an appropriate social, economic and political order of life in accordance with the human personal value of the workers, in justice and brotherliness' was a demand of 'human nature in the perspective of a fruitful life of grace in justice and love' (31f.) Nevertheless, at the same time he thought that 'at the present historical moment' collaboration with the Communist party 'is in fact an effective contribution' to the 'success of its whole programme, which nevertheless objectively attacks the basic principles of Christian life', because of the materialism and the exaggerated collectivism that stubbornly remains, 'despite all loyal recognition of what is valuable in Communism' (34f.). He emphatically acknowledged the right of the hierarchy to condemn a collaboration which could not simply be called internal, *'propter maius bonum ecclesiae*, i.e. for a greater good of the church's life of grace in a particular state'. In a very traditional way he finally appeared to think that by virtue of the fact that it represented this life of grace, the church had to defend its influence and interests, and that the church leadership had the authority to subordinate to this other interests which were so necessary.

Thus, with all the renewal that his striving for a theology of culture represented, in the 1940s Schillebeeckx continued to maintain the conviction that the church needed to have a central place in culture. The openness of culture to supernature ultimately had to be guarded by the church, and that was possible only from a position of power. On the basis of a similar conviction Cardinal Suhard had emphatically turned against people who thought 'that their conscience was sufficient for working out what Christian moral teaching ... requires'. That would

> make the conscience of the Catholic so autonomous that it would no longer recognize the mediating role of the church in the order of human action and in practice it would deny the lordship of God over the whole of social life.[144]

That the recognition of the role of the church in defining good action is automatically coupled with the recognition of the lordship of God over the whole of social life would really disappear from Catholic thought and feeling only with the Second Vatican Council. Schillebeeckx, too, made this connection. He made a direct link between following the guidelines of the church authorities, of which one did not immediately see the importance, and the 'supernatural exclusivism' for which he stood. In his view, the history of the UCP made it clear

> how, in our enthusiasm for the ordering of life within the world, we nevertheless have to leave a perhaps effective means for the moment unused for the sake of higher interests, the *unicum necessarium*. Such an attitude certainly requires both humility and asceticism. But it also seems

wholly within the perspective of the Christian life, which will always sow a spot of unrest in the order of life within the world (30).

Despite all the talk of a theology of culture, readers here again get the impression that for Schillebeeckx supernature and nature are two detached spheres of reality.

DOMINICAN RELIGIOUS LIFE

In 1946 Schillebeeckx was officially appointed to give lectures in dogmatics to the Dominican theological students in Louvain. He was to continue to do this until 1957. He gave the four-year cycle of lectures on fundamental theology, the doctrine of creation, christology and eschatology almost three times. In these courses and in his book *De sacramentele heilseconomie*, which took the same line, he made full use of facts from the history of the church and theology in the way that he had learned in France, and also adopted in his own manner the French orientation on the contemporary situation. In 1947, at the same time he became the successor of his teacher De Petter as spiritual director of the students. In retrospect he said that in this period he carried through a number of important reforms. The French influence, all that he had seen and heard in France and what he had read about theological responsibility for a missionary view of the apostolate, seems to be at work here. With his students he sought a form of the religious life which was adequate for working in the midst of contemporary culture.

At all events, later retrospects give the impression that he identified strongly with his students in their quest of a form of Dominican life that suited them.[145] For example, he said:

I did not want to be a superior but the oldest among brothers. I was convinced that the religious life of students needed a certain flexibility, in the sense of an intense humanization of the religious life without a reduction in its theological or religious depth.[146]

The fact that he lived with his students in their own quarters – the fairly independent community formed by the students in a Dominican convent – as was usual for a *magister* of the students, brought him 'more freedom to take part in society'. It made the religious life 'less isolated'.[147] By his own account he also experimented with forms which were akin to those of the French worker-priests. He spoke a good deal with his students about their work, and a number of them also wanted to join in practically: there even seem to have been plans to begin a community in which practical work and theological reflection were combined and in which Schillebeeckx was to be responsible for the latter. For however much he was attracted emotionally

117

by the strategy of 'not talking about God and the church but just being there, among people, in the hope that they would become aware of something – a deeper mystery – because of one's Christian praxis, one's way of life', he continued to attach great importance to praxis being followed by theological reflection: 'If it doesn't, praxis becomes too vague.'[148]

Schillebeeckx's reflections in this area were expressed above all in some articles about Dominican spirituality in the internal magazine for Flemish Dominicans, *Dominikaans Leven*, but ultimately in a duplicated text of 74 pages, illustrated with drawings, which was widely disseminated in Dominican circles and simply entitled 'Dominican Spirituality'.[149] It is striking how clearly he stated as early as in the foreword that he was not concerned with how the Dominican tradition deriving from the Middle Ages had to be adapted to 'the demands of modern times'. He was not concerned to make a modern translation of the tradition, in order to assess the viability of regulations and forms. In his eyes the question was: 'How shall we give form in our time to the original idea of the order in all its wholeness and its authenticity?' He connected this with the fact that on their profession Dominicans do not profess obedience to the constitutions of the order but to the 'superiors who give orders "according to the constitutions"'. And he interpreted this as follows: 'Not a dead, general legal text to which the conscience is bound but any concrete command given in the spirit of and in line with this law' (9, 38).

Schillebeeckx, following many others, saw the specific mark of Dominican piety in the comprehensiveness of the gracious presence of God which precedes all human efforts and supports them. Therefore, in his view Dominican life was a matter of putting into

> practice in the spiritual life what St Thomas indicates at the level of Christian thought as the basic attitude of the theologian, namely to consider everything *sub ratione deitatis*, i.e. from an all-prevailing sense of God, theocentricity (17).[150]

According to Schillebeeckx, the renewal represented by the foundation of his order by Dominic lay in the combination of contemplative religious life and a priestly orientation on preaching, a notion that he took over directly from Clérissac. In his view, the 'tension' which emerged here 'between the essentially contemplative orientation of the *religious life* and the essentially apostolic attitude of the *Dominican order*' gave Dominican spirituality 'a proper physiognomy which is usually summed up in the sentence taken from Thomas Aquinas, *contemplari et contemplata aliis tradere*, contemplation and handing on to others what is contemplated (43).

From two sides, Schillebeeckx now demonstrated that this tension does not amount to an internal contradiction. On the one hand, in his view the encounter with God in contemplation was itself 'social' and 'expansive': he thought that Dominican spirituality was a matter of making the love experienced in the personal encounter with God 'blossom in activity'. In fact, he thought, in the Dominican sense acting with a view to the salvation of others was part of contemplation itself. 'Contemplation remains ... a matter of inspiring what is done, and really does not disappear during the apostolic work: the psychological target is merely shifted from one's own soul to the community on which the preaching and teaching apostolate is focused' (44–6). Thinking along these lines, on the other hand Schillebeeckx can say that 'the being-in-and-with-the-world, the "*présence au monde*", [is] a co-essential complement of the *contemplata aliis tradere'*. The world was not just a place where insight arrived at in private needed to be put into practice; it was a Dominican task to realize a 'dialogal presence in the present-day world' and thus hear

> the language of truth which, perhaps disguised, detected and entangled in a net of untruth, nevertheless rings out from the events of the time. The [Dominican love of the truth, the] *amor veritatis* thus sets out with serene daring to grasp the elements of truth and consistently to apply the appropriate therapy of the time *ad salutem animarum* [to the salvation of souls] (49–50).

He summed all this up by saying that the foundation of the apostolate in the Dominican sense lay in 'the God-centred hope for the others', in the hope for the kingdom of God as the reality which embraces the whole creation and all human being. Or, put in more concrete terms, the apostolic work was 'the active manifestation of our hope' (58).

Schillebeeckx's duplicated paper on Dominican spirituality was a striking contribution to the rediscovery of the specific nature of the Dominican charisma, even if little notice was taken of it in the wider discussion. Growing historical insight and reflection on the religious situation of modern times together meant that this charisma was increasingly sought in the central place of preaching in the religious life. At the same time it is not difficult to point to all kinds of views in the text which are characteristic of Schillebeeckx. Thus, great emphasis is placed on study, specifically also as a link between religious experience and insight into the tradition on the one hand and the contemporary world on the other. Philosophy in particular should be in a position to bridge the potential gulf between receptivity to the world (*capacitas mundi*) and receptivity to God (*capacitas Dei*, 53–4). Moreover, in a strikingly matter-of-fact way, here Schillebeeckx also noted that in the Dominican order there was initially a certain antipathy to the study of 'pagans and philosophers' with all the danger of clericalism and the failure to recognize the 'autonomous earthly domain'. According to Schillebeeckx, Albertus Magnus's statement that in medical matters he trusted pagans like Galen and Hippocrates and in the natural sciences Aristotle – whose recently rediscovered text represented the cutting edge of science at the time – more than Augustine was 'progressive language' in his time and marked a break. But at the same time the 'intellectual humanism' of Albertus and – in his footsteps – of Thomas Aquinas was at a deeper level loyal to the intuition that had led Dominic to found his order, namely the intuition that a milieu of study is indispensable for good preaching (50–2).[151] It also fitted Schillebeeckx's approach in the 1940s and 1950s that in 'Dominican Spirituality', for all its attention to historical details, he above all leaned towards what Thomas Aquinas had brought out in his systematic reflections on the mission of an order of preachers.[152]

Schillebeeckx finally described Dominican spirituality as 'the spiritual attitude of one who with a sense of God and with human openness approaches events in contemporary life and the world *ad salutem animarum*, with a view to the spiritual salvation of human beings' (54). It was clear that the developments in France lay behind such a formulation. It bore witness to his sense of being bound up with the worker-priest project and the work of theologians like Chenu and Congar. In his exposition of the Dominican ideal of poverty, Schillebeeckx referred to the view of one of the authors of *La France, pays de mission?*, the writing which stood at the beginning of the worker-priest movement. Henri Godin was said to have discovered in practice that for many people 'a fundamental sobriety of life in a priest' was the first necessary step to his approach, a step that had also been taken practically by the worker-priests. By immediately adding to this remark that Dominic brought to 'the idea of preaching in poverty' 'identically the same conviction' of the 'apostolic dignity of a sober evangelical life', Schillebeeckx connected the Dominican project very closely with that of the worker-priests. However, in a way which has by now become familiar, he warned against the threat of a 'concealed laicizing of the supernatural' and a 'levelling down of the mystery of the religious', and he urged his students to be aware 'that the harmony between nature and supernature here on earth is only *in the making*, and needs a good dose of asceticism' on the basis of letting go of oneself with a view to God. Nevertheless, in his view it was equally necessary to make a break 'between what I would call notional knowledge, intellectual culture and, on the other hand, the religious experience of reality' (65f.).[153] In his eyes it was Dominican not to allow oneself to be led astray into 'flat actualism' and not to be driven by a 'butterfly'– again! – desire to be 'up-to-date'; as always, for him it was important to be completely bound up with real life:

The order allows itself to be guided by the seriousness of its principles in confrontation with concrete historical reality; but these last have to be examined to a degree which includes their accidental connections (68).

120

But above all there was a need to avoid Dominicans becoming colporteurs of religious ideas, 'attractive speakers who hawk religious thoughts, just as there are people who hawk carpets and bootlaces'; Schillebeeckx thought, with Clérissac, that Dominicans had to be 'witnessing heralds' of what they themselves had experienced. Schillebeeckx only began to write down his reflections for *Dominikaans Leven* in 1952, and his stencilled discussion of Dominican spirituality was dated 'Christmas 1954'. Thus, strictly speaking these texts fall outside the period with which this chapter deals. But they seem to offer a good summary of how he regarded himself as a Dominican even in the period before 1950, also under the influence of what he had seen at close quarters of new developments in France and was to continue to follow later.

However, for those who look carefully, traces can also be found of a conflict around what he defended, without it becoming clear precisely what this conflict was about.[154] 'Put in charge of the students', was written on the third page, '*in spe meliorum dierum*', in the hope of better days! And on the same page 'Father Master' had put a cry which has solemn connotations even in the typography, '*Ad vos, O Juventus*', 'To you, young people!' It was certainly connected with the further complications surrounding the worker-priests, which will be discussed in the next chapter, and ultimately led to the experiment being stopped on orders from Rome. But these complications then evidently had repercussions on the life of Schillebeeckx and his students. In 'Dominican Spirituality' he alluded to a stricter application of the rules, greater emphasis on asceticism and more frequent intervention by the authorities. 'This is not an ideal, but can be demanded for the moment by the more sober way of living,' he wrote cautiously. He insisted that due attention should be paid to the opportunity for particular actions and for respect for authorities 'who because of their office are more concerned with the question of opportunity than perhaps with the objective matter itself' (64, 67). However, the way in which Schillebeeckx addressed his students through the initial assignments makes it clear how difficult he himself found it. Evidently he had the feeling that he could only hope that his students would allow themselves to be inspired by his reflections ('*ad vos, O Juventus*') to put them into practice in better days ('*in spe meliorum dierum*').

The duplicated paper on Dominican spirituality is typical of Schillebeeckx's work in the 1950s, especially in this ambiguity. In the period from the appearance of *Humani generis* to the Second Vatican Council his theology was to know great tensions. After 1950 his work began increasingly to look like a kettle with a lid which has been fastened down, so that the pressure in it constantly increases. What he thought he had to say theologically on the basis of his insight into the data of faith was in tension with the limits within which he thought that he could move as a Catholic theologian. The next chapter is about this question.

Chapter 3

The View of the Church as a Form of the Theology of Culture in the 1950s

'Christianity is the basis for a cheerful but serious optimism in life which is nevertheless fraught with tensions'

BETWEEN CULTURAL CHALLENGE AND CHURCH PRESSURE

In the years immediately after the Second World War, France was to a considerable degree at the centre of the European cultural discussion. French existentialism attracted attention all over the world, above all, it seemed, because it gave the impression of wanting to see the world of the second half of the twentieth century without any illusions and to find a way of living in it. For this world, on the one hand the anonymous social structures were important: they were no longer experienced by people as meaningful bonds which provided order and support for a meaningful life, but as arbitrary hindrances to freedom. On the other hand there was the experience of the war and the complex moral questions which this raised, especially about the possibility, the need and the basis for morality and for opposition to evil.[1] In France more than elsewhere, church and theology formed part of a culture in which these questions were being discussed. In the previous chapter it became clear that Schillebeeckx was taking part at a distance in the discussions which were being carried on in the French church and in French theology.

In a general sense, in the 1940s and 1950s his work was strongly marked by the existentialist way of posing problems, by the categories in which the existentialists thought and by their style of thinking. Through De Petter's philosophy Schillebeeckx's theology was bound up with the existentialist idea that everyday life was the place where people always already lived in and with the world and were in contact with it. In his view of human knowledge De Petter in fact stood quite close to the view of the atheist philosopher Maurice Merleau-Ponty (1902–62). Over against Sartre, who emphasized the impossibility of really bridging the gap between one's own subjectivity and the 'other', Merleau-Ponty thought that each time a concrete phenomenon was seen as part of the world in which we live, a concrete synthesis of being and consciousness came about. Thus, in his eyes the possibility of knowledge and experience was given with the fact that human beings are part of the world, and conversely knowledge and experience are the outcome of this 'being in, with and of the world', this *'être au monde'*.[2] The fundamental difference between the thinking of Merleau-Ponty and that of De Petter lay above all in the latter's conviction that the horizon which made life 'in, with and of the world' possible was ultimately the representation of a metaphysical ground of being and meaning. According to De Petter, 'being in the world' pointed to God, whereas in his philosophy Merleau-Ponty emphatically wanted to keep to naked, finite human existence itself.[3]

More than other existentialists, the writer Albert Camus (1913–59) explored in concrete terms and images the world of contemporary men and women, and the way in which these gave themselves form in the midst of their world. His novel *The Plague* was published in 1947. The book gave an impressive picture of human existence after the outbreak of violence in the Second World War and at the time of the threat of violence from the Cold War between the Soviet Union and the United States, and the moral questions that this existence raised. In *The Plague* Albert Camus described the course of a plague epidemic in the city of Oran, cut off from the outside world. In this way he mapped the reactions of people to this irrevocable evil, the existential and moral way in which they dealt with it. His ultimate interest was in how and on what basis people could and must live in a world which was inevitably marked by an inescapable evil that affected all. Camus arrived at the basic conviction that, as one of the figures in *The Plague* put it, 'on this earth there are pestilences and there are victims, and it's up to us, so far as possible, not to join forces with the pestilences'. He wrote about this choice in terms of holiness without God: 'It comes to this, what interests me is learning how to become a saint.' At the same time he was concerned with the inconspicuous, naked basis of humanity itself: 'What interests me is – being a man.' Eye to eye with overwhelming evil, according to Camus all meaning or guarantee of happiness fell away and there was hope only for 'a very old, grey hope, that hope which keeps men from letting themselves drift into death and is nothing but a dogged will to live'.[4]

In 1951 Camus was to work out his view of hope as an unalienable part of human life and as the source and expression of opposition to evil, suffering and death systematically in his essay *The Rebel*.[5] In the second half of the 1960s the thoughts developed here were to begin to have a great influence on theology, especially that of Schillebeeckx. What he was to write from 1968 about the experience of contrast, the experience that a particular situation is inhuman and therefore calls for opposition, and thus pictures the good in a negative way, is closely related in its style of thinking to the ideas of Camus.

In his work Camus adopted an emphatically anti-religious attitude. Nevertheless, Schillebeeckx met him with the Paris Dominicans and was to remember him as someone who said that he thought Christianity abominable 'but Christians were his best friends'.[6] The same paradox is evident in the fact that Camus himself regarded *The Plague* as his most un-Christian book,[7] but in it describes a change in the thinking of the Jesuit Paneloux which could be a model for the development in parts of the French church in the post-war period.

According to the narrative in *The Plague*, Paneloux twice gave a sermon during the plague epidemic on the situation in which the city of Oran found itself. First he interpreted the epidemic eloquently and with impressive imagery as a sign that God had lost patience and had turned away, in this way summoning people to conversion. 'The same pestilence which is slaying you works for your good and points your path.'[8] He gave the second sermon after he had seen a child dying in a heart-rending way and had exclaimed, 'My God, save this child' – of course in vain. In this sermon he interpreted his own impotent gesture of opposition as grace, and turned against

> moralists who told us to sink on our knees and give up the struggle. No, we should go forward, groping our way through the darkness, stumbling perhaps at whiles, and try to do what good lay in our power. As for the past, we must hold fast, trusting in the divine goodness, even as to the death of little children, and not seeking personal respite.

Soon afterward, Paneloux himself died. Paradoxically enough, however, here he showed a tranquillity and an indifference to his own fate through which he differed most deeply from those who shared his lot.

It is not difficult to see in Paneloux's second sermon a description of the standpoint of solidarity which the worker-priests and those of kindred spirit adopted, faithful as they wanted to be to their 'Master [who] knew all the pangs of suffering in his body and his soul'.[9] Camus' story of Paneloux's death is to be read as the desperate question how far this solidarity really went. Did not the appeal that they made to God in their 'mystique of incarnation' ultimately mean a fundamental break with the world, despite all the desire for a link with it?

Schillebeeckx's work from the 1950s can be partially interpreted as an attempt to answer this question. In line with what he had said in earlier articles, he tried to demonstrate that to follow the Christian tradition did not conflict with proximity to concrete life in the midst of the world. Quite far-reaching changes were taking place in the context, in the Belgian cultural climate, as a result of the question of the monarchy, but especially in the church climate, because increasing pressure was being exerted on theological currents and on individual theologians with whom he felt related. But there is a good deal of continuity in Schillebeeckx's theological development up to and including the Second Vatican Council.

Still, the shifts in the church-political context, and especially the increasing concern of the Catholic hierarchy to make a distinction in principle between church and world, also had a great influence. Schillebeeckx's interest shifted particularly as result of this. Instead of constantly turning towards theological reflection on culture, which had seemed an obvious course in view of his writings from the 1940s, he tried to show that the tradition, the organization and the liturgy of the church already really embodied the theology of culture that he sought. They only needed to be understood properly. If the wealth of the Catholic tradition were seen in all its breadth and depth, that is, if a complete picture were to be had of its history and development, then it would become clear that the church is in fact the living form of the synthetic Catholic view of life of which the editors of *Kultuurleven* spoke with such verve in 1945. Thus the emphasis came to lie more markedly on the conviction that modern culture needed to listen to the church if it was to be able to get out of its impasse. But the message remained just as much that the church itself, too, really needed to begin to behave as the embodiment of the culture that was necessary for human salvation, which sometimes implied strong criticism of its current practice.

The well-known pattern of the history of Catholic theology as a whole seemed to be repeated at the level of the development of one theologian. From halfway through the nineteenth century to the Second Vatican Council there was the constantly recurring experience that fundamental criticism of Catholic teaching and far-reaching efforts to reform theology on the basis of this criticism led to condemnation and marginalization. They got nowhere, and the only way which remained for Catholic theologians was the renewal of prevalent views from within.[10]

In this light it seems significant that Schillebeeckx deviated from his original plan. Rather than producing a treatment of the theology of culture or a fundamental definition of a standpoint on the relationship between 'nature and supernature', viz. 'religion and the world', at Le Saulchoir in 1952 he presented a thesis on the sacraments of the Catholic Church as *the* places of encounter between God and world: the dissertation was to appear under the title *De sacramentele heilseconomie*.[11] There were primarily

125

practical reasons for this choice, which ultimately was also to be the reason why later he was called to the Netherlands as a theological specialist in liturgical questions. After only a year in Paris Schillebeeckx again became lecturer for the Dominicans in Louvain. He had to give lectures on the whole of dogmatics, and what was more obvious than that he should try to get his doctorate on a subject that he had to study? But the choice of the sacraments also brought to light a certain reorientation.

This chapter tries to map the tensions which characterized Schillebeeckx's work in the 1950s, in fact from 1950 up to his arrival in the Netherlands at the beginning of 1958. Then, with the move to Nijmegen and the announcement of the Second Vatican Council a year later, a new chapter also begins in the metaphorical sense.

The encyclical *Humani generis* and its consequences

The reorientation in Schillebeeckx's theology to which *De sacramentele heilseconomie* bore witness can be understood only against the background of the growing tensions between the Roman authorities and the sectors within the French church which stood for an open confrontation with modern culture.

The publication of the encyclical *Humani generis* in 1950 can be regarded as a result of this development. In it, Pius XII emphatically opposed tendencies in the church which had been guided by what he called an 'imprudent zeal for souls' and here raised the question 'whether theology and theological methods ... should not only be perfected, but also completely reformed, in order to ensure the more effective propagation of the kingdom of Christ throughout the world, among men of every culture and religious conviction'.[12] Such a suggestion was regarded as unacceptable, for together with the traditional theology, Rome felt that the identity of the church was also fundamentally being put in question. For contemporaries it was crystal clear that in *Humani generis* the pope was turning particularly against the developments in France, especially those around the worker-priests, and against the theology which was growing in dialogue with these developments. This was confirmed once again when a short time later the document *Menti nostrae* appeared, in which Rome made it clear that the primary task of the priest was to represent the supernatural in the natural world, as a separate sphere. The main concern of the text was that if the life of priests became too like that of the people who were entrusted to their care, their priestly dignity would not be sufficiently visible, nor would be the dignity of the church as the place of divine presence within a godless world. Here the 'mystique of incarnation' of the worker-priests and those who thought along the same lines was unambiguously rejected. The document turned against them as priests who were said to have adopted the views, or a lifestyle, or a type of clothing

> alien to both their dignity and their mission, priests who allow themselves to be led astray by the mania for novelty whether it be in their preaching to the faithful or in combating the errors of adversaries, priests who compromise not only their consciences but also their good name and the efficacy of their ministry. [13]

This statement seeks to prove Camus unambiguously right in his doubt about the ultimate Christian solidarity with the life of men and women in the world. It will not have surprised him, but it made a deep mark on many others.

Menti nostrae represented the beginning of the end of the worker-priest project. In 1951 a prohibition on the recruitment of new worker-priests followed. In 1953 restrictions on their activities were announced which in fact amounted to making it impossible for them to work: thus factory work had to be limited to at most three hours a day. In 1954 a number of Dominican theologians were condemned for their involvement in the worker-priest movement and 'progressivism', including Chenu, Congar and the church historian Henri-Marie Féret, and the superiors of the French province of the Dominicans were removed from office.

The appearance of *Humani generis* also affected Schillebeeckx. The religious and theological movements with which he felt connected and which set out to express the content of the Christian faith in new ways, in contact with contemporary theology, in which he saw the beginnings of a new Christian culture, a 'new Christianity', were set down in the encyclical as so many signs that 'the very principles of Christian culture are being attacked from all sides'. According to the document this attack was the consequence of an invasion of the church by the world; here the 'disunity and error' which had constantly prevailed outside 'the fold of Christ' were also said to have penetrated the church. According to the encyclical there was no lack of 'those desirous of novelty' or who, 'fearing to be ignorant of recent scientific findings', tried 'to withdraw themselves from the Sacred Teaching Office and are accordingly in danger of gradually diverging from revealed truth and of drawing others along with them in error'. *Humani generis* mentioned the desire to allow themselves to be dictated to in a far-reaching way by 'the circumstances and needs of today', an ill-advised orientation on unity between church and world, an 'imprudent eirenism'.[14]

In his work Pius XII was particularly opposed to any attempt to detach Catholic teaching from the philosophical notions in which this was contained within neoscholastic thought. He saw theologians dissociating themselves from 'the words and concepts which are in use among scholastic theologians' in favour of 'conjectural notions and ... some formless and unstable tenets of a new philosophy, tenets which, like the flowers of the field, are in existence today and die tomorrow'. In his eyes this was not only 'supreme imprudence' but also made 'dogma itself a reed shaken by the wind'. He warned especially against the philosophy of existentialism, because 'it neglects the unchangeable essence of things and is concerned only about the existence of the singular'. The language of the encyclical becomes almost shrill with the accusation of theologians who

> seem to consider as an obstacle to the restoration of fraternal union, things founded on the laws and principles given by Christ and likewise on institutions founded by Him, or which are the defence and support of the integrity of faith, and the removal of which would bring about the union of all, but only to their destruction.[15]

According to the familiar papal approach and in a way which strongly recalled the standpoint of Pius X towards modernism at the beginning of the century, in *Humani generis* Pius XII thus rejected any suggestion that the Catholic faith was subject to history and that the church and its doctrine could be subject to change. Indeed, the designation *'nouvelle théologie'* for the theological approach which was condemned in the encyclical was meant in a pejorative sense.

Pius XII regarded any notion that faith and theology had to change in view of the contemporary situation as an affront in itself. For, he asked rhetorically, 'what then becomes of the ever unchangeable Catholic dogmas of the unity and the immutability of faith?' To which he replied: 'Let no one bring confusion or diversion in the things which are unchangeable.' As early as 1946 he had protested in these words against what was said in different ways about a 'new theology' which was supposed to be necessary, in other words about a theology which – and antipathy clearly glimmers though in the formulation – 'would also have to change with everything else that constantly changes; it would have constantly to be on the way without ever reaching its destination'.[16] *Humani generis* even sees the establishment of the fact that in the course of its history theology has made use of different philosophical systems – 'so that it should give human expression to divine truths in various ways which are even somewhat opposed'; the task of the dogmatic historian should be 'to report the various forms in which revealed truth has been clothed' – as a sign of 'dogmatic relativism'.[17]

'We cannot allow ourselves,' Congar wrote in 1951 with what seems to be real pain in his heart, 'to comment on *Humani generis* in a theological chronicle which as an act of scholarly life claims free criticism as its law.' The encyclical was an expression of the supreme magisterium of the Catholic Church and as such 'requires and receives our respectful submission with mind and heart'.[18] In these words, which now sound somewhat pathetic, Congar was doubtless expressing the view of by far the majority of Catholic theologians. Schillebeeckx, too, like his teachers Chenu and Congar, against whose work the document was after all directed, refrained from public opposition to the encyclical.

But in a 1959 article one can still glimpse how much he identified with what in *Humani generis* is condemned as *'nouvelle théologie'* and how much he must have felt attacked by the document. In it he reviews a book *De nieuwe theologie* written by a Dutch Dominican, Andreas Maltha, with whom he also lived after his move to Nijmegen in 1958. Maltha lectured on dogmatics for the Dutch Dominican students and gave an unprecedented maximalist interpretation of *'nouvelle théologie'*, and thus of the papal condemnation, in which he accused a very large number of theologians and church journalists of largely self-constructed heresies. He accused them of a departure from abstract concepts and 'a predilection for a concrete, immediate and affective knowledge', which he called 'intuitionism'; he saw in them an intertwining of nature and supernature, philosophy and faith, essence and manifestation, which he labelled 'confusionism'; and everywhere he pointed to the 'evolutionism' challenged by Pius XII, in other words the notion that conceptual expressions of the faith were time-conditioned.[19]

From his own far more dynamic approach, Schillebeeckx could no longer recognize all Maltha's 'sheer summing up, a long row' of standpoints, as an authentic form of doing theology: 'this book makes a very awkward impression'. But he also vigorously opposed the way in which in *De nieuwe theologie* Thomism was brought forward as a criterion for the Catholicity of a theological approach. Although on precisely this point Maltha could rightly appeal to *Humani generis*, Schillebeeckx asked rhetorically: 'Which Thomism? ... of the sixteenth, eighteenth or twentieth century? And in this last case the Thomism of Garrigou-Lagrange, or Manser, Sertillanges, Gilson, Kreling, De Raeymaecker, Febro, Hayen or Maltha?' Schillebeeckx also emphatically opposed the notion characteristic of the encyclical that influence from outside could be a contra-indication of true Catholicity from a theological standpoint.

> What author says this? Under what, above all suspect [Protestant, schismatic, apostate, atheistic], influence do these Catholics stand ... ? This seems to be the main question. Not: is it true? Under whatever influence these people arrived at this truth.

Confronted with Maltha's dry summing up and 'eternal *yes* and *no*', Schillebeeckx argued for a way of doing theology along the lines of what had been made suspect as *'nouvelle théologie'*. He characterized this as doing theology 'with a steady feeling for the sources of faith, the tradition of faith, the church's magisterium, and with whatever truth is to be found in the present-day philosophical explicitation of the experience of existence'. Moreover, Schillebeeckx made quite clear his antipathy to the suspicious detection of theological deviations in itself. Here of course he was specifically attacking Maltha, but one must presuppose that he was also expressing his dissatisfaction about the Roman authorities. He finally depicted theology as a 'majestic forest which burgeons in its spring glory, and through its inner power ... itself brings forth wild shoots'. In his view this forest was certainly under the care of the 'pruning forester', the magisterium of the church, but in principle loyalty to the dynamic of contemporary theology was a prime requisite for an adequate judgement. He himself thought that through the 'steady renewing synthesis' which in his view was growing in contemporary theology, 'the sickliness that is unmistakably expressed here and there in some rather butterfly attempts at modernization would be corrected automatically'.[20] In his view, rather than intervening, the magisterium should support this dynamic.

Of course, the church magisterium acted in quite a different way: the condemnations of people very close to Schillebeeckx must have made that clear to him. Nevertheless, he seemed to be driven by the firm resolve to understand the interventions of the hierarchy as support for the dynamic of theological development itself. In his public statements about it he in fact presented *Humani generis* as an attempt to prune lovingly the spreading forest, which was renewing itself, and to cut off the shoots that were too wild. It was clear in the 1950s where the boundaries for a Catholic theologian lay, and particularly for anyone who strove for the renewal of church and theology from within it was important not to go beyond these unnecessarily. On the other hand it was not just a tactic. Schillebeeckx felt that as an expression of the church's magisterium the papal documents *had* to be an authentic contribution to the development of church and theology. And since he could only see them in this way if he understood them in a certain sense, they also *had to have been* meant in that way.

Schillebeeckx saw in the document's opposition to relativism a possibility of taking up *Humani generis* positively and thus giving it the place in his theologizing which according to the then current Catholic view it was due. In a 1957 article for the *Theologisch woordenboek* he discussed the encyclical and wrote that the text was primarily directed against 'dogmatic and theological relativism'.[21] That also met up with his own concern for the objectivity and rationality of theology and his antipathy to a way of doing theology which was directly based on feeling and experience that had not been reflected on. That the background of the opposition to relativism in his own case differed markedly from that of Pius XII did not emerge in his reflection on the document. He simply took over the rejection of 'the thesis that our concept of faith has a purely pragmatic value and possesses no abiding truth value, and in connection with this turned against the failure to recognize the church's obligation to engage in speculative reflection on faith'. According to his interpretation, *Humani generis* was not about a positive solution to 'the problem of the relationship between the experience of faith and the conceptuality of faith'; here he denied that the encyclical brought to the fore the continuation of neoscholastic thought and method as the only valid starting point for theology, and in reaction to the new circumstances in which theology was done simply allowed its 'perfecting'. In his eyes the document indicated 'the limits *within which* a solution can be sought' for this relationship.[22] In this sense he supported the encyclical.

'Dogmatic relativism is always the core which is censured by the encyclical in different tendencies [within the current theological discussion]: no more and no less.'[23] Certainly he tried to show that, contrary to what the document suggested, the problem of 'the relationship between experience and concept' which had already been put on the theological agenda at the beginning of the century by modernism was real and had not been resolved by the condemnation of the modernist solution to it. In his view 'it [had] remained the task of theological problems to the present day'. Schillebeeckx was never one to seek a direct confrontation with the magisterium, even in his later career. But at a time when modernism was regarded as the deviation *par excellence*, the main threat to the Catholic faith in modernity unless the church protected itself sufficiently against influences from contemporary thought, it was striking that a Catholic theologian should write: 'The modernists discovered ... a real problem, namely the unmistakable difference between the truth in itself and the truth as a spiritual possession of man.' Though he immediately went on to add that modernism was a failure to recognize the 'integral essence' of the act of faith and therefore 'unavoidably ends up in unorthodoxy', Schillebeeckx made it cautiously but unmistakably clear that to hold firm to the abstract conceptuality of neoscholasticism alone, which is what *Humani generis* in fact wanted to make theologians do, was not a solution. On the contrary, the neoscholastic idea that truth was to be found only in abstract concepts – which Schillebeeckx, following De Petter, called 'conceptualism' – had in his view given believers the feeling that the dogmatic statements of the Catholic faith had nothing to do with experience and thus led to an impasse.[24] There was therefore a new, modern theological problem that called for a creative and contemporary solution, and this solution was not to be found in *Humani generis*.

But in his view this solution was in fact present in principle, in De Petter's philosophical epistemology. This needed to be adapted to theology. According to Schillebeeckx, De Petter's epistemology made it possible to maintain the objective value of concepts and at the same time to leave room for their shortcomings in respect of God himself. It showed that over against

God as mystery, concepts had only a relative significance and that therefore there was a possibility of 'growth in our reflection on the faith'.

The typical epistemological value of our conceptual knowledge of God therefore lies in a projective act in which we in-tend God via the content of the concept. We cannot comprehend him conceptually, but we can know that God is present precisely in this objective, definite direction which is indicated by the content of concepts.

In the direction in which the concept pointed, God could not be comprehended, but could nevertheless really be experienced. 'Experience and conceptuality ... together make up our one knowledge of reality.'[25] According to Schillebeeckx, De Petter's view contained 'the right perspective in which we can affirm both the absoluteness of the truth of faith and the great margin of relativity'. But that was not all. According to him, this view was also to be found, 'although in a way which has not been completely worked out', in the work of the prototypical Catholic thinker whose authority had been endorsed once again in *Humani generis*, namely Thomas Aquinas. In 1952 Schillebeeckx wrote a long and very technical article for *Tijdschrift voor Philosophie* on 'The non-conceptual element of knowledge in our knowledge of God according to Thomas Aquinas'. In it he showed that in Thomas's exemplary synthesis of faith and reason, too, the basis of all theological thought was a knowledge implicitly given in the living experience of faith. This knowledge of faith ultimately and most deeply remained unexpressed, but it did form 'the matrix ... of the conceptual elements in our knowledge of God'.[26]

Doctrine was real, but not absolute, knowledge of God. Not only did Schillebeeckx succeed in basing his theological epistemology on the supreme authority of Catholic thought, the work of Thomas Aquinas, and was able to concede that the modernists and their followers were right without abandoning the church's teaching about the objectivity of the knowledge of faith. At the same time he evidently succeeded in constructing a starting point from which an approach to the Catholic tradition was possible that was fruitful for his own time and culture, without coming all too clearly into conflict with the views of the church's hierarchy. The fact that in his Flemish period Schillebeeckx's theology never aroused the suspicion of Rome was also probably connected with the fact that he wrote in Dutch. His work simply seems not to have been noticed.[27]

The church in the centre

The theological approach which Schillebeeckx developed following De Petter's epistemology ultimately also made him remain fundamentally faithful to his sympathy for the worker-priests, while the church-political circumstances became increasingly grim. In 1952 and 1953, while the Roman conflict with the project was already in full swing, but before the experiment was definitively stopped, he gave 'various lectures' on this question. Ultimately these were published in an article which appeared in the Dominican student journal *Biekorf* in the spring of 1953.[28]

With great caution Schillebeeckx moved through the minefield of loaded and intertwined discussions at the level of church politics, pastoralia and theology. From a theological perspective his view was highly innovative. The central intuition which bound him to the worker-priest movement was the conviction that religion and a sense of God were not completely under the control of the hierarchical church: 'I do not believe in the absence of religion from the working-class world, although I do believe that it has fallen away from the church.' He called this statement 'one of the clearest lines of guidance in the orientation of our apostolate'. 'People must be personally addressed by their God.' It was a thought that he had already developed in his student days and to which he had returned in the series of articles on 'The Christian Situation'; what was new was that on the basis of this he now argued for an inductive proclamation of faith, arising from life itself. In his view it was indeed the task of priests 'to show men the way to the depths of God, but this way goes towards God *through the depths* of man himself!' Therefore he thought that use had to be made of the fact that priests are 'not only teachers, we are also first and foremost, believers. In preaching ... we are expressing our own deepest experience.' Now this was more than a simple plea for the existential involvement of priests in what they preached. It implied a clear choice of position in church politics. In the same sense Chenu had defended the authenticity of the content which the worker-priests gave to their priesthood. Starting from the notion that the central task of the priest was to teach the faith, Schillebeeckx stated that it was not enough to proclaim the teaching of the church. In his eyes the priest must also in fact realize the church as a whole at the personal level: 'The distinctiveness of our specific priestly apostolate ... lies in the fact that throughout the history of the church we actually link men with Christ's mysteries, his historical acts of redemption.' In his view priests had to show what it was to believe in a reality which since God's initiative to become man is at the same time both worldly and godly, natural and supernatural. If that succeeded, the Christian culture appeared in them in a personal way.[29]

The standpoint that Schillebeeckx proclaimed here, about the relationship between natural and supernatural life and about the way in which the supernatural can be known, differed radically from the view still prevalent everywhere at that time. 'Our humanity is the "matter" and our divine life is the "form"', he wrote in 1953, and five years later, in a review of a book on

133

the religious situation among workers, he developed this thought in more detail:

> The church never brings people a complete novelty or something 'alien'. It is simply concerned to clarify and to bring to its true fullness the anonymity of the sense of God addressed by faith which is being sought in any human existence. The church is never the first breakthrough in human beings. It only puts the wine in the vessels which had already been filled with 'water'. It brings to 'self-awareness': it works out what was already brewing or is still brewing in human life.[30]

So this is a church which came into being and indeed has to come into being from below, from human existence. That was also the deepest conviction of the worker-priests. Therefore they wanted to abandon the existing forms of the church in order again to discover what was needed among workers.

Schillebeeckx, too, spoke of 'founding the church' and of a new establishment of the church in the working-class milieu. With the worker-priests and the theologians associated with them he pointed to the involvement and the middle-class origin of a number of church customs which workers 'may not like or easily accept'. These latter, however, were largely external matters: 'for example collections of money during mass, special devotions which are alien to them, class difference in the case of nuptial masses or funerals, the celebration of mass in the morning instead of in the evening, which would suit them better, and so on'. Schillebeeckx saw the special apostolate in the workers' milieu above all as a supplement to existing regular pastoral work. For him, the ultimate goal of all special efforts was the complete participation in the sacramental life of the church in its existing form and obedience to all valid laws and commandments. Remarkably, in 1953 the possibility that the worker-priests could discover in their work that the church had to be changed fundamentally lay outside his perspective.

> Of course, the church is not a church of workers, any more than she is a church of respectable citizens or middle-class people. But because she is at the moment the church of many people with the exception of the workers, this special pastoral care of the workers is quite legitimate.

In the *Biekorf* article he therefore no longer spoke of worker-priests but of priests of the workers.[31]

Now the relationship between the worker-priests' activities and their pastoral work in regular parishes was one of the more explosive points in the conflict over the movement. The Roman authorities feared that the worker-priests would have too much autonomy and were afraid of their inclination to experiment in seeking a form of the church which was adequate to the situation. Under pressure from Rome, the standpoint therefore gained ground that their approach must not appear as an alternative to the regular exercise of the priesthood.[32] Schillebeeckx seemed to go along with this argument. He emphasized that he was not concerned with 'a "dogmatic" or "theological foundation" to the apostolate of the worker-priests': this was a particular response to a particular emergency. The issue was beyond doubt the defence of the worker-priest project against suspicion by showing that a concrete form of the priestly task *par excellence* was to 'found and to form church fellowship'. But the effect of this attempt to show its legitimacy in terms of the classical doctrine of the church and the priesthood was ambiguous. It also reinforced the authority of this doctrine. In the years around the appearance of *Humani generis* the message of Schillebeeckx's theological work was increasingly that the synthesis between God and man, between nature and supernature, which he and others sought was realized in the existing Catholic Church. Provided that it was seen and experienced in the right way and made accessible to everyone, in his view as a living community the church was the Christian way of dealing with the world and culture that was being sought.

In 1952, in his book *De sacramentele heilseconomie* Schillebeeckx was to give a scholarly substructure to the notion that the heart of this synthesis is formed by the sacraments, and especially by the eucharist.[33] But he had begun on this as early as 1949. At that time he set out in a brief article all the thoughts that he was to work out in detail in *De sacramentele heilseconomie*. He argued that it was fundamental to the sacraments that they brought about a synthesis between the human longing for salvation and the divine will for salvation, a synthesis which had first of all taken form in the life, death and resurrection of Jesus Christ. In his eyes the sacraments are a concrete embodiment of the paradox of the Christian message of salvation that man, thrown into the midst of a chaotic world which has succumbed to the greyness of sin, is promised salvation; this is the paradox of a hidden God who wants to be visibly, audibly and tangibly present.[34] He began from the classic conviction that believing in the Christian sense must at its deepest be 'discipleship of Christ'. For him, from a psychological perspective the key to 'the mystery of Jesus's exultation in the Father' lay in 'the unbreakable contact in prayer that Christ had with the Father', and the 'buoyancy of Christ's revelation' lay in his 'religious experience'. So in his view the believer had above all to follow Christ here. 'To be full not of himself, but of God, in order to fill others with this inner fullness; that is witness, apostolate,' he said to his students who as Dominicans were considered to have chosen a witnessing, apostolic life.[35] Along these lines, receiving the sacraments was the form of our 'personal adherence to the redemptive acts of Christ', an adherence which was ultimately aimed at in fact transforming the old sinful man.[36] For him, Christian faith was ultimately bound up most deeply with the whole person, body, heart and mind, 'to enter into the sacramental economy of salvation' as the church represents this.[37] He spoke in terms of 'subjectively becoming involved in the objective value of the prayer of the church's act of worship'.[38]

In his emphasis on the church, Schillebeeckx was in a sense taking up the 1943 encyclical *Mystici corporis*. In it Pius XII, engaging in the theological discussion about the church which was topical at the time, clearly laid down the unity of the church as a visible institution. This unity was said to consist in the one hierarchical leadership and the one well-defined church doctrine, and the encyclical was especially directed against theologians who saw an opposition between the inner fellowship of the many members with one another and with Christ on the one hand, and the external unity guaranteed by the hierarchy on the other.[39] But like any text which chooses a position in an ongoing debate and tries to adopt or refute the good arguments of an opponent, the encyclical, in Schillebeeckx's words, was 'fraught with tensions'. This made it possible for theologians to adopt the notions of the document within the framework of their own theology, even if this was fundamentally different from that advanced by the pope; we already saw something of this approach in Schillebeeckx's use of *Humani generis*. In the case of *Mystici corporis* he especially linked up with the emphasis on the church as a coherent whole made up of different elements: 'for this reason above all the church is called a body, that it is constituted by the coalescence of structurally united parts'.[40] Along these lines Schillebeeckx above all put the emphasis on the social aspect of faith, on the importance of belonging to the community of the church. He concentrated less on the believer as the image of Christ than on the believer as part of a social body founded by and through Christ which, as a body, was an image of Christ, and formed his 'mystical body'. However, Pius XII saw this unity realized primarily in social submission to the leadership of the hierarchy and the one Catholic teaching as laid down by this leadership. For Schillebeeckx, on the other hand, who here took up a notion of Congar's, this unity is above all realized in the sacraments as living signs of the bond between believers and, through the story of Jesus, with God. In *Mystici corporis* the sacraments are seen above all in an instrumental way. They are the means by which the faithful 'as though by an uninterrupted series of graces ... should be sustained from birth to death, and that generous provision might be made for the social needs of the Church'.[41]

Shortly before the encyclical came out, Congar had argued that the church is constituted as a mystical body and that its unity is realized in sacramental actions. Baptism made people members of the body of Christ and 'the eucharist makes us all one single body, his body'.[42] Along these lines Schillebeeckx regarded the sacraments as an expression and foundation of the church and its function in the world. He described them as at the same time the 'metaphorical expression of the human need for God' and the 'external expression of God's condescending encounter with our religious longing for God'. For him they were thus 'the sacramental place of encounter where the human need for God and God's love for man come together', and in the light of the sacraments that also applied to the church in which they were celebrated. The sacraments continued, and the church continued through the sacraments, the divine–human – 'theandric' was the term that he used at this time – synthesis established by divine initative in what in this period he usually referred to for short as 'the mystery of Christ'. By this he meant the union of the divine and the human which according to tradition had taken place in the person and history of Jesus Christ.[43]

In the background to all this stood the rediscovery in the French theology of the 1930s that the faith is an all-embracing reality. According to Congar, the faith was 'total by nature' and indicated the establishment of a comprehensive ordering of life. However, in his view the defensive attitude of the church towards culture and neoscholastic theology orientated on polemic and segregation had lost this insight, and he regarded this as an important cause of contemporary unbelief.[44] With others he therefore argued for an 'incarnate faith', a faith that was completely rooted in the world and assumed a living and synthetic form which was visible in a new way.[45] The hope for such a revival of faith as a living reality was also the background to thinking about the church in terms of the 'mystical body of Christ'. This description rapidly spread through the Catholic world after the First World War and was characteristic of the atmosphere of Catholic theology between the two world wars.[46] The term marked a break with neoscholastic thinking about the church which put the emphasis above all on a number of static characteristics and a church structure which was laid down by law. Over against this, 'mystical body' fixed attention first of all on the living faith and the organic contact between believers. In 1937 Congar expounded the idea of the church as the body of Christ like this:

> The community of Christians, inspired by the same Spirit and acting on the authority of, and moved by, the same Lord, forms one single whole, the Body of Christ. What does 'body' mean? It seems to mean this: just as our body is animated by our soul, makes it visible and expresses it in different activities, so the church is animated by Christ, makes him visible and expresses him in different activities.[47]

The church as a living whole, animated by the spirit of Christ, had a central place. Here Congar saw the hierarchy as one of the means by which Christ guides his church: in his view the church is not only held together from within, by the activity of the Spirit; it is also held together 'from outside', by the work of the totality of the pope, bishops and priests.

According to Congar's image of the church, Christ had called the apostles, and through them the hierarchy, to a threefold ministry: to instruct in the faith, to preside at the 'sacred mysteries', viz. the celebration of the sacraments, and to lead the communities of the faithful.[48] However, for Congar the form of the leadership was not the decisive factor and to a large degree belonged to the domain in which the church was an organization like any other. It had sub-divisions and structures of the kind that were also to be found in other organizations: public functions, a legislation or regulation with sanctions on transgressions, public actions, a people that was governed.[49] Certainly Congar said in the terms of traditional Catholicism that the hierarchical structure of the church showed how everything in the church came 'from above', emanating from God and the glorified Christ, but at the same time he emphasized that the church does not just become a unity through an external order or the mutual collaboration of the various sub-divisions. In his view that applied in 'natural' communities, but he saw the church as a 'living unity', 'in a sense, that is, like a living body'. Christ did not found it on a constitution or legislation but promised that truth and life would be found in it because he himself, who is the Truth and the Life, would live in it through his Spirit. The Law to which it owed obedience did not govern it from outside but guided it from within.[50]

Here the importance of the hierarchy in the church was fundamentally relativized, at least by comparison with the central place that it occupied in the official Catholic doctrine of the church, especially since the first Vatican Council of 1869–70. In the dogmatic constitution *Pater aeternus*, Vatican I had derived the mission of those who held office in the church directly from Jesus Christ. Their mission was analogous to that of Christ himself through God the Father and it was their task to build up the church in which, 'as in the house of the living God, all believers are held together by the bond of the one faith and love'.[51] In Congar's view of the church this notion of things was in fact reversed. It was the Spirit of Christ as the inspiration of the community of the faithful who indicated the divine origin of the church, and the hierarchical leadership first of all showed that the church was also a human reality, although the hierarchical form indeed indicated its divine origin.[52]

Mystici corporis was opposed to this reversal. The encyclical gave a distinctive content to the term 'mystical body'. According to the encyclical it was not the believer as an individual, nor the church as a living community, but the church as a hierarchical institution that was a second Christ.[53] The thought of the document was wholly in terms of the hierarchy and it emphasized that the threefold office which Christ held according to scholastic theology had passed over to the church hierarchy: therefore 'for all times' its members exercised the function of teacher, king and priest.[54] They were those who consolidated the church with 'supernatural gifts' by using the 'life-giving means of salvation', the sacraments; they were appointed 'to

138

offer the Sacrifice of the Eucharistic Victim, to nourish the flock of the faithful with the Bread of Angels and the food of doctrine, to guide them in the way of God's commandments and counsels'.[55] Only the Second Vatican Council would break through this fixation on the hierarchy and the *de facto* identification of the hierarchy with the church as a whole by regarding the whole church, as God's people, as bearers of the threefold office of Christ.

This would not have been possible without the work of theologians like Congar and Schillebeeckx. They found a point of contact for working out their different views of the church in the passing remark in *Mystici corporis* that the organic building up of the body of Christ was not limited to the hierarchy, although the encyclical said in so many words that those who in the church 'exercised sacred power' were among 'its most prominent and eminent members'. However, the text also spoke in a positive way not only about the religious who 'pass their lives either actively among men, or hidden in the silence of the cloister, or who aim at combining the active and contemplative life', but also about the laity. There is extensive praise of those who

> though living in the world, consecrate themselves wholeheartedly to spiritual or corporal works of mercy, and of those in the state of holy matrimony. Indeed, let this be clearly understood, especially in our days, fathers and mothers of families, those who are godparents through Baptism, and in particular those members of the laity who collaborate with the ecclesiastical hierarchy in spreading the Kingdom of the Divine Redeemer occupy an honourable, if often a lowly, place in the Christian community.[56]

Congar in particular, and Schillebeeckx to an important degree in his footsteps, intensively occupied themselves with the place, the role and the function of the laity in the church, along the line of this argument. *Humani generis,* with the climate from which it emerged and which it further strengthened, compelled theologians to put the church and its teachings at the centre of their thought. But by taking up the increasing importance of the lay apostolate and the lay spirituality which went with it, it was possible for Schillebeeckx to continue to reflect on the questions which he faced when he took the way towards a theology of culture.

THE LAITY CENTRAL

In the background of Schillebeeckx's concept of cultural theology stood the broad, organic view of faith and church developed especially by Congar in the footsteps of Chenu's intuition. When, around 1950, Schillebeeckx began to turn his theological attention more emphatically to the church, he also remained faithful to this view, except that he presented it in a way which took account of the conditions in the church. It seemed to him to remain formally within the framework laid down by the magisterium and at the same time to break through a number of its presuppositions.

Here the sacraments played a key role. In Schillebeeckx's view the sacraments made it clear that faith was not primarily and at its deepest about the revealed knowledge which can be contained in a collection of true statements; it was not about what he called 'word revelation' but about 'revelation of reality'. This revelation of reality is expressed in language, and reflection on it gave access to the knowledge implied in it.[57] Schillebeeckx's great study on the sacramental economy of salvation can also be read as an attempt to demonstrate that the church rituals of baptism, confirmation, eucharist, confession, the anointing of the sick, marriage and ordination, which in the official theology appeared so much as visible manifestations of the unique power of the hierarchical church to represent the supernatural, were forms of the church as a whole in which a connection was made between Christ and the Christians. They were places of encounter between God and human beings 'in the holy and sanctifying milieu of the fellowship of the church'.[58] Schillebeeckx could therefore say, 'The church, that is the sacraments'; in his view they contain 'the reality of revelation as a reality which is constantly present'.[59] Especially in the eucharist he saw human openness to and desire for God uniting with God's love for human beings. In the symbolic sacrifice of bread and wine, in his view believers offer 'God the poor water of [their] good will and human sacrifices' and subsequently Christ himself made this water the good wine of his redemptive offering of himself. By identifying himself with them, Christ transformed the humble human work of the sacrifice of bread and wine to complete 'the mystery of his sacrifice'; in this way he changed the human expression of request for redemption into 'the sun of hope which has dawned on our disastrous situation'. In the light of this realized synthesis of divine and human reality, in Schillebeeckx's eyes believers could 'renew the face of the earth'.[60]

Here Schillebeeckx was not only interpreting the Catholic theological tradition across the grain but was also opposing a view of the sacramental power of the priesthood which in the 1950s seemed to him to be already in retreat but nevertheless still to exist. According to this view, the priest – in Schillebeeckx's words – was 'a magician, a muscleman *in sacris*' and the sacraments were realities in what a priest author described as 'a magic forest' in which it was no longer surprising 'that the deer speak, that the bread is flesh, that my poor hands are suddenly called holy and venerable'. This author wrote in a little book about the help he gave in a terrible train disaster and in so doing focused everything on his hands, which blessed so many dying people, forgave them their sins and opened up the way to heaven for them. In a discussion of this, dating from 1960, but characteristic of his approach to priesthood and sacraments in the 1950s, Schillebeeckx accused him with great indignation of 'unworldliness, not penetrating to the awful problem of [the] unspeakable suffering of his fellow men and women'.[61] And that was precisely the opposite of what in his view the sacraments were about: the synthesis of human life in all its fullness and mutuality with the divine sublimity and holiness. Thus the sacraments showed that church and faith have to do with all aspects of human existence, of human nature and the human world. For Schillebeeckx, this also implied that a priest must not stand over against the world but must be 'among men', though as a priest, in other words, 'formally as a mediator between God and men'.[62]

But as I have already indicated, at the end of the 1940s and the beginning of the 1950s the Roman authorities increasingly regarded the involvement of priests in worldly questions and problems as a threat to the image of the church as the representative of a supernatural order. At the same time there was growing attention to the task of the Catholic laity in embodying the Catholic faith in modern society. For those concerned about the way of being the church that the worker-priests were trying to realize, this offered a possibility of conceding to the highest church authorities that their work was not a specific priestly activity, yet maintaining that it was an important task of the church. It was a task that really fell to lay people, but had to be performed by priests 'for lack of lay workers who are thoroughly trained and who bear witness'. This was the course that Schillebeeckx took, in important respects in the footsteps of Congar.[63] In the short term and seen pragmatically, it was doubtless a sensible choice. But it would ultimately lead to an extensive theology of the laity, whose position in the church was defined as fundamentally different from that of the priests (though this aspect was still hardly seen); this ultimately reinforced the separate position of the priest. This was to have an influence even on the documents of the Second Vatican Council.[64] After the Council the ambiguity of this position became clear. In the closing document of the 1987 Synod of Bishops about the mission of the laity in the church, formulae which previously offered scope and had seemed liberating, and had made clear the importance for the faith of the activities of people in the world, were used as an argument to identify the tasks within the church that the laity could perform without objection, as distinct from the really priestly tasks. The synod represented the restoration of the very notion that people were trying to break through in the 1950s with the development of a theology of the laity: that the holiness of the church was represented by the hierarchy, and that the laity then had to put this holiness into practice in the world.[65]

The mission of the Catholic laity

In opposition to Protestantism, the starting point of which was that within the new covenant all participate in the priesthood to an equal degree and which regarded church office as a temporal authority, from the Council of Trent onwards the Catholic Church had put all the emphasis on the fundamental difference between the universal priesthood of believers and the hierarchical priesthood that was conferred sacramentally with ordination. In 1943 Pius XII had once again endorsed this standpoint in *Mystici corporis,* and again in 1947 in a rather more pointed form in the encyclical *Mediator Dei*.[66] This defined the climate in which in 1949 Schillebeeckx began to write about the nature of the church, in the footsteps of Congar's publications on the subject.

Congar had already been preoccupied with the distinctive position of the laity in the church since 1947, and this long labour made it possible for him to set out some 'markers' for a theology of the laity in 1953 in a thick book of 700 pages: *Jalons pour une théologie du laïcat*.[67] It was in fact a theology of the church which differed at essential points from that of the papal documents. Congar began by stating in principle that the term 'lay' was derived from the Greek *laos*, people, a word which in Christian terminology had the meaning 'people of God'. In this sense, for him 'lay' was a comprehensive term for both members of the clergy and 'laity' in the technical sense; he thought that the difference between the two groups was subordinate to the fact that they formed part of the same people. As members of the people of God, all Christians together shared in the threefold office of Christ as king, teacher and priest: as 'people' they represented men before God and made God present among men. In 1970, looking back on the development he had undergone in his thinking about the laity and the ministry, Congar stated that despite everything, in 1953 he had still held too firmly to the pattern of thought that the mission of the laity in a technical sense in fact derived from Christ's mission to the apostles, and through them from the hierarchy. According to this view, the laity indeed shared in being sent by Christ, whether through the sacraments of baptism and confirmation or through fulfilling by explicit command a specific task in so-called Catholic Action, but in his words of 1970, the initial view remained 'principally and spontaneously clerical ... '[68] Despite all his efforts to give the laity a place of their own, the Congar of *Jalons pour une théologie de laïcat* 'found it easier to imagine the church without laity than without a hierarchy'.[69]

Schillebeeckx was strongly influenced by Congar in his theological reflections on the place of the laity, and in connection with this on the significance of the church and the priesthood. But he differed from Congar at precisely this point. Traces of the dominant 'clericocentricity' can also be found in Schillebeeckx. But from the beginning, more than Congar, he emphasized that clergy and laity fulfil different functions within the church which cannot be reduced to each other. In a more concrete and more consistent way than Congar, he thought in terms of the church as a whole and the different tasks in it. This led to a view of the priestly office which in substance was quite traditional, but at the same time Schillebeeckx's clearly functional approach marked a break. In the course of history, people within Catholic theology had begun to see the priesthood increasingly as a dignity indicating a specific person, a capacity to perform validly certain actions of the church which was conveyed by ordination. Schillebeeckx saw the ministry not only in principle, but also in its concrete sub-divisions as a ministry to the community of the faithful. The laity, too, had their own task within this community. Their task was to build up a culture which was open to God and the preaching of the church: 'They are responsible for the ordering of human life as a basis for the life of grace.' Again it seemed that this preaching, which for Schillebeeckx in the 1950s was one of the intrinsically priestly tasks, was the real task of the church, and that the building up of a 'Catholic culture' was only at the service of that. However, for him this was an independent task of the church:

> Through the laity the church is engaged ... in the temporal, earthly ordering of life, and since the 'earthly facts' constantly evolve, the Catholic laity here will have to fulfil a never-ending, autonomous creative function ...[70]

Ultimately his efforts were to issue in what, in the first instance, he called 'lay spirituality'. At the same time this was a renewed attempt at reflection on the ecclesiological and theological significance of human existence in the world.[71] In his first article on 'Theological Foundations of Lay Spirituality' he wrote that through the laity the church lived in the world, in the midst of culture.[72] In accord with what had been advanced on the Roman side, he assigned the members of the church hierarchy the role of leaders and teachers in the church, but at the same time made it clear that the church did not live exclusively, or even primarily, from this leadership.

In 1953 Schillebeeckx gave a lecture in the Netherlands which in fact sketched the outlines of his theology of the church and made it clear how he assimilated the ecclesiology which was promulgated by Rome and had been laid down especially in the encyclical *Mystici corporis*. The study conference at which he gave the lecture had been specially organized by his own *Tijdschrift voor Geestelijk Leven*, in collaboration with its sister journal *Carmel*, with a view to the development of a lay spirituality.[73] At this conference Schillebeeckx had the at first sight quite thankless task of showing that an authentic evangelical person 'is at the same time a man of the church, and a man of the church is a true member of the church only to the degree that at the same time he is evangelical': his lecture was entitled 'Gospel and Church'. But although the thought that gospel and church are indissolubly connected was still hardly controversial among Catholics in the 1950s, he was not content to repeat theological commonplaces. To make his position acceptable, he wanted to 'analyse the sound, religious nature of the mystery of the church'; he wanted to show 'how this heavenly form embodies itself in our earthly world, as it were "becomes man" with all the ambiguity of that'.[74]

The sacraments played a central role in defining this 'religious essence' of the church. According to Schillebeeckx they bridged the distance between 'heavenly form' and 'earthly world'. He began by saying that the faithful are the church and the church 'is the *congregatio fidelium*, the community of faith of all who confess Christ'. But he immediately added that to belong to this community implied that one had entered the 'inner, evangelical community of grace with Christ'. In his eyes the visible church was not only a pointer to 'an invisible presence in this world of a divine community' but at the same time 'the organ of salvation through which Christ calls to life the evangelical community, extended in breadth and internalized in depth'. Just as during Jesus's lifetime the encounter with God took place through the encounter with his humanity, with his words and actions as man, so, according to Schillebeeckx, after his ascension the encounter with God takes place through the sacraments. And at the same time that means that this encounter takes place through the 'sacramental church in which Christ's sacred humanity encounters us by way of the sacraments' (96–8). On the basis of this he could conclude that the church was thus the gospel and 'the living relic of the sacred manhood of Christ that has ascended to heaven ... which allows us over space and time again to touch the hem of Christ's human garment' (102f.).

In this way he identified the Catholic Church which really existed with the mystical body of Christ in a way which was hardly less than that in *Mystici corporis*. Because for him this identification went through the sacraments and not directly via the hierarchical leadership of the church and its doctrine, he also left more room for historical change and necessary corrections. But he did not hesitate to put belief in the holy and Roman Catholic Church – *credo in unam sanctam ecclesiam catholicam romanam* – on the same level as faith in God as Father, Son and Spirit. He identified the breaking of visible church community as 'the great sin of the division of the Reformation and a heresy' (111f.). Schillebeeckx indeed recognized the gulf 'between the external church community and the internal church community, in other words that in many of its members visible membership of the church community is no longer the meaningful expression of their individual communion in grace with Christ', but nevertheless the 'earthly church' was and remained for him 'the evangelical church, an unassailable, effective sign of God's will for salvation'. According to him it was right to 'continue to believe in the saving fact that weak men may be the organs of Christ's love' (108f.). This led him on the one hand to emphasize the need for the commitment of believers to the reform of the church. But on the other hand, at the same time he thought that 'abuses and false beliefs' could never be remedied by 'resounding pamphlets and mutiny'. In his view the true Christian should never 'rise up against authority or appeal to a so-called "filial opposition"' (116–18).

This last is of course striking in view of Schillebeeckx's later defence of a loyal opposition in the church. But in 1953, too, the question of the legitimacy of opposition within the church was highly topical for him, given the pressure under which his fellow Dominicans Chenu and Congar were placed. Schillebeeckx thought that what they were in fact doing was the only right thing: 'if in our honest striving for an evangelical church we are not understood by those who hold authority in the church and are worked against, so that the hoped-for reform does not come', nevertheless 'the only attitude of the truly evangelical man is obedience to the church hierarchy'. In an argument which still shows the pain which he and kindred spirits felt during the church-political troubles, he stated:

> This, then, is no failure of our evangelical effort, but its highest evangelical act of love: such an act of sacrificial love to the church, the highest evangelical action following the ... self-denial or self-emptying of Christ, who through his sacrificial love redeemed men and gave birth to the evangelical community of love ... Then, at least in us, through our sacrificial love the church will be reformed and its purely evangelical face will be shown. And through the saving reality of the 'communion of saints', what happens in us has its unavoidable repercussions on the whole community of the church (117).

Worthily bearing misunderstanding as an evangelical value, and accepting the failure of the attempt to bring the church more into accord with the gospel as a way of still having success probably offered the necessary comfort.

But it was not a sign of resignation. Perhaps it was a response to the objections of kindred spirits; perhaps it was also a reaction to the ecclesiastical measures which meanwhile had affected Chenu and Congar. At all events Schillebeeckx sharpened his remarks further on the publication of his lecture in *Tijdschrift voor Geestelijk Leven*. He emphasized that the acceptance for which he argued must not be passive, and indicated that disciplinary measures could be 'objectively unfortunate' through all kinds of circumstances, that 'all kinds of human, all too human influences' could play a part in them. In his judgement it was not *per se* more imperfect' to want to gain insight into these mechanisms than 'blindly to obey'. In a kind of echo of Chenu's remark that obedience is only a minor virtue, which has become well known, Schillebeeckx argued for 'understanding obedience', since

> a Christian who is serious about his obligation to take initiatives [will] with an honest sense of the painful factors which because all kinds of spheres of influence have led superiors to a less happy intervention or even sometimes have compelled them to take measures ... not in a contrary love of self throw in the sponge: Christ's love continues to constrain us, and even after the unfortunate intervention his redeeming love remains an urgent reality. Calmly, but daringly, he will have to continue his zeal for the kingdom of God within the reduced boundaries.

According to Schillebeeckx the 'context of a commandment or a prohibition' also determined 'the scope of its content', and therefore its concrete significance and 'meaning' had to be investigated 'in one's conscience' against the background of what one had learned to see as Christian duty. And then in a strikingly sharp way:

> For example, not a single church measure can conflict with the right and the duty honestly to seek the truth, which, as St Thomas says, is a natural duty (118).[75]

It is evident from the fact that Schillebeeckx makes these remarks that his view of the church ultimately differed quite essentially from that of *Mystici corporis*. Granted, the identification of God's presence on earth with the church meant that it was inconceivable to him that a church regulation could perhaps make no sense at all, but at the same time it emerges that in his eyes the hierarchical church was not solely responsible for faith. The church is the form of the evangelical truth and the place to encounter God, but this refers to the whole church in the mutual interconnection of its members: 'The whole of the church, the laity as well as the priests, each in his own way, is the active organ that hands on the living content of the gospel faith through time.' Along the line of Congar's ecclesiological studies, Schillebeeckx stated with Thomas Aquinas that 'the church is raised up on the faith and the sacraments of the faith'. It was the function of the hierarchy to support and build up this church and keep it in being, and that made its task an essential one. Moreover, in this church the hierarchy was responsible for contact with the divine element: Schillebeeckx here after all ultimately called the 'priestly hierarchy' the 'source of the church's life', and the faithful owed obedience to it. But in his eyes the hierarchy nevertheless performed its function supported by, and in the service of, a greater whole. He did not hesitate to speak almost directly against *Mystici corporis* – though without saying so – and to claim: 'The evangelical saving power of

Christ lives on *in the whole of the visible church community*, in its lay members as well as in its hierarchs: they all form the one "priestly and royal people of God'"; faith lived and was expressed in this people as a whole (98–100: my italics).[76]

According to Schillebeeckx there were fundamentally three clearly different functions in the church, performed by three different church 'estates'. The 'priestly hierarchy' had a 'transcendent, other-worldly task' and was 'directly related to the kingdom of God'. Alongside this was the 'religious state', which 'pointed both laity and priest to the "one thing necessary", the gospel as the vocation of all men'. But above all he saw it as his task to take up all the impulses, including those from the pope, and to urge the 'Catholic lay community' to perform its own function. For him that meant that it had to take account 'of the way of life within the world in the light of its evangelical view of Christ' (119).[77] Here he took up in a new way his old notion that nature was there for the sake of supernature, 'which is therefore already prepared for in nature'. With an intriguing image he called the church 'the radar' which 'tracks the "inner call" by God to souls which could be lost in the tumult of life and emphatically brings it into the consciousness of believers'. However, he now said that the task of doing this fell especially to 'the lay members of the Catholic Church'. It was their task 'not only to humanize the world through their animation by the gospel, but at the same time to permeate the order of life within the world with a Christian spirit. The laity must build up a Christianity around the core which is the church (104f.). The aim of their work was to permeate culture, not with a view to a positive Christian programme, but out of a sense that the

> inner usefulness of earthly culture for the religious life of the church is directed towards the Mystery, so that the ultimate significance of the service of these earthly factors to the church slips into this Mystery by which it is constantly put in question and relativized (107).

In short, all the themes of the earlier project of a theology of culture returned in Schillebeeckx's attempt to formulate the mission and the task of the laity.

Lay people in Flanders and the Netherlands

Of course Schillebeeckx's reflections on the mission and spirituality of lay people did not stand alone. In general, in the immediate post-war period the laity enjoyed a special importance, in the eyes of both church leaders and theologians. Among other things this was connected with the acceleration of the industrialization and modernization in Western Europe which had been taking place under the influence of the American Marshall Plan, and the integration into the world market that this reinforced. In a situation defined by 'the growth and unification of the population of the globe, scientific, technological and cultural progress, the institutions and structures to which they lead, which are becoming increasingly broad and complicated', the leadership of the Catholic Church saw a growing influence of 'materialism ... and all false ideologies which strive for totalitarianism'; in using this last word the authorities in fact particularly had in view the Communism which immediately after the war was a significant factor in many countries. In these circumstances it was more urgent than ever to influence the situation in a Catholic direction, and there were efforts to do this with renewed zeal by the active presence 'of lay apostles in all sectors of modern life'.[78] Here, however, the thought on the official side was still along the lines of the views of Pius X and Pius XI about Catholic Action as the participation of the laity in the mission of the hierarchy. For Pius XII, too, the hierarchy remained the church in the real sense and the laity participated in the church's mission only in so far as the hierarchy involved them.[79] Therefore, to give the laity a mission of their own, as Congar and Schillebeeckx did, was in itself a breakthrough in principle.[80]

Despite the restraint of the hierarchy over the official recognition of the competence of lay people, life was regularly stronger than teaching. In fact Catholic lay people took active responsibility for the world upon themselves. Here in practice they needed a certain degree of freedom of action and thought: they were actually able to gain this for a while, but after a time the freedom was again limited and the church government once again emphasized that the laity had received the authority to convey the message of the church in contemporary society from them.[81] For their part the laity found the constant anxiety of the hierarchy about the legitimacy of their activity and the orthodoxy of their standpoints a restriction on their freedom and a failure to recognize their own expertise. They felt that they were being hindered in what they now saw as their task as Catholics in modern society: to give form to an active social presence. In Belgium the growing self-awareness of Catholic lay people clearly came to light around the National Congress on the Lay Apostolate in 1956, on the theme 'The Layman in the Modern World Crisis'. This was drawn from a wide range of people and had an attendance of almost 2,000. A number of burning national and international social questions were discussed, and a group of Catholic spokesmen formulated as their task a contribution towards 'the building up of society as responsible fellow-citizens'. They noted a 'need for an open dialogue with those of other views' based not on rivalry and strife between ideological currents but on 'shared good faith and a common striving for higher humanity'. The journal De Maand appeared for the first time in 1958. It was focused on such a dialogue and emphatically described itself as the first 'general cultural, social and political monthly' in the Catholic sphere to appear 'under the full responsibility of lay people'.[82]

In the Netherlands the view that was given a voice in Flanders in *De Maand* had already gained some publicity. The journal *Te Elfder Ure* had been appearing since 1950: it expressly presented itself as a 'progressive Catholic journal'.[83] Like many others, its editors found inspiration in the developments in France. Initially, the monthly Dutch journal presented itself less emphatically as a *lay* enterprise, and in fact there were also a number of priests on its editorial board. Earlier, *Te Elfder Ure* had been the voice of the so-called 'breakthrough' thought, opposing the confessionalist structure of Dutch Catholicism, a structure within which in fact the clergy dominated many spheres of life. In this way the journal, with its largely lay editorial board, bore witness to a growing sense of the responsibility of 'the Christian' for 'the world in which he lives'. In the face of the 'stifling formalism' which was dominant everywhere, it made a case for daring and élan as the appropriate way of making Catholic faith present in the rapidly changing world.[84] When *Te Elfder Ure* was in a sense refounded in 1954, now as a monthly, the editorial board testified to its plan to

> approach all serious contemporary questions *with openness* and *without prejudice*, without fear and without suppressing certain problems out of a mistaken concern for orthodoxy.

It emphatically added that the journal was open to contact with 'those who think otherwise'. The journal addressed itself explicitly to the shaping of society:

> It is in particular 'the world' by which the Catholics of *Te Elfder Ure* are intrigued and fascinated, and the ordering, Christianization and redemption of which they see as one of their tasks.

In this sense *Te Elfder Ure* was thus also programmatically a lay journal: it addressed itself to the task of Catholics in the world, and this was regarded as a lay task *par excellence*. In order to be able to fulfil this task well, the journal wanted to deal not only with social but also with religious and church problems.[85]

De Maand and *Te Elfder Ure* were both orientated on a more adequate Catholic presence in the world and therefore on breaking down confessionalization. In the Netherlands this effort did not go unopposed. In 1954 the Dutch bishops published a statement on 'The Catholic in the Public Life of this Time'. In it they committed themselves – as it would prove, for the last time – to subject Catholics by force to the discipline of the confession. They tried to compel the laity to take part in social life only under the leadership of the church and organized into associations approved by the church. They forbade Catholics to become members of a number of organizations on pain of excommunication: these included the Communist Party of the Netherlands (Communistische Partij van Nederland, CPN) and its trade union (Eenheids VakCentrale, EVC), the socialist trade union (Nederlands VakVerbond, NVV), the socialist broadcasting association (Vereniging voor Arbeiders RadioAmateurs, VARA) and the Dutch Association for Sexual Reform (Nederlands Vereniging voor Sexuele Hervorming, NVSH). They also banned membership of the Social Democratic Workers Party (Partij van de Arbeid, PvdA), which had become particularly prominent after the war as a party focused on breaking down the confessional structures; a number of prominent Catholic laity had been involved in it since its establishment.[86] These had their own working party within the PvdA which had its own journal. The bishops did not want to threaten this relatively small group with excommunication. They limited themselves to calling on its members to go back on their tracks.[87]

Thus formally, the bishops allowed those whom they addressed some leeway. However, that these in fact made use of it was a clear sign of the changed conditions among Dutch Catholics and of a growing self-confidence among Catholic lay people. Thus the president of the Catholic Workers Association within the Workers Party, J. N. Willems, said in a radio broadcast immediately after the appearance of the bishops' statement that he thought that he had a responsibility not only as a Catholic, but also as a member of Dutch society. In this last capacity he felt that heeding the call of the bishops would have such dire consequences for the position of Catholics in society that he did not dare to take responsibility for this.[88] Soon afterwards *Te Elfder Ure* came out with a special issue on how Catholics should regard the bishops' statement. Here a prominent lay member of the editorial board, the philosopher Bernard Delfgaauw, unreservedly opposed a Catholicism which imprisoned itself in its own confession; with new verve he called for a personal Catholic witness in the midst of society by laity who were well equipped to do this.[89]

In the second half of the 1950s a climate developed among Catholics in the Netherlands which a contemporary described as 'a complete crisis of authority'. In his view the growing tension between the laity and the church leadership was only apparently 'the traditional and quite harmless anti-clericalism'; in fact it was an expression of 'a deep-rooted mistrust'.[90] This climate explains to an important degree the specifically Dutch attitude to the Second Vatican Council. Socially active Catholics – lay people but also younger priests – with expertise above all in management and the humanities, felt frustrated in their attempts to give form to post-war society as Catholics by the existing church structures, the dominant conditions and the attitude of the hierarchy. This was less a philosophical and theological debate than it was in France, but in the Netherlands, too, two groups were opposed: those who wanted to allow the church to play a role in modern society and to influence modern developments indirectly and through culture, in which automatically the laity too would play an important role, and those who maintained a closed Catholicism under the strict leadership of the hierarchy. At all events, halfway through the 1950s the Dutch bishops represented this second standpoint. They were loyal to the spirit of the Roman activity against 'progressive' movements in France, but in this period particularly also the Netherlands.

In 1954 and 1955 the Jesuit Sebastiaan Tromp (1889–1975) visited the Dutch major seminaries and the Catholic University of Nijmegen in the name of the Roman Congregation of Seminaries and Catholic Universities. The Dutchman Tromp was a well-known teacher at the Gregorian, the Roman university of his order, and the spiritual father of the ecclesiology of *Mystici corporis*. Moreover, he was a prominent advisor to the Holy Office, the Roman authority which safeguarded the purity of Catholic teaching. On the one hand his purpose in the Netherlands, too, was evidently to remove from positions of church leadership those who sympathized with the *'nouvelle théologie'* and its programme. Thus the dogmatic theologian Klaas Steur of the major seminary of Warmond, who after *Humani generis* had continued to teach on the *'nouvelle théologie'*, lost his job and was appointed a village pastor. But on the other hand the whole operation started as a result of a specific case, the Terruwe-Duynstee case. This Dutch case was comparable with the French conflict over the worker-priests and their intellectual leaders, in so far as here Rome was convinced that the church was not adopting an appropriate distance from the world and thus was bearing all too little witness to its holiness and lofty position.

The Terruwe-Duynstee case was symbolic of the growing opposition among Dutch Catholics in the 1950s.[91] The Catholic psychiatrist Anna Terruwe (1910) had demonstrated in her doctorate that modern psychology, and especially the theory of neuroses, including those in the sexual sphere, was not in conflict with the Thomistic anthropology from which the church's magisterium and moral theology began. Thus, from a Catholic standpoint, psychology could be quite useful.[92] In practice, however, this meant that modern science was brought within a sphere in which the church had always thought that it had a monopoly, namely that of the human soul. Here psychology made it clear that the usual Catholic view of sexual morality and celibacy, in which very great importance was attached to sexual continence, could not be maintained intact. A passionate conflict began. When Terruwe, in collaboration with the Redemptorist lawyer and pastor Willem Duynstee (1886–1958), on the basis of her psychological insights also began to treat priests and student priests, this gave the Psychological Institute of Nijmegen University a bad name. It began to be regarded as 'the sinful Riviera of Catholicism' in the Netherlands.[93] Rumour had it that the rules about sexual morality and sexual behaviour which were so strictly maintained within Catholicism were being abandoned there, and in the treatment of celibate priests at that. Opponents brought this to the attention of the Roman authorities, who thus finally sent Tromp.

The strict admonitions which were published in 1956 as an outcome of Tromp's visitation in fact contained a condemnation of Terruwe and Duynstee: as a woman she might no longer be consulted by priests, and despite protests from Nijmegen University, Duynstee was transferred to Rome.[94] In content the admonitions were one great attempt to safeguard the traditional sexual morality of the church and its views about continence and asceticism, evidently seen as pivotal signs of the detachment of the church from the world, from the influences of modern science, which threatened to relativize all limits.[95] In Rome the fact that (moral) theology was seeking to make contact with psychology was evidently seen as an expression of the imprudent eirenism, the senseless seeking for reconciliation with modern thought condemned in *Humani generis*. Here, more than the reputation of individuals was at stake. The minor Roman offensive around Terruwe and Duynstee was in fact an attempt to reverse a strong tendency in Dutch Catholicism at that time. To an increasing degree the pastorate was beginning to be concerned not just with the practical implementation of the church's rules for behaviour but also with human welfare. Here in particular pastors began to make use of a contemporary scientific approach and especially of psychology.[96] Tromp's whole operation was thus directed against what from the Roman perspective could only be seen as a laicizing of church theory and practice from within. The same also applied at quite a different level to the measures against the French worker-priests.

When Schillebeeckx spoke for the first time at a so-called 'theological week' of the Nijmegen theological faculty in 1957, as the one expected to become professor of dogmatics there, this was the climate in which he found himself. This week was about the church and the place of the various groups in it, which at the time was in itself already an explosive topic. But to some degree Schillebeeckx found himself right in the middle of the dispute, because he had been brought to Nijmegen by the dean of the theological faculty, Willem Grossouw. Grossouw was a priest of the diocese of 's Hertogen-bosch and a prominent champion of a more open Catholicism, which would include greater lay influence. He was a clear supporter of Terruwe and Duynstee during the case. He organized the theological weeks as a deliberate attempt to make the faculty, which at that time was still small and quite isolated, more outward-looking, so that it addressed a wider public than the 40 students, all priests, who were there in 1957. Grossouw became involved in what according to him was the growing 'interest of the laity in the basic questions of theology'. Among the 200 participants in the first theological week there were indeed a considerable number of lay people, and Grossouw reckoned that their theological interest was a sign of the 'growing awareness of the laity and their sense of a real share in responsibility for the fate of the church'. Here he bore witness to a view of theology which in its openness to contemporary questions and its sense of its own uncertainty was very striking, at any rate in 1957:

> All of us, including the theologians among us, ... are seeking light in the darkness, clarification in confusion, certainty in the midst of all our fear. Like Peter we want to listen to 'the words of eternal life' and to try to understand these again for ourselves and our time ... Theology itself and thus also our faculty can only profit from an attitude which can combine obedience to God's word and the magisterium of the church with openness and boldness. *Vox temporis vox Dei*: God speaks to us through the time in which we live.[97]

'Openness and freedom' seemed a direct echo of the 'open and unprejudiced' in the preface to the first issue of *Te Elfder Ure*: Grossouw was closely associated with this journal.

Evidently Grossouw saw Schillebeeckx as a potential ally in the quest for a theology with these characteristics: he himself said that he regarded the 'theological week' as a welcome occasion to 'promote Edward's nomination to our faculty', an effort which was ultimately crowned with success.[98] Of course he will have based his judgement of Schillebeeckx on his publications, but he also may have seen his recent nomination as professor to the Higher Institute of Religious Sciences as an indication that Schillebeeckx shared his desire for an open theology which was also accessible to the laity and was in keeping with the spirit of the time. This Higher Institute of Religious Sciences, set up in 1942 at the Catholic University of Louvain, had the aim of providing theological instruction for lay people – including non-ordained religious – who at this time were not yet admitted to the Catholic theological faculties.[99] For Schillebeeckx it was like a consolation prize: at this time only diocesan priests could become professors at the theological faculty of the University of Louvain. Nevertheless, the nomination to an institute orientated on the laity fitted his theological position well. As a result of Schillebeeckx's lectures at the Higher Institute of Religious Sciences his book *De Christusontmoeting als sacrament van de Godsontmoeting* appeared; this was at the same time a concentrated summary of his major study *De sacramentele heilseconomie*, which had been primarily limited to historical theological analyses, and a more systematic sequel to it.[100]

During the 1957 theological week the development of a view of the place of the laity in the church was entrusted to a lay person. On the basis of the literature most topical at that moment, though not uncontroversial,

Bernhard Delfgaauw argued that all believers shared in the role of priest, teacher and king which according to current Catholic teaching pertained to Christ and had been handed on by him to the church. He took up the growing interest in the universal priesthood of all believers, a thought which was based on 1 Peter, in which the whole church is addressed as 'a royal priesthood, a holy nation, God's own people, that you may declare the wonderful deeds of him who called you out of darkness into his marvellous light' (1 Peter 2.9). Delfgaauw went on to state that the Catholic laity had its own apostolate 'in its own place in the world, not as participation in the apostolate of the hierarchy but as an apostolate on its own responsibility, because of its own bond with Christ'.[101] These thoughts were in line with Congar's *Jalons pour une théologie du laïcat*, which moreover had already indicated that there was ultimately only one true theology of the laity: a comprehensive theology of the church, *'une ecclésiologie totale'*.[102]

The same was true of an authentic theology of the ministry. This was what Schillebeeckx was asked to speak about during the theological week. In the framework of this week, of course, he did not develop such a comprehensive ecclesiology, but he did draw a very broad outline in his lecture. Beginning with some fundamental reflections on the nature and significance of redemption by Christ, he arrived at a picture of a church in which the members of the hierarchy and the laity each had their own place. But the question is how far that became completely clear to the assembled public at the time of the meeting itself. Schillebeeckx had intended emphatically to say that

> actions set on foot by Christian lay people and stemming from their Christian conviction ... [are] authentic church activity, even when the laity completely has the initiative in them ... Alongside the hierarchical institution there is in the church ... an essential church mission entrusted to the community of faith.[103]

For lack of time, however, he could not deliver the very part of his discussion which dealt with the relationships between 'the hierarchical apostolate' and the 'task of the Christian lay community within the world'.[104]

Bishop, priest, layman: different functions within the church

Schillebeeckx's views on the clergy and the laity were characterized by concentration on the different functions which the various groups fulfilled in the service of the church as a whole. Here from the very first his approach put another emphasis from that of the French authors whom he largely followed. French thinking about the priesthood was strongly influenced by an image that ultimately went back to Francis de Sales (1567–1622): the priest as the one who personally takes upon himself the role that originally belonged to Jesus Christ. The priest was an '*alter Christus*', and in his person had to be the divine representative. This idea could lead to a view of the priesthood as representative of the holy, with an emphasis on the priest's role in the cult, which Pius XII worked out in the encyclical *Mediator Dei*. However, the idea of the priest as *alter Christus* could also take the form of the bringer of the message of the gospel of mercy in an insensitive world, who to human appearances is powerless, and who comes to grief through his own mission: this picture of the priest was painted by the French novelist George Bernanos in 1936 in his *Diary of a Country Priest*, a novel which proved attractive to many people in this period. And the fact that in worker-priest circles the participation by the priest in the living conditions of the workers was spoken of in terms of 'incarnation' also pointed to a view of the priest in this spirit. The French discussions of the position and role of the laity were prompted in the first instance by the question whether the laity could not also represent Christ in this sense. However, Schillebeeckx approached the priesthood primarily as a special task in the church, a special responsibility for building up the people of God.[105]

In his lecture at the Nijmegen congress Schillebeeckx mentioned 'administering the sacraments, the service of the word and pastoral and organizational leadership of the people of God' as specific priestly tasks. That did not mean that in his view the laity could play no part in these tasks; but they did not do so as laity. If the laity took part in the leadership of the church, in his view this meant that they had clearly received a special mission from the hierarchy and in their own way shared in the authority of the hierarchy. Here he argued that a traditional pattern was being repeated: on the basis of the results of what was then recent research he stated that the ministerial priesthood had arisen gradually in the early church as an auxiliary ministry of the bishop, who in turn by his consecration shared in the authority given by Christ himself to the apostles.[106] Schillebeeckx thought that the origin of the presbyteriate – in the historical description he prefers the terms 'presbyteriate' or 'presbyterate' to 'priesthood', in order to avoid the prevalent unintentional identification with the priesthood – disclosed the true theological structure of the ministry in the church. The fullness of power lay with the bishops, and their office was the central office in the church; priests shared in that office:

> The episcopate is ... consecration to be a successor of the apostles with their apostolic authorities which they exercise *potestate propria et ordinaria*, in unity, however, with the whole of the apostolic college and with the pope. The presbyteriate is not this in any respect. By virtue of his ordination the presbyter is simply the priestly aide of this episcopal

priesthood, and so he can do everything (on the basis of his ordination) to which he is mandated by the apostolic office.[107]

With its matter-of-fact functionalism this view broke through the mystical atmosphere which surrounded the priesthood and the clerical state in the church. It was not the cultic priesthood that had a central place in the church but the role of pastor and leaders as exercised by the bishops, with the help of others to whom they delegated tasks. This view of the structure of the ministry was to be adopted generally and endorsed in the Vatican II Constitution on the Church.[108]

Apart from recent insights into the early history of the church, in a sense this view of the structure of ministry in the church also took up that of Pius XII, which strongly emphasized the teaching office of the bishops. At the beatification of Pope Pius X in 1954 he praised the latter above all as a famous champion of the church and a providential saint for his own time. All the emphasis was put on the fight against modernism in the church.[109] In his own fight against what he labelled 'nouvelle théologie', the author of Humani generis clearly identified himself with the author of the encyclical Pascendi and the 1907 decree Lamentabili that went along with it, in which 65 standpoints attributed to modernism were condemned. Two days after the beatification of Pius X in 1951, Pius XII received 39 cardinals and around 450 bishops from all parts of the world in an audience and addressed them at length on the significance of the magisterium in the church, a magisterium that Pius X had exercised in so exemplary a form. In his address he emphatically stated:

> Apart from the apostles or their lawful successors, namely the pope of Rome for the whole church and the bishops for the believers who have been entrusted to their care, there are no other teachers in Christ's church who are appointed by divine law ...

Pius XII was especially concerned to confirm 'the right and responsibility' of the bishops 'for the flock which has been entrusted to you to feed with the unfalsified teaching and the truth of Christ'. All those who were allowed to act as teachers in the church did so in permanent dependence on the pope and the bishop who bestowed the teaching authority on them; they did not teach 'on their own authority, or on the basis of their theological knowledge, but by virtue of the mission which they have received from the legitimate magisterium'. Their authorization therefore always remained subordinate to this magisterium and could 'never be exercised arbitrarily or independently'. This magisterium in turn had the duty to guard over their instruction.[110]

When Schillebeeckx emphasized that the office of bishop is the central office in the church, he did not mean that the bishops had to exercise more supervision of preaching. He wanted above all to emphasize that all the offices in the church, especially the priesthood, were orientated on the service of the church as a whole; however, in his view that whole was represented by the college of pope and bishops. Departing from the customary approach, he did not see personal ordination as the central element of the priesthood, but the mission to fulfil a task in the church and in the service of the church. He put within this mission the specific ordination that the priest received personally, which made it possible for him to administer the sacraments in Christ's name.[111] Thus the difference between priest and layman was relativized by being functionalized.

Another implication of Schillebeeckx's view of the priesthood was that it has a collegial character. In his view the bishops formed part of an apostolic college and had actively to attach themselves to 'the whole apostolic body'. However, in 1957 he still mentioned that as it were only in passing; only some years later, during the preparation for the Second Vatican Council, was the question of 'episcopal collegiality' to occupy a central place in the discussions in the church. In 1957 it was evidently more important for Schillebeeckx to point to the need for the priesthood to take form in 'a co-ordination of collaborating priests under the leadership of the episcopal body'. In Schillebeeckx's view the episcopate has as it were become collective in the priests and bearers of other possible offices which might arise in answer to specific questions and needs. 'Only the whole gives a picture of a presbyterial apostolate,' he stated, 'so that at the same time not every priest has to do everything', and also 'rivalry between presbyters becomes a contradiction of the very nature of ordination as presbyter'. That was a consecration to take part in the fullness of episcopal office and fellowship with others who bore office.[112]

According to Schillebeeckx the legitimate differences in exercising the presbyteral office also included the difference between priests who fall directly under the local bishops and priests who are members of a religious order or congregation. From a theological perspective, in their priesthood these last, too, were members of the corps that supported the college of bishops, the *coadiutorium ordinis episcopalis*, even if in their priestly work they did not fall under the jurisdiction of the local bishop in terms of canon law.[113] Contrary to the picture which was almost universal at that time and anticipating the reflections of the Second Vatican Council on the religious life, according to Schillebeeckx the religious life was not completely orientated on 'the sanctification of the self', on a life that because of its voluntary renunciation of 'low' earthly values like marriage, possessions and self-restriction was superior to the lives of lay people. In his view, celibacy, poverty and obedience were the expression of the 'appreciation of the surplus value of God's being God' beyond all values of creation, however much in his view these also pointed to God.[114] He rightly thought that this was in line with his teacher De Petter, who had written that for the religious the promises of obedience, poverty and celibacy 'at least in principle' close off the way to 'any *natural* self-development or self-realization, however exalted may be the level of life at which these are seen'. To expect everything from God was thus still the only possible thing. In Schillebeeckx's words, the religious is completely orientated on the 'transcendent appreciation of God' and therefore voluntarily detaches himself from the possibility of realizing 'the three basic values from which the order of values within the world can be derived: worldly possessions, the companionship of marriage and the right to self-determination'.[115] But he put the emphasis rather differently from De Petter by emphasizing that the religious life embraces a public witness. It functions as a kind of counterpoint. From his perspective on the theology of culture he thought that for Christians 'the earthly also [entered] into the *mystery* of the supernatural life, in which the divine possibility completely surpasses all earthly possibilities within the world'. But within a church which has to realize this it was the task of a religious to make visible this surplus value of the supernatural life.

> As an organ of the life of the church the religious life has a typical social function; it is the living signal, *in facie ecclesiae* – before the face of the church and the whole world – the admonitory sign of the surplus value, of the 'one thing needful' of the supernatural life of grace and the calling of every man to salvation.[116]

This was certainly also the message that he gave to the Dominican students entrusted to him in order to support their further spiritual training.

In a sense the functional view of the religious life was along the lines of the Dominican religious ideal. Here at any rate personal orientation on God – contemplation – and service of the church's task of preaching are directly connected.[117] In his duplicated text on Dominican spirituality Schillebeeckx described contemplation in the Dominican sense as becoming detached from the immediately visible world. The aim of this detachment was to bring out the presence of God hidden in the world. 'If the living God appeared to us as the bright advertisements in a big city', he wrote, that would not be necessary, but 'our God is a hidden God who no longer appears on the stage but reveals himself in all the actors to those who look and listen with interest'. In order to make this looking and listening possible, in his view it was necessary to be permeated by the 'contemplated God', in other words by 'God who has also become a psychological reality in our life'. He thought that this did not lead to a permanent distancing from the world, but to a new *'présence au monde'* – he deliberately took up this expression – because in his view the divine truth contemplated had within it a synthesizing force which incarnated itself in the world. In the light of the 'God who has become a psychological reality', it was possible in the contemporary world to listen to 'the language of truth which, perhaps caught up and entangled in a net of untruth, nevertheless resounds from the events of the time'.[118]

Being a Christian in the world

Distancing oneself from the world and emphasizing God's absolute superiority on the one hand and being present and incarnate in the world in the experience of this superiority on the other were two attitudes which according to Schillebeeckx belonged together. For him, together and in connection they made up the fullness of the Christian life. In his view they had found a synthesis in the Dominican life. In the typological-functional division of work which he constructed in the 1950s, this in fact implied that the Dominican life was a synthesis of the religious life and lay life. For whereas it was the function of the religious life to be the 'living signal' and the 'admonitory sign' of the superiority of 'the supernatural life of grace and the calling of every man to redemption', according to him, there it was the special vocation of the laity

> in appreciation of God and in apostolic zeal for the kingdom of God to exert themselves for the natural value which the religious in fact renounces. He takes into account the fundamental statement of the Old and New Testament that 'the world is there for man' (and man for God).[119]

As in the 1940s, so also in the 1950s and at the beginning of the 1960s Schillebeeckx wrote articles about the relationship between God and human life in the world and about Catholicism as humanism, in discussion with existentialism.[120] Questions of this sort continued to remain of central importance to him with a view to the adequate attitude of the church in the contemporary situation. But in the 1950s he increasingly began to discuss questions connected with the place of Christians in the world under the heading 'lay spirituality'. This was how he justified his abiding efforts on this subject in the eyes of the hierarchy, and at the same time he was responding to signals from the laity that they indeed wanted such a spirituality. Of course it was of little importance that Schillebeeckx himself was not a layman. Both in his own eyes and in those of the laity whom he was addressing, reflection on the place of the laity in church and world was manifestly part of his task as a theological teacher.

From the moment that he first went into it at length in 1949, Schillebeeckx described 'lay spirituality' very broadly. He speaks of 'the Christian situation' – in fact using the same expression as in his articles in *Kultuurleven* – of 'the lay person in the world', of 'the total situation of the Christian lay person, his integral attitude to life, the "being" and "doing" of a baptized person in the world'.[121] And the question on which this particularly turned was the specific way in which this 'person-in-the-world' had to be faithful in his situation to God's calling 'to intimate fellowship with God and finally to experience of God'. According to Schillebeeckx, that amounted to considering the possibility of bearing a twofold responsibility. On the one hand, lay people have to devote themselves to their work and task with the required dedication and professional knowledge – 'a mother is Christian as a housewife, a father as a breadwinner and father, a teacher as a lecturer, etc.' – and so help to build up earthly culture. 'In this Christian view of the lay state the seriousness of the earthly worldly task is fully accepted.' On the other hand the laity must give form to an authentic faith in the midst of contemporary culture and by participating in it. Schillebeeckx summed it up like this:

> The distinctive lay living out of the apostolic faith of the Christian in the world is primarily ... to realize soundly the inner orientation of the natural on the supernatural through expert implementation of the values of nature and at the same time embodying authentic Christianity in this structure of creation ... which is thus permeated with it like dough.[122]

For Schillebeeckx the foundation of a lay spirituality was the same as that of his theology of culture: the unity of God's plan of salvation in which the earthly reality and earthly values are brought within the kingdom of God. In 1952 he himself also made an explicit connection between his articles on the position of the church and his earlier articles on 'The Christian Situation' and interpreted the articles by Jan Hendrik Walgrave in *Kultuurleven* which were orientated on the development of a Christian humanism as attempts to work out a lay spirituality.[123]

But at the same time this indicates that Schillebeeckx always had an ambivalent attitude to the discussion on lay spirituality which was being carried on everywhere in the 1950s. Here he was not concerned with what was important for a group within the church but with an analysis of the basic structure of what he regarded as Christian existence as such. In 1962 he stated that 'the discussions around a distinctive spirituality of priest, bishop and lay person' had got bogged down in recent years. He argued that this indicated a fiasco that also had to be recognized and demonstrated that 'we were searching in a dark room for a black hat that wasn't there'. But he had never been concerned with a lay spirituality in the limited sense of the concrete experience of lay people. What he now set down in so many words he had always known at the back of his mind:

> Spirituality is neither lay nor clerical, but every believer has to experience the one Christian perfection in a *situational way*, and one of these situa-

tions is for example to be in a secular profession or, for those who hold office, to be entrusted with apostolic office.[124]

According to Schillebeeckx, in the end there were two levels in the theological discussion about the laity in the 1950s. He objected to the statement that the laity were the church, because this confused the two meanings: of 'lay' as a member of the people of God – the Greek *laos* – and as distinct from someone holding office. '"The believers are the church" is the more correct expression', he thought; by this he meant the 'whole of the community of faith' which comprises lay people, priests, bishops and popes.[125] Nevertheless, his own standpoint ultimately came close to what is expressed in the controversial expression 'the laity are the church'. In fact he regarded the laity, the believers in the world, as the representatives of what being a believer in the Christian sense really was, those who give the church a face.

> In the hierarchy and the community of lay faithful together the church is the earthy manifestation of Christ's redemptive grace … Within this whole the hierarchy has a function of authority, which is therefore exercised for the sake of the community of lay faithful: the apostolic office is a diaconia or service to Christ and to the faithful.[126]

This function of the hierarchy as an authority was there 'for the sake of the community of lay faithful'!

Like other theologians at this time, in his concern with the discussion of a lay spirituality Schillebeeckx made creative use of the ambiguities of the term 'lay' so as to be able to think about the church in an innovative way at a time when it had become impossible to take the ordinary ways. Starting from what he himself later called the 'historical bond between so-called secularization or the discovery of the "laicity" of the world and the discovery of the "lay person in the church"', he developed a view of the church in which the position of lay people in the world was of central importance.[127] In his first publications about a 'theology of culture' he had developed ideas about 'a truly Christian attitude to laicity within the world', in other words the world in its worldliness. In the 1950s, in the light of this he gave a central place to those who as Christians in the world had the task of making the divine redemptive grace present. It was the laity who specifically ensured 'that encounter with people … could become for fellow human beings specifically the sacrament of encounter with God'.[128] Another practical consequence of this high estimation of the specific task of lay persons in the world was that Schillebeeckx argued for lay influence on the governance and teaching of the church. He put this in a restrained way, but in fact what he said was quite revolutionary in the conditions in the church before the Council:

In certain cases a lay person can also have a distinctive message to bring to the church, even in its own sphere of faith. The *lay experience* of faith can illuminate aspects in the datum of revelation which otherwise would remain implicit or would be capable of expression only much later.[129]

According to Schillebeeckx, the church thus needed to occupy the place that the worker-priests had vicariously occupied for it. It was of fundamental importance for Christianity to take form in the midst of everyday culture, alienated as that was from church and faith. However, this needed to happen not through priests but through lay persons.[130] He attached great importance to 'making holiness actively present among people where they are to be found'. It was completely clear to him that here not just mutual interest but the Christian message of redemption itself was the issue: 'The "presence in the world" of a Christian ... is always a presence in terms of redemption, and thus with and in the living God; a redemptive presence.' At the same time, in his view this was not sufficient. He continued to maintain the classic notion that 'by divine institution' there is an essential difference 'in the one great saving sign of the church between the hierarchy of those who hold office and the faithful people of God'.[131] His theology of the church in the 1950s was indeed 'fraught with tensions', tensions which arose as a result of the interference on the one hand of the dynamic of his theological thought in interaction with contemporary culture and on the other of official Catholic doctrine. When in the first half of the 1960s the boundaries which this thinking imposed on his thought to an important degree fell away, an enormous amount of theological energy was released – and not just in him. In the 1960s, radically new theological theories and insights followed one another at a previously unimaginable speed.

The ultimate foundation of the distinction that Schillebeeckx continued to make in principle between the faithful people of God and the official hierarchy lay in the image of Jesus Christ as the origin of the church. On the one hand he adopted the classic view that in Jesus Christ God has become man, which for him meant that the divine and heavenly has revealed itself in the human and earthly. 'In Christ the glory of God enters our world in a personal way.' On the other hand, in his view Jesus Christ as a human being was also 'personally in his human manifestation the supreme realization of religion' and represented human beings before God. In other words, for him Jesus Christ was both 'the realizing revelation of the gift of God to man' and the revelation of 'the restoration of man to God'. Here too he took up a classic theological theme, namely that of Jesus Christ as head of the church, the first of humankind to receive the grace of redemption, who made all those who believe in him share it. But the way in which he worked this out was unusual. However, Schillebeeckx thought that the dominant conception fell short and stated that Jesus Christ was 'head of humankind, redeemed and to be redeemed', by calling humankind to a fellowship which emerged from 'the unity of the destiny and the value of this community'. And he thought that this unity, 'like all that is authentically human, [was] not a fact, but a task, a reality to be realized'. Thus, according to Schillebeeckx, Jesus Christ was not just an object of faith but also had this function as an exemplary believer. He had called the church to life as a fellowship of believers by being an exemplary human being and calling on others to follow him. The tradition made it impossible for Schillebeeckx to speak about Jesus in so many words as a believer, but he came close to doing so:

> In this respect the whole of Christ's earthly life is a living out of being the incarnate child of the Father, in the human situations in the world in which he came to be entangled. In obedient love of the Father the messiah will accept the whole of his concrete human life and live it out as the religious expression of his attachment to the Father despite everything. Through this supreme religious cult we are redeemed.[132]

Christians are redeemed because in Jesus Christ they have a perfect forerunner on their way of faith to redemption. Conversely, this means that according to Schillebeeckx, the redemption in Christ was not yet completed as long as the whole of humankind was not glorified with him in God. As Christ glorified by God, he brought together all human beings, 'in principle and objectively', into the *qahal* of Yahweh: into the *ecclesia Dei* or 'the ecclesial people of God'. But, Schillebeeckx said,

> this gathering of all men in God around his messiah, which in principle objectively has already come about, must then be achieved by us personally. What is achieved in Christ, 'the one who is representatively redeemed', must antitypically become an actual reality in us which is personally achieved and appropriated in the dimensions of space and time.[133]

According to Schillebeeckx, the church was now on the one hand 'the earthly visibility of Christ's glorious body', and as a 'saving institution' it gave form within the world to his 'glorified power, but by giving human form to earthly weakness'. This manifestation 'of the Kyrios in his capacity as head of the people of God' now took place, in his view, '*exclusively* in the apostolic office or in the church's hierarchy'. The hierarchy exclusively represented the church as a saving institution, a continuation of the visible presence of God's lordship as this had entered the world in Jesus Christ. On the other hand, the notion that what had taken place in the glorification of Jesus Christ becomes complete reality if it is appropriated by the faithful in their lives meant that for Schillebeeckx the church was not a static datum. It embodied 'a rising movement from the victory that has already been won to the full encounter with Christ ... It is a church in eschatological movement and unrest: it does not yet possess its lasting abode.' According to Schille-beeckx, this second aspect of the continued presence of Christ, the aspect of 'being the incarnate child of the Father', which constantly needed to be realized further in believers, is embodied in the church by the laity.

> Thus the lay community manifests the same Christ [as the hierarchy], but in so far as Christ himself is representative of the whole assembled people of God, and typically realized what the church's community of faith has to achieve antitypically. Here at the same time it is being said that the lay community has to perform an active role in the so-called apostolic co-redemption.[134]

The hierarchy had the role of representing the divine worth of the church, but the laity had the task of making a place for this divine reality in the earthly reality.

Especially the way in which Schillebeeckx took up the classical idea of 'the whole Christ', the *Christus totus*, was surprising. Paul had called the faithful members of one body (1 Cor. 12.12–31) and Christ the head of the body, the church (Col. 1.18). At the same time he formulated the notion that Jesus Christ brings all to perfection from heaven and supports 'the saints' until 'they attain to mature manhood, to the measure of the stature of the fullness of Christ' (Eph. 4.13). Taking this up, Augustine spoke of the *Christus totus* as the head and the members together: the glorified Christ as head and the church as his body.[135] In the history of Catholic theology this idea of the *Christus totus* served above all to emphasize the unity between the church and the glorified Christ, living with God. It emphasized that the church, and in fact the ecclesiastical hierarchy, really represented Christ on earth: that is also how the idea functioned in *Mystici corporis*.[136] However, Schillebeeckx expounded it in terms of making the significance of the laity clear for the life of the church. For him, the fact that Christians did not just believe in Jesus of Nazareth as the Christ but in 'the *complete Christ*' meant that this was ultimately about 'Christ with all his flowering of the saints', Jesus Christ as he manifested himself in the communal life of all the faithful; this idea meant that any 'free and personal acceptance of grace [occupies] an irreplaceable position in the divine dispensation of grace'.[137] In other words, the history of every believer is of the utmost importance and an irreplaceable part of the history of human beings with God.

Until halfway through the twentieth century almost the whole history of piety and theology had put all the emphasis on the fact that God had redeemed humankind in Jesus Christ. Nothing and no one can add to or take away from that. The church hierarchy had control over this redemption and the authority to speak about it authoritatively and to distribute its fruit. In this light it was a fundamental and surprising breakthrough that in the 1950s Schillebeeckx called every believer a 'co-redeemer',[138] although ultimately this went unrecognized because he equally defended the view that Jesus Christ was represented as *Lord* over the faithful by those who held office. Schillebeeckx was to work out the 'lay line' further in his theology after the Council. Not only was he to devote extensive attention to the theological significance of 'work' in the world; he was also to make concrete attempts to work out what it meant for the ordained ministry in the church to be at the service of the believing community as a whole. Moreover, he was to put all the emphasis on Jesus Christ as 'being an incarnate child of the Father'. But above all he was to present Jesus as the one in whom the lordship of God entered our world in a personal way, and that would make it possible to think of the church as above all an assembly of the faithful who precisely as such made present the man Jesus, glorified to be the Christ.

LIFE ORIENTATED ON GOD

However, in the 1950s this was not yet the issue. Certainly in this period Schillebeeckx increasingly saw faith and spirituality as dynamic life in the midst of culture, orientated on God. In 1949 the essay on 'Theological Foundations of Lay Spirituality' appeared, and this thinking on the position of lay people clearly gave his reflections on spirituality a new impulse. It resulted in a series of articles on what in the French Thomistic tradition were called the 'theologal' virtues, those orientated on God: faith, hope and love. From 1950 these articles appeared in *Tijdschrift voor Geestelijk Leven*. In the theology of the magisterium, faith, hope and love were regarded as the 'ground of unity' which binds all Catholics 'most inwardly with one another and with God'.[139] In the series of articles Schillebeeckx used this as the basis for a dynamic view of spirituality, of Christian life in the midst of the contemporary world. In the previous chapter it became clear that in the 1940s his view of the spiritual life put the emphasis on the openness in principle of the creation to God, on the indissoluble and intimate relationship between 'nature' and 'grace'. However, at that time his view of this relationship was ultimately static. In the four articles which were published between 1950 and 1952 in *Tijdschrift voor Geestelijk Leven* on faith, hope and love, the dynamic of human life and human history was far more central. The emphasis shifted from what used to be called 'the creaturely awareness' towards what later was called 'the economy of salvation', in other words to the way in which human beings are taken up into God's movement, which sought to lead them 'in and through Christ' to 'redemption', 'holiness' and 'salvation'.

Belief in a history

In the first article of the series, 'I Believe in the Living God', Schillebeeckx once again made the statement which coloured all his articles on spirituality. According to him, faith was more than holding particular statements to be true:

> Faith is not just a matter of the mind ... Faith is also this, and indeed is so to an important degree ... But this acceptance ... is possible only if it is surrounded with an atmosphere of trust.

For him it was ultimately a matter of 'a view of life and an attitude to life which human beings adopt towards things, persons, the world, life, everyday life, because it is an attitude towards God, who is the Everything of all this'.[140] However, what was new in this 1950 article was that he did not work this out philosophically but connected it directly with the history of God with human beings as narrated in the biblical writings and interpreted in the first centuries by the church fathers. For Schillebeeckx, as for many Catholic theologians in this period, the rediscovery of the dynamic theology of the church fathers was of great importance. He saw them as 'the initiators of church theology or of the intellectual awareness of faith', as the first who 'tried to resolve by theological reflection the problems which arise as a result of the confrontation between the apostolic kerygma and contemporary problems'. He saw their theology as 'laying foundations' and thought that an 'urgent study' of their work was necessary for contemporary theology, alongside 'fundamental reflection on scripture'.[141] In certain conditions he saw above all that their dynamic concept of 'mystery' as the real presence of the glorified Christ in the church's liturgy made it possible to work out further his own need for a living, dynamic concept of faith. The way in which he was finally to develop this in 1952 in his major study *De sacramentele heilseconomie* will be discussed at length in the next chapter, but as early as 1949 he said that faith was a matter of 'entering into the sacramental economy of salvation, in the firm conviction that personal contact with the "mystery", the saving event, with Christ, comes about there'. Schillebeeckx now saw believing as trust and as surrender to the history with which God took human beings up into the movement of redemption. It was a matter of putting trust in

> the reality of the person and the work of Christ, in other words in the economy of salvation, in the good news that we are redeemed by God who becomes man and died for us, but rose again that we should live.[142]

In the period after the Second World War the terms 'salvation history' and 'economy of salvation' resounded throughout Catholic theology. On the one hand this was an attempt to take account of the growing sense that human existence was 'historical' and bound up with space and time. In particular Karl Rahner's philosophical and theological reflections on the 'historicity' of human existence played a key role. At the same time there was a desire, in contrast to the static neoscholastic way of thinking, to take account of the fact that in the biblical writings no immutable truths were revealed, but events were narrated. These events made it clear that human events are taken up into a divine movement and dynamic. In this connection the church fathers spoke of a divine 'economy'.[143]

An important factor here was the turn that the Catholic approach to the Bible had taken after 1943. In his encyclical *Divino afflante Spiritu* Pius XII broke with the restraint towards historical–critical biblical exegesis which his predecessor Pius X had opposed so strongly in his hostility to all 'modernist' tendencies. In 1920, in the encyclical *Spiritus paraclitus*, Benedict XV had still given an emphatic warning against the use of the methods of the profane sciences in the investigation of holy scripture, but after 1943 it was possible for Catholic biblical exegetes, too, to use the modern methods of historical and textual investigation which had already long been current in Protestant theology. Here Catholic theologians certainly kept in view the continuity between the results of exegetical investigation and church teaching, and it was very important for them through responsible exegesis to be able to regard the Bible as inspired by God's Spirit. The approach of the Protestant exegete Oscar Cullmann, which he himself called 'salvation-historical', was important in this respect. Since the 1920s, Cullmann had been occupied in breathing new life into the trend that had long existed in German Protestantism; here the biblical revelation was regarded as a history driven by the dynamic of the divine Spirit. Catholic theologians saw an affinity to the way in which the church fathers used the Bible in this, and many of them thought that to an important extent they could follow their approach.[144] In the 1950s Schillebeeckx was in agreement with them: the term 'salvation-historical' crops up often in his texts.

In 1953, in a lecture to Flemish theologians, he explicitly went into the question of attention to salvation history and the historicity of revelation. His reaction to this was very similar to his reaction to kerygmatic theology at the end of his student days. He rejected the 'complete depreciation of speculative thought' which he perceived in some champions of a salvation-historical approach, and by means of the work of Thomas Aquinas defended the theological necessity of 'the distancing from life which is characteristic of any science'.[145] Nevertheless, his view of theological procedure changed as a result of insight into 'the salvation-historical basis of theology'. He stated that 'the real object of theological science', namely 'God himself according to his inner mystery', could be known only 'at the level of the economy of salvation situated in history'.[146] With the terseness of a lexicon article, some years later he put it like this:

> Since revelation runs its course on the basis of a salvation history, history has an extremely important function in faith and theology ... The whole of Holy Scripture describes a bit of human history to us. But through this history there comes about a divine *Heilsgeschichte*: it is an account of ... what God does for us in and through men ...

But Schillebeeckx's acceptance of historicity was ambiguous. In his view, what salvation history was about was supra-historical: he literally said that revelation was 'the historical accomplishment of a supra-historical divine act and word of salvation'. Although he thus called history 'a *locus auctoritatis* in theology', in his view in the 1950s that was only as an externalization, a sign of the divine truth which remains the same. 'Thus Christianity is about the triune God, as manifested in a history of salvation.'[147]

At the end of the 1960s he was also to describe in historical terms the salvation from God that came to light in salvation history. For Schillebeeckx himself 'the sacramental structure of revelation' was still the important thing. He was primarily concerned with 'the fact that the divine manifests itself in figures and forms of our earthly reality'.[148] The appearance of Jesus Christ as the 'effective expression of God's concern for men' was the central element of this manifestation, and it was especially his 'human deeds and words contained in history [which veil] a divine mystery that escapes the grip of sheer history and can be approached only in faith and in the context of the church'.[149] The Old Testament pointed forward to this, and the church lived from it with a view to, and in fact already as part of, the final consummation which is announced with this event.

> The three great phases of salvation are: the *Old Testament*, in which God chooses a 'non-people' as his people in order to be the witness to the other peoples of God's saving purposes; the *New Testament*, the phase of the incarnation in which God himself enters history, really *becomes history* and completes divine redemptive activity in human, historically situated actions; and the *history of the church*: at the conclusion of revelation the period begins which will only be ended at the parousia: the history of the new people of God that lives by the once-for-all fact of redemption.[150]

It is nevertheless clear that in the 1950s Schillebeeckx's openness to history and historical change grew and also became more concrete. He continued to maintain the Catholic conviction that faith always remained the same and that there was development only in the *understanding of* faith; he spoke about the 'church's consciousness of faith which always remains identical but grows'. In his view the third phase of the history of salvation, the phase of the church, was not a history of revelation in the strict sense: this phase did not bring to light any new things about God and our salvation. However, he added to this the fact that in the church, too, there was 'a historical

168

saving event that is fed by the unique reality of the mysteries of Christ or revelation'. It was a matter of what elsewhere he was to call the 'total Christ': what happened in history after the beginning of our era was indeed still important. Time and again salvation needed to be made present. In his view, that happened especially in the sacraments as they were celebrated by the Catholic Church, in which 'the redemptive mystery of Christ' was made present in such a way that the people who had not seen Christ could still live by that historical mystery of Christ.[151] But in his view this also happened in the history of the church's faith.

In the footsteps of Chenu and Congar he concluded from this that so-called 'positive theology', the study of the views of faith and theology in the biblical and post-biblical period, was of essential importance for theology: 'The theological exploration of the growing belief throughout the history of salvation ... is one of the foremost tasks of speculative theology itself.' Here Schillebeeckx was not concerned with 'instructive facts': as a systematic theologian he was concerned with the historical reconstruction of views of faith from the past – which had really taken off in Catholic circles in the first half of the twentieth century[152] – and ultimately with 'the element of witness' in the life of faith from the past.

In Le Saulchoir he had learned quite specifically to see the texts from the history of theology as expressions of concrete, historical forms of the life of faith and also to study them in that light. As far as he was concerned, thinking in terms of salvation history made the theological importance of this study clear:

[Positive theology is] really about a better understanding of the thing itself, namely the mystery of salvation, in which Holy Scripture, patristics, high scholasticism and all the later periods of the church were intellectually interested. From all sides, illuminated by different perspectives of time, the mystery of salvation betrays more clearly its inner, above all integral, content, whereas any expression and synthesis of faith bears the exponent of its own imperfections of expression and its own perspectives.

In Schillebeeckx's eyes this imperfection and limitation also applied to a theology based exclusively on statements of the magisterium. According to him, 'the definitions of the church, usually occasioned by heresies and errors ... [were] only crystallizations, at some points, of a life of faith which extended much further'.[153]

And that was not limited to the past. With a surprising matter-of-factness and almost in passing he expanded the concept of 'positive theology' to embrace the investigation of contemporary forms of faith. In the same breath, he simultaneously gave an explanation of his involvement in some contemporary developments:

The positive function of theology [includes] a survey not only of early expressions of the life of the church but equally of those of the present day, like those of former times: the lay institutions, the growing sense of the place of the layman as a Christian in the world and as a layman in the church, the liturgical movement, the observable shift of religious life towards the world, etc.: all this also forms a *locus theologicus* for theological reflection on the faith. Wherever a possible witness to authentic faith is to be found, the theologian stands in his own territory.[154]

When Schillebeeckx was nominated professor in Nijmegen and in 1958 summed up the result of his development hitherto in his inaugural lecture there, he described theology along these lines as thought 'in search of the living God'. In his view, in faith 'the world of man's history-creative freedom is now taken up into personal living relationship with God' and it was the task of theology to reflect on that personal intercourse as it took concrete form in its own time.[155]

The distinctive character of Schillebeeckx's theology becomes yet clearer through the way in which he took up the term 'salvation history'; this was comparable to the role that the term played in the work of the German Jesuit Karl Rahner (1904–84), which had a very great influence especially on German Catholic post-war theology. After the Council, Rahner was to begin to work it out into a large-scale 'salvation-historical theology'.[156]

There is a striking affinity in development between Rahner and Schillebeeckx. At the end of the 1930s Rahner himself developed an anthropology by means of his own reading of the work of Thomas Aquinas, which was influenced above all by the philosophy of Martin Heidegger. Rahner saw human existence as the existence of a 'spirit in the world', consciousness clad with a body and thus with the world, which was therefore at the same time bound up with historicity.[157] Building on the work of his fellow Jesuit Joseph-Maréchal (1878–1944), Rahner saw human existence as orientated on God in longing. In his view, faith in the Christian sense meant that a particular word spoken in human history is accepted as God's word and the fulfilment of the human longing for God. Here he emphatically stated that the necessity for this word cannot have a human foundation but rests on a free action of God, on God's free decision to disclose himself.[158] This showed a good deal of agreement with the way in which Schillebeeckx took up De Petter's philosophy theologically and tried to bridge the gap between nature and supernature while at the same time holding firm to the freedom of God's revelation.

However, at the same time there was a fundamental difference in approach. In Rahner all the emphasis was on the basic structure – in technical philosophical terms the transcendental structure – of the human consciousness. The important thing was that man as question was open to God's self-revelation, which in Rahner was in fact represented by the teaching of the church. By contrast, already in his student days Schillebeeckx insisted on a clear link between the concrete content of the human questions and that of the church's proclamation, which after all claimed to be a response to them. Along these lines, in 1950, in his first article in the series about faith, hope and love, 'I Believe in the Living God', he wrote that faith presupposed a 'longing for redemption' that was already present in God, a 'hankering after religious happiness'.[159] In Schillebeeckx's view the active, dynamic longing was an essential element of humanity. It was ultimately through the concrete human longing that people came into contact with God's economy of salvation.

Life redeemed by hope and love

Schillebeeckx expressed the nature of this longing at more length in the second article in the series about the theologal virtues, that on hope. In it, he said in a sentence which in fact summed up the whole article, albeit cryptically, that hope 'transfers the focus of the present to the future by virtue of the past', and does so 'by virtue of the mysteries of Christ which have already been completed'.[160] The striking feature of this sentence at the time when it was written was not its second half. That the incarnation, the death and resurrection of Jesus Christ in the past was the basis of redemption from sin and reconciliation between God and human beings had now for centuries been an indisputable starting point, both for the faithful and for theologians, and in the 1950s this starting point was still valid. However, theologians still differed over how this connection could be envisaged. Schillebeeckx, too, tried to do justice to his conviction:

> We believe in the historically accomplished fact of Christ's redemptive life and death, because we ... believe that almighty God himself has taken our life into his hands in Christ, has committed himself personally to it and is constantly devoted to it ... Sanctifying grace, as the fruit of Christ's atoning death and resurrection and as the beginning of the realization of the final redemption, is the rock-hard foundation of the Christian hope (8f.)

According to Schillebeeckx, the faithful came into contact with the divine commitment and sanctifying grace through the church, and in particular through the sacraments. However, it was striking that in his work this did not lead to the unshakeable certainty of being redeemed. On the contrary, for him sanctifying grace led to a reinforcement of the feeling of the need for redemption, to a 'commitment to God' which corresponded to that and even to 'aggression' against 'all those many things that Christ's triumph seems to speak against'. Of course, Schillebeeckx was not concerned with a 'human conquest of God', and for him the basis of Christian hope was not 'self-confidence'; given the state of things and the weakness of human beings, hope based on this would lead only to disappointment and despondency. Christian faith was about 'trust in God, relying on the redemptive work of Christ ... At a deeper level winning God means being won over by God ... ', allowing the dynamism of one's life to be linked up with God's power (13f., 18f.).

But the striking thing about the article on 'The Hopeful Mystery of Christ' was the degree to which it was concerned really to take seriously the evident situation of the world:

> Modern man is very aware that life is almost impossible to understand, that life remains a perplexing possibility ... He feels thrown into the fetters of a damaged world.

By comparison, according to Schillebeeckx it was impossible simply to maintain that this world has been redeemed by Christ, as the mainstream of the Christian tradition from Augustine had in fact done; that would be in flagrant contradiction with '"the sighing of this world", and in particular with the moral and bodily woes of humankind'. In his view believers were given a life to live 'of security with God', but that life could only assume the form of 'a hidden urge and a hidden growth of the kingdom of grace in a world and culture which are visibly not yet redeemed' (3, 6, 5). And he did not hesitate to draw what theologically were quite far-reaching conclusions:

> We ourselves, baptized, are indeed redeemed but not yet fully; our final redemption is still not an accomplished fact ... The complete and visible triumph of Christ over the world is ... still in store. Therefore in the Christian earthly attitude of faith and love there is still a necessary demand for the specific attitude which we call hope (5).[161]

Redemption is not yet complete, and therefore hope is the central theological virtue.

According to Schillebeeckx, thinking in terms of hope at the same time brought religious consciousness 'into closer connection both with Christian eschatology and with all kinds of currents of earthly expectations within the world'.[162] It opened up the possibility of a salvation-historical reading of tradition and an understanding of contemporary humankind which mutually reinforced each other. The salvation-historical reading of the New Testament made it clear to him that the church does not just live after the resurrection, but equally in expectation of the second coming: 'the ultimate act of redemption, which still has not taken place ... is brought about by a last mysterious action of incarnate love: the mystery of *the return of Christ* at the end of time. This historical fact still lies in the future' (5).[163] For Schillebeeckx, this biblical image of time then discloses human existence as an active and concrete hope for salvation and redemption. Precisely here it was open to the Christian message of salvation. But according to him this message of salvation did not proclaim that the hope was already fulfilled. The Christian message was that the human hope bound up with the world – ' "we hope to receive from God our whole lives, even the material element in it", says St Thomas'[164] – was confidently possible, despite the experience of failure which returns again and again.

> Thus the Christian hope ... gives all [our] life a tranquil but indomitable dynamic. Suffering and the miseries of life, formerly a sign of our lack of redemption, now become the effective symbol of our redemption-in-action (23).[165]

Of course, Schillebeeckx's approach to Christian redemption as a redemption in hope had clear roots in the New Testament: according to Paul we are saved in hope (Rom. 8.24). But in the 1950s his view marked a fundamental break within the thought and self-understanding of the Catholic Church. Only when redemption was complete could it be understood as complete confidence in the rule of the church, and could entry into the church also be regarded as both a necessary and a complete condition for participating in this redemption. By making the apparently laconic statement that the members of the church, the baptized, are indeed redeemed, 'but not yet completely', Schillebeeckx raised a fundamental question: what is the fundamental role of the church in redemption? In the second half of the 1960s this question was also to come to define his theological agenda. In the 1950s, alongside his emphasis on hope as the main Christian virtue stood the statement that 'Christ's historical mysteries of redemption', especially his death and his resurrection, the significance of which the church proclaimed and with which it maintained a living contact in the liturgy, were 'the anchor of our hope':

> Thus the future final consummation of the mystery of Christ and of redemption is the prospect that our hope longs for; on the other hand the already completed phase of this mystery is the foundation by which this ardent yearning is supported.

So the church had the task of guaranteeing the contact of humankind with redemption. It guaranteed 'the real possession of Christ in and through his Holy Spirit' (7f.).

'We are already in heaven, "because Christ, our head, is already there" ... and we are "members of Christ"', said Schillebeeckx (9).[166] But in his eyes at the same time we are not yet there, because we have not yet been 'fully' redeemed. Here he touched on what he had already been mentioning in connection with his interpretation of the idea of the *Christus totus*, 'the Christ with all his flowering of saints' in the still incomplete history of the church. Halfway through the 1950s he developed this thought further, along the lines of the classic dogmatic distinction between objective and subjective redemption. Objective redemption was to be understood as the redemption which, according to traditional doctrine, had taken place through the suffering and the death of Jesus Christ: through this act of obedience to God's will, as a handbook put it, God's honour, which had been damaged by human sinfulness, was restored, 'because it glorified God more than our sin dishonoured him'. However, for human beings this redemption did not yet mean that they too were really redeemed, but rather that redemption was once again a possibility for them. In current scholastic theology, subjective redemption embraced the further working out of this objective redemption on the particular person by means of the sacraments of the church and the living faith of believers.[167] Taking this up creatively, in 1955 Schillebeeckx wrote that 'objective redemption' is to be understood as 'the redemption of mankind in its head'; in Jesus Christ 'the redemption of mankind is an established fact'. He defined subjective redemption as redemption as this is 'actually realized in our lives'. Here, however, he made a closer distinction between the 'gift of Christ to and in us' – with a rather difficult term he calls this 'the objective aspect of our subjective state of redemption' – and the 'human and personally free consent' to redemption. And by this last he did not just understand the acceptance and awareness of the redemption that had already been achieved. Something new really has to take place: 'The redemption which the God-man brings is a redemption to which the recipient, man, freely consents in living faith, strong hope and submissive love.' In this sense he could speak of every believing human being as 'co-redeemer' – which is therefore something more and different from one who affirms a redemption that has already been achieved.[168]

Thus for Schillebeeckx the church was not just 'the visible instrument of the heavenly Christ' through which he brought into being on earth 'the community of faith and love' that already existed in him. As we saw, he thought that this aspect was particularly cherished by the church hierarchy. In his view the church was just as much the *'congregatio fidelium*, the community of faith and grace, composed of all those who belong to Christ and hope for the glorious *parousia* of the Lord'.[169] This aspect of the church is realized especially through the laity.

Again Schillebeeckx's explicitation of faith remained full of tensions. On the one hand he wanted to give the human hope for salvation and the clearly incomplete character of redemption a place in his theology; on the other he continued to think in terms of appropriating a redemption which had essentially already taken place, though that hope for salvation was one of the ways in which this appropriation came about. In his view in the 1950s, people, and especially lay people, were 'co-redeemers'. But in what sense? Did they ultimately add anything to redemption?

'The mystery of Christ-in-us finds its birth in faith, its viability in hope, but only love makes it an authentic life.' That is how Schillebeeckx began his third article on the theologal virtues in 1951. Again he linked up with what he felt to be the contemporary experience of reality. 'Whenever we reflect in a Christian way on the great human tragedy which is being played out in the course of time, we understand that its deepest meaning lies in the fact of human weakness.' Here he had in view above all the human inability to love God, to give God the love that he required of human beings, 'the highest love, unlimited and perfect love, without conditions and without reservation'. In the 1940s Schillebeeckx had always tried to illuminate the human situation from the theological thought of Thomas Aquinas. In the framework of his more salvation-historical approach of the 1950s, he tended, rather, to begin from the biblical texts. He showed that according to these texts 'God has come to meet [the] terrifying need for love in human beings.'[170] Therefore in his view – and this accorded completely with what he said in the 1940s – human love of God must in the first place be a matter of 'allowing oneself to be swept off one's feet by God', allowing oneself to be touched 'by his love for us'. Christians were the beloved, the *agapetoi* of God, he said with a reference to Paul in Romans (1.7), and he interpreted the sentence from the Gospel of John, 'I no longer call you my servants but my friends' (15.15), as 'Christ's great declaration of love' (616f.). In his view, God's love called for a response from the human side, for 'God thirsts for thirsty men ... to love God is the very mission of man in this world.' An aspect which is in a sense new by comparison with his views about faith and spirituality from the 1950s and a product of his salvation-historical approach emerged in his statement that according to the biblical writings God's love is above all saving love and therefore implies mercy towards human beings and a commitment to redemption. On the basis of this he concluded that 'the act of love is directly connected' with the human obligation to respond to God's love. In his eyes, loving God was 'not just confessing God', was not just expressed in religious actions in the usual sense of the word: to love God meant just as much to 'live out this confession in the faithful performance of daily tasks' (613, 619). Here Schillebeeckx took up his approach in terms of a theology of culture and was concerned with an authentic 'life in the sphere of faith' in all aspects of human existence, in which 'faith has become a seeing in faith' (621).

How important practical action in faith was for Schillebeeckx emerged once more from the fact that he devoted a separate article to the religious significance of love for other people; at this time, in which almost every view within the Catholic church was still totally pre-feminist, he still had no problem in calling this 'brotherly love'. In this fourth and last article from the series on theologal virtues, in connection with the religious significance of this love orientated on human beings and their salvation he came to a conclusion which in the theological climate of the 1950s was quite far-reaching:

> In the most precise sense of the word God's love comes to and in us and becomes 'flesh' in our love of neighbour, which is the ultimate consequence of ... the incarnation or the mystery of Christ: brotherly love is the *sacramentum*, i.e. the manifestation of the *mysterium* hidden in it which simultaneously veils and unveils, namely God's love for us as persons in a community of salvation.[171]

Thus, for Schillebeeckx love of neighbour was not an incidental matter, important only with certain restrictions. For him practical love of other people was a form, an embodiment, of God's gracious presence in the world. In neoscholastic theology, action on behalf of others was not in fact seen as a value in itself. It was good in so far as it was a consequence of faith. Christian love of neighbour had to find its motive in God; it was Christian to love the other for God's sake.[172] In a sense Schillebeeckx argued the other way round: 'if we ... love one another, then God is revealed in us' as the loving God who brings salvation (601).[173] In his eyes, dedication to others was the Christian faith in active form:

> What a Christian does is to love. That is the barometer of the depth of his life of faith. Therefore Christian brotherly love is essentially a religious event, a religious task and not simply 'morality'; it is not profane, however much it may embody itself in the reality that is this world.

Schillebeeckx also distanced himself from what he called 'the modern "love of man"', the motive for which is human needs and not, if one may put it that way, God's 'need' (611). However, he interpreted the orientation of the love of neighbour on God as the substantive orientation of involvement with other people. According to him 'Christian love' was a love which has no respect for persons and takes no heed of the supposed 'dignity or lack of dignity of the fellow man'. Here he demonstrated practically that its motive lay with God and not with human beings; in his view, only of such a love could it be said that God's love of human beings – of which Paul said that we were already loved 'when we were still sinners' (Rom. 5.8) – 'breaks through in temporal human relations' (607). His statement that the motif of Christian love must lie in 'God's "need"' at the same time implied that its starting point has to lie in the divine longing for comprehensive human salvation, that it must be connected with this and orientated on it. What was important for him was the commitment to 'the perfection of redemption' (611).

Thus, according to Schillebeeckx in 1952, the very heart of Christianity was the 'earthly beginning of the future glory'. He saw Christian 'brotherly love' as a 'breakthrough of a divine reality in visible earthly form. Here the later (eschatological) glory is all the time in it and advancing: it is the coming of the kingdom of God' (619, 617). The same thoughts about human existence, the incompleteness of redemption and the human desire for salvation, opened up broad perspectives. For example they made it possible to think about faith as inner participation in the 'joy and hope, sorrow and fear' of humanity as this would be formulated during the Second Vatican Council in the constitution *Gaudium et spes*. Elements from the later 'theology of hope' shine out, as does the announcement of what Schillebeeckx would later, in the footsteps of Johann-Baptist Metz, call orthopraxy: 'right' faith by doing right actions. But in the 1950s these were only perspectives, and these insights did not yet really break through the existing frameworks. Schillebeeckx felt obliged to hold firm to the notion that redemption had essentially already taken place and was mediated by the hierarchical church, and continued to think in terms of taking part in this redemption in faith. That ultimately kept his thought static, however much of an eye he had for the dynamic of human life.

This became clear once again in the article that Schillebeeckx also presented explicitly in *Tijdschrift voor Geestelijk Leven* as a sequel to the articles on faith, hope and love. He said that the theologal virtues consisted only in the grace of 'the state of holy existence which lies at the basis of the divine life of the believer'. For him they were 'the personal realization of what is usually called sanctifying grace', so in 1954 he published an article on 'Sanctifying Grace as the Sanctification of our Existence'.[174] According to the view current within scholastic theology, sanctifying grace was the gift of God to believers as an abiding determination of human existence. Schillebeeckx took up this idea in terms of 'precisely this new sense of life which God has given us and through which we can pursue him lovingly and directly as the supreme value in life'. Here he emphasized that this encounter with God came about through creation and culture. It was not something special or extraordinary, something that lay outside everyday life; rather, the encounter with God put everyday life in a radically different light. 'God as God cannot be reached through one of the many senses with which we as human beings are of course actively equipped and through which we can evaluate all facets of the world'; in this sense it is a gift and a break with the 'earthly order of life within the world' (10f.). For Schillebeeckx, grace meant that people experienced life as coming from God's hand and all that happened as being from God. 'Grace brings us into a new sphere, a situation-in-God.' Here he again took up his familiar theme of the harmony between nature and grace, where, nevertheless, asceticism in respect of natural values was necessary.

Grace does not put a line through nature or culture, but it does take its definitive resting point from it: our homeland is in heaven, no longer in a situation-in-this-world, in which this heavenly life must nevertheless be experienced and lived out. The breakthrough of God into our life takes us out of ourselves. The life of grace is not the independent unfolding of created human forces through sheer receptiveness in active docility and availability. The God of grace, the living God, cannot be conquered, but breaks through ... (14).

That leads him to say that the life of grace, the life of sanctifying grace, is ordinary life – 'a life of toothache, stomach upsets, family worries, disputes with particular fellow men and women, a life of praying, praying on time and sleeping' – but the experience of this life in grace. 'For the lay person, the fine adventure of the life of grace lies above all in his daily life' (21).

So the spiritual life is daily, ordinary, unspectacular life. In his thoughts about this, Schillebeeckx was clearly influenced by the spirituality of Thérèse Martin, St Thérèse of Lisieux, which was very influential in this period. Schillebeeckx expressed the conviction of many, which was also shared by the highest church leadership, when he called her a saint 'whom God has given deliberately for our time' (22).[175] Thus, for example, Cardinal Suhard was also inspired by her spirituality of the 'little way', of doing God's will in everyday life, to attempt by means of special projects to bring God and living faith back into the daily life of ordinary people.[176] In a sense one can call the spirituality of 'little Thérèse' an inspiring force behind the worker-priest movement. In saying that a situation which is meaningless and without insight remains what it is, namely 'intolerably meaningless', but that the believer living in grace 'knows that in Christ such a situation is still meaningful, although he does not sense how', Schillebeeckx was thinking along these lines and bearing witness to a deep insight into both the gospel message and human psychology. But the view of the relationship formulated here between human beings and the world on the one hand and God on the other is ahistorical. For him, longing for the abolition of meaninglessness was after all theologically less important than fitting it into a meaningful framework:

We suffer ... no less than non-believers, but we suffer the same suffering in a different way: it makes an enormous difference whether suffering is merely experienced ... or is an event that may come to us 'from outside', or something that we connect meaningfully with an active, personal activity (26).[177]

And in fact this meant that Schillebeeckx also tried to give the human experience of meaninglessness a place in the sense-giving milieu which in his view was offered by the church's teaching and the church's liturgy.

178

This emerged once again in his remarks about death. In his view, the paradoxical nature of the existence of the believer came most explicitly to light in the experience of death. On the one hand he did not trivialize the terror of death: 'Of course for human beings death is an absurd phenomenon, incomprehensible and meaningless, something that destroys and makes intrinsically hopeless all the promises which human beings carry around with them during their earthly life.'[178] This was confirmed for him by the fact that in the biblical writings death is presented as a punishment for sin (cf. Rom. 5.12), and by the statement that God did not create death and derives no joy from the destruction of believers (Wisdom 1.13).[179] But he illuminated what he thought was the other side of the Christian view of death by pointing out that Jesus, in the spirit of his surrender to the death that was inflicted on him as man, abandoned himself completely and entrusted himself to God, who could transform death into the 'supreme religious experience of God' and the 'actual confirmation of God's superiority'. Along this way,

> the lostness and the absurdity of death is inwardly reinterpreted as an event which although intrinsically disastrous and as it were annihilating, yet becomes the way to the encounter with the living God: the Father receives the soul in mercy.

According to Schillebeeckx, to die was thus to lose the natural space of life and contact with persons and things. For Christians this was indeed a catastrophe, but at the same time it meant a 'revival in the sphere of God's life'. To be redeemed from the fear of death was to learn to see death within the framework of church doctrine: by virtue of the fact that 'Christ as the holy man who is God has lovingly entered death, death has taken on a saving significance, a redeeming value'.[180] For Schillebeeckx the theological importance of death lay especially in the pressing call to forsake the self which issued from it, to abandon trust in anything but God.[181] Earlier we saw how he brought into the foreground the notion that according to the New Testament the return of Christ is still to be expected above all as confirmation of the notion that Christian faith is above all hope. In his theology of death, remarkably enough the notion of new creation and resurrection from the dead, as a response to a confirmation of human unrest in the face of death and the longing for life, played little part.

MARY AS THE IMAGE OF THE BELIEVER

The view which Schillebeeckx developed in the 1950s about the existence of the faithful is vividly expressed in a book which was published in 1954, under the title *Maria, Christus' mooiste wonderschepping* (Mary: Christ's

Most Beautiful Miracle).[182] In the 1950s these theological views about Mary were welcomed as very innovative, successful attempts to demonstrate the significance of the figure of Mary for contemporary men and women. They were an attempt to address readers in their own life of faith and to make it clear to them that in Mary they had an exemplary fellow believer, someone who was in the same position as they were, but who was ahead of them on the way of faith and by whom they could rise spiritually.[183] In 1957 Schillebeeckx once again summed up the results of his investigation into Mary in a long article in the *Theologisch woordenboek*, from which it emerges that in his view mariology also needed to be taken seriously in the technical theological sense.[184] In fact Schillebeeckx's concerns came together in his occasional works on Mary. In them it became evident how much the ultimate motive for his theologizing was pastoral, even when he was not afraid to raise technical questions. Everything remains focused on human beings and their questions in faith. Likewise it becomes clear here how throughout the 1950s Schillebeeckx tried to remain within the given and to a large degree prescribed frameworks. On the one hand this produced acute and creative interpretations of the tradition of faith and theology, which also opened up really new perspectives. On the other hand it made his theology rather confined and static, as if its dynamic was blocked before it could really take shape.

Immaculate conception

On 8 December 1953 Pius XII officially proclaimed the church year that had just begun a Marian year. Many needs in Marian devotion which in the church's eyes were serious were addressed in the special prayer composed for this year.[185] But the church leadership did not just have the prayers of Mary or the obtaining of heavenly favours in view. As early as 1925 Pius XI had emphatically laid down the didactic aim of great and comprehensive church celebrations like that of such a Marian year:

> Man is composed of body and soul, and he needs these external festivities so that the sacred rites, in all their beauty and variety, may stimulate him to drink more deeply of the fountain of God's teaching, that he may make it a part of himself, and use it with profit for his spiritual life.[186]

In order to further this progress in the spiritual life, in 1953–4 priests were repeatedly to preach about Mary, and in support of this the Flemish Apostolate of the Rosary was looking for a theologian to give them some background. Schillebeeckx undertook this investigation, and *Maria, Christus' mooiste wonderschepping* arose out of the lectures that he gave.

Now mariology in a new way put Schillebeeckx in the minefield of church

180

politics and theology in which he had already constantly found himself when doing theology in the period before the Second Vatican Council. The Catholic doctrine about Mary as formulated in papal documents and laid down in two declarations of dogma – that of her immaculate conception in 1854 and her bodily assumption in 1950 – was indissolubly bound up with the course of the Vatican in this period. Leo XIII wrote nine encyclicals encouraging the veneration of Mary in support of the offensive that he launched against modern society in the various spheres of modern culture. In the footsteps of his predecessor Pius IX (1846–78) he regarded this as the inner force which propelled the mission of the church to modern society. Leo XIII saw the rosary above all as a powerful weapon against the unbelief that was cropping up everywhere.[187] Traditionally, Mary was especially regarded as mother, but in the presentation of the papal documents, above all halfway through the nineteenth century, Mary was by no means primarily gentle and caring. Pius XII himself thought that an 'army in battle order' (*acies ordinata*) was an appropriate symbol for her, though he hastened to add that Mary did not of course have a 'martial disposition', but 'strength of soul'.[188] Mary took on the form of a spiritual leader in the battle which according to this pope the church had to wage against modernity. To conclude the Marian year of 1954 Pius XII instituted the feast of Mary Queen of Heaven, in order to increase the confidence of the faithful that 'a new era may begin, joyous in Christian peace and the triumph of religion'.[189]

In this militant mariology the dogma of the immaculate conception played a central role. Mary's miraculous preservation from original sin, as the only one of the human race, symbolized the infinite difference between the sin which holds the world in its grasp and the redemption from it represented by the church. The church was reflected in the image which she creates of the 'all fair and immaculate one who has crushed the poisonous head of the most cruel serpent and brought salvation to the world', as Pius IX put it in the declaration of the dogma.[190] On the fiftieth anniversary of that dogma in 1904 Pius X presented it as a kind of concentration of all the questions which were important in the confrontation between the church and the modern spirit. In his eyes, for people to believe in the immaculate conception directly implied

> that it is necessary that they should admit both original sin and the rehabilitation of the human race by Jesus Christ, the Gospel, the Church and the law of suffering. By virtue of this, Rationalism and Materialism is torn up by the roots and destroyed.

That from the very first moment of her existence Mary was without the stain of original sin made it clear that there was 'an infinite opposition and division between sin and God' and thus conflicted with the ideas of 'the enemies of the faith' that the world was not under the rule of sin and did not need any saviour, saving message or the church as the institution that mediated salvation in order to be freed from it. Moreover, according to Pius X it was precisely in its incomprehensibility and irrationality that this dogma was a weapon against the rejection of 'reverence and obedience to the authority of the Church'. Faith in this dogma required people ready to 'recognize an authority in the Church to which one must subject not only the will but the mind'.[191] The dogma that Mary has been taken up into heaven soul and body along these lines showed believers 'for what a lofty goal our bodies and souls are destined', in the words of the encyclical with which the declaration of the dogma was coupled.[192]

The period of the history of the Catholic Church which is marked by the pontificates of Pius XI and XII is called the 'Marian era'. In this period something qualitatively new happened to the figure of Mary. In the first six centuries of Christianity the church had solemnly established that Mary could truly be called 'mother of God' and that she had remained 'ever virgin', before and after the birth of Jesus. However, both statements were not primarily about Mary but, by a detour, established the doctrine that Jesus Christ was 'truly man and truly God' and God's only-begotten Son. In other words, the early church spoke about Mary in order to say something about Jesus. But the dogma of the immaculate conception and the dogma of the bodily assumption were directly about Mary herself, certainly in terms of her relationship to Jesus, but in relative independence.[193]Above all after the Second World War theologians once again began increasingly to put the emphasis in their talk of Mary on her relationship with her Son. On the one hand this was connected with the return to the sources which took place in Catholic theology from the 1920s. In the writings of the church fathers and in the New Testament it is abundantly clear that everything that is said about Mary depends on what is believed about Jesus Christ. The quest for a more patristic and biblical view of Mary was also important for ecumenical dialogue, which was hesitantly beginning. On the other hand the approach to Mary through the church fathers and the biblical writers provided a picture of her which could inspire believers in their quest for God. The shift in mariology was connected with the shift away from the triumphant impregnable church – Mary had always also been an image of the church – to the human life of believers in the midst of the world.

Schillebeeckx began the introduction to *Maria, Christus' mooiste wonderschepping*, along the lines of the renewal which took place in mariology after the Second World War, with the sentence:

The mystery of Mary can only be expressed in its authentic Christian depth as a sure and sound expressiveness if it does not develop into a separate treatise, but comes to full flourishing in organic unity within the treatise of the mystery of Christ.[194]

His justification for this statement was primarily dogmatic. In his view, without this foundation there was a great danger that concentration on Mary broke up what he called 'the basic Catholic dogma', namely that 'we are redeemed by God and by God alone in and through his earthly form of appearance, in other words through the incarnate God Christ Jesus'. But at the beginning of the first chapter he put the emphasis on another aspect of the return to the sources of mariology. He stated that anyone who wanted to see 'the universal significance of Mary for our salvation from the beginning and in a proper perspective' must 'in the first place remain aware that like us she is a redeemed human being'.[195] From the beginning he put all the emphasis on the likeness between Mary and the other believers and thus on her function as a model for believers.[196] On the one hand he was concerned to demonstrate that what the church tradition says about Mary was in fact compatible with this view, but on the other hand he wanted to make it clear that precisely as the redeemed human being, Mary has a saving significance for other human beings. By trying to achieve these two goals at the same time, his mariology was as 'fraught with tensions' as the rest of his theology in the 1950s. For as I have said, the dogmas of Mary's immaculate conception and her physical assumption to heaven served specifically to emphasize the qualitative difference between her and the rest of humankind. Papal mariology was about her exalted status and thus that of the church, which in the eyes of the magisterium she embodied.

Schillebeeckx evidently felt this to some degree. He began his book on Mary immediately with a discussion of the dogma of the immaculate conception. In his view this dogma meant above all that Mary was redeemed like all believers, although there was also a 'fundamental difference': 'The hatefulness of sin was never in her; in us it was.'[197] Making use of his interpretation of the classical distinction between objective and subjective redemption, Schillebeeckx moreover stated that the dogma of the immaculate conception related to Mary's objective redemption; that was unique. But in his view the subjective appropriation of redemption came about through the ordinary process of human awareness and related wholly to Mary's 'conscious life of faith, hope and sacrificial love', as was the case in the development of every believer. In his view Mary had to become a believer like everyone else and make her non-sinful way through a sinful world.

The privilege of the immaculate conception in no sense implies that Mary was not subject to the normal process of human development, or that even in relation to the system of salvation she had a kind of omniscience, could not make any mistakes (in the non-moral sense) or did not know any spiritual progress. Mary was in no sense exempt from the *consequences* of original sin in so far as these themselves are not sinful, just as Christ himself did not take them upon himself voluntarily.[198]

Thus, the dogma of the immaculate conception in particular becomes an incitement to regard her history of faith as exemplary. She really succeeded in leading a life withdrawn from sin, which is a task for every believer.

A model of Christian life

Schillebeeckx then illuminated some central theses from the Marian tradition in a way which showed Mary as 'the prototype of redeemed life, the full and perfect realization, model of any Christian life'.[199]

First of all he interpreted Mary's virginity – which he saw along the lines of the traditional Catholic view as a *choice* of virginity – as an 'expression of her deep longing for God and as the culmination of her messianic expectation'. Her virginity indicated her openness to God's initiative and made her the prototype of the orientation of the believer on God, the transcendent example of the Jewish expectation of the Messiah.[200] Then Schillebeeckx presented Mary's answer to the message of the angel, her so-called *fiat*, as her receptiveness to the actual initiative of God. 'She *allows* the redeemer to give himself,' he wrote; she accepted this as a gift and that is what every human being is in a position to do in the awareness of human limitations. 'In her is accomplished in a sublime way what takes place in all those who are redeemed: the gift of the redeemer and the free acceptance of it.' Then he portrayed Mary as one who shares in the suffering of Jesus, as *socius passionis*; here too he emphasized that she shared in this at a certain distance and in her child, and thus is 'a participant in sheer reciptivity'. Here her love was supremely what according to Schillebeeckx in this phase of his thought Christian love has to be: 'sacrificial love'. Finally, in his view all this comes to a climax in the sending of the Holy Spirit at Pentecost, also to Mary. The Spirit gave her full awareness 'of her place in the very heart of the young church', just as the Spirit gives believers an awareness of their own place in salvation history.[201]

Thus, according to Schillebeeckx Mary was the believer *par excellence*. And in *Maria, Christus' mooiste wonderschepping*, faith was in fact a matter of being open to God in the midst of the sinful closedness of the world, and being tempted by it. Here little was to be found of the more dynamic, salvation-historical view of faith which he developed at the beginning of the 1950s in the articles on faith, hope and love in *Tijdschrift voor Geestelijk Leven*. Evidently this approach needed time to take its place in the reflections about Mary, for in the very thoroughly revised reprint of his book on Mary which appeared a year later under the title *Mary, Mother of the Redemption*, it was recognizable, and relatively clearly at that.[202] The original text was very markedly expanded, not least with a first chapter about the 'scriptural image of the mother of Jesus'. The first section of this chapter was entitled 'God's action in human history' and the first sentences immediately made it clear that the approach to the figure of Mary was to be in terms of salvation history.

> As revelation Christianity is not simply a doctrine. First and foremost it is an event ... in which a divine reality impinges upon human realities in an earthly, visible form. It is thus a history of salvation.[203]

In the later 1950s, that the divine reality impinges on human reality increasingly became the central meaning of the revelation in Jesus Christ. In him God had appeared 'in humanity', and as a result all aspects of human life were divinized and placed in the right perspective: 'in the encounter with God's worshipful love, we already encounter what God's love loves: the whole of the world, all human beings'. In the revelation of God by the man Jesus, men and women can find 'the religious dimension of the universe and above all of this dear world of human beings': 'In him *everything* becomes home for us', and then with surprising radicalism: 'If the heaven is our home, then since Christmas Day the world of human beings is also our home, for heaven has become earth.'[204]

In *Mary, Mother of the Redemption*, Schillebeeckx spoke first of all about 'history' in terms of 'two dimensions' of the stories which are told in the Gospels, including those about Mary. There is what he calls the 'historical–human dimension' which makes it possible 'to consider the history of Mary at the level of a pious, simple woman of the people whose view of life is steeped in the Old Testament and Jewish tradition and who lives at the moment in history of a Roman occupation'. In quite a long exegetical exposition he called the spiritual attitude which Mary showed in the so-called Magnificat (Luke 1.36–55) a concentration of 'the whole of the Israelite "*anawah*" piety as utter trust in God the Helper and Redeemer'. In his view Mary is the glorified poor woman and as such 'the mother of the long-awaited justice'.[205] However, for Schillebeeckx, more important than the specific characterization of Mary's world and her existence in the midst of it was the fact that the 'tangible, visible and historical aspect [was] a suprahistorical dimension which affects the salvation of all human beings'. The supernatural, the redemptive, the divine was present in human history: that is the conclusion that he drew from this salvation-historical theology.[206] Moreover, he then stated that this hiddenness of the supernatural significance of history also applied to Mary herself. Here too she shared in the situation of all believers. In his view the true greatness of Mary was that she did not know what she was beginning when she said to the angel, 'Be it to me according to your word'; she said this out of a 'faith which neither saw nor comprehended' and surrendered herself to 'an uncomprehended mystery and an unknown future'.[207] According to *Mary, Mother of the Redemption*, it was not the abstract and general 'being open to God' that was decisive in Mary's life, but her surrender to the future in faith. He pointed to the paradoxical nature of this trust. As mother of Jesus, Mary was confronted with events that contradicted her expectations, the nadir of which was of course his death on the cross, yet nevertheless, she continued to believe and trust in the future from God.[208]

Here Schillebeeckx returned to the question of the relationship between subjective and objective redemption. In the first version of his book on Mary there was room only for the acceptance in faith and the awareness of the redemption that had already been completed in Christ, though this acceptance had to grow and mature in the course of life. In the revised edition he made the statement already quoted that even after the life, death and resurrection of Jesus Christ, the redemption still had to take place for believers. Therefore, taking up a title for Mary which was being vigorously discussed at this time, he could speak of every believer as a 'co-redeemer', and present Mary as the one who also had given form to this role *par excellence*.[209] In his view Mary, too, still had to expect her subjective redemption during her life. Not only did she laboriously have to attain insight into her own role in the economy of salvation, but she was also at the mercy of the sinful, unredeemed world, although dogma says that she herself was not sinful. In this way he deepened what he had already said in the first edition.

From the other side, in the second edition Schillebeeckx also added the notion that the dogma of Mary's assumption soul and body implied that what the earthly church still expected had already taken place completely for Mary. 'For Mary, for her alone, the parousia, the glorification and the spiritual and bodily togetherness of Christ in triumph has already taken place.' Whereas in Schillebeeckx's account the life of Mary is an image of the struggle of the faithful and the church, the Mary who is taken up to heaven and glory is the image of the church and the faithful as this is ultimately intended.[210]

The central notion in Schillebeeckx's mariology is expressed with a quotation from Augustine: 'Mary is a part of the church, a holy member, an excellent, prominent member, but still a member of the church.'[211] He tried to express her special nature, which had always been stressed so strongly in the Catholic Church, emphatically along the lines of her bond with other believers. For him, Mary's uniqueness lay above all in her place in the history of salvation, in the uniqueness of the object of her 'Yes' to the message of the angel. '"*Getting* a child" becomes for her the *giving* of God's child to the world'; in this way she in fact made possible the incarnation of the divine word and thus objective redemption. According to Schillebeeckx it was this that made her mother of grace and the redemption, as the church says of her.[212] Moreover, but emphatically *after* this, in his view Mary was unique because of her really complete openness to the divine initiative. She truly committed herself unreservedly in faith, hope and love to the history of salvation; in this sense, for him she was the exemplary believer. In the second of his books on Mary he made this an emphatic theme by interpreting her assumption as a sign 'that Mary's life-sacrifice was fully accepted by God'.[213] And according to him, this glorified state was the third aspect of her uniqueness, a state which also implies that Mary 'committed herself personally so that what was realized by Christ "typically" in her life should also be accomplished in the other members of the community of the church'. From heaven and as a glorified believer she is abidingly mother of the church and of all peoples.[214]

In her motherhood, moreover, according to Schillebeeckx Mary embodied an essential and irreplaceably personal contribution to the redemption, which really adds something to what has taken place in Christ. So in this sense, too, she was the exemplary believer. In a very striking passage he writes:

> Mary's state of being Christ's and our mother explicates something of Christ's redemption, an element which is not explicated itself in Christ's act of redemption and which even cannot be explicated in this act. This is the feminine and maternal quality of goodness. The goodness of God's redemptive love is both paternal and maternal . . . This maternal quality of mildness, this particularly feminine tenderness, this *quid nesciam* which is the special mark of the mother cannot, however, be explicated as such in the man Jesus. It can become explicit only in a mother who is a woman. God chose Mary so that this maternal aspect of his love might be represented in her person.[215]

As I have said, Schillebeeckx's texts on Mary reflect the ambiguity of his theology in this period. On the one hand they express a pastoral concern for the human situation and his desire to do theology beginning from human history. Especially in *Mary, Mother of the Redemption* he wrote impressively on the weakness and fragility of human existence and the longing for God.

In a passage entitled 'An argument for the "fringe manifestations" in the religious life of the people', in this framework he opposed, too, great emphasis on a return to the biblical and theological source of the faith.[216] Anyone who wanted to banish the 'O so human fringe manifestations of the religious life of the people by a cold rational appeal to return to "authentic" religious practice' would in his view kill off the life of the people and would possibly be able 'to kill the deep pith of the religious life of a people'. He emphasized that God is in a position constantly to 'see beyond the almost superstitious and sometimes disturbing credulity of certain practices and expressions of popular piety' and through them perceive 'the good intentions of his poor, inadequate creatures, who are not able to express, in the right words and in fitting actions, their deep longing for God which, until they are finally capable of surrendering unconditionally to God, must inevitably result in restlessness in their lives'. Here he showed a striking sensitivity to the importance of rituals. 'The candle, left burning quietly, in timid humility, in front of the statue of Mary after the pilgrim has gone away from the shrine, can be seen as a symbol of the Christian's presence. He leaves this candle behind because he is not yet fully capable of surrendering completely in faith to God's dispensation, of letting his heart melt away in the glow of this total submission.' According to Schillebeeckx, it was the non-rational nature of popular religion that was important; it split open all rationality and was a reminder that faith was about 'giving credit to God, contrary to all human calculations and appreciations'. Popular devotion to Mary was in his eyes ultimately orientated on putting the whole of life in the framework of the dynamic towards redemption. This made him almost lyrical at times:

> Life is love, a love which gives. The gift which we make of our love, our life, must be made in a spirit of pure self-forgetfulness. If we do this, our suffering will become a relic of Christ's redeeming death, a priceless relic which will find its resting-place, like the crucified Christ's, in the arms of Mary ... She is the great Pietà who casts her mother's cloak of mercy over our suffering humanity. She is the living womb in which, as in a second act of bodily motherhood, we are carried for the nine long months of our lives until we at last come to the glory of redemption and resurrection.[217]

As in any form of religion, so too in devotion to Mary, in his view, we have to give the basic themes of the human situation a 'Christian perspective' so that they are stripped of their 'human superficiality and human disappointment'.[218]

Here an eye for human religious need was coupled with an apparently unproblematical reverence for the church's mariology and the forms of veneration of Mary approved by the church. In his view these offered an adequate form for 'the intense concern with the "mystery of Christ"' which is a necessary part of religion and is also longed for by people; it could make believers aware 'of our place and our concrete vocation in the redeemed world'. He thought that the daily praying of the rosary in the family was a particularly suitable means of seeing one's own everyday life without great effort in the light of God's presence:

> While the prayer pursues its steady, rhythmic course, the many family problems which beset him are passing fleetingly through the father's tired

mind and the mother is thinking of the baby she is carrying or of the children around her, each with its own particular difficulty. All this can be seen. In the light of the redeeming mystery of Christ, and in peaceful simplicity, the family learns to entrust everything to the mother of the miracle of Cana and of the whole redemption of mankind.[219]

His matter-of-fact treatment of the rosary as an aid to prayer for 'those occasions when the spirit is weary, dull and listless' was striking. It liberated Catholics from the oppressive thought that they had to pray the rosary at the cost of 'titanic efforts' completely in accord with the complicated rules. But here, too, what remained was ultimately the giving of new meaning to an existing practice which in this way was in fact propagated without real qualifications.[220]

Only after the Second Vatican Council was there to be a real change in Schillebeeckx's attitude to the formation of Christian faith in the existing Catholic Church. Here, under the inspiration of John XXIII, the relationship between the church and the world was discussed in all openness among bishops and theologians. Laboriously but unstoppably the tendency broke through no longer to play these two spheres off against each other and to associate faith and theology closely with 'the joy and hope, the sorrow and fear of the people of today'. Only all this made it possible for Schillebeeckx – like other theologians – to be more independent of the hierarchy and its thought and action, which was strongly orientated on the church.

Nevertheless, Schillebeeckx's thought in the second half of the 1950s was already evolving in the direction of the breakthrough after the Council. Or perhaps it is more accurate to say that the tension which he wanted to expound as a Catholic theologian and the dynamic of openness to human life and the orientation on understanding and inspiring contemporary culture constantly increased. Thus, an article that he wrote for *Kultuurleven* in 1955 about hope is striking not just because of the occasion (it was a reaction to the documents of the Second Assembly of the World Council of Churches in Evanston in 1954, the theme of which was Christian hope). This made it Schillebeeckx's first ecumenically orientated publication.[221] In the light of the theological history that was to follow it is therefore certainly striking that in this article – a long time before Jürgen Moltmann was to attract worldwide attention with his *Theology of Hope* and to have great influence on the theology of the 1960s, and also on that of Schillebeeckx – Schillebeeckx was speaking of a 'Catholic "theology of hope"'.[222]

In the midst of keeping the well-known balance so as on the one hand to hold to the traditional view that the final consummation comes wholly from God and on the other hand to emphasize the importance of human activity, Schillebeeckx made an attempt to understand the activity of human beings in creating culture as an active waiting for the parousia, the return of Christ. On the one hand,

> the innermost, deepest tendency of any human earthly value ... and of any human basic hope is ultimately messianic – and is thus also taken up into the Christian expectation of the parousia as hoping, active commitment.

On the other hand, for him the coming of the final kingdom has to be received actively, in a concrete way, by commitment to a humane culture:

> As the radiance of the eschaton, a Christian culture ... will always be recognized by its moral and religious tone: a kingdom of justice, peace and love as the core of an integral civilization and culture.[223]

And challenged by the markedly apocalyptic tone of messages which were attributed to Mary in her appearances, some years later Schillebeeckx sharply stated that because of belief in God as creator, the final phase of history could not be a violent breaking through of God's power in the course of earthly developments. This phase 'lies along the lines of what makes up the basic pattern of the whole of church history as an ascent to the parousia of Christ'. God is present in and with history and does not suddenly come from outside; people do not live in a world which is completely unredeemed and forsaken by God. 'The history of the world itself grows slowly from within towards the end time.' Here, moreover, he held firm to the insight that as long as it continued, history remained ambiguous and in this sense developed in the direction both of the anti-Christ and of the coming of Christ.[224]

Salvation history as a concentration of history, faith as a way of looking at this history and at the vicissitudes of human beings within it, and theology as a thematization of what is perceived in this perspective:[225] this was the basis on which Schillebeeckx's thought was to develop further after the Council.

Chapter 4

The Louvain Theological Synthesis

'... on the basis of St Thomas, in the light of the previous tradition and the problems of today'

A SYNTHESIS

When Edward Schillebeeckx moved from Louvain to Nijmegen at the beginning of 1957 and effectively made a new beginning as a Dutch theologian, his theology was a rounded whole. 'His view of the task and functioning of theology, his talk of God, his thinking about human beings and the world have been well thought out.'[1] It is an exaggeration to speak of a system, but his theology was certainly a synthesis, a coherent vision worked out down to the different partial aspects. This chapter is about this synthesis, the coherent view which is expressed in the theological monographs published in the period covered by this book, specifically between 1952 and 1963; in the articles published in the *Theologisch woordenboek*, which appeared in three big volumes between 1952 and 1958 under the editorship of Dominicans well known at this time and in collaboration with Catholic theologians from a large number of seminaries then abundant in the Netherlands,[2] and in extensive lecture notes. Throughout the period he was working in Louvain, Schillebeeckx gave lectures on the different sub-divisions of dogmatics. The text of these lectures was circulated in duplicated form, and time and again when a topic came up again he added new material. The Louvain lecture notes were never formally published, but they were disseminated widely, and for many years used and consulted by students in Louvain and Nijmegen. They form an indispensable source for anyone who wants to gain a total picture of Schillebeeckx's theology. The papers of these lecture notes, which grew organically, are now rather yellowed; here and there they are difficult to read because the same stencil has

191

been used so many times, and the original structure is hidden under the many accretions and expansions, but especially in them the activity of the 'Louvain Schillebeeckx' can be captured.

Systematic theologizing on the basis of Thomas Aquinas

In the middle of the period during which Schillebeeckx was lecturing in Louvain and shortly before the publication of his first big book in 1952, the first volume of the *Systematic Theology* by the German-American Protestant theologian Paul Tillich (1886–1965) appeared. In 1919 Tillich had for the first time explicitly come to the fore as a theologian of culture who ultimately regarded theology as a cultural science. In his view theology did not have its own object alongside other objects: the 'object of theology is what concerns us ultimately' and according to him 'what concerns us ultimately' ran through the whole of human culture. It was as it were the soul of culture, the core, what he called the *Gehalt*, and it was expressed in other external forms which announced themselves at a concrete historical moment as culture, the *Gestalt*. It was not Tillich's purpose in following this way to make theology dependent on the subjective feeling of the theologian for the importance of cultural phenomena: in his view 'what concerns us ultimately' was 'that which determines our being or non-being'.[3] Tillich saw that it was the central task of a systematic theologian to show that what he called 'the new being' as this offered itself according to the Christian tradition in Jesus Christ can also be known in the contemporary situation as 'ultimate concern'. Thus he wanted to show that the Christian message, which could not be derived from human existence, itself formed the answer to the question posed, in his view, by human existence as a whole.

At that moment neither of the two knew it, but this view in fact brought Tillich close to Schillebeeckx. In his thoughts about being human as a question, like Schillebeeckx, Tillich was strongly influenced by philosophical existentialism. On the basis of their affinity, Schillebeeckx, once he got to know Tillich's work in the second half of the 1960s, could explicitly adopt what Tillich called the 'method of correlation', which connected human question and Christian response.[4] Thinking further about this method of correlation, Schillebeeckx was to come into intensive contact with the neo-Marxist theories of the so-called Frankfurt school, with which Tillich was closely associated when he worked in Germany in the 1920s.[5] Tillich always indicated that the focus of his own approach was the way in which the strict division that he found in Catholic theology between the sphere of the religious and the supernatural on the one hand and the sphere of the world, the natural and the secular on the other made thinking about a theology of culture impossible.[6] In his project of a theology of culture, the Catholic theologian Schillebeeckx was likewise concerned to break through this division.

Now at first sight what is most striking is the difference between Tillich's *Systematic Theology* and Schillebeeckx's books and lecture notes from the 1950s. In particular, the strict and really schematic coherence of Tillich's *magnum opus* contrasts with the fragmentary nature of Schillebeeckx's *oeuvre*. Tillich wrote in the preface to his *Systematic Theology* that it had always been impossible for him to think 'theologically in any other than a systematic way'.[7] This certainly also applied to Schillebeeckx; however, the systematic way of thinking did not express itself in a systematic whole but in a range of articles about different subjects, wide-ranging lecture notes, and studies on the sacramental economy of salvation, on Christ as the sacrament of the encounter with God, and on marriage as an earthly reality and a saving mystery. Two of his books presented themselves as the first part of a diptych, the sequel to which was ultimately never published.[8] Internally, too, Schillebeeckx's texts do not stand out for their complete concentration on the main line, as Tillich's do. Rather, they impress by their multiplicity of excursuses and detailed investigations. It was characteristic of the approach of the Louvain Schillebeeckx that in all these details he saw a main line which he tried to bring out for his readers and hearers; however, at the same time this came through only in confrontation with all the theologians and church documents from the past and present which he discussed. Still, when he wrote that in theology he was not concerned with the system but 'with the contact with reality itself' and indicated that he wanted to put his systematic power of thought at the service of this, he again came close to Tillich.[9]

The most striking agreement between the theologies of Tillich and Schillebeeckx from the 1950s presents itself in the first instance as their most fundamental difference. In the introduction to his *Systematic Theology* Tillich opposes the tendency of theologians to present their own views and conclusions as the message of the gospel itself. According to Tillich, the orthodox suffered under an illusion which also constantly lurked for great theologians. They had the idea that the significance of the Christian proclamation could be laid down in a theological doctrine that remained the same and that they, or the church in whose name they spoke, had discovered this doctrine. In so doing they failed to recognize that theology was always historical, deriving from and orientated on its own time.[10] This insight into historicity, this conviction that the task of theology was to disclose the significance and the importance of the Christian proclamation to contemporary men and women, made Tillich's theology in principle modern: in modernity a theologian does not carry conviction by demonstrating that he is interpreting the tradition faithfully, but by making clear the relevance of his work, and thus, indirectly, of the tradition on which he is basing himself.

Now Schillebeeckx's position in his Louvain period at first sight seems still trapped in what Tillich regarded as the illusion of orthodoxy. Like all other Catholic theologians in this period, Schillebeeckx starts from the assumption that there is a true Christian doctrine, that this is preserved by the Catholic hierarchy and is expressed by its statements, and that this teaching is best explored in depth through the *Summa theologiae* of Thomas Aquinas. After the dispute over modernism at the beginning of the century it was clear that a renewal of Catholic theology could come about only if these starting points were accepted in the first instance. The open confrontation with modern thought which the modernists had envisaged was condemned in principle in 1907 on the authority of Pius X in the decree *Lamentabili* and the encyclical *Pascendi domini gregis* as 'the sum total of all heresies'. Like the other theologians who subsequently proved to be important renewers of Catholic theology in the twentieth century – Marie-Dominique Chenu, Yves Congar, Henri de Lubac, Karl Rahner and Piet Schoonenberg – in his Louvain period Schillebeeckx went the way of an internal return to the sources of the scholastic theology of the church.[11] Here, on the one hand, he subscribed to the orthodoxy and truth of the official church statements, but on the other hand he put them in the context of a broader and longer theological development and thus tried to find a new access to their thought.[12] He had learned this procedure of historicizing theology from Chenu and Congar, but he developed a great mastery in it. Readers, despite any antipathy that they may feel to the theological presuppositions which dominated Catholic theology in the 1950s, are still impressed by his apparently exhaustive knowledge of the history of theology. 'I learned from Schillebeeckx that you ... must not pass over anything in the history of faith and theology', wrote an old pupil in retrospect, apparently somewhat exhausted.[13] This intense attention to history made it possible for Schillebeeckx to say new things in the only way in which this was possible in Catholic theology at this time, by demonstrating that they were not new at all, but really the authentic teaching of the church – provided that this was understood properly.

But that is not everything. Tillich explicitly argued that a modern theologian could not speak in the name of the tradition, but only in terms of the contemporary situation, and had to bring this into contact with the tradition. The important thing was to express the significance of the Christian message in the situation. In his inaugural address as professor in Nijmegen, Schillebeeckx expressed a similar conviction when he told his students that doing theology presupposed 'inserting the living self into the tradition, not in order to be subject to it but in order to recreate it and to test it again by the present-day experience of faith and reflection on it'.[14] Here he was in fact summing up what he had done in his Louvain period. But in Louvain he still allowed himself to be led to a considerable degree by Thomas Aquinas. Just as Tillich was convinced of the importance of the message of the gospel for contemporary men and women, and precisely for that reason argued that theology must not presuppose this meaning but demonstrate it, so Schillebeeckx was convinced of the importance of a theological approach along Thomas's lines, precisely in order to be a theologian in the midst of modern culture. In 1943, on his first public appearance as an independent theologian, he had already made a distinction between a Thomistic theology and doing theology on 'purely Thomistic principles'; this last was particularly important to him.[15] In his Louvain lectures, along the same lines he stated that theology was not about a system in itself. For him the central question was whether 'a particular theological system, for example that of St Thomas', was a good guide for 'penetrating deeper into the theological event itself', in other words into God's history with human beings. Here above all 'the basic view' of the relevant system and the openness that it had to supplementary insights was the important thing.[16]

In the texts from which this chapter attempts to reconstruct his Louvain synthesis, Schillebeeckx was concerned time and again to learn from Thomas in his systematic theological thought, on the basis of Thomas's fundamental view. This was not just because in his milieu Thomas was regarded as the authority *par excellence* but because he took this claim to authority seriously, in a sense more seriously than ecclesiastical Thomism did. Along the lines of the programme of Leo XIII, in the 1950s Schillebeeckx was in fact convinced that Thomas's thought offered the best possibilities for finding an adequate Catholic answer to contemporary questions. But completely in line with his theological temperament and the trust in the power of the truth that he had found among the Dominicans, for him this was a reason not to treat Thomas's thought as a closed system, a bulwark from which the errors of modernity could be effectively combated. Schillebeeckx read Thomas's work through the spectacles of the philosophy of Domien De Petter and, moreover, based himself on more recent historical investigation into the thought, the development and the characteristics of mediaeval theology.[17] He was convinced that the dynamic that he thus perceived in Thomas's thought could break through the impasses in which the Catholic theology of the 1950s had become bogged down, or constantly threatened to get bogged down. In his view the Thomistic textbook theology was based only externally on Thomas's work, whereas closer attention to the movement of his thought could renew theology from within and correspond better to the situation and the experiences of contemporary believers.[18] He was especially convinced that a correct view of the pattern of Thomas's thought helped to break through the dominant division between 'nature' and 'supernature' which blocked the development of a theology of culture. He continued to use these words, which suggested two separate, static realities, but through Thomas he devoted himself to making clear that faith and theology were ultimately about a nature which was exalted so that it became supernatural. According to Schillebeeckx, theology on the basis of 'pure Thomistic principles' showed its superiority in producing a fruitful contemporary understanding of the faith.

Given the degree to which, in the 1950s and 1960s, Schillebeeckx's theology formed a synthesis, the most striking thing about his development was that from 1963 onwards he could throw everything up in the air again. The Second Vatican Council in the first half of the 1960s marked the end of the anti-modernist attitude of the Catholic Church. Among other things this meant that to an important degree Thomas Aquinas lost his philosophical and theological authority, at any rate in so far as this was based on the conviction that his thought formed a bastion from which the heretical fight for freedom waged by modernity could best be combated. From the beginning of Schillebeeckx's theological development, however, he had dissociated himself from this view of Thomas's thought. In a sense he read Thomas as a modern theologian *avant la lettre*, as someone who tried to overcome the division between the world and God, between nature and supernature, by making clear the significance and the relevance of a believing view of reality.[19] The theological openness which Schillebeeckx found in Thomas, via De Petter, and which in his view was endorsed by the Council, was more responsible for the growing distance between his theology and that of Thomas than the fall of Thomas as an intellectual champion of church anti-modernism. From 1963 Schillebeeckx saw himself intensively confronted with questions which had no place in the theological thought-form which he perceived in Thomas. Secularization and the exodus from the church not only sharpened the question of the religious and theological significance of reality outside the church, but for the first time also confronted him seriously with the question of the significance of dealing with ideological and religious pluralism. His quest for an answer to this question led to discussions with hermeneutical philosophy and theology, with the neo-Marxist thought of the Frankfurt School, and with the historical–critical exegesis of the New Testament. These developments will be discussed at length in the second and last part of this study, but at all events it is certain that Schillebeeckx departed almost completely from the intellectual tradition based on Thomas in which he stood in the 1950s.

Schillebeeckx also noted this subsequently. He gave an explanation for it which at the same time represented a sealing of the break. In his view, the starting point of the tradition which ultimately went back to Thomas, a tradition in which in his view not only De Petter but also philosophers like Louis Lavelle and René Le Senne stood (these attracted him greatly in the 1940s), was that whenever people experience meaning in reality, this experience is evoked by a comprehensive sense of the reality in which the particular experience participates. This starting point was plausible in a world in which – as in mediaeval society or in the closed Catholicism of before Vatican II – 'the one (Christian) destiny of human beings', namely the blessed vision of God, was taken for granted as the horizon of human existence and also expressed in the social structures. But the plausibility to a large degree disappeared in a situation in which 'divergent views of life are on offer on the "common market" of what happens in the world'. Ultimately, Schillebeeckx was to conclude from this that 'the participation idea, as it is called, has to be replaced by the idea of anticipation of a total meaning amid a history still in the making'.[20] However, I think that the opposition that he constructed in this way is too schematic. What he discovered as the basis for his theology in his Louvain period through Thomas Aquinas and Domien De Petter certainly continues to be present in his later work. The way in which this basis functioned changed quite considerably here, as will emerge in the next volume.[21] But at the same time in my view this constant basis, and the theological orientation on culture and the public which was the result of it, still make Schillebeeckx's theological approach very important. I shall return to this in the postscript to the present volume.

For this chapter this means that in my experience the sometimes very dated discussions and formulations of Schillebeeckx's Louvain synthesis still offer present-day readers – after some effort – the possibility of penetrating deeper into 'the theological event itself', God who gives himself to be known. I hope to show that this is plausible, not by justifying it as a statement but by the manner of my presentation. Here I feel that I am treading in Schillebeeckx's own footsteps.

The aura of the mysteries of faith

In 1958 Edward Schillebeeckx emerged as the editor of a collection of theological articles which set out to make the recent developments accessible to a wider public. It was aimed not only at the laity, who in this period were becoming increasingly interested in theology, but also at Catholic students for the priesthood and priests who had completed their studies. They still were primarily given, or had been given, lectures from theological textbooks which presented the content of faith as unchangeable and dry systematic teaching. At the end of the 1950s it was clear to many how unsatisfactory this situation was, and Schillebeeckx tried to allude to it. In the preface which he added to the book he stated that theology was 'not a question of "what do the textbooks say about this problem?"' He saw the aversion to textbook theology as an opportunity to develop a lively theological sensitivity: 'Theology is alive to the degree that it is always confronted with the sources of revelation and keeps a feeling for growing human experience'.[22] Years earlier, in the preface to *De sacramentele heilseconomie*, he had mentioned the 'almost universal complaint that "the class material" does little to arouse the enthusiasm of the young clergy'. Although he defended the need 'for one's own technical scholarship in the positive and speculative theological study of the data of faith', he went on to emphasize that good, theological reflection 'wells up from the life of faith itself and in its turn serves the life of faith'. However, he was convinced that 'an appropriate theological, scholarly reflection on the faith inspired by the structure of the datum of faith', of the kind that he himself was undertaking, would best meet contemporary needs.[23]

For Schillebeeckx, theology was thought 'in search of the living God'.[24] That is how he put it in 1959 in the title of his inaugural lecture as professor in Nijmegen, but by then he had already in fact been doing theology for around fifteen years. In the previous chapters it will have become clear that Schillebeeckx's theology was always closely related to the current situation in culture and the church, and also changed in reaction to it. This did not just apply to the texts which were written for a specific occasion; a clear confrontation with the spirit of the time also took place in his technical and scholarly work. As I have said, Schillebeeckx did this on the basis of the work of Thomas Aquinas, but he put this emphatically 'in the light of the [further] tradition and of present-day ... problems', to quote the subtitle to *De sacramentele heilseconomie*. It was precisely in this way that he thought that it took on true meaning. This was because for him, as for Tillich – and he had doubtless learned this from Chenu – theology was an enterprise situated in history. In 1958 he still had to formulate this with due caution:

> Outside God, truth and the possession of truth are never completely identical. It is not the truth that changes, nor even the inevitable conceptual element in the knowledge of truth, but the perspective from which the finite believer sees reality and truly knows it through the conceptual, albeit not purely conceptual, changes in the course of time. Where this happens, the possession of the truth grows, and so do our theological concepts of the faith.[25]

For Schillebeeckx there was no disputing the value and the objective importance of the traditional concepts of faith: no other standpoint was possible for a Catholic theologian in the 1950s. But the way in which the concepts of faith were sounded out and understood was time-conditioned.

The most striking thing is that as a theologian Schillebeeckx was not simply concerned with the eternal truth, but with the time-conditioned penetration of the concepts of faith. In his view the '*objective* being itself of the mysteries of faith' was not a static reality, but an 'irradiation: emanation and value in life'. It was the task of theology to demonstrate this emanation and value in life, and that could be done only by making clear their significance to contemporary men and women.[26] Here, in his view, much was to be learned from theologians of the past and the way in which they had understood the faith.[27]As his hearers remembered, unlike the usual textbooks he succeeded in demonstrating that theology was not about dry and ultimately insignificant regulations which were presented on the authority of the church hierarchy 'to be believed'. These were important things which could stir up passions and about which there was still something new to discover. As one of them was to write much later:

> One of Schillebeeckx's greatest gifts is . . . his capacity . . . to bore through traditional terms and concepts to the original meaning. By being connected with related concepts and known experiences and then being put in a new context, these are given back as new.[28]

That is how this chapter sets out to portray Schillebeeckx's theology.

'THE SACRAMENTAL ECONOMY OF SALVATION'

Schillebeeckx's theology is rightly characterized as 'theology about reality', and reflection on this reality as God's creation is said to be his central theme.[29] The previous chapter made it clear that in the course of his Flemish period discussion about the meaning of the sacraments began to serve him as an approach to these problems. In the liturgy, and especially in the action around the central symbols of baptism and unction, eucharist and marriage, in Schillebeeckx's eyes Catholicism showed itself as culture that was lived out, as a meaningful human way of dealing with reality in which, in contrast to culture in its dominant form, there was room for God's presence. He worked out the first basis of this in *De sacramentele heilseconomie*. Then what he discovered in this way about the presence of God in the hiddenness of human existence became the starting point for detailed reflections on the most important themes in the Louvain lectures for Dominican theological students. All the 'definitive' versions of the lecture notes date from after the completion of his first major book and are also clearly influenced by the standpoint adopted there. In 1963, when he had already been in Nijmegen for some time, he was finally in a sense once again to resume his approach in terms of a theology of culture within the framework of a study of the most earthly, most profane sacrament: *Marriage: Human Reality and Saving Mystery*.

One of the few concrete reminiscences of his youth that Schillebeeckx passed on in interviews was that at an early stage, 'in my sixth or seventh year', he served at mass, and that he was strongly attracted by the holy, more than everyday, nature of the liturgy:

> Serving at Mass was something that was quite different from ordinary life. There was something sacral about it, something that was not present

in ordinary life, but gave meaning to everyday experience. It was above all a religious emotion that I experienced. In comparison with the other emotions that I felt, at home, at school, with my friends, in everyday life, this one had something special about it, something that attracted me especially.[30]

He described it as something personal, something that came about in his soul, as it were by chance. But the power of attraction of the liturgy, the suggestion that more than everyday reality was visible in it, had for a long time deliberately been worked on in the Catholic Church.

Halfway through the nineteenth century, in the wake of Romanticism, the first beginnings of the so-called liturgical movement developed. The liturgical movement tried to rediscover the historical wealth and organic coherence of the church's liturgy and make it fruitful for its own time. From the beginning, liturgy was then seen as a possibility of gaining access to the 'soul' of the church through experience. People saw the possibility in a revived liturgy of departing from the fixation on organization and legal formulation into which the church had allowed itself to be forced in its confrontation with modern society; liturgy was to make it possible not to experience 'the absolutely obligatory demand of the [Catholic] view of the church' as an external obligation imposed by the hierarchy, but to see it as something that emerged from the very nature of faith in an organic way. Thus the liturgical movement formed part of the broad Catholic revival, including the ambiguity in it which has already been indicated on several occasions. On the one hand the church sought its own appropriate place within modern culture, and on the other hand it did this on the basis of a questionable anti-modernist attitude, being prominently an authority with a sense of tradition and authority from which the world increasingly threatened to become detached, with disastrous consequences.[31]

The beginning of the liturgical movement in the strict sense is usually put in 1909. In that year the abbot of the Benedictine abbey of Keizersberg in Louvain, Lambert Beauduin, gave a lecture at a mass meeting of Belgian Catholics in which he announced that the primary and indispensable source of the true Christian spirit was to be found in the active participation of the faithful in the church's liturgy. There the Catholic faith took form in a living symbolism. In the period which immediately followed, a programme directed towards the whole of Belgium was developed under the inspiration of Beauduin and with the support of Archbishop Mercier. The results of the first 'archaeological' phase of the liturgical movement, the period in which all kinds of source material were rediscovered through historical research, now had actually to bring the faithful into the liturgy and its spiritual world. The programme provided for the translation of liturgical texts, the provision of training in liturgy, and the publication of both a French- and a Dutch-language scholarly journal on the liturgy. Apart from the influence that it had on Benedictine abbeys in other European countries, this programme had a quite direct influence on the liturgy in Belgian, and also in Dutch, parishes.[32] In the 1920s, as a boy, Schillebeeckx was confronted with the results of this programme. And it evidently had the intended effect on him.

The mystery theologies of Odo Casel and Edward Schillebeeckx

Schillebeeckx's major study on the sacramental economy of salvation, the dissertation with which he gained his doctorate in Paris, can only be understood within this history. The book was written in a climate in which liturgy, understood in a new way and practised with a new verve, again became the starting point for theological reflection. This last began especially with the so-called 'mystery theology' of the German Benedictine Odo Casel (1886–1948). Although Casel's approach was highly controversial both in its starting point and in its influence and consequences, without doubt it was extremely significant for the rethinking of the liturgy and the sacraments. In a sense, *De sacramentele heilseconomie* is to be regarded as a critically modified development of Casel's theology of the mysteries.[33]

But Casel's theology was not only, or even primarily, a theological interpretation of the Catholic liturgy, though his work was usually read in this way. Casel himself was primarily interested in a theology of culture – but not in the same way as Schillebeeckx. Casel's liturgical theology was a comprehensive attempt to reverse the consequences of the individualizing and associated subjectivizing of human experience in modern times, which many people had found to be disastrous during the period between the wars in Germany. Casel formed part of a broader movement in German culture which sought a basis for life and thought in what was organic and transcended the individual, in what was placed as the objective over against the subjective. This intellectual tendency had in fact already been present since the beginning of the century, but really broke through only after 1918. Catholic theologians like Karl Adam, Romano Guardini and Erich Przywara (1889–1972), and thus also Casel, tried to connect with it theologically. They saw in this movement an opportunity to be both contemporary and fully Catholic, and presented the Catholic Church as the objective authority sought by so many people which made possible a break between the modern experiences of meaninglessness, uprooting, fragmentation and conflict over issues which could not be resolved.[34] Thus, in their own eccentric way, they implemented Leo XIII's programme.

Casel set out the basic outlines of his conservative critique of culture in 1932. He began by stating that for modern man, 'the mystery of God, in infinite majesty enthroned above man and intervening in all earthly fortunes, his exalted and incomprehensible wisdom and his all-conquering power', had become a burden from which he tried to rescue himself. As a consequence of this exaltation by human beings of themselves, in his view nature had lost its mystery to economics and technology, and the human soul had been profaned by 'the sober spotlight of psychoanalysis'. Casel saw the humanism which from the twelfth century onwards had increasingly dominated the history of Western culture as a penetration of this desecration right down to the domain of religion, church and piety: the authority and mystery of the church lost their influence to subjectivity and the disfiguring 'thought-patterns of mathematics'. For Casel, all these effects of modernity were in fact an ongoing repetition of the first sin of mankind, rising up against God and his commandments. In his view, 'now' was precisely

> like the primordial beginning of the history of mankind: when man believed that he had become like God in his own power, that his own light made him know good and evil, that he had come of age and that he no longer needed any paternal guidance – then he knew that he was naked, a king who had been put to shame, a dethroned ruler.

The fortunate result was that people were again seeking an exalted image of God:

> People are again seeing that God is all in all and that his power fills all things, his will dominates all things, his love permeates all things, that people become great in God precisely when they become nothing in themselves. The mysterious harmony of God and creation is felt again. The world again becomes a scene of divine powers, a symbol of supernatural ideas. In a word: the divine mystery again stands before us in an awesome way, luring us and challenging us at the same time.[35]

Casel saw the liturgical movement with its practical orientation, the attempts once again to make the liturgy the heart of church life, as an expression of the desire to return to the mystery of God and the love of Christ.[36] He went on to base his attempts to describe the liturgy as the living presence of the mystery on the results of this movement.[37]

Casel spent his whole life far from the turmoil of the modern world: at the age of 19 he entered the Benedictine abbey of Maria Laach, studied there and in the Benedictine house of studies in Rome, and from 1922 was spiritual director of an important Benedictine nunnery in Herstelle, where he died. In his view God was 'no friend of proud cities'. For him, God led 'his faithful outside, into solitude, into the wild nature where his breath of life blows and makes people dependent on it'. Of course, as he knew from the psalms, which have such a central place in the church's liturgy, God also built cities, but they were the prefigurations of God's heavenly city. Casel argued to his contemporaries that the church community was 'the true city of God', 'God's fortress against the spirit of the world'. In his view it was important above all to hold firm to what this city had to offer within its gates.

> Anyone who has become a citizen of this [city] should never more forsake her; he should never again go outside. Outside, baseness and impurity prevail. You are within, remain there! You are at your destination, stay there! Hold firm to the salvation of your soul.[38]

That Casel put so much emphasis on the church as a refuge from the prevailing 'baseness and impurity' did not imply that in his view the church had no significance for wider culture. On the contrary, for him the church, through its liturgy, was also of great significance for the politics of culture. Casel regarded the liturgy as the heart of Catholic Action, understood properly, which in his eyes needed to make the animated community that arose in the liturgy around the presence of the divine mysteries radiate on society as a whole. The true Christian spirit is made present in the liturgy and could thus permeate Catholics, and through this true Catholic Action was possible: 'only the true Christian who bears the Christian spirit within him can act in a Christian way'. Moreover, in his view this action was especially a matter of giving a central place to the principle of community which dominated the liturgy: 'all for one and one for all'.

To get a good picture of Casel's view of the relationship between church and culture it is important to remember that for him liturgy, 'properly understood', was also the 'highest church politics'. In his view the liturgy made clear the place of the laity in the church over against the clergy. The priest performed the central role and functioned as a mediator of the divine life. Through him the liturgical action of the church became the place of 'the presence of mystery':

> Nowhere does the authority of the hierarchy emerge in such a clear and attractive way as in the liturgy, where the priest appears as the father in the pneuma, as the procreator of the supernatural life and thus as the greatest benefactor.

According to Casel, it was the task of the laity to join this father, procreator and benefactor and be subordinate to him, not only in the liturgy but also in appearing before society and culture as a whole:

> [The] work [of the Catholic laity] also intrinsically has a priestly character because they are living members of the body of the true and only high priest of the new covenant, not only through faith but also through

sacramental incorporation into this body; however, their position in the church, that is as the receptive bride of Christ, is revealed in their sub-ordination to the priesthood.[39]

In Casel's view the liturgy of the Catholic Church was ultimately the place where the anonymous mass of solitary individuals in the midst of a soulless world reduced to matter transformed themselves into a hierarchically ordered organism in the midst of a creation that pointed to God. In this sense his thought was related to that of others who in Germany between the wars strove for a return to the solidarity of the people on the basis of the recognition of authority.[40]

Evidently Schillebeeckx was strongly attracted by Casel's basic conviction that Christianity was not a 'religion' or 'confession' in the narrower sense of the word, in other words not a 'system of more or less dogmatically stated truths which one accepts and confesses, and of moral commandments which one observes or at least recognizes'. Over against this Casel empathically pointed out that Paul regarded Christianity as 'a mystery'.[41] In *De sacramentele heilseconomie* Schillebeeckx quoted Casel almost literally on this point: 'The Christian revelation is not only the communication of a collection of truths preached by the prophets and Christ; it is, more fundamentally, a *mysterion*.'[42] But their views differed fundamentally, especially their attitudes towards modernity.

What springs most directly to view is the difference between the attitudes of the two of them to theology as an academic discipline. As we know now, Schillebeeckx thought that the scholarly character of theology was very important, whereas Casel's antipathy to modernity also led him to reject academic theology. He vigorously opposed the philosophical and rationalistic orientation of scholasticism and neoscholasticism,[43] but unlike Schillebeeckx he set over against it *theoria* in the mystical Platonic sense: the immediate contemplation through which a reality becomes present to the observer. Casel wanted to go back to the approach of the church fathers, who in his view were orientated on gnosis, in other words knowledge on the basis of the 'contemplation of the only true being'; union with the divine truth was the ideal of true theology for patristics.[44] Here Casel followed the thoughts of Georg Koepgen, which Schillebeeckx had fundamentally criticized as early as 1943.[45] In the light of this basic conviction he presented the liturgy of the church in its various forms time and again as 'the presence of a mystery' and did not develop a theology of the sacraments. That is what Schillebeeckx tried to do in *De sacramentele heilseconomie*. Through close analysis and specialist study of the church tradition and by 'careful theological argument on the basis of St Thomas', he sought to answer in a rational way the question whether and above all in what sense there was a real presence of the divine redemption in the church's sacraments.[46]

In this attempt at an answer it proved that the difference between Casel's and Schillebeeckx's view of modernity had a theological consequence. Schillebeeckx began his analysis of the tradition in *De sacramentele heilseconomie* with a study of what the church fathers had written during the first three centuries on what they called in Greek *mysterion* or in Latin *sacramentum*. Casel had taken over from historians of religion the idea that the structure of early Christianity corresponded to that of the mystery religions of late antiquity, though there were a number of decisive differences. For Casel the concept of mystery in these religions offered access to the proper understanding of Christian faith as this took shape in the liturgy.[47] Casel defined the mystery along the lines of the mystery religions as 'a sacred cultic action in which a fact of salvation is made present in the rite; at the moment that the cultic community performs the rite, it takes part in the saving act and thus acquires salvation for itself'.[48] On the basis of the patristic use of the idea of mystery he thought that he could say that early Christianity belonged to the same type as the mystery religions and took over this idea of mystery, but on this point he was heavily criticized. Schillebeeckx shared this criticism. With due scholarly accuracy he tried to discover the different shifts in the ancient concept of *mysterion* and *sacramentum*, and also the way in which the church fathers used these terms. He connected this with the way in which the term *mysterion* is used in the New Testament and the Septuagint, the Greek translation of the Old Testament.[49] He finally concluded that in contrast to the mystery religions, in the Christian view the liturgical mysteries were not shut up in themselves, but were mysteries precisely in the way in which they referred to a unique event of salvation, namely Jesus's life, death and resurrection. So he focused the problem on the idea of a 'presence of mystery' in the Christian liturgy. Here the closed nature of Casel's view of liturgy had already in a sense been broken through. The distinctiveness of the liturgical ritual was not that it introduced believers to a world of its own which contained all that they needed; the significance of the liturgy lay in the way in which it pointed to something that lay outside the ritual. 'The mystery of Christ ... is the primordial sacrament from which the Christian sacrament can be understood' was his technical way of putting it.[50]

Moreover, for Casel the concept of mystery which he had reconstructed from patristics was the only norm. He regarded the religion of the mystery religions as 'the golden bowl ... into which the church can pour the wine of Christ';[51] for him, a departure from the modern understanding of reality and a return to the ancient reverence for nature as pointing to God's majesty was the only way to an authentic Christianity. In Schillebeeckx's view, on the other hand, the patristic concept of mystery expressed in a time-conditioned way the universal truth that 'nature, for all its autonomy, [was] still ordered inwardly on supernature which, although transcendent, finds its providential prestructure in the complex of nature, above all in accordance with its natural religious character'.[52] Throughout the history of human-kind, longing for God's redemption found its expression in various external religious symbols. In the Christian sacraments the human longing for God was brought into synthesis with God's redeeming descent into human history. In his view this matched the statement in the phenomenology of religion that the Christian liturgy had adopted universal human religious symbols, but that these took on specific meaning within it. In Casel's view the liturgy, in the midst of a modernity which had been stripped of any sense of mystery, was the only place where God's holiness was still experienced and venerated. However, in Schillebeeckx's view the liturgical celebration of the sacraments was ultimately a concentration of the human quest for God and at the same time contact with God's redemptive love as that had taken concrete form in Jesus Christ.[53]

Like Casel's work, but less explicitly, *De sacramentele heilseconomie* in fact contained a theological view of human nature, modern culture and the significance of the Christian tradition. However, the book was received above all as both a specialist and comprehensive study of the theology of the sacraments. In this specialist area the book was regarded as a monumental synthesis; one commentator argued that the fact that it 'bewilderingly enough' remained untranslated meant that 'Dutch is a language which all contemporary theologians have to know'.[54] The importance of this major study was also seen in the Netherlands. Its power lay especially in the way in which it combined the tendency to understand the sacraments as liturgical actions in which God's redemption was really present – along Casel's line – with a precise reading of Thomas Aquinas's theology of the sacraments. Here it used the method of existential phenomenology, which at the time was thought to be markedly innovative.

From the beginning of the century Catholic theologians had been making furious attempts to overcome the aporias of textbook theology by returning to the text of Thomas himself. In neoscholastic theology, sacraments were seen primarily as means of salvation, the central question being how they could effectively mediate grace to believers. By putting this question and by writing about the sacraments in this way, chance manners imposed by God on human beings proved to be ways of attaining a 'sanctifying grace' which was understood in the abstract and was almost quantifiable. The place of the sacraments in the life of the faithful seemed to be completely overshadowed. Only in the twentieth century did a greater awareness develop of their place in salvation history and the role that they needed to play in the life of the faithful. In 1925 the English Benedictine Anscar Vonier (1875–1938) arrived at a pioneering view of Thomas's theology of the sacraments which came close to the concept of mystery that Casel derived from the church fathers.

Vonier began from Thomas's statement that faith and sacraments were the two different ways in which the faithful were bound up with the redemptive power of Christ's death: in faith through 'an act of the soul', and in the sacraments through 'the use of external things'. Vonier's clarification that in Thomas's view the sacraments were 'sacraments of faith' was an important one. They did not work by themselves in an isolated way but had their place in the life of believers and were orientated on that: both 'faith and the sacraments have the divine effective power which will open up for men the treasury of Christ's redemption'.[55] Schillebeeckx was to take up this notion in his theology of the sacraments.

The sacraments as human and divine reality

Schillebeeckx dated the 'Preface' to *De sacramentele heilseconomie* 7 March 1951. That was a confession of faith: before the reform of the calendar of saints in 1969, 7 March was the feast day of Thomas Aquinas. In his introduction Schillebeeckx said that the basis of his study lay in 'St Thomas's writings, analysed historically and doctrinally and also situated in the perspective of the tradition of faith which went before, came after and is still alive now',[56] and he paid extensive attention to Thomas's theology of the sacraments. He did so as the specialist on Thomas that he was, with great erudition and technical skill, but he aimed at more than an accurate presentation of Thomas's views. In a sense he made an attempt at a literary effect. He presented Thomas in such a way that the question of the place of the sacraments in his work almost coincided with the question of the place of the sacraments in the life of Catholics, which was topical when he wrote. In this way the analysis of the significance of the sacraments in Thomas at the same time appeared as a possible solution to the contemporary theological and pastoral problem.

'For a long time there was a dispute over the fact that the construction of St Thomas's *Summa theologiae* is almost complete before there is any mention of Christ and his sacramental economy of salvation,' wrote Schillebeeckx in what was at first sight a matter-of-fact statement in the introduction to *De sacramentele heilseconomie* (2). This could give the impression that the sacraments were arbitrary, as it were a chance historical element in the life and faith of Christians, with no relation to what was essential for Thomas: the way in which human beings start from God and return to God. By going on to indicate how the different parts of the *Summa* hang together, including the part on the sacraments, Schillebeeckx was also talking about the significance of the sacraments in Christian life. In his view Thomas distinguished in the 'one indivisible Christian reality of salvation ... different aspects of the human ascent to God'; these permeate one another and cannot be seen apart from one another. Schillebeeckx formulated the connection between the different aspects like this:

> Foremost is the determination of man's salvation [in Christ]. This salvation is attained by free human dedication, at least in so far as this is supported by grace, and precisely by a specifically Christian grace, as participation in Christ's fullness of grace with which we are brought into contact through the sacramental economy of salvation (5).[57]

According to Schillebeeckx, the structure of the *Summa theologiae* could be understood only by starting from the fact that Thomas tried to treat these actions one after another, but at the same time was fully aware that it was impossible to detach them from one another.

From the beginning of his theological career Schillebeeckx had asserted, on the basis of the insight that was formulated anew here, that the natural aspect of reality could not be seen apart from the supernatural. Now he went a step further and argued that the theological and the salvation-historical aspects of the existence of faith could not be detached from the sacramental aspect. Thus sacraments were not quasi-fortuitous extras, but embodied the synthesis of all levels of the life of faith. Schillebeeckx called them 'the ultimate saving organs through which human beings [could] reach their destiny', the forms in which the human ascent to God was formally accomplished. They took the faithful up into God's movement, which descended to human history and also led this back to God, from whom everything came: the sacraments made possible 'the ascent of man-in-the-world to heaven', 'his homecoming', the '*accessus ad Patrem*' which is firmly fixed on the coming of the Son within the limits of our world' (16). In short, for Schillebeeckx the sacraments were the places where in a concentrated way the deepest element of faith was consummated: the union of God and human beings, nature and the supernatural. This made it clear to him that the sacraments were of central importance in the life of faith and at the same time that reflection on the sacraments was of central importance for theology.

According to Schillebeeckx, the basis of what took place in the sacraments was the history of Jesus, to which they point. He reconstructed the history of theology from before Thomas in such a way that it ended up with a question which also preoccupied sacramental theology in the first half of the twentieth century. Thus he persuaded his readers to focus on what Thomas had to say on this point. According to Schillebeeckx, the discussion which was topical both for Thomas and for his readers regarded the sacrament on the one hand as a sign, a pointer to something else, and on the other as an instance that brought about the salvation that it expressed. The question was how these two views were related. According to Schillebeeckx, Thomas's important contribution to the theology of the sacraments was that he found a principle of unity from which he could reconcile both these aspects, the 'sign value and the efficiency value' of the sacraments.

In an analysis of Thomas's early work, especially his commentary on the *Sentences* of Peter Lombard which was composed between 1253 and 1257, Schillebeeckx demonstrated that 'Thomas junior' first regarded the sacraments as 'means of grace', institutions that mediated grace. This was also the aspect that was central in the neoscholastic view of the sacraments, and thus Schillebeeckx claimed implicitly that neoscholastic theology was based on the work of a Thomas who was not yet completely mature theologically. But Schillebeeckx at the same time made it clear that in his commentary on the *Sentences* Thomas had really already located the principle of the unity of the sacraments in the history of Jesus understood in faith, in other words in 'the mystery of Christ' or the *'passio Christi'*. In Schillebeeckx's eyes, for Thomas this was the fundamental cause of the salvation that is given to man in faith: 'the sacrament is a sign *of* a saving cause, viz. in the first place of ... the redemptive mystery of Christ' as the first cause of human sanctification.[58] He thought that this emerged to a heightened degree in the third book of the *Summa theologiae* (1272–3), in which Thomas had abandoned the idea that the sacraments were means of handing on an abstract quantum 'salvation' in a mysterious way.

It is striking that Schillebeeckx attached so much importance to the fact that Thomas had not included the specifically Christian significance of the sacraments in his definition of them. According to his interpretation, Thomas would have deliberately limited himself to 'the nature which is *capable of definition*' and then located that in the anthropological element: 'Sacraments are essentially the *cultual* [we would say cultic] *symbolic actions of a religious community'*, is the way in which he summed up Thomas.[59] In this respect the Christian sacraments were no different from what mediaeval scholasticism called the 'Jewish sacraments', the central elements of Jewish worship as expressed in the Old Testament which were regarded in the Christian tradition as pointers to Jesus Christ. Nor did they differ from what Schillebeeckx called 'the sacraments of nature', in other words the religious significance that according to the historians of religion some phenomena and actions had in all cultures and religions.[60] That Thomas's approach concentrated so strongly on the anthropological aspect made it possible for Schillebeeckx to regard the sacraments as utterly human phenomena. Their essential feature was not what distinguished them from all other forms of human behaviour but precisely what linked them up with other human behaviour. In the somewhat technical and detached language of *De sacramentele heilseconomie* Schillebeeckx put it like this:

> The *propter homines* of the sacramental economy of salvation is thus also revealed in the fact that Christ has taken natural symbols from truly

concrete everyday life as the subject of sacramental symbolism and precisely in so doing has given them an appropriate, similar but transcendent significance ... The sacraments are not pure signals, but real symbols. This nature symbolism, as exalted by the specifically Christian significance of salvation, is thus also part of the beginning of the sacrament as *signum* (140).

In other words, by being bound up with ordinary human life, the sacraments could fulfil what according to Schillebeeckx was their distinctive nature: they made present the salvation of God, hidden but orientated on human salvation, and were an 'external, eloquent, tangible view of God's goodness and redemptive love', just as God is visible in Jesus Christ to those who 'know how to treat him, guided by the gaze of faith'.[61]

For Schillebeeckx this went on to open up the possibility of thinking about the sacraments with the theory of symbolization developed by De Petter. According to De Petter's anthropology, human action in and through the body was the beginning of a comprehensive process in which, in Schillebeeckx's paraphrase, the 'material process of nature ... is taken up into a specifically human finality' and 'is elevated into a free practice of life with a spiritual perspective'. Through human action the world of phenomena becomes a space for human symbolic activity and the giving of meaning, and ultimately 'objectified spirit', culture (394–7).[62] In Schillebeeckx's eyes this also applied to symbolic, sacramental action within Christian worship. He emphasized that the significance of symbols was not arbitrary – in a twofold sense. First the phenomena were given, including their function in reality as it was lived out, and their historical significance arose on the basis of this. 'The anchor holds the ship fast; hope as a spiritual reality gives firmness and security to human life. Thus in human experience the anchor becomes the symbol of hope' (397). Secondly, symbols were active attempts to clarify the human situation, to get a grip on the intangible by means of evocative images. According to Schillebeeckx, they were aimed at 'making an "already" present but only vague, "evasive" knowledge of reality *clearer* and through this making it "explicit"' (399). Thus, in his view symbols actively disclosed reality, and set people against a comprehensive, meaningful horizon; however, they disclosed only what was there. The anchor as a symbol bore witness to hope as a human attitude, and at the same time embodied the experience of reality as ultimately hopeful.

In this sense, according to Schillebeeckx the sacraments were symbols. In this case they were objectified forms of a culture, of a believing, Christian, Catholic culture. Indeed he understood the doctrine solemnly laid down by the Council of Trent (1545–63) that the sacraments worked 'by the power of the action itself' – *ex opere operato* – in this sense. The sacramental action was not the expression of a prescribed formula and the making of an isolated gesture. In his view the action comprised both the intention of those who administered the sacraments and the readiness of the recipients to accept them in faith; understood in this comprehensive sense, the sacraments in fact contain within themselves the salvation to which they point – *continere gratiam, quam significant* – to quote the Tridentine formulation.[63] The seven sacraments of the Catholic Church were then specific focal points of the Christian way of dealing with reality (398–400).[64] In Schillebeeckx's view the sacraments give the diffuse and still indeterminate human experience of reality a form and a significance by putting them in contact with the mystery of Christ and its redemptive significance.[65] This happens through a universally human religious gesture – breaking bread and sharing wine, immersing in or pouring water on, anointing .

In 1957 Schillebeeckx wrote the article on the sacraments for the *Theologisch woordenboek*. In it he once again took up the position that he had defended in *De sacramentele heilseconomie* and set this out more clearly and in a more synthetic way. There was a passage in this article – a quotation – which is remarkable to find in a lexicon article, precisely because of its everyday character. In it the sacraments are compared to the handshake which people offer one another in daily life as an expression of friendship or affection.

> I meet a friend and shake him by the hand. My friend sees this gesture as a 'sign' of friendship: he makes the abstract and logical connection that there is between the external gesture and the spiritual reality which is called friendship. However, in this action that I perform the spiritual reality of which the handshake is a sign is also really *brought about* in and through this sign. The handshake 'is' really a sharing of friendship.[66]

Schillebeeckx's point was that the sacraments were as everyday and human as that. It was first of all a polemical point, made to theologians who could not see the anthropological depth of the symbol and therefore had to resort to complicated theories to explain the significance of the sacraments. But he was also concerned with a theological point which was of fundamental importance for his approach.

Man's outreach to God and God's descent to man

According to Schillebeeckx, the fundamental mystery of faith represented by the sacraments was that the divine grace of redemption is present in the prayerful and symbolic, utterly human, action of a faith community.[67] In order to maintain this mystery he emphasized that the redemptive significance of the sacraments is not a specific characteristic of these symbols. The saving significance of the sacraments does not emerge from the sacraments in themselves but from the divine grace which takes these human symbols into service and transforms them into the 'saving organ through which the grace merited by Christ's redemption is also in fact communicated to us in an instrumental and effective way'.

According to Schillebeeckx, Thomas Aquinas made precisely this clear by on the one hand regarding the 'mystical efficacy of salvation' as 'the most essential basic feature of the Christian nature of the sacraments', but on the other hand keeping this essential basic feature outside his definition of their 'essence which is capable of definition' (142). According to Schillebeeckx, what in the first instance could appear to be a discrepancy bore witness to a fundamental insight.

> This solution of St Thomas's is in my view brilliant theology. It is a typical expression of his authentically theological attitude, as a result of which he attempts to grasp from the mystery what is really comprehensible within it while at the same time leaving its transcendence completely intact (142).

That was a surprising reading of Thomas, and at the same time extremely important for Schillebeeckx's theology of the sacraments. For by distinguishing between the anthropological structure and the theological significance of the sacraments, he could go on to see that the two coincided as the central religious event. In his view the sacraments were the synthesis of the human outreach to God and God's descent to human beings. Thus he kept the divine mystery in the sacraments intact in his theologizing on them – though that did not mean that he then lapsed into silence, any more than Thomas did. He thought that by bringing together the different mysteries of faith in a rational way, Thomas arrived at 'a deeper knowledge of faith'. The realization that this led to remained a perception of faith, 'but faith living in the reflexive thought of the believer' (174); for Schillebeeckx this was the definition of a theological insight.

In Thomas's footsteps, Schillebeeckx also tried to get a deeper insight into the way in which the redemptive grace contained in the history of Jesus Christ could still be present for people centuries later in the sacraments. He strictly maintained that the sacraments functioned as pointers and emphatically distanced himself from Casel by stating that time was 'irreversible'. What happened could not in his view 'in any way, not even through God, be once again made present in the world, not even *in mysterio*'.[68] In a complicated analysis of Thomas's train of thought, he went on to show that the sacraments contained the grace that they signified precisely by pointing actively to what has taken place in Jesus Christ. In his view, for Thomas the classic doctrine that Christ united God and man in one person and thus could bring salvation and redemption to human beings meant that the man Jesus in his bodily appearance was God's tool, God's instrument, and that God's redeeming love manifested itself at the different moments of his history. 'The whole of the human appearance of Christ on earth was an effective manifestation of salvation, the visible reality of a gracious God' (164).[69] Because Christ's humanity was at the same time the divine manifestation of salvation, in Thomas's view his human actions had more than local and temporal significance: their abiding actuality, even for people of later centuries, lay in the fact that – in Schillebeeckx's words – 'they are permeated by a divine force'. In the sacramental cult of the church these acts are made symbolically present, and therefore this actual significance, which was thus an aspect of the original actions of Jesus Christ and not of the sacraments, becomes present. In Schillebeeckx's view the sacraments thus, ultimately, have 'saving power in so far as they are related to Christ through their sacramental signification', and it is through the way in which they point to him that the faithful come into contact with God's effective saving will, which includes them.[70]

Because of the emphasis which thus came to lie on the link with the actions of Jesus Christ himself, Schillebeeckx was firmly attached to the traditional Catholic notion that the sacraments were instituted by Jesus during the time of his earthly life. In 1957 he went into this point rather more closely. He proved to be well aware that it could not be demonstrated historically in the strict sense that the seven sacraments which the Catholic Church identifies as instituted by Christ were explicitly willed by him during his earthly life. But in his view this was not the issue. The important thing was the link between the sacraments and the earthly Jesus, who lived on in the church after his death in the sacraments. Schillebeeckx maintained that it had to be possible to derive the sacraments from 'Christ himself ... before his departure to the Father', but in his view there was 'an implicit, confused yet nevertheless real manifestation of the will' of Jesus of which 'the fundamental institution of the church itself, as a sacramental sign of salvation', was the deepest core. Therefore, ultimately what the church itself had instituted as a sacramental sign of salvation had been instituted and willed by Jesus Christ himself in an indirect but no less real way.[71]

Schillebeeckx then tried to demonstrate that each of the seven sacraments 'involves us in a characteristic of the church as the earthly presence of the messianic salvation' in Christ and makes the central elements of human life 'moments of salvation in which God manifests himself through Christ in a gesture which belongs to our human, earthly reality'.[72] Here baptism, confirmation and ordination to the priesthood had a key function for him. They incorporated the faithful into the fellowship of the church – this was his explanation, on the basis of a historical reconstruction of their origin, of the traditional notion that on receiving these sacraments the recipients had a 'mark' put on them – they were given authority to participate in the worship of the church in their own way. Again carefully interpreting the texts of Thomas, he regarded baptism as the recognition of an 'active cultic capacity'

– a capacity to worship God – 'on the part of a non-qualified member of the church'; confirmation as the transformation of this into a 'qualified, non-priestly membership of the church'; and ordination to the priesthood as the handing on of the capacity to celebrate the sacraments. In his view, these three sacraments were not just about the attribution of an external authority, but about becoming involved in and taking part in the high-priesthood of Christ himself, in three different ways. 'The one who is sent, who is deputed by Christ in his church to perform certain actions in the church's cult or to take an active part in it', had to receive 'real "consecration", so that it became possible for his action really to be the action of the heavenly Christ.'[73]

An important concern for Schillebeeckx in his theology of the sacraments was to lay no other foundation than that which has already been laid, Jesus Christ (to paraphrase a sentence of the apostle Paul, in 1 Cor. 3.11). In his view the sacraments brought about the grace to which they point, which from of old had been the Catholic tradition, but he made it clear how much the sacramental liturgy was a summary and making present of all of Christian faith as it took form in the church. He certainly called the church the primordial sacrament of the glorified Christ within the world and said that in its visibility 'in sacramental and thus inadequate identity [it was] the "body of the Lord" or redemption as visibly addressed to human beings', but here he proved in particular to be thinking of the church in so far as it celebrated the sacraments as pointers to Christ's redemptive grace.[74] He presented the 'initiation' through baptism, confirmation and priesthood of those who took part in the sacramental liturgy as a condition which alone made this 'the real action of the heavenly Christ', but he likewise took great pains to show that the intention in faith of the minister and the recipient really to celebrate the mysteries of Christ determined the effect of the sacraments on the recipients. In his view, in principle this effect was part of the sacraments themselves.[75] He patiently analysed the structural elements of the church's understanding of the sacraments themselves as these are objectively visible in the history of theology and the liturgy, but at the same time emphasized that the sacraments are ultimately about a reciprocal personal encounter with Christ.[76] By all this he made it clear that in theology he was concerned with what is called the *nexus mysteriorum*, clarification of the connection between the different mysteries of faith. He was not concerned to explain the sacraments or base them on the authority of the church, ordination to the priesthood or the correct performance of the ritual. He was concerned with the power of the sacraments themselves to point in the direction of Jesus Christ, whose life formed their true origin, true foundation and true content.[77]

In the Thomistic perspective that Schillebeeckx used in the 1950s, the history of Jesus Christ was an encounter between God's descending love of man and man's desire to rise to God. 'God was in Christ reconciling us to himself,' he said, following Paul (2 Cor. 5.16), but this reconciliation took the form of the obedience of a human being to God in the midst of a broken situation and as part of a fallen humankind.[78] According to Schillebeeckx, the sacraments were about this synthesis, the symbolic repetition of this event, and he tried to demonstrate by the liturgical form that they had been given that in fact each in its own way made the link between the human question of God and God's orientation on human salvation, so that the natural human desire for God, which time and again takes concrete form, also receives a concrete response. Given the nature of the church's tradition and the scholastic assimilation of it, in which Christ's death played a great role as a vicarious offering to God the Father for the sins of mankind, Schillebeeckx emphasized strongly that the earthly reality needed to be offered to God, in other words that its independent significance had to be abandoned: only then could it take on the sacramental significance that was its deepest characteristic. Thus, the ambiguity of Schillebeeckx's theological position in the 1940s and 1950s which I have already indicated also appeared in his theology of the sacraments. But at the same time, in his studies of the sacraments he had the same comprehensive goal as in his whole project: the theological integration of nature and the supernatural. At the end of *De sacramentele heilseconomie* he summed up his view as follows:

> One and the same objective form, appearing in veiled cultic symbols, viz. the sacramental mystery of the cult, becomes ... both the expression of and the descending *agape* of God and the human being who reaches out above himself. Thus the sacrament is the intersection between a divine and a human commitment; only in it is God's act of salvation given complete priority (662f.).

Here, in the language of sacramental theology, he in fact once again expressed the focus of his whole theology of culture.

The degree to which Schillebeeckx in fact meant his theology of sacraments to be a theology of culture would perhaps have become visibly clearer had the planned second volume of *De sacramentele heilseconomie* actually appeared. According to the table of contents included in the first volume, he had planned sections in it on the 'sacramentality of the material world' and the 'sacramentality of Christian humanism' (XX). But although in 1957, shortly after his arrival in the Netherlands, he wrote to a fellow-Dominican that the second part was almost ready and that finishing it off was 'only a matter of writing it all out', it never appeared. Two studies did appear in which he expounded in a synthesis and to some degree a popularization what he had already presented in outline in *De sacramentele heilseconomie*: the article 'Sacrament' for the *Theologisch woordenboek* and the little book which in fact contained the substance of a lecture that he had given at the

Higher Institute of Religious Science established by the University of Louvain to make it possible for non-priests also to study theology: *De Christusontmoeting als sacrament van de Godsontmoeting*, later published in English in an expanded version as *Christ the Sacrament*. The additions to this last version, which appeared in Dutch in 1959, included a long section on the Christian life as animating presence in the midst of culture, a presence which Schillebeeckx himself also regarded as 'the sacrament of the encounter with God'.

For in his view the church was not exclusively about the reception of the sacraments. These took on their true meaning only in the context of a Christian 'presence in the world' with a broader significance. 'The sacraments are flashes of light within the whole of Christian life, which has a wider sphere of influence', he wrote, and he saw the real key to gaining access to them in 'the real treatment of human beings, but then as an expression of our love of God'.[79] This resulted in the following sentence, which though a summary, is in quite broad terms:

> The sacraments, the Word, all Christian conduct which proceeds from grace, the entire world of man – all these are, in their various ways, visible realities in this world of which the Lord avails himself, using his rich fund of inspiration in the most diverse means, to orientate man existentially towards God in Jesus Christ.

For, he added later on, 'the Son's incarnation admits the world into a personal relationship between God and man and man and God'. And in his view that becomes visible both in the sacramental economy of salvation in the strict sense and in the Christian way of dealing with the world that creates culture.[80]

In Schillebeeckx's view, 'the sacraments, the Word, all Christian conduct which proceeds from grace' and in a certain sense in fact 'the whole human world' came together especially in Christian marriage. He was to be extensively concerned with this sacrament when he lived in the Netherlands and was intensively involved in the Second Vatican Council. In 1963 his labours were to issue in the publication of the first volume of a 'dogmatics of marriage', planned in two volumes under the title *Het huwelijk, aardse werkelijkheid en heilsmysterie* (*Marriage: Human Reality and Saving Mystery*). I shall be returning to this study at the end of the chapter.

THE THEOLOGY OF THE LOUVAIN COURSES

The most important approach to Schillebeeckx's Louvain synthesis is through the notes which formed the basis of the lectures which he gave in his

Louvain period. To a certain degree one can say that lecture notes were the most appropriate form of his way of theologizing. It has rightly been pointed out that in all his texts he was primarily addressing an audience, and that the way in which he produced texts was more that of a speaker than of a writer. This also applied to the texts which were published. Schillebeeckx did not compose his texts carefully nor did he build them up in sentences which were formulated as precisely as possible. Even when he was writing, his approach was rather to talk 'until everything has been said – but not in a few words'.[81] This approach can be found in its purest form in the lecture notes.

According to his own later testimony Schillebeeckx taught in Louvain in a curriculum spread over four years 'from what used to be called "the treatise on God", the theology of creation and salvation – man and nature, world and the world of angels – christology, church and sacraments, up to and including eschatology',[82] but at all events this framework does not seem to have been followed very strictly. The precise framework within which a number of parts and fragments of the extant lectures duplicated for his students function is not always clear. After his arrival in the Netherlands, however, at the request of his students, Schillebeeckx made four sets of lecture notes available: on the structure of the act of faith and the nature of theology, on christology, on eschatology, and on creation. In each case these notes formed a more or less consecutive text of around 500 pages. They were collected for the last time that he lectured on the relevant subjects in Louvain, but also contain parts which clearly date from an earlier period. The texts were doing the rounds, both in Flanders and in the Netherlands, until well into the 1960s, and can be regarded as the account of Schillebeeckx's theologizing in Flanders which to a degree was also authorized by him.[83] That is also how I shall treat them in this chapter. I am not concerned to reconstruct the various layers from the history of the texts, but shall discuss them in their final form, as one of the forms of Schillebeeckx's thinking in his Louvain period. The intellectual history from which they emerge has been discussed in the previous chapters.

Thinking about the God who is manifest in salvation history

Schillebeeckx's study on *De sacramentele heilseconomie* appeared in 1952, but had already been completed in March 1951. The duplicated course 'Introduction to Theology' dates from the following academic year, 1951–2. In it he not only expounded the basic principles of the theological approach, but in Chenu's footsteps went at particular length into the structure of the 'act' of faith, God as object of this faith, the Bible and tradition as access to this object, and the possibility of a growing conceptual insight into the faith.[84] He developed his thoughts about theology, which he was convinced is born from the structures of faith itself, *'ex ipsa structura fidei'*, on the basis of his reflections on faith as a human activity.[85]

A remark which Thomas Aquinas seemed to make almost in passing in his *Summa theologiae* was important for Schillebeeckx's view of theology: 'Now the act of faith,' Thomas writes, 'is not orientated on a statement but on the thing': *actus autem credentis non terminatur ad enuntiabile, sed ad rem.*[86] Faith is thus directed not towards what is formulated in the biblical texts or the church's confession of faith, but towards what emerges from these statements and what they point to. According to Schillebeeckx, the 'thing' at issue was visible in the light of faith: 'Through the *lumen fidei* the *res* itself is attained' (171). But what is this 'thing'? What in his view is the object of faith? The whole of his theology is in a sense contained in the answer to this question. According to Schillebeeckx, 'what we believe' is not just God, but the history of God with human beings as the revelation of God himself, what he called 'the history of salvation as theophaneia'. For him, Christians believe in the 'mystery aspect of a saving event', in the reality of God 'as appearing for us in historical saving events'. These events and their significance for salvation are put into words by formulations handed down in the Bible and the church tradition. However, according to Schillebeeckx, even what is presented in and through these formulations, the 'material subject of our faith', was not 'the material form of our faith'; it was not just God in a general undefined sense. In his view belief was in 'the *Deus salutaris*, in other words, God who bears witness to himself as God as a reality which encounters me directly'. For him the deepest core – 'which is what is at issue' – of all statements about the content of faith in the Christian tradition, 'the innermost material object of faith', was 'inner union with God' as the God of salvation and as the supernatural goal of humanity. In other words, for him it was 'God as our God' (215).

Here Schillebeeckx thought that he had grasped the most fundamental insight of Thomas Aquinas, the pivot of his whole theological *oeuvre*. Thomas stated right at the beginning of his *Summa theologiae* that the truths of faith were orientated on salvation, that these were truths of faith which presented to human beings the orientation of human existence. Faith makes it clear what human beings must strive for. In this way of thinking theology was

> not a system ... of metaphysical truths concerning God as God, but a *religious system of salvation*: a reflection on an economy of salvation in which a glimpse can be caught of God's innermost being, in and through his loving treatment of human beings. We have no other more direct view of God-as-God (16f.).[87]

According to Schillebeeckx, God's nature came to light in the history of salvation, which in its turn was the 'historical consummation' of the 'divine initiative of salvation'. God could be known only through history as this is related in the biblical writings, but above all as it took place in Jesus Christ. According to Schillebeeckx, the classical christological view that God had become man in Jesus Christ meant that a 'fragment of human history' became 'a radical theophany' and that had made history the vehicle of a suprahistorical message and transformed it into a divine mystery in a veiled unveiling. 'History is transfigured into a theology', and in this history God made himself known as essentially a God of salvation (12).

As a consequence of this, according to Schillebeeckx God could be known only through human experience in faith. As we saw in the previous chapters, from the beginning of his career as a theologian he attached great import-ance to intellectual penetration into the mystery of God. As intellectual activity, as a science which brought to light conceptually the internal logical and conceptual bond between the mysteries of faith, for him theology had saving significance. This conviction also permeates all his Louvain lecture notes; the consequence was that for him, systematic reflection on the reve-lation as this is given in the history of salvation must always have a central place in theology. Thus, for example, he thought that all that is said theo-logically about human action must begin from a reflection on grace.[88] At the same time Schillebeeckx could say this because in his view theology was an experiential faith related to reality, but had this character 'as living in reflective thought'. In theology faith was 'clearly aware ... of its faith content', and this content was then integrated into the whole of human spiritual life (218, 265).[89] For Schillebeeckx, this emphasis on the link with experienced faith relativized any form of systematic theology. For him, any theological system, even the best of them, like that of Thomas Aquinas, presented a view in faith of the absolute from a specific standpoint in that reality. The way in which any standpoint is bound to a system made it clear 'that the issue is not the system but contact with reality itself'. As far as he was concerned, the system as system was 'the defective expression of reality; one cannot attach any intrinsic value to it'. From this, he drew the very striking conclusion for the beginning of the 1950s that complete unanimity among theologians was therefore 'impossible', not only 'in the course of time' but also at 'one historical moment': everyone looked at reality from his own perspective. Surprisingly enough, however, he did not see this as a problem but as a source of the enrichment and renewal of theology: he thought that the differences in the view of the one 'thing' made the growth of knowledge in faith possible (260–4).

So according to Schillebeeckx, the faith, and thus theology as the faith 'in scholarly form' did not live by a truth which was contained in a dense edifice of doctrinal statements. Faith lived by 'contact with reality itself', and by contact with God which came about through that and in that. In a way which involved all kinds of technical theological points of discussion, he worked this out more closely in his Louvain 'Introduction', especially in his discussion of what he regarded as the different 'structural elements of the act of faith'. The first part of these lectures was entitled *De structura actus fidei* and ran to almost 250 duplicated pages.

The structure of the act of faith was determined first of all by the texts from the Bible and the church's tradition from which faith derived the specific knowledge of the history of salvation, which in turn made it clear who God was. First of all Schillebeeckx investigated the classical debating point of the mutual relationship between Bible and tradition. According to the customary Catholic view, the Bible and the tradition were two separate sources of the knowledge of faith. In the course of the nineteenth and the first half of the twentieth century, however, a variety of Catholic theologians argued that this juxtaposition was unsatisfactory. In his lecture notes Schillebeeckx discussed a number of their proposals in order to see the relationship in a different perspective; he also discussed the views of theologians from the past to which the authors of the proposals thought that they could refer in their turn.[90] He finally followed the tendency to put the Bible and tradition above all on the same wavelength and for this referred to the Council of Trent, which according to the neoscholastic interpretation had laid down the notion of the two sources. According to the Tridentine formulation, revelation was contained 'in written books and unwritten traditions which, received by the apostles from the mouth of Christ himself, or dictated by the Holy Spirit, have been passed on as it were from hand to hand and have come down to us'. Schillebeeckx showed, however, that this view in particular presupposes that there is ultimately only one source, namely the revelation in the gospel proclaimed and lived out by Jesus Christ. According to Trent there are two witnesses to this source, the biblical writings and the tradition of the church. The First Vatican Council stated that the magisterium of the church was the normative interpreter of 'the written and unwritten word of God'.[91]

Schillebeeckx quoted with approval the ecumenist Willem van de Pol – whose colleague he was later to be in the theological faculty at Nijmegen. As early as 1947 van de Pol argued that 'the idea that there are two independent sources of knowledge from which the knowledge of revelation is drawn, so that one part of the revealed truth can be drawn from the holy scriptures and the other from the tradition' was a thing of the past.[92] At the Second Vatican Council the Catholic Church was officially to depart from the idea of two sources and also formally to say that 'holy tradition and holy Scripture' were closely connected and shared in each other: according to the dogmatic constitution *Dei verbum*, 'holy tradition and holy Scripture' were 'one sacred path entrusted to the church'.[93] In the 1950s Schillebeeckx's thoughts were moving in the same direction. But whereas the Council document halfway through the 1960s was to emphasize that the tradition was the way in which the Bible, the correct understanding of the Bible and access to the Bible in history were handed down, at the beginning of the 1950s Schillebeeckx argued the opposite. 'Scripture is one form of tradition, namely its literary form.' Here he quoted the Anglican theologian Lionel Thornton, whose book on revelation had evidently made such an impression on him that he added a reference to it at the end of the duplicated lectures, which were really already complete.[94]

Schillebeeckx derived his view of the relationship between Bible and church tradition to an important degree from the work of Congar. Like him, Congar and Chenu had also taught that faith is first of all a living way of dealing with reality and indeed lives by it. This way of dealing with reality takes shape in the church as a living community and then, but only secondarily, also in institutional forms and formal statements. In Congar's view the norm for living faith is what he called the objective tradition, namely the tradition as what was and is handed down in the life of the church. And at the heart of this tradition the biblical writings – in fact especially the writings of the New Testament – functioned as an objective normative rule. According to Congar, their special place in the tradition had two aspects. First, the constitutive elements of church life and church organization were laid down in the New Testament. Secondly, the biblical writings in fact formed the starting point for the further development of faith: according to Congar, the ongoing interpretation of 'the prophetic and apostolic writings' is an important part of the teaching church.[95] Thus he emphasized the special place of the Bible in the church and at the same time embedded the biblical writings in the 'living reality of Christianity'.

Schillebeeckx thought that in this way Congar was in fact returning to the comprehensive concept of tradition in the church fathers. This was still at work in Thomas Aquinas, but in his view, theologians lost sight of it, above all in the controversies after the Reformation.[96] According to the patristic view the tradition was the very life of the church and faith. The documents which had been handed down were then to be seen as attempts by the church to decipher its identity from the past, and therefore the further development of the content of these documents represented the explicitation of the living faith of the church. In Schillebeeckx's view, Congar's approach overcame the constant tendency to set over against the living present what had been institutionalized, laid down and established in the tradition in the past. For Congar, faith still alive here and now did not stand over against the objective tradition, but was its living soul: for him the tradition certainly did not consist only of texts, but equally of the sacraments, the liturgy and the hierarchical structure of the church. Schillebeeckx summed up Congar's view by saying that 'the Holy Spirit is ... like the soul of the tradition' in this broad sense.[97] Thus, this was a view which stood close to the one which he himself had developed in *De sacramentele heilseconomie* and which made it possible to regard the active tradition, the faith as it had already developed, as a living culture, a constantly evolving way of dealing with the tradition and the world.

The leading principle of this culture of dealing with the tradition was the so-called light of faith, the *lumen fidei*, which made it possible for believers to see reality from the perspective of God, or the urging of the Holy Spirit as the working of God in human beings, the *instinctus Spiritus Sancti*, which in Schillebeeckx's eyes, and in his view also in Thomas's eyes, was ultimately the same thing.[98] For him, a statement of faith was an attempt to formulate what is visible of God in the light of faith and also to teach others to see this. Statements of faith were not expressions of objective reality, but forms of 'address'. In a statement of faith one believer invited another to believe what he was imperfectly trying to point to with the help of language, to 'what I signify to him by bearing witness'. This applied not only to contemporary statements of faith but also to those from the past. Thus the tradition changed from being a collection of authoritative definitions to which believers must subject their behaviour and thought into the linguistic expression of attempts of believers to express to others their view of reality in the light of faith; in other words, attempts to teach others to believe (100D).[99]

Here, incidentally, something was also being said about the second question with which Schillebeeckx was very much occupied in his 'Introduction to Theology': the development in the tradition of the faith. Just as with the relationship between Bible and tradition, there was an old and animated discussion on this question. The Catholic Church had always maintained that the faith was fully present in the church from the beginning, but at the same time it was clear that in the course of time doctrine had developed and that some truths of faith were formulated as such at a relatively late date. A return to the Bible or the faith of the early church was ruled out here. Schillebeeckx first demonstrated that this problem was in fact felt only in modern times, and then went on to demonstrate that neo-scholastic attempts to explain the developments of tradition or dogma with reference to conclusions from revealed truths at which theology had already arrived by thought and speculation were inadequate. He then entered into discussion with above all contemporary attempts to understand the development of dogma as the expression of the evolution of living faith.[100] He took up these attempts in his own way, making use of De Petter's idea of 'implicit intuition', which he now connected with Thomas's *lumen fidei*. In his view the light of faith colours experience and ensures that believers experience existence within a religious, Christian horizon. According to Schillebeeckx, this horizon is the living God himself, who is the one whom the Christian tradition is ultimately about. A direct view of this horizon is impossible, he remarked, following De Petter, but this horizon is implicitly known in any knowledge of what is known within this horizon. With the help of this argument he could hold together the abiding identity of faith and the changes in it: faith proves to be the same, in the sense that the horizon proves to be same, but it develops because the experience of faith within this horizon changes. These constantly new experiences also kept giving a different view of the horizon, and in Schillebeeckx's view that made possible a growth of insight into the significance and implications of faith in God and Jesus Christ.[101]

Thus, according to Schillebeeckx it was possible to understand how new insights of faith could come about and new statements of faith could be made which, when the reality of the light of faith converged 'over time ever more markedly on one point', could then be laid down authoritatively by the magisterium. He thought that this had happened with the recent declarations of the dogma of the immaculate conception and the assumption of Mary, but he was not concerned to legitimate relatively recent statements by the magisterium. What was most important for him was that this train of thought made clear the importance of the experience of the believers which in this way emerged as the embodiment of new insights into the divine truth. He stated emphatically that

> in the bosom of the community of faith and sometimes especially of the Catholic lay community, experiences of faith could mature which did not go back to an explicit teaching of the church's magisterium ... the Catholic lay community [can], by virtue of its specifically lay experiences and its lay experience of faith in the world, by degrees illuminate aspects of the deposit of faith and gradually make them ripen into explicit awareness. Thus the Christian lay community is also a vehicle of the active tradition (153).

However, according to Schillebeeckx, to state that the active tradition as conveyed by the Christian lay community was indeed authentic was solely a matter for the hierarchy: he regarded the magisterium of the hierarchical church as the authority which 'on the basis of the charisma of infallibility' authoritatively stated whether 'a particular collective reaction of faith did in fact take place in the power of the light of faith ... and not on a human basis' (147).[102]

Ultimately, in his view what was called the 'development of dogma' was none other than 'the totality itself of the life of faith as determined by its object', effective in the whole church (150).[103] He thought that the written and oral tradition in the church were embraced by 'a *traditio vivens* which *in mysterio* contains the whole content of revelation'. Here a 'collective sense of faith' is at work throughout the church, the experience guided by the light of faith which is ultimately the 'principle of continuity' in the development of the conceptual explicitation of the faith (150f.). This meant a break with the neoscholastic view, which in fact asserted almost the opposite and located the continuity in the formulations and what could be derived from them: in this view faith could only be submission to given formulae. In Schillebeeckx's texts, however, faith appeared as an open, dynamic view of the world.

Concepts of faith and the reality of faith

In fact here we have the third question, which was ultimately most important for the specific character of Schillebeeckx's Louvain synthesis: his view of the relationship between the reality of faith and concepts of faith. In developing this view he directly took up the work of Thomas Aquinas, but read Thomas through the spectacles of De Petter's epistemology.[104]

That he leaned so heavily on Thomas on precisely this question seems connected with the fact that it was very loaded and controversial. In fact since the Council of Trent, the leaders of the church had presented the Catholic faith above all as a doctrine, a doctrinal system which they thought that they had to impose. The church saw this doctrine as a treasury of faith given in the Bible and tradition, but entrusted to the hierarchical church to preserve. Halfway through the nineteenth century this tendency was reinforced and extended. Neoscholastic theology regarded revelation as in fact an 'embryonic theology' – as the theologian George Tyrrell, who was condemned for his 'modernism', put it – from which the theologians under the supervision of the infallible magisterium derived the dogmas and doctrines dialectically.[105] In the fight against the liberal spirit of the time, which was seen as relativistic, the Catholic hierarchy presented itself with increasing firmness as the guardian of a system of absolute truth. In 1950 this ended up with Pius XII's encyclical *Humani generis*, with its condemnation, already mentioned earlier, of 'some theologians' who were said to think that the mysteries of faith 'are never expressed by truly adequate concepts but only by approximate and ever-changeable notions, in which the truth is to some degree expressed, but is necessarily distorted'. According to Pius XII the relativizing of the scholastic form of Catholic theology evidently necessarily led to a relativizing of doctrine itself and to 'a neglect of and even contempt for' the church's teaching office.[106]

For Schillebeeckx, the relationship between concepts of faith and the reality of faith was one of fundamental importance. He began his discussion with a general survey in which he discussed modernism from the beginning of the twentieth century; in his view it had put the problem on the agenda. He investigated the polemics which had developed around the so-called *'nouvelle théologie'* that had come under fire from *Humani generis*.[107] Moreover, he presented at great length to his students – and this was very striking for a Catholic theologian at this time – the work of the Protestant theologian Rudolf Bultmann, who wanted to detach the biblical proclamation from the mythical picture of the world within which it was contained and interpreted it as addressed to the most inward element of human existence: according to Bultmann the central Christian message was that human existence is meaningful in all its fragmentariness (167A-167M).[108] In modernism, the *'nouvelle théologie'* and Bultmann, Schillebeeckx ultimately saw similar attempts to emphasize the saving value of the experience of faith at the expense of the truth-value of the concepts of faith. Over against this he brought forward the opposition of *Humani generis* to such relativism and the emphasis that the encyclical put on the truth-value of concepts. To some degree he identified with the standpoint of the encyclical, but interpreted it above all as a theological duty to outline further for oneself the truth-value of the concepts of faith. For 'without giving a positive solution to the problem, the encyclical indicates ... the limits within which a nuanced solution must be sought' (168f.).

In finding this solution Schillebeeckx relied explicitly on De Petter. According to De Petter's epistemological theory, any judgement was ultimately based on a knowledge of reality as a whole which was implied in the experience of the world and of objects within this world. Any statement, any judgement, isolated an aspect from the implicit intuitive knowledge of totality and as such, compared with concrete reality, was an abstraction and thus inadequate. But at the same time the implicit intuition of reality was expressed by this; in this sense a statement pointed to reality and a verdict had truth value. Along the lines of De Petter, he argued that having an experience was never a matter of coming upon brute factuality but a form of dealing with reality in the midst of the totality of the world, of fathoming out and seeing through this totality by means of a concrete part of it. For Schillebeeckx, following De Petter, experience was therefore also always intellectual experience; the intellectual element of it was expressed, inadequately and only partly, but in a real way, in the concepts with which this experience was expressed. Quoting his teacher with approval, Schillebeeckx argued that

> no concept can be present in knowledge which is not capable of being expressed in one way or another. But on the other hand ... the presence in knowledge of a content and the expression of this same content may not just be identified with one another. A context which is less perfectly expressed will then, although present in knowledge, to a certain degree remain alien to the activity of knowing and incapable of being grasped by it. Rather than grasping it, the epistemological activity will as it were reach out to it from a distance.[109]

Schillebeeckx now transposed this view of human knowledge into the sphere of faith and theology. Through this he was able to do justice both to the value and to the relativity of the concepts of faith.

In his view the concept of faith was not a concept, a dogmatic or doctrinal formulation, but God himself as God of salvation, *Deus salutaris*. Conversely, the concepts of faith were 'the mystery of faith grasped in faith as to a certain degree made conscious in the explicit awareness of faith'. In his view, as an expression of the perception of reality in faith, the conceptuality of faith really 'grasps' something of the content of faith, 'however inadequately', and concepts of faith were 'to some degree transparent to the mystery itself'. In other words, they were 'the experience of faith itself according to the moment of its expression' (177, 179).

Now Schillebeeckx read this back into the texts in which Thomas Aquinas investigated the possibilities of speaking about God in human concepts. This brought him directly into a fundamental discussion with neoscholastic theology, which on the basis of a specific reading of Thomas's discussion of this problem in the *Summa theologiae*, along the lines of the statement by the First Vatican Council that the mind enlightened by faith can gain some insight into the divine mysteries through an analogy with what is naturally known, had developed a very complicated and extremely technical doctrine of this 'analogy'. With ingenious distinctions and lucid analyses, an attempt was made to discover how human language, tailored to creation, could be transferred to God and what the basis of this transfer was.[110] In the footsteps of De Petter and De Petter's teacher Balthasar, Schillebeeckx rejected the idea that the basis of the analogy could be a concept of being which is common to God and creatures.[111] The whole structure of the neoscholastic doctrine of analogy was based on this presupposition, including the classification of the different logical operations which were necessary for transposing a word from one terrain to another. In Schillebeeckx's view, by contrast, the analogy was the expression of an experience in faith of reality itself. In his interpretation, the basis for this experience in Thomas was the participation of the creation in God as creator. The goodness in creation was an emanation of the goodness of the creator God, and creaturely goodness pointed in its inadequacy towards a goodness which transcended it, but in which it shared in its limited, finite way. Believers know – this is the way in which Schillebeeckx, using De Petter's epistemology, interpreted Thomas's answer to the question whether it was possible to make statements about God in human language – God's goodness implicitly through their faith in the goodness of creation that they experience, and can therefore rightly say that God is good. The human concept of the good which is bound up with creation certainly cannot be transferred to God, but anyone who uses the word 'good' in fact intends a reality which is not of this world but can be found in completeness only in God. As origin of the good, God is really on the wavelength of earthly goodness.[112]

Schillebeeckx himself thought that this reading of Thomas in the light of De Petter represented a step forward by comparison with the neoscholastic reading of Thomas in the light of Vatican I:

> It seems to us that this view contains the right perspective for affirming both the absoluteness of the truth of faith and the great margin of relativity and therefore growth in our reflection on the faith ...[113]

The satisfaction which could be heard in these words also had a background in church politics. First of all Schillebeeckx had succeeded in presenting the very authoritative Thomas as a witness to the theory of implicit intuition, a theory which was suspect in the church, as is evident from the measures taken against De Petter in 1942. Secondly, he thought that by his theological adaptation of De Petter's thinking he could do justice to the intention of the church's condemnation of modernism and 'nouvelle théologie', and strangely enough ultimately also to that of the condemnation of De Petter himself. In contrast to the epistemological theory of Maurice Blondel, who was regarded as a modernist, and of Joseph Maréchal, who in his view followed the same lines, in Schillebeeckx's eyes De Petter did not relativize the intellectual importance of concepts. This epistemology made it possible to do justice to the truth-value of concepts of faith and doctrinal statements, and in his interpretation that was precisely the intention of the Roman interventions which ultimately resulted in Humani generis.[114]

But as a third point, Schillebeeckx thought that via De Petter and Thomas he could also resolve the impasse in which theology found itself as a result of ecclesiastical Thomism. For him that was ultimately the most important thing. In his view the neoscholastic over-concentration on conceptuality had led to an 'impoverished theology of faith' in which people had begun to regard the act of faith as something like 'the conclusion of a successful argument'.[115] In this way faith had become completely isolated from experience and thus from the life of believers and the developments in the world in which they lived. Schillebeeckx was convinced that De Petter's epistemology made it possible to break through this isolation and, as we saw, to emphasize how important experience in the world, and thus the 'Christian lay community', was for the development of faith.

Theological reflection on faith as living culture

Ultimately the importance of the view of theology which Schillebeeckx developed with the help of De Petter's philosophy and through Thomas transcended the advantages that it offered in church politics. It made it possible to see faith as 'culture', as a culture-creating activity in the form of a lived-out and knowing way of dealing with reality. In Schillebeeckx's view theology was reflection on this faith as living culture and in this way in a comprehensive sense a 'theology of culture': in his 'Introduction to Theology' he called theology emphatically one of the 'humanities', albeit a 'discipline of a distinctive kind' (218). Statements of faith functioned as a species of moments of intellectual concentration of the living culture of faith as a whole, just as the sacraments were the cultic moments of concentration of it. He regarded judgements of faith as the expressions of specific aspects in concrete terms, but at the same time as expressions of an implicit total acceptance in faith (180). The whole of faith was present and intended in every statement as living contact with God. In his view, the concepts used functioned in the same way as the symbols in the liturgy or the parables in the New Testament: they were time-conditioned and culture-conditioned signs pointing to the mystery that is known in the experience of faith.[116] According to Schillebeeckx, the fact that they were tied to a context did not relativize their importance but gave them their significance as the concentration of living faith on a specific place and time. In his view, what he said explicitly about the official doctrinal statements of the hierarchy, in a language taken directly from his theology of the sacraments, in fact applied to all authentic faith judgements: the descending love of God coincides with the loving response to this love by the believing church. Thus his statements of faith are the confirmation in faith of the 'good news of Christ's redemptive love' and the totality of faith in a particular form (197).[117]

At first sight he was making a reduction here, as with his treatment of the sacraments. In his theology of the sacraments the special character of the seven official sacraments of the Catholic Church was kept out of the discussion, as was their form. The existing sacraments and the form given to them were the starting point for further theological reflection. It was the same with his discussion of the development of the church's explicit awareness of faith out of the legitimacy of the actual development of Catholic doctrine, expressed in the doctrinal statements of the hierarchy. But Schillebeeckx did not only, or even primarily, develop an apologia for the official doctrine of faith, with the recent declaration of the dogma of Mary's assumption as the *pièce de résistance*. The text regularly and clearly expressed the desire to make room for actual dynamic in the awareness of faith, for new insights that were coming to light. To demonstrate that this was in fact possible, he then pointed to the doctrinal development in the recent past which were regarded as authentic.

It was also important that Schillebeeckx tried to make room for the possibility that the doctrine of the church, once accepted, could not just develop further but could also be changed and in certain aspects opposed.

This was an extremely sensitive matter, for here the impression was at least given that the former doctrine contained errors, and that conflicted with the current idea of the infallibility of the church's magisterium.[118] But by locating the truth of concepts and statements in the fact that they expressed conceptually how reality is known in the experience of faith, he could also connect the ongoing developments in the awareness of faith with a growing awareness of the limits of particular intuitions which in themselves point in the right direction. In his view it could gradually become clear that because of the historical conditioning of the conceptual apparatus used, in earlier expressions things were also defined, in the first instance imperceptibly, which on closer inspection had nothing to do with the content of faith or which even proved to be in conflict with it. This then had to be corrected; in this connection he spoke, using a creative term, of 'development as it were by taking away', an *evolutio quasi per subtractionem* (182f.).[119]

For this, Schillebeeckx referred in the first instance to the development of Catholic doctrine as this had taken place: in his view, in the study of the development of dogma the theologian must in fact establish 'evolutions as it were "by subtraction"'. But a number of the examples that he gave made it clear that the notion of an *evolutio quasi per subtractionem* was not completely innocent. Thus he thought that the opposition which had spread widely among Catholic faithful and theologians 'at least twenty years ago' to the view that the human body had arisen by evolution bore witness to an uncritical attitude towards time-conditioned elements in their own beliefs. This verdict was certainly not uncontroversial at the beginning of the 1950s, though it remained well within the limits of the talk about evolution which were set by *Humani generis*.[120] This applied to Schillebeeckx's suggestion that the mediaeval doctrine of the two swords put forward by Boniface VIII (1294–1303) should definitively be abandoned. According to this doctrine, the church had received through Christ from God's hand both the spiritual and the worldly power – symbolized by the two swords spoken of in Luke 22.38. It gave the latter to the emperor, who was thus to exercise power in the name of the church. This doctrine no longer had any direct practical significance, but in the 1950s to a certain degree it still underlay the attitude of the Catholic Church towards states. For example, it influenced the official Catholic standpoint that the task of the state was to facilitate access to the spiritual goods controlled by the church. In 1955 Pius XII was certainly to contrast Leo XIII's doctrine that church and state are sovereign, each in its own sphere, with the mediaeval doctrine of two swords, which he called 'a child of the time', but only in the documents of the Second Vatican Council was the church really to work out a different view of its relationship to the state.[121] Schillebeeckx's statement that the conceptual content of the doctrine of purgatory had nothing to do with the 'whole phantasmagoria of a pool of fire' was not revolutionary, but it was nevertheless striking by comparison with the preaching still customary in the 1950s.[122] Finally, to take leave of the confusion 'among many contemporary Christians between Christianity, capitalism and the bourgeoisie', as Schillebeeckx did, was by no means as customary at the beginning of the 1950s as it was around twenty years later.

But Schillebeeckx went a good step further, a step in which he in fact distinguished in principle between the doctrine of the church as laid down in decisions of the magisterium and Catholic theology. In the 1950s this was extremely unusual, but Schillebeeckx does not seem to have been fully aware of the far-reaching consequences of his standpoint.

Having described the origin of the contemporary term 'dogma' as a solemn proclamation by the hierarchy that particular doctrines were authentic expressions of Catholic teaching, and having made it clear that this concept of dogma had not always existed in the church (192–7), Schillebeeckx stated that definitions of dogma in this sense were usually reactions to images which were regarded as heretical.[123] The foundation of a heresy was usually a Christian truth of faith, but 'detached from the totality of dogma' and as it were set at too great a distance and interpreted in too one-sided a way. However, in reaction an anti-heretical definition of dogma put the emphasis specifically on the aspects of faith which were denied by the heresy, and therefore had a tendency to distance itself from the truth of faith on which the heresy was based. 'A theology which is only "dogmatic"', in other words a theology which is 'only based on what in fact is declared dogma', therefore threatens to become one-sided. 'Integral Christianity is not anti-Nestorian, anti-Lutheran, anti-modernist' but a 'positive acceptance of the totality of faith' (196).[124] Therefore, in his view the church's explicit statements of faith could not just be regarded as the starting point of theology, as was customary in neoscholasticism. As an alternative he proposed that theology should be based in a specific sense on what according to Thomas Aquinas were 'the articles of faith'.

Traditionally, an article of faith – *articulus fidei* – was understood to be one of the twelve sections into which the Christian creed was divided. Now in his Louvain lectures Schillebeeckx stated that in Thomas the word 'article of faith' took on a rather different meaning during his theological development and that in a sense he dissociated himself from the pure factuality of the creed. 'Materially he was still concerned with the twelve articles of faith', but Thomas went on to look for 'the ground inherent in the facts of faith', the reason why these particular twelve articles should have been included in the creed (198f.). Schillebeeckx pointed out that Thomas connected the word 'article' with the Greek word *arthron*, 'arm', and on the basis of this regarded the articles of faith as joints, hinges of faith. For Thomas they were ultimately underivable statements of faith from which all other formulations of faith flowed. According to Thomas, these statements were essential parts of the articles of faith which expressed either the means by which we participate in eternal life – the statements about God – or how we are brought to that eternal life – the statements about salvation history and the stipulations for human action which flow from it. Schillebeeckx concluded from this that in Thomas's view the *articuli fidei* are the elementary and central saving truths of Christian faith, in their mutual interconnection (200f.).[125]

As a man of the Middle Ages, according to Schillebeeckx Thomas still thought that the creed which in the tradition is called 'the Apostles' Creed' was really a summary of faith by the apostles themselves. However, a twentieth-century theologian could not fail to know that this creed had grown up in history, with all the chance characteristics and one-sidednesses that this involved. So from then on there was 'something forced and artificial' in the connection between Thomas's normative idea of the 'article of faith' as an element that bound faith together and the twelve articles of the Apostles' Creed which had in fact been handed down. According to Schillebeeckx, it was no longer possible to see the articles of faith, in the sense in which Thomas understood them, as just given. In his view 'a synthesis of faith which theology must be able to draw on from as exhaustive as possible a survey of the whole of the tradition of faith' was the only thing that did justice to Thomas's description of a coherent whole of '*articuli fidei*' which expressed the basic truths of the faith. The two core elements in the synthesis were God as the basis of human salvation and the saving history handed down in the Bible and tradition as access to this. It was a matter of God's hiddenness and the mystery of the humanity of Christ, of the 'temporal system of salvation as directly concerning the *mysterion* of the divine realities within us', 'the temporal economy of salvation with the Trinity as its eternal background' (202f.).[126]

With this interpretation of what Thomas said about the *articuli fidei*, Schillebeeckx was in fact bringing about a quiet revolution in the Catholic concept of theology. As a result, theology came to be much more loosely connected with the statements of the magisterium than had been customary hitherto. Schillebeeckx continued explicitly to emphasize that theology as 'thought bound up with faith' always presupposed a 'reference to the magisterium', and in practice behaved completely consistently with this. Nevertheless he noted that the constant reaction of the magisterium to doctrinal deviations had given rise to a distinctive theology of the magisterium, with its own one-sidednesses. In his view it was the task of the theologian not to reproduce these one-sidednesses, but to correct them in the light of as complete as possible an investigation of the data of the faith in the tradition (228 and 196f. respectively). The notion actually implied here that theology has a critical function over against the magisterium of the hierarchy was unprecedented in the 1950s. But the ultimate consequences of what Schillebeeckx was saying about theology were even more radical. By comparison with what was current in the 1950s, in fact the whole basis of doing theology shifted. With his view of the *articuli fidei* he broke with the presupposition that theology should be based on a collection of normative truths which were already given. The starting point for theology was the tradition of faith as a whole, and the synthesis of faith implied in it. The *articuli fidei* in the normative sense were no longer the starting point for doing theology, but in Schillebeeckx's view in fact had to be discovered in the doing of theology. It was the task of the theologian to look at the connection between the facts of faith, to see them as 'one synthesis, which in human reflective knowledge is the recasting of Christ's view of salvation' (226f.).[127]

During his Louvain period Schillebeeckx continued to presuppose that this synthesis was indeed implicit in the Catholic tradition and not the free creation of the theologian. In this way he maintained the traditional notion that the task of theology is to unfold the implications of the revelation which it has received, a revelation which, however, is given only in the living tradition of faith that runs through to the past. Only critical discernment can therefore trace the divine truth. Schillebeeckx saw theology as a service to the church as a living culture of faith, focused on its contemporary and future form. In his view theology was an 'organ of the church's life'; it was 'the human critical authority of church life, of the church's preaching, of spiritual life, etc.' (258–60).[128] Just as human culture was, in Schillebeeckx's view, reflected in philosophy, so the culture of faith in the church was reflected in theology, and to a large degree with the same means (227). Thus, theology was a reflection on faith 'in search of the living God', the title that he was to give to his inaugural lecture in Nijmegen. In faith, in his view, the earthly 'world of man's history-making freedom is now taken into a personal living relationship with God', and the theologian needs to reflect on that move.[129]

In the experience of many of his students from his Flemish period and the beginning of his time in Nijmegen, this basic conviction gave Schillebeeckx's theologizing a dynamic which the work of other theologians usually lacked. By comparison with the rigidity of neoscholasticism, his theology was extremely exciting, and working along his lines made it possible to discover new and surprising things when doing theology. However, as long as the existing church culture continued firmly to shut itself off from the world, and 'personal relations with God' in the Catholic world were largely homogenous, the radical consequences of this view of theology which he had developed were largely hidden. Only when with the Second Vatican Council the question of the most adequate form of Catholicism in the present and the future was raised, did the space offered by his theology open up to the full.

The mystery of Christ: a synthesis of nature and supernature

'As a science of revelation, theology ... is a christology which nevertheless remains theology.' With this sentence in the introduction to his lecture notes on christology Schillebeeckx showed his students how important he thought the content to be. In the theology of the Louvain Schillebeeckx, Jesus Christ ultimately embodied the synthesis of nature and the supernatural which was the deepest source of Christian faith, which it constantly actualized, and for which it ultimately hoped. According to Schillebeeckx, theology in the sense in which he understood it, in other words as dealing with God as the God of human salvation, was possible only as reflection on Christ:

> The character of 'our direct attainment' of God's divinity is manifested to us meaningfully by the incarnation of God, that is, by the appearance of God in our time and in gestures and forms which belong to our human, earthly reality. In Christ it proves that God is *totus in suis, totus in nostris,* the God who is interested in all things. In Christ, God shows himself to us as really at home in our earthly human world, so that we may be at home in the divine reality. Revelation is essentially the sanctifying manifestation of the divine reality of salvation in Christ ... (IV).[130]

In the lecture notes on christology which have been handed on in a text dated to the academic year 1953–4, he tried to demonstrate that the core of christology is the merciful and redemptive love of God – 'the redemptive incarnation shows us the true face of God: *Deus caritas est*' – over against sinful humankind. Here Schillebeeckx was convinced that the same love was to be found which at its deepest was also the origin of creation and which ensured that the natural order was directed to the supernatural.[131]

Schillebeeckx thought that first he had to draw the picture of Christ from tradition, so that contemporary men and women – 'we' – could 'reflect on that mystery of salvation in faith ... with all our intellectual culture'. It is evident from his introduction that his plan was first of all to rethink Thomas Aquinas's theological synthesis on the point of christology in order then 'on the basis of a broad positive theology to rediscover its sources and enrich it, and thus arrive at a perhaps deepened speculative synthesis'. In fact, however, in his lecture notes he did not arrive at such a new synthesis. The 'analytical reflection on the mystery of Christ, on the basis of St Thomas in the light of the ongoing tradition and the problems of today' filled by far the greatest part of the manuscript, and the integration of data from the tradition which had been forgotten or underestimated was largely omitted. In his christology in particular, he remained quite close to Thomas, although the contemporary theological discussions and questions left a clear stamp on the way in which he read Thomas's christology.

233

For example, Schillebeeckx went at length into the nature of Jesus's consciousness and psychology, a question which did not really play a role for Thomas, but which, halfway through the twentieth century, was an important point of discussion in theology.[132] For a long time Christ was described in theology above all as Son of God, second person of the divine Trinity. Usually people argued from this that as God-man he also shared completely in the divine knowledge: Jesus was said to have had God's knowledge of the world, of his fellow human beings, of the course of the history of salvation and of the nature of God. In the nineteenth and twentieth centuries this notion encountered increasing opposition.[133] There was an increasingly acute awareness that the biblical narratives presented Jesus as first of all a human being, with all the limitations in knowledge, emotions, wonder and possibilities of experiencing and learning new things which that involved. Within the traditional framework of theological thought this could really only be understood as a kind of divine masquerade, an 'acting as if' on the part of Jesus. For an increasing number of theologians this was unsatisfactory. The church's hierarchy was, however, vigorously opposed to everything that in its eyes infringed the exalted nature of Jesus Christ and his unity with God, for this similarly seemed to infringe the infallible truth of what he had said and taught, which the church regarded as the legacy that it had received from him. On a number of occasions the leadership of the church condemned attempts to relativize the significance of Jesus's direct view of God and innate knowledge of the world for his human life.[134] However, theologians who made these attempts emphatically defended Jesus's true humanity and from their side emphasized that it was of great importance to take this with the utmost seriousness.

Schillebeeckx attacked very fiercely the tendency to emphasize Christ's deity at the expense of his humanity, which was still very strong in the 1950s.

[Jesus] acted as an ordinary Palestinian of the time – which is what he was. His judgement on the nature of the sickness of the people who were brought to him was the same as that of other Jews, and medically perhaps quite incorrect, but he healed with other means and purposes than a doctor! ... I do not believe that when – like any carpenter – he was struggling with a recalcitrant, stubborn plank his *visio beata* or *scientia infusa* suddenly gave him a hand, so that he could slyly wink at his amazed teacher. That is not gospel, but apocrypha (II, 242).

Over against this 'apocrypha' he emphasized that the incarnation of the second divine person was real and complete. Certainly in his view the human activity of Jesus Christ was 'the divine life itself', but it was this life wholly in human form: 'an exercise of the Godhead in and according to the human-ity'. For Schillebeeckx this implied that from the human side Jesus's self-

234

awareness awoke 'in precisely the same way in which our self-awareness awakens', in other words by experience and action in the world. In his view, this was 'the breakthrough ... in human awareness of his divine self-awareness that was already present' (II, 256). In other words, the incarnation of God in Christ did not take place at a single moment but came about 'through the growing humanity of Christ'. In Schillebeeckx's view the breakthrough of Christ's divine self-awareness in Jesus's human self-awareness was an ongoing incarnation (II, 161f.).[135]

Thus, for Schillebeeckx the human being Jesus and his life, his words and actions – in the Thomistic tradition called *mysteria carnis* – were of fundamental theological importance even in the 1950s.[136] It is obvious that here we should see a foretaste of the extensive attention that he was to pay to the historical man Jesus in the 1970s. In his Louvain lectures he already gave a summary sketch of Jesus's person and activity, including his activity as a 'holy, religious man', and thus in fact as an exemplary believer who has to be followed by other believers. In summing up the picture of Jesus that he had given he quoted Karl Adam with approval: 'No man understood so profoundly the old biblical saying, "You shall love the Lord your God with all your heart and all your soul and all your mind"' (II, 118f.).[137] But in the 1950s the focal point of christology was clearly elsewhere than in the 1970s. In *Jesus* in 1974 and *Christ* in 1977 Schillebeeckx wanted to make clear to contemporary men and women the relevance and significance of Jesus's message, and thus that of the God whom he proclaimed. In the Louvain lecture notes, too, he stated that the Christian significance of the statement 'God is good' can be seen from 'the good man Jesus' who was the epiphany 'of the divine goodness in earthly visibility'.[138] But in the 1950s the emphasis did not lie on an analysis of the goodness which took shape in Jesus's life. Central to Schillebeeckx's Louvain lectures on christology was the conviction that through theological analysis of the mystery of Christ it was ultimately possible to reach 'the human heart of God himself'. It was of fundamental importance to him that in Jesus Christ God becomes visible as the most profoundly human God, involved in human history, a *Deus humanissimus* (II, 266).[139]

Specifically in order to fathom God's involvement with human beings, Schillebeeckx steeped himself in Thomas's christology, where Thomas tried to grasp the saving significance of the dogma that Christ is one person in two natures, God and man. Probably thinking of his students, who found it difficult to imagine that this abstract doctrinal statement, with which, moreover, they had been routinely familiar since their youth, could have any existential value, surprisingly he began with a quotation from Martin Luther. Luther suggested that the speculative-theological constitution of Christ had no saving significance whatsoever; this is how Schillebeeckx translated Luther's lamentations:

Christ has two natures. What concern is that of mine? ... that he consecrated himself to his ministry and poured out his love as my redeemer and saviour, therein lies my comfort and my salvation ... Believing in Christ does not mean that Christ is one person who is God and man at the same time; that doesn't help anyone! To believe in Christ means to believe that this person is 'Christ', that is, that he went out before us from God and came into our world (II, 115).[140]

At this point, too, Schillebeeckx remained faithful to his basic conviction that 'the value of dogma' for life ultimately lay in 'its meaningful truth value'. Over against Luther he stated that the correct understanding of what is technically called the hypostatic union of the human and divine nature in Christ is 'fundamentally none other than a deeper fathoming of the very meaning of our redemption' (ibid.).[141] In his view, that Christ was God and man expressed the significance of the Christian redemption. Convinced of this, he thought that he was supported by Thomas, in whose christology he believed that the question of the meaning of the incarnation, its redemptive significance, came first. Fathoming the nature and possibility of the union of the two persons in the one person of Christ was not a matter of understanding a 'purely metaphysical problem' but of fathoming God's 'faithful human love which stops at nothing' (II, 4).

According to Schillebeeckx, it was especially where Thomas spoke of 'the meaning (*convenientia*) of the incarnation', at the beginning of the third part of his *Summa theologiae*, that he demonstrated how he approached the mystery of the incarnation of God in Christ.[142] First of all he expounded the logic of the incarnation as in his view this applied from God's side. It was evident from the whole creation how much God in his deepest being is self-giving love, *bonitas subsistens,* in Schillebeeckx's words, 'sheer giving self-communication' and 'lavish generosity'. Now incarnation is the most radical form of surrender and self-communication, and since according to Thomas God is the *summum bonum,* this *summum* of self-giving love was very appropriate for God. According to Schillebeeckx, the importance of this argument emerged only when it was read, so to speak, across the grain. Then it proved that the incarnation made clear to Thomas that 'God's love for man' as a consequence of 'God's loving nature' was the root and core of faith and theology, and everything turned on it (II, 5–8).[143] Next, according to Schillebeeckx, Thomas analysed the human significance of the incarnation as liberation from the sinful situation in which human beings were imprisoned. It offered a basis for the human desire to return to God from this situation of alienation from God: 'As man, Christ is our way to God.'[144]

But Schillebeeckx directed his attention above all to the third point of Thomas's treatment of the incarnation. Here he considered what at first sight was the very abstract and speculative question of whether the incarnation would have taken place even if 'Adam had not sinned', in other words, if the Fall had not taken place and human beings had therefore not lived in sinfulness from which they had to be freed. From as early as the church fathers this question had led to great differences of opinion between Eastern and Western Christianity. In fact the correct concept of redemption was at stake. Did the redemption on which Christian faith turned at the outset bring about the redemption of humankind from sin, or did it first of all have to be understood as its exaltation to God, as deification? On Schillebeeckx's reading, Thomas tried to adopt a kind of intermediate position on this question. Because the biblical writings indicated so abundantly clearly that the sin of the first human being was the reason for the incarnation, he thought that a negative answer to the question whether the incarnation would have taken place even without the sin would be advisable. But at the same time he made it clear that the incarnation was more than the restoration of the situation before the Fall. As Paul showed, God allowed the evil so that something better should come from it (cf. Rom. 5.20).

After Thomas, the different solutions to this question were to divide the two main schools in Catholic theology, the Thomists and the Scotists. The Franciscan theologian John Duns Scotus, who came from Scotland (c.1265–1308), began from the conviction that the incarnation was God's supreme action, and thus the highest action conceivable. Since according to mediaeval metaphysics dependence meant imperfection, this conviction led him to the conclusion that the incarnation could not be dependent on anything else, even the Fall. Duns Scotus, Schillebeeckx said, saw Christ above all as the 'crowning fruit of the creation and holy *par excellence*' (II, 26). In his lecture notes, Schillebeeckx went at length into the origin of the dispute between Thomists and Scotists. He stated that the Bible and the church fathers knew no opposition between Christ as the redeemer from sin and as the crowning fruit of creation: both notions played a role. There was ongoing emphasis on the effect of the incarnation in redemption from sin, but likewise he started from the standpoint that everything was created in Christ and with a view to him.[145] Schillebeeckx described Thomas's standpoint at length: he investigated the changes that Thomas underwent in the course of his life and also explained Scotus's standpoint in a differentiated way. He demonstrated that the views of the two theologians were not as diametrically opposed as the later formation of schools might suggest; that for Thomas, too, Christ was the crown of creation; and that Scotus, too, saw him, the holy one *par excellence*, at the same time as the head of a humanity given grace and redeemed from sin.[146] Nevertheless, Schillebeeckx thought that the standpoint of Thomists and Scotists were ultimately irreconcilable, and resolutely opted for the Thomistic view. Although it was hardly conceivable that as a Dominican he could make any other choice, the reason he gave for this was striking. In his view Thomas could do more justice to the historical situation of Jesus Christ and his history. For Schillebeeckx it was a fundamental inconsistency that God should have willed that Christ 'as "the man of sorrows" ... has to die on the cross' not because of sin, but as an end in itself, purely as the supreme expression of God's goodness. Schillebeeckx did not say so in as many words, but evidently already in the 1950s he was convinced that the *Deus salutaris* could not want any human suffering. For him Christ was 'the crowning fruit of the whole of creation', but as the one who has died for the redemption of sinful human beings and thus has become head of the new humanity (II, 26).

Schillebeeckx's intensive study of the dispute between Thomists and Scotists led him to conclude that theology was about Christ 'as "*capax humanitatis*" and not as ontologically a *summum*-being regarded in himself' (II, 29). Specifically in his concrete history and its effect on human beings, in his view Jesus Christ was the supreme expression of God's self-communicating goodness, which was also the deepest ground of all creation. For him the incarnation made it clear that, as God, God is bound up in his very being with our human history (II, 31).[147] Herein lay the saving significance of the dogma of the incarnation: in his eyes this divine bond constituted human redemption at its deepest.

The primordial sacrament of the *Deus humanissimus*

Thus for Schillebeeckx, that God had truly become man in Christ indicated that God is pre-eminently a human God, a *Deus humanissimus*. Therefore, in his discussion of the classic doctrine of the hypostatic union of two natures in one person he put all the emphasis on the incarnation. Contrary to the custom of regarding Christ as ultimately and above all a divine person, and tending to avoid the designation 'human person' for him, Schillebeeckx sketched him as 'truly man ... in a divine way'. In his view, it was precisely thus that Christ's human existence was the 'expression of divine life in human actions' and his whole history up to and including the crucifixion embodied 'God really becoming human' (II, 126 and 132f.).

In elaborating this view, he again leaned heavily on the work of Thomas Aquinas. He almost suggested that at the end of the day Thomas was the only theologian who really, consistently and in a satisfactory way had avoided the two deviations from orthodox christology which always threatened: confusion and division of the divine and human nature in Christ, which according to the dogma of Chalcedon were unconfused and undivided.[148] In his lecture notes Schillebeeckx went into a long and complicated discussion of Thomas's terminology, especially the different terms relating to personhood; he concluded that Thomas would not see person and nature as detached from each other. A human person had a human nature, but a human being was an individual by being a person and could only exist as a person (II, 76–99). He read in Thomas's christological texts that the second person in Jesus Christ existed in his divine character precisely by making his human nature a person. He adopted this notion. On the one hand, in this way human nature is taken up into the second divine person – the Son or the Word – as the orthodox standpoint wanted. On the other hand, according to this train of thought the human nature really existed as a human person, without one having in fact to assume that there were two persons in Christ, one divine and one human. The human person is personified by the divine Word; the 'person function' of this man is 'exercised by the divine person itself'. In other words, Schillebeeckx was convinced that Jesus Christ was man in a divine way. But what was really even more important in his Louvain synthesis was the opposite notion, which finally formed the basis of his view of God, as *Deus humanissimus*. At its deepest a 'humanization of God' took place in Christ: 'God himself is man', and allows himself to be known as God in the form of a concrete human life (II, 102f., 120–5).[149]

In the theology of the Louvain Schillebeeckx, this meant that Christ is a special sacrament, the primordial sacrament of the encounter with God, the sacrament in which the divine and human reality are bound together in the most intimate way: he spoke of a 'hypostatic sacrament' (II, 125). This first of all implied that Jesus Christ in his history was 'the manifestation and revelation of God', a thought which he was to formulate around ten years later like this:

> The form of God's revelation is the man Jesus. God's being reveals itself in the humanity of Jesus. We must not look behind, above or below the man Jesus for his being God. The divinity must itself be evident in his humanity ... Jesus's human form is the revelation of God.[150]

Conversely, however, this also meant that Jesus's humanity was taken up into God. In this way his human actions were removed from their human limitations, took on universal validity and lived on in the sacraments.[151] It was as God the Son that he led the life of someone who was wholly and utterly filled with grace, as Schillebeeckx said, following Thomas, and thus also with virtue (II,172–8).[152] This perfection made him the supreme representative of humankind; all human beings were called to fellowship with God and to virtuous living. By sharing in the human situation and as a fellow human being realizing human existence in the best possible way, through and in his life Jesus created new, redeemed and redemptive possibilities which could then be shared with others. Thus not only was he himself filled with grace, but as such he was also the source of grace, to quote the classical expression. By becoming human to the extreme as divine Word and unreservedly entering the human situation of sin and taking it upon himself, according to Schillebeeckx he becomes 'representative of the whole sinful human race' and thus 'head of all men, both saints and sinners'. In his view Jesus's humanity primarily meant a universal offer of redemption, 'the offer of divine life to all men' (II, 178–94).[153] This conviction matched the basic method of the whole of Schillebeeckx's Louvain theology. Its starting point was that while revelation could not be derived from natural human life, this natural life – and the philosophical analysis demonstrated this quite clearly – did in fact make revelation comprehensibility as an offer of salvation. It was the task of theology to bring out this comprehensibility.[154] In his view that evidently also applied to the focal point of revelation in the Christian sense, Jesus Christ himself.

In reaction to Jesus's 'offer of divine life to all men', according to Schillebeeckx the church came into being as the fellowship which is animated by what he called an 'incarnate spirituality'. This meant that it lived by contact with the continuations of Christ's incarnate divine existence, 'his living relics here on earth: the seven sacraments' (II, 202f.).[155] As we saw, for Schillebeeckx the basis of the sacramental life was the concrete event of Jesus's life, death and resurrection, his *mysteria carnis*. It was here that the supreme worship of God the Father took form, 'lived out in our universal human and concrete situations in life', and in this way orientated on the whole of the human community. Jesus's life resulted in his own self-surrender to death, a death which Schillebeeckx interpreted as being on the one hand a dying to sin, and thus a supreme solidarity with humankind, living under sin and suffering under its consequences. On the other hand, Jesus's voluntary surrender was the perfect offering of himself to God. As presented by the Louvain treatise, Jesus gave up his life and thus allowed 'God to be really . . . God'. In the resurrection this sacrifice is accepted by the Father, and as head of fallen humankind Christ then becomes head of redeemed humankind, directly bound up with God and sitting at God's right hand. Because Christ was truly human and formed part of human history, and therefore human history also formed part of him, according to Schillebeeckx human beings could then enter into the mystery of his life through faith and the sacraments, and follow and take part in his ascent to God. In this way they shared in his redeemed glory.[156]

Thus everything came together, and christology proved to be the basis of Schillebeeckx's Louvain synthesis. Being a Christian becomes visible as being human as a result of and with a view to redemption; the church becomes the place where the new way of being human which has become possible through redemption takes form in the world. Under the influence of the discussion about the relationship between church and world which was to take place during the Second Vatican Council, especially in view of what was finally to become the Pastoral Constitution *Gaudium et spes*, Schillebeeckx was constantly to stress the notion that the whole of human history is taken up in God. To give form to life in this history is to give form to life with God in the light of this conviction. Thus Schillebeeckx's speculations on the union of God and man in Jesus Christ laid the foundation for a view in which the effect on human culture is seen to be of fundamental theological importance:

> The 'hypostatic union' [of the divine and human nature] of Christ, on whose riches we can draw, teaches us that the whole of the history of mankind is contained in the love of God. The history of this world is therefore not sacralized, because it preserves its specific quality, but sanctified, included in the absolute and gratuitous presence of the mystery.

In this notion, which dates from 1964, life in the world was 'a distinctive, non-sacral, but sanctified expression of man's living community with the living God'. For its part, the church 'with her communal confession of faith, her worship and her sacraments, is the set-apart, sacral expression of this'.[157]

Both on the way to God and united with God

According to Schillebeeckx's Louvain theology, the hypostatic union of the divine and human nature in Christ meant that at the same time he was on the way to God, like all other human beings, and *in* so doing was already united with God; he was *simul viator et comprehensor*.[158] Or – a better way of putting – as *viator* he was *comprehensor*; as a human person on the way to union with God, and precisely by being on the way, he was united with his destiny and one with God his Father. In Schillebeeckx's view that was redemptive, because it made it possible for other people, after him and in his footsteps, also to be united with God in the midst of life and on the way to God. Christ made it possible to be redeemed on the way to redemption. With this view, which he worked out in his lecture notes on eschatology, Schillebeeckx maintained the classic notion that the life of the believer is a redeemed life, but at the same time he could dissociate himself from the triumphalism which saw the Catholic Church as the embodiment of redemption and regarded it as withdrawn from the unredeemed state of the rest of humankind. In fact the lecture notes on eschatology were at the same time a theology of man, a theological anthropology and a theology of redemption, a soteriology.[159]

According to Schillebeeckx, the problem of eschatology was that its origin had been lost sight of in the course of the history of theology. Scholasticism had turned the doctrine of 'the last things' into speculation about heaven, hell and purgatory as independent realities, and had paid no attention to the origin of these ideas. Schillebeeckx was by no means alone in this judgement; around the time when he was giving his lectures in Louvain, his Dutch fellow-Dominican I. W. Driessen pointed out that the biblical view of eschatology differed fundamentally from that of the 'current theological textbook'. This was to the detriment of theology, because according to Driessen the least essential additions theology had made to the biblical data were in the treatise on eschatology. Scholasticism had put central biblical data in second place, while secondary matters – 'like purgatory and the nature of the risen body' – were discussed at length.[160] On the basis of a similar assessment, in his lectures on eschatology Schillebeeckx went back to the New Testament notions of the ultimate future of human beings and the cosmos. He reduced them to a twofold origin: the apocalyptic tradition and the tradition which would ultimately issue in rabbinic Judaism (253).[161] In his view, the notions of apocalyptic – cosmic disasters at the end of this age and at the same time the birth pangs of a new age, a new heaven and a new earth – and those of rabbinic Judaism on a divine judgement on human life and the retribution of moral actions after death both came from ultimately the same desire: to connect actual existence and all that belonged to it, its suffering and trials and moral dilemmas, with God.

But in his discussion of eschatology Schillebeeckx did not avoid theological speculations either. He made no attempt to return to an original biblical view. As always, he was concerned to discover what theologians had tried to say in the past. In his view it was the task of the theologian to understand them and thus to renew theology from within. Here the personalistic anthropology that he had borrowed from De Petter was an important support, not in terms of content, but formally. In his view this made it possible to regard the concrete life of human beings in the world, which at the same time was always bodily and spiritual, as the starting point and goal of every theological notion. As we saw, in Schillebeeckx's view every theological statement was made as an imperfect but real expression of an intuition implicitly present in the life of believers, an attempt to fathom the existence of the believer in faith. By thus investigating statements of faith from the past he regularly succeeded in illuminating the logic hidden behind the multiplicity of technical theological distinctions, thus giving a new view of the relevance of the great theological themes.

Theologically his starting point was that eschatology was not primarily about life after death or events at the end of history. According to him, the whole idea of the 'last things' had taken on a specific emphasis in Christianity as a result of the conviction that in Christ the ultimate determination of man was already present among us 'by way of a prelude':

Our treatise begins with Christ, the eschaton. We confirm that with [Christ as] the kyrios [after his resurrection and glorification] eschatological times have already begun. Thus the eschata are already a reality, but have different phases. What happens after that is the continuation in our created world of what in Christ is already reality: the kingdom of God [2f.].[162]

This made it possible to regard heaven, hell and purgatory as images of a final outcome of human existence, images that shed new light on that existence. Heaven, hell and purgatory were a kind of summary of the corresponding human project of life and earthly life in God's grace. Schillebeeckx regarded the so-called blessed vision of God – *visio beata* – in heaven by the souls of the righteous departed and the resurrection of the body at the end of time as different phases in a development of increasing fellowship with God in Christ.[163]

Schillebeeckx began his lectures on eschatology with a discussion of the so-called dispute over grace. He went at length into the discussions on the relationship between God's grace and the human effort which must be made to get to heaven, and the related question of the divine election of some to eternal bliss and the damnation of others.[164] As always, so too in his eschatology, Schillebeeckx wanted to be faithful to Thomas Aquinas, and in this case especially to his basic intuition that divine grace determined everything in the history of the redemption of human beings and the world. He showed how the whole of thought about grace in Catholic theology had taken a wrong turn in the dispute with the Reformation, as a result of which it lost sight of the fact that redemption was ultimately about a qualitatively new bond between human beings and God.

The conviction that the whole Counter-Reformation dispute over grace was based on the wrong starting points did not prevent him from resolutely taking sides. He strongly opposed the efforts of the Jesuit Luis de Molina (1535–1600) to distinguish between God's grace and the free human response and sided with Domingo Báñez (1528–1604), the most important Dominican opponent of so-called Molinism. In Schillebeeckx's view, Báñez 'fundamentally' handed on Thomas's teachings in his work, but 'in and through a polemic (in the spirit of the time) which is formulated in such a conceptualistic and technical way that the subtle spirit of St Thomas gets a little breathless as a result' (125).[165] In his discussion of the positions of Molina and Báñez, Schillebeeckx was intent on rejecting any suggestion that God and man were or could be in any way rivals. God, fellowship with God, was the purpose of human life, and in his view grace was the human choice which realized this fellowship, a choice which was a gift of God, but from the human perspective at the same time remained completely free. The dispute over grace between Molina and Báñez turned on the question of how human freedom and God's power could go together, but according to

Schillebeeckx that was the wrong question. He had learned from Thomas that God's creative and redemptive activity was the basis and support of human freedom and not its rival. Fellowship with God was a personal fellowship based on God's love, and love 'does not compel, does not force, does not "predetermine"', but 'calls, woos, invites'; therefore, fellowship with God was necessarily free (149). So man's freedom in relation to God did not comprise an arbitrary choice to do one thing or the other. At the deepest level it was a freedom to choose the good and to choose God without compulsion from outside, in other words on the basis of inner conviction and out of the goodness and Godness of God himself (144–6). Schillebeeckx was convinced that freedom in this sense was not the rival of divine grace but its fruit, and the effect of redemption in Christ. It was Báñez's emphasis on the comprehensive significance of God's grace that led Schillebeeckx to opt for his position.

Schillebeeckx attached so much importance to the comprehensive understanding of grace because he wanted to see human life in the world and faith as an interconnected whole. In the end, the human choice for God in a religious perspective was implied by the way in which human culture dealt with the world. As he saw it, God's final judgement on the history of the individual and human history as a whole was not based on a kind of book-keeping which took account of specific religious actions, but was what he called a 'resounding of final history'. Individual or collective history was recapitulated in this. Judgement, as he put it with a term borrowed from existentialism, was about the endorsement of the 'fundamental option' for or against fellowship with God which was embodied in the personal project of a person's life (142). Turning to God is confirmed or, if it has not taken place, is definitively ruled out. In other words, in Schillebeeckx's view believers, like Christ, were redeemed on the way to redemption: definitive redemption was the unveiling of what had happened on the way to this redemption.

Heaven, hell and purgatory

This represented an important correction to the traditional theology of 'the last things'.[166] In Schillebeeckx's approach, the starting point for all thought about the last things was the concrete human person as a whole, as a unity of spirit and body; he consistently opposed any tendency to introduce a division between soul and body. In his view human existence was an embodied existence, and that continued to apply, even in theological reflection on ongoing human existence after death. Over against what he called a Platonic interpretation of human existence before and after death, he therefore argued for an 'existentialistic' view, a view 'which regards human beings as spirits which are in the world through their own corporeality'. Here he took up the Aristotelian elements in the thought of Thomas Aquinas which were more strongly orientated on the bodily side of existence than the Platonism which had hitherto been dominant in theology. But in his view Aristotelianism, too, fell short.

In his lectures on eschatology he wanted to allow himself primarily to be guided 'by the data of revelation and on the other hand the datum "human reality" as spirit which through its own corporeality lives with fellow human beings in an earthly world and thus not as a "soul imprisoned by the body"'. In his view, this last image was the hidden starting point of much theology about 'the last things'. As in the rest of his theology, he was concerned 'throughout the reflection [to] allow himself to be guided by the kerygma, the word of God living in the church', but in such a way that 'we try to clarify the inner meaning or the comprehensibility of this revelation event by means of an interpretation of man founded on phenomenology and philosophy' (5f.).[167] His existentialistic-phenomenological view of human existence led him to break completely with the influential and tenacious notion that the dying of the body meant the liberation of the immortal soul from the mortal body and a first step towards heaven. 'Dying *as such* brings no greater nearness to God than here on earth; on the contrary,' he remarked: death was a catastrophe which happened to human beings in their bodies, but which through the body also affected the soul. For him, the immediate vision of God enjoyed by the departed righteous in heaven certainly meant that hope had given place 'to the secure possession of God', but as long as the last judgement, the resurrection of the body and a new heaven and earth were still to come, their situation was still incomplete. For the 'divinization [did] not yet involve the integral human subject', but still only the departed soul (274).[168] In this last argument he was directly following Thomas, who thought that in the resurrection of the dead the bodies of the saints took part in the bliss which up until then was enjoyed only by their souls.[169]

On the basis of his approach, which was strongly coloured by existentialism, Schillebeeckx arrived at a remarkable interpretation of two central data of tradition associated with the ultimate human fellowship with God. The first, the expectation of 'a new heaven and a new earth where righteousness dwells' (2 Peter 3.13), which as an apocalyptic notion had rightly found its way into the New Testament, had become the Cinderella of the history of faith and theology. The shift towards salvation history in theology had once again focused interest on this expectation of cosmic salvation, and Schillebeeckx too was intensively occupied with it in his lectures on eschatology. He connected the traditional picture of the future and of a new heaven and earth with his thoughts about man as a being who creates culture. In De Petter's footsteps he began from the view that being human in the world means and is orientated on the humanization of this world. In itself the 'material world' is not a perfect world, but requires to be given meaning by man, who exalts it 'above its own capacity and assumes [it] ... in the process of the actualization of man's own person' (398).[170] Thus, human self-fulfilment took the form of a cultural transformation of the world and, conversely, culture appeared as the realization of a desire for humanization which was alive in the world. According to Schillebeeckx, this argument fitted with the way in which the Bible always saw the fate of the world as bound up with that of man. Man was taken from the earth, and was appointed 'lord and master' over creation, and creation in turn again appeared as the mirror of human fate.

From this perspective Schillebeeckx could give a good place to the expectation of a renewed harmony between man and the world, beginning with the prophets and issuing in the image in Paul's Letter to the Romans and the Revelation of John of a world pregnant with hope (394–8).[171] He interpreted this expectation theologically as radical reliance on God's faithfulness to man: this faithfulness took the form of a divine involvement in the human task *par excellence*, that of giving meaning by cultivating and transforming the world. Thus his eschatology is a sub-division of his theology of culture:

> The world which God offered to mankind by creating it will be glorified in the eschatological act of God's creation and the eschatological giving of meaning by holy humanity. In this sense the renewal of the world is inevitably a consecration of earthly culture.

He emphasized that this did not mean that the products of human culture took on eternal value, but that through grace God would bring about the comprehensive synthesis between spirit and nature which was ultimately aimed at in the formation of culture. The image of a new heaven and a new earth announced the situation in which 'the glorified world is the pure, crystal-clear reflection of divinized human life and in which indeed it can be completely used by the saints'. Thus it is not that human claims are bathed in a sacral aura; rather, what man builds on a culture is brought into the eschaton, which had already taken on a 'veiled beginning' with the coming of Christ, since in Schillebeeckx's view the 'activity of creating culture has something "in the making" which in a transcendent way will be consecrated in the eschaton' (398–401).

Schillebeeckx wanted to make clear above all that 'the *human* in us is redeemed and brought into heaven'. The human means the bodily, the worldly, the humanized world, the activity of humanizing and human society. By means of his existentialist-inspired anthropology he also used the image of a new heaven and earth to interpret the traditional notion of the 'communion of saints', and did so in a surprising way: in his view this was a real human fellowship. And although he maintained the Catholic conviction that the saints are now already in contact with the living and their cares – 'a holy Mother in heaven also lives with her children on earth helping them, a St Dominic with the Dominicans, etc., and above all Mary with all of us and with each of us in particular' – only the bodily resurrection can lead to mutual relationships in the full sense. 'Only through openness to one another through the risen body does the human community begin interpersonal relations again on a heavenly plane through the resurrection.' Schillebeeckx even speculated on whether this also implied that there would be 'special friendships' with particular people in heaven. In his view there would be: although he thought that in heaven a number of earthly limitations would fall away, even glorified men and women would not be in a position to maintain intersubjective relations 'equally with the billions of saints'; even a risen body was not omnipresent. And in the choice of particular friendships which would therefore be as necessary as on earth, 'redeemed and holy' but nevertheless 'natural' affinities would play a role. 'These are *human beings, who are in heaven.*'

One might think that here he was allowing himself to be lured on to the path of idle speculation, but in fact what he said, for example in his remark that in heaven it would be quite visible that 'brotherly love is the representation, on a human level, of our love of God', turned on the religious and theological significance of the interpersonal sphere. With his notion of 'special friendships which are always a form of *caritas* and the experience of God' and would last in heaven, he was opposing a view still widespread in the 1950s, that the cultivation of personal ties is in conflict with a radical orientation on God. So 'special friendships' were often strictly forbidden and even punished in seminaries and religious houses, and also usually strongly discouraged in boarding schools run by religious. As we saw in the first chapter, in his time at college Schillebeeckx had found this difficult to take. At that time he interpreted the fact that in 1933 Mannes Mathijs sent him a picture of Francis and Dominic embracing as a sign that the Dominicans had a different view of friendship from the Jesuits. In his lectures on eschatology he tried to demonstrate the theological legitimacy of this other view.

In his lectures Schillebeeckx also talked about hell as a counterpart to heavenly bliss.[172] Whereas for him heaven was fellowship with God and as such also a reality for human beings who are still on the way to heaven, he understood hell as separation from God, which at the same time meant exclusion from the communion of saints – and in this sense isolation – and the failure of the natural striving for harmonious humanity. 'All harmony of life is lacking; the innermost capacities of human beings which as the other side of fellowship with God are integrated into perfect "humanism", have disintegrated in the damned.' According to his interpretation of the tradition, this last culminated in the notion of hell as a fire that eternally torments the bodies of the damned. He regarded the image of bodily suffering in hell as the counterpart of bodily bliss in heaven bound up with earth:

> For the damned, the new heaven and earth is itself the bodily reality which, because of their unadapted unglorified corporeality, pains them fearfully. The whole of their bodily environment, both their corporeality which is also damned and the glorified world, is like a fire which burns in the bodies of the damned ... Being in the world through one's damned corporeality is a fierce torture of which we can have no idea, and therefore we grasp at the image of the most fearful pain, fire (441f.).

Schillebeeckx tried on the one hand to accept the statements of the church's magisterium which explicitly declare that hell is an objective reality and may not be interpreted as an image or as a psychological reality. On the other hand he was convinced that the notion that hell as a place of torture was created separately by God could not be reconciled with God's nature, which is love and mercy. Therefore he emphatically did not regard hell as divine retribution – 'God does not take vengeance' – but as a consequence and continuation of a person's free choice to turn from God 'through sin upon sin', 'until his heart is turned to stone and his spirit is blinded', and thus to cut himself off from any possibility of salvation. In Schillebeeckx's view, the punishment represented by hell was that people realized this situation, including their own guilt for it and its consequences. Refusal of fellowship with God itself '*is* hell, but in the clear sense of the absurdity of this refusal which, however, has grown with their whole being'; hell is the 'hellish raging of despair, extended for ever'. So he could understand hell as an expression of the 'mystery of God's love', as 'God's love itself for a man who hates this love for eternity' (441).

As an image of the constant threat of the overwhelming power of evil in the face of which human freedom no longer has power, in existentialism hell was a powerful symbol of the human situation. Especially in his play *Huis Clos* (Closed Doors, 1945), the existentialist philosopher Jean-Paul Sartre had given hell a place in the post-war imagination. Of course, Schillebeeckx did not adopt Sartre's notion that hell is 'others' – in his remarks about heaven as a place of fellowship he clearly dissociated himself from such a thought – but he saw hell especially as a symbol for the importance of human choices, along the lines of Sartre's usage. Like many other Catholics in this period, Schillebeeckx was struck by the remark of St Thérèse of Liseiux that she believed in hell, but at the same time thought that it was empty. This conviction was in line with Schillebeeckx's theological concentration on God's comprehensive will for salvation. Now the doctrine of the ultimate redemption of all human beings – the so-called *apokatastasis panton* – had been emphatically condemned by the church as early as the sixth century, but it seems that Schillebeeckx wanted to choose a way which was both doctrinally and philosophically safe by writing in his lecture notes on eschatology that even if no one was damned – a statement which at the same time he said he did not want to endorse – nothing in the structure of creation was changed. In other words, in his view the reality of hell did not lie in its existence as an independent place or as a state in which particular human souls were to be found. Hell was real as a human possibility. Human beings remained free spiritual and corporeal beings, and for such beings hell was really a possible ultimate consequence of the choice of a literally godless mode of existence (442).[173]

We get the impression that in his theology of 'the last things' Schillebeeckx in fact developed a theological anthropology and that 'heaven' and 'hell' were important for him above all because of what they suggested about the relationship between human beings and God. This impression is confirmed by what he said in his lectures on eschatology about purgatory. Like heaven and hell, for him purgatory denoted 'an eschatological stage' of the return to God – the *reditus ad Patrem* – of 'the redeemed children of God' (533).

The existence of a 'place' of purification for the souls of believers after their death and the nature of this purification has always been disputed among the various Christian churches, and Schillebeeckx investigated this dispute. The Protestants rejected the existence of purgatory as unbiblical and in conflict with the basic conviction that reconciliation was brought about only by the sacrifice of Christ's death on the cross. They maintained what in their view was the biblical doctrine of a resurrection from the dead on the last day, which would be sealed with a once-for-all and definitive judgement on the life of individuals. The objections of the Eastern churches to the notion of purgatory were of an earlier date and related above all to the idea of the expiation of sins and the ongoing purification of the human soul by fire. Schillebeeckx certainly conceded openly that 'scripture, outside the tradition, has no explicit doctrine of purgatory' and also agreed in being opposed to the more dubious – 'sadistic' or 'superstitious' – aspects of ideas about purgatory, but nevertheless resolutely opposed the objections. In the face of the Protestant view he was concerned to demonstrate that purgatory was not a new reality but a development of the saving work of Christ. He thought that the opposition of the Greek church to purgatory derived from the strong emphasis on purgatory as a punishment in the West, whereas the East, in his view rightly, gave a central place to the healing effect of God's love.

Schillebeeckx based his exposition especially on the dogma of purgatory that the Latin church had formulated, in the first instance, in dialogue with the Greek Church at the Council of Florence (1439–45), which sought to be a Council of reunion. He thought that this Council remained outside the dispute between East and West over the precise nature of purgatory and simply limited itself to declaring that:

> Anyone who dies in the love of God but has not yet done satisfaction in true *metanoia* for sins he has committed or for his sins of omission must after death ... be purified by cleansing punishments: the suffrages [= intercessions] of believers (namely the sacrifice of the mass, prayers, alms, good works, along the guidelines laid down by the church) are healing for these souls in purgatory, namely to be rescued from these punishments (485).[174]

In his judgement this formulation was acceptable to both Latin and Greek Christianity. In his further reflection in this dogma, which the Catholic Church had once again advanced against the Protestants, especially at the Council of Trent, Schillebeeckx tried once again to demonstrate above all that purgatory must not be regarded as a 'temporal hell'. He saw it, rather, as a 'shining prelude to heaven where one can talk only of the fire and the glow of love' and then in the form of 'purifying love' (452).[175] In this way he felt that he had removed the central objection of the Eastern church to the idea of purgatory.

In the idea that Schillebeeckx had of purgatory, what in fact took place during the whole life of the faithful happened there in a concentrated way. The faithful were not given the task of worshipping God outwardly in the form of spiritual or physical offerings or sacrifices, which was the customary notion in popular pious Catholic literature up to the 1950s. Schillebeeckx thought that human beings could not enrich God, certainly not through suffering, and he was vigorously opposed to the idea that purgatory was a place where sin needed to be expiated and that the pain suffered there restored the equilibrium which had been damaged. For him, serving God meant really making God seen as God in one's own life and giving God his due. In this light, faith was a matter of directing one's own will to God, with the ultimate aim of holiness, through which everything in a man was grasped by the love of God and nothing escaped it. If all went well, this holiness came about during the life of faith on earth; however, to the degree that this process had not yet been completed at death, it was continued after death. For Schillebeeckx, purgatory was the further permeation of God's loving presence in the faithful; that is why he could say that it was the place of God's fire and glow of love. Because real openness to God meant that one needed to let go of self-love, and because, given the way in which human beings sinfully cling to themselves, this was a painful process, purgatory involved penance and suffering. It was not a matter of suffering but of letting go of the orientation on oneself of which suffering was a symptom; Schillebeeckx explicitly said that pain did not purge, but that the detachment from sin caused the pain (494–500).[176]

However, consignment to purgatory also meant that God had in principle found a person worthy of union with him. As we saw, according to Schillebeeckx the faithful during their earthly life are already redeemed on their way to redemption, but in purgatory this applied to a heightened degree. Once admitted to purgatory the believer's attention was in his view 'fixed' – 'the fundamental basic will is for ever what it is at death' – and the soul had nothing more to dread from the doubt and wavering that had always lurked during earthly life. For Schillebeeckx this meant that the soul in purgatory was a kind of ideal type of the believer, as too was the mystic. 'One could call purgatory the "mystical church"', he wrote. Purgatory was the place where believing souls did in a concentrated form what was essential for a believing existence: they broke with their attachment to the world and themselves, allowed themselves to be freed by God's grace, and took a penitentially-active part in the suffering that emanated from this:

> The penance is 'imposed' in the sense that it stands for the unavoidable fact of a purification that still has to take place. But on the other hand it is freely accepted, even with eager love: the penance comes from their deepest personal conviction, which is no longer contradicted by a still wavering will that still secretly hankers after evil.

This led Schillebeeckx to the striking conclusion that the souls in purgatory were fundamentally happy 'in their love of God', although this love was at the same time their pain, because 'God's glorious splendour' scorches 'what is still unholy in them'. That, he said – with a reference to the link between the Dutch word for purgatory, *vagevuur,* and the verb *vagen,* to sweep away, remove – 'and that alone is what purgatory is: the fire of love sweeps away the last remnants of sin in them' (504–12).[177]

In Schillebeeckx's view, the souls in purgatory in fact form part of the fellowship of the church, along with the souls in heaven. Through their definitive relationship with God they are bound up with the saints; in their suffering from what is still unholy in them they are bound up with the distress of the earthly church. Schillebeeckx interpreted the Catholic practice of saying masses, doing good works and praying for the souls in purgatory as an expression of this bond in fellowship beyond death (512–17). In particular, he went at length into the possibility of the church granting so-called indulgences, in other words reducing temporal punishments for sins committed. Although he said that he provisionally wanted to refrain from passing a final judgement on indulgences, the view of purgatory that he had developed told against there being a place where souls were subjected to all kinds of punishments. In his view, what in the history and theology of piety was often regarded as a punishment was suffering that was the consequence of the necessary intrinsic purification of the soul; therefore in his view it was *impossible* – he wrote this word in capital letters! – for the church to be able infallibly to remit these punishments on the basis of a God-given right. Reflecting on recent historical investigation and at the same time confronting explicit statements by the church in this area, he concluded that what had taken the form of a legal act in which the church remitted a punishment was really a prayer of the church. The indulgence was a 'supreme appeal' for God's mercy on the souls in purgatory to give them the grace that they needed for further purification. By the utterance of the prayer, the soul in purgatory was again consolidated in the fellowship of the church and thus in the community of grace in the Spirit with God in Jesus Christ. That prayer was – and this was how he interpreted the power of the church to grant indulgences – 'as made by the whole communion of saints' in the church 'who pleased God', and as such was 'of course well-pleasing to God' (517–34).[178]

According to Schillebeeckx, the purification of souls in purgatory was 'actively supported by the redemptive activity of the Father in and through Jesus Christ in the perfecting power of the holy and sanctifying Spirit' (511). His eschatology was ultimately concerned to show faith as fellowship with God. The life of faith orientated on God and bound up with God, the 'theologal' life, is taken up as human life into the divine life, and that is the case even beyond death.

Creation theology as theology of culture

For Schillebeeckx, the deepest basis of the communion between God and man lay in creation. In the lecture notes entitled 'Theological Reflections on Creation Faith' he investigated the significance of belief in God as creator. In their final form, the notes are dated '1956–7', and thus chronologically form the conclusion to his activities as a theological teacher in Louvain. However, in content, too, they are in a sense a summary of his Louvain theological synthesis. In these notes Schillebeeckx again used the phrase 'theology of culture' for the first time since his article in the 1950s. According to the table of contents, in the penultimate section of the lectures 'outlines of a differential theology of culture' had to be sketched out, ending in a 'theology of material culture', in other words of economic, technological and scientific values, a 'theology of personal culture', a 'theology of social culture' and a 'theology of history'. All this had further to result in a section on the eschatological glorification of the world and a closing section on Christ as head of the church and king of the world (*caput ecclesiae et rex mundi*). However, the text for this never seems to have been written, nor was that of the planned section on the place of priests, religious and laity in the church – 'the evangelical counsels and laicology' – and on the 'significance of the earthly branch of culture in the Christian order of life'; the notes on the theological reflection on creation faith as delivered break off in the middle of a sentence after around 650 pages.[179] Be this as it may, the whole manuscript makes it clear that in his theology of creation Schillebeeckx took up the themes that he had envisaged in 1945 when he was in search of a theology of culture, which he then regarded as a necessary new sub-division of the theology of creation. 'Theological reflection on creation faith' is in a sense to be regarded as a theology of culture in the form of a theology about creation.

Schillebeeckx himself was convinced that this did not mean any diminution of creation theology or a reduction to its pragmatic importance. By comparison with neoscholastic theology, his approach made possible a broader view and a reinforcement of the theological content of statements about creation. Under the influence of the statement at the First Vatican Council that the one true God, our Creator and Lord, as the origin and goal of all, can be known with certainty on a creaturely basis with the help of the light of human reason, in neoscholasticism faith in God as created is here reduced to the formal insight that cosmos and man are finite and owe their existence to their creation by God. That God is the creator of heaven and earth thus in fact meant no more than that God has produced all things after their whole being and that all that exists owes this existence utterly and completely to God.[180] Schillebeeckx thought that this was not a theological view of the dogma of creation or reflection on it in faith. In his view, neoscholasticism was stuck in philosophy: in philosophical reflection on created reality God indeed came indirectly into view, as origin and cause of all, as *principium objecti*. In faith and thus in theology, however, God himself was the object of knowledge and was known as the God of salvation (I, 25). In Schillebeeckx's view creation faith was a religious view of reality as a whole, in the light of the encounter with God. He regarded the biblical liturgical confession that 'our help is in the name of the Lord who has made heaven and earth' as a summary indication of 'an all-supporting element in our supernatural experience of God and in our sense of salvation as believers', namely that the God of salvation permeates the whole of reality (I, 1–4). He never said this in the lectures in so many words, but it is clear that for him creation faith made it possible to do theology as he wanted to, 'on the basis of St Thomas', as relating to everything and seeing everything from God's perspective.[181] For Schillebeeckx, all theology was ultimately creation theology in this sense; even more than in his other lectures on the great theological themes, in 'Theological Reflections on Creation Faith' he had difficulty in outlining his subject.

The lectures on creation again turned on the relationship between nature and supernature, as in an important part of his theological *oeuvre* since the 1940s. By an intensive confrontation with the biblical texts on the basis of recent exegetical insights he arrived at a new and focused insight into this relationship. For him, the starting point was a conviction which quickly gained ground in exegesis, that belief in God as creator had arisen on the basis 'of the experience in faith of the God who acts in salvation history'. Not only was it important that 'revealed creation faith came chronologically after saving faith and welled up out of saving faith'; the very meaning of creation faith itself was at stake (I, 2). For Schillebeeckx, the fact that salvation history was the basis of creation faith was first of all significant formally. In his view creation faith showed that in the light of the personal encounter with God everything changed, and that the 'reality of salvation' of the 'God experienced personally' had an effect on the believer 'even when he is speaking about "worldly things" and is confronted with profane, even stupid and trivial, human matters' (I, 3). But in his view, the fact that creation faith had a basis in salvation history showed especially that creation faith itself has a soteriological significance and is redemptive. The biblical texts on the cosmos as creation, in polemic with the surrounding cultures, characterized reality as a place where God's covenant with Israel has comprehensive significance. Biblical creation faith expressed the conviction that the powerful and gracious God who had liberated Israel, who had 'united a band of Bedouins, made up of all kinds of tribes ... politically around the name "Yahweh"', who had made the 'outcasts' 'elect' and had gathered them together to be 'one people, the people of God', was the God of heaven and earth (I, 63–4).[182] This on the one hand meant that this God could be recognized in all kinds of phenomena and events in nature and history, and on the other implied that the God of heaven and earth revealed himself in the particular salvation history with this people, and that therefore this history was of universal significance. 'Theologically, here we stand before this revelation of God; creation is functional to Israel's calling, which itself is functional to Christ' (I, 64–5); in the 1950s this last was a starting point which had hardly yet become a particular problem in Christian theology.

'Deus salutaris est creator'

According to Schillebeeckx, the new element in biblical creation faith is not the conviction 'that one God created everything' but the view that everything has been created by the God who has revealed himself in the history of Israel. In other words, 'the *novum* lies in the Old Testament idea of God itself'. 'The fundamental creed of Israel' expresses trust in 'the mighty act of Yahweh who made a great mass of fugitives from Egypt (a popular migration of the time) into *one people* and indeed *God's people*', but he thought that this particular election was about the revelation of a 'God with ethical and religious qualifications', who at core was universal (I,51).

Schillebeeckx regularly indicated his reservations about the idea, which in his view had been adopted above all by Protestant exegetes, that creation faith was the product of Israel's prophets, but he thought that this insight into the unity of exodus and creation definitively broke through in so-called Deutero-Isaiah, the author of which is hidden behind the second part of the biblical book of Isaiah:

> This unknown prophet intensely feels the unity of the creation of the world and Israel's salvation history, as this had previously been expressed – but less strongly. Precisely because Yahweh is the Lord of history, He is also the Lord of nature, which is indissolubly bound up with this history (I, 68).[183]

According to Schillebeeckx, this led to the conviction that the creation is 'an unfathomable wonder of the wise, good and omnipotent Yahweh'; hence the idea that 'human existence and the world' are 'governed and "made" by the unfathomable action of God, the creator and saviour' becomes 'the shrine of the whole of Old Testament religion' (I, 69). That the redeeming God of Israel is the creator of heaven and earth was the 'dominant dogma', the determinative view in faith of reality as a whole from which 'nature, history and salvation can be understood' (I, 122) and which formed the basis 'of trust in Yahweh's saving system' (I,70).[184] He was prompted by Deutero-Isaiah to say that 'creation faith here is not a *preambulum fidei* but one of the fundamental creeds of ... faith' (I, 73), and that creation faith as it is expressed in the great Christian creeds can also be found in the New Testament and has 'completely the same scope' as that of Deutero-Isaiah (I, 184).[185] In his view a rediscovery of Christian creation faith in this sense would have far-reaching consequences:

> The authentic sense of God is aware of God's presence also in the normal process of nature and life, and when the order of creation is incorporated into the order of salvation, which is basically the biblical view, it is clear that natural phenomena can take on a special significance for those who live in a bond with the *Deus salutaris* (I, 90).[186]

According to Schillebeeckx, an authentic creation faith puts human life in this context and makes it possible to experience the world as God's world.

In Schillebeeckx's view, biblical creation faith had a productive dialectic. On the one hand the special bond between God and the people had a central place and emphasized that the Mighty One of Israel is the God of heaven and earth (I, 63). On the other hand, precisely as creation faith it put Israel's election in a wider framework. According to Schillebeeckx, creation was 'itself a kind of "covenant"', of which God's covenant with Israel was a special realization, and creation faith implied the view of 'one world, one humankind, one great family of "children of God"' (I, 62). In his view, the first chapter of the book of Genesis was ultimately a creation hymn 'to the glory of the Mighty One of Israel who created heaven and earth and made this creation culminate in man, who has been called to worship' (I, 63). He saw a development in the Old Testament in which Israel's covenant morality of doing right, remaining faithful and walking humbly with God (Micah 6.8) was based increasingly on creation and therefore was increasingly seen as having universal validity (I, 62).[187] This universality again has two sides: first, all human beings are addressed by the moral appeal, and secondly, in principle God's kingdom embraces the whole world. According to the Old Testament, 'all things are created to the glory of Yahweh', and this glory will ultimately break through definitively and then prove to be the salvation of Israel and all humankind (I, 97–103).

According to Schillebeeckx, the focus is on human beings. In his view the Old Testament idea of creation did not so much seek to be an explanation of the world, but was 'the foundation ... which dominates the existentialistic relationship between God and man' (I, 104). In this relationship human beings are the image of God; in other words, human responsibility is the reflection of the divine worth and makes human beings co-creators: 'for man, creation is a task' (I, 103–8). In Schillebeeckx's eyes the Old Testament idea of creation was the horizon spanning history from primal time to end time and making it comprehensible as God's history. As was also evident from his lectures on eschatology, the ever more focused expectation of the end time in the later strata of the Old and New Testament did not bring about any change. The sense of 'the sinful old world' and the good news of the new creation, which according to the Christian witness had begun in Christ, were forms of the belief that the God of salvation and salvation history was the creator (I, 108–10).[188] For Schillebeeckx, God as creator spanned even the situation of 'original sin' which, Christians were convinced, governed human existence before any deliberate choice of good or evil. In his view, what the existentialists called 'situated freedom' was in fact a freedom in the midst of an objective and subjective, a social and personal, history which tended towards evil and sin. In this situation, to opt for the good meant to break with the existing logic (II, 366–84).[189] The Old Testament story of the fall of Adam as an expression of the sinful situation in which human beings found themselves made sense only in the perspective of salvation history within which the creation story also stands and which it at the same time expresses.[190] According to his interpretation of the Old Testament, the human situation of disaster in particular made it clear that 'man is compelled to expect all salvation only from God' (I, 116):

Through man, creation is made a history of disaster, but the Creator turns this into a history of salvation, so that the motif of creation, namely the reciprocal nature of the love of God and man, explicitly, despite everything, can still be brought into being (I, 117).

In this sense, in Schillebeeckx's view, biblical creation faith, even in its apparent pessimism about the human situation, has an ongoing undertone of optimism.

For Schillebeeckx, the Old Testament conviction that the God of heaven and earth is a 'God of salvation', a *Deus salutaris*, a 'God with us', even helped in a certain sense to explain the notion of a divine incarnation. He saw this as the overwhelming trend of the divine presence which was already so evident in the Old Testament: 'Yahweh is a God who is so "humanly human" that he truly appears among us in bodily life, *creator incarnatus'* (I, 127). He regarded the New Testament sense of creation first of all as an 'extension or continuation of the Old Testament sense' (I, 134), above all also in the basic conviction that 'the whole situation of life', even if 'from a human perspective it is intolerable', is in depth a situation of grace 'because it is linked with the most personal concern of the *Deus salutaris creator* for religious man' (I, 135f.). Nevertheless, in his view creation faith showed its true face 'in and through the confession of Christ' in the New Testament, 'which in the Old Testament is revealed only in veiled form' (I, 134). It got a new centre, namely redemption, the restoration of the intimate relationship between human beings and God in Christ. The conviction that the God of salvation is the creator of heaven and earth was expressed in the New Testament in the belief that 'the God who reveals himself in Christ is the creator of heaven and earth' (I, 143).

At the same time, for Schillebeeckx an important difference in tone remained between the Old Testament and the New. For the New Testament authors the new age had dawned in Christ, the end time, and he noted that the old world and the existing cosmos were almost demonized in the light of it: 'In the light of the redemption brought by Christ, the world which does not confess Christ appears as a dark background' (I, 138). He explained this line in the New Testament scriptures, which formed the basis for the detachment of the Catholic Church from the world in general and modernity in particular and in many respects its downright hostility to them, 'in the light of the unknown joy at the fact of the redemption by Christ in which one shared'. This brought about a 'fundamental dissatisfaction with the world'. Schillebeeckx wanted to maintain this dissatisfaction and eschatological tension. He was opposed to the notion influential among exegetes that Christians had initially still expected the speedy return of their Lord, but when this failed to materialize, directed their attention towards the church as the place of Christian life in the midst of the world. He thought that the New Testament was not about 'the quantitative nearness of the kingdom of God – namely that the parousia would come soon' – which would make the marked orientation of some New Testament passages on a new heaven and earth only of passing importance. By contrast, in his view the key issue was 'the qualitative nearness, the importance of the kingdom of God', which resulted in 'a new experience of time' (I, 140). And this was of abiding significance.[191] In this connection he also pointed to the difference in emphasis that there was, in his view,

> between the realistic preaching of Christ, which is shot through with a fresh, healthy and at the same time reverent tone towards the world and life as God's creatures, and the apostolic preaching of the primitive church, which, following Christ, only longs for his return (I, 139).

But he did not argue for any return to Jesus himself. He was concerned that the New Testament pessimism about the existing world should not embrace the whole of creation, 'as if the creaturely world is essentially evil'.

In his eyes the apostolic church remained faithful both to Jesus's preaching and to its own desire for his return by ultimately making the same move that he had reconstructed in the Old Testament writings. With the help of arguments based on the exegesis of the Christ hymn in the Letter to the Colossians (1.15–20), the Letter to the Hebrews, the Revelation of John and the so-called prologue to the Gospel of John (1.1–18), he tried to demonstrate that according to the New Testament view, 'in the person of Christ we have the christological extension of the Old Testament unity of creation and salvation' (I, 164). Here he followed exegetes who had shown that the background to the texts about the cosmic Christ in the New Testament was not one of Greek cosmological speculations, as had often been claimed, but was in line with the ongoing development of Old Testament thought.[192] He perceived a 'christologization' of thought-patterns from the so-called wisdom literature, especially from the wisdom books, Proverbs and Ben Sirach, as a defence in particular against Gnostic speculations about the origin and structure of the world and the cosmos. At the same time, however, he emphasized that the *origin* of the New Testament ideas about Christ's role in creation did not lie in the wisdom literature but in the 'experience of Christ itself'. However, the material with which the far-reaching consequences of this experience could be expressed in a vision of creation was found in the Old Testament (I,149). 'He argued that 'the experience of Christ itself is explicitated by Old Testament data, prompted by pagan speculations about the cosmos'.

As I have said, in Schillebeeckx's view the Old Testament pattern was repeated in the New Testament. There the 'idea of salvation' was again the origin of 'the ... idea of creation' (I, 153), which made it clear that the whole cosmos existed with a view to creation and thus was most deeply salvific. However, this fact for the moment remained hidden from the experience of the New Testament writers. It still came to light only in their own new dependence on God. According to Schillebeeckx, they saw life as a 'being-towards-God' of the kind that makes itself known in Christ as the God of salvation, and as such was meanwhile the beginning of a new creation. 'Later', this new creation-in-the-making was to become visible, in their conviction, 'down to the newness of the bodily world' (I, 166). In Schillebeeckx's view, not only the doctrine of redemption but also eschatology was part of a theology of creation.

Creation as a basis for culture

In fact, throughout his Flemish period Schillebeeckx was convinced that two main lines can be recognized in Christian faith. There is the rising line from creation to consummation, a consummation which was always already present in creation 'by way of prolepsis' through, for example, grace, sacraments and miracles; he called this the 'humanistic' line. Alongside this is the line which emphasizes that God's glory reveals itself through suffering and detachment from the world (I, 171). In his lectures on creation faith he indicated that these two lines are not synthesized in the New Testament, and argued that this synthesis still had to mature 'in the living life of the church'. He himself clearly wanted to contribute to this maturing.

Here he maintained the basic conviction that the New Testament rejection of any dualism in creation left open 'the door for a distinctive kind of "humanistic Christianity"' (I, 141); in his view, Christianity was 'humanistic' in its own specific way, and in his theology of creation he tried to track down precisely what this was. He was concerned with Christian humanism, which is why from the beginning he put so much emphasis on the fact that the God of salvation history is the creator. In his view, the Christian-humanistic perspective emerges whenever God is seen as creator of heaven and earth, and especially of human beings, in the light of his revelation as God of salvation in Jesus Christ. Schillebeeckx thought that in him God has demonstrated how much he loves humankind, and that creation faith in the Christian sense represents the conviction that this love underlies the whole of creation (I, 4). However, at the same time he thought that this conviction was not purely based on a decision of faith. If the loving God who revealed himself in Jesus Christ is really the creator of the cosmos and human beings, then human beings living in this cosmos must already see this God, 'emphatically or not emphatically, to some degree in sorrow', at least in the form of an 'essentially important desire for divine intersubjectivity'. In his view that was the significance of a philosophical doctrine of God on the basis of human experience in the world, although the philosopher could not know the deepest significance of what he arrived at – here he joined up with the classical Catholic conviction:

> He knows that the unknown God who is really the God of Christians actually exists and casts his shadow over all the world, but standing in this shadow he immediately knows that this unknown God dwells in an inaccessible light which his human thought cannot penetrate further (I, 5).

This seems traditionally Catholic, but it is striking that by this approach Schillebeeckx in fact made the possibility of natural knowledge of God a conviction *of faith*. It was part of creation faith that through his creatures God provoked the search for him in man as his creature *par excellence* (I, 6). 'The natural knowledge of God ... is the recognition of the creator of things' through these things (I, 9).

Here Schillebeeckx was convinced that he was taking up the declaration of the First Vatican Council 'that God, origin and goal of all things, can be known with certainty from natural things with the natural light of human reason'.[193] He was even clear that the church could declare something of this kind, though he was convinced that 'the church has no authority over natural truths which are of no significance for the religious life' (I, 13). But although he continued to retain the scholastic terminology in which the philosophical doctrine of God is regarded as guidance towards faith (*preambulum fidei*), in an extensive commentary on the texts of Vatican I he in fact developed a quite distinctive view of the importance of philosophy within the framework of theology. According to Schillebeeckx, the First Vatican Council did not set out to support the philosophical proofs of God with conciliar authority. In his view the Council was not rejecting the idea that in concrete terms it is impossible for human beings to know God through creatures as their cause and purpose; moreover, he pointed out that a 'purely natural' idea of God as creator 'hardly exists, if at all', and was not even present in Israel before God revealed himself to this people as the God-of-the-covenant (I, 17). The revelation of the God of salvation in fact always preceded faith in God as creator and led to a purging of the spontaneous consciousness of God given with life within creation. He thought that the First Vatican Council defined 'only the possibility of knowing the existence of God' (I, 19): the possibility, not the actuality. And the meaning of the declaration that God can be known through the natural light of reason is that the truth of the Christian awareness of God is not simply an assertion which has to be accepted on authority; it is an insight founded on reason. Or, to paraphrase Schillebeeckx's own words: because it is the Christian conviction that 'concrete reality has really been taken up into God's system of grace and can be completely understood only there', and because this reality is 'the philosopher's field of reflection', it is possible 'to construct a "Christian philosophy" which on the basis of reason can show that it is better than other philosophies' (I, 20). He thus regarded the emphasis of the church on the possibility of natural knowledge of God as a form of solidarity with 'the modern self-awareness of humankind', which can only accept an invitation the meaning and importance of which is also credible to those with a critical turn of mind.

From this it would be right to conclude that according to Schillebeeckx a contemporary theology of creation needs to take the form of a 'Christian philosophy' which thinks on the basis of the Christian revelation of salvation, but at the same time does not allow 'the critical demands of philosophy ... to fade', with the secret conviction 'that we "know it already" through faith' (I, 20). Schillebeeckx did not develop such a philosophy systematically in his lectures on creation. But he did demonstrate that the typically human participation in creation through the creation of culture, the conscience and religion ultimately have their place within 'being created' and therefore most deeply within the sphere of the human relationship with God (I, 249).

Thus, like his eschatology, the creation theology of the Flemish Schillebeeckx was especially an anthropology. In working it out further, the anthropology of existentialist philosophy was his sparring partner. In particular he investigated the conviction of Maurice Merleau-Ponty that a religious perspective on reality is incompatible with human freedom; the believer is already certain of the saving course of history. For Merleau-Ponty this removed from human freedom its characteristic uncertainty and simply left the obligation for the believer to submit to the will of God. In response, Schillebeeckx did not repeat what he had said in his lecture on eschatology about the relationship between grace and freedom, but remained on the existential level. He tried to make it clear that God's providence for the believer is not a clear 'divine plan', but the mystery that the real dialogue between God and man is ultimately embraced by God and guided for the good. In his view, faith in providence did not mean a 'knowledge of its content' to which human beings must submit, but 'belief in a personal Mystery', within which people tried to work out the project of their own lives – laboriously, but at the same time in all faithfulness and in any case in all freedom (II, 262–71).[194] Ultimately he thought that he could counter Merleau-Ponty only by – as he said – concretely proving the existence of God: in other words, by demonstrating that free human action in responsibility for the world necessarily implies 'the mystery of God', 'and this amounts to showing that we stand in the Mystery' (II, 267). To gain sight of the depth dimension of one's own existence, in the project of one's own life, as part of the comprehensive reality of creation and salvation history, was ultimately at the same time a personal encounter with God (II, 269).

According to Schillebeeckx's picture, God is not proved by an abstract philosophical argument. He remained faithful to his starting point that creation is a theological idea based on belief in the *Deus salutaris* as creator, and from here he undertook an analysis of human freedom in terms of a theology of creation – he called it 'ktisiological', after the Greek word for creation, *ktisis*. In his view, this freedom was situated, had ethical norms and made history. Along De Petter's lines he first of all emphasized that from a philosophical perspective human beings are always already involved in the situation, biologically and socially, and are more inclined towards freedom than already completely free. Freedom is not a starting point but a possibility, because human beings can distance themselves intellectually from their situation:

> Standing in a situation in which he is already entangled through all kinds of instinctive drives, and to which the human drives react in a whole variety of ways, man can make this situation an object as situated freedom (II, 240).[195]

Human freedom is a matter of allowing freedom to reign, not 'in a vacuum', but with respect to man's own natural inclinations and situation (II, 240f.). In the first instance Schillebeeckx emphasized strongly that the human spirit stands apart from this situation, has the capacity to know objectively and disinterestedly. For him, access to God and his saving will meant liberation from 'the determination of nature' and insight into what is absolutely good. However, for finite human beings this in fact amounted to an assessment and a choice. 'I make the objective norms my own, because I see that they have this intrinsic character, and do so absolutely'; in his view insight into the good took the form of what he called 'the ideal sense', the sense of what is good in one's own life and one's own situation (II, 242–5). He thought that these norms and this acquisition of a personal ideal provide the basis of the way in which human beings can give form to their lives. Because human beings as bodily beings are bound up with the world, at the same time they give form to the world with their own lives; they give meaning to material reality by doing good, by taking it up into a project that is ultimately orientated on God as the absolute good.[196] Schillebeeckx's anthropology ended up with a statement about the fundamental importance of culture for being human: 'In and through the humanization of the world' – in other words in and through the creation of culture – 'man humanizes himself' and arrives at 'spiritual self-possession' (II, 246).[197]

In this way, at the same time Schillebeeckx got away from the contrast that he seemed to be making between being situated and freedom. Ultimately, after all, Schillebeeckx proved to think that God addresses the human being as a free person not when the human being stands apart from his situation, but in his human involvement in it (II, 251). Good shines out in the situation itself, with all its aspects. In a way which seems to anticipate what he would say around ten years later about 'experiences of contrast',[198] in 'Theological Reflections on Creation Faith' Schillebeeckx described the conscience as the capacity by which human beings experience the situation as a personal call to a particular way of behaving. In his view the conscience is not a place of feelings, but primarily a capacity for perception; perceiving reality with the help of the conscience means seeing through one's own situation in the light of a sense of the ideal and from there knowing what had to be done. For him, the participation of human beings in the divine Mystery given with creation assumes its concrete and specifically human face in the conscience.

> In the creaturely reality which is called man, what outside man is only an objective participation in God becomes a personal participation and collaboration with God in forming the face of the world and the human face.

In his view, God's plan for the world presented itself to the conscience as a personal challenge-and-obligation freely to become involved and to accept the norms given by God, 'so that in my human activity I accept my honest conscience as the norm; I do concretely, and freely, what God asks of me'. He saw the conscience as the guiding authority of the human project of life, the basis of 'the fundamental option of life' in the midst of the situation in which a person lives. He regarded this option as an answer to God's claim made by the situation, even if that is not recognized as such and 'at the limit' is coupled with 'a certain negation of God'. Because God is creator, the fundamental option for every human being is 'to adopt a position over against (for or against) the living God and total reality, and thus in real confrontation with the living reality of God'. That applies even to those who say that they do not believe in God. However, if it is experienced in complete religious maturity, for Schillebeeckx action on the basis of the insight of the conscience into reality was at the same time 'an intimation in faith, a hopeful inclination towards [the] Mystery and loving affirmation of it'. 'Ktisiologically', 'a good deed of the conscience' was 'an "entry" into God's creative love' (II, 251–5, 257).[199]

In Schillebeeckx's view, all this becomes truly theological only if the perception of reality is taken up by the conscience in the perspective of God's will for salvation. Only then does created reality itself become 'a moment of conversation' in the believer's attitude to God. Only then can what the world requires of human beings through the conscience be listened to 'in intimacy with God' and be understood as an inner address from God (II, 258).[200] For him, this divine claim had two elements. First of all there was 'the challenge to submit' and accept totally 'the facts, that is, ultimately my specific humanity, with all the inevitability and the concrete situatedness that this comprises'. The God of salvation is the creator of every situation, and through this situation seeks contact with human beings, who here are challenged to 'give to God without holding anything back' (II, 260). But Schillebeeckx did not stop there. He indicated as a second element of the way in which God's free creative activity addresses the conscience the task of 'recreating' the existing situation as 'a milieu worth living in'. Precisely in their desire to 'renew the face of the earth', in his view human beings are being faithful to the *Deus salutaris creator*. In the second half of the 1950s this argument was by no means taken for granted, and Schillebeckx clearly took trouble to make it theologically credible. He argued that the concrete situation as human beings find it did not come directly from the gentle hand of God but was also the result of 'already sinful, free attributions of meaning by human beings'. Therefore – he suggested with great caution, but nevertheless resolutely; the full scope of this notion would come to light only in the 1960s and 1970s – 'faithfulness to God ... can also *coram Deo* imply opposition to the situation'. As if he recoiled from his own statement, he immediately added that in concrete cases within the church, as a 'form of the Christian system of redemption', sacrifice is brought into the centre of the effort at commitment , 'so that at times ... the effort at obedience itself must bend and, subjected, becomes accepting obedience'. Here he emphasized that this obedience must not be capitulation to evil but must be a form of discipleship of Christ, 'of Christ who, condemning evil, for higher ends gently "allowed" people to crucify him' (II, 261).

With this last statement Schillebeeckx returned to a well-known theme in his theology throughout his Louvain period. Time and again he emphasized that Christian faith also meant that it was necessary to stand back from creaturely reality and the commitment to creation, something that had become visible above all in the crucifixion which Jesus as Christ had voluntarily taken upon himself. Along the lines of this basic notion, in his lecture notes on the theology of creation he stated more emphatically than before that the God who resolutely wants only to be loved is at the same time the creator of heaven and earth. For him this implied quite radically that 'in and of itself ... suffering remains an evil', a curse which has not been made by God. From a Christian perspective, in his view suffering was important as a sign of God's refusal to give human beings the opportunity to nestle in the 'security within the world'. But he thought that this must not lead to the notion that 'social structures of reform' were of no value from a Christian perspective in diminishing suffering or even doing away with it entirely. The human obligation, which was also a Christian obligation, to 'order life within the world', in other words to create culture, remained fully in force (II, 417f.). Even more strongly, in his view Christians found the creature 'in its original value' in particular in the God whom they must love above all and only – in his words, 'in the midst of the jealous inexorability of his being all in all'. For Schillebeeckx, believers stand, united with God, 'at the source of everything, and then go with God ... to the world' of human beings and things. On this way they are completely with God, their 'task giving meaning in the world'.

Schillebeeckx saw the central paradox of salvation history, that God's salvation is made manifest in the suffering of Christ, as in fact lying back in creation itself: God has committed himself unconditionally to the finite and highly conditional. 'The conditional that we ourselves are' was in his view 'that which is unconditionally loved by God', and this gave 'the creaturely an inviolate validity'. In that light, the supreme love of God was no longer to be seen as the sacrificing of creaturely reality in honour of God's abso-luteness, but automatically took the form of loving creation with God (II, 255f.). In his books on Jesus from the 1970s he was also to describe Jesus's history and ministry, including his suffering, death and resurrection, con-sistently along these lines: 'God wills to be the origin ... of the worldliness of the world and the humanity of man. He wills to be with us in and with our finite task in the world.'[201] In the 1950s this view announced itself, as it were, increasingly loudly, but in the end did not completely break through.

Creation and grace

Schillebeeckx's lectures on creation were deeply marked by his constantly developing discovery of 'our finite task in the world'. Granted, the view that he developed earlier about the relationship between nature and the super-natural was repeated at some length in it, and he again spoke of the positive but passive openness of created human nature to the life of grace, which comes from God freely and in a way that from the human perspective is impossible to explain (II, 465–508). He also again proclaimed that the sacrifice of the values and desires given with created human nature was the necessary condition for being given grace (II, 509–13). But by comparison with his earlier publications the perspective had changed; above all because with greater resolution, in the conviction that 'human nature [is] created for a true and effective supernatural destiny', he drew the conclusion that this destiny was indeed 'the uniting principle of nature'.

This meant that for Schillebeeckx human nature could be understood authentically only in terms of the grace into which human nature is taken up through salvation. Not only did grace presuppose nature, as the classical scholastic adage ran – *gratia supponit naturam* – according to Schillebeeckx it was 'even more true that grace is the condition for the existence of nature', and *natura supponit gratiam*. This was in fact a translation into the technical theological jargon of the time – which was scholastic – of the central starting point of his lectures on creation, namely that creation faith expresses a total religious view of reality. According to Schillebeeckx's theological view, human nature as it came to light in human life was not the abstract *natura pura* which neoscholasticism tried to describe, nor the reality with which the grace controlled by the church linked up. Human nature as this in fact showed itself was human nature on which grace had been bestowed; human beings actually living were always already taken up in to salvation history (II, 513–17). 'If we want to regard the concrete real historical man as he is given to us in experience – and after all this is the only real standpoint – we face a man with an effective supernatural destiny' (II, 455f.).[202] Therefore, in his view, as we saw, a proof of God was possible from the accurate analysis of human existence. That meant that only a theological perspective on this existence could be comprehensive; even a philosophical approach to man was in fact orientated on human existence under grace, but it could not explicitate that. For that reason, finally he could say more decisively than before that the human creation of culture – 'let us say humanism, *to anthropopuesthai*, to use a saying of Aristotle's' – was a task of creation orientated on the true, good and beautiful in reality and thus on God'.

'Culture is the world which man himself . . . brings into being, on the basis of the world of nature in the function of the optimal deployment of his own human possibilities of life', in which man transforms both himself and the world (II, 455–64). For Schillebeeckx, in the perspective of the actual bestowal of grace this meant that man humanizes himself and the human world in the perspective of grace and redemption. Here too we see him shift towards the standpoint that from the perspective of faith the creation of culture also meant taking part in redemption and therefore in principle did not compete with being orientated on grace as a completely free gift of God. Nevertheless, in his view a fundamental ambiguity kept clinging to the actual human creation of culture:

> The whole of culture with its development down the centuries, 'world history', is thus inwardly tuned to the kingdom of God; but in the light of the very mystery of this kingdom of God as the Christian principle of redemption, the ambiguous value will remain a value of this inner ordering will become clear (II, 515f.).

That was the background to his argument, which has already been indicated, that the believer needed to sacrifice everything for the exclusive love of God, but that 'in the midst of the jealous inexorability of [God's] being all in all, the creature [was] to be found in its original character', in which it then once again asked for support and dedication.

For all his orientation on the concrete man and the salvation history narrated in the Bible, Schillebeeckx continued to speak in the quite abstract and static terms of neoscholasticism, which, in the 1950s, were simply part of theology. Nevertheless, his lecture notes on creation heralded the far-reaching metamorphosis that theology was to undergo after the Second

Vatican Council. In his lectures this remains only a beginning, but in the chapter on 'evil in creation' it is possible to discover the basic features of a new way of thinking about the relationship between the human situation in the world, misery, and the suffering bound up with it, and God's redemptive involvement in it. Clearly under the impact of the existentialist critique of the usual Christian view of suffering and death, and referring explicitly to the appearance of the Jesuit priest Paneloux in Albert Camus' novel *The Plague*, he remarked:

> It is appropriate to speak of the problem of suffering, sin and death only with reverence. The reality of suffering is too terrible for us, even as Christians, to have a clear solution for it (II, 352f.). Suffering in itself is not a problem, but *my* suffering, *your* suffering, the suffering that is built into life that is *my life*, is. To be entangled in suffering is fundamental for the problem of suffering (II, 353f.).

He then went on to construct with almost essayistic boldness a conflict between the contemporary question 'which from the experience of suffering puts the existence of God in question' and the mediaeval attitude which still lived on in contemporary neoscholasticism. For this way of thinking the reality of God was certain, and in his view the question arose, rather, 'whether evil is a real fact'. Thomas Aquinas actually asked himself 'whether evil is to be found in things' – and moreover went on to answer this question in the affirmative[203] – and Schillebeeckx seems deliberately to abandon 'the basis of St Thomas' so as to be able to go fully into 'contemporary problems'. He wanted to maintain what he called the 'ktisiological optimism' that in his view formed part of the classical Christian view, deriving from Augustine, namely that evil is not anything in itself but consists in the absence of good. At the same time he felt that this approach to evil as *privatio boni* did not seem to take evil seriously enough. With a capacity for empathy he expounded the experience that evil is so overwhelming in history that it almost seems to come from an active, independent personal power. This helped him to understand why the tendency towards dualism arises time and again in human religious and intellectual history (II, 352–6). He was convinced that there was no solution to 'the serious problem of suffering' except in 'belief in the mystery', but in his view that was precisely the opposite of the usual solution.

Despite his plan to take the concrete experience of suffering seriously, Schillebeeckx engaged in quite extensive speculations about the origin of evil in general, about its relationship to human freedom, and about how something that God had not willed could clearly have so much power. But he was not concerned to offer a metaphysical explanation of evil. He was concerned to maintain the notion that from a theological perspective even evil and the human choice of evil cannot go outside God. This implied for him that God is 'not checkmated by sin and its consequences' (II, 384). He incorporated into this framework the notion that he had developed in his lectures on christology: that Christ as redeemer from evil and sin is the 'crowning fruit of all creation'. In his view, that meant saying that precisely by being the redeemer Christ was the embodiment of God's faithfulness to his creation, in other words to God's ultimate motive for creation: comprehensive salvation and happiness, bringing everything into God's glory (II, 389f.). Schillebeeckx concluded from this that the whole history of humankind pointed to the redemptive history of Jesus Christ and was contained by the divine redemption as this is expressed in his history: if this was true, then that must also be the case for evil and sin, and for the suffering which was the consequence and expression of it (II, 387f.). This was Schillebeeckx's interpretation of the age-old Christian conviction that God did not want sin and evil, but allowed them. In contrast to the usual idea, here in his view it was not a matter of passiveness from God's side; rather, God's allowing of human evil and human sin was the expression of his abiding love and faithfulness, despite and in human unfaithfulness. In Schillebeeckx's view, God persisted with man, although man had abandoned God and this led to the domination of evil. Therefore the possibility was always open for human beings to return to God (II, 385–7).[204]

Following this train of thought, Schillebeeckx argued first – and this was in line with what he had said in another context about the Christian task of discipleship – that human suffering which was meaningless in itself took on meaning in the history of the suffering of Christ. That did not mean that suffering in itself took on meaning; suffering took on meaning through the way in which Christ transformed his suffering into an expression of God's abiding love and at the same time into a way of remaining bound up with this suffering as a man, to the point of unmerited and excessive suffering.[205] In Christ, for believers suffering becomes a possibility of showing the truthfulness of their surrender to God. Secondly, Schillebeeckx's train of thought also implied that one must not seek contact with God by becoming detached from concrete suffering, but by accepting it as a situation which in all its incomprehensibility nevertheless comes from God. According to the Schillebeeckx of the 1950s, painful though it might be, suffering was ultimately meaningful in the pedagogy of salvation, and in a paradoxical way made God's redemptive presence visible. Suffering made the painfulness of the human situation of entanglement in evil and sin an unavoidable experience and thus at all events broke through 'the illusion "that all is well", simply because things go well within the world'.[206] In the 1970s Schillebeeckx would become constantly more hesitant about the possibility of any meaningful Christian explanation of suffering. Suffering was intrinsically meaningless. But already in his lectures on creation he maintained the insight that 'a mystery [continued] to hang over suffering, above all when it affects innocent people or people who are inwardly advanced in the love of God' (II, 395–9). Ultimately, one could only hold firm to the meaning of suffering and the fundamental conviction that in one way or another this had to be, because it was taken up by Christ's suffering into God.

Schillebeeckx firmly rooted this conviction in his christology of this period, which was based on Thomas Aquinas. From a Christian perspective, in his view the mystery was ultimately the fact that in the history of this man who in his humanity is at the same time God, 'suffering which is intrinsically absurd' is borne up by God himself and by the one who by divine mission is 'the ultimate meaning of creation'. 'God, absolute meaning, here endures the absurd and therefore, hidden in God, suffering must be meaningful.' In his view Christians can therefore experience as a situation of salvation what in the first instance is only a situation of disaster: 'There is no less suffering, death continues to remain bewildering, but this bewilderment itself becomes a state of redemption.' In this way 'a spirituality of surrender to the mystery of God' becomes possible (II, 401–3). Redeemed in Christ, according to Schillebeeckx, Christians could paradoxically experience suffering as meaningful 'and in lostness cleave to God above all – and at the same time in all' (II, 406). Thus, specifically in suffering, Christ proved to be the form of 'God's glory itself', precisely in his radical love for human beings which expressed itself in the unreserved divine readiness to share the human situation of disaster and suffering. The aim was to transform it from within and to orientate it on human salvation: Schillebeeckx quoted the church father Irenaeus of Lyons: God's glory is the living man, *Gloria Dei, vivens homo* (II, 407).[207] On the basis of the conviction that even absurd suffering was not outside God's presence, in the 1970s, with great obstinacy, Schillebeeckx could continue to ask the theological question: at what precise point does this presence shine out in the midst of suffering? As I have already indicated, he ultimately began to speak of suffering as a contrast experience, an experience which provokes opposition, and precisely in so doing points to the situation of human salvation willed by God and thus, in hope, makes this already present.

MARRIAGE AS A SAVING MYSTERY

But that was still to take ten years, ten years in which the context of Schillebeeckx's theologizing was to change fundamentally, and therefore with it likewise his theology. At the beginning of 1958 he moved to the Netherlands, and a year later the Second Vatican Council was announced. This was to make him world famous, together with a number of colleagues who were likewise closely involved in this gathering and its epoch-making discussions. The Council would put special emphasis on the church as the sacrament of God's salvation for the world, and after the Council Schillebeeckx would concentrate on the question how, in a Western society which was becoming increasingly secular, the Christian faith could indeed be presented as a message of salvation. But before all this could really get going, even during the Council he was to publish a book which can be regarded as a closer focusing of the sacramental theology of culture in his *De sacramentele heilseconomie*. It was in line with the kind of thinking which he developed in his Flemish lectures. *Het huwelijk, aardse werkelijkheid en heilsmysterie* (*Marriage: Human Reality and Saving Mystery*) appeared in Dutch in 1963 and was written in Nijmegen. In this sense the book falls outside the scope of this chapter. But because it is so completely along the lines of the Louvain part of Schillebeeckx's work, it does form part of the 'Louvain synthesis'. So I shall discuss it as the end of this chapter.

The Catholic discussion of marriage and sexuality

Schillebeeckx was in no way exaggerating when in the Foreword he said that what he envisaged as a 'dogmatics of marriage' had 'become, especially since the last war, the object of a great deal of lively discussion which has concerned itself both with the experience of marriage and with our thinking about it'. He loosely summed up the 'contemporary problems of marriage' with which the church authorities found themselves confronted in their pastoral care:

> The psychological and social aspects of marriage, the question of 'mixed marriages', the secular dimension of marriage and (linked to this) the question of civil marriage, celibacy (considered both on its own and in connection with the secular priesthood) and marital difficulties and the allied problem of responsible parenthood.

Almost forty years later these have become strange words, but at the end of the 1950s and the beginning of the 1960s this passage pointed in an understandable way to the questions which were certainly at the centre of interest among Catholics. At this period, in the Netherlands, a quite concrete reality corresponded to the picture sketched out here, that 'above the heads of married couples' all kinds of expert views clashed with one another, particularly those of psychologists on the one hand and theologians on the other. According to Schillebeeckx, these clashes were to an important degree due to the tendency of experts to overstep the limits of their competence: 'Theologians, for example, would like to regulate human psychology according to their own theological views, while psychologists are often inclined to think that what they have to say completely invalidates the *dicta*

270

of the theologians.' He himself was therefore concerned to develop a theological view of marriage which was also supported by 'an anthropological understanding of marriage and sexuality', in the conviction that such a view, like any theology, had a chance of success only 'if it manages to clarify both the word of God concerning man, and man's experience of his own existence in the light of demands made by the situation in which he finds himself living today'.[208]

In fact while paying attention to these questions about marriage and sexuality as they were in the late 1950s, Schillebeeckx was also concealing something. Marriage, sexual experience and above all dealing with fertility had been important and loaded questions for Catholics since at least 1930, the year in which Pius XI's encyclical *Casti connubii* appeared. In this encyclical the pope opposed modern developments like the separation of civil marriage from church marriage and the conditional allowance of divorce; the efforts toward women's emancipation from submissiveness in traditional marriage; birth control and abortion, and he emphasized that marriage is a divine institution, holy and indissoluble. In its offensive against modernity, the leadership of the Catholic Church emphasized that marriage is primarily ordained for the procreation of children. As late as 1944 the Roman authority which guards over orthodoxy, then called the Holy Office, emphatically decreed that mutual conjugal love must not be elevated to become the prime goal of marriage and that having children must not be seen as the mere consequence of it; moreover, according to the pronouncement of the decree there could be no talk of two equal main purposes of marriage, though the Second Vatican Council was to state exactly this.[209] This decree of the Holy Office, and also the encyclical *Casti connubii*, was part of a series of Vatican reactions to the discussion on marriage and sexuality which the Catholic Church could not ward off, despite all its efforts. In the course of the first half of the twentieth century, in Catholic circles, too, there was an ever stronger and wider effort to replace the textbook morality surrounding marriage based on laws, commandments and prohibitions with an approach which took account of concrete human desires and needs. The so-called 'marriage distress' caused by the church's absolute prohibition on the use of contraception, which put sexual practice under enormous pressure, was a special issue here.

After the Second World War, sexuality, and especially the non-neurotic or psychologically healthy way of dealing with it, became an important theme in the Western world. The years 1948 and 1953 saw the appearance of the notorious and pioneering studies by the team of researchers around the American sexologist Alfred C. Kinsey, who demonstrated how much the actual sexual experience of men and women differed from the restrictive sexual morality which was still dominating the public sphere.[210] The presentation of the results of the investigations made the reports powerful pleas for greater openness and boldness in this sphere, and that is in fact how they were read. In Catholic circles the longing for more openness and boldness was expressed in publications like those of the German psychiatrist Ernst Michel, who, in 1948 in his book *Ehe: Eine Anthropologie der Geschlechtsgemeinschaft* (Marriage: An Anthropology of Sexual Relationships), developed a philosophical vision of marriage in which human sexuality was seen as a positive value and which offered an alternative picture of anthropology to that of the handbook of moral theology. And 1952 saw the publication of the study *Vie chrétienne et problèmes de la sexualité* by the French psychiatrist and priest Marc Oraison, in which in principle he left the dominant Catholic morality intact, but for practical and pastoral reasons tried to find room for a solution to the sexual problems with which Catholics in practice seemed to continue to fight, often precisely because of this morality. Both books were put on the Index of Prohibited Books by the Holy Office, but this did not prevent them from having an influence on Catholic intellectuals and pastors.[211]

As elsewhere, in the Netherlands during the 1950s there were a growing number of conflicts between a psychological approach to sexuality and procreation and an approach from neoscholastic moral theology. However, there more than elsewhere these were connected with the growing practical influence of psychology as a separate discipline, especially also in Catholic circles. In the course of the 1950s a broad movement for Catholic spiritual health care grew out of the Catholic marriage bureaux, which had originally been set up as a form of special pastoral care. It stood for spiritual freedom, personal responsibility and a spiritually sound life of faith. This programme was based on the ideas of a limited group of opinion-making Catholics – including a number of professional lay people, which was still striking in this period – about the need for a new tangible form of church action in post-war society. Their ideas about a healthy and harmonious human existence, which were especially based on the phenomenological psychology of F. J. J. Buytendijk, spread rapidly among key figures in the Catholic Netherlands during the second half of the 1950s.[212] Obviously, in this framework the actual problems of Catholics in their experience of marriage and sexuality were a central point of attention.[213]

On the combined initiative of the National Centre for Catholic Action and the Catholic National Bureau for Spiritual Health Care – in other words the national centres of both the official Catholic lay movement and the Catholic organizations active in the sphere of spiritual health care – in 1959 a broad investigation was begun into the problems that Dutch Catholics had in connection with marriage and the family, and into the views about this held by the authorities active in this area. Those who took this initiative succeeded in getting an endorsement from the episcopate.[214] In the autumn of 1960 this investigation presented a provisional report

272

to the bishops and the authorities which had collaborated in the investigation. In it, the fundamental questions surrounding a renewal of pastoral care for marriage and family were discussed, and a survey was given of the views of Dutch Catholics on the subject. The report indicated a current in preaching and pastoral practice which maintained the traditional morality of marriage and family, a second current which wanted to combine the continuance of integral preaching with a degree of mildness in its application, and a third current which started from the notion that pastoral care needed to guide couples lovingly towards the ideal of a healthy loving partnership. Supporters of this last standpoint did not want to abandon the traditional morality in principle, even where it prohibited the use of contraceptives, something that Catholics found very oppressive at a time when the contraceptive pill had become available for broad layers of the population. However, their starting point was that the faithful had to grow into accepting this teaching in freedom, and here they argued the need for respect for the decisions which the faithful took on the basis of their consciences.

The working committee that produced the 'Investigation into Marriage and the Family' – in fact its spiritual father and the motive force behind it was the priest, moral philosopher and pastoral psychologist Hein Ruygers, who by his own confession had edited the report 'very extensively and boldly' – clearly supported this last view. It was thought that the results of the investigation showed that it was necessary to develop a pastoral approach which began from the understanding of actual people, their difficulties, their hopes and their discouragements.[215] In the discussion of the report by the theological steering committee a voice was heard which went even further. The account of the discussion sent to the bishops with the report made summary mention of 'question-marks and doubts about the correct interpretation of the standpoint of the church', but a very fundamental discussion underlay this. In fact Fons Wijers, formally professor of exegesis at the major seminary of the diocese of Den Bosch, and at the time of the discussion rector of the St Radboud hospital in Nijmegen, had defended the view that morality was part of a historical process of development. On the basis of this, he had then raised what was at that time the quite sensational question in Catholic circles whether a morality which virtually no one could put into practice could be right.[216]

In their reaction, the bishops said that they valued the phenomenological and psychological approach to the problems in the draft report that had been sent to them. However, they found the investigation one-sided, and were particularly shocked by the commentary by the theologians, even though in the account of the discussion that they saw this had been put with great restraint. They evidently felt that 'question-marks and doubts about the correct interpretation of the church's standpoint' was opposition to the statement made by Archbishop Bernard Alfrink shortly beforehand to a congress of Catholic doctors to the effect that anyone who expected that 'the church would declare *coitus interruptus* and the use of contraceptives permissible' would be disappointed, because it was the conviction of the church in all times and all places that these practices were wrong.[217] The bishops therefore went in search of people with the synthetic capacity to put the data of the 'Investigation into Marriage and the Family' in a theological framework which seemed more convincing to them. They asked the moral theologian Theo Beemer and Schillebeeckx to write the definitive final report, after consultation with the commission which had given the report theological substance, and also on the basis of the reactions to the provisional version of the report. For Schillebeeckx this was in line with developments. As we shall see in the next chapter, in this period he became one of the most important advisers to the Dutch bishops and appeared whenever they needed someone who would connect the church tradition with contemporary questions. Moreover, he seemed to subscribe to the standpoint that Alfrink had adopted towards the Catholic doctors. In a lecture in 1960 he had called the prohibition against contraceptives 'the unanimous teaching of the world episcopate', so in his view there was 'no way back' on this point.[218]

In this report for fellow-theologians, Schillebeeckx had emphatically left room for a further development of the church's standpoint on the basis of new contemporary insights. In this connection he gave an interpretation of the teaching of Thomas Aquinas on natural law in which, along the lines of De Petter's philosophy, he gave a central place to human beings as complete persons who also had bodies, rather than to a human *natura* which was to be explored separately.[219] However logical this may have been in the framework of Schillebeeckx's development, it also meant a fundamental break with the dominant way of thinking about marriage and sexuality in moral theology, which tried to base itself on insights into sexual actions as expressions of the natural human orientation on procreation. He called such an approach 'physicistic' and strongly opposed it, regardless of whether it had a 'progressive' effect – in some circumstances in favour of birth control – or a 'conservative' one. Moreover, he rejected out of hand 'situation ethics' – which was condemned by the church – with its view that the moral content of an action was strictly dependent on the situation, and also the notion that there was an absolute natural law which could be and had to be relativized for practical and pastoral reasons.[220] The provisional report on the 'Investigation into Marriage and the Family' which was brought out later would move in this last direction.[221]

Rather than a pastoral adaptation of the prevalent morality of the church, Schillebeeckx wanted a fundamental theological reflection on marriage and sexuality. With a view to this, in his technical theological report, on the basis of De Petter and in line with contemporary discussions in moral philosophy, he made a distinction between the *project* of marriage, which according to him the church taught inescapably and with the full weight of its infallible authority, as being incompatible with the positive exclusion of having children, and the various *acts* of marriage – moral-theological jargon for sexual intercourse – in which in some cases the use of contraceptives could be permitted.[222] Schillebeeckx clearly hoped for new developments in official church statements on this last point; he evidently saw room for this. But as long as these new developments had not taken place, he argued for loyal obedience and faithfulness to existing church teaching, since 'an ecclesiastical document [can] be interpreted in an authentic way only by the church itself and not by theologians'.[223] Here he was falling short of his own views on ecclesiology and was identifying 'the church' with the magisterium of the hierarchy.

This whole question ultimately fizzled out like a damp squid. When, in June 1963, Schillebeeckx and Beemer brought out their final report on the 'Investigation into Marriage and the Family' for the bishops, many Dutch Catholics felt that the liberating words about contraceptives had already been spoken. As a result of this, the theological discussion on marriage and sexuality had lost much of its urgency. In a notorious broadcast in March 1963, Willem Bekkers, the popular Bishop of 's-Hertogenbosch, had said in his monthly television talk that 'in its loving concern' for the covenant between married couples and God the church indeed taught 'that children are a blessing, a gift', but that questions relating to the number of children could 'never be treated apart from married life as a whole'; here it was possible to recognize the line that Schillebeeckx stood for. Within this framework Bekkers called decisions about birth control 'matters of conscience' for married persons themselves 'in which no one may interfere'.[224] For many Catholics, in connection with the broader social developments in this sphere, this meant the beginning of a freer way of dealing with sexuality and contraception, without burdening the conscience. Initially, prompted by the report, the bishops worked on a pastoral letter on marriage and family, but this never appeared. Probably there was not sufficient time to do the necessary preparatory work, especially because the Second Vatican Council was now under way, with all the work that it involved. But in addition, in the meantime a papal commission in Rome was working on an encyclical on the church's teaching about marriage, and it was then customary for 'lower authorities' in the church not to make further statements on the matter.[225]

The Pastoral Council of the Dutch Church Province that was meant to adopt the results of the Second Vatican Council to the Dutch situation was to devote a report to 'marriage and family'. The planned encyclical appeared a year before this was discussed in Noordwijkerhout at the beginning of 1969. How much the situation in the Dutch church had changed, also as a result of the Council, was evident from the statement by the Pastoral

Council, with the approval of the Dutch bishops, that the prohibition of all methods of birth control with the exception of the so-called rhythm method, again firmly urged in *Humanae vitae*, was 'unconvincing'. The Pastoral Council emphatically backed the line taken by Bishop Bekkers and said that the regulation of the number of children in a family was 'a free and inalienable personal decision for the married couple'.[226]

Marriage as a human reality elevated to become a sacrament

So this was the climate in which Schillebeeckx wrote his 'dogmatics of marriage'. Simply by giving his study this name he seemed to want to break with the approach of moral theology, which in the case of marriage classically kept close to church law.[227] However, before the end the study was to run aground, like the discussion on sexuality in the Dutch church, and thus never became 'the most comprehensive work on this topic' which according to a commentator it could have developed into.[228] Perhaps Schillebeeckx thought further reflection on marriage less important after the appearance of the Second Vatican Council Constitution on the Modern World, *Gaudium et spes*. He himself was involved in the preparation of the section on marriage, and according to a later commentator he also found his ideas in the final text.[229] He also once confided to people close to him that in his view further theological writing on marriage should be done by a married man. Be this as it may, in the 1960s other questions were to require so much of his attention that he simply did not return to the second part of his study on marriage.[230]

However, from the beginning it had been quite clear to him what the direction of his work on marriage had to be. As early as February 1960, in other words relatively early in the intensive and fundamental philosophical and theological reflection manifestly provoked by the 'Investigation into Marriage and the Family', 'commissioned by the bishops', in the season 1960–1 the Association of Catholic Theologians in the Netherlands devoted five lectures to it and discussed it intensively. In the same season the Association of Thomistic Philosophers devoted its annual meeting to the subject, and in 1960 two hefty monographs appeared on the theology and dogmatics of marriage respectively.[231] Moreover, the progressive weekly *De Bazuin*, addressed to a broad public, came out with a special issue completely devoted to marriage. *De Bazuin* was published by the Dutch Dominicans from the house in which Schillebeeckx was living, and the issue on marriage was written completely by him.[232] In it he offered a relatively succinct sketch of his theological views on marriage, including sexuality and birth control, and he had wanted to work out this sketch further in his planned study on marriage. The starting point was the notion the essence of which he expressed in September 1960 like this:

Marriage is a human reality which is elevated to a sacrament. One of the fundamental decisions of human life, a decision in the midst of all kinds of concrete situations and social ties, is thus a religious event.[233]

This notion is indicated even more succinctly in the subtitle to his book on marriage: 'Human Reality and Saving Mystery'.

The special issue of *De Bazuin* was entitled 'The Blessings of Sacramental Marriage', and according to the brief explanation by the editors, in their view Schillebeeckx had succeeded in developing a new perspective on marriage. They remarked that they realized that the text called for 'much serious attention and readiness for reflection', but at the same time they thought that 'honest study' would 'bring forth its fruits one hundredfold', because for anyone who penetrated it 'often a totally new perspective [would] be opened up on the saving reality of Christian married life'. It was not only the Dutch bishops who thought that in this period Schillebeeckx had evidently succeeded in arriving at a theological framework within which there was room for reflecting fruitfully and in a refreshing way on current questions while at the same time remaining faithful to the tradition of the church. In fact, for example, the boldness with which he wrote that people who got married did not go to the altar to 'detach their human love from its humanity' was refreshing. And in the midst of all the anxious statements by pastors, church leaders and theologians about the developments surrounding marriage, it was without doubt a relief to get a 'dogmatics of marriage' which unrestrainedly began by saying that the 'modern type of marriage', in which the married couple were no longer held together by economic necessity or the pressure of their surroundings, and the bond of love came to have a central place between the couple, was 'an opportunity for grace'.[234]

But *Marriage* had little that was downright shocking to offer, even by the standards of the early 1960s. Only in the second part was Schillebeeckx to go into 'the concrete problems of marriage' and to discuss with the tradition 'the relationship between interpersonal relations in marriage and having a family, and between married love and sexuality', and from here to draw attention to 'the urgent modern problems of marriage' (211). The first volume was pioneering, especially in the theology in the strict sense which it offered.

According to the general approach that characterized his scholarly work in the 1950s, Schillebeeckx investigated the tradition of faith and theology at length. 'Although the subject of marriage is examined in this book on a broad basis of positive theology, I feel that this basis is still too narrow and insufficient', he wrote in the Foreword (xvii). He went on to sketch the development of the theological view of the sacramental nature of marriage.

But what was most striking was the way in which he approached marriage theologically on this basis. The fact that in the 1950s contemporary discussions about marriage as an interpersonal and socio-cultural relationship and about sexuality as a psychological phenomenon found their way into the church and theology showed that the secular, worldly perspective was also gaining strength in Catholic circles. The perspective on reality of lay people who lived within the world and tried to live out their faith there was finding a voice. And Schillebeeckx saw that it was the task of a contemporary theology of marriage to take particular account of this perspective and to assess it positively. In his book, his theological interest in the position of lay people and their contribution to culture and his theological view of the sacraments as effective signs of the divine grace within the world influenced each other. For him the specific nature of the sacrament of marriage lay 'in a reality secular by origin which has acquired a deeper meaning in the order of salvation in which we live and which, for this reason, points to something higher' (18). For this reason he argued emphatically for an interdisciplinary discussion as part of theology, at least as part of the theology of marriage:

> Precisely because [the] human reality [of marriage] is itself a sacrament, everything that can be said from a natural standpoint about marriage has enormous significance for the theologian. Psychologists and sociologists, philosophers of culture and psychiatrists, even historians, have made a tremendous contribution to a deeper knowledge of the reality of marriage.[235]

In the wake of what the Second Vatican Council stated about the close connection between church and world, and prompted by new developments in culture, Schillebeeckx himself was increasingly and more intensively to enter into discussions with these contributions, in ever more theological areas.

As in *De sacramental heilseconomie*, so in *Marriage* Schillebeeckx did not directly identify himself as a Thomist. Certainly he gave himself the profile of a pupil of Thomas, but he did so especially by indicating the similarity between Thomas's situation and the questions with which he saw himself confronted as a theologian. In this situation he then tried to adopt a standpoint analogous to that of Thomas in his situation.

The Catholic view of marriage was heavily influenced by the declaration of the Council of Trent that for baptized Christians only a marriage in the presence of a priest and two witnesses was valid in law. In the wake of this, the notion had developed that sacramental marriage was identical with marriage contracted in church in this sense. In connection with this the Catholic church leaders were strongly opposed to any state influence on marriage, and especially the possibility of a civil marriage independent of the church.[236] On the basis of an investigation of the history of marriage, however, Schillebeeckx boldly stated that church jurisdiction over marriage was a chance fact of history and not an expression of theological necessity. In his view the 'church's jurisdictional monopoly in connection with matrimonial matters' which in fact developed later became a 'theological thesis' (214). He argued that from the eleventh century, in both the West and the East there was a tendency to locate the sacramentality of marriage in the celebration of the marriage liturgy, but he was convinced that until then the experience of marriage was rightly seen as a natural human reality which was experienced 'in the Lord'. It was sacramental in this experience. He thought that the view that marriage was a sacrament in the strict sense, one of the seven central signs of divine salvation in Christian life, developed between the eleventh and the thirteenth centuries. It was out of this growing *awareness in faith* of the unique sacramental significance of marriage' that theological reflection on it then began; he was convinced that the sacramental theology of the time did not determine the concept of marriage as a sacrament, but that this concept came about on the basis of the experience of marriage in faith (108–35, quotation 134). With this interpretation of the history of theology, at the same time he suggested a quite different kind of theological reflection on marriage from the one customary at that time. In his view, the view of marriage as a sacramental reality did not arise out of a moral theological approach which took up church law, but could form only as theological reflection on the experience of marriage among the faithful.[237]

According to Schillebeeckx's view of the history of theology, it took quite a long time for mediaeval theology really to understand marriage in a convincing way as a sacrament in the technical sense, as an effective sign of God's grace.[238] Certainly it was already a biblical tradition to see marriage as an image of God's covenant with his people and then of Christ's bond with his church. This last in particular was regarded as the inner ground of the conviction that Christian marriage was indissoluble; its external origin lay in Jesus's statement that man might not put asunder what God had joined together (Matt.19.1–8; Mark 10.1–12; Luke 16.18; 1 Cor. 7.10–11).[239] But in his view, the negative view of sexuality, which had been widespread in the church since the church fathers, had blocked an integral view of marriage from this perspective. People could not see that marriage which allowed 'such things' could be a source of grace like the other sacraments, and marriage was regarded more as a 'medicine against desires', aconcession to those who could not live in sexual continence. During the 1950s experts and counsellors were particularly opposed to the view of sexuality as a necessary evil, good only in so far as it led to procreation and allowed on strict conditions as a way of countering human sinfulness. According to clinical and pastoral experience this view was highly likely to lead to neuroses. For Schillebeeckx, theological reflection on Thomas Aquinas offered the possibility of getting rid of this negative view of marriage and sexuality.

In his interpretation, for Thomas the sacramental reality of marriage was its authentic fellowship. It was an 'association of man and wife directed towards sexual intercourse and everything connected with it', in other words having children and bringing them up. In Schillebeeckx's view 'the real actuation of this community of marriage [was] the sex act' (127).[240] Convinced that he was walking in the footsteps of Thomas, Schillebeeckx thus regarded sexuality as a positive human possibility. However, this was not sexuality in itself, but sexuality in the framework of a fellowship which was open to the reception of children – and in his view that was what marriage needed to be. Within this framework he thought that sexual activity expressed the firm will 'to share the whole of life with a partner' and thus became 'the expression of a lasting union of two *persons* – a *human*, sexual relationship' (210).[241] This very 'living union of two persons', the 'mode of existence of married love which has grown up inwardly', became an effective sign of God's faithful love for his people in sacramental marriage. Lasting human love is a sign of 'a divine redemption which grasps our humanity down to its corporeality'.[242] In this view, however, sexuality remained focused on procreation, for especially in its orientation on children – in other words on the continuation of the world – and their upbringing – the continuation of the Christian message

> sexual intercourse [was] by definition the expression of a personal decision to serve the kingdom of God in a secular way ... This decision by which man opens himself, through the other person, to the kingdom of God, is irrevocable, since it is in this decision that the mystery of the *henosis*, or the union of Christ with his church, is achieved (208).

In his view, as an expression of openness to having children, sexuality was openness to the coming of the kingdom of God. As a distinct person the child was not just the fruit of the love of its parents but a mystery, a gift of God that the parents received. So in his view it also had to be kept away from 'desecrating human hands'.[243]

Those who read Schillebeeckx's texts on marriage and sexuality around 35 years after they were written will be struck above all by the great hesitation over interpreting sexual experience itself as a positive value, regardless of its possible aim or function. This hesitation seems to derive from a concern to give the church's statements about marriage and sexuality a meaningful place in his theology. Not only did he not want to contradict the magisterium, but his whole approach bore traces of the traditional preoccupations with what make a marriage an authentic marriage and with the connection between sexuality and procreation, however much he also tried to see them in a broader perspective. Thus, the statement about the positive significance of sexuality, which in the context in which he wrote was by far his most revolutionary remark, came to stand almost in brackets: to the statement that a child comes as a gift of the living God, as an aside he added that 'marital love and its passion' were 'also gifts from God'.[244] Had he written his theology of marriage on the basis of this observation and thus used as his starting point the increasing dissociation of sexuality and procreation, he would have taken more seriously his conviction that the 'modern type of marriage' is 'an opportunity for grace'. He would have been better able to pay attention to what in his view was the task of the theologian: to take account of contemporary insights from the philosophy of culture, sociology and psychology. But at the beginning of the 1960s doing theology from this perspective was in fact still unthinkable.[245]

Marriage seems important for the later development of Schillebeeckx's theology above all because in this study he took up his project of a theology of culture. In the footsteps of Thomas he distinguished three aspects of marriage. First there was the natural dimension of the conception and upbringing of children, the *officium naturae*. Secondly there was the *officium civilitatis*, which he interpreted as the interpersonal, social and cultural dimension of marriage. And thirdly there was marriage as a sacrament. According to Schillebeeckx, the first two dimensions were taken up in marriage as a sacrament, and in these dimensions a mystery of salvation came about without their losing their character. Because of the character of the civil dimension – it is worth mentioning in passing the prevalent church opposition to any state influence on marriage – in his view a certain preoccupation with marriage on the part of the state was legitimate, since the church was concerned with the social dimension of human existence (141–8, 210). Moreover, he was convinced that this view of marriage, as sacramental precisely in its secular character, brought him near to the Protestant view of marriage: according to him Protestant theology did not deny the holiness of marriage but only the church's jurisdiction over it (113). But the most important thing was that in his view of the sacramentality of marriage the natural and socio-cultural dimension of human existence was taken up into the divine economy of salvation as such, and therefore without losing its distinctiveness.

In [the sacrament of marriage] a human reality which is deeply rooted in the earthly world is redeemed. And the family arises out of marriage. Thus the marriage bond is the source of the closest community, namely family community, from which all further human community gradually develops. Philosophers of culture have rightly said that marriage is the foundation of the whole creation of human culture. Now through the sacrament this source, namely marriage fellowship, is sanctified and brought 'into the Lord'.

According to Schillebeeckx, through the family, and through efforts by parents on behalf of the family, the grace of marriage ultimately worked through into the whole of society.[246]

This meant that in his view the deepest reason for Christians to be concerned with the world was not that 'being a Christian must also be experienced in and with what happens in the world' and did not lie in the task of the lay apostolate to renew the face of the earth. For him the deepest reason for religious effort with the world – and here he used thoughts especially from his lectures on creation – was that 'the secular reality, which has been taken up into salvation, has itself become sacramental in the technical sense', in other words has become an effective sign of God's gracious presence (217). On the basis of this conviction, in the period after the Second Vatican Council Schillebeeckx was to intensify his theological reflections on earthly reality, especially cultural and social reality, and give them a new turn.[247]

However, that became possible only through the Second Vatican Council, which was announced a year after Schillebeeckx came to the Netherlands. He was immediately enthusiastic about the idea, and the period between 1959 and 1960 was largely shaped by activities which had directly or indirectly to do with this gathering. The next chapter investigates that period. The content of his theology was not to change markedly at this time, but, as we shall see, his image as a theologian changed, both for himself and for others. After the Council he was to be *the* Dutch theologian, and people almost forgot his Flemish origins.

Chapter 5

A Dutch Council Theologian

'... *Christianity* ... *must also be an event in which authentic salvation history is achieved*'

BREAKTHROUGH OF CHANGES

It was not immediately striking at the time, but in retrospect the last quarter of the 1950s was a time of great change. It was the time in which the post-war period in Western Europe came to an end, and there were signs of the era which under the designation 'the 1960s' would come to be regarded as a turning point in the social and cultural history of the twentieth century. The sober period of recovery was followed by years of great hope. Along with the success of the reconstruction, great optimism arose over the unlimited possibilities of modern technological developments, and there was a broad concern for a fundamental renewal of society and culture. In the 1960s the people of the United States were to elect the charismatic and youthful senator John Fitzgerald Kennedy (1917–63) president, and he embodied these feelings *par excellence*. In 1958 the United Nations unanimously re-elected Dag Hammaskjöld (1905–61) Secretary-General; during his first period in office he had become almost a legend as a result of his successful peace missions. That same year the European Parliament chose as its pres-ident the French statesman Robert Schuman (1886–1963), who had always been committed to economic collaboration with a view to a permanent peace in Europe. This project had been crowned the year before with the establishment of the European Economic Community. In short, at the end of the 1950s the world seemed full of hope and expectation.

This dynamic of expectation and hope was echoed in the Catholic Church. In 1958 the cardinals chose the disarming Angelo Giuseppe Ron-calli (1881–1963) as successor to Pope Pius XII. During his pontificate of

283

almost twenty years, Pius XII had increasingly become the symbol of unshakeable Catholic steadfastness in the face of the influences of modernity. An era ended with his burial; many people felt that more was taken to the grave than the material remains of Eugenio Pacelli, who was then 82 (1876–1958).[1] For in fact the process had already long been under way in the Catholic Church which in 1965 was to lead to the official declaration that it was no longer shutting itself off from modern times. After an amazing U-turn in the heads and hearts of its leaders, it solemnly stated that its task was to associate itself with the 'joy and hope' – *gaudium et spes* – which were so clearly expressed in the spirit of the age, although in the same breath it would also mention the sorrow and anguish – *luctus et angor* – of the people of this time and identify with it. In January 1959, Roncalli, who had become John XXIII barely three months previously, surprised everyone by announcing an 'ecumenical council for the universal church' – as he himself remarked, 'with some trembling but still in humble resolution'. It was to be concluded seven years later, on 8 December 1965, with this declaration of the solidarity of the church with contemporary men and women as its apotheosis.[2]

Between January 1959 and December 1965 the Catholic Church was to change fundamentally. All kinds of developments and thoughts emerged which had necessarily been forced underground in the previous period. During the time of the Council, Catholics got another image of their church. It became clear even to outsiders that this church was entering into a new relationship with the modern world and that its internal culture had fundamentally changed. Above all it had become more diverse. Catholic theologians acquired greater freedom – and took this, if necessary against opposition from above, which would have been almost inconceivable in the previous period – and did pioneering work in a number of theological areas. By no means all Catholic theologians saw things in that way, but in this period a sizable and eloquent group developed the conviction that the church did not need to be a static structure but had to take form in reaction to and in interaction with what the Council, using a phrase of Marie-Dominique Chenus called 'the signs of the time'.

It seems obvious that as a result of this development, Edward Schillebeeckx's project of a theology of culture entered a new phase. Beyond doubt it was a more modern phase. In a sense the Second Vatican Council represented a modernization of the Catholic Church and Catholic theology. The insight broke through that the church unavoidably formed part of modernity, even if it opposed all kinds of modern developments, and once this became clear the question had also been raised whether an attitude of opposition was right. Was standing apart from democracy and the efforts to achieve freedom and prosperity the most effective and most adequate way of proclaiming the gospel message of hope and redemption for the world?

In fact, when the Council stated that this proclamation had to be based on responding to the joys and cares which were alive among men and women, to a large degree it was adopting the alternative that theologians like Chenu, Congar, Rahner and Schillebeeckx had developed in the period before the Council. The way in which the Council did this, and the expectations that it raised among people, were strongly influenced by the optimistic spirit of the middle of the 1960s. But the Council was certainly not just an adaptation of the church to progress and the ideology of progress, as was claimed later.[3]

Schillebeeckx has spoken in connection with the Council of the historical irony that it gave religious and ecclesiastical legitimation to the spirit of modern times at a moment when this spirit was fundamentally coming under criticsm.[4] But the bold criticism of unjust conditions is also an especially important characteristic of the intellectual culture of modern times. Precisely as a result of the renewal brought about by the Council, the criticism of modernity which developed at the end of the 1960s could be taken up within the church. There was fundamental theological reflection on this. In this sense the Council did not just represent the breakthrough of a development which had already taken place in theology, and among the faithful and the leadership, but also really produced a new phase in this development. From the end of the 1960s until halfway through the 1980s a flood of criticism of the Western idea of progress and prosperity, of the Western view of the world and the Western domination of the world, was to emerge. It came both from groups within the Western world and from peoples who learned to see themselves as the victims of its progress and development. The openness to the 'signs of the time' meant that this criticism gained a firm footing in the church and theology. Especially representatives of so-called political theology, of liberation theology, and rather later of feminist theology, and also a number of other theologians who were influenced by these trends but were not really part of them, were to realize just how contextual Christian faith really is. Faith and theology always form part of a particular culture and take shape within it, but within this culture Christian faith calls for a partisan option for the poor, the oppressed and the outcast.[5] In a later phase Schillebeeckx was to belong among the theologians who made an active contribution to this development.

Schillebeeckx's move to Nijmegen

Of course Schillebeeckx did not have the slightest suspicion of any of this when, on 7 April 1957, he wrote a letter to Willem Grossouw, the dean of the Nijmegen theological faculty. This was not a letter of application – at this time senior professorial posts were not applied for, certainly not professorial posts in theology – but it did have to do with the vacancy in the chair of dogmatics at Nijmegen. Grossouw had gone to Schillebeeckx in search of a successor to the Dominican G. P. Kreling (1888–1973), who for health reasons had asked for early retirement from the beginning of September of that year (at that time professors did not usually retire until the age of 70). For Schillebeeckx a chair at Nijmegen was a unique opportunity, since at Louvain only secular priests could become professors of the university, and the chair which Schillebeeckx had held since 1957 at the newly founded Higher Institute for Religious Sciences, an institution which offered theological training to those who were not priests, was in some respects regarded as a substitute. He will have accepted Grossouw's invitation to send in his curriculum vitae and list of publications with some eagerness, but evidently he also saw some of the complications which might arise. In a covering letter he advised discretion: 'For my part I am not saying that I am sending this ... so that I can never be accused of having wanted to desert our Flemish Dominican province.' It seems as if he hardly dared hope that any good would come of it, as he added that he personally left 'the whole question to the good guidance of the Above'.[6]

In fact there were two complications. First of all the Dutch Dominicans had used their right of recommendation – which dated from the time when their lecturers taught at the University of Nijmegen without receiving salaries – to put forward Andreas Maltha, the dogmatic theologian whom they themselves had trained and who had a strongly neoscholastic orientation. Kreling thought that the traditional scholastic theology was a 'game of chess with terms alien to the world' and had found his own way to 'the divine mystery' in the texts of Thomas. He continued to stand by this: he was a 'man of one book', as Schillebeeckx was later to put it in a study of his predecessor, at the same time also indicating the sense in which his own approach differed fundamentally from that of Kreling.[7] However, the nomination of Maltha as Kreling's successor would have been a retrograde step. Schillebeeckx was not the only one to see Maltha's theology as 'just a summary, a list' of standpoints which was always anxiously concerned with the question who had put forward the standpoint under discussion and especially under 'whose, above all suspect (Protestant, schismatic, apostate, atheistic) influence'.[8] Kreling evidently also thought that further theological innovation was needed, although he himself was not in a position to provide it. Like Grossouw, he too seems to have wanted Schillebeeckx as his successor, though Schillebeeckx was later to recall that immediately after his appointment a conflict broke out over the central place that salvation history occupied in Schillebeeckx's theology at this time.[9] Be this as it may, there seems to have been little opposition from the Dutch Dominicans to Schillebeeckx's possible nomination.

The real objections came from Flanders. Twenty-five years later, in his memoirs Grossouw was to recall how 'one day at the beginning of April 1957' he went to Brussels to discuss Schillebeeckx's possible move to Nijmegen with the provincial of the Flemish Dominicans, L. Camerlynck. Camerlynck pointed out that the Flemish Dominicans did not recruit members from a secondary school which they ran; most of them had been inspired by the members of the Flemish province. Therefore Domien de Petter, Jan Hendrik Walgrave and also 'the new star', Edward Schillebeeckx, were indispensable. Grossouw's threat that a Jesuit rather than a Dominican would get the chair, in the person of Piet Schoonenberg (who, however, in 1964 was to be given a chair in theology alongside Schillebeeckx), failed to have any effect. Only after Grossouw, with the complicity of Schillebeeckx, had turned to the superior of the Dominicans could the nomination go through. It is ironical that after his period as Master General the Irishman Michael Browne would become a Curia cardinal, and emerge as one of the most conservative theologians at the Second Vatican Council (he opposed Schillebeeckx directly over the church). But Browne was convinced as a matter of principle that if a Dominican had the opportunity to become professor in theology at a university, this opportunity needed to be grasped, and he told Camerlynck so. Camerlynck concluded that broader interests had to be served than those of his own province, and in September 1957 Schillebeeckx was nominated to Nijmegen.[10]

In January 1958 Schillebeeckx moved to Nijmegen and occupied a room there in the Albertinum, the religious house in which the theological training of the Dutch Dominicans was also based, and where Maltha was and remained a lecturer. Looking back later, Schillebeeckx several times observed that to begin with he did not feel at all at ease in the Netherlands. 'Everything was new for me, even the language,' he remarked, and in his view the transition verged on a new 'inculturation'. Like many Flemings he found the Netherlands 'more formal, stiffer, more principled'. Moreover, his latent nostalgia for Flanders was kept alive by the fact that for a year he remained magister of the Dominican students in Flanders and every three weeks travelled to Louvain for a long weekend of conversations with them.[11] But as he later remembered it, Schillebeeckx was above all disturbed by what in his view was the somewhat inferior state of Dutch theology. He thought that Nijmegen university with its relatively short history – dating from 1923 – compared unfavourably with the far older Catholic university of Louvain, which had 'a centuries-old ... above all philosophical tradition' and was world famous for its historical theology.[12]

Now of course there were good reasons why Grossouw took so much trouble to get this Fleming to the Netherlands. But his estimation that Schillebeeckx could give an important stimulus to Nijmegen theology at the same time pointed to a climate of renewal in the Catholic Netherlands at the end of the 1950s. The connection with the international theological renewal came about especially through the new pastoral questions which the rapidly changing post-war society was unavoidably putting to the church and through the ecumenical dialogue which got moving after the Second World War. For a long time the climate in the Dutch minority church had been one of apologetics, but after the war a new generation of theologians arose who were clearly more open both to society and culture as a whole and to the Protestant churches and theology in particular.[13] There were mature Catholic laity who had been very active in the reconstruction of the post-war Netherlands. Various Dutch theologians – and Grossouw himself was a prominent example of them – saw that in this situation renewed reflection on the sources of faith was necessary, that a new view was needed of the liturgy as a living presentation of the reality of faith expressed in these sources, that the church had to have a new dynamic way of existing in contemporary culture, and that this presupposed a view of the church as a living community.[14] Whereas the faith was previously experienced as a doctrinal system, now it was seen above all as an experience. That an ecumenical publication could appear in 1951 under the title 'The Content of Faith and the Experience of Faith', aimed at bringing Catholics and Protestants more closely together by focusing their attention on the experience of their faith, says a lot about the changed climate in the post-war Netherlands.[15]

In this manner the vocal élite of the Dutch church joined in international developments in Catholic theology in their own way, while a number of Dutch theologians, led by Piet Schoonenberg, who has already been mentioned, also worked on making theology theoretically more profound.[16] For the Dutch theologians, Schillebeeckx embodied the wider international discussion on which they wanted to orientate themselves more strongly because of their practical concerns. Grossouw brought him in as the champion of a dynamic theology which in a new way was orientated on the sources, the champion of a church in which the laity had a clear place and which through the laity itself had a clear place in the world. Moreover, Schillebeeckx came as a theologian who had shown in *De sacramentele heilseconomie* that he had a pioneering view of the liturgy. However, Schillebeeckx was not only to represent the international theological discussion to his colleagues, although he himself evidently had this primarily in view. Later he said with disarming clarity:

In Nijmegen I wanted to continue the work that I had begun in Louvain ... So in Nijmegen I wanted to do ... precisely what I had been doing in Louvain. And although it seems somewhat arrogant – but I have to say it – I really came less with expectations than with my own message.[17]

But relations were not to be as one-sided as that.

Especially in the first years, Schillebeeckx travelled all over the Netherlands. He was asked for lectures and articles on all sides; people expected a new contribution from him. The result was that soon he 'had to travel on a number of evenings each week, sometimes to quite improbable places'. In that way he met all kinds of people and after a few years he himself had become 'a bit of the Netherlands'. Not only did he know what was going on among Dutch Catholics, but he had also learned from the Dutch directness and involvement in concrete questions and problems: in his own way he had turned into a Dutch theologian.[18] That makes it seem somewhat less incongruous that in the 1960s and 1970s Dutch theology became internationally famous above all through this Fleming.

An innovative contribution

In the first months of 1958 Schillebeeckx immediately began giving lectures, although he was only really to take up his task as lecturer at the beginning of the new academic year. In the first years of his Nijmegen period he used material from his Louvain courses, but he again expanded this quite considerably.[19] This combination of old and new also characterized the lecture with which, almost eighteen months later, on 9 May 1959, he officially accepted his professorship. It was clear throughout that the Flemish Schillebeeckx was speaking. Not only did he emphatically confess his roots in his conclusion, but he thanked his teacher De Petter and his Flemish fellow Dominicans in the person of Jan Hendrik Walgrave, and remarked that he had mixed feelings about moving to Nijmegen. He described theology as thought 'in search of the living God' and once again set out the main idea of his theology of culture. In his view, in faith 'the world of man's history-creative freedom . . . is now taken into personal living relationship with God' and theology was reflection on that personal relationship. Here, theology has two different but ultimately connected aspects: one that he calls the philosophical aspect, in which human life makes itself visible in creation and culture as a question of religious fellowship with God, and one that is more theological reflection in the strict sense on salvation history as this is remembered in the Old and New Testaments and in the traditions of the church and kept alive in the existence of believers. But ultimately, in his view there had to be a synthesis between these two aspects, for 'the real life of man in its dialogued relationship with the God of our salvation is the treasure-mine and workshop of authentic and vital theology'.[20] The Louvain Schillebeeckx is also clearly recognizable in the words that he addressed to his students. In them he showed an understanding of the youth of the day, wary of 'a lifetime of scholarship, which is what after all theology must be *par excellence*, if this can only be practised somewhere in an oasis of solitude without even any repercussions for the life of man and of religion', but he accompanied this with the warning that 'the professional practice of theology is a serious matter, in which there is no place for butterfly-like dilettantism'.[21]

But the tone of this message, which had meanwhile become familiar, had to some degree changed. For it was being given in a new context; or rather, it was formulated with a clearly increased awareness of the distinctiveness of the context. In the very first sentence of his lecture Schillebeeckx made it clear that he was aware of living in a context of secularization, of the demystification of the world and the obscuring of God. He said that 'theology, which claims God himself as its subject, has every reason to be modest nowadays. For everywhere his non-existence is proclaimed as an almost existential experience.'[22] He thought that precisely in this situation an adequate theological approach to reality was of the utmost importance. In his view the 'laicization and emancipation of man's outlook' contributed to purging of faith because they made it unavoidably clear 'that God transcends this world; that God is really God, that he is wholly other than the world, and that whenever we come clearly and definitely into contact with something, this reality cannot ever be God himself', but must time and again be called 'world'. God was therefore accessible only indirectly, through the reality which was taken up in him, and especially through 'the security of our human existence in the living God'.[23] In order to make that clear, it was necessary to relate tradition and situation actively, and it was precisely here that in his view the theologian had a special task. At the end of his address he told his students:

> By virtue of his vocation the theologian stands at a risky crossroads: where faith comes into contact with modern thought and with the whole of the new situation of thought, where no synthesis has as yet come into being but this is what is expected of him . . . [T]he condition for the growth of theology lies in a living involvement in the tradition, not however submitting to it but recreating it and testing it again by the present experience of faith and reflection on it.

Perhaps because the Council casts its shadow, here Schillebeeckx seems to be distancing himself from the idea which in a sense held him captive in his Louvain period, that the theologian only needs to 'reflect' on the synthesis which already exists in the church. He returned to the notion that lay at the basis of his quest for a theology of culture in the 1940s, the notion that the contemporary situation was the Christian situation. The theologian is again, and more emphatically, seen as a creator of tradition, as the one who in his own person makes the link between the contemporary situation and the tradition hitherto.

One of the first things that Schillebeeckx undertook in Nijmegen was to attempt to create a forum for the theology that he envisaged.[24] At the faculty he quickly came into contact with the journal *Studia Catholica*, formally since 1925 the successor to the aggressive ecclesiastical polemical organ *De Katholiek*, officially a theological journal addressed to the Netherlands, and edited from Nijmegen and the major seminary at Warmond, but in fact to a considerable degree the somewhat withered house journal of the Nijmegen theological faculty. For Schillebeeckx it exuded the dustiness and formalism to which at that time he had such antipathy, and initially he tried to found a new theological journal as a counterpart. However, Grossouw and the other members included him on the editorial board of *Studia Catholica* and at the same time indicated to him – 'rightly', he was to say later, 'as yet I knew nothing of the internal workings' – that 'a parallel journal [was] unthinkable'. Instead of beginning a new journal, with some effort *Studia Catholica* was transformed into what Schillebeeckx called 'my dreamed-of *Tijdschrift voor Theologie*'. This name showed that Schillebeeckx wanted to give new impetus to Dutch-language theology, just as his teacher had given an impulse to Dutch-speaking philosophy by founding *Tijdschrift voor Philosophie*. Schillebeeckx thought that to fulfil this function the journal had to be a joint Dutch–Flemish enterprise. However, part of the editorial board wanted to dispel any impression that something new was being started, and that hurt Schillebeeckx. He did, though, finally succeed in renewing the editorial board completely – a number of people were invited who were far more active than the members of the old board and therefore put a strong stamp on the journal – and in 1961 the first issue of the first year appeared under the new name. *Studia Catholica* remained only as the name of the foundation which financed the journal.

It was striking that in the first issue of *Tijdschrift voor Theologie*, which was clearly meant to be programmatic, three Flemings presented the recent renewals in exegesis, dogmatics and moral theology; the last two themes were covered by Schillebeeckx and Walgrave respectively. In the other three issues of the first year, however, there were also articles by well-known Dutch theologians like Willem Duynstee, Lucas Grollenberg, Frans Haarsma, Ansfried Hulsbosch and Piet Schoonenberg. Apart from Duynstee, all of these were also to spend some time as editors or on the editorial board of the journal. In the first issues of *Tijdschrift voor Theologie* Schillebeeckx was called 'secretary to the editorial board', and from the fourth issue of the second year it was mentioned that the practical secretariat was in the hands of Ted Schoof. In preparing the first issue for the press at the end of 1960, Schillebeeckx's health had been weakened under the burden of the many speaking engagements and articles, the lectures and now also the technical editing of issues of the journal. The church historian Reinier Post, at that moment acting president of the faculty, ensured that Schoof could be nominated as Schillebeeckx's assistant. From issue two of year six the actual circumstances were indicated accurately: there Schillebeeckx is said to be chief editor and Schoof officially editorial secretary. Schillebeeckx had little feeling for the technical work of editing, and Schoof's efforts made a major contribution to the high reputation of *Tijdschrift voor Theologie* at home and abroad, not least for its broad and abundant reviews.

The accounts of the editorial meetings for the first years show how much Schillebeeckx put his stamp on the discussions of the course of the journal and the authors to be sought; they indicate that he had an important voice in the assessment of articles. In the first ten years he himself had 23 articles published. He also devised the aim and formula of the journal, and was the author of the 'Orientation' section in the first issue, which was signed by 'the editors'. Here, in a manner typical of Schillebeeckx emphasis was put on the importance of 'scholarly reflection on the faith', but on the other hand it was said that

> precisely because the divine revelation is expressed in words, images and concepts derived from the human experience of existence ... theological reflection on the mystery of revelation can be scientific only to the degree that it keeps pace with the constant progress of reflection on this natural experience of existence.

Later this is summed up as 'scholarly reflection on current problems' or, as an expression of the distinctive formula of *Tijdschrift voor Theologie*, as 'topical and scholarly'. If theology was scholarly in this sense and reflected on the particular situation and 'the place of the mystery of revelation' within it, the editorial board had high hopes that the journal would really prove to be an important voice in contemporary culture, and that by its nearness to life but at the same time its clear-sighted theological scholarship *Tijdschrift voor Theologie* would really make the faith a constructive element in our human society.[25]

To begin with, 'topical and scholarly' were seen above all as giving information on current developments and shifts within theology. After the preparations for the Second Vatican Council were well under way, current problems of church and society were to get a more prominent place. The first real thematic issue of *Tijdschrift voor Theologie* was dedicated to the secular significance of the faith, at that moment a burning topic internationally, though Schillebeeckx had also presented it five years earlier in his inaugural address. 'The Secularization of Religion: a Grace or a Temptation' was the title of the third issue of 1963, still put in traditional language.[26]

In his own contribution to the first issue of *Tijdschrift voor Theologie* under the title 'The New Trend in Present-day Dogmatics', Schillebeeckx in fact sketched out the differences between the traditional theology as it appeared primarily in *Studia Catholica* and the theological approach that he had developed in Louvain. He tried to demonstrate that from 'the new

anthropo... ...
...return to ...
with Anglican, Roro...
theology was coming into being... ...
the sphere of moral theology.[28] Neith...
strate that what they indicated as dynamism in...
of theology to reality could also really be found in ...
literature; they hardly referred to other publications. The message that they wanted to convey seems rather that the theological discussion was indeed topical, provided that it was described properly.

Schillebeeckx began his article with a basic account of the historicity of theology and went on to investigate the growing theological attention to the human experience of existence. He then went on to show that it was indeed about questions which were of great interest to many people at that moment. In dogmatics, which in his view was to be understood as 'the faith of the thinking person' and 'the thinking community of faith', for him everything ultimately turned on the question how, for contemporary people in the present world situation, authentic faith meant that 'we live in God, as in our own home'. Schillebeeckx also especially demonstrated that the questions of believers were also the questions of theology. In a situation where Catholics were being confronted with secularization and did not know what to make of it, but at all events also discovered positive aspects in it, dogmatics was also occupied with the phenomenon and recognized 'the legitimacy of a degree of secularization'. And where Dutch Catholics had increasingly had the experience of being in dialogue with 'those who believe and think otherwise', he pointed out the ecumenical character of present-day dogmatics.

In short, theology is topical and has something to say in the current situation. *Tijdschrift voor Theologie* set out to show that, and in this respect was born under a favourable star. The first issue appeared in the midst of the period of preparation for the Second Vatican Council and there was widespread interest in developments in theology and the church. Church and theology wanted to renew themselves in the light of the contemporary world, and the questions that this raised made Catholic theology unusually lively. And there was great interest in the Council. Soon after the appearance of the first issue, *Tijdschrift voor Theologie* had an unprecedented number of subscriptions for a scholarly theological journal: just under 4000.

THE PREPARATION FOR THE COUNCIL
The announcement

On 25 January 1959 the world was surprised by the papal announcement of an 'ecumenical council for the universal church'. The reactions to this announcement and the skirmishes over its significance and scope in fact formed a first phase in the conciliar discussion. The Catholic Church immediately began to ask itself what it wanted to be, where its place was in the world, and what the burning questions really were for it in the second half of the twentieth century.

In the first instance only a very summary communication about the announcement of the Council was available to the press. It explained the pope's plan to organize a Council as follows:

> In the thought of the Holy Father the celebration of the ecumenical council not only aims to strengthen the Christian people but also sets out to be an invitation to the separated communities to seek the unity for which at present so many souls all over the world long.

The text had far-reaching consequences. Many journalists did not know that 'ecumenical council' was a technical term for a gathering of the Roman Catholic bishops from all over the world, and by far the majority of the first reactions to the idea of the Council referred to its presupposed 'ecumenical' character.[29] Even the General Secretary of the World Council of Churches, the Dutchman Willem Visser 't Hooft, thought this. Immediately after the announcement he indicated his interest, but stated that much would depend on the way in which the Council was convened and the spirit in which the question of Christian unity was approached. 'The question is: how ecumenical will the Council be in composition and spirit?'[30] Although a short time later it became clear that the Second Vatican Council was certainly not intended as a council of reunion, the first misunderstanding was productive. The Council was to prove very significant for ecumenical awareness within the Catholic Church. A couple of years later Schillebeeckx rightly wrote that the initial confusion around the term 'ecumenical' had ultimately proved fruitful, and 'also through the reactions of Reformation, Anglican and Orthodox Christians' the attention of the Roman authorities, of the bishops and the whole Catholic Church had been directed more firmly to 'the modern ecumenical problem'. Nevertheless, in his view

> The coming Council should be primarily a reform council ... an internal reform and revival of Roman Catholic church life; and this Catholic reform would then at the same time be the best preparation for later developing closer relations between the different Christian churches.[31]

Schillebeecxk's own insight into the 'modern ecumenical problem' seems only to have come with his move from the homogenous Catholic Flanders to the religiously divided Netherlands, but whereas his predecessor worked actively for more intensive contacts between Catholic and Protestant theology, the ecumene hardly played a role as a theme for Schillebeeckx, though he had contacts with Protestant theologians and was to have good relations with Hendrik Berkhof and Harry Kuitert.[32] For him, work on Catholic theological reform was the best way of furthering Christian unity, and he would later point quite emphatically to the ecumenical character of theological discussion after the Council. In his view it had not to be about compromises between the churches but about a common reflection on the faith in the light of the biblical witness and the contemporary situation.

Pope John XXIII in fact seems to have envisaged reflection on the place of the church in the contemporary situation from the very first announcement of the Council onwards. In his announcement he also went into the state of the world. In the press release his words were paraphrased as follows.

> As Bishop of Rome the Holy Father spoke about the great expansion of the city in recent decades and the great problems associated with spiritual support for the population. As supreme pastor of the church he pointed out the dangers which threatened above all the spiritual life of the faithful, for example the errors that arise here and there and the disproportionate attraction of material goods, which with the progress of technology have increased more than ever today.[33]

However, this was a misleading summary. The text could easily be read along the lines of the traditional anti-modern attitude of the church: the church warned against the dangers of all kinds of developments and thought it necessary to oppose them as far as possible. But, when, on 27 February, the complete text of the pope's address was published, it became evident how much John XXIII was thinking in terms of direct pastoral involvement.

This had really already come to light at his coronation. At that time Roncalli had said that the authentic ideal of the papacy was not to be a statesman or a diplomat or a man of learning or a governor. It is difficult not to interpret this as dissociating himself from the image of the papacy embodied by Pacelli, although Roncalli made it clear that he also did not want to be the pope, long awaited by some, who was open 'to all the progress of modern times, without any distinction'. In his eyes the ideal of the papacy was to be a pastor in the way in which Christ himself was a pastor. And that primarily meant that he wanted to share in the cares of his fellow pastors, the bishops, and aimed at brotherly dealings with them. The special character of the words with which he did this were immediately noted world-wide when he said to the bishops present – as usual, speaking of himself in the third person:

> in the vicissitudes of this life the new pope is like the son of Jacob who encountered his brethren in a miserable state, opened his heart to them in all tenderness, and burst into tears, with the words, 'I am Joseph, your brother.'[34]

Eventually, the brotherly relations between pope and bishops would become a point of profound discussion at the Council under the term 'collegiality'.

This was also the background to what the pope said in his address on the announcement of the Council. As the press report also indicated, he had first of all spoken emphatically as Bishop of Rome, and this in itself was striking and seen by commentators as a revaluation of the office of bishop. Here he had gone into the problems which in his view the rapid growth of the city had brought with it, but he had referred far less in the familiar terms to the known shortcomings of modernity than the press release suggested. He was really expressing his pastoral desire in order to allude adequately to the changed situation of the modern world. This is how he described the situation of Rome:

> Here and there people still see the old fundamental outlines of her architecture, but it is sometimes hard to discover them, above all at the periphery, which has grown into an accumulation of houses and families who have come together here from all over Italy, from the surrounding islands, indeed one could almost say from all over the world. It is a true beehive full of people from which a constant buzzing of confused voices arises, in search of a unity which easily arises and then falls apart again.[35]

In the 1940s and 1950s the new pastoral questions which arose as a result of the accelerated modernization of societies and increasing urbanization had been formulated in France in a way which had found broad acceptance. Raising these questions had become almost suspect as a result of the measures which Pius XII had taken against the '*nouvelle théologie*' in the wider sense. That is why it was so striking that now the pope himself referred to these questions and moreover announced a diocesan synod for the city of Rome which was to reflect on a more co-ordinated commitment 'to an order which corresponds to the demands of the religious, civic and social life of Rome'.

John XXIII's plan to convene a Council for the church was along the same lines. Many times he emphatically called the Council 'pastoral'. This may also have given rise to misunderstanding, but at all events it indicated that in his view Vatican II had to be a different kind of Council from Vatican I.[36] In 1869/70 all the emphasis had been on Catholic doctrine, and in the subsequent period the popes also concentrated on this. However, for

John XXIII what came first was the spiritual renewal of the church, the form of its appearance in society and its presence in history. In the first encyclical of his pontificate – *Ad Petri cathedram*, which appeared on 29 June 1959 – he wrote:

> [The Council will] consider, in particular, the growth of the Catholic faith, the restoration of sound morals among the Christian flock, and appropriate adaptation of Church discipline to the needs and conditions of our times. This event will be a wonderful spectacle of truth, unity and charity.[37]

He said this even more clearly six weeks later in an address to the presidents of Italian Catholic Action; it was important to purge 'whatever humanly could hinder the church on its way' and to allow it to be seen 'in all her splendour, "without spot or wrinkle"'.[38] And in the sermon during the celebration of the eucharist which had preceded the announcement of the Council the pope had made clear how closely the reforms within the church were connected with the saving presence of the church in the world. He spoke lyrically of the gladness that would come over all the world 'through the perfect unity in faith and in the practical realization of the teaching of the gospel, at least as far as this is possible on earth'.[39]

On 27 June 1959, Charles de Gaulle, the French president, was received in audience by the pope. According to his later memoirs he was well aware of what inspired Roncalli in his proposal to convene a Council. He wrote that while John XXIII saw great problems in the church and society, he regarded these as signals of

> yet another crisis which in our times is being added to the long series of crises that the church after Jesus Christ has already experienced and surmounted. He believes that if only the church can make productive use of its own values of inspiration and investigation, this time, too, it can again restore its equilibrium.[40]

The pope was ultimately concerned to reform the church in the sense of restoring it to what it should be, convinced that this in particular represented a service to the salvation of the world.

It is striking how much from the beginning the texts of John XXIII undermined the presupposition that the church and the world stand over against each other as two static entities. In the pope's eyes, the church has above all to be on the way, to go forward on the way of life. He saw it emphatically as his task to lead it on this way and not to 'guard it like a museum'.[41] And this picture of a church on the way was matched by a picture of a world in conflict. In the address in which he announced the Council, the pope put it like this:

If the Bishop of Rome lets his gaze roam over the whole world for which he bears responsibility as a spiritual leader ... what a scene he sees! On the one hand there is a delightful prospect where the grace of Christ permeates the fruits and wonders of spiritual revival in the world, multiplying them so that they bring salvation and holiness. And on the other hand there is the sorry prospect of the misuse of freedom by people who do not know that heaven is open, who refuse to believe in Christ the Son of God, the Redeemer of the world and Founder of the holy church, and who therefore cast themselves wholly on the so-called goods of this earth ...

So the church did not have to defend itself against the world, but to develop suitable instruments for seeing and furthering 'the grace of Christ' active in the world. This was quite a different tone from that expressed in the official press release. Perhaps the Vatican officials did not immediately see that Roncalli's position differed from that of his predecessor. Perhaps, too, they had deliberately tried to give another twist to the pope's words.[42] Certainly the pope had also said in his address that 'the progress of modern technology' made the attraction of the 'advantages in the material order' even greater. Ultimately, in his view,

man holds back from striving for higher goods, paralyses his spiritual energy, and undermines the structure of discipline and the good old order, to the great detriment of the capacity of the church and her children to resist the errors which in practice in the history of Christianity have always led to fateful and dire division, to spiritual and moral decay, to the downfall of whole peoples.

Those who composed the press report had clearly based themselves on this well-known anti-modern rhetoric. But even here John XXIII had another surprise in store. He proposed to 'restore some old forms which serve to consolidate faith and to take wise measures of church discipline', but by this he did not mean something like sharpening the moral guidelines, imposing a stricter asceticism, or calling for greater obedience to the supreme authority in the church. By 'old forms' Roncalli proved to be referring to an 'ecumenical council for the universal church'! A pope who had no administrative measures in view and did not want to increase discipline within the church, but first of all wanted intensive reciprocal consultation among those involved and spoke of 'measures of church discipline which the Spirit of the Lord' would inspire 'in the course of time', in other words *during* this deliberation, was unprecedented. And to begin with, many people could hardly believe it.

But John XXIII meant it very seriously. When the preparations for the Council actually began, at his request a world-wide enquiry was set in motion so that the urgent questions and problems about which the Council needed to speak could be listed. But already when announcing the Council he himself tried to set reciprocal discussion in motion. In his address he asked the cardinals present, and through them the other cardinals, for a reaction to his plans and for suggestions about how to carry them out. But he received hardly any answers, and two and a half years later he remarked euphemistically that his proposal was received by the cardinals with a 'devout and impressive silence';[43] they were struck dumb. In view of the confusion which arose immediately after the announcement of the Council, it is amusing that the pope said that he did not believe that he needed to explain the significance of his plans to his 'venerable brothers and beloved sons'.

The figure of John XXIII

Now the confusion among the cardinals and other leaders within the Catholic Church was of course directly connected with the fact that the papal initiative was so unexpected. On 10 August 1961 Roncalli rightly wrote in his spiritual diary, looking back on his pontificate hitherto, that when he was elected at the age of 77, everyone was convinced that he was a caretaker pope. With amazement, almost four years later he noted that now, aged more than 80, he faced carrying out 'an immense programme of work ... before the eyes of the whole world'. Shortly before the opening of the Council – 'on the slopes of the holy mountain' – he wrote, again looking back, that he had first spoken about the Council with his secretary of state Domenico Tardini on 20 January 1959, 'without any forethought'.[44] This last remark has given rise to much confusion and strictly speaking seems to conflict with the facts. Roncalli always emphasized that the plan for the Council was not a thought which had matured over a long period, and that too seems to fit. In his eyes it was 'an inspiration which we, in lowliness of heart, spontaneously felt coming over us as an unforeseen and unexpected contact from above'; as he was to say later, it was the spontaneous opening of the flowers of an unexpected spring.[45] For him, spontaneity and unexpectedness were signs of the guidance of the Holy Spirit, which he clearly felt at that point. This seems to have influenced his memory. For John XXIII seems regularly to have given inklings of the notion of a Council in confidential conversations, albeit in dribs and drabs.[46] And from the discovery of a note which he made on the evening of 20 January 1959, it proves that on this day Roncalli had the clear intention of getting Tardini's reaction to his idea to convene a Council and announce it publicly five days later. He may have at first been 'hesitant and uncertain', but after what he interpreted as a positive reaction from Tardini, evidently all his doubts fell away.[47]

Besides, the idea of a Council was not completely new. Ever since the First Vatican Council had to be broken off prematurely because of the Franco-Prussian war, there had been calls to take its agenda further. As only became known later, both Pius XI and Pius XII also investigated the possibilities in secret, but their attempts to convene a new Council got prematurely stuck.[48] The idea that Vatican I needed to be rounded off was also generally known in principle. That certainly does not mean that it was also generally shared: when John XXIII announced a new Council, a number of theologians in particular were hesitant because they were afraid that in fact it would be a continuation of the First Vatican Council, in other words that again all the emphasis would be put on papal authority and doctrinal unity. This fear was reinforced in the first instance by the press release in which the announcement was made, and with the exception of the few striking remarks at the beginning of his pontificate, there were few indications in Roncalli's career hitherto that he really had something quite different in view. But this was the case. All the indications are that the announcement on 25 January 1959 was the direct and unilateral initiative of the pope himself, taken on the basis of a personal conviction which had grown and matured in conversations with others. There were no prior diplomatic negotiations or formal consultations, as there had been with previous Councils, and precisely what he wanted now also became clear to Roncalli in the course of the extensive preparatory process. On 17 May he announced a pre-preparatory process in which all the bishops would be consulted about what they felt to be the urgent problems.[49] The announcement was thus in every sense 'a gesture of serene audacity and inspired trust'.[50]

The question how the Catholic Church of the 1950s, which was so closed in on itself, could change thoroughly within a few years here became concentrated on what is called 'the Roncalli mystery'. Before his election he had given little indication that anything special could be expected of him. In the circles of those who under Pius XII had tried to reform the church so that it could take its place in modern society, often at great personal sacrifice, he was regarded as at best an untroubled dilettante and at worst a skilful conservative.[51] But he set in motion a process which was to bring the leaders of the church and the ordinary faithful all over the world into passionate and open dialogue with one another in the Catholic context. As an all-embracing event Vatican II has no equal in modern church history. It seems that the two-track history of the Catholic Church found expression in the person of Roncalli. Whereas little changed on the surface, either in the structure of the church or in the form of piety and church teaching, the awareness grew that these were no longer sufficient for the contemporary situation. The gap that existed between the church and the world, which for a long time had been deliberately kept in place by the church, was no longer felt to be a sign that the church was exalted above the turmoil of the world but to be a hindrance to the proclamation of the gospel. From his address immediately after his election – 'Hearing your words I shake with fear; what I know of my insignificance is sufficient to explain my bewilderment' – the feeling rapidly grew that the special character of this pope was hidden in his simplicity.[52] As Pius XII, especially in the later period of his pontificate, Pacelli had become an icon of the church's steadfastness and dignity in difficult times.[53] As John XXIII, in the brief period during which he was pope, for countless people Roncalli became the symbol of mobility and openness to the signs of the time which the church seemed to want to develop from the end of the 1950s onwards. For people from all estates of the church, spread all over the world, as a person and a church leader he was 'a man sent by God', and in a special way 'a witness to the light', as Cardinal Leo Suenens was to put it a few months after his death.[54]

Schillebeeckx, who in the period of the Council was to acquire the reputation of being *the* Dutch theologian and was regarded as most knowledgeable about everything to do with the Council, had an article published three and a half weeks after John XXIII's death about the significance of 'Pope John' for the church. This especially investigated his significance for the Council.[55] With a play on words which he took over from Karl Rahner, he argued that John XXIII, 'rather than being a transitional pope, had become the pope of a church in transition' by convening the Council, and that in the different phases he really had known how to make it a Council of the whole church.[56] In this connection he speculated briefly on the background to the idea of holding a Council. Without detracting from the spontaneity of the initiative on which the pope himself put so much emphasis, but also without letting himself be distracted from other questions, Schillebeeckx looked for 'psychological and situational factors' which explained the origin of this idea. The prime psychological factor that he mentioned was Roncalli's great sensitivity to 'the present situation of the church'. According to Schillebeeckx:

> the most important contributions of Pope John to the Second Vatican Council ... are a psychology which questions the situation of the world church, in which and from which the charisma of God that always works silently could develop into clear speaking. From this it is evident that it [the convening of the Council] was not a wild idea nor even the conclusion of a long argument but ... a first *interpretation* by grace of a question which was put to him by the situation of the church and the world.[57]

As papal nuncio in Paris, a function which he occupied from 1944 to 1953, by his own account Roncalli had been asked to be 'the eye, the heart and the hand of the pope': an eye that was open to observation of the moral, religious and social situation of France; a heart that was sensitive to the needs of the people of Christ, 'as hungry for spiritual food as for spiritual satis-faction'; and a hand that pointed the right way and that 'supports, encourages and blesses' the French Catholics 'in the name of the Lord'. At this time the French saw him more as 'the eye and ear of the Holy See', who out of a sense of duty had emphatically undertaken not to 'conceal out of politeness the shortcomings and true state of affairs of the oldest daughter of the church', and who spoke to the French about their religious practices, their lack of priests, the dominant laicism and the widespread Communism. However, given his later attitude, his stay in France seems to have brought about more in him than irritation about the French arrogance, about which he complained several times.[58]

In Schillebeeckx's view, John XXIII embodied in person at the deepest level the church as he wanted to bring it together at the Council, above all by entering into conversation with everyone and being open, by being modest and listening. He thought that in convening the Council, John XXIII was ultimately concerned to

> show the pure nature of the church as a visible presence of grace and love in this world. For he knew that if goodness and holiness become invisible, the world lives in the mist. Therefore we can say that although in purely theological terms Pope John adhered to the old ecclesiology, through the practice of his Christian life he implicitly defended the new ecclesiology – in a way which no single theologian matched![59]

In practice, John XXIII had already made the transition from the hier-archical, closed teaching church to the collegial, open and listening church. According to Schillebeeckx, he listened at the Council 'to the "voice of God" which could be heard in the "voice of the bishops"'. In Schillebeeckx's estimation the origin of the idea of the Council itself also lay in this open, listening attitude and the insight that he could not tackle 'the problem of the church and the world alone'.[60] It was born of an urgent insight that a number of questions were arising unavoidably and of the intuitive certainty that the answers could be found only by consulting the church widely about them. Schillebeeckx put it figuratively like this:

> It is as if in the [first] three months [of his pontificate] John was looking for a specific word which was burning on his lips but which he did not want to utter, until suddenly from the old magic book of theological jargon the word *council* ... occurred to him.[61]

Here at the same time he was suggesting that Pope John understood 'the word "council"' in his own way and gave it content with a view to specific contemporary needs and possibilities. The result was that gradually, and to a degree which no one had foreseen, the questions, problems, intuitions and thoughts which had remained latent under Pius XII, actively repressed and harshly oppressed, emerged; and the whole church, in Schillebeeckx's words, turned into 'a state of council'. At the end of the 1950s and the beginning of the 1960s it seemed for a while that the Catholic Church was indeed reforming itself after the image of the charismatic supreme pastor who so surprised it.

Reactions to the plan for the Council

John XXIII's plan to hold a Council rested on the insight that far-reaching reform of the church was necessary and at the same time on great trust in the purifying power of the church's tradition. This met up with the basic conviction of those who before the Council had already argued for changes, including Yves Congar and Edward Schillebeeckx. In the period which directly followed, the pope's announcement of a Council was received particularly favourably by those who in the previous decades had devoted themselves to renewal within Catholicism.[62] They saw their opportunity.

It was striking that immediately after the announcement, in an article which he could not sign because of the ban on teaching and publishing that he had had imposed on him in 1954, Congar thought it necessary to say: 'With the announcement of his decision to convene a Council, His Holiness John XXIII has aroused immense interest and a great hope.'[63] The great stream of reactions within the Catholic Church still had to start, and many members of the hierarchy, for example, had some reservations about the idea: perhaps they complained in secret about a pope who did not know what he had started and waited until the direction things would take had become rather clearer. To their detriment they had learned in previous decades that it was best to react with restraint to the dictates of Rome. Most of them indeed took this course until they could no longer keep silent.[64] And most theologians also seemed to wait until it became clearer what they could expect. However, the press immediately saw the announcement of the Council as an initiative of great importance. Journalists realized that something very striking had happened on 25 January 1959 and tried actively to discover its background, purpose and implications. For lack of facts, now and then they resorted to speculation.[65] Of course, this left marks on their readers and led to the rise of expectant curiosity among Catholics.

But in his article of February 1959 Congar had in fact spoken above all of his own 'immense interest and great hope'. At the accession of Pope John he had argued along the lines of Cardinal Suhard for the abandonment of the pomp and paternalism in favour of a more prophetic activity by the pope.[66] And it is not difficult to see in the article surprise at the unexpected opportunity for something of this suggestion to be realized so soon afterwards. 'Aren't the events of the moment like the first snowdrops of an ecumenical spring?', Congar asked himself. 'Don't they announce the coming of a time of mercy?' These seem to be the words of a much-tormented man who hopes that the tide will now finally turn, but dares not believe the signs that it might. However, Congar's attitude in this article was in no way naïve. In retrospect he himself wrote of his commitment to the preparation for the Council:

> I devoted myself to the task of stirring up public opinion, so that the many should expect and demand. I never tired of saying, wherever I was, that we would get perhaps only five per cent of what we asked for. All the more reason to push up our demands. The pressure of public opinion had to force the Council to become a real Council and to achieve something.[67]

Congar estimated that the Council offered a decisive opportunity to change the church, a possibility that a number of his ideas and those of his like-minded colleagues would in fact achieve a breakthrough. For a while he put his own theological projects in second place and as a theologian devoted himself entirely to the Council, so that the chance of success should be as great as possible.

Something of the same thing applied to Schillebeeckx. In a sense he was even shrewder than Congar, and even before Congar's article appeared he wrote a striking piece in the weekly *De Bazuin* under the title 'The Grace of a General Council'.[68] The title itself makes the tone clear: he regarded 'a general assembly of the church,' as a positive possibility for the church to look at its own situation, and urged those involved, especially the bishops, above all not to be afraid of taking a stand. In his view a Council was not an already-existing manifestation of unity but 'shared deliberation under the good guidance of the Holy Spirit', from which 'explicit unanimity about the problems on the agenda could then grow'. In the end, the voice of everyone in the church should be uttered and had to be heard:

> A general assembly of the church [must] also be an act of the prayer of all the faithful. *Nostra res agitur*! It is our business! We can only wish that the world episcopate, supported by the consultative help of theologians, pastors and, God willing, also intellectual laity, will really allow their voice to be heard. That is what they are convened for. And it is for that that the whole of Christianity will urgently pray.[69]

Like Congar, Schillebeeckx was concerned to compel the Council to become a real Council through the pressure of public opinion.

There were more striking agreements between Schillebeeck's article and that by Congar, which was to appear about a week later. Both Dominican theologians expounded the nature of a Council at relative length and made it clear that a Council was the expression of what Schillebeeckx called the 'apostolic collegiality of the bishops'. He formulated with the utmost brevity a theology of episcopal authority which during the time of the Council was still to stir up a good deal of dust: 'Essentially, by Christ the authority of the church is put in the hands of a college, a body, with the pope as its supreme head.'[70] Moreover, both Congar and Schillebeeckx indicated what in their view were the evidently unintentional but unfortunate consequences of the declaration of the infallibility of the pope at the First Vatican Council. Congar thought that it had distracted attention from the doctrinal significance of the episcopate, but that this one-sidedness could without doubt have been put right if the Council could have been finished as originally planed. The question of the power of the bishops in the church had been on the original agenda of Vatican I.[71] Schillebeeckx presented his theory that a declaration of dogma in justified opposition to an error always meant that there was a one-sided emphasis on one aspect of Catholic faith. There was a possibility that in this way – and we can see from the way in which he put it that here he was balancing on the edge of what could still be said – 'it could "distort" the practical experience of faith a little, above all … if this emphasis is made at the theological level and there leads to the development of one-sided syntheses'. Now in his view this was the case with the dogma of infallibility:

> This dogma was and is a blessing for the church … In practical experience this truth of salvation is spontaneously detached from the whole in which it essentially belongs. So much attention is paid to Peter that we forget the other eleven apostles. In practice, by so doing we damage the apostolic structure which Christ instituted.

He then sketched out how the relationship between Peter and the apostles, viz. the pope and the bishops, was in his view well intended: Peter in the midst of the apostles, the bishops bound up in faith with the pope. 'The reciprocal relationship between pope and bishops is essential.'[72]

But Schillebeeckx added a distinctive, and in a sense Dutch, emphasis. Congar's article was above all doctrinal and historical. Schillebeeckx made a connection between the coming Council and the practical fact that the church is always also a collection of local communities of faith, each with its own colouring. The bishops are primarily the pastors of these communities. And it is this very diversity which makes consultation between them extremely important:

> There is only one faith. But the faithful in India experience and think the one faith in a different way from those in southern Europe, England or South America. The problems too are different on either side of the ocean … In an exchange of ideas, the specific needs actually experienced by a church province can open the eyes of the bishops of other countries where these needs are perhaps just as strong but not yet recognized.[73]

Here was an indication of an important extension of Schillebeeckx's view of a theology of culture. The Catholic faith did not just mean a view of culture and a distinctive cultural way of dealing with the world which was experienced by the faithful 'in God', as he had indicated from the 1940s on. To an increasing degree it became clear to him that, conversely, the faith, the way of life of the faithful and any contact with the living God was also determined by culture. However, he would not be exploring the far-reaching consequences of this notion further until after the Council.

Insight into the importance of the local communities of faith meant that for Schillebeeckx the question of episcopal collegiality was no abstract ecclesiological principle. His commitment to this during the Council formed part of his constantly evolving project of a theology of culture. Episcopal collegiality, in union with the pope but not under him, was so important for Schillebeeckx because only the local bishops could really see what was going on in the church and therefore how it could be reacted to in faith. The pope's task was to hold together their different views:

> By an exchange of standpoints it can indeed emerge that, however necessary Roman centralization is for a world church, this centralization at the same time needs to have a clear eye for the decentralized authority of the resident bishops, who are in the midst of the actual problems and know the feelings of their own church province.[74]

A year later, when he had already been extensively occupied with the Council, he could formulate more accurately the idea of the Council as an expression of episcopal collegiality and as a quest by the whole church for what the Holy Spirit had to say to it. He did so particularly in connection with an episcopal letter on the subject which he in fact wrote. In an article for *Elseviers Weekblad*, a completely secular journal with an interest in developments in religion and the church – evidently in 1960s such a journal was interested in the Council and even in very technical theological information and discussion about it – Schillebeeckx explained the interaction between pope and bishops in a long sentence which is very typical of him:

> The personal infallibility of office ... is also supported by the infallibility of the world episcopate which is unanimous in the faith, which in its turn is buttressed by the living practice of faith of the whole faith community which is infallible '*in credendo*', i.e. in its believing confession of faith which can always be understood only from the Spirit of Christ.[75]

The Spirit does not guide only, or even primarily, the hierarchy, but first of all the believing people of God, and through the people of God the hierarchy! Now according to Schillebeeckx this becomes concrete in the Council. That John XXIII always insisted that the faithful should be consulted as widely as possible over the Council and should be given plenty of room to say what was on their minds further emphasized this aspect of the convening of the Council. A Council also arrives 'at a more expressive awareness of what the Spirit itself suggests in the life of the whole church' by 'tracing the breath of the Spirit in the whole of Christ's church'.[76] The Council documents would ultimately follow this line by placing the bishops as pastors within their own local church as the people of God, and the pope as pastor within the college of bishops. However, the texts ultimately also remained ambiguous on this point.[77]

THE DUTCH CONTRIBUTION TO THE PREPARATION

In 1963, Congar indicated that 'the idea of episcopal collegiality' had made lightning progress. In a few months it had conquered theological opinion, and the word 'collegiality' had 'almost taken the form of a magical talisman'.[78] The elevation of this word to become a sign of hope for an open, more democratic and more pluriform church was possible because of the theological work that had already been done before the Council. That it also came to have a prominent place in public awareness was partly due to the Dutch contribution to the preparations for the Council and at the first two sessions. Here too Schillebeeckx was closely involved on a number of occasions.

On 17 May 1959 John XXIII appointed a commission which had to prepare for the Council which had been announced shortly beforehand, or rather had to prepare the preparations for the Council. Its task was to investigate what questions and problems there were in the church and what it was thought that the Council should investigate. This commission, consisting almost entirely of Curia prelates, worked for some time on a list of questions to be sent to the bishops. At the same time it wanted the different departments of the Curia already to begin writing the texts which the Council would then have to approve. However, this was manifestly so much in conflict with the conciliar discussion which Pope John had in view that on 30 June he intervened personally at the plenary assembly of this so-called *commissio antepreparatoria*. At his instigation all the bishops were sent a letter in which they were simply urged

> to send to this papal commission the criticisms, suggestions and wishes which your pastoral concern and your zeal for souls prompts you to present in connection with the possible questions and subjects for discussion at the coming Council, and to do this in complete freedom and honesty.[79]

The Dutch bishops, too, received this request at their office and were to discuss it at length there.

A similar letter, but focused on their specific responsibility for study and research, was sent to the Catholic universities, and thus also to the Roman Catholic University at Nijmegen. Schillebeeckx made a substantial contribution to the composition of the list with wishes and desires – in conciliar jargon called 'vota' – of Nijmegen University, in harmonious collaboration with his fellow-Dominican, the exegete Jan van der Ploeg.[80] The final result betrayed his influence, especially in the layout and division.[81] The text was subdivided into four sections, the first of which related to the 'mystery of the church'. It called for further reflection on the relationship between pope and bishops and between bishops and priests, and on the place of the laity in the church. The second section was about 'the attitude of the church towards the task of humankind within the world', an expression typical of Schillebeeckx. The third section raised some specific practical problems, and the fourth was devoted to proposals in the area of church law. However, there is no indication at all that the Nijmegen vota which were eventually sent to Rome on 19 April 1960 had any special impact on the further course of the Council. No connection can be established between the suggestions made by the Nijmegen professors – that perhaps the permanent diaconate needed to be restored or that in the framework of the investigation into the place of the hierarchy in the church an answer needed to be found to the question whether the exclusion of women from hierarchical offices was or was not a matter of divine law – and the later discussions and developments.[82]

Perhaps the most important thing about the Nijmegen vota was that on 27 April a copy was sent to the archbishop. In the covering letter the rector magnificus of the Catholic University proposed that the Dutch episcopate should elect a member of the theological faculty as a counsellor. The Nijmegen senate, at that time the highest governing body of the university, was here thinking especially of Schillebeeckx.[83] It is not clear whether or not there is any direct connection between this suggestion and the fact that Schillebeeckx very quickly indeed became an advisor to the Dutch bishops before the Council, but at least it is a striking coincidence which shows how fast his authority was growing.

As I have said, the Dutch bishops, too, had received the invitation to give their criticisms, suggestions and wishes at the Council in all freedom. Originally they wanted to send in a joint text, but at a second stage each resolved to send in his own vota. That gave scope for specific emphases. In different ways and in discussion with different people the bishops of Utrecht, Groningen, Haarlem, Rotterdam, Breda, Den Bosch and Roermond in fact arrived at clearly different texts.[84] But what came through all the vota that were sent in was a shared feeling, which also grew rapidly in the period before the Council, that changes were urgently necessary.

We stand as if between two worlds on the threshold of a new age, which seems to have dawned for the whole world. Changes and renewals are called for in all areas. And indeed in the sphere of the church far-reaching changes must be made all over the world and also in our fatherland.

That is how the Bishop of Haarlem, Johannes Huijbers, expressed this common feeling in an address on 6 April 1960, on the occasion of the return from Rome by Bernard Alfrink, Archbishop of Utrecht, after he had been made a cardinal.[85]

Episcopal collegiality and the faith of the believers

Commentators have judged that the vota sent in by the Dutch bishops were on a strikingly high level. Above all the quality of that sent by Cardinal Alfrink is famous.[86] This differed strikingly from that of his colleagues and was the product of intensive collaboration between him and especially Herman (H. J. H. M.) Fortmann, and through him some other professors at the archdiocesan major seminary.[87] The unsolicited contribution of the president of the National Centre for Catholic Action, Ludolf Baas, who thought 'a theological, legal and pastoral reflection on the place, task and function of the laity in the church to be of capital importance' also seems to have influenced the archbishop's vota. They contained a substantial section on the laity, which ended up with a plea for a discussion of the place of the church in the world of a kind which was indeed to take place at the Council. Here, among other things, Alfrink recommended further reflection on the significance of human work and on economic prosperity.[88] However, the most striking feature of Alfrink's answer to the question of the papal commission was that it was conceived with a consistent and clear theological view of the church, into which recent theological developments had clearly been incorporated.[89]

Especially after 1953, the centenary of the restoration of the church hierarchy in the Netherlands, the office of bishop was intensively studied by Dutch theologians.[90] On the basis of the results Alfrink had already spoken of in his first pastoral letter as archbishop, in 1955, about the communion of the bishops with the pope 'and with his brothers in the episcopate all over the world'.[91] In the vota that he sent to Rome on 22 December 1959, Alfrink developed this thought further. In his view, bishops were not appointed to govern part of the church in dependence on the pope, but shared in the power and governance of the universal church. The governance of the church was the task of the college of bishops under the guidance of the pope. What was explosive for church politics in Alfrink's vota was that in this way they indicated theological opposition to the centralistic way in which the church was governed. There was resistance to the unbridled and uncontrolled power of the curial organs among many bishops, but it usually remained their painful experience, as it was that of Alfrink, that the local bishops were given too little scope, 'to the detriment of their moral authority'.[92] However, Alfrink went a step further and indicated in his wish-list for the Council the need to create organs which would also implement practically the bishop's responsibility for the church, under the leadership of the pope. He argued for a permanent council of bishops from all over the world, who would exercise legislative power over the church in conjunction with the Roman Curia.

The bishops and their collaborators will probably have read Schillebeeckx's *De Bazuin* article on 'The Grace of a General Council', but this played no further role in the composition of their vota. However, the formulation of the role and significance of the episcopate in Alfrink's vota did largely correspond with views which had been and were being developed especially by Congar and his pupils.[93] Congar thought that Alfrink's view was of great importance for church politics. In Schillebeeckx's ecclesiology, episcopal collegiality had played only a marginal role up to the Council, but his views about it were along the same lines as those of Alfrink and Congar.

Towards the end of the Council, Schillebeeckx wrote a portrait of Bernard Jan Cardinal Alfrink for an American publisher, in a series of brochures on prominent figures at the Council. In it he analysed Alfrink's attitude at the time of the Council, and at the same time identified strongly with it.[94] As a result of everything that had happened at and around the Council, at that moment Schillebeeckx had become *the* theologian of the Dutch bishops, and now in turn he showed publicly how much he regarded Alfrink as *his* bishop. He especially praised Alfrink's pastoral attitude as leader and representative of the Dutch church, and the way in which he dealt with the 'will for renewal which [was] also animated by the Council'. He reported with great admiration the way in which Alfrink defended his faithful whenever they were put in a one-sided light by the international press.[95]

Schillebeeckx portrayed Alfrink first of all as someone who had devoted himself heart and soul to the Council and to involving as many of the faithful as possible in it. Awareness of just how important the Council was had dawned on Alfrink a year later than it had on him. Schillebeeckx did not write that in so many words, but he emphasized that in Alfrink's 'preaching, addresses and lectures' before 1960 'virtually no allusions are to be found to the coming Council'. But after Alfrink had been made cardinal in March 1960, and probably also under the influence of the meeting that he had had there with Pope John XXIII, he got a great campaign for the Council under way in the Netherlands. Its climax was an address with which the cardinal archbishop personally travelled round all the Dutch dioceses in

1962. In a French translation this came to the attention of the pope in Rome, who valued it very highly, and some quotations from it were published in *Osservatore Romano*.[96] For his part, Schillebeeckx thought that 'at least from the side of the episcopate there are few countries in which the Council is being prepared for as intensively' as in the Netherlands.

According to Schillebeeckx, Alfrink became a really personal enthusiast for the Council during his work on the so-called 'Central Commission'. This was appointed by the pope on 5 June 1960 after the conclusion of the pre-preparation for the Council, in order to co-ordinate the preparatory activities. However, it was to be almost a year before this great company of around fifty cardinals, twenty archbishops and around another ten superior generals of religious orders and congregations met for the first time. In the period leading up to the opening of the Council on 19 October 1962 they were to meet seven times, each time for a full week. According to Schillebeeckx, in this commission Alfrink discovered in practice the episcopal collegiality which theologically he defended so urgently. He felt that the 'Central Commission' was a 'reflection of the totality of the church', as the whole church *in nucleo* and the 'Council itself *in forma contracta*'.[97]

Within the 'Central Commission' Alfrink increasingly developed into an important representative of the opposition to the power of the Curia and to the preparatory texts. These bore the stamp of the powerful Curia Cardinal Alfredo Ottaviani, who as secretary of the Holy Office had the task of guarding over doctrinal orthodoxy. Together with the Dutch theologian and Jesuit Sebastiaan Tromp, Ottaviani was the most prominent spokesman of the conservative Roman faction, which thought that the Council had to content itself with condemning the serious errors of its time and consolidating the most important points of Catholic doctrine.[98] Despite the quite broad opposition to them within the 'Central Commission', the texts were to find their way to the Council. In the last phase of preparation, at the request of Bishop Willem Bekkers of Den Bosch, Schillebeeckx was to write a comprehensive theological critique of them. This was very much along the lines of what Alfrink had produced in writing in his vota and verbally within the Central Commission.[99] Schillebeeckx's remarks and observations went the rounds in duplicated form all over Rome during the first session of the Council and were translated into French, German, English and Latin. In this way he had an important influence on the formation of opinion, even if this is difficult to trace precisely.[100] However, more important for Schillebeeckx than the specific skirmishes before and during the Council was his 'experience of the church's interest in a universal contribution, in which from all corners of the world church the church is discussed "in great freedom and openness"'.[101] In his view this applied to Alfrink, but it certainly also applied to him.

Schillebeeckx found especially congenial what he was later to call the 'basic notion' of Alfrink's pastoral activity, namely that 'the views of the faithful people form the basis for the responsible decisions of the episcopate'. It was not that Alfrink was developing a distinctive ecclesiology, but this view was expressed in his practice, which Schillebeeckx regarded as the 'responsible consequence of his view of the church'.[102] He quoted with approval Alfrink's summary of the image of the church which had broken through at the Council, the image of 'one people of God within which each has his own responsibility and his own task'. Here the norm was 'loyalty to the authentic message of the Lord's gospel, which one may not violate or evacuate'. In the tumultuous and polarized situation of the Dutch church after the Council, for Alfrink this led to an ongoing call for dialogue, and great restraint in judging how far practices and standpoints, or the groups that they represented, were loyal to the church.[103] Not only did Schillebeeckx share his attitude during this period in his own way and on the basis of his theological responsibility, but he evidently also had the feeling that he could fulfil his own responsibility and task as a theologian particularly well under the gentle guidance of Alfrink. Schillebeeckx, who from his youth had so emphasized the importance of theological thoroughness, had the experience during the Council that 'scholarship, remaining itself, [becomes] insignificant compared with the content of [an] upright Christian leading an authentic life'. This led him to strive with renewed intensity to support such a life, and under the leadership of Cardinal Alfrink he had much scope for this.[104]

If Schillebeeckx regarded Alfrink and also Bekkers emphatically as his bishops, as I have said, the Dutch bishops under the leadership of Alfrink regarded him as their theologian. When in 1968 Schillebeeckx got into difficulties with the church and the first investigation was made into the orthodoxy of his views, in an address at Nijmegen university Alfrink emphatically expressed his antipathy to 'the mistrust that is being sown and the suspicions that are being voiced'. He reminded his audience that he had to suffer this just as much as 'those who practise academic theology', and although 'as pastor to the whole of the Dutch community of faith' he argued that it needed to be noted that some fundamental theological discussions were the cause of 'much uncertainty, much unrest and much fear' among the faithful, at the same time he resolutely defended the freedom of theological investigation. For Alfrink the task which theology had of illuminating the tradition of faith critically did not conflict with its obligation to remain faithful to the authentic faith of the church:

... it seems to me that the critical situation of this time lies in the fact that contemporary theology sees itself confronted with the question what precisely constitutes the authentic faith of the church – of the exact meaning and content of what the ordinary and extraordinary magisterium of the church that we all want to respect proposes that we should believe, as the old formula runs. I thought that was a legitimate question . . .[105]

In the second half of 1960 the Dutch bishops decided to ask Schillebeeckx for theological support in their efforts to involve the faithful more closely in the preparations for the Council, and he accepted the task. This had far-reaching consequences for both parties. It is not clear how the bishops arrived at Schillebeeckx, but it is most probable that they were particularly keen to involve the new Nijmegen professor, of whom much was expected on all sides; moreover, as chancellor and ex-professor of exegesis Alfrink had a close link with the University of Nijmegen.[106] The collaboration ultimately led to Alfrink and Schillebeeckx coming under fire because of their view of the episcopate and its relationship to the papacy. It made them together the face of the Dutch church, which in the same process came to be known all over the world as 'progressive'. Schillebeeckx was later to put it like this:

[E]very word of Cardinal Alfrink [is] on the one hand seen as a liberating blast of the trumpet, while on the other hand he is spied on from all sides in the hope that he can be trapped in a deviation from Catholic orthodoxy.[107]

Here Schillebeeckx was also sketching out indirectly the way in which he himself was regarded when he went to Rome with the Dutch bishops in 1962.

In 1960, little of this could yet be seen. The whole process was only beginning. For a number of reasons, in the course of that year it became clear to the bishops that specific activities were needed to involve Dutch Catholics more in the Council, and in a better way. Now the involvement began to grow of its own accord. Even the commentary in which it was indicated that there was a critical and expectant attitude to the Council in the Dutch church was above all a contribution to the discussions about its significance which were under way:

Now that the church is making the proclamation, really a sublime proclamation, of an ultimate reflection on the tasks of today, people do not believe the church. The church must have gone badly wrong to have so little credit.[108]

This was a disguised call to the bishops to show that commitment to the Council was worthwhile. In 1960 the organization for Catholic intellectuals, the St Adalbert Association, began to publish contributions to the preparation for the Council by lay people in its own journal. When one of these contributions took what the bishops felt to be too bold a tone, and Alfrink protested against its publication, the editors defended the importance of making public 'disquieting thoughts' as these were entertained 'among broad circles of the clergy and laity'. With a striking self-confidence the intellectual Catholic laity demonstrated that they wanted, through the bishops, to make a contribution towards the preparation of the Council, but on their own terms: 'Ask, we are ready ... but then also accept us, even if some of us speak in a rather recalcitrant way, even if we are a burden ...'[109]

But the bishops were pleased neither by indifference nor by boldness, and on 8 July in an address about the Council Alfrink tried at the same time both to stimulate the involvement of all the faithful and to defend himself against all too critical voices. With the latter in view he put great emphasis on the distinctive and inalienable responsibility of the bishops:

> The bishops together, assembled round the Bishop of Rome, are the successors to the college of apostles, assembled around Peter. By virtue of their apostolic office the bishops around the Bishop of Rome at a general council are witnesses to the faith of the Church empowered by the Lord of the Church. There is a place for others here only in so far as by church law they are involved as witnesses to the faith of the Church, often still only with a consultative voice.

At the same time, in his view the bishops had a special responsibility for their faithful. For the bishops were not only successors of the apostles but also 'the witnesses to the faith of their church people', and this meant that they had the task of 'listening carefully to the testimony and the desires of their church people and noting them faithfully'. This implied that 'the church people [should] be able to have the freedom to bring their bishops up to date with their thoughts and desires about the general council', but that this had to be done calmly. Freedom needed to be coupled 'with the respect which everyone in the church, whoever he may be, owes to the authority set over him'; this remark was generally regarded as a warning to those from the circle of the St Adalbert organization engaged in the discussion. Alfrink ended by urging his audience not to wait until the Council began but to realize that the Council had already begun, and to pray 'for the illumination of the Holy Spirit for all those who are now occupied with the Council'.[110] In 1960 Alfrink found it hard to see that the fierce discussion of which he was so afraid as a church leader was also part of this 'being occupied with the Council'.

The main lines of this conflict between the St Adelbert Association and Alfrink were to be repeated two years later. At the annual congress of the association which took place in Rotterdam on 29 and 30 September 1962 under the title 'Freedom – conscience – magisterium', the student chaplain and Jesuit Jan van Kilsdonk argued for the need for a loyal opposition in the church and here emphatically made himself the spokesman of the generation which had grown up since the Second World War. In his view an opposition was loyal which was 'perhaps not tempered but constantly opened up by love, by the need always to remain within the bond of the church'. And he suggested that 'the awesome crisis which is raging in the world of the young Catholic intelligentsia and the annual silent loss of faith or diminution of faith among a large number of gifted scholars, also in the Netherlands' was connected with the activity of the Roman Curia, which usually showed little sensitivity.[111] And with many people in the Netherlands he was anxious about the great influence of the Curia on the preparation of the Council, especially on the preparatory documents; the question of the Curia's influence on the Council was to remain an important topic in the Netherlands. Alfrink felt that this speech thwarted his strategy of cautious diplomacy and subtle argument. A report of it was broadcast on television, so that the statements, which in the current conditions were extensive, reached a national audience. A week later he reacted to Van Kilsdonk by pointing out that one ran

> with un-nuanced public cries of despair, even if they are born of love of the church ... the risk of working up a mood, but little prospect of bringing improvement closer. Rather, they arouse new opposition and a stubbornness which seems justified.[112]

The history of relations between the Dutch church province and Rome were to justify this anxiety. But gradually it was to become increasingly clear to him that for more and more Dutch Catholics, the airing of the frustrations and the expression of the desires of which Van Kilsdonk had made himself the spokesman were the only way of preserving the faith. Schillebeeckx seemed to feel this when he admonished his fellow-priests: 'Let us first learn to listen before we want to be listened to.'

Schillebeeckx was originally to have appeared as the speaker at the Adalbert congress, but he declined at the last moment; Van Kilsdonk was his replacement. Schillebeeckx agreed with him that Catholics could expect a hearing from their bishops. From his youth he had been convinced that the word of God 'must not be thrown at people like a stone at their heads ... but [must] be experienced as a value by the listeners'. In a lecture on communication between priest and layman, also given in September 1962, he concluded from this that members of the hierarchy also had the obligation to listen to 'what they themselves think wrong or half-baked ideas':

> If some of the ideas that are going the rounds are 'way out', priests must not simply brush them aside with a disdainful gesture, but take them seriously and try to analyse them. Surely experience has taught us that there is almost always an element of truth even in the most rash sounding

views, and priests should not take any immediately defensive attitude towards them but make use of the germ of truth they contain.[113]

When halfway through 1965 part of the press, above all the Italian press, had turned against the developments in Dutch Catholicism and even the pope himself condemned the way in which the decisions of the Council were received there, Alfrink was to react along the lines that Schillebeeckx indicates here. Alfrink was to point out that all were driven by love of the church. 'Ultimately their sole aim is, for love of the church, according to the saying of Paul which Pope John gave this Council as a motto, to remove every speck and wrinkle from the church's garment.' And he pointed out that 'the interest of the faithful in everything to do with the church', especially in the Council, was 'extremely great and deep' and extended to 'all levels of the population'. For Alfrink what were seen in Rome as signs of disobedience had clearly become signs of life.[114]

'The Bishops of the Netherlands on the Council'

At the beginning of 1961 a brochure appeared under the title 'The Bishops of the Netherlands on the Council', aimed at the involvement of Dutch Catholics that the bishops wanted. This was in fact largely written by Schillebeeckx.[115] In it he drew on his wide knowledge of the tradition and current theological discussions about the nature of the church, the place of the laity and the hierarchy in it, and the relationship between pope and bishops. In collaboration with his fellow dogmatic theologians Jan (J. C.) Groot from the major seminary of the diocese of Haarlem at Warmond and Frans Haarsma of the major seminary of the diocese of Utrecht at Rijsenburg, he produced a text which because of its content and theological jargon was regarded as 'difficult' but at the same time also as inspiring.[116] The skirmishes which had preceded the publication of the text made it logical that most attention was paid to the question how far in the letter lay people were really regarded as conversation partners of the bishops. Some commentators picked out the admonitions: that the laity's criticism of the church must emerge from 'true love of the church', a love which pointed out faults in it 'only with caution', which was tactful in advancing its 'childlike remarks and comments', and which did not undermine the obedience of faith. This passage, which had been added on the urging of the Haarlem chaplain J. M. Groot, reinforced among some laity 'the bitter feeling' that they were being treated like 'irresponsible children'.[117] Nevertheless, according to most reactions, 'The Bishops of the Netherlands and the Council' was a 'lively, inspiring and visionary word'; the text 'clearly [kept] in contact with reality in an all-embracing theological foundation' and offered 'perspectives on our being as church in the world'. There was no request

> just for our prayers ... [but] also for our competent collaboration by joining in the search for solutions to the problems, sharing in thought about renewal and adaptation, and by making our opinions known with great boldness, in love for the church and in thorough and knowledgeable reflection.

One commentator christened the episcopal brochure the 'new mandate'.[118] It in fact broke with the notion that Catholic laity needed above all to gather behind their pastors *en masse*, a view which was still expressed in the episcopal mandate 'The Catholic in the Public Life of this Time'.[119] It is questionable whether the theological content really penetrated to the Dutch Catholics, but the openness of the text to the laity met with a broad response. It was the same with the brochure's picture of the church, indicated by a statement by the co-author, Groot, that 'the church as a community of love has the character of a conversation'.[120] In the wake of this letter, stimulated by the discussions of the Council and what got through from them into the press, and encouraged by the Dutch bishops, in the 1960s and 1970s dialogue groups formed in the Dutch church everywhere and at every level. In them the faithful took up recent ecclesiastical and theological developments and tried to connect them with developments in society and in their own personal lives.

'The Bishops of the Netherlands on the Council' tried above all to make clear the importance of a Council. As a gathering of the world episcopate, such a general assembly of the church was not made superfluous by the promulgation of papal infallibility. Along the lines of early formulations of Schillebeeckx, Alfrink and also Groot, it was said that 'papal infallibility [is] also involved in the ministerial infallibility of the world episcopate'.[121] The text even went a step further and stated – certainly along the lines of earlier remarks by Schillebeeckx but less so along the lines of those by Alfrink – that 'the ministerial infallibility of the world episcopate' in its turn was 'also borne up by the infallible faith of the whole of the community of faith'. Each of the bishops went to the Council 'as bishop of this specific church', and in each of them was heard 'the voice of the whole community of faith for which he is responsible'. Therefore, all the faithful were also involved in a council, and its results were the product of 'the active faith of the whole community of faith'.[122] The real point of the brochure was that indeed the community of faith in turn needed to be actively involved in all areas of the Council. It emphatically stated that the 'difference in the church between the clergy and the laity' may not be understood to mean that 'the clergy have the care of the kingdom of the God, whereas the laity, as the passive objects of this priestly care, are characterized by a worldly task'. It emphasized the shared responsibility of all the baptized 'for the church and its function as a sign in the midst of the world'.[123]

'The Bishops of the Netherlands on the Council' was a special document, and not just in retrospect, though of course it is striking that generally speaking the statements that the Council was later to make about the position of the bishops and the laity in the church took the same line as those in the brochure.[124] But what made the text unique among the other preparatory texts was the consistent way in which it was constructed out of a theological reflection on the nature and function of the church. Moreover, in terms of content this reflection was quite remarkable within the Catholic world. With an abundance of quotations from the New Testament, the church was not derived from the sending out of the apostles by Jesus and thus from the institution of the church's hierarchy. Central to the church was its sight in faith of the dawn of the kingdom of God in Jesus, and the way in which it put the whole of reality within that new perspective. Where the faithful did that, they realized the church. This view in fact offered an alternative to the picture of the church in *Mystici corporis*, which at that time was still the official one. To this degree 'The Bishops of the Netherlands on the Council' is also an important breakthrough in Schillebeeckx's own development.[125] From the beginning we can see in his work a clear tendency to break through the existing doctrinal limits. In the second half of the 1950s the tension between this tendency and what were in fact immovable limits clearly grew. The preparations for the Council reinforced this tension, making clear with renewed force how necessary a real breakthrough was, but for the first time it also offered possibilities here. The writing of 'The Bishops of the Netherlands on the Council' and the need to present a clear message in fact led Schillebeeckx to formulate the basic features of the new ecclesiology, which made it possible not just to tolerate the initiatives of believers and the renewing impulses of theologians with due difficulty, but to regard them as pleasing signs of a living faith.

We also find already announced in this brochure the great themes of Schillebeeckx's theology in the period after the Council. There is, for example, his concentration on the significance of the man Jesus, which was to attract theological attention from all over the world through the two major studies of Jesus which he wrote in the 1970s:

In [Jesus's] words, his actions – healings, miracles and exorcisms – , in the forgiveness of sins, it above all becomes clear that God is manifesting his lordship through the overwhelming power of grace in a visible way ... The people of God, the people which lives in the presence of God's domain, is a people of the faithful who 'know' the kingdom of God; in other words, they experience God's kingdom as it takes historical form in this earthly world and moreover are given the task of making this kingdom known to others.

In the view of the brochure God had called the church as a whole, all the faithful, in Jesus Christ, 'as those who have been redeemed, to be the visible manifestation of the kingdom of God in this world' and thus to show their knowledge that the kingdom of God has appeared in Jesus.[126] At the same time the brochure indicated that the thought that people were called in this sense to become, as he would put it much later, the 'story of God' for 'us, believers' made a deeper reflection necessary 'on what our faith contains about life in a modern world'.[127] This reflection runs like a scarlet thread through the whole of Schillebeeckx's theological work, but in fact already in the course of the Council, and to an even greater degree after it, it would command the greater part of his intellectual attention. This will be discussed at length at the beginning of the second volume of this study.

It is often said that in the views which the Dutch episcopate expressed during the Council it was ahead of the Council. To support this judgement, reference is then made not only to 'The Bishops of the Netherlands on the Council', but also to a number of contributions to the discussion at the Council by Cardinal Alfrink. But there is a difference between the view in the brochure and that of Alfrink. This is immediately evident if one sets beside the brochure the text of the address with which Alfrink tried to convince the Dutch clergy of the importance of the Council in May and June 1962. In 'The Bishops of the Netherlands on the Council' could be heard the voice of a theologian who already saw the church changing in the course of the discussion. Despite all its enthusiasm about the work in the 'Central Commission' in preparation for the Council, the voice heard in the speech was primarily that of a conservative reformist administrator who hoped that the Council would remove a number of blockages to the proper functioning of the church. Alfrink saw this as his responsibility: 'The mobility which develops in the church is important ... '[128] Beyond doubt Alfrink's view corresponds more to Roncalli's intentions than to what in fact were the far-reaching ecclesiological views expressed in the brochure, and as I have said, Pope John in fact indicated his agreement with the content of Alfrink's address. What emerged from all the commotion around the bishops' brochure was a certain vindication of Alfrink.[129]

Almost immediately after the Council Schillebeeckx would note that the Council documents did not consistently and explicitly connect the place of the laity in the church with the mission of the church as a whole. In his view, in the constitution *Lumen gentium* the Council fathers had not really succeeded in getting away from the clerical concept of the church. He thought that the history of the church showed that the hierarchy had grown out of

319

the concrete needs of the whole people of God, and that in this sense the laity did not 'need to be related to the hierarchy', as in the document. Rather, the hierarchy needed to be related to the laity, and the church's ministry needed to be justified 'on the basis of its service to the people of God'.[130] Especially also in view of later discussions on the relationship between priests and laity in the church, it proves extremely striking that as early as 1960 'The Bishops of the Netherlands on the Council' already sketched a picture of the church in which the ministry emphatically took a place within and at the service of the community of faith. This text also continued to emphasize the special character of the ministry, but it did so precisely by emphasizing the function that it had for holding the church together as people of God: in the 'perspective of the church as "body, nourished and knit together through its joints and ligatures" (Col. 2.19), the apostolic ministry, extended into the church's hierarchy, also has its own place in the people of God'.[131]

THE COUNCIL AS A BREAKTHROUGH

The publication of the brochure of the Dutch bishops on the Council had great consequences for all concerned. Because of the striking theological position expressed in it, the text attracted wide international attention, and translations into German, French, English, Polish and Spanish appeared. However, difficulties arose when an Italian translation also appeared in February 1962. Ultimately, it was withdrawn from sale, in all probability on the prompting of theologians associated with the Holy Office – which formerly had been called the Inquisition and was later to become the Congregation for the Doctrine of Faith – and with the official theological commission which was then still dominated by the Roman Curia, in which the texts to be approved by the Council were prepared.[132] Both Alfrink, who as cardinal archbishop was the first signatory, and Schillebeeckx, who was emphatically thanked by the bishops at the end of the text, were to become internationally famous as spokesmen of the progressives within the church. Neither of them liked this – bishops and theologians were not supposed to take positions but to represent the Catholic centre – and for Schillebeeckx this meant the beginning of a series of conflicts with the Roman authorities.

Schillebeeckx's work on 'The Bishops of the Netherlands on the Council' was also the immediate reason why he was not appointed an official theological expert – *peritus* – by the Council. This did not happen, despite all his efforts to further and deepen the discussions at the Council: according to an eye-witness, as a regular adviser to the bishops during the time of the Council sessions he had 'steadfastly worked in his rented room in the Dutch College on advice, commentaries and interventions for the bishops and on preparing drafts and meetings'.[133] Schillebeeckx was most unpleasantly affected by this veto, which came from very influential Roman circles, above all the powerful Cardinal Alfredo Ottaviani, who was not only secretary of the Holy Office but also president of the theological preparatory commission of the Council. For Schillebeeckx, it was a symbol of all the opposition from Rome that he was also to encounter after the Council. The conversation with Pope Paul VI that took place in 1965 with the aim of rehabilitating him did not alter this. Almost 30 years later he was to write that he always found it 'very painful': 'the people "up there at the top" seem to be living in another world'.[134]

The breakthrough of a renewing theology

At the same time, the problems surrounding 'The Bishops of the Netherlands on the Council' also made Schillebeeckx an internationally known figure. During the time of the Council and as a result of his public appearances, especially also on Dutch radio and television, he became *the* theological expert for the Dutch public, especially on the developments at the Council. Because he was not a *peritus* he was not sworn to secrecy or involved in time-consuming committee work, so he could respond widely to the increasing number of invitations. In Rome he gave a large number of lectures to bishops and journalists, and after the Council he travelled all over the world as a speaker; many of his works were translated into a variety of languages.[135]

As a theologian who was highly controversial in the church in the 1950s, but who in the 1960s suddenly became a much-sought after and valued expert, Yves Congar stated with bewilderment that at the Second Vatican Council 'all the work that had been done over 30 years, sometimes in difficult circumstances ... suddenly [issued] in a great gathering of the supreme teaching authority'.[136] This gave a new status and a far wider public to that work and those who were doing it, the intellectuals and thinkers within the church, and especially the theologians.[137] The question of the relationship between contemporary thought and church tradition which had already been occupying them for a long time and for which they had found provisional answers became a question for the whole church. At the time of the Council it was even a question for the whole of Western culture, which from the end of the 1950s had become aware that it was in a period of intensive change and was reflecting on its relationship to the traditions that hitherto had been normative. That explains why the theological discussions were reported in the press all over the world and theologians sometimes became stars. Great tours were arranged for the Council theologians, especially in the United States, and their lectures were attended by thousands of people. And on the modest Dutch scale, the Catholic theological faculties which had been formed in the 1960s, partly as a result of the concentration of seminary training – the Nijmegen faculty, which hitherto had offered training after study at seminary, became a place for training undergraduates – opened their doors to the laity and enrolled unprecedented numbers of students.

Moreover, now that theologians who had previously only read one another's work could meet in person at the Council, they could discover a shared mission in the church. A bond developed between them which later Schillebeeckx was to describe as 'a close bond of friendship'.[138] The time seemed ripe to realize an earlier plan of the Dutch publisher Paul Brand to start an international Catholic journal addressed to a wide public. Brand was a publisher of current theological literature; among other things he had published Dutch translations of books by Karl Rahner and Hans Küng. He regretted that it took so long for his readers to get to know about new theological developments abroad. In 1958, for the first time he put to Rahner the idea of a theological journal edited and published internationally, but Rahner did not think that something of that sort made sense in the existing situation in the church: 'In such a journal we could not write what we want to and have to write.' Brand repeated his request for collaboration on a number of occasions, but it was always turned down until in 1962 the breakthrough of the progressive trend at the Council ensured that there was the necessary institutional and intellectual space. Yves Congar, Hans Küng, Karl Rahner and Edward Schillebeeckx met and discussed what was to be the foundation of the journal with Brand and Marcel Vanhengel, who was the first editorial secretary. In 1963 it proved possible to attract well-known specialists from the various theological disciplines to head up the different sections of the new journal and back this up with the support and regular collaboration of around 450 theologians from all over the world. The necessary finances were arranged, along with the complicated organization which by definition was necessary for such a large-scale international project, and the publication of editions in the different language areas. The journal *Concilium* was officially founded in Saarbrücken on 20 July 1963.[139]

Concilium was established on the basis of a declaration of intent, signed by Schillebeeckx and Rahner, and published in the first issue, which appeared in January 1965, after a trial issue in autumn 1964. The text bears witness above all to the new self-confidence that Catholic theologians had acquired as a result of their work at the Council. As well as being a council of bishops Vatican II had also been a council of theologians. The founders of the journal were convinced that a theology was in the making which in particular could be a support to 'those who carry out the pastoral task within the church'. It is clear that the authors primarily had in mind those who governed the church, especially the bishops, and through them the priests in the pastorate, although they said that they did not want to exclude 'laymen with responsibilities in the church'; evidently women were still outside their perspective. It was to be especially this theology, which was practical in a new way, that would appear in the journal. According to Rahner and Schillebeeckx the Council had made it clear 'that the pastoral work of the Church and the preaching of the Gospel has something to learn from the science of theology, just as this theology has to learn from pastoral practice', and according to them the central issue was the same in both practice and theory, namely

> a theology which is deliberately based on Scripture and the history of salvation. At the same time it has the humble courage to confront the new problems arising from the human conditions of today. It seeks, on the basis of our contemporary situation, a better understanding of the word of God for man and the world of our time.

Such a theology was in their view 'necessary for anyone who, acting in faith, is actively engaged in the Church and in the world'; according to them, it was in line with the Council and called for the collaboration and discussion of 'an international group of professional theologians'. In their view this discussion had already been begun on the periphery of the Council.[140]

Throughout the Council, but especially also during the period of preparation, there were disputes about the direction the church had to take.[141] On the eve of the opening it seemed that those who wanted to make Vatican II the definitive seal on Vatican I would come out on top. The drafts for the final text as they then were exuded the atmosphere of a Catholicism which set itself against the modern world. But during the preparation these drafts had provoked widespread opposition. The fact that the dispute between different currents in the church emerged was itself a powerful blow to the myth of the church as an indestructible bulwark within which an ever immutable truth was revered.

In a commentary on the eve of the first session Schillebeeckx spoke openly of a conservative and a progressive camp, since 'it would be unrealistic to want to deny this fact of the two trends'. It was quite clear on which side he himself stood, but he took a good deal of trouble to maintain the idea 'that on both sides thought is governed by concern for the church'.[142] Moreover, he clearly felt uncomfortable with the contrast made between progressive and conservative, between those who were up with the times and those who were not. In his view it was more a conflict between different views of the truth of faith. The essentialist-conceptualist view regarded truth as a timeless essence and tried to formulate this as exactly as possible in a clear doctrine; the existentialist view to which he himself adhered regarded theological truth as a saving value for historical people living in the world. Thus, in his view of the Council, too, Schillebeeckx maintained the conviction that basic theological views were of decisive importance in pastoral questions and that pastoral orientation and concentration on the truth did not conflict with one another. The truth of faith was intrinsically pastoral, and in his view the Council was ultimately concerned to maintain *this* truth.[143]

But he could do little to alter the fact that, as he was to remark later, in the corridors and in the press the Council was felt to be 'a kind of tournament'.[144] In the experience of many of those who were involved, the period from 11 October to 8 December 1962, during which the Council fathers met in St Peter's, Rome, for the first session, were 'sixty days that changed the church'.[145] Shortly after the Council had really begun, Schillebeeckx spoke about it in terms of 'hope and concern'; he urged Catholic journalists above all to have an eye for 'what can be realized in this Council' and he admonished the readers of the Dominican weekly *De Bazuin* increasingly to develop into a voice for conciliar renewal, to show themselves 'good winners, but in individual matches (for the moment) also good losers'. 'For life goes on after the Council.' However, in January 1963 he could note that the course of the first session had 'exceeded all optimistic expectations'. He conceded that officially no decisions had yet been taken, and there were still always anxieties about the future course of the Council, but he thought that with 'the turn that the Second Vatican Council has taken in its first phase' it has 'already reached ... its climax'.[146] What was generally regarded as the 'progressive wing' had won a decisive victory: 'The majority has spoken for a different course. This fact can no longer be undone.' However, in his view 'the open wing' had not won 'because it now represented progressiveness, but because it has really brought out aspects of reality which evidently the so-called "closed wing" has continued to fail to see'. He was very well aware that the Council fathers had not suddenly become adherents of progressive theology. They had simply taken their pastoral problems seriously. Therefore they turned away from the narrow schemes of Roman theology and recognized themselves in what so-called progressive theologians put forward.

> It was heart-warming to be able to see how, for example, Chilean, Brazilian and Indian bishops ... on hearing the exposition of one or another theological theme reacted spontaneously as if in connaturality: 'that speaks to us'. The living contact with human reality gave them this openness, which only needed to be 'filled' or sometimes even just 'put into words'.

And here the theology known as progressive evidently succeeded. In Schillebeeckx's view, the central event of the first session of the Council was the breakthrough of reality into the traditional theological categories. On the basis of this he hoped that in the following phases, too, the Council would not orientate itself on keeping the faith pure but on keeping it vital and alive.[147] He was convinced that this would manifestly and automatically also mean great freedom for the theology which he himself championed, and which understood itself to be thinking in the historical situation 'in search of the living God'.

To a not unimportant degree, the decisive change of climate during the first session of the Council was the result of the appearance of Pope John XXIII himself. In his address at the opening, which made a great impression everywhere, the pope immediately seemed to be taking sides in the conflict that was going on. Thus, he broke with the tradition of Catholic anti-modernism by emphatically dissociating himself from those who 'in the situation of our modern time simply say decline and disaster'. He described the period as a situation in which people were already automatically inclined to turn away from 'forms of life which despise God and his laws' and become more and more aware 'of the dignity of the human person'. In his view, in these circumstances the church had to point to the power of its teaching and not utter condemnations. It had to show itself to be a 'loving, benevolent and patient mother to all, merciful and good to the children who are separated from it'. There was more need for 'the cure of mercy' than for the 'weapons of strictness'.[148] He emphatically told the Council fathers that Catholic teaching had already been laid down with all desirable clarity, especially at the Council of Trent and Vatican I. Therefore, Vatican II did not need to have any special anxieties about doctrine. The issue was now a different one:

> This certain and unchangeable doctrine, which must be maintained faithfully, needs to be studied and expounded according to the method which is appropriate to our time. For a distinction must be made between the heritage of faith, or the truths which are contained in our sacred doctrine, and the way in which these truths are formulated, of course in the same sense and with the same meaning. Great importance must be attached to this manner of formulation and it must be developed with due patience. Here a method must be followed which is appropriate to a predominantly pastoral magisterium.

Here a different concern was being expressed from that in the markedly scholastic and doctrinal draft texts which the theological commission had produced. According to the pope, faithfulness to the Catholic tradition did not mean preserving doctrine as if it were an interesting antique, but energetic and fearless dedication to 'the work called for by modern times', in other words, 'progress on the way that the church has now taken for almost twenty centuries'.[149]

Only three days later, at their first real working session, the Council fathers made it clear that they could not just accept the draft texts. After all the preparations they now had to elect the members of the different Council commissions, and for this purpose were given a list of the members of the different preparatory commissions responsible for the draft texts that had been introduced. However, obviously contrary to what had been expected of them, the Council fathers did not choose the members of the preparatory commissions, who could have efficiently turned the proposals for texts into constitutions of the Council. Then Cardinal Liénard of Lille presented a motion to postpone the elections because of the need to discuss the commissions first in the different national conferences of bishops, and Cardinal Frings of Cologne agreed in the name of the German-speaking cardinals. This was followed by applause, whereupon it was decided that there was no need to vote on the motion. Consequently, in the space of half an hour 'the fortunes of the Council were largely determined': Vatican II could go its own independent way. This was confirmed in the feverish deliberations which immediately began, and led not only to Council commissions which, by comparison with the preparatory commissions, 'reflected far better the different trends of thoughts and nationalities', but also to the first more intensive contacts between bishops from different parts of the world.[150]

In the second half of November the revolution was complete. There was a discussion on an intended Council document which would speak of 'the two sources of divine revelation': alongside the Bible also and independently the apostolic tradition, which according to the draft text was entrusted to and embodied by the hierarchy. The intervention by Cardinal Alfrink on the first day of the discussion of the text may be said to be representative of the criticism which the mass of the Council fathers had of this. Alfrink began by reminding the assembly of the pope's remark that the Council did not need to discuss church doctrine and criticized the text because it did not do anything but repeat at length 'what can be found in all the theological textbooks about the sources of revelation, about holy scripture, about the tradition and the church's magisterium'. Instead of this, he would like to see in the text

> the essential contribution made by theological studies in recent times to a
> clearer and more precise insight into, for example, the very term 'divine
> revelation' in the relationship to holy scripture and the church's magis-
> terium, in the terminology in which one can speak of two sources of
> revelation – a terminology which the Council of Trent lacked: its members
> preferred to talk about the two ways in which the one truth of faith, the
> gospel itself, was handed down.

The hand of Schillebeeckx and the view of tradition which he had developed in his Louvain courses can clearly be recognized in this text.[151]

The final text of the Constitution on Divine Revelation, *Dei verbum*, was in fact to speak in this spirit.[152] After a week of intensive discussion, on 21 November there was a vote on a proposal to have the text rewritten by a commission; 1,368 Council fathers voted for this proposal and 822 against. However, because of the way in which the proposal had been formulated, which favoured its opponents – 'must the discussion of the schema be broken off?' – a two-thirds majority was needed, and the plenary discussion of the text continued. Nevertheless, on the next day the decision came down from the pope that the text had to be rewritten, by a new commission in which there were also representatives of the secretariat for the unity of Christians, which was regarded as progressive. In a commentary on the first session Schillebeeckx spoke of 'the climax of the Council when the pope – this great figure – had the theological schema on the sources of revelation removed on the wishes of the moral majority'.[153] Much later he was to write in retrospect that the general feeling was that the Council really began after this intervention. In the euphoria of the moment he himself wrote in a letter home that 'the new direction in theology has from now on become the official direction of the church ...'[154]

In the course of the first session the assembled Council increasingly took things into its own hands. Key Council fathers also criticized the draft for a constitution on the church because it spoke too much in legalistic terms and structures and too little about the church as the people of God, within which the hierarchy had the task of serving rather than governing. Moreover, the text did not develop any theology of the episcopate, although there were questions about this from many sides during the period of preparation. In this framework Cardinal Alfrink also noted the lack of co-ordination in the Council's activities and argued that better co-ordination was now vital for everyone, 'so that the Council does not have different schemas proposed on the same subjects'.[155] The Belgian Cardinal Archbishop Leo Suenens joined in here and suggested a specific programmatic approach: whereas at Vatican I the primacy of the papacy had been central, in his view Vatican II had to concentrate on the church as the 'light for the peoples'. He argued that the preparatory texts for the Council should be looked at again from two aspects: the church internally as the mystical body of Christ and the church externally as the proclaimer of the gospel.

Suenens had already presented the broad outlines of his view on the programme and structure to John XXIII in the preparatory phase, and the reaction had been very favourable. According to Suenens the Council had to bring the whole church 'into a state of mission'. He spelt this out in the Council aula by announcing:

The church must enter into a dialogue with the world and adopt clear standpoints on the great problems of the world like the inviolability of human rights, procreation and population policy. It must stand up for social justice, bring a redemptive message to the poor and state its position on war and peace.

Many supported Suenens' proposal, including Cardinal Giovanni Batista Montini of Milan, who at that time was generally seen as the heir apparent to John XXIII and who was in fact to become Pope Paul VI. And once again Roncalli reinforced the voice of the majority which developed. The Council fathers were given a revised list of subjects to be discussed on the basis of Suenens' proposal, and a co-ordinating commission was formed which included Suenens among its members.[156] This happened on 6 December. Two days later the first session closed; at it a clearly sick pope expressed the hope that the Council could be concluded by Christmas of the following year. He called on everyone to prepare for the new task which awaited them after that: to carry out the message of the Council and give it form in the world of this time. He had very great expectations:

> Then may we really see the new Pentecost that we desire, which will reinforce the spiritual powers of the church and make its motherly influence and saving activity penetrate more deeply in the sphere of human activity. Then the kingdom of Christ on earth will blossom again.[157]

Roncalli himself concentrated heavily on the message of peace among the nations. 'The efforts of these four years of our humble service as we see this and understand it to the end is service as servant of the servants of the Lord, who really is *the Lord and the prince of peace*', he said shortly after the end of the first Council session.[158] On 11 April 1963 he added deeds to words and published the encyclical *Pacem in terris*, the first papal message in modern history which was not just addressed to the faithful but to 'all men of good will'. It was to become his testament. A month later Cardinal Suenens as his representative was able to present the plea for peaceful dealings between the nations at the United Nations in New York; the pope himself was too sick to do this. As his representative Suenens offered the leaders of the nations the choice between 'the arms race with the constant risk of a collective nuclear suicide emerging from this rivalry' and a 'growing trust as a basis for a stable peace'.[159] This papal message was received everywhere as an event of the greatest importance. Schillebeeckx spoke of a gesture 'which made Christian rulers shudder and atheistic rulers rejoice'.[160] *Pacem in terris* was seen as a document in which the church had indeed associated itself with the joy and hope, the sorrow and fear of the people of today, as Vatican II was finally to describe its new attitude towards the modern world.[161] The dynamic of the Council seemed unstoppable.

Concern for doing the Christian truth

Pope John XXIII died on the Monday after Pentecost, 3 June 1963. The Dutch bishops expressed the feelings of a great many when they described him on his death as the one who had again given scope for the Holy Spirit in the church. In their view he was the vehicle of the vision to which they too in the meanwhile had come to adhere:

John understood that being an ideal Christian is not bound up with a pattern which is unchangeable for all times, but that this being a Christian is very closely connected with the time in which the Christian lives ... He saw that the church was no longer up with the times and made the decision to hold a gathering of the church to bring the church up to date – to make the church understand the language of the world and the world understand the language of the church.[162]

At the opening of the second session of the Council, on 29 September 1963, Montini, who had been chosen to be his successor, commemorated him at length. In a long address, which replaced the usual first encyclical in which a new pope expounds his view of the situation of the church, Paul VI praised John XXIII very personally:

Beloved Pope and revered Pope John! We thank you, we praise you for having prescribed this Council as divine inspiration to open up new ways for the church and to make new and beneficial but still hidden streams of the teaching of Christ our God flow over the world.[163]

Montini indicated that he was willing to walk in Roncalli's footsteps, and that is indeed what he was chosen for. In a statement for Dutch television Cardinal Alfrink rightly said that 'the college of cardinals which has chosen the new pope ... did not doubt at any moment that Paul VI will continue the work of Pope John, but in his own way'.[164] In the speech which Cardinal Suenens gave in Pope John's memory in the Council aula, he compared him with John the Baptist, the witness to the light, and established him as a historical figure: 'From the standpoint of history without doubt it will be legitimate to say that he opened a new period for the church ... '

In his '*in memoriam*' Suenens at the same time indicated the considerations which had led to the choice of Montini: the spirit of Pope John now needed to be firmly rooted, and he believed that 'providence [had] given His Holiness Pope Paul to the church in order to lend form and structure to the prophetic view of his predecessor'.[165] The hope that Paul VI would translate the spirit of John XXIII into concrete structures and administrative proposals grew when on the eve of the second session of the Council he announced a reform of the Roman Curia. This central administrative apparatus of the church had been vigorously criticized at the Council for its tendency towards centralization and its high-handed attitude. The increasingly strong emphasis that the college of bishops under the leadership of the pope is the supreme organ in the church was not just a correction to the one-sided emphasis that the First Vatican Council had put on the power of the pope. It also represented opposition to the power which the Curia had in fact acquired. For those who know with hindsight how little came of these reforms, what Paul VI said to the Curia does not seem much; it was a prime concern of his to make it clear that the Curia was the instrument 'which the pope needs and which the pope uses to fulfil his divine charge'. Nevertheless, many drew hope from the fact that this pope had listened to the criticism of the Curia, from his proposal to make the Curia less Italian and Roman and to give it a more international orientation, and from his statement that unfocused and no longer healthy forms of centralism had to disappear in favour of 'the episcopate'.[166] On the eve of the second session of the Council Schillebeeckx concluded from this that 'Pope John brought the spirit and let the spirit blow on the Council. But as long as the spirit is ahead of the structures something is wrong. This pope wants to tackle the structures.'[167]

However, there was soon a change in the evaluation of Montini. He certainly was to take a number of measures which were very much along the lines of conciliar renewal, including giving away the triple papal crown on behalf of the poor and elevating two women, Catherine of Siena and Teresa of Avila, to be teachers of the church, the first in church history. But by his death in 1978 he was generally regarded as the one who had blown out the spirit of the Council. Above all, a great many Catholics all over the world saw his 1968 encyclical *Humanae vitae* as a return to the rigid anti-modernist attitude of before the Council.[168] Moreover, the encyclical had been composed in a way that violated the democratic ethos which had grown, thanks to the Council. In the Netherlands this negative image was to be reinforced by the conflict over the way in which the Dutch Catholics thought that they should take up the stimuli of the Second Vatican Council in their own context, a conflict which was to result in the nomination in 1970 of Adrianus Simonis to be Bishop of Rotterdam and in 1972 of Johannes Gijssen to be Bishop of Roermond, against the wishes of the Dutch Catholics and the majority of their bishops.[169] But in a sense the image of Paul VI as the opposite pole to John XXIII was already established at the end of the Council or even earlier. His cautious and careful activity and his concern to preserve the unity of the church made many people feel that the conservatives had regained the initiative they had lost under John XXIII.[170]

The so-called 'black week' in 1964 at the end of the third session of the Council was very important in forming this picture. During it, especially the final phase of the very long and intensive discussion of the intended Council document on the church caused great resentment among many people. In the course of two sessions the original draft text, which was very much along the lines of *Mystici corporis* and *Humani generis*, had been changed into a document in which the church is first of all described as the people of God and only after that as a hierarchy. Moreover, in the second session the vast majority of the Council had supported a fundamental revaluation of the episcopate. This had come about at the cost of a vigorous conflict about procedures and the competences of the different conciliar authorities – which, as Schillebeeckx wrote in a commentary,[171] 'may be reckoned as the blackest shadow side of this session of the Council because of the opposition and obstruction practised' by the conservative minority. Each had interpreted this revaluation at the appropriate moment as confirmation by the Council of the approach that had been developed shortly before and during the Council. Schillebeeckx had followed these discussions intensively and now and then will have been very worried by them, but after the outcome he noted with grateful amazement that 'throughout the history of the development of dogma' he did not know of 'any case in which a particular datum of faith was accepted so quickly and with such an apt formulation, almost unanimously by the world episcopate'.[172] In principle the Council fathers agreed with a number of specific consequences of this theology. The consecration of bishops was the highest degree of the sacrament of ordination, and every bishop who had been lawfully consecrated formed part of the college of bishops, which was the successor to the college of the apostles and which, in union with the pope as its principle of unity, had complete and supreme power over the universal church. This represented a rejection of the view – which had been put forward especially by the Roman Curia – that the pope alone had supreme authority in the church and that he could involve others in exercising this power at his discretion, although the Council maintained that while the pope could act without the bishops, the bishops could not act without the explicit and free agreement of the pope. In his commentary on the second session Schillebeeckx indicated the inconsistency of this standpoint. He argued for consistency and for seeing the pope really as primate within the college of bishops, evidently on the presupposition that such a plea made sense:

> If the college of bishops possesses a legitimacy directly from God, it must also be able to exercise this from God. However, the role of the primatial rights of the pope lies in the fact that the pope moderates this exercise of rights; in other words he also leads and guides them, precisely as head of this college.[173]

In the period between the second and third sessions the text of the Council document was rewritten in the spirit of the deliberations. The shock came during the third session, when on 14 November 1964, shortly before the definitive vote on the relevant chapter, the text of a so-called *nota explicative praevia* was presented. This was an explanatory preface, which some days later proved to be meant as an authoritative papal exposition of the text. It stated that the college of bishops was dependent on and remained dependent on the initiative of the pope, and the pope was unambiguously set above the bishops.[174] It was generally recognized that this did not conflict with the draft text about the church, and in general it was also recognized that this *nota* represented an attempt to get as wide a consensus as possible and to persuade the small group of opponents of the text also to vote for the constitution. Nevertheless, above all the way in which this interpretation was imposed on the Council fathers from above provoked opposition. In a lecture which he gave in Rome immediately after the approval of the constitution on the church on 18 November, Schillebeeckx remarked:

> The dynamic of the Council has been stopped in its tracks as far as the collegiality of the world episcopate is concerned. The *nota praevia* which serves as a kind of illumination of the third chapter of the schema on the church has laid down something that the Council specifically did not want to define ... But fortunately this Council is only one link in the history of the councils and the church. We may trust that the thinking about collegiality which has grown up in modern theology will spread further.[175]

Soon afterwards, the disappointment which can clearly be heard here, precisely when he tries to see the matter in proportion, would be repressed. But Schillebeeckx himself let his disappointment show only briefly, where he thought it his duty to try to temper the wave of fury and disappointment among Dutch Catholics.[176]

With good reason the closing week of the third session was called a black week: further incidents took place, with the nadir on 19 November, 'black Thursday'. On this day the Council was for the first time confronted with the news that the vote on the Declaration on Religious Freedom, which had been announced a day earlier, would be postponed to give more time for discussion; given the approaching end of the third session this mean postponement to the fourth and last session, which was to take place in autumn 1965. Many Council fathers saw this as an attempt by the conservative minority to gain time, and the same day an express letter was sent to the pope asking 'with the greatest urgency ... that the vote on the Declaration on Religious Freedom should take place before the end of this session, so that we do not lose the trust of the world, both Christians and non-Christians'. The majority wanted the rapid publication of this text with its high symbolic value for the new open attitude of the Catholic Church, and had the feeling that the credibility of the Council depended on it. However, with a reference to the rules of the Council and with the support from the commission which had to supervise the implementation, on 20 November the pope stated that he could not accede to this request. Nevertheless, during the fourth session, on 21 September 1965, after renewed efforts at delay,

Paul VI was to ensure that there was a vote on the tenor of the draft text which was then available. In the end the final text of the declaration on religious freedom, *Dignitatis humanae*, did not suffer as a result of these troubles. But the psychological damage at the end of 1964 was no less.

Also, on 19 November 1964 there was to be the last vote on the document *Unitatis redintegratio* on ecumenism, now as a whole; the separate sections had already been approved by an overwhelming majority on 10 November. Shortly before the vote proper, the Council was confronted with the news 'from above' – clearly from the pope himself – that the printed text was still not definitive. The Council fathers were presented with a list of nineteen new changes, all clearly aimed at meeting the wishes of the extremely small group of opponents. Many people felt that here Pope Paul was making it clear that he attached too much importance to the conservative minority. The mood became extra bitter when it was clear that for formal reasons he did not want to appear as a defender of the majority interest. Although in terms of content the changes did not undermine the tenor of the document on ecumenism and there was still sympathy for Montini's efforts to preserve the unity of the church, this papal intervention caused a crisis in the Council which was to last until the beginning of the next session.

This crisis was further deepened when in his address at the conclusion of the third session Paul VI also solemnly proclaimed Mary 'Mother of the Church'.[177] Here again many people felt that he was going against the clear tenor of the discussion at the Council. With some difficulty the Council had resolved not to produce an independent document on Mary, but to speak about her within the constitution on the church. In the eighth chapter of *Lumen gentium* as it was finally accepted by the Council there was a break with nineteenth-century Marian theology, which had made the mother of Jesus Christ an independent object of veneration. Mary was described as being redeemed by Christ and following Christ, a model believer, who as mother of the redeemer was also mother of the other redeemed.[178] This was thus a mariology along the same lines as Schillebeeckx's publications on Mary in the 1950s.[179] The title 'Mother of the Church' for Mary was deliberately not included in the text of the constitution, although a number of Council fathers had argued for it. Here above all there was an awareness of the ecumenical problems that this would cause. Yet now, after all, at the end of the Council the pope gave Mary this title. And although he did so with a view to devotion and not as a dogma, it was nevertheless perceived as the fourth gesture within eight days in support of the conservatives at the Council. Evidently for Montini the approval of a small but powerful minority in Rome was more important than the threat that the Council would 'lose the confidence of the world, both Christians and non-Christians'.

As I have remarked, on 19 November Schillebeeckx gave a lecture on the results of the third session. It was the evening of 'Black Thursday', but his judgement on the results of the final session was very positive. He was convinced 'that the consequences of the definitive decisions already taken in this Council will prove to be unmistakably great'.[180] As always, he emphasized not so much the concrete documents as the infectious dynamic of the Council. In a retrospect on the second session he had already arrived at the surprising statement that

> this Council ... in all kinds of areas [produces] such openness that after it the church can begin to live at an accelerated pace; so much will burst out that – and this seems to me to be the wonderful thing about this Council – in fifteen years it will already seem antiquated, though compared with the time before the Council it represents a greater step forward than to my knowledge any Council has ever taken.[181]

In his review of the third session he developed this notion further. For him the main thing about the Council was the rediscovery of Christianity as an event. In his view this of course corresponded to the theological insight developed in the 1950s into the salvation-historical character of the Christian faith, but the new thing was that this dynamic was again becoming a living reality in the church through the Council. The 'worry about *how* the Christian truth must be done stands in the foreground for the bishops [at the Council]; how can it become an event in the present-day concrete human world?' What he saw in his reflections on a theology of culture as essential for Christian faith, namely that it was a dynamic into which people were taken up by faith, made the Council a reality that could be experienced. 'The so-called pastoral character of this Council is none other than a new *dogmatic* sensitivity' to this.[182]

In his view, this linked in with a wider theological and social discussion. In March 1963 a book by the Anglican Bishop of Woolwich, John A. T. Robinson, had appeared under the title *Honest to God* which then 'went through Europe like a whirlwind'.[183] In a way which evidently many people recognized, it signalled the gulf between present-day people living secularized lives and the classic religious and theological formulations and ideas. Robinson argued for a form of religion which did not construct any supernatural edifice, but in which belief in God was regarded as radical trust in the supportive power of love. The problems indicated by Robinson were to lead Schillebeeckx in the period between 1963 and 1970 to occupy himself urgently with the secularized world and the question what in this radically new context could be the contours of a 'theology of culture' as he imagined it. At the end of 1962 he also signalled the same concern at the Council:

> Beyond doubt, in the Council aula not a single bishop presented the problem of life as described, for example, by Bishop Robinson of

Woolwich, and apart from him as felt in a concrete way by many Christians. It was nevertheless felt that this problem played a part in some interventions: the Council fathers wanted to bridge the break between church and world.[184]

It was along the lines of his orientation on a theology of culture that Schillebeeckx said that the 'global significance of the Second Vatican Council' would stand or fall by the result of the discussion on what would ultimately become the Pastoral Constitution *Gaudium et spes*; in 1964 this was still called 'Schema 13'. In it the Council tried to formulate the task of the church within human culture. In 1964 Schillebeeckx gave an extensive account of it, since in his view this Council document in particular should make it clear whether the church in fact understood itself as 'an organ to serve the whole of humankind subjected to Christ'. In his view, this 'Schema 13', 'without lapsing into humanly false optimism, should [become] the Magna Carta of the Christian hope which also carries along all human expectation in its purifying and elevating dynamic'. Carried along by enthusiasm himself, he sketched out what he had in view:

> The church sees man's ambitious attempt to transform the world situation into a truly human situation. It also sees the wonderful success of these ambitious undertakings today and their failure tomorrow. Yet, despite this cycle of success and failure, man always continues to set about this task again and again and to begin anew the arduous work of building up the world in a humane way. A veiled *hope* seems to inspire and support this world, a hope that stands firm despite signs of despair and a sense of the absurd in the history of the world. In 'Schema 13' the church ... must seize hold of this concealed hope and invite the world to its explicit hope.[185]

This was in fact a reformulation of his own project of a theology of culture. He was to be intensively occupied in developing it further in the period after the Council.

However, in the autumn of 1964 a remarkable paradox also developed, which in a sense was to become characteristic of his theology from halfway through the 1960s. Precisely because he had this broad vision before him, Schillebeeckx took very much to heart the progress of the dynamic of the Council and concentrated closely on the discussion within the church. He saw this progress threatened by the commotion which had come about in the Dutch press as a result of the events in the last week of the third session.[186] Many Catholics had got the feeling that the dynamic of the Council had come to a standstill, that the powers that be had again taken the reins firmly in their hands, that it no longer made sense to work further for a good outcome of the Council, and that the best thing to do was to dissociate oneself inwardly from the events in Rome. Schillebeeckx thought that this could become a self-fulfilling prophecy and therefore felt it his duty to explain to a broad public what he saw as 'the truth about the last week of the Council'. By his own account he did not want to calm things down, but he saw the threat of 'at least an *internal* schism in the spirits of the faithful' and therefore thought that he could no longer look on passively 'after what has appeared in some Catholic and non-Catholic papers'. In an article in *De Bazuin*, he tried first to show that the papal interventions did not represent any real departure from the documents presented by the Council. Secondly, he explained that nothing contrary to the regulations had happened, and so the Council had not been diverted from following the line that had gradually developed. His conclusion was that, 'reduced to their precise historical proportions', the events in the 'black week' amounted to some psychological mistakes which the bishops, 'after their first bewilderment and anger – we do not want to conceal this – have swallowed ... ' And rightly so, he evidently felt.[187] This prompted the author of a letter to *De Bazuin* to react mockingly that 'Schillebeeckx has made it clear that nothing at all happened in the so-called black week' and to accuse him of failing to take sufficiently seriously the pain that these psychological mistakes caused people. But Schillebeeckx's interpretation seems to have been substantially correct, though he was over-optimistic, especially about the effect of the *nota praevia*.[188] In a second article, moreover, he explained that he had deliberately not tried to comfort people, because this is impossible 'when the body of the dear departed is still in the room'. He felt that he could only keep silent and suffer with people, and thought it 'very sad that I have to write two articles with all kinds of theological distinctions and expositions in order to bring some sort of clarity'.[189]

However, Schillebeeckx did not stop at a matter-of-fact analysis of the actual course of events, as a correction to sensational newspaper reports. Moreover, he tried – and in view of the letters which had been sent in, this was especially difficult for the *De Bazuin* readers to take – to discover a deeper spiritual significance in the papal intervention. Paul VI was both 'pope of the majority and of the minority in the world episcopate' and in his view had rightly attempted to bridge the opposition between the conservative minority and the progressive majority, which was dangerous for the church. In his view this attempt was meant to lead the progressives in the church to examine their consciences; then, like him, they would discover that 'in a disguised way a new form of triumphalism had also arisen with the majority position in the world episcopate: the triumphalism of the breakthrough and the existential church which could give new *prestige* to the Catholics'. He therefore said that the last week of the Council session was 'a catharsis of spiritual purification for the whole Council'.[190] Many *De Bazuin* readers could not accept especially the suggestion that the progressives needed a lesson in humility – a thought which also seemed to Schillebeeckx, in view of a second article in which he reacted to responses which had reached him, to arise out of indignation at the lack of loving understanding for opponents and faith in their honesty.[191] They no longer shared the starting point which in fact was the basis for the whole of Schillebeeckx's argument and no longer began from the assumption that a statement by the pope was by definition aimed at the salvation of the church.

Those *De Bazuin* readers who wrote letters felt that Schillebeeckx passed over the fact that they really experienced the renewal as a renewed discovery of what the church should be about in the light of the gospel. They emphasized that the church of the gospel also had to be visible and tangible for all; otherwise it would lose all credibility. Schillebeeckx did not disagree with this, but he wanted to save the Council as a process at whatever cost. During the Council he had increasingly had the feeling that the church was occupied in breaking out of its isolation and really becoming the church in the world of the time. His commitment was therefore not to endanger this dynamic and not to disappoint people prematurely, with the result that they switched off: everyone's contribution would be needed in the open church that would come into being. In this period he was still formulating the insight that the church did not live by its own tradition and the way in which this was transformed into a living culture of faith, but also by the new experiences and views which arose within the independent developments of secular culture. In 1964, on the basis of his Louvain theology of creation, he developed the standpoint that living in the world was also living 'on holy ground'. A year later he was also to distinguish between what he called somewhat confusingly 'the *sanctifying tendency towards secularization* in the church', the movement in which the church realized in the world the salvation given to it in Christ, and a '*tendency* of the world *to become the church*': there was a tendency in the world and humankind to bring to light the salvation that the church was trying to express.[192] A faith and a theology which trust in this last movement know in principle that the future life of the Christian and the Catholic tradition does not depend on developments within the church as an institution. The insights that Schillebeeckx was to develop along these lines during the Council to some degree released him from his concern about developments in the church, but on this point his theology was to remain fundamentally ambiguous.[193]

Theology of the eucharist

At the end of the third session of the Council Paul VI was beyond question concerned to reduce the oppositions between progressives and conservatives in the church. But the way in which he did this rebounded, and during the course of 1965 the oppositions were only to get more acute. Moreover, during this process Dutch Catholicism came strongly under fire. In the Netherlands, during the time of the Council, the church was seething with activity and some were wondering whether things were not going too far. At the beginning of 1965 the pope made himself the spokesman of these doubts and indicated his concern at what he saw as a lack of respect for the hierarchy and the rise of opinions which were difficult to reconcile with Catholic doctrine. He also thought that the liturgical renewal in the Netherlands was not disciplined enough. The pope's approach was diametrically opposed to the lead given by the Dutch bishops, and according to the recollections of the then auxiliary Bishop of 's-Hertogenbosch, Jan Bluyssen, his words hit them particularly hard. In their answer the Dutch bishops expressed their sorrow. They wanted especially to give a chance to the good things which had also emerged in what in their view were the turbulent developments, and were trying to stand in the middle of the developments, 'guiding them very attentively and cautiously'. They maintained this line, promised to produce pastoral letters on a number of points of faith, and finally asked for trust, indicating by this last comment that in fact they could no longer take such trust for granted.[194] It was to be the beginning of a long series of confrontations.

A first climax was reached shortly afterwards.[195] In the wake of the renewal of the liturgy, which had already been intensively discussed during the Council along the lines of the constitution accepted on 4 December 1963, among other things there was a vigorous discussion in the Netherlands about the significance of the eucharist. This discussion was also echoed internationally and attracted widespread attention.[196] When on the eve of the fourth and last session of the Council Paul VI published an encyclical on the eucharist, the Italian press in particular reported that it was directed against theological tendencies in Belgium, France and above all the Netherlands.[197] Although the Vatican officially denied that the pope 'had in view the clergy of this or that church province', but as always was addressing 'all the children of the church', and although no persons were condemned, it was in fact striking that Dutch translations were available when the text was presented. All the commotion in the international press, in which church life in the Netherlands was compared with the situation of modern art, 'formless and chaotic', caused Cardinal Alfrink to state:

> the press reports generalize, offer half truths, are one-sided, often wrong and accuse the whole community ... their core and climax is to announce the danger or more or less the certainty of an impending schism. They give a description of [the] Dutch Catholic community which is nothing short of a caricature.[198]

Schillebeeckx tried to show this too in his own way. He was concerned to demonstrate that the views which the Dutch theologians had in fact developed on the eucharist did not fall under the condemnation of the encyclical.

However, this was not so easy. The papal brief stated emphatically that it was insufficient to understand the eucharist in terms of 'transsignification' and 'transfinalization', and these were the very words used in the Dutch discussion to shed new light on the significance of the eucharist. But in Schillebeeckx's view the encyclical was concerned above all that the notion that after the consecration there were no longer 'ordinary and natural' bread and wine, but the presence of 'the Lord himself in the presence of bread and wine' should be central to the theology of the eucharist. And he thought that no Dutch theologian had wanted to deny that in the discussion.[199]

Here, first, he was ignoring the fact that according to the pope it was necessary to maintain the traditional way of speaking about the eucharistic mystery. According to Paul VI, 'in a centuries-long work and not without the support of the Holy Spirit', the church had stated that the eucharist needed to be spoken of in terms of 'transubstantiation'; this was established with the authority of the councils and had often been a 'sign of recognition and a banner' of orthodox faith. Therefore it was intolerable – and the fierceness of tone is striking here – for 'anyone on their own authority to meddle with the formulations with which the Council of Trent has presented the mystery of the eucharist to be believed'.[200]

In the conflict surrounding the theology of the eucharist, in fact a difference came to light between two views of the identity of the church. As presented by the encyclical *Mysterium fidei*, the church remained faithful to itself by maintaining the formulations of faith approved by the hierarchy and hallowed by time. By contrast, the theologians whom Paul VI was targeting here thought in terms of the living practice of liturgy and eucharist. They looked for formulations in contemporary thought to express what happened there and to a certain degree to make it understandable – there was a strong sense that the eucharist is a mystery. Schillebeeckx was right in saying that none of them criticized the formulations of Trent. They did not dispute that Jesus Christ is 'truly, really and substantially present' in bread and wine or that the word 'transubstantiation' is an appropriate term for expressing the change of 'the whole substance of bread into the body and the whole substance of wine into the blood' of Jesus Christ.[201] But this way of thinking was too static for them, not sufficiently liturgical, and did not do sufficient justice to the fact that Jesus glorified as Christ willed to be present to his church specifically under the form of *bread and wine*. They were concerned in their own way to safeguard the church's teaching, but in such a way that 'the people of God, and especially the clergy, who are increasingly being trained in a non-scholastic spirit, can experience him in a more authentic and as it were more existential way'.[202]

In the article which was to a large degree the direct occasion for all the commotion, the Capuchin Luchesius Smits used a domestic picture to make clear what in his view the eucharist was about. However, it was precisely the domestic nature of the image that was an important cause of the opposition that his view provoked:

Whenever we pay a visit to someone, the lady of the house will express her welcome by offering tea and a biscuit, a universal human sign of food and drink. So far this biscuit and this tea were significant only as a means of sustaining bodily functions. But the moment that the biscuit and the tea are used as gifts, they change: they have become signs of friendship.

According to Smits, that is also how the gesture made by Jesus at the Last Supper and remembered and repeated in the eucharist is to be understood. By breaking bread and sharing wine at the last supper, in his view Jesus did not make the bread and wine symbols, but the incarnation of the friendship that they expressed, just as tea and biscuits are not symbols but forms of the reality of friendship itself. However, because Jesus Christ was not just man but God, bread and wine express 'not only what is happening inwardly in him as man but also what is happening inwardly in God'. Thus, according to Smits, in the eucharist 'God's love ... is "tangible"'. For him, the true union in Jesus Christ of divine and human nature was the model for understanding the eucharist in such a way that bread and wine become the body and blood of Christ, not by a 'demolition' of their distinctive character, but by 'incorporation into a higher totality of existence'; just as Jesus's life, placed in a higher totality of existence, shows the nearness of God, so 'transubstantiation is none other than the extension of the unity of Godhead and manhood in Christ'.[203]

Here Smits was continuing provocatively a line which had already been taken by Dutch theologians. Already before the Council the philosopher Johan Möller, who would be consecrated Bishop of Groningen in 1969, had developed the notion that in the eucharist the risen Christ used bread and wine as instruments of his self-offering. And also already before the Council Piet Schoonenberg had begun to understand Christ's presence in the eucharist starting from his presence in the community celebrating the eucharist. According to Schoonenberg it was Christ's presence in the community of the faithful which in the liturgy made bread and wine signs of this presence, and of his self-offering. He regarded transubstantiation as 'transfinalization', a change of purpose, and as 'transsignification', a change of significance.[204] In the calm before the Council all this remained almost unnoticed, but during the Council there was a vigorous commotion because some of the formulations were felt to be radical. The issue here was after all the eucharist, which in everyone's view was a sign that defined Catholicism *par excellence*. Rumours went the rounds that on the basis of the theological innovations priests were feeding left-over consecrated hosts to the chickens. Schillebeeckx saw happening around the eucharist in the Dutch church what had happened in the early church at the time of the great controversies over the christological and trinitarian dogmas: even the man (sic) in the street was being involved in theological discussion.[205]

With his encyclical *Mysterium fidei* Pope Paul VI wanted to put an end to the confusion and unrest which in his view were damaging to the church. However, the result was that the fronts of the discussion were fixed, to the detriment of the church and the development of theology. There was no chance of developing approaches to thinking about the eucharist and the presence of Jesus Christ in it in a way which really gave a central place to its significance for salvation, while the traditional doctrine of transubstantiation seemed 'to describe the holy event in consecration as a physical process of which the supernatural character, the miraculous, seems to exist only in its strangeness'. The doctrine of transubstantiation was put forward as an abiding norm.[206]

From his side, in the framework of the troubles around the eucharist, Schillebeeckx tried to rescue its dynamic. Shortly before *Mysterium fidei* appeared he wrote an article on the debate that had arisen which with hindsight seems almost to be polemic against the encyclical. Above all he emphasized the need to express the same truth of faith differently in a different time:

> I cannot appreciate at its true value the dogmatic significance of the Council of Trent – a historical close-up set in a history that is constantly moving forward – if I act as though history had ceased to move forward since Trent; as though I, still as a believing Catholic, had not become, as a twentieth-century man, a different person from medieval man, even as a believer; and as though the Catholic faith had remained outside the process of history.[207]

Along the lines of the development of dogma that he had already formulated in the 1950s, for Schillebeeckx, remaining faithful to the Catholic Church meant holding firm to time-honoured formulas, but 'in a concern ... [to] make the old and unassailable church dogma attractive again ... for present-day believers, by detaching it from an outdated framework of thought within which faith can no longer flourish'.

However, in his view the time-conditioned formulations were not just a shell which covered a timeless nucleus of truth. He thought that 'expressions like the "clothing of dogma" ... are fundamentally misleading', since they 'give the impression that we can clothe and unclothe a dogma with the ease with which children play at dressing dolls'. In his view, theologians who tried to express the significance of the eucharist in a new way were not being careful enough. He thought that a responsible reinterpretation of the dogma of Christ's real presence in the eucharist especially called for a detailed investigation into what had taken place at the Council of Trent around its establishment.[208] He made an attempt to do this in his article, though at the same time he said that it was really necessary to reflect on the whole mystery of the eucharist through church history, rather as he had done in the 1950s in *De sacramentele heilseconomie* with the sacraments in general, and as in the period immediately before the Council he had begun to do with *Marriage*. According to his interpretation the Council of Trent was concerned to establish 'a specific and distinctive eucharistic presence' of Christ. The Council itself 'was unable to express this eucharistic real presence in any other way than on the basis of a change of the substance of bread and wine into the substance of Christ's body and blood', a change which according to the Council was 'very suitably' called transubstantiation. From this formulation he inferred that the statement about transubstantiation did not add anything new to the statement that there was a specific and distinctive eucharistic real presence. It only indicated the way in which this could be meaningfully understood by the majority of the Council fathers.[209]

At the same time, however, he thought that according to the Council of Trent, during the eucharist an ontological change took place which affected the very nature of bread and wine. As far as he was concerned this was a fundamental Catholic principle:

> The cosmic reality does not remain outside this process of grace, nor is it involved in it simply by an extrinsic word of God – the consecrated bread itself is the grace that is conferred here; that is, Christ himself in a sacrament to be eaten as a sacrificial meal, nourishment for the whole man.[210]

But in his view the scholastic interpretation after Trent had a tendency to look for 'the ontological "in depth"', as it were *behind* the phenomena. Schillebeeckx wanted to break with such a 'substantialist metaphysical view' and sought an alternative to thinking in schemes of natural philosophy, an alternative to an approach which in fact sought the 'ontological dimension' of the eucharist 'outside its sacramentality' and objectified it apart from faith.[211] He also felt that this associated him with the authors who so came under fire in 1965.

In the lecture immediately after the appearance of *Mysterium fidei* which has already been mentioned, Schillebeeckx pointed out that there have always been controversies over how Christ's real presence in the eucharist could be understood. He referred to the attitude of Thomas Aquinas and Bonaventure towards what in their eyes was an exaggerated view of the real presence in popular belief, and with obvious satisfaction pointed out that the post-war discussion, of which the Dutch offshoots were causing such a sensation, had in a way begun in Italy.[212]A year later, as a sequel to his article on the significance of the Tridentine dogma, he produced a study which put these recent discussions in the context of the history of twentieth-century theology. This ended with an attempt to define his own position. But Schillebeeckx wanted above all to normalize the situation and return to what he thought to be the normal theological process of reflection on the reality of faith: a formulation of it, the reception of this formulation in the awareness of the faithful, and due correction of the formulation. Without explicitly criticizing the pope's position, he made it clear that his reaction was exaggerated, by pointing out that there was little new under the sun: 'when I was studying in France in 1945 and 1946, transubstantiation was a subject of animated discussion among the students'. He also thought that the discussion in principle represented a step in the direction of a real sacramental understanding of the real presence.[213]

He located in 1951 the beginning of the actual tendency to start from the change in function, purpose and significance which the bread and wine took on in the eucharist – in the technical terms which were valid at that time: transfunctionalization, transfinalization and transsignification. Schillebeeckx saw this discussion fanning out widely: to France, Belgium, Germany, England and of course the Netherlands. He saw the best summary of this approach in the analyses by Schoonenberg, which he regarded as the most adequate for contemporary thought. 'One could say that it is as natural for the picture of human beings and the world today as by and large the Aristotelian picture of human beings and the world was in the theology of the second half of the thirteenth century.'[214] But Schillebeeckx himself at the same time proved emphatically to maintain that the Holy Spirit recreated the reality of bread and wine, and that the new way of dealing with bread and wine in faith was a reaction to what was ontologically present in the eucharistic bread and the eucharistic wine. For him as a believer it made a big difference 'whether Christ is merely giving me a present in which I . . . can taste his love, or whether he is giving himself to me as sacramental nourishment'. In his view, approaches along the lines of Schoonenberg and Smits ultimately did too little justice to this difference: 'I have struggled with the interpretation of this *mysterium fidei*; . . . I cannot personally be satisfied with a *purely* phenomenological interpretation without metaphysical density.'[215]

Now it has been pointed out that this distinction makes no sense within a phenomenological ontology. Such an ontology begins from the assumption that the human activity of giving meaning to and dealing with physical reality is the only accessible level for thought and speech, and that thus from a phenomenological perspective the shift in meaning – 'transsignification' – is the ontological change.[216] At this point, however, Schillebeeckx never went along with phenomenology. From the beginning a constituent element

343

of his project of a theology of culture was the conviction that human dealing with reality was a reaction to what was given in reality, and that this also applied to the way in which the believer dealt with reality and to theology as the intellectual expression of this. Therefore, he thought that dogmatic views could not just be imposed on reality but had to prove to be meaningful interpretations of human experiences of reality. But the striking thing is that in the case of the eucharist Schillebeeckx spoke in terms of replacing one ontological essence with another and did not think in terms of sign and (re)interpretation. Throughout the discussion in the 1960s the central question remained how the change of bread and wine into the body and blood of Christ could be understood. The way in which the dogma of transubstantiation was again put forward in Paul VI's encyclical *Mysterium fidei* further strengthened this. After it every theologian tried to demonstrate even more explicitly that dropping the term transubstantiation did not mean that the miracle of the change was undone. Schillebeeckx was no exception on this point.[217]

In a sense, though, it was more in keeping with *De sacramentele heilseconomie* to see the eucharist along the line of what happens among people at any meal time. There Schillebeeckx had written that the Christian sacrament uses symbols taken 'from quite concrete, everyday life to which the significance given is not alien and arbitrary' but 'appropriate, equal, yet transcendent'. 'The sacraments are not pure signals but authentic symbols', he argued, and their natural symbolism was also part of their essence, though 'elevated by the specifically Christian significance of salvation'.[218] Along these lines he also uncovered a variety of levels in the eucharistic liturgy. He pointed out that bread and wine were primarily products of human culture and were made 'for human use' by 'an activity of giving meaning'. Hence, in his view it was logical that they took on a symbolic significance: bread becomes a symbol of life, wine a symbol of the joy of life, and the meal a symbol of the human bond of friendship. All this in turn had a place in what he called the 'cosmic liturgy' of the 'nature religions', which in Israel was transformed into the paschal meal as 'anamnesis of the exodus from Egypt, Israel's redemption'. In the eucharist, according to Schillebeeckx, all these lines came together and found in it their 'inward but transcendent consummation'.

> What the gospels say is, This bread – both the symbol of life ... and the paschal bread ... – is my body. My body is a paschal sacrifice which I give you here to eat. 'I am the Life' – this is what is really experienced in the Eucharist: in *anamnesis* of the Lord who died, but is living.[219]

In the discussion in the 1960s a saying was regularly quoted which was attributed to the Swiss reformer Huldrich Zwingli. He was said to have remarked that he did not want to kneel before the tabernacle because at home he did not kneel before the bread bin, a remark that was regarded as the expression of an extremely spiritualized view of the eucharist. But if it was thought through consistently along the lines of Schillebeeckx's theology of culture, in my view the problem with this statement would not be in the identification of bread bin and tabernacle but in the way in which it assumes that it would be nonsensical to kneel before the bread bin. Just as in the Thomistic sense grace does not destroy nature but elevates it to a higher level, so the religious and ritual interpretation does not do away with the profane significance of a gesture. With retroactive force it sheds a different light, which from a theological perspective makes visible the true nature of the gesture. In this sense the question of the relationship between real presence and ontology is ultimately one of the relationship between theology and ontology.[220]

But instead of thinking through Christ's presence in the eucharist in terms of the presence of the gracious God in and through the whole of creation which is brought out in the sacrament, concentrated and set on a higher plane – that seems in a true sense to be the 'metaphysical density' with which in his own words Schillebeeckx was concerned in his reflections on the eucharist – he broke away from this line of thinking and thus became unfaithful to his own intention of thinking about the real presence in consistently sacramental terms.[221] Here he lost an opportunity really to take a step further in thinking about the eucharist – or perhaps it is fairer to say that this chance had already been lost with the appearance of the encyclical *Mysterium fidei* and that Schillebeeckx's ambiguity on this point was the expression of that.[222] Only when the reform of the liturgy by Vatican II had been carried out everywhere and the eucharist was also really celebrated and thus experienced in a different way, and only after the commotion over *Mysterium fidei* had died down, could there once again be reflection by a Catholic theologian on the real presence in a fundamentally renewing way.[223]

THE RESULT OF THE COUNCIL

Shortly before the opening of the fourth session of the Council on 14 September 1965, the Dutch bishops had a pastoral letter read out in the churches in which the purpose of the Council was described as 'giving form for the people of today ... to the goodness of Christ, to the grasp that Christ had for every need of humankind'. During the fourth and last session in fact a great deal of attention was to be paid to the document which for a long time was called 'Schema 13' but which during the fourth session began to be referred to officially with the newly-coined term 'pastoral constitution'. This document was addressed not only to the faithful but to all people. In content but above all also in tone it attempted to convey that the church was seeking the way 'to do service to the Lord and humankind "by putting itself at the service of spiritual well-being and material prosperity, for the sake of the peace and true happiness of the world"'.[224] It already became clear that in the course of the period of the Council, for Schillebeeckx this document had become the criterion by which to measure the success of the Council as a whole, and he was not the only one for whom this was true. After the conclusion of the Council he was to publish a 'reflection on the final result' in which he describes the documents which it had produced as an expression of a renewed and comprehensive project of a theology of culture. He emphasized especially the pastoral constitution *Gaudium et spes* as the prime example of the method of a theology of culture as he now saw it. Just as according to mediaeval theology nature was taken up into the sphere of grace, so in his view in modern times human existence with its existential experiences needed to be taken up into the church and faith, and this in his view was precisely what *Gaudium et spes* tried to do.[225]

Verve and conflict over giving form to the church

It seemed that Pope Paul VI had planned during the fourth session to make people forget the 'black week' with which the third session had ended. At the opening on 14 September 1965 he reminded the Council fathers that the church was not an end in itself but was at the service of all men and women. 'It is the messenger of love, the promoter of real peace,' he said.[226] And deliberately treading in the footsteps of John XXIII, who had not been able to carry out his plan himself, to the applause of his audience he concluded by announcing that he would visit the United Nations with this message of peace. During his ultra-short stay in New York on 4 October 1965 he presented himself as a messenger who at the end of a long journey was really handing over the message that had been entrusted to him. It made a great impression that he emphatically presented himself as the interpreter not of church teaching but directly of the dead and the living. As he himself put it:

> Of the dead who have fallen in the terrible wars of the past, in the hope for harmony and peace in the world. Of the living who have survived these wars and who are already a priori uttering their condemnation of any attempt to start a new war. Of yet others alive, the younger genera-tions of the present, who are entering on their lives with confidence and who rightly hope for a better humanity.

He also said that he wanted to be the representative of the poor, the mal-treated, the sufferers, in short of all those who longed for righteousness, human dignity, freedom prosperity and progress. The Council welcomed the pope on his return with a long ovation.[227]

This journey once again fixed the attention of the Council on the importance of the relationship between the church and the 'modern world'. Next, the pope also announced in his opening speech the institution of a synod of bishops which for the most part would be nominated by the episcopal conferences of the different countries. Whenever the pope thought it necessary with a view to the 'general well-being and benefit of the church', he would convene this synod. A detailed regulation reached the Council the very next day. Although this synod was not the permanent council of bishops which fervent champions of episcopal collegiality like Cardinal Alfrink had always envisaged, although the pope retained supreme power at all points, and although the Curia was again spared – Paul VI emphatically said in his opening speech that the synod would be 'particularly useful for the daily activities of the Roman Curia' – the proposal was favourably received. It was regarded as a good beginning.[228] And it seemed that Paul VI wanted to seal his renewed commitment to a good outcome to the Council when on the evening of 20 September he intervened personally the moment that the discussion on the Declaration on Freedom of Religion threatened again to get stuck as a result of the actions of the conservative minority. Realizing that this would make his position lose all credibility for the adherents of other religions in the United Nations, the pope forced a vote. An overwhelming majority supported the direction of the text, and he was able to travel to New York with extra backing.

But this was not to be the atmosphere of the whole of the last session of the Council. The pattern of the black week of the year before would in fact be repeated twice. The first time was on 11 October. Pope Paul had heard that some bishops planned to put the question of celibacy as a condition for the priesthood on the agenda. He had a letter read out in the Council aula which stated that he thought that a public debate on this theme, which in his view required 'the utmost caution', was 'completely inopportune'. He announced an encyclical aimed at 'not only maintaining this holy and providential law with all our power but also enforcing the observance of it'. Although the Council fathers applauded when this message was read out, and shortly beforehand an overwhelming majority had agreed with the highest appreciation for celibacy expressed in the Conciliar Decree on the Training of Priests, a significant proportion of them found this manoeuvre difficult to take. Again the pope seemed to be making a concession to the conservative minority, which was afraid of all too much public discussion, and to be trying to replace the dialogue which had been going on hitherto with a papal monologue. At all events, if it was the purpose of the pope to avoid publicity over this question, his intervention went wrong.[229]

It was more than a matter of detail. The changed view of faith and church

347

developed by the Council unavoidably raised the question what the consequences of this were for the role, the identity and the lifestyle of priests. Schillebeeckx also made this clear in an article in 1965. In his view, the idea that there should be a necessary bond between priesthood and celibacy was directly dependent on the traditional image of the priest: as the representative of the holy he needed to keep a distance from the world. The Council broke with the notion that the sacred and the profane, the divine and the human could be in conflict with each other. A new picture of God and holiness arose, and logically that had consequences for the image of the priest:

> In all attempts at the reorientation of the priesthood in the present-day world, there is always a doubt about celibacy, whether explicit or not: does it not become irrelevant in the present-day evaluation of earthly reality, especially of marriage and sexuality? The traditional arguments for this celibacy seem to collapse, and the reality itself seems to totter.[230]

Schillebeeckx continued to think that there was an inner affinity between celibacy and the service of the priesthood, because the basic pattern of both was 'total and special availability for God and fellow human beings'. However, this affinity could not lead to a strict requirement of celibacy, and therefore in his view the possibility could not be excluded that 'the church will always emphasize for priests and deacons only the positive challenge of the ministry, or its inner appeal to the conscience of the candidate ordinands to accept religious celibacy'. As far as he was concerned, celibacy could only be accepted in freedom 'as a charisma'. Now the option for priesthood including celibacy was indeed free in a formal sense, but the problem was that as a result of the coupling, 'candidate priests *put up with* the celibacy connected with the office'. His conclusion was that 'the law of celibacy, the urging of a challenge which is given in ordination itself, still presents difficulties in practice'.[231]

The document signed by 81 Catholic intellectuals from various parts of the world, including fourteen from the Netherlands, went further. It was published during the fourth session of the Council in Latin, French, German and English but circulated for much longer. It sometimes even seems as if Schillebeeckx was reacting to it in his article, which was meant to be part of an issue of *Tijdschrift voor Theologie*. The views in this twenty-page 'booklet on the celibacy of priests'[232] went back to the debate on the value of corporeality and sexuality which, as we saw in Chapter 3, had flourished strongly in Catholic circles in the 1950s. The text argued for the possibility 'of holding office out of free choice, as married or unmarried', but cited as the main objection to the existing situation that the obligation for priests to be celibate 'a priori removes the possibility of inter-personal sexual maturing'. It was pointed out that the Council had broken fundamentally

348

with the view that connected holiness directly with forsaking the world, and that 'the recognition [by the Council] of the value and significance of corporeality' must have consequences for the image of the life of the priest, as being 'for the believer ... the most direct human sign of the face of the church'. Here the 81 intellectuals tabled a question which was not explicitly formulated in their text, let alone answered: what could be a priestly way of life appropriate to their own time which was in a credible way 'the most direct human sign of the face of the church'? Even Schillebeeckx had no answer to this question, but continued to hold to a liberalized form of the traditional idea that there was an inner affinity between priesthood and celibacy.[233]

Since Paul VI had made his authority felt at the Council on this point, discussion of this question was avoided in the Catholic Church. For the central leadership of the Catholic Church it was a priori certain that the priest living a celibate life was the most authentic 'human sign of the face of the church'. In 1970 the Dutch Catholics, the majority of whom in that year put forward a variety of statements at the 'Pastoral Council' of Noordwijkerhout in favour of the uncoupling of priesthood and the obligation for celibacy, and found a hearing for these among their bishops, encountered the irreconcilable opposition of the Roman authorities. This permanently damaged relations.[234] Since the Council it has in fact proved impossible to discuss any of the questions surrounding the nature, structure and form of the church's ministry, and in the meantime the confrontation has hardened completely. Schillebeeckx would ultimately conclude from this that the theology of the ministry can develop further only when it can link its reflections with the alternative practices which have grown up nevertheless and are often illegal.[235]

However, in 1965 very few were really ready for a fundamental discussion on celibacy and the adequate form to be given to the church's ministry. In the Dutch church, too, which had the image of running ahead on this point, doubts about the need for the coupling of priesthood and celibacy were to become general only after the Council, and this happened primarily because a notable number of prominent and respected priests were forced to leave the ministry because they married. Theological considerations and big words slowly lost their significance, and there remained the sober practical observation that the existing combination of priesthood and celibacy was preventing many 'from accepting the call to the ministry'; for others it was more a hindrance than a support in performing that ministry, and often skilful and experienced pastors had to leave office. In 1966 a group of Dutch priests presented these observations to their colleagues and asked for support for the conclusion that 'the breaking of the legal connection between the priesthood and celibacy [was] an urgent task'.[236] That is why

349

the conciliar reactions to the papal intervention of 11 October were as yet
not so vigorous.

Things were different about six weeks later. The commission which was
charged with the definitive revision of the text of the Pastoral Constitution
on the Church in the Modern World met to discuss the part of the text
which related to marriage and sexuality. The relevant section was the only
one in the official Council texts to which Schillebeeckx made a direct contribution. After the third session he was adviser in the sub-commission on
this part, though except for his own testimony there are no indications that
he in fact composed the text concerned, 'above all with Professor Victor
Heylen and Bishop Heuschen'. But although this remark does not seem to
give a good account of the workings of the sub-commission, it does show
how much Schillebeeckx identified with the final text that was proposed.[237]
This was also completely in line with the theology of marriage that he had
begun to develop at the beginning of the 1960s. It was inevitable that in the
relevant chapter something should also be said about birth control and
contraception, although Paul VI had already appointed a commission in
June 1964 to investigate the permissibility of using the contraceptive pill and
thus in fact had imposed 'a kind of pause on the discussion of this question'.[238] However, the secretary of the commission caused great amazement
when he read out a message from the pope which not only asked for no
interference with a text the discussion of which was already closed, but also
gave an indication of the result of the work of the papal commission. The
Council commission was exhorted forcefully to refer to the rejection of any
form of contraception by Pius XI and Pius XII, and Paul VI thought it
'absolutely necessary that the methods and means which destroy conception
– in other words the methods of contraception which are discussed in the
encyclical *Casta connubii* – are openly condemned'.[239]

This was a hard blow, for when the pope had announced that a commission was going to study the question of birth control, many people hoped
that this would be a first cautious step towards changing the church's
standpoint. On 24 November 1965 the suspicion began to arise that the
opposite might perhaps happen. Those who had produced the draft text on
marriage in the pastoral constitution had carefully tried to give married love
and procreation equal status as 'purposes' of marriage, and the Council had
adopted this view after intensive and sometimes difficult discussion. Had the
balance now to be disturbed, and was the idea laid down by Pius XI – that
the purpose of marriage was to have children – to be reinstated?[240] With
great prudence, making use of the freedom that had been granted it, the sub-
commission succeeded in keeping the equilibrium achieved in the chapter on
the subject, remaining loyal to the view of by far the majority of the Council
fathers. At the same time the pope's concern was met by quoting early
church documents on the subject in a positive way and thus bearing witness

to the continuity of the church's teaching. As is well known, this would prove a stay of execution, and a short time later the champions of a broader view on sexuality and birth control were definitively to lose at the official church level. The view of the encyclical *Humanae vitae* which was published on 25 June 1968 was completely in line with the papal intervention of 24 November 1965. All the complications surrounding the papal commission which prepared the document and the composition of the text itself gave the impression that according to Paul VI this was also the only possible outcome.[241]

It does not seem an exaggeration to say that the appearance of *Humanae vitae* marked the end of the period of the Council. The notion that the Catholic Church was concerned all along the line to encounter 'the modern world' openly, and really wanted to make its own the 'joy and hope, the sorrow and anguish of people' lost its credibility. For countless people, at all events in the Western world, the document was an occasion for leaving the church, or at any rate for no longer following what they thought it had to say about their lives. Internally, after 1968 all over the world attitudes within the church were to become strongly polarized.

Keeping the spirit of the Council alive

However, when the Council closed on 8 December 1965, little polarization could yet be noted. Certainly, many saw the danger of a further growth of the oppositions which had begun to appear during the Council, but that seemed to have been exorcised. It seemed possible to tread the golden middle way which Pope Paul VI had marked out for the period after the Council and which consisted in doing away with the sluggishness 'of these who refuse to adapt to the new course of things in church life' and the signs of impatience 'of others who wrongly go for special novelties and thus could damage the work of renewal that has been undertaken'.[242]

In his review of the results of the Council, Schillebeeckx indeed foresaw the 'possibility of an integralist reaction', but not the fundamental disruption of communication which was in fact to develop between groups of Catholics, and especially between the Dutch province and the supreme leadership of the church. He certainly foresaw that the formulations in the Council documents, which were sometimes diplomatic and aimed at compromise, could cause difficulties, but when he wrote that 'merely to fall back on the letter of Vatican II and regard this as the ultimate norm for judging coming theological thought ... [can] only be reactionary', he in no way sensed how real this possibility would prove to be. At the end of the Council it seemed possible to him that the renewal of the communication between the periphery and the centre of the church was still in practice irreversible.[243]

Despite all the incidents and difficulties, there was a feeling of great unanimity among all those who had been involved in the Council, after the effort that they had put in and after working under great pressure of time. Because of this feeling, the church could face the world with great self-confidence. As the pope said during the closing ceremony, 'From our long contemplation of Christ and his church at this moment, the first thing that must be said to the many who have been waiting is an announcement of joy and happiness', and after his introduction spokesmen from the Council came forward with messages to governments, to intellectuals and scientists, to artists, women, workers, the poor, the sick and all those who suffered, and finally to young people.[244] Thus, the Council itself made it clear that it regarded as its climax and the most authentic expression of the conciliar spirit the document which had cost it the greatest effort and which had been something completely new in its history: the Pastoral Constitution on the Church in the Modern World, *Gaudium et spes*. This could not fail to make an impression, both within the church and outside it.

At the end of the Council everyone seemed to realize the importance of maintaining its spirit and dynamic. Pope Paul VI solemnly announced a period of rejoicing from 1 January 1966 to Pentecost in which all the dioceses – the pope referred emphatically to the new emphasis that had been given during the Council to the episcopate as 'the axis of unity, consecration, jurisdiction and real authority' – had to organize activities to disseminate the results of the Council among the faithful. The faithful had to be given a renewed understanding of the mission of the church in the world, and 'the hearts of believers' had to be touched by the conciliar spirit of renewal and deepening.[245] At Christmas 1965 the Dutch bishops wrote a letter to their faithful in which they thanked them for their 'constant involvement in the Council' but at the same time told them of the new task: 'Now that the Council is finished, we face the great task of making the insights of the Council live.' Taking up the pope's message at the end of the Council in their own way, they thought that it was not enough to resolve to implement the Council – although the bishops said that they would do this as well as possible; the ultimate issue was the spirit of the Council as contained in the Council documents:

> This spirit must come alive. We must give form to the basic insights of the Council in the practice of the Christian life and in the human community. Not only must the insights of the Council become flesh and blood among all of us, but they must also become the basis of our episcopal government.

Here, then, the bishops were thinking of things like respect for the human person and the beliefs of others, of the link between priests and laity in the church, or the 'ordered democratization of practical government', the responsibility of the church for the world and attention to the relationship between Catholics and 'fellow Christians and non-Christians'. All this would need time, and unanimity over pluriformity, and inevitably there would be moments of 'sorrow at disappointments, which the Council sessions have sometimes already experienced'.[246]

The passage at the end of the bishops' Christmas letter was to be very significant for the immediate future of the Catholic Church in the Netherlands:

In the short term we are thinking about beginning preparations for a provincial council. That is a council for the Dutch province. At it, the main points of the life of the church in our land must be discussed in the spirit of the Vatican Council.

On 15 March 1966 the preparatory commission for what officially began to be called the Pastoral Council for the Dutch Church Province met for the first time. The Pastoral Council was officially opened on 27 November of the same year. This large-scale 'joint consultation of all the faithful of the whole Dutch church province' about the adequate form of the church in contemporary circumstances – in the jargon: about 'the self-realization of the people of God according to the charge given by the gospel, the new insights of the Second Vatican Council and the needs of our time' – was to change the Dutch church deeply and irrevocably. As Schillebeeckx had already predicted in 1964, the documents and decisions of the Council would quickly become outdated for Dutch Catholics as a result of the stormy developments.[247] The growing oppositions within the church and the opposition of Rome to what was happening in the Netherlands, especially after 1970, made an increasing number of Catholics feel thwarted in the initiatives which they took, and which they were convinced were faithful to the spirit of the Council and the insights that they had been able to derive from it. In 1985 the frustration and disappointment over this was to lead to a massive protest against the exclusion of a number of spokesmen and important organizations from involvement in the visit of John Paul II to the Netherlands. 'The other face of the church' was presented in a separate demonstration. The abiding faith in the dynamic which had been set in motion with Vatican II resulted in a platform of more than one hundred Catholic organizations 'for the renewal of church and society'; these called themselves the Eighth of May Movement, after the date of this demonstration. On 8 May 1985 Schillebeeckx gave an address in which he put this movement in 'the already long, noisy and sometime sleeping life of the great Christian traditions of experience, of which we are all the heirs and the future'.[248]

Schillebeeckx was also to play a notable role at the Pastoral Council. But his own reception of the results of the Second Vatican Council meant that he was not very happy with what in fact was the quite pragmatic and organizational course of the discussions. In 1967 he produced an article, according to a note 'written by the author after a dialogue among some theologians', in which he argued that the Pastoral Council should issue what he called a 'fundamental document'. Here he envisaged a text which

> illuminates faith in a secularized world, in other words makes it *understandable* and *clear* why the world has thoroughly changed and why this is a test for the church, which is thus challenged to stand 'differently' in the world of faith.

Over against the direct solution of the pressing problems with reference to sociology and psychology, he emphasized the importance of 'listening theologically to the Dutch situation'. For although in his view theology fails 'when it does not take the insights of sociology and psychology into account', he thought that without theological illumination these disciplines lacked the necessary orientation on human salvation, understood theologically.[249] Apart from the controversial epistemological and scientific organizational position that he adopted, here an important tension emerged in the reception of Vatican II and the interpretation of its spirit.

In general, in the Dutch Catholic church the Council was seen above all as a stimulus to internal reform in the church, and to the adaptation of church structures, religious behaviour and language to the demands of modern times. Here the Dutch Catholics stood closer to Pope Paul VI than they usually realized. For the pope, too, to continue along the lines of the Council meant above all to carry through organizational reforms like the establishment of the synod of bishops, the revision of canon law and the reform of the Curia. Moreover, towards the end of the fourth session he had already declared that after the Council the term *aggiornamento* introduced by Pope John XXIII would have the meaning of 'a deep immersion in the spirit of the Council and the faithful adaptation of the guidelines which it has laid down in such an excellent way'.[250] However vigorously they might be in conflict with the pope over precisely what the authentic spirit of the Council was and what it meant to implement the guidelines of the Council, the Dutch Catholics in the period after the Pastoral Council wanted just as much as he did to leave the theoretical discussions behind and draw the practical conclusions from them.

For Schillebeeckx, however, the Council was important above all because of the new relationship between the church and the world which it made possible. For him the Council documents drew the contours of a theology of culture along the lines of what he had proposed from the beginning of his theological career. In his view Vatican II was above all the renewed beginning of a project, of an open-ended quest. The Council documents formulated no more, but also no less, than a 'historically situated profile' of 'the apostolic spirit of holy Scripture' and as such created new possibilities of sounding out the world theologically.[251] In his view this theological grounding of the world was the central task for the time after the Council. At all events, he himself had already made a beginning on this during the Council, although he would also take up this beginning from the new conditions in society and the church, and interpret the results of his work in the 1950s in a new way. In the second volume of this study I shall be discussing precisely how he was to set about this.

A renewed start to the project of the theology of culture

According to Schillebeeckx, 'the distinctive feature of Vatican II' was its perspective on the theology of culture. In the personal final evaluation of the Council published in 1966, he described all the Council documents as a contribution to reflection on this basic theme. It is striking how loosely he sat to the historical course of events in his description. During the first session the progressive theologians had all held their breath and had had the feeling that they could sell their theological books if the schemas of the theological preparatory commission were accepted, especially that on revelation. During the first session Schillebeeckx had given numerous lectures aimed at convincing the Council fathers of the need to reject the draft. Later the discussion of the constitution on the church, and the degree to which this indicated that the hierarchy was in the service of the church as the people of God and the bishops together with the pope formed the supreme leadership of the church, gave him many sleepless nights.[252] But little of this is to be found in his evaluation. During the Council his own perspective also shifted.

At the end of the Second Vatican Council Schillebeeckx stood amazed at the way in which things had taken off:

> Anyone who browses in the progressive literature of the four years which elapsed between the announcement of the Council by Pope John XXIII on 25 January 1959 and the solemn opening in October 1962, and then looks at the desires, wishes and petitions which were produced then, will be bewildered at the 'conservatism' of even the most avant-garde journals of that time. The Council has gone so much further that the final result has left these desiderata far behind.[253]

He himself had also undergone a far-reaching development. Before the Council actually began, he hoped that at all events a number of barriers which had made theological developments stagnate for so long would disappear. But the concentrated work within the church on the preparation for the Council and reflection on it had ultimately led him to take up a new position as a theologian. No longer was the church the starting point and criterion of his thought, and no longer did he regard it as the realization of the authentic culture which as a theologian of culture he wanted to provide a basis for and disseminate further. In the period after the Council the world and God's presence in the world came to take an ever more central place in his theology. He had become convinced that the starting point must no longer be the questions internal to the church, but that the issue was 'the experience of religious existence in a changed, above all in a desacralized and humanizing, world'.[254] With retrospective force he also regarded this as the 'real basic theme' of the Council.

From this perspective the Council's Declaration on Religious Freedom was fundamental. From Schillebeeckx's point of view, *Dignitatis humanae*, over which there had been so much conflict at the time of the Council, indicated that for Catholics the supreme value was not supposedly being right, but 'respect for the dignity of the human person, including personal convictions'. Here he readily admitted that humankind did not owe the idea of religious freedom 'to Catholic or Reformation theologians, but to lawyers and secular positive law, and ultimately to the modern democratic idea of the state'. For him the fundamental importance of the document was that in fact by accepting modern democratic thought by way of religious freedom, the Catholic Church had removed the basis of the modern world's mistrust of it. He then found the relevant picture of human beings in the Conciliar Declaration on the Relation of the Church to Non-Christian Religions, *Nostra aetate*. The religious dimension was thought to be constitutive of human beings, and from here all religions were evaluated in principle as the expression of a 'pre-reflective, intimate religious awareness' that was characteristic of human beings. On the basis of this, the concrete historical religions were to be seen as an expression of the human quest for an answer to fundamental questions about existence 'in accordance with the diversity of the peoples'. With foresight, here Schillebeeckx indicated that the notion following from this that anyone who went over to Catholicism did not need 'to deny the religious heritage of his people' implied a completely new view of mission and would also have great consequences for ecumenical relations. In his view Christianity, too, was ultimately put on this line in *Nostra aetate*, but as 'the fullness of religious life'.[255]

He thought that in the Constitution on Revelation, *Dei verbum*, the Council quite emphatically declared that 'religious experience, thematized in a variety of religions ... first [gets] its authentic, explicit content in the Old Testament revelation and finally in Christ, who has established the church among the nations to extend his work of salvation'. He saw here confirmation of the fundamental theological and anthropological starting point for his theology of culture: 'the religious assumes its basic form willed by God in the "church of Christ": Christianity in the form of the church is objectively the fully-grown manifestation of all true religion'. Thus, in his view, the openness of the Council to humanity as a whole in the constitutions on revelation and on the church and in the decree on the missionary activity of the church, *Ad gentes*, went along with an emphasis on 'the absolute uniqueness of the Christian religion'. Here Schillebeeckx emphasized that according to the Council documents the church was not unique in its possession of the truth, but was unique as what is called the universal sacrament of salvation. In fact this meant that in his eyes it was the embodiment of a qualitatively new culture and a pointer towards it. 'The unity in peace, justice and love, that great powerless desire of present-day men and women, is realized in a transcendent way in the church as a sign that has already been shown and in fact is significantly realized in this.' It is striking that he put the conciliar view of relations within the church in this framework. For Schillebeeckx, the shift from the hierarchy to 'the people of God on the way under the leadership of the hierarchy', and from the pope to the collegial leadership of the bishops, ultimately had to do with the discovery of the church as the sacrament of salvation. In his view the Council had discovered and made it clear that the unity desired by humankind which the church needed to embody would be better expressed in relations of collegiality and community than in structures of hierarchy and obedience. He would later work out this train of thought in a powerful plea for 'a democratic church'.[256]

At an existential level, the whole period of the Council seems above all to have meant for Schillebeeckx that he identified less directly with the Catholic Church as it really existed. Its structure was not a priori the best, and decisions by its hierarchy were not a priori right or justified. His involvement in the conciliar discussion had given him the concrete experience that when problems arose, alternatives were conceivable. And if conditions in church politics made it possible, the alternatives could also be realized. For him, the Council documents also indicated that the Catholic Church had given up its 'exclusive patent' not only to the religious as such – *Dignitatis humanae* – but also to the Christian, in the Decree on Ecumenism, *Unitatis redintegratio*. However, for Schillebeeckx the most important thing about giving up this claim was not that it offered more scope for interchurch approaches or for dialogue with representatives of other religions. The most important consequence for him was that the church now constantly had the burden of proof. The Council made it clear that it had to show that it was indeed the church that it claimed to be. From now on it was unavoidably bound

> to make its own religious form shine out more purely in the light of the gospel, so that the church of Christ can also make its legitimate dogmatic

claims existentially true in the sight of all. This calls for a religious *aggiornamento* throughout the church, in its depth and breadth.

According to Schillebeeckx's reading, the final message of the Council documents was that the Catholic Church was really itself only if it succeeded in giving credible form to God's salvation for the world in its structure, its speech and its action. Therefore it was of central importance for him that in its Constitution on Revelation the church put itself 'more consciously than ever under the critical authority or the criticism of the original apostolic church with its scripture' and thus was shown a norm for judging its actual form. In his final evaluation of the Council, he spoke of an 'attempt to re-evangelize the historical phenomenon of the church' which was expressed in different Council documents on different areas. He thought that thanks to the constitution *Sacrosanctum Concilium* the liturgy could develop into the form of the spirit of the conciliar church. It could incorporate believers into the living movement of the spirit of the Council and give them a share in it.

But above all, in Schillebeeckx's view the Council made the 'relationship between the earthly future and the absolute future of humankind, between the ordering of life within this world and the kingdom of God', the central theological question.[257] For him, after the Council the theological ground *par excellence* was 'the ground of the Pastoral Constitution on the Church in the Modern World'. And it was precisely here that in his view the Council did not end with its closure. He thought that the Pastoral Constitution *Gaudium et spes* above all marked off an area. It bore witness to what for an official document was a new

> 'worldly' spirit, supported by faith in the Creator God who at the same time is our unmerited salvation, so that the whole of the concrete reality in which we live comes to us as a grace in the ordinary things of every day, in the face of our fellow human beings and in the great aspirations of present-day humanity.

In his view, after the Council this spirit needed 'in fact and also practically' to penetrate to the faithful.[258] And its far-reaching theological consequences needed to be thought about, including the consequences for the life of the faithful, church structures and the liturgy. Schillebeeckx was particularly to devote himself to this reformulated project of a theology of culture after 1965. In truth, he made an unmistakably new start to his theology of culture as early as 1964, challenged to do so by John Robinson's book *Honest to God*, which has already been mentioned and which was notorious in 1963. In it the difficulties of contemporary, secularized men and women about traditional beliefs and traditional theology were described and largely affirmed.[259] After a first respectful but ultimately dismissive article about it, a year later Schillebeeckx wrote an article in which he made Robinson's questions to an important degree his own, although he envisaged another solution.[260] The next volume of this study will discuss the way in which Schillebeeckx continued his theology of culture after the Second Vatican Council and after this new stimulus from the world-wide debate over Robinson.

But the renewed orientation on the secularized world to a degree also took up a development in his thought which had already been under way for a long time. From the moment that Schillebeeckx came to the Netherlands, he was regularly asked to shed theological light on questions with which Dutch Catholics and their organizations found themselves confronted. Often these were questions on the frontiers of society and faith or the church.[261] By accepting the requests to speak about them he developed his theology of culture in supplementary fragments. Above all he worked out further the notion of hope as a central virtue, building on the thoughts that he had formulated about this in the first half of the 1950s, and clearly stimulated by the atmosphere of social optimism which characterized the end of those years.

Most curious, probably, is the speech that he gave at the opening of the animal laboratory at Nijmegen University. This began in a strikingly ironic way:

> I have been asked to throw a little light on the problem of man in his relationship with the animal. In theology-minded Holland, we are anxious to let the liberating light of faith penetrate into the darkest corners of the university animal laboratory where, in an otherwise splendid and humane environment, 'evil' men are busy torturing 'innocent' animals in a subtly refined scientific manner.

As might have been expected, after the tone had been set like this, he resolutely supported the doctors: 'Creation is fine and good. It is also good for man who, serving the salvation of his fellow-men, experiments with animals in an animal laboratory.' He expressed a radically Christian humanistic standpoint and made the value of creation central for human beings. On theological grounds he defended the view that things, plants and animals 'have no distinctive value of their own in the strict sense of the word', but are part of 'a continuous cosmic development'. Therefore, in his view, 'from the philosophical point of view, there can be no possible objection to laboratory tests, in which man has deliberately to cause pain to animals in order to test various reactions to pain for the benefit of human medical science'. However, the needless torturing of animals was beneath the dignity of human beings as ethically sensitive persons with empathy for others, and of believers who know that the whole creation is God's.[262] The article in which under the neutral title 'Philosophical and Theological

Reflections on Man and Woman' Schillebeeckx gives a commentary in terms of his view of human beings as freedom situated in a body, is also quite curious. It was prompted by a notorious operation in the Netherlands in which because of her psychological need the body of a woman was changed to make it look as far as possible like that of a man. Along the lines of the views customary at this time Schillebeeckx reacted in a negative way to the first Dutch case of a sex-change, but in the text he was still clearly looking for the right way to reflect theologically on this question. He did his very best to demonstrate that he understood the psychological need of the person concerned, but nevertheless finally thought that such an operation should be rejected because it damaged the integrity of the human being as a unity of spirit and body.[263]

More important for Schillebeeckx's theological development were his reflections on the responsibility of human beings and believers for the future, which were published from 1958 on. On the one hand he emphasized that human responsibility for the world was not an absolute task and an intolerable burden but a challenge from God to human beings to arrive at unconditional submission through the circumstances. In his view, to take responsibility had as a necessary pendant 'the divine virtue of hope'.[264] Here he maintained that the Christian hope was first of all directed towards God and the coming kingdom of God, but 'within this transcendent expectation of the future, human freedom also hopes for a future for this world'. For him, to take responsibility in faith for the earthly future was to take a personal place in God's saving history. The charge to 'humanize this world' is not about taking the world into one's own hands but 'a mysterious anticipation of the eschatological glorification'. Here, according to him, it was very important to bring the whole of world history, and especially the changes taking place at the end of the 1950s and beginning of the 1960s, which many people felt to be dramatic, into the circle of light that embraced believers and theology.

> Far too often we talk to God about the petty difficulties of our lives and never discuss with him the most important development of the modern world – the birth of the new society and mankind's becoming one as an enormous and new possibility for the universality of genuine Christian love.[265]

Here he was clearly anticipating *Gaudium et spes*, in both content and tone.

For Schillebeeckx, the intensity of contemporary changes evidently also made it clear that the Christian tradition found it difficult to take history with all its vicissitudes and uncertainties really seriously. Along the lines of what he had written earlier in the 1950s, but with a notably greater boldness and at the same time a certain implicit self-criticism, he pointed out in 1959 that 'in the modern type of religion' the world is certainly experienced anew as the place where the God of salvation reveals himself and 'the world of creation [is] taken up into living personal dialogue with God'. However, this evaluation of the world often got stuck in the 'personal individual "existential" practice of piety'. He argued in favour of regarding the 'history of the world, church and mankind as a collective salvation history'. To speak of the theological significance of history after the life, death and resurrection of Jesus Christ in terms of the growth of subjective redemption was evidently no longer enough; he now spoke of 'a theology of the history of the church'. Granted, he maintained the basic conviction that 'the basic pattern and the ultimate sense of our human history' has been revealed 'in Christ the Son of Man', but he added emphatically that God is not only knowable in the tradition of the words and actions of Jesus:

> Faith itself summons us to active, expert and laborious commitment to the history of the world and development in every sphere, the distinctive structure and relative independence of which is accepted: for the believer, the will and at the same time the glory of God becomes manifest in the earthly structure of things.

God could also be known in the world and in history. And that ultimately had consequences for the way of doing theology. When Schillebeeckx spoke about a 'theology of history' which urgently needed to be developed if theology was to be capable of playing more of a leading role in building the future of the church and world, he was not envisaging any speculative structure but was concerned with the insight that something could be said 'about the future and about the eschatological significance of the world event' only by reflecting on one's own religious situation in life. And that meant:

> [The] task of theology does not lie only or primarily in a revision and superficial modernization of mediaeval terms, but has to grow out of the awareness that God's message of salvation must time and again be brought into contact with a humanity living here and now with its own concrete experience within the world. Theological reflection on the revealing word of God must then be undertaken again within the framework of the awareness of faith that has already been achieved though the experience of contact with the contemporary experience of life.[266]

In the period after the Council he was to devote himself above all not just to seeking a theology of contemporary culture but to doing theology as a reflection in faith on contemporary culture, in the midst of it and in concrete contact with it.

This view of theology as a subdivision of culture in a sense reflected the deconfessionalization which began at the end of the 1950s and was to continue in intensified form in the 1960s and 1970s. The tight structure of organizations which together were realizing something of the Catholic 'counter society' long envisaged by the church leadership since Leo XIII was falling apart. The different subdivisions were being taken up into the welfare state, which was growing explosively. In this situation Catholic organizations again sought the interests of their ideological identity, no longer as standing outside modern society and culture but as consciously part of it.[267] In a lecture at a congress for the Association of Catholic Hospitals as early as 1958 Schillebeeckx explained that in his eyes Catholics could only endorse the idea of the welfare state. He spoke of a 'grandiose' plan for a society which tried to guarantee greater equality of opportunity in life for all men and women. What had previously been done to support people out of mercy was now recognized to flow from the social demand for justice; according to Schillebeeckx, the construction of the welfare state indicated that 'man's awareness is becoming increasingly interior, profound and spiritual'. In his view, the secularization of, for example, health care, in other words the organization of health care on the basis of the autonomy of the social sphere, was the necessary consequence. From a theological perspective this secularization was not a loss, and needed to be the starting point for any other reflection on it.[268]

Around four years later, Schillebeeckx reiterated this standpoint even more sharply in a text for the National Centre for Catholic Social Work. In his view, the welfare state in its objective structures was an expression of love for fellow human beings: 'Love requires ... a technical skill and professional expertise which is as perfect as possible, precisely because it has in view the real good and welfare of the other and not the satisfaction of the giver.'[269] At the same time Schillebeeckx maintained the notion that 'all man's organization of life in this world ... finds its ultimate significance only in a religious view of life'. In other words, the precondition for a correct view of the care and healing of the sick was not a confessional organization – 'the question of a specifically Catholic hospital ... is not a matter of principle but one of a practical pastoral nature' – but an adequate theological view of human existence as a whole and of human culture and history in particular. First of all, according to Schillebeeckx, this view needed to ensure the necessary animation of workers in health care or social work. Without such inspiration 'the expert outwardly perfect care of the sick' would remain 'asocial' at the human level. He felt that this inspiration was particularly important in the case of social work, since that was done in a sphere where social need also becomes personal and existential need. Therefore, he was convinced that subtle intuition was required to see and hear what was really going on among people.

But ultimately, in Schillebeeckx's view, from a Christian perspective health care was 'not just an instrument' but equally a 'holy sacrament', in which the bond of love, 'the unity of *caritas* between God and man and among human beings', is experienced in 'an appropriately incarnated way'. He did not work out the practical consequences of this view completely, but he did suggest what in his view were its far-reaching implications. Because active Christian love for other people, the 'Catholic *caritas*', was not immediately directed towards suffering human beings but has God's love as a motif, according to Schillebeeckx its service was disinterested. It stood apart from whether specific people were 'loveable' or 'unloveable'. Therefore, it could be a love – and needed to be a love – 'which goes beyond ingratitude, sin and hostility and by preference goes out to those most in need of help'.[270]

At the end of the 1950s and in the first half of the 1960s Schillebeeckx was at the point of evidently still seeking the social significance of the Christian faith. In a sense, the formulation that he found in 1965, towards the end of the Second Vatican Council, in an article meant to be programmatic, represented a breakthrough. The article appeared in the first issue of *Concilium* and in it Schillebeeckx expounded how he saw his task as a theologian after the conclusion of the Council. He indicated that on the one hand he wanted to look for 'the tendency in the church of Christ towards sanctifying secularization, that is, the tendency which aims to make the salvation of the church incarnate in the secular reality of the world itself'. Secondly, he wanted to 'investigate the tendency in the church of Christ towards sanctifying secularization, which aims to make the salvation of the church incarnate' in the world. In their way, church and world are both places for being 'with God'.[271] With a 'feverish urgency', Schillebeeckx was to devote many articles to the question precisely how the two ways of relating to God were connected; only in 1968 did he think that he had now 'achieved a formulation which is satisfactory in principle'.[272]

But his return to the Netherlands after the Council represented the conclusion of a phase in his theological development and the dawn of a new one. On 7 March 1965, the feast day of Thomas Aquinas, he gave a sermon in the Albertinum in which this clearly emerged.[273] By the way in which he portrayed Thomas it emerged how much he had begun to see theological thinking as a religious task, a sacramental service. 'Rarely does human thought become religious worship, as it did in the case of the Dominican Thomas Aquinas,' were the words with which he began his sermon, and he went on to speak of the life of a theologian as a 'priestly doctorate', in other words 'a priestly service of the word in a well-thought-out form, expressed specifically for this time' – the same sentence appears twice, word for word, in the printed version of the sermon. 'For Thomas, thought is the human material which he sanctifies as a Christian and dedicates to God and at the same time that with which he seeks to be of service to his fellow human beings.' Schillebeeckx presented this form of priesthood, which he clearly also regarded as his own, as *par excellence*

> the distinctive Dominican form of the religious life, a form which is pure dedication to the Sacra Pagina, the Sacra Doctrina, to which everything in the Order is subordinated: the saving content of human life.

Here, according to Schillebeeckx's view at this time, Thomas was fighting against 'a variety of forms of conservative integralism'; he was concerned not to let the word of God go into what are in fact 'human, time-conditioned clothing or thought forms'. To this end he studied with great concentration the books which for many of his contemporaries were suspect: 'the latest studies of the pagan philosophers and of Jewish and Arabic thought, the modernism of the Middle Ages'. On the other hand Schillebeeckx saw in Thomas an opposition which could not be more passionate – he asserted that in the work of the usually very serene Thomas terms like *stupidum, absurdum* or *stupidissimum* occur exclusively in this context – 'against all forms of brazen progressiveness'.

The reason that Schillebeeckx gave for this fierceness says much about how he must have felt in this period. In his view, Thomas got so agitated because the extreme standpoints 'put the progressiveness of Thomas himself in discredit' since they threatened to block any true theological renewal along the lines of the tradition and almost inevitably provoked a conservative counter-reaction; thus, 'his life work in the service of the truth came under suspicion'. For Schillebeeckx, many radical proposals during and after the Council went too far, and he was anxious about the reactions that they could provoke among certain groups of believers and among the church authorities. At the same time he continued to regard it as his duty also to listen to proposals which in his view went too far, to consider them, and to think them through theologically. This would ultimately lead him after all to adopt some proposals in the course of time, but he then did so because they were theologically convincing. For after the Council he was to become a theologian with renewed dedication. With obvious satisfaction he related in his sermon that Thomas was afraid that the elevation to cardinal which awaited him at the time of his unexpected death in 1274 'would have made it impossible for him to continue his life's plan of priestly learning'. Perhaps it is not just a projection to feel here a glimmering of a certain relief on the part of the preacher that the Council was approaching its end and that before too long he would be able to devote himself whole-heartedly to theology again.

Towards the end of his sermon Schillebeeckx becomes very personal in an indirect way about his dedication to theology. He quotes the exclamation that traditionally Thomas is said to have made at the end of his life: 'Jesus, for the love of whom I have studied, lain awake at night, preached and given lectures ... ' As a commentary on this he adds:

> No closet learning, no ambition or sheer intellectual curiosity explains this life of study. But loving service of a living Someone does: the Lord Jesus Christ ... Because he loved. Love in the form of the priestly and serving doctorate.[274]

'Love in the form of the priestly and serving doctorate.' That suggests a great deal about Schillebeeckx's own experience of his theological work as a distinct kind of liturgical worship. After the Council, with renewed resolution he was to make this the centre of his life.

And as I have already indicated, he was to do so out of what was clearly a broad vision. His assertion that 'being occupied in religious thought with God, human beings and the relationship between them' was 'liturgical worship' for Thomas already indicates something of this, and some years later he was to speak of 'worldly service and the church's liturgy' as two different but equal activities.[275] Both thought and prayer were equally ways of devoting the world as a whole and in parts to God. And by thought he meant not only theological thought in the strict sense but thought in all its breadth. As early as 1958 he wrote that, from the perspective of Christian theology, thought and the practice of science are forms of *caritas* towards God and humankind.[276] In 1965 he emphatically located theology within the university as a community of sciences and scientists – *universitas scientiarum* – in which theology is in contact with all the disciplines through different realms of experience. It is its task to see them 'in the light of faith'. This article was the beginning of an intensive concern with the discussion of the place and function of the university which was to break out fiercely in the second half of the 1960s.[277]

But it was also above all a new step in his ongoing attempt to arrive at a theology of culture. In this way he tried to clarify the place of theology in a culture in which the different spheres of life and realms of experience were becoming increasingly autonomous from one another. He sought eventually in this society, too, with all its brokenness and plurality, to create a distinct place for 'critical thought about faith as worship and apostolate'.

Postscript

Notes on the Theological Yield

We 'must always insist that it is not a matter of the system but of the contact with reality itself'

In the 1920s and 1930s, as a boy, Edward Schillebeeckx greatly admired his older brother Louis. He wanted to become a Jesuit in his footsteps so that he could go as a missionary to foreign lands. However, Edward became a Dominican, a specialist theologian, and continued to live in the Low Countries. Nevertheless, in the second half of the 1960s in a sense he proved to have conquered the world, and in any case his relationship with his brother was completely reversed. When the famous American Trappist and author Thomas Merton visited Louis Schillebeeckx in 1968 during a trip round India at the invitation of the Jesuits in Kuseong, where Louis was lecturing, according to the notes in his diary Merton clearly saw him as 'the brother of Fr Schillebeeckx OP', and Louis Schillebeeckx advised Merton to go and see 'his brother in Nijmegen'.[1] In general, in the second half of the 1960s Schillebeeckx was included in the company of the important modern theologians who had prepared for the Second Vatican Council and had had a direct influence there. The wider public now wanted to get to know their pioneering views better.[2] Schillebeeckx gave lectures in a number of places. Articles by him were collected to document his development and grouped together in four volumes of 'Theological Soundings' under titles which refer to the themes which had been of great importance at the Council: *Revelation and Theology* (ET 1967), *God and Man* (ET 1969), *World and Church* (ET 1971) and *The Mission of the Church* (ET 1973); these collections of articles were translated into various languages and found readers all over the world.

Originally, more volumes of 'Theological Soundings' were envisaged.[3] However, the feeling that the Council represented a fundamental break-through was so strong that in the period after the Council Schillebeeckx himself above all felt that he should make a new theological start. Increasingly he found his earlier articles only of documentary interest. Certainly in his eyes it remained important to know 'what specific possibilities for the future . . . were seen on the fracture between past and present by theologians before Vatican II', but this was only background information for what in his view was really important in the situation after the Council: new, daring theological projects, orientated on the future.[4] In 1964 he still indicated that 'nowadays' the conviction was becoming ever clearer that man's salvation comes about within his daily life '"in the world", in his relationship with the strictly "secular"', and he clearly thought that in principle his earlier articles, which marked and explored this discovery, were still topical.[5] In subsequent years, new questions which in his view followed this discovery demanded his attention, and he lost interest in his earlier writings. With 'almost feverish urgency' he produced new articles and had his hands more than full with them.[6]

At the end of this book the question inevitably arises whether Schillebeeckx was right when he lost interest in his former work during the 1960s. Have I, and has the reader, been occupied in the previous pages with texts, views and arguments which at best are intriguing as a preamble to the Second Vatican Council, but no longer have any real relevance since the change in faith and theology which is marked by this assembly of the church? Were the 1945 articles on 'The Christian Situation' worth the attention that has been paid to them in this book, although as early as 1965 Schillebeeckx remarked that at most they were still significant as an expression of a clear enthusiasm for the world and 'being human' after a period when this had been impossible for the faithful, an enthusiasm which, moreover, he was convinced, was expressed 'in an adolescent style that we now find distatsteful'?[7] What can still be the significance of Schillebeeckx's view of the relationship between priests and laity, now that the clerical image of the church has in any case in practice lost all credibility with the collapse in the number of ordained priests? Isn't the discussion on the worker-priests and *Humani generis* too much a thing of the past still to have significance? Isn't Schillebeeckx's theology from his Flemish period interesting exclusively as an attempt to break out of the frameworks dominant at the time, and hasn't it largely lost its significance since these frameworks disappeared? Does it still make sense to investigate a theology like that of the Flemish Schillebeeckx, the starting point of which is that Thomas Aquinas is the central theological authority, now that his authority is no longer taken for granted by Catholic theologians as the starting-point?

In the introduction to this book I made it clear that it aims to be a contribution to the current theological discussion. In this postscript I shall try to indicate what I think to be the yield of the previous chapters for systematic theology.

THEOLOGY AS A HISTORICAL ENTERPRISE

Schillebeeckx's development from the 1930s to halfway through the 1960s primarily makes it clear that theological speaking and writing is radically historical. His work can be understood only from and in relation to the context in which it came into being. Anyone who reads a book like *De sacramentele heilseconomie* as a self-contained argument that derives its persuasiveness from its internal coherence will not really grasp the true significance of the work. For this lies in the power of its reference to what lies outside the text: the historical–cultural situation in which people were living at the time when it was written, the structures and images within which they thought, felt and believed. This does not mean that the book – or any other of Schillebeeckx's texts from the period to which this study relates – can no longer make a contribution to present-day discussion, but it does mean that it is necessary to build a bridge between the situation in which it was written and the situation now. In the present study this link is made in principle by interpreting Schillebeeckx's theology as a theology of culture.

The definitive discovery of the historicity of theology within the Catholic world is to an important degree the work of the generation of theologians to which Schillebeeckx belongs. The church's condemnation of modernism could not prevent the mounting knowledge of history from making progressively more incredible the view that the church was unchangeable in its structure and its doctrine. Study of the church fathers and the Bible unavoidably led to the conclusion that the biblical and patristic writings not only spoke about God by telling a salvation history, but, moreover, did so in the midst of and bound up with a history. Intensive historical research into Thomas Aquinas brought to light the fact that he was not the creator of a rigid system of thought aimed at defying time, but on the basis of contemporary questions had tried to understand in what sense the Christian tradition indeed contained a message of salvation.[8] The philosophy from the period between the two world wars, and to a heightened degree from after the Second World War, showed that human beings are not just thinking spirits, but that through the body, thinking and the spirit are indissolubly bound up with in the world in which they live, with all its historicity and vicissitudes. In short, whereas on the one hand it has become increasingly clear how much modern times are characterized by a constant bombardment of changes in all spheres of life, on the other hand an insight developed into how thoughts, convictions, forms of organization and experiences are bound up with these spheres of life.

Now all this radically confronted church and theology with the question how in this situation they could think about the God of salvation credibly and adequately. In a time when the Catholic Church as a whole and the representatives of its hierarchy in particular were constantly seeking the relevance of the church in its capacity to be a certain and unchangeable place of refuge in the midst of confusing changes, theologians like Schillebeeckx were in search of links with topical questions and the contemporary sense of life.[9] In their view, the church fathers, the biblical writings, Thomas Aquinas, the church's tradition, had saving significance for living people precisely in their historicity; or, in this historicity they demonstrated that what they said about God was really connected with the questions of their own time, and thus with concrete human existence in the form that it assumed in the period concerned. It is therefore very much in line with Schillebeeckx himself to connect the significance of his work directly with its historicity. It is of fundamental importance that from the beginning he strove to develop a 'theology of culture', a theological view of the historical form of human existence in dealing with the world and its religious significance. His 1964 remark which I have already quoted, that 'the conviction is increasingly [gaining] ground that salvation comes to meet us from our daily life and activity "in the world", from our dealing with "the earthly"', was an adequate summary of his development up to that point.[10] The abiding significance of his work lies primarily in the consistency with which it bears witness to the desire to theologize with this conviction and the evident possibility of doing so. That is why the preceding chapters have primarily emphasized how much in his work Schillebeeckx focused on bringing out the actual significance of tradition and the theological significance of the present day.

However, the optimism to which Schillebeeckx's 1964 formulation bears witness proved premature. The conviction that God can be known only from contact with concrete everyday life and the desire for and the experiences of salvation that are alive within it are still a matter of controversy. After the Council, not least within the Catholic Church, there were those who again began to seek the relevance of faith and theology in the possibilities that these were thought to offer of escaping the increasing confusion and uncertainty.[11] This view was presented by the Vatican with hierarchical authority and sealed with disciplinary measures. But although it derived a degree of plausibility from the collapse of Communism in 1989, above all given the consequences that this had for the lives of people in Eastern Europe, in the Catholic Church this did not lead to a revival of the time before the Council. In a number of places the faithful refused, and still refuse, to let go of the mandate extended to them by the Council to interpret the signs of their own time in the light of the gospel. Schillebeeckx also constantly gave them theological support in this refusal.[12] He did not seek publicity on this point, but he did publicly support the group of German-speaking colleagues who in 1989 protested in the so-called 'Cologne Declaration' against the declaration by the church authorities that the faithful and theologians were not yet 'of age', and declared that they saw the church in whose service they had put themselves, along the lines of Vatican II, as the 'people of God' on the way. They emphatically did not want to see it as a 'beleaguered city which raises up its bastions and firmly defends itself within and without'.[13] If the salvation with which the gospel is concerned really encounters people from their daily life and work 'in the world', the church which is called to preserve the message of the gospel needs to open its eyes to what resounds from this life and work and to give theologians room to reflect on it.

So the dispute which still goes on all over the world in the Catholic Church, and the internal polarization which is the result of it, is far more than a matter of church politics. It ultimately turns on the very question which was at stake in the 1950s and was raised in all openness at the Council: in what form do faith, the church and theology bring salvation in the present situation? In principle the notion that a strong church which in all circumstances powerfully puts forward one uniform and undoubted doctrine could be the true soul of culture, and could preserve modernity from succumbing to its internal contradictions, seems more incredible than ever. It is an unavoidable fact that we live in an untidy situation which we cannot grasp, a 'postmodern' situation. In the midst of the still ever-growing differentiation and pluriformity it is impossible for us to return to a 'great ideology', of whatever brand. Even theologians, philosophers and social scientists who think that modernity is heading for destruction and that the task of the Catholic Church is to protect it from this do not usually begin by presenting the teaching of the church. Instead they concentrate on its liturgical rituals, its narrative tradition and the living bond which it has as a community with the past. In their view this should make possible redemption from the meaninglessness, the atomization and the loss of direction which are said to threaten a modernity left to itself.[14]

In short, theologians find themsleves confronted with the kind of questions which Schillebeeckx and those of his generation faced in the 1940s and 1950s. What is the significance of the Christian and theological tradition in the midst of a bombardment of changes that is becoming increasingly intensive? What is the adequate theological attitude towards (post) modern culture? Again, and in my view more unavoidably than ever, we face the task which Schillebeeckx set himself in 1945: the development of what he called the 'foundations of a theology of culture'. This insight does not suddenly make his theology a secret treasure trove of answers to topical questions, since these questions are quite new and require a theological reflection and way of dealing with the tradition which is truly tailored to the new situation that is raising them. Nor does it just make his theological course through history a model that needs to be followed as well as possible, for this course too was largely determined by concrete conditions which are no longer ours. But it does mean that with his theological development Schillebeeckx also suggests a possible way in which one can be a theologian today. Contrary to a widespread scepticism inside and outside theology, he shows that an open, unprejudiced and at the same time critical theological attitude towards the history that surrounds us and permeates us is a real and meaningful possibility. The whole of Schillebeeckx's work from the period covered by this book makes it clear that the Catholic tradition can become surprisingly significant, precisely in confrontation with the contemporary situation and contemporary culture. It is a stimulus and a challenge to engage in a personal quest for a theological way of dealing with the situation today.[15]

It has been repeatedly made clear in the course of this book to what extent the ambiguous attitude which Leo XIII adopted towards modernity determined the history of Catholic theology up to and including the Council; his influence in fact even extends over the period after the Council. Leo XIII made it clear that Christian faith needed to be significant for life in contemporary culture: in this sense there is a direct connection between his 1891 encyclical *Rerum novarum* and the 1965 Pastoral Constitution of Vatican II, *Gaudium et spes*. But there is equally a straight line from *Inscrutabili* of 1878 – Leo XIII's first encyclical, which called for submission to the Catholic Church as a remedy against the chaos that the modern ideology of freedom was said to cause – via *Rerum novarum* and *Gaudium et spes* to the encyclical *Veritatis splendor* which John Paul II issued in 1993 on the teaching of the Catholic Church as the only saving truth. At the end of the twentieth century, dominated by the modern spirit of agnosticism and scepticism, according to the present pope 'the temptation to despair is one of our greatest threats'. The remedy against despair is for people to bring to it 'both their capacity to discover knowledge of the truth and their desire for the ultimate and definitive meaning of life'; and in both cases that means that they must be instructed in Catholic teaching.[16] Thus, two lines run from the standpoint of Leo XIII. In one the Catholic tradition is seen as intrinsically bound up with the joy and the hope, the sorrow and the fear of people and as lying on the same wavelength. In the other line the sorrow and the fear are regarded as signs that a modernity which is left to itself does not just lead to disaster, and the task of the church is thought to be once again to give people joy and hope. In the first line the salvation of human beings is broadly seen as the central criterion for the significance of insights in faith and theology, starting from the Christian claim that the gospel and the church's tradition proclaim a truth that makes people free. In the second line it is an axiom that the official interpretation of the tradition brings salvation, and disaster is interpreted as a sign and result of a lack of readiness to listen to the official proclamation of the church.

Now we could regard this second line of thought as the obsessive ideology of a religious institution which is increasingly losing power and cannot be reconciled to the decline in its influence. But that is too simple. It is not only the pressure from the central authority of the church which makes it so difficult for the faithful and theologians really to break with this line of thought. It is not only in the Catholic Church that there is a fear that a failure to keep human drives in check, the pursuit of self-interest without the limiting effect of moral traditions and views which are diverging further and further, will bring chaos. It is not peculiar to Christianity or even to religion to think that salvation can come only from a (renewed) submission to authority. There are countless forms of fundamental pessimism about the state of the present, and hence a desire for drastic authoritarian solutions: religious and non-religious, conservative and progressive.[17] Here we come up against the divergent expressions of a paradox at the heart of modernity itself.

The French philosopher Michel Foucault has pointed out that the modern consciousness is characterized by both a belief in the autonomy of man and an insight into the unavoidability of human heteronomy. The modern ethos requires people, on the basis of weighing up arguments, to be their own judges of what is true and good, while modern reflection on the self at the same time makes it clear how much they always remain dependent on what is already given. Their judgement is defined by their position and their culture; they are tied to their biological needs, they are shaped by their history and their parents. But even more important, despite and often even through the attempts to increase human autonomy and liberate people from what holds them captive, involved in suffering and alienated from themselves, at the same time ever new forms of subjection, suffering and alienation seem to arise. One way of breaking through this paradox is to proclaim a specific, particular tradition to be the authentic representation of the truth and goodness which is sought, and to regard submission to this tradition as the supreme form of autonomy.[18] This makes it possible to escape the intellectual confusion and the moral uncertainty that goes with a life of responsibility, while at the same time having a sense of one's own limitations. In this light it is not surprising that in all kinds of places there is regularly a call for a renewed submission to a tradition. This can give rulers the feeling of having a basis for their regulations; it can free activists from their doubts about the purpose of their actions; and it can again offer intellectuals a view to proclaim to the world. It is no less natural that religious leaders regularly try to show that the tradition that they represent is by far the most suitable for fulfilling the need for a view which is comprehensively clothed with authority.

However, the theological course through the history of Edward Schillebeeckx that has been reconstructed in this book points in another direction.

372

His constant emphasis on the scientific character of theology is also a refusal to let the Christian tradition function as the authority which should measure modernity. The view that theology is a scientific discipline presupposes that the truth and moral justice of the Christian tradition must be supported by arguments and tested in discussion. Here it is implicitly being said that no single truth-claim, not even a religious truth-claim, can escape the (post)-modern clash of views and opinions and the resultant relativization of its authority. This can look like a capitulation to the modern spirit of the time. In fact this position prevents the content of the Christian tradition of faith from being made subordinate to its authority and thus becoming an instrument for getting or maintaining power. It is a core conviction of the Christian tradition that the truth makes free (John 8.32) and that morally just action implies living in God's light: 'Who may stand in the holy place? He who has clean hands and a pure heart' (Psalm 24.3–4). This obliges all believers, and theologians in particular, not just to submit to a religious claim to authority but instead to investigate the spirits, 'whether they are of God' (1 John 4.1). Therefore choosing a theological position over against (post) modernity cannot be an authoritarian rescue from its paradoxes.[19]

In the course of his theological development Schillebeeckx was increasingly to discover that religion, church and theology do not stand outside modern culture but can take form only by living through and thinking through this culture, with all its questions, dilemmas and paradoxes.[20] The previous chapters on the one hand make it clear how his project of a theology of culture led him to a comprehensive interpretation of the tradition and on the other hand show that from here a theological view of the contemporary situation is possible. Schillebeeckx's theology of culture is so to speak 'the suspension of culture in culture',[21] the creation of room for reflection in the midst of existing human attempts to give form to the good life. In this space, his interpretation of the Christian tradition opens up the prospect of a culture in which true, right and meaningful humanity is possible. At least, that is ultimately my theological interpretation of the history that has been reconstructed in the previous chapters.

HUMAN HISTORY AS THEOLOGICAL TERRAIN

Schillebeeckx's theological work is in the end built on the presupposition that human existence has a theological dimension. His project of a theology of culture is ultimately a persistent attempt to bring human history, and human culture as a historical manifestation of being human, into view as the theological terrain *par excellence*. For him theology has no reference to a reality which lies behind things and to which access is to be had only through the Catholic tradition. Theology points to the horizon within which human life and dealing with the world are played out. Therefore, human existence, with all its questions and dilemmas, always already has theological significance. That means that theology is not to be done in the utmost remoteness from this reality, with the help of abstract speculations. It proved that Schillebeeckx presents this view, like many of his insights in the period covered by this book, as primarily coming from Thomas Aquinas. So I cannot avoid a brief investigation of Schillebeeckx's interpretation of Thomas's work, and of the role that the philosophy of his teacher Domien De Petter plays here. This role is and remains of great importance for what Schillebeeckx himself was also to say later.

Schillebeeckx's interpretation of a text of Thomas in which Thomas says that human reason is not in a position to know God in himself is of fundamental importance for his theological approach. God can be known only by the things that can perceived by the senses of which God is the cause. Schillebeeckx read this as an indication that 'creatures are and remain the podium of the human knowledge of God'.[22] Here he was opposing what he called the 'conceptualism' of the neoscholastics, who thought that a concept could be applied to God through abstraction, in other words to the degree to which it no longer referred to creatures.[23] They, too, could refer to Thomas to support their view, since for Thomas by his own account the speculative vision of God was the supreme human happiness.[24] Neoscholasticism in fact began from the assumption that the traditional church doctrine of God expresses this speculative vision precisely in its abstraction. Therefore, it concentrated on analysing the internal logic of this doctrine, in the belief that in this way it could participate in the vision of God. For Schillebeeckx, by contrast, the vision of God was 'implicitly but really' present in life in the midst of creatures and the knowledge of them. To this degree the notion derived from De Petter of an 'implicit intuition' of God is in fact fundamental to Schillebeeckx's approach. In his interpretation, this notion states that God can be known only implicitly, but at the same time it claims that this implicit knowledge of God is real knowledge of God. In his view it is via the creatures in their concrete needs and historicity, via creation and history, that human beings within their finite and historical existence come into contact, not with an abstract supreme entity, but with a living God who reveals himself and at the same time conceals himself in his mystery. Here theology has in principle changed from being a science about a well-determined church tradition which argues rationally, as it is in neoscholasticism, into a deciphering of human existence in its different aspects, under the view of God as this is expressed in the Christian tradition.

Here in fact Schillebeeckx brought about a real revolution, although in the period covered by this book the implications were somewhat hidden: I think that they were also to remain to some degree veiled in his later career. But slowly, during the history which has been reconstructed in the previous chapters, more and more consequences of this change have been formulated, with all the difficulties that it caused and the ambiguities with which it was coupled. The most obvious result of Schillebeeckx's conviction that the foundation of theology lay in God's traces in creation and history was that theology was withdrawn from the exclusive say of the magisterium and could no longer be regarded as the reflected mode of the teaching formulated by the hierarchy. In the first three chapters of this book it emerged how complicated Schillebeeckx's view was of the relationship between theology, culture and church, and within the church between theology and hierarchy, but one can nevertheless say that in the period between 1945 and 1957 to an increasing degree he realized the church-political consequences of his theological starting point. Chapter 4 showed that this resulted in his conviction that the theology which the hierarchy developed in its official statements on the basis of its responsibility for combating divergent views of faith was one-sided. Theologians had not to reproduce this one-sidedness but to correct it.[26] That on the basis of his own view of the Christian faith and its 'conjunctures'[27] this needed to happen made it clear that the way in which he distanced himself from doctrine in the form which was still dominant was directly connected with his specific view of the task, function and object of theology.

In the address with which he officially accepted the post of professor in Nijmegen, Schillebeeckx said: 'The real life of man in its dialogued relationship with the God of our salvation is the treasure-mine and workshop of authentic and vital theology.'[28] This was an adequate summary of his view of theology as a theology of culture, in the midst of culture and reflecting on it in dialogue with the Christian tradition, bringing to light the intuition of God which is implicit in this culture, and so arriving at a theological view of this culture and of human existence within it. The first three chapters of this book showed above all how this view of a theology of culture emerged in the concrete questions which occupied him in his Flemish period and in the various questions with which he saw himself faced. In a constant exchange, he reflected on the position and task of faith, church and theology within the contemporary cultural and social situation. He involved himself in the ecclesiastical and pastoral questions connected with it, put them in a theological light, and developed a view of culture, the world and humankind in general, along with insights into different theological spheres. In a complicated way, all his activities formed a coherent whole in which the different parts had an influence on one another: the discussion with Karl Adam and Jacques Maritain, the study of the existentialists, of Thomas, of Marie-Dominique Chenu, Yves Congar and Domien De Petter, the reflection on the post-war situation, his work for *Kultuurleven* and *Tijdschrift voor Geestelijk Leven* and his task of guiding students towards achieving a Dominican spirituality, his involvement with worker-priests and his quest for a lay spirituality, his interest in the sacraments and sacramentality, and the little books on Mary, and all the other things which arose.

All this ultimately comes together in Schillebeeckx's Louvain lecture notes. These disclose the link between insights developed earlier, and work out his own interpretation of the Catholic tradition in detail, often in extensive discussions with others. But above all – and this makes his theology unique and ensures that even where the questions, terminology and some standpoints are dated, it can still always prove attractive – they demonstrate that the Christian tradition can function as the explication of a horizon within which contemporary human existence with all its possibilities and difficulties can be illuminated and interpreted. More than anything else, Schillebeeckx's Flemish lecture notes suggest that images (for example, hell, heaven and purgatory), thought (God as creator of heaven and earth), and theories (Jesus Christ as one person in two natures) which at first sight seem strange can provide insights into human existence, help to further a meaningful life within a meaningful culture and thus bear witness to the God of salvation of which the Christian tradition claims to speak. In particular the lecture notes make clear the implications of the revolution which began with Schillebeeckx's adaptation of De Petter's philosophical theory of the implicit intuition in the sphere of theology. Finite historical, worldly human existence is the place where God is to be seen in an indirect way, and theological treatment of the tradition is orientated on making visible this existence as such.

Schillebeeckx felt that with the Second Vatican Council this insight broke through in broad circles within the church. He thought that in convening the Council Pope John XXIII was concerned to 'show the pure nature of the church as the visible presence of grace and love in this world', and that the main conciliar question was what role the church plays in culture and history.[29] During the discussions at the Council and above all in reporting them, the assembly often proved to be a 'kind of tournament' between the conservatives and those who wanted to renew the church, as Schillebeeckx put it, and after the Council the view which saw the Council as a battleground within the church would be further strengthened. However, Schillebeeckx's activity in this period, described in Chapter 5, makes clear how much in all this dedication to church renewal he was ultimately concerned with the ability of the church to represent God's salvation in the midst of the contemporary world. That this meant a fundamental reorientation of the church and theology as a whole was not always clear to everyone. Many people, in the footsteps of Pope John XXIII himself, continued to make a sharp distinction between the internal organization of the church and its activity in the outside world, the former then being regarded as doctrinal and dogmatic and the latter as primarily pastoral and practical. This was a productive misunderstanding, since it meant that the Council fathers could

376

speak relatively frankly and freely, by the standards of the time, about the relationship between the church and the world. But Schillebeeckx rightly indicated that the true dogmatic significance of the Council lay in its sense of the extreme importance of these pastoral questions for church, faith and theology: ' ... Christianity ... must also be an event in which the authentic salvation history is accomplished'.[30] In his view the Pastoral Constitution *Gaudium et spes* drew the right conclusion by trying to 'bring into the daylight', with the help of the Christian tradition, the veiled hope which inspires and guides humankind – 'a hope which seeks to sustain and strengthen this world in spite of certain signs of despair on all sides and a sense of the absurd in the history of the world', and in this way invites people to appropriate 'the Christian hope'.[31] The tenacious human hope is here seen as a hidden form of the Christian hope, the Christian tradition as a thematization of this hope which derives its value from the degree to which in this thematization it succeeds in bringing the hidden hope to light as a form of the vision of God.

This is the indication of a new theological way. At the beginning of this way a number of new questions would arise, and a number of old questions would present themselves in a new manner. Schillebeeckx himself began to explore these questions with 'an almost feverish urgency' even during the Council, at that moment doubtless with the thought that this *first* had to happen so that *then*, and on the basis of that, he would be able to work further on his theology along the lines of what he had developed in his Flemish period. It was soon to prove, however, that a theology which seeks to read the Christian tradition as clarification of the contemporary situation and with an eye to the salvation of contemporary men and women, a theology which in this way is 'in search of the living God', can never just go on building on a foundation that has already been laid. A theology which really puts itself 'at the centre of culture' and from there reflects on the world, human beings and God in the light of the Christian tradition, always in a sense begins at the beginning and is constantly at risk. In the period after the Council, what Schillebeeckx already in fact practised in his Flemish period was increasingly clearly to prove to be a principal characteristic of theology in modernity: going on means beginning at the beginning once again.[32]

For Schillebeeckx himself, a number of his original starting points would come under discussion in the ongoing process of the analysis of current developments, the re-reading of documents from the tradition and the renewed consideration of basic questions. The confrontation with secularization and with the plurality of views of life led him to begin to detach himself from a central starting point of his early theology. In it he had in fact presupposed that God's presence could be known in an unambiguous way through creation. In his later theology, too, for Schillebeeckx God remained present and knowable, but this presence began to be coupled with absence, and the possibility of knowledge with hiddenness.[33] During this process, Schillebeeckx was in particular to become critical of the epistemology of De Petter, which through the criticism of a number of critical young fellow-Dominicans he learned to see ultimately as a hidden legitimation of the church's tradition.[34] In 1968 he was to indicate the gulf which in his view immediately separated him from De Petter by saying that the conviction that human life and human culture imply an implicit intuition of God as this is expressed in the Christian tradition can 'at best be a responsible final conclusion of an analysis of human existence', but cannot precede it.[35] However, this amounted to a radicalization of his starting-point that God is not directly accessible through speculative thought but only indirectly by dealing with the world and history, a starting-point which he had developed with the aid of De Petter's theory of implicit intuition. In the second half of the 1960s Schillebeeckx then abandoned not only De Petter but also the 'Thomistic principles' which, since the beginning of his career, had so much formed the starting point of his theology. Certainly after the Council he was to drop the custom of first asking in connection with any theological question what Thomas Aquinas thought about it, but by his constant reading of Thomas he had developed for himself a way of theologizing in which 'the saving content of human life' had a central place. After the Council he found notions in other thinkers which in his view provided a better support in the present context than ideas from the work of Thomas.[36] In the end he was above all to turn intensively to the text of the Bible and also to begin to steep himself in the details of biblical scholarship. In his publications and in his year-long lectures on philosophical and theological theories of interpretation, he thought extensively about the relationship between the interpretation of biblical texts and that of human existence, and about the fundamental fact that for finite human beings meaning and significance can never just be present in a finite world, but can only come to light through interpretation.[37] In the period after the Council, hermeneutics was to assume the role in Schillebeeckx's thought that De Petter's philosophy had had in the period discussed in this book. At least that is my provisional hypothesis.

One of the basic insights of hermeneutics is that no single interpretation exhausts the significance of texts, things, events or happenings. On the basis of a new situation and with a changed awareness of the problem, a new look at something from the past provides new insights. And anyone who now, seeking to contribute to the progress of theology, looks at Schillebeeckx's earlier work will learn new things. That applies at all kinds of specific and subordinate points, as I hope readers have learned while reading, but it also applies at the level of this book as a whole. Even while writing it, I had the feeling in the same movement not only of developing an interpretation of Schillebeeckx's work between 1936 and 1965 and bringing out the historically situated effect of his theology of culture, but also of offering an interpretation of the theological situation of that time, which now requires to be worked out further and adapted by such a project of a theology of culture. And here, in this reflection of past and present in each other, I am convinced that this book is not just a book about a theologian in his history but a theological book. In his Louvain lectures Schillebeeckx stated that theology is not about reconstructing thought-systems as such, however venerable they may be. For him the central question was whether 'a particular theological system' – he mentioned that of 'St Thomas', but why shouldn't it be applied to his own theology? – was a good guide to 'penetrating deeper into the theological datum itself', in other words to God, in so far as he is present in bringing salvation to men and women of today, and thus of the present, in so far as it is the place of God's saving presence.[38] At all events, in what the previous chapters also bring to light, to me at any rate they suggest that Schillebeeckx's theology is in principle indeed a good guide here.

BIOGRAPHY AS THEOLOGICAL AUTOBIOGRAPHY

According to Schillebeeckx, the God of salvation encounters people in their 'life and work in the world' and from our dealings with earthly things. On the basis of a similar conviction, his friend and colleague Johann Baptist Metz has emphasized how important the biography of the theologian is for theology.[39] A theologian has to find God in her or his biography; only then is a credible theology possible. Theology must indeed be living reflection on a reality that is experienced as living, which shows itself in life. But conversely, it is equally necessary for the biography of a theologian to be a biography of thinking, seeking and finding God, of living-as-a-theologian. One's own biography must take the form of a theological autobiography. Theology is credible whenever theologians do not just talk about God but while speaking about God also speak about themselves, and while writing, (re)write their own life as a place where God comes to light. In short, theological writing has to be autobiography – not in the sense of *writing about oneself* but in *writing oneself*; and in this sense this book, in its reconstruction of the history of the one theologian that I regard as my teacher in the full sense of the word, is a form of autobiography. By following Schillebeeckx's development, analysing his writings, and investigating how when doing theology in confrontation with his context and the changes in it he rewrote his own situation as a theological situation, at the same time I found a mirror which helps me to see my own situation as a theological situation that also requires to be thought through theologically.[40] I hope that my description has also served as a mirror for readers of the previous chapters. In this indirect way this book is then a contribution to promote Schillebeeckx's work in our context.

There is no more direct way. It is part of our situation that because of the way in which modernity changes, the questions with which one generation is also confronted differ markedly from the questions of a subsequent generation, and this later generation can often understand them only after an extensive analysis of the context in which they arose. Therefore, it is impossible just to follow thinkers of a previous generation, however great they were or are. The situation of their thought is no longer ours. But that in itself does not mean that time and again theology must be recreated out of nothing. Theologians from a previous generation can certainly still challenge those of the next in the way in which they sought and found their theological way within their context, and above all in the view to which this bears witness. I think that Schillebeeckx can still be an example to a younger generation in this sense, above all because he himself was already so clearly confronted with the instability of the modern situation and reacted to it. The First World War marked the end of the stability of the preceding period, and for church and theology that created the need to situate themselves in the midst of a world which had become fundamentally uncertain and changeable. Among other things, this situation meant that statements of faith and theological positions were no longer accepted because of the status of those who put them forward, but had to show their plausibility and relevance precisely in this changeable situation. Schillebeeckx saw this not only as a problem but in principle also as a source of new possibilities for faith and theology. That is also how I would want to regard the present situation, knowing from experience that this is still far from obvious among theologians. Here, in general and in the various different questions, I have often been put on the way, regularly challenged and sometimes surprised in a productive way, by parts of Schillebeeckx's work.

A new book is needed to show that parts and fragments from Schillebeeckx's work can do good service in making all this clear in the theological reconnaissance of the situation at the end of the second millennium and in the present-day quest for the presence of the God of salvation. One day I hope to write such a book. It cannot be other than a book which takes readers from the actuality of the church and views of life to an analysis of the place and function of religion, faith and theology; from the social implications of the Christian tradition to the religious significance of social questions; from concrete religious expressions of the human quest for liberation and redemption to reflection on the Bible, Christian tradition and the figure of Jesus Christ; from the existential questions of individual people to the ultimate nature of the world and the cosmos as God's creation. In short, it will have to be as broad and as comprehensive as Schillebeeckx's own work, which has also made this book so broad and comprehensive. But it must nevertheless be quite different from Schillebeeckx's writings, especially by constantly taking as the goal of theology the disclosure that our own situation is the place where God's presence is to be found, and starting from the fact that the importance of theology becomes clear in the importance of what comes to light.

Theologians need to abandon the fiction that the truth of the tradition and the authority of the church form a firm foundation on which they can build further, up to and including the last remnants and traces. Theology has no other foundation than the God of salvation, whose mystery it may and must constantly decipher and clarify. If it takes that completely seriously, it will inevitably change fundamentally, time and again.[41]

In Schillebeeckx, too, theology changed decisively after the Second Vatican Council. This change is directly connected with the fact that, more urgently than the period which has been discussed in this book, the post-conciliar period confronted him with the need to sound out his own time theologically. In the second volume of this study of *Edward Schillebeeckx: A Theologian in his History*, it will become clear how much rethinking this calls for.

Notes

INTRODUCTION

1   Cf. E. Simons and L. Winkeler, *Het verraad der clercken: Intellectuelen en hun rol in de ontwikkelingen van het Nederlands katholicisme na 1945*, Baarn 1987.

2   For the first 'Schillebeeckx case' cf. R. Auwerda, *Dossier Schillebeeckx: Theoloog in de kerk der conflicten*, Bilthoven 1969; here it also becomes clear how much Schillebeeckx was regarded as a representative of Dutch Catholicism. For the second 'Schillebeeckx case' see *The Schillebeeckx Case*, ed. T. Schoof, New York and Ramsey, NJ 1984. There is an extensive account of the reactions to this second 'case' in T. M. Schoof, 'Getuigen in de "zaak Schillebeeckx": Theologische lijnen in de publieke en persoonlijke reacties', *TvT* 20, 1980, 402–21.

3   For a general introduction to Schillebeeckx's theology, addressed to a wide public, see P. Kennedy, *Schillebeeckx*, London 1993; cf. also R. J. Schreiter, 'Edward Schillebeeckx: An Orientation to his Thought', in *The Schillebeeckx Reader*, ed. R. J. Schreiter, New York 1984, 1–12; *The Praxis of Christian Experience. An Introduction to the Theology of Edward Schillebeeckx*, ed. R. J. Schreiter and M. C. Hilkert, San Francisco, etc. 1989. More technical accounts are T. Iwashima, *Menschlichkeitsgeschichte und Heilserfahrung: Die Theologie von Edward Schillebeeckx als methodisch reflektierte Soteriologie*, Düsseldorf 1982; P. Kennedy, *Deus Humanissimus: The Knowability of God in the Theology of Edward Schillebeeckx*, Freiburg 1993.

4   For a survey of his work during this period see Schoof, 'Aandrang' ('25 Years').

5   See Borgman, *Sporen*.

6   The editors, 'Ter oriëntering'; *TvT* 1, 1961, 1–2: 2. I make an attempt to investigate the current significance of this in 'De kerk als schijnbaar fundament: Over het zwijgen van de theologie, en het doorbreken daarvan', *TvT* 35, 1995, 358–72.

7   Cf. especially my *Alexamenos aanbidt zijn God: Theologische essays voor sceptische lezers*, Zoetermeer 1994.

8   That does not mean that Schillebeeckx's theology has not been researched. For an overall account of the around 200 studies of Schillebeeckx's work which he has listed cf. T. Schoof, 'Werk van en over Edward Schillebeeckx', *TvT* 34, 1994, 430–8. However, most studies prove either to be very general or to go into just one part of Schillebeeckx's work.

9   This has proved to be the case in the courses which the Edward Schillebeeckx Foundation has offered on his work in recent years. To support these courses some books have appeared which open up part of his work for a wider public: P. Valkenberg, *Leeswijzer bij 'Mensen als verhaal van God' van Edward Schillebeeckx*, Baarn and Nijmegen 1991; H. Snijdewind, *Leeswijzer bij 'Jesus, het verhaal van een Levende' van Edward Schillebeeckx*, Baarn 1994; I. D'hert, *Een spoor voor ons getrokken: De Jezustrilogie van Edward Schillebeeckx*, Baarn 1997.

10 Cf. the article by A. R. Van de Walle, 'Theologie over de werkelijkheid: Een betekenis van het werk van Edward Schillebeeckx', *TvT* 14, 1974, 463–90, which is still worth reading.

11 The title of the middle of three consecutive articles which appeared under the common title 'Christelijke situatie' (in *Kultuurleven* 12, 1945, 82–95; 229–42; 585–611) has as a subtitle 'Basic Principles for a Theology of Culture'.

12 Pastoral Constitution *Gaudium et spes*, 1965, no. 53. 'Culture' is an extremely complex concept, cf. the classic A. L. Krober and C. Kluckhohn, *Culture: A Critical Review of Concepts and Definitions*, New York 1952. It is inconceivable that there would have been such an extended coverage in *Gaudium et spes*, taking up the relationship between church and culture (Part I, chapter 2, nos 53–62), without the Catholic theologians who from the late 1920s had devoted themselves to a new confrontation with culture and theological reflection on it; in the 1950s Schillebeeckx was one of them.

13 For a summary of my view of Schillebeeckx see Borgman, 'Cultuurtheologie'. For an earlier position on his work, see Borgman, 'Universiteit' and 'Identiteit'.

14 J. B. Metz, *Glaube in Geschichte und Gesellschaft*, Mainz 1977, 195–211: 'Theologie als Biographie?', esp. 196.

15 J. and A. Romein, *Erflaters van onze beschaving: I: 14de-16de eeuw*, Amsterdam 1947, 7–8.

16 Here I am indebted to the contextual approach to theology and the history of theology developed by the dogmatics section in the Nijmegen theological faculty in the 1980s: cf. especially A. van Harskamp, *Theologie: Tekst in context*, Nijmegen 1986; *Tussen openheid en isolement: Het voorbeeld van de katholieke theologie in de negentiende eeuw*, ed. A. van Harskamp and E. Borgman, Kampen 1992. The present study also differs from other biographies of theologians by virtue of this approach. Here are some examples: E. Busch's well-known book *Karl Barth. His Life from Letters and Autobiographical Texts*, London and Philadelphia 1976, does not do more than document the external events in Barth's life and put them in chronological order; the same goes for the book by W. and M. Pauck on Paul Tillich, *Paul Tillich. His Life and Thought*, New York 1976, personal fortunes and historical events simply form the 'frame' for the theological work; E. Bethge's biography, *Dietrich Bonhoeffer: Theologian – Christian – Contemporary*, London and New York 1970, investigates Bonhoeffer's personality with the overwhelming amount of information which he presents; H.-B. Gerl regards her study of Guardini (*Romano Guardini, 1885–1968, Leben und Werk*, Mainz 1985), explicitly as an investigation of 'who he really was'; I. Ker's book on Newman (*John Henry Newman: A Biography*, Oxford 1989) stands clearly in the tradition of English literary biography and interprets Newman's life, personal development and theological work in the light of one another in order to portray a great spirit, so I am not concerned with any of this. For an approach which is in some way comparable to mine see T. Ruster, *Die verlorene Nützlichkeit der Religion: Katholizismus und Moderne in der Weimarer Republik*, Paderborn 1994.

17 For J. Romein's ideas on biography see his *De biografie: een inleiding*, Amsterdam 1946.

18 Cf. Schillebeeckx, *Theologie*, 1958, 71–121, esp. 84–7: 'The positive-historical function of the one theology: positive theology.'

19 Ibid., 86f. The text at the head of this introduction is also taken from this passage.

20 Letter of 7 May 1997 to me, in which Schillebeeckx also wrote that '*in globo*' my inter-

pretation of his work and development as presented in the first three chapters of this book seemed right.

CHAPTER 1

1   Edward Schillebeeckx's letters home are in Arch. 699.
2   See 'De christen en zijn politieke partijkeuze', in *Archiv. v.d. Kerken* 27, 1972, 186–99.
3   Puchinger, *Toekomst*, 121–59: 130.
4   Ibid., 123.
5   For the course of the German invasion see S. de Schaepdrijver, *De Groote Oorlog: Het koninkrijk België tijdens de Eerste Wereldoorlog*, Amsterdam and Antwerp 1997, 67–102.
6   A copy of the document was given to me by Ted Schoof. It is undated but according to him seems to come from after the appearance of Oosterhuis and Hoogeveen, *God New*, as a correction to the version given there.
7   M. van der Plas, 'Een verering die vriendschap werd: Edward Schillebeeckx over zijn vader en het geloof der vaderen', *Elsevier* 44, 1988, 136–41: 136. It is also in Schillebeeckx, *Testament*, 15–16. As early as 10 October the fortress which the Belgians thought to be impregnable had surrendered.
8   K. Marx and F. Engels, *The Communist Manifesto* (1848), Harmondsworth 1967, esp. 83.
9   For the situation on the Yzer and its significance for the Flemish movement see de Schaepdrijver, *Groote Oorlog* (n. 5), 173–214.
10 For the culture of mobility which definitively broke through with the First World War see M. Ekstein, *Rites of Spring: The Great War and the Birth of the Modern Age*, Boston 1989. For the consequences for Catholicism and its reaction see E. Fouilloux, 'Der Katholizismus', in *Die Geschichte des Christentums*, ed. J.-M. Mayeur et al., *XII: Erster und zweiter Weltkrieg. Demokratien und totalitäre Systeme (1914–1958)*, Freiburg, Basel and Vienna 1994, 134–302. For the political and cultural situation in Belgium after the First World War see de Schaepdrijver, *Groote Oorlog* (n. 5), 289–314; for the church situation see A. Tihon, 'Belgien', in *Die Geschichte des Christentums* XII, 649–66.
11 H. Schillebeeckx, 'Humaniora en humaniora', *Biekorf*, 1936–7, nos 1,10. The pages of the original article are not numbered; page numbering has been added in pencil on the copy in Arch. 3203. In the following discussion the page numbers are given in brackets in the text. See text, p. 35, for an explanation of the different names and initials found on Schillebeeckx's publications.
12 A summary and climax of this opposition can be found in the 1931 encyclical *Casti connubii* of Pius XI.
13 Puchiger, *Toekomst*, 127; cf. Schillebeeckx, *Testament*, 16.
14 A. W. Willemsen, *De Vlaamse beweging, II: Van 1914 tot 1940*, Hasselt 1975, 149–50; H. Gaus, 'Het cultureel-maatschappelijk leven in België', in *Algemene geschiedenis der Nederlanden, XIV, Nederland en België 1914–1940*, Haarlem 1979, 256–84: 264–8.
15 The quotations are from van der Plas, 'Een verering' (n. 7), 136.
16 Ibid., 137.
17 Puchinger, *Toekomst*, 131.
18 Ibid.
19 H. Schillebeeckx, 'Het waarheidskarakter van de studentenbeweging', *Biekorf* (1937, Arch. 3205); id., 'Purisme en purisme', *Biekorf* (1937–37), no.1 (Arch. 3206). The influence of his then teacher D. M. De Petter is clearly evident in this last contribution; De Petter argued strongly for a Flemish intellectual culture and established the *Tijdschrift voor Philosophie* with a view to this.

20   Puchinger, *Toekomst*, 127–9 (where the Jesuit in question is called 'Pater De Witte'); Oosterhuis and Hoogeveen, *God New*, 7. Schillebeeckx also mentions the names of his teachers as Seeldraayers and Nootebaert. Unfortunately issues of this journal are no longer to be found.

21   E. Witte, 'Déchristianisation et sécularisation en Belgique', in H. Hasquin, *Histoire de la laicité principialement en Belgique et en France*, Brussels 1979, 149–73: 163.

22   J. Art, 'Kerk en religie', in *Algemene geschiedenis der Nederlanden, XII: Nederland en België 1840–1914, eerste helft*, Haarlem 1977, 168–78.

23   Cf. H. Righart, *De katholieke zuil in Europa: Het ontstaan van verzuiling onder katholieken in Oostenrijk, Zwitserland, België en Nederland*, Meppel and Amsterdam 1986, 132–88: on 'the origin of Catholic deconfessionalization in Belgium from the second half of the 1880s to 1921'. The paraphrased text on the anti-religious spirit in streets, trams, etc. (quoted ibid., 154), comes from 1909.

24   See K. Walf, 'Die katholische Kirche – eine "societas perfecta"', *Theologische Quartalschrift* 157, 1977, 107–18: 107–10.

25   M. N. Ebertz, 'Herrschaft in der Kirche: Hierarchie, Tradition und Charisma im 19. Jahrhundert', in *Zur Soziologie des Katholizismus*, ed. K. Gabriel and F.-X. Kaufmann, Mainz 1980, 89–110; K. Gabriel, 'Die neuzeitliche Gesellschaftsentwicklung und der Katholizismus als Sozialform der Christentumsgeschichte', ibid. 201–25; for the effect of this in Belgium see S. Hellemans, *Strijd om de moderniteit: Sociale bewegingen en verzuiling in Europa sinds 1800*, Louvain 1990, 57–78.

26   É. Poulat, 'Préface', in P. Thibault, *Savoir et pouvoir: Philosophie thomiste et politique cléricale au XIXe siècle*, Quebec 1972, ix–xix: xi–xii; id., *L'Église est une monde*, Paris 1986, ch.10: on 'the Roman church, knowledge and power', esp. 218ff.

27   Leo XIII, encyclical *Inscrutabili* (1878), nos 2 and 3.

28   B. McSweeney, *Roman Catholicism: The Search for Relevance*, Oxford 1980, 61–91.

29   Fouilloux, 'Der Katholizismus' (n.10), 135. J. Roes ('In de kerk geboren: Het Nederlands katholicisme in anderhalve eeuw van herleving naar overleving', in *Jaarboek Katholiek Documentatiecentrum 1994*, Nijmegen 1994, 61–102), defends the thesis that this opposition ultimately brought about the downfall of deconfessionalized Catholicism in the Netherlands. However, his restriction to the Netherlands seems strange.

30   Hellemans, *Strijd om de moderniteit* (n. 25), 107–8.

31   Belgium had had a multiple universal vote for men: a man had one, two or three votes depending on how much tax he had paid.

32   Van der Plas, 'Een verering' (n.7), 139.

33   Puchinger, *Toekomst*, 127.

34   Letter of 9 March 1928.

35   Ibid. However, that did change later; Schillebeeckx relates (ibid.): 'when I was in the top class, and when we were moved to a new college building on the edge of the city ... there were rooms in which brothers could sleep together ... My younger brothers have quite a different recollection of their time at college from mine.'

36   Oosterhuis and Hoogeveen, *God New*, 8.

37   Puchinger, *Toekomst*, 130.

38   Ibid., 11.

39   Ibid., 20.

40   Originally *From Evangelical to Catholic by Way of the East*; it appeared in 1920 as an article (in *The Catholic Herald of India*) and shortly after that in book form (Calcutta); it was translated as *De l'Évangelisme au Catholicisme par la route des Indes* (Brussels 1921) and *Lang Oostersche Paden: Van evangelisch tot katholiek* (Louvain 1925).

41   J. J. ten Berghe, introduction to Wallace, *Lang Oostersche Paden* (n.40), 7–30.

42   Wallace, ibid., 134.

43 Ibid., 171–80.
44 Puchinger, *Toekomst*, 128.
45 Oosterhuis and Hoogeveen, *God New,* 6.
46 Ibid., 8.
47 Schillebeeckx, *Testament*, 10. Around fifteen years after the retreat he was to write an article in which he tried to relativize the methodical rigidity of the *Spiritual Exercises* and their approach, which was apparently so voluntaristic and activistic, and to put them within a view of prayer as the orientation of human beings on God brought about by God's grace. He had great difficulty in doing this (see 'Beschouwingen rond de "Geestelijke Oefeningen"', *TGL* 4/1, 1948, 202–11).
48 Gaus suggests – with great caution – that the episcopal prohibition against the secular clergy engaging in social questions could be an explanation why the religious orders were evidently more attractive than the secular priesthood, 'Het cultuur-maatschappelijk leven en België' (n.14), 259.
49 From 1861 to 1958 there was one Belgian province of Dominicans; in 1958 this was split into a Flemish and a Walloon part. From 1923, however, what later became provinces each already had their own novitiates; from 1929 they had their own philosophical centres, and from 1948 their own theological centres. Cf. A. M. Bogaerts, *Bouwstoffen voor de geschiedenis der dominikanen in de Nederlanden, A: Dominikanen in België 1835–1958*, Brussels 1969, esp. 188–9.
50 H. Clérissac, *L'Esprit de Saint Dominique: Conférences spiritualles sur l'Ordre de Saint-Dominique*, Saint-Maximin 1924, ET *The Spirit of Saint Dominic: A Retreat for Dominicans*, London 1939.
51 Puchinger, *Toekomst*, 130.
52 D. Lacordaire, *La vie de Saint Dominique*, Paris 1841.
53 Clérissac, *The Spirit of Saint Dominic* (n. 50), 38.
54 Ibid., 50.
55 Ibid,. 51–2; for the Dominican view of grace according to Clérissac cf. ibid., 110–121; here especially 115–19.
56 Ibid., 69; for the respect for individual responsibility and the relativizing of the rules which emerge from it, cf. ibid., 86–8.
57 Thus the title of Schillebeeckx's inaugural lecture as professor at Nijmegen (1958), in which in fact he sums up his theologizing to date; cf. Borgman, 'Cultuurtheologie', esp. 336–41.
58 Matthijs' letter is printed in Schillebeeckx, *Testament*, 193–5.
59 Letter from Mannes Matthijs to Constant Schillebeeckx, dated 10 June 1933 (Arch. 699, among Schillebeeckx's letters home).
60 Oosterhuis and Hoogeveen, *God New*, 9; cf. Schillebeeckx, *Testament*, 21.
61 Letter from the house in Ghent, 31 July and 1 August 1933.
62 Puchinger, *Toekomst*, 130: 133–4.
63 For this development see O. Steggink and K. Waaijman, *Spiritualiteit en mystiek, I: Inleiding*, Nijmegen 1985, 47–54; see R. Garrigou-Lagrange, *Perfection chrétienne et contemplation selon S. Thomas d'Aquin et S. Jean de la Croix*, Rome 1923.
64 Van der Plas, 'Verering' (n. 7), 139.
65 Puchinger, *Toekomst*, 133–4; cf. van der Plas, 'Verering', 139–40.
66 Schillebeeckx, *Testament*, 23. Of course the provincial's remark is a reference to Eccles. 9.4: 'A living dog is better than a dead lion'; Schillebeeckx will have remembered the remark wrongly.
67 Leo XIII, encyclical *Inscrutabili* (1878), nos 2 and 3.
68 Cf. also R. Aubert, 'Die Enzyklika "Aeterni Pastoris" und die weiteren päpstlichen Stellungnahmen zur christlichen Philosophie', in *Christliche Philosophie im katholischen*

Denken des 19. und 20. Jahrhunderts, ed. E. Coreth et al., II. *Rückgriff auf scholastisches Erbe*, Graz, Vienna and Cologne 1988, 310–32.

69 Thibault, *Savoir et pouvoir* (n. 26).

70 For Matthijs' philosophy cf. Struycker Boudier, *Wijsgerig leven*, II, 207–8.

71 Schillebeeckx, *Testament*, 22.

72 M. Matthijs, '"Gods Beeld in den Mensch" voorwerp van de Theologie', *Kultuurleven* 7, 1936, 515–31: 522 and 526.

73 W. G. Gobert, 'Algemene kroniek', *TvF* 34, 1972, 386–97: 387.

74 For the history of philosophy there see Struycker Boudier, *Wijsgerig leven*, VII, 71–5.

75 For the history of the Institut Supérieur de Philosophie/Hoger Instituut voor Wijsbegeerte, see L. De Raeymaeker, *Le cardinal Mercier et l'Institut Supérieur de Philosophie en Louvain*, Louvain 1952; Struycker Boudier, *Wijsgerig leven*, V, 77–146.

76 G. Van Riet, 'Kardinal Désiré Mercier (1851–1926) und das philosophische Institut in Löwen', in *Christliche Philosophie im katholischen Denken* II (n. 68), 206–40.

77 Id., 'L'epistémologie de Mgr Léon Noël', *Revue philos. de Louv.* 52, 1945, 394–415; Struycker Boudier, *Wijsgerig leven*, V, 147–52.

78 N. Balthasar, 'Intuition humaine et expérience métaphysique', *Rev. neo-schol. de philos.* 41, 1938, 262–6. This summarizes a standpoint that Balthasar developed at length in unpublished courses, cf. Struycker Boudier, *Wijsgerig leven*, V, 152–60. For De Petter's picture of Balthasar see his 'In memoriam kan. prof. dr. N. Balthasar', *TvP* 21, 1959, 567–9.

79 J. H. Walgrave, 'Petter, John de', in *Encyclopedie van de Vlaamse Beweging* II, Tielt and Amsterdam 1975, 1242–3: in his commitment to Flemish-language philosophy De Petter trod in the footsteps of his teacher Noel, who drafted the Dutch-language programme of the Higher Instiute of Philosophy.

80 D. M. De Petter, 'Het "Tijdschrift voor filosofie" 1939–63', *TvP* 26, 1964, 303–11; cf. also C. E. M Struycker Boudier, 'Tijdschrift voor filosofie vijftig jaar', ibid., 51, 1989, 64–95.

81 'Verantwoording', *TvP* 1, 1939, 3–4.

82 The articles on implicit intuitition are collected in D. M. de Petter, *Begrip en werkelijkheid*. See also D. Scheltens, 'De filosofie van p. D. M. De Petter', *TvP* 33, 1971, 439–505; Struycker Boudier, *Wijsgerig leven* II, 78–90; S. van Erp, *Intentionaliteit en intuitie: De Petters formuliering van de realistische metafysica tegen de achterground van de 'traditionele' metafysica en de husserlianse fenomenologie* (doctoral script, theological faculty), Tilburg 1995.

83 Puchinger, *Toekomst*, 135.

84 Ibid.

85 Oosterhuis and Hoogeveen, *God New*, 13.

86 'Als de ziele luistert ... ', *Biekorf*, 1936–37. 3: the pages of the original article are not numbered; page numbering has been added in pencil on the copy in Arch. 3204. In the following discussion the page numbers are given in brackets in the text.

87 Dating from 1859; see G. Gezelle, *Verzamelde dichtwerk* II, ed. J. Noeta, Antwerp and Amsterdam 1980, 180.

88 Ibid., 2–3: Schillebeeckx quotes, in Greek, from Aristotle, *Metaphysics* XII, 1072 b. 24–27.

89 It is along the lines of 'When the soul listens' when in a later article ('Zijnsbewustzijn en rationaliteit', *Biekorf,* 1938–9, no. 3, 109–71: 118; Arch. 3208) he explicitly calls philosophy a *scientia subalternata*, in other words a science which is dependent on the sense experience which precedes it and constantly 'lingers'. Thomas Aquinas emphatically called theology such a dependent science (*scientia subalternata*), based on faith and the linguistic expression of faith in the biblical and church tradition, cf. *Summa theol.* I, q. 1, art. 2.

90 H. M. Schillebeeckx, 'Voor-socratische denkers', *Biekorf*, 1937–38, no. 3, 22pp.; id., 'Voor-socratische denkers (slot)', ibid., no. 4, 22pp (copy – some of which is very difficult to read, Arch. 3207).

91 Cf. Oosterhuis and Hoogeveen, *God New*, 26. The reference is to H. M. Schillebeeckx, 'Zijnsbewustsein en rationaliteit', *Biekorf*, 1938–39, 109–71 (Arch. 3208); in the following discussion the page numbers are given in brackets in the text.

92 'Impliciete intuitie' (1939), in De Petter, *Begrip*, 25–43. Struycker Boudier calls this 'one of the most influential writings of neo-Thomism in the Low Countries by the Sea', which also became known 'far outside the frontiers of the Netherlands and Belgium' (*Wijsgerig leven* II, 80).

93 No names of contemporary philosophers are given in the article, but one should probably think of thought along the lines of the French philosopher Henri Bergson (1859–1941), who was especially influential around this time.

94 So to my mind there is a difference between the approaches of De Petter and Schillebeeckx from the very beginning. Whereas the former above all addressed the *possibility* of knowledge of God, the latter was above all concerned with the *comprehensiveness* of knowledge of God and thus of the breadth of the awareness of God, philosophy orientated on God and – later – theology. This also explains why at a later stage their ways parted. Both De Petter and the Edward Schillebeeckx of the period in question are idealists in the sense that for them being is ultimately spiritual, and direct spiritual contact is possible. Moreover, both begin from the assumption that, as Schillebeeckx writes ('Zijnsbewustsein', 139), 'in the consciousness of being, the being-known of what is known is "totally identical" with what is known'. The first represents a neglect of the importance of the material and the historical and sees the whole of reality as an embodiment of what are in principle static 'ideas'; Schillebeeckx would later try to correct this by attaching great importance to historical human praxis, which is always concrete and material. The second implies that at the deepest level criticism of sense experience is impossible and superfluous, that knowledge cannot really grow or change, and that what would later come to be seen as necessary 'ideological criticism' is unthinkable: Schillebeeckx would later correct this with the idea of the experience of contrast. In connection with the increased importance of praxis and the experience of contrast in his thought he would emphatically dissociate himself from thought along the lines of De Petter (*Jesus*, 618).

95 Puchinger, *Toekomst*, 136; the letter quoted is dated '28 October 1938'. His recollection that he had his first ecumenical contacts in this camp – 'because before that I had never met a Protestant Christian' – thus seems to be a poetic exaggeration.

96 Cf. 'Persoon en genade (1)', *Biekorf*, 1939/40, no. 2, here 58–61 (Arch. 3209). In the following discussion page numbers are again given in brackets in the text.

97 In Puchinger, *Toekomst*, 135, Schillebeeckx speaks of his 'final essay on philosophy', which was about the 'correlation between word and answer'. 'Persoon en genade' is the only text preserved in the Schillebeeckx archive to which this characterization can relate, but the dating of it, the framework and the fact that a second part which never appeared is announced at the end make it improbable that this is in fact the essay. Schillebeeckx talks at the same point about an essay 'on *ousia*, the term for substance in Aristotle'. Here he seems to be referring to 'When the soul listens', but this nowhere has the characteristics of an essay.

98 Cf. Thomas, *Summa theol.* I, q. 12, art. 8.

99 Cf. A. H. Maltha and R. W. Thuys, *Katholieke dogmatiek*, Roermond and Maaseik 1951, 59–61.

100 Cf. already 'Zijnsbewustzijn' (n. 91), 167: ' ... in my view the *praeambula fidei* lies not so much in the rational aspect of our integral consciousness as in the intuitive transcendental consciousness of it. Only on the basis of this awareness of transcendentalia – as a whole, relating to the *verum, bonum* and *divinum* – can we speak of a *desiderium naturale*.' 'Persoon en genade' works out this notion.

101 Ibid., 113–16; for 'nature' as 'advent: a preparation for the coming of God', cf. ibid., 101.

102 H. M. Schillebeeckx, 'Oorlogsmenschen', *Biekorf*, 1940–41, 236–43 (Arch. 3210).

103 Schillebeeckx, *Testament*, 24.

104 Puchinger, *Toekomst*, 133.

105 Struycker Boudier, *Wijsgerig leven* II, 150; see also R. Vanlandschoot, 'Perquy, Jules', in *Encyclopedie van de Vlaamse Beweging*, II (n. 79), 1194.

106 Leprieur, *Rome*, 23, 25; cf. Schillebeeckx, *Testament*, 196 n. 2. For Rutten, see C. Van Gestel, 'Rutten, Georges Albert', in *Encyclopedie* II (n. 79), 1371; Struycker Boudier, *Wijsgerig leven* II, 150–1.

107 Cf. Puchinger, *Toekomst*, 137; Schillebeeckx, *Testament*, 25. For Martin, see Struycker Boudier, *Wijsgerig leven* II, 191–3.

108 Oosterhuis and Hoogeveen, *God New*, 13; moreover, as early as 1939 Schillebeeckx mentioned Adam as a theologian whom he admired because of his capacity to do justice to human experience in theology, 'Persoon en genade (1)' (n. 96), 97.

109 R. Aubert, 'Karl Adam', in *Tendenzen der Theologie im 20.Jahrhundert*, ed. H. J. Schultz, Stuttgart, etc. 1966, 156–62; H. Kreidler, *Eine Theologie des Lebens: Grundzüge im theologischen Denken Karl Adams*, Mainz 1988.

110 Oosterhuis and Hoogeveen, *God New*, 13; for Schillebeeckx's attitude to Karl Adam's theology cf. K. A. Krieg, *Karl Adam: Catholicism in German Culture*, Notre Dame and London 1992, 81–3, 102–6.

111 Thus, J. H. Walgrave, 'In memoriam pater J. D. Maes', *TvP* 7, 1945, 209–11: 209; cf. also id., 'Een levenswekker, pater J. Maes', *Kultuurleven* 12, 1945, 272–5; Struycker Boudier, *Wijsgerig leven* II, 45–7.

112 P. Rousselot, *L'intellectualisme de Saint Thomas*, Paris 1924, 1936; for his view see J. M. McDermott, 'Pierre Rousselot (1878–1915)', in *Christliche Philosophie* II (n.68), 437–52.

113 Oosterhuis and Hoogeveen, *God New*, 13.

114 The measure against De Petter was part of a greater offensive by the Holy Office of the time against unscholastic, 'modernist' and 'subjectivist' Catholic thinkers, among which it included M.-D. Chenu, R. Draguet and L. Charlier. For the background cf. E. Fouilloux, 'Le Saulchoir en procès (1937–42)', in M.-D. Chenu, *Une école théologique: le Saulchoir*, Paris 1985, 37–59.

115 Quotations from Puchinger, *Toekomst*, 138; Schillebeeckx, *Testament*, 26.

116 Puchinger, *Toekomst*, 137. Here Schillebeeckx wrongly gives the title of Adam's speech from memory as 'Christianity in the New Order'. The text of the speech was distributed by the former 'Government Counsellor' Baron Leopold von Nagal, who agreed with Adam's position; cf. J. Aretz, *Katholische Arbeiterbewegung und Nationalsozialismus: Der Verband katholischer Arbeiter- und Knabenvereine Westdeutschlands 1923–1945*, Mainz 1978, 225–6. It is no longer possible to discover how and precisely when the text came into Schillebeeckx's hands.

117 Cf. H. Kreidler, 'Karl Adam und der Nationalsozialismus', *Rottenburger Jahrb. f. Kirchengeschichte* 2, 1983, 129–40; Krieg, *Karl Adam* (n. 110), 107–36.

118 K. Adam, 'Deutsches Volkstum und katholisches Christentum', *Theologische Quartalschrift* 114, 1933, 40–63: 41–2; however, the sequel to his article which was announced never appeared. Cf. K. Scholder, *The Churches and the Third Reich*, I: *Prehistory and Time of Illusions, 1918–1934*, London and Philadelphia 1985, 427–30.

119 Adam's speech appeared in two parts in *Deutsches Volksblatt* of 23 and 24 January 1934. Here I am quoting from Kreidler, *Theologie des Lebens* (n. 109), 133.

120 That is indeed suggested by Scholder, *Churches and the Third Reich* (n. 118), 427–30. For the conflict between Adam and the Party see Kreidler, 'Karl Adam' (n. 117) and K. Scholder, *The Churches and the Third Reich*, II, London and Philadelphia 1988, 106–8.

121 Quoted from Kreidler, 'Karl Adam' (n. 117), 137.

122 Puchinger, *Toekomst*, 137–8.

123 H. M. Schillebeeckx, 'Natuur en bovennatuur', *Biekorf*, 1942, and ibid., 1943, nos 4 and 5. I am quoting the paginated version from Arch. 523. On the page after the title page, as a sub-title, there are the words 'A theological value judgement on today's renewed interest in the values of nature and culture'. In what follows page references are given in brackets in the text.

124 Thus Kreidler, 'Karl Adam' (n. 117), 138.

125 For this characterization of Adam as a 'master of presentation' see F. Hoffmann, 'Geleitwort', in K. Adam, *Gesammelte Aufsätze zur Dogmengeschichte und Theologie der Gegenwart*, Augsburg 1936, 5–16: 5; for the characterization of his rhetoric see Karl Barth, *Church Dogmatics* I/2, Edinburgh 1956, 145.

126 Quoted from 'Die geistliche Lage der deutschen Katholizismus', after Kreidler, 'Karl Adam' (n. 117), 207.

127 Ibid., 70, 131, 140–2.

128 Ibid., 150–5. Five years earlier, in 1937, Schillebeeckx had written an article for *Biekorf* under the title 'The Character of Truth in the Student Movement', in which he took over from the militant Flemish Dominican L. J. Callewaert (1886–1964) the ideal of 'the harmony between a healthily normal natural Flanders and a healthily normal super-natural Flanders'. From this he concluded that there had to be an effort to achieve a 'Dutch order' in the state as well, 'so that in it the supernatural could flourish to the highest degree, for a nature which is not shrivelled up or contorted is the most submissive possibility of sparkling supernature'. So here to some degree he revised his earlier standpoint.

129 Id., 'Persoon en genade (1)' (n. 96), 92.

130 For the shift compared with the 1939/40 article cf. ibid., 58 n. 1.

131 Though Karl Adam had a view of modern culture which one can certainly call theological: taking the romantic conservative line of Catholic Tübingen, he thought that modernity meant decay, loss of fellowship and religious feeling (cf. T. Ruster, *Die verlorene Nützlichkeit der Religion: Katholizismus und Moderne in der Weimarer Republik*, Paderborn, etc. 1994, 197–201; Krieg, 'Karl Adam' [n. 110], 159–78). He recognized precisely this criticism and the synthetic force of what in his view should be the Catholic answer in National Socialism, and that attracted him. However, in Adam this positive integrating force of Catholicism is not given any theological content, and that is precisely what Schillebeeckx was criticizing.

132 Puchinger, *Toekomst*, 138.

133 H. M. Schillebeeckx, *De zondige voor-geschiedenis van het christendom volgens Sint Paulus*, 1941–2 lectorate thesis, Louvain; the foreword is dated 11 November 1942 (Arch. 753). Again page numbers are given in brackets in the discussion in the text.

134 Id., 'Natuur en bovennatuur' (n.123), 60–1.

135 *De zondige voor-geschiedenis* (n.133), III and II.

136 Especially after the appearance in 1943 of Pius XII's encyclical *Divino afflante spiritu*. For the history of Catholic exegesis cf. F. Mussner, *Geschichte der Hermeneutik: Von Schleiermacher bis zur Gegenwart* (= Handbuch der Dogmengeschichte I/3c), Freiburg, Basel and Vienna 1970, esp. 22–34.

137 For this idea among people within Catholic Action and the Catholic workers' movement see E. Tisserant, 'Préface', in F. Amiot, *L'enseignement de Saint Paul*, I, Paris 1938, vii–x: vii.

138 Id., 'Natuur en bovennatuur' (n. 123), 25.

139 The text of this address ('Naar een levenstheologie?') is in Arch. 358. In the discussion the page numbers are given in brackets in the text.

140 For this picture of developments in Catholic theology cf. Schoof, *Breakthrough*, passim; for kerygmatic theology or the theology of proclamation see 101–2. For the contemporary

discussion cf. E. Kappler, *Die Verkündigungstheologie: Gotteswort auf Lehrstuhl und Kanzel*, Fribourg CH 1949.

141 J. A. Jungmann, *Die Frohbotschaft und unsere Glaubensverkündigung*, Regensburg 1936, 60.

142 H. Rahner, *Eine Theologie der Verkündigung*, Freiburg im Breisgau 1939, 10–11.

143 See almost 15 years later his 'Kerugmatische theologie', in *Theologische woordenboek* 2, 1957, 1779–81.

144 G. Koepgen, *Die Gnosis des Christentums* (1939), Salzburg and Leipzig 1940, 9–10.

145 Cf. A. van Harskamp, *Theologie: tekst in context. Op zoek naar de methode van ideologiekritische analyse van de theologie*, Nijmegen 1986, 326–52; cf. J. A. Möhler, *Die Einheit in der Kirche* (1825), ed. J. R. Geiselmann, Cologne and Olten 1957.

146 Schillebeeckx, 'Naar een levenstheologie?', 1 (n. 139).

147 Ibid., 0; the pages of the typescript in the Schillebeeckx archive are numbered in pencil from 2 to 21. Before them are two unnumbered sheets which I refer to as pp. 0 and 1 respectively, also in the text.

148 The description of faith as *cum assensione cogitare* comes from Thomas, *Summa theol.* II–II, q. 2, art.1. It looks very much as if Schillebeeckx bases his analysis of Thomas in 'Naar een levenstheologie?' on an article by M.-D. Chenu, 'La psychologie de la foi dans la théologie du XIIIe siècle: Genèse de la doctrine de S. Thomas, IIa, IIae, q. 2, a. 1' (1932), in id., *La parole de Dieu*, I: *La foi dans l'intelligence*, Paris 1964, 77–104, which he does not identify.

149 The quotation comes from *I Sent.*q. 1 art. 2; the analysis is above all based on *Summa theol.* I, q.1, art.2

150 In this way Schillebeeckx himself (ibid., 11–13) indicated that he also wanted to follow Thomas's argument (*Summa theol.* II-II, q.1, art. 2) that, seen from the object, faith only has a simple, non-composite object, namely God, but seen from the believer it has a composite object, namely the different statements which are made about God. Here he refers to M.-D. Chenu, 'Contribution à l'histoire du traité de la foi: Commentaire historique de IIa IIae, q.1, a. 2' (1923), reprinted in *La parole de Dieu*, I (n. 147), 31–50. Without explicitly saying so, he also takes up Thomas's conviction (ibid., I, q. 1, art. 4) that theology is at the same time both a practical and a speculative science, but more a speculative science because it is orientated more on the knowledge of divine things than on human action, and sees the latter only as a means and a way to the perfect knowledge of God, in which human bliss consists.

151 'Naar een levenstheologie?' (n. 139), 19–20. The last sentence originally contained the word 'break'; this has been crossed out and altered to 'tension'.

152 For Chenu's view of Thomas cf. Van den Hoogen, *Chenu*, 195–213.

153 Schillebeeckx, *Testament*, 27.

CHAPTER 2

1 E. Canetti, *Auto-da-fé* (1935), London 1995.

2 W. Mehring, *Die verlorene Bibliothek: Autobiographie einer Kultur*, Düsseldorf 1978.

3 J. P. Sartre, *Nausea* (1938), Harmondsworth 1990.

4 J. P. Sartre, *Being and Nothingness: An Essay in Phenomenological Ontology* (1943), London 1990.

5 A study which puts existentialism in the context of developments in European culture has yet to be written. For want of anything better see the location of existentialism within the context of the history of modernity, as this appeared in intensified form after the Second

World War: W. Barrett, *Irrational Man: A Study of Existential Philosophy* (1958), London 1972, 3–57. For the attempts at a Christian (re)interpretation of existentialism cf. C. E. M. Struycker Boudier, 'Fenomenologie en existentiefilosofie in Nederland en België', *Ons erfdeel* 26, 1983, 340–8.

6   H. Van Herreweghen, 'Getuigenis 1950: De poëzie', in *V. E. V.-Berichten*, August 1950, quoted in H. Brems, *Analyse van een malaise: Het jongerenprobleem in de Vlaamse poëzie 1945–1950*, Louvain 1988, 28, 59–60.

7   G. Walschap, 'Wat willen de jongeren?', *Dietsche Warande & Belfort* 45, 1945, 161–4, quoted in Brems, *Analyse van een malaise* (n. 6), 10, 31; cf. id., 'Waar blijven de jongeren', ibid. 36, 1936, 3–6. Walschap explained his public departure from Catholicism in *Vaarwel dan*, Rotterdam 1940.

8   P. Van Keymeulen, 'Wij, jongeren', *De faun* 1, 1945, no. 1, 1–3; quoted in Brems, *Analyse van een malaise* (n. 6), 13.

9   Quotations from G. Michiels, 'Het standpunt der jongeren', *Nieuwe stemmen* 1, 1944–5, no. 2, 26–9; H. Brands, 'Wij, jongeren', ibid., no. 4/5, 58–9; G. Michiels, 'Wat de jongeren willen', ibid., 2, 1945–6, no. 1, 6–12; H. Schoofs, 'Idealisme en romantiek', ibid., no. 2, 48–50, quoted in Brems, *Analyse van een malaise* (n. 6), 19–21, 33–5.

10   Schillebeeckx, 'Situatie', 84: in the discussion of this text which follows, page references are given in brackets.

11   Ibid., 88–9: 'Although the life of grace is infinitely more precious and although great holiness has flourished in wrecks of human nature, now we must emphasize the value of the natural, its intrinsic value, but also its value as a vehicle of grace. Therefore we unreservedly accept earthly life in all its goodness and all its beauty.'

12   Cf. 'Natuur en bovennatuur', *Biekorf*, 1942, 9.

13   For this discussion cf. F. W. Graf and K. Tanner, 'Kultuur II: Theologiegeschichtlich', *Theologische Realenzyklopädie* 20, 1990, 187–209. For Tillich's theology of culture cf. especially his article 'Über die Idee einer Theologie der Kultur', in id., *Die religiöse Substanz der Kultur: Schriften zur Theologie der Kultur*, Stuttgart 1967, 13–31; also 'Religion und Kultur' (ibid., 82–93); 'Über die Grenzen von Religion und Kultur' (ibid., 94–9); 'Aspekte einer religiösen Analyse der Kultur' (ibid., 100–9), from 1948, 1954 and 1959.

14   G. Thils, *Théologie des réalités terrestres, I. Préludes*, Bruges 1947; *II. Théologie de l'histoire*, Bruges 1949; for Thils' work cf. R. Gibellini, *Handbuch der Theologie im 20. Jahrhundert*, Regensburg 1995, 254–8; Schillebeeckx reviewed Thils' book in *TGL* 6, 1950, 430–1.

15   A. Dondeyne, 'Religieuze en aardse mystiek', *Kultuurleven* 12, 1945, 35–41. For Dondeyne's philosophy cf. Struycker Boudier, *Wijsgerig leven* V, 204–12. Schillebeeckx later expressed great appreciation of Dondeyne: 'Ter school bij prof. A. Dondeyne', *TvT* 2, 162, 78–83, in fact an extensive, largely positive review of his *Geloof en wereld*, Baarn 1961. B. J. DeClercq informed me that at this time Dondeyne regularly came to the Louvain Dominicans 'to say mass'.

16   P. Wust, *Die Rückkehr des deutschen Katholizismus aus der Exil*, ed. K. Hoeber, Düsseldorf 1926.

17   J. Maritain, *Art et scolastique*, Paris 1920; id., *Primauté du spirituel*, Paris 1927; id., *Integral Humanism* (1936), Notre Dame 1996. For this cf. above all Schoof, *Breakthrough*, esp. 72–145; C. Moeller, 'Die Theologie angesichts der Entwicklung der Literatur und des Menschenbildes', *Bilanz* I, 108–45; R. Aubert, 'Die Theologie während der ersten Hälfte des 20. Jahrhunderts', ibid. II, 7–70. For the French theology which influenced Schillebeeckx most strongly and for French Catholicism see A. Louis, *Le renouveau catholique en France*, Paris 1949; C. Frey, *Mysterium der Kirche. Öffnung zur Welt: Zwei Aspekte der Erneuerung französischer katholischer Theologie*, Göttingen 1969, 28–90; C. Moeller, *Littérature du XXe siècle et christianisme*, I-V, Tournai 1953–75.

18 'Ter school bij prof. Dondeyne' (n. 15), 82.

19 For the Council as a reorientation of the relationship between the Catholic church and modernity cf. *Vatikanum II und Modernisierung: Historische, theologische und soziologische Perspektiven*, ed. F.-X. Kaufmann and A. Zingerle, Paderborn 1996, and especially F.-X. Kaufmann, 'Zur Einführung: Probleme und Wege einer historische Einschätzung des II. Vatikanischen Konzils' (9–34).

20 G. Vandewalle, 'De economische ontwikkeling in België 1945–1980', in *Algemene geschiedenis der Nederlanden, XV: Nieuwste tijd*, Haarlem 1982, 116–58: 116–17.

21 Cf. J. Beaufrays, *Les parties catholiques en Belgique et aux Pays-Bas, 1918–1958*, Brussels 1958, 129–32, 360–5; T. Luykx, *Politieke geschiedenis van België, II. Van 1944–1977*, Amsterdam and Brussels ⁴1978, 431–40; E. Witte, 'Het maatschappelijk-politieke leven in België 1945–1980', in *Algemene geschiedenis der Nederlanden*, XV (n. 30), 240–68: 205–12; E. H. Kossmann, *De lage landen 1780–1980: Twee eeuwen Nederland en België, II: 1914–1980*, Amsterdam and Brussels 1986, 210–20; *Tussen staat en maatschappij: 1945–1995 Christen-Democratie in België*, ed. W. Dewachter, Tielt 1995, esp. 13–42.

22 Quoted in R. Vermeire, 'Katholieken en politiek: Na de tweede wereldoorlog', in *De kerk in Vlaanderen: Pastoraal-sociologische studie van het leven en de structuur der kerk*, ed. J. Kerkhofs and J. Van Houtte, Tielt and The Hague 1962, 585–601: 589.

23 Luykx, *Politische geschiedenis van België II* (n. 21), 452–7; Witte, 'Het maatschappelijk-politieke leven in België 1945–1980' (n. 21), 214–17.

24 For a survey of the developments at the time of the monarchy question cf. Luykx, *Politische geschiedenis van België II* (n. 21), 441–52; Witte, 'Het maatschappelijk-politieke leven in België 1945–1980' (n. 21), 217–22; Kossmann, *De lage landen 1780–1980* (n. 21), 224–30.

25 For this cf. J. Stengers, *Léopold III et le gouvernement: Les deux politiques belges de 1940*, Paris 1980; J. Girard-Libois and J. Gotowitch, *Leopold III: L'an 40 à l'éffacement*, Brussels ²1991; J. Velaers and H. Van Goethem, *Leopold III: De koning, het land, de oorlog*, Tielt 1994. For the view of the king among Catholics see M. Van den Wijngaert, *Een koning geloofd, gelaakt, verloochend: De evolutie van de stemming onder de katholieke bevolking ten aanzien van Leopold III tijdens de bezetting (1940–1944)*, Louvain 1984.

26 Van Herreweghen, 'Getuigenis 1950' (n. 6), quoted in Brems, *Analyse van een malaise* (n. 6), 28.

27 *Thomistisch Tijdschrift voor Katholiek Kultuurleven* I, 1930, 3–4.

28 Pius XI, *Quas primas* (1925), 45; for 'Christ the King' see no. 42.

29 Pius XI, encyclical *Ubi arcano Dei* (1922), esp. nos 55–6.

30 Pius X, encyclical *Il fermo proposito* (1905), no. 13.

31 Ibid., no. 12.

32 Ibid., no. 38; for the church-political background see R. Aubert, *De kerk van de crisis van 1848 tot Vaticanum II*, Bussum 1974, 167–72.

33 Cf. Pius XI's letter to Cardinal Van Roey, Archbishop of Malines (15 August 1928), in *AAS* 20, 1928, 295–6; id., letter to Cardinal A. Bertram, Archbishop of Breslau (13 November 1928), ibid., 384–7; id., letter to Cardinal P. Segura, Archbishop of Toledo (6 November 1929); ibid., 21, 1929, 664–8; for these letters, emphatically meant as further instruction on the establishment of Catholic Action, cf. P. de Haan, *Van volgzame elite-strijder tot kritische gelovige: Geschiedenis van de Katholieke Actie in Nederland (1934–1966)*, Nijmegen 1994, 20–2.

34 E. Gerard, 'Aanpassing in crisistijd (1921–1944)', in *De christelijke arbeidersbeweging in België*, I, ed. E. Gerard, Louvain 1991, 172–243, esp. 186–90, on 'Catholic action with or without initial capitals?'

35 Here Cardijn trod in the footsteps of the famous Adolf Daens, the priest who under the inspiration of *Rerum novarum* in 1893 established the Christian Popular Party in Okegem

near Ninove out of discontent with the social conservatism of the Catholic Party and out of indignation about the fate of the workers. As a result he got into difficulties with his bishop and with Rome; cf. F.-J.Verdoodt, *De zaak Daens: Een priester tussen kerk en christen-democratie*, Louvain 1993. Cardijn had applauded Daens in Halle, where he grew up.

36 For Cardijn's biography cf. M. Fievez and J. Meert, *Cardijn* (1969), Brussels 1978, and M. Van Roey, *Cardijn*, Brussels 1972; both are written out of admiration. Cf. also F. Hugaerts, 'Cardijn, Josef Léon Marie', in *Encyclopédie van de Vlaams beweging* 1, 1973, 274–5.

37 Cf. L. Vos, 'Het maatschappijbeeld van Cardijn tussen twee wereldoorlogen', in *Cardijn: een mens, een beweging/un homme, un mouvement*, Louvain 1983, 149–79, who goes at length into the shifts in Cardijn's view of society and the role of theology in it; there are also quotations of Cardijn, often from unpublished works or works published only in KAJ circles. At the same time cf. L. Preneel, 'Kerkbeeld en kerkbeleving in de publicaties van Cardijn', ibid., 45–63; E. Gerard, 'Cardijn, arbeidersbeweging en katholieke actie (1918–1945)', ibid., 119–45.

38 J. H. Walgrave, 'Oriënteering', *Kultuurleven* 12, 1945, 16.

39 Editorial, 'Kultuurleven', ibid., 6.

40 Ibid.

41 For biographical details see 'Biografie', in J. H. Walgrave, *Selected Writings –thematische geschriften*, ed. G. De Schrijver and J. Kelly, Louvain 1982, IX–X.

42 J. H. Walgrave, *Kardinaal Newman's theorie over de ontwikkeling van het dogma in het licht van zijn kennisleer en zijn apologetiek*, Antwerp 1944; for Walgrave's view of Newman see G. De Schrijver, 'De theoloog Walgrave', in Walgrave, *Selected Writings* (n. 41), XI–XXVI: XVIII–XXI, Struyker Boudier, *Wijsgerig leven* II, 94–5.

43 Walgrave generally follows De Petter's interpretation of Thomas in his 'Zelfkennis en innerlijke ervaring bij Sint-Thomas', *TvP* 9, 1947, 3–62: 61 n. 132. Cf. also his 'De benadering van de Godsvraag door Thomas van Aquino', where he points out that in the use that Thomas makes of conceptual notions 'he always thinks beyond them', *Alg. Ned. ts. v. wijsbeg.* 66, 1974, 279–86: 284.

44 He found this synthesis in Newman and was to work it out systematically only much later by means of a precise interpretation of the work of Thomas Aquinas; cf. especially his study 'Het natuurverlangen en de Godsaanschouwing bij Thomas van Aquino', *TvF* 36, 1974, 232–66, and 'The Use of Philosophy in the Theology of Thomas Aquinas', in *Aquinas and the Problems of his Time*, Louvain 1976, 181–93; cf. De Schrijver, 'De theoloog Walgrave' (n. 42), XV–XVIII; Struycker Boudier, *Wijsgerig leven* II, 96–9. Whereas twenty years earlier Schillebeeckx had looked for openings in Thomas's work to human experience and the world, in the period of Vatican II Walgrave evidently again sought orientation in Thomas's work in what he saw as a crisis situation for faith and theology, as is evident from his *Geloof en theologie in de crisis*, Kasterlee 1966.

45 Cf. the collection of a number of these articles under the title *Op menselijk grondslag: Christelijke verantwoording van de cultuur*, Antwerp 1959. The 'Humanus' rubric was clearly modelled on a similar one in the sister journal *La vie intellectuelle*, in which the commentary at the time appeared with the signature 'Christianus'.

46 Struycker Boudier mentions as those who were closely involved with *Kultuurleven* the Dominicans M. Goetstouwer (cf. ibid., 171) and V. Walgrave (cf. ibid., 174) , the Capuchin M. Wildiers (id., *Wijsgerig leven* III, 71–5) and the secular priests V. Leemans (ibid. VII, 231–7) and A. Kriekemans (ibid. V, 161–2).

47 Walgrave, 'Oriënteering' (n. 38), 16 and 19.

48 Ibid., 9 and 15. For Walgrave as a social philosopher cf. Struycker Boudier, *Wijsgerig leven* II, 170–4; T. Salemink, *Katholieke kritiek op het kapitalisme 1891–1991: Honderd jaar*

debat over vrije markt en verzorgingsstaat, Amersfoort and Louvain 1991, 131–6.

49   J. H. Walgrave, 'Humanisme', in *De katholieke encyclopedie* 12, 1952, 766.

50   Ibid., 'Dienst aan het Woord in de spanning tussen gezag en vrijheid', in 'De positie van de theoloog: Sonderingen – voor Schillebeeckx' (= *TvT* 14, 1974, no. 4), 432–8.

51   H. Schillebeeckx, 'Pogingen tot een concrete uitwerking van een lekenspiritualiteit', *TGL* 8, 1952, 644–56, 655–6; here he reviews Walgrave's *Op menselijke grondslag* (n. 45).

52   P. Hoogeveen and F. Maas, 'Ik hoop op nieuwe dingen: Een gesprek met Edward Schillebeeckx', *TGL* 50, 1994, 181–90: 184.

53   In *Keesings historisch archief* 12, 1958, 13975.

54   J. Semprun, *Schrijven of leven: Autobiografie,* Amsterdam 1996 (originally 1994), 131.

55   Cf. also S. Dresden, *Vervolging, vernietiging, literatuur,* Amsterdam 1991.

56   'Situatie', 586: in the text, page references are given in brackets.

57   For the anthropology of neoscholasticism cf. Maltha and Thuys, *Dogmatiek,* 276–93. For the quotation see 'Persoon en personalisiering', in De Petter, *Begrip,* 186–208: 204. In this article, which dates from 1948, De Petter develops a view of culture very akin to that of Schillebeeckx's 'Situatie'.

58   On 23 September 1995, in a lecture in Bruges, (published as 'Cultuur als grensverleggende beweging', in *Cultuur als grensverleggende beweging,* n.d., n.p., 9–30: 12), Schillebeeckx disclosed that 'noble and good humanity' (in Dutch this was a single word, 'schoon-menselijkheid') was a translation of the Greek *kalokagathia,* literally 'beautiful and good'. According to Aristotle (*Magna moralia* $1207^b 20 - 1208^c 4$), *kalokagathos* denotes someone who is perfect in the moral sense, in other words someone for whom things are noble which are also noble in the absolute sense, and things are good which are also good in the absolute sense.

59   For original sin cf. Maltha and Thuys, *Dogmatiek* (n. 57), 309–27.

60   It is part of the classic Catholic definition of original sin at the Council of Trent that as a consequence of Adam's transgression of God's commandment human beings 'as a whole have arrived at a worse condition in soul and body' (Denzinger 1511). Schillebeeckx thus in fact changed this into the positive statement that through grace human beings arrived at a better condition 'as a whole in soul and body'.

61   H. M. Schillebeeckx, 'Natuur en bovennatur', *Biekorf,* 1942, no number, and 1943, no. 4/ 5, here p. 196.

62   The quotation at the head of this chapter is also taken from here. Following Thomas Aquinas (*Summa theol.* I-II, q. 6, art. 4; q. 28, art. 2; q. 65, art. 5), here Schillebeeckx transposes Aristotle's reflections on friendship (*Nicomachean Ethics* VIII–IX) to *caritas* as friendship between God and human beings.

63   The subtitle of 'Christelijke situatie III' is 'Towards a solution: supernatural exclusivism'.

64   H.-M. Schillebeeckx, 'Considérations autour du sacrifice d'Abraham', *Vie Spirituelle* 75, 1946, 45–59: 47–8.

65   H. Schillebeeckx, 'Humble Humanism' (1949), reprinted in *World and Church,* 19–31: 28–31.

66   The article 'Humble Humanism' (n. 65) is to be understood as an attempt to give the ascetic elements in the Christian tradition a place within Schillebeeckx's project on the theology of culture; the article 'De ascetische toeleg van de kloosterling' (*TGL* 3, 1947, 1,302–20) is an attempt to do the same thing with the ascetic elements in the monastic tradition.

67   Cf. A. Rigobello, 'Jacques Maritain (1882–1973)', in *Christliche Philosophie im katholischen Denken des 19. und 20. Jahrhunderts,* II, ed. E. Coreth et al., Graz, Vienna and Cologne 1988, 493–528: the quotation from N. Berdyaev appears in *Essai d'autobiographie spirituelle,* Paris 1958, 331.

68   Pastoral Constitution *Gaudium et spes,* nos 53, 57. Maritain is mentioned twice (nos 17, 44)

in Paul VI's encyclical *Populorum progressio* (1967) on the development of the peoples, alongside other authors like L. J. Lebret and M.-D. Chenu, and his view of integral humanism is in fact adopted as the starting point of church doctrine on the relationship with culture. For Maritain's influence on church doctrine see M.-J. Nicolas, 'Jacques Maritain ed il Magistero della Chiesa', in *Jacques Maritain e la società contemporanea*, ed. R. Papini, Milan 1978, 36–49, esp. 42–9.

69 J. Maritain, *Art et scolastique*, 1920; id., *True Humanism*, London 1938.

70 J. Maritain, 'Quelques réflexions sur l'art réligieux', *De gemeenschap* 1, 1925, 10–11, 63–6 (it appeared earlier in *Les cahiers catholiques* 5, 1924, 2943–9) is the essay included from the third impression on in *Art et scolastique*, Paris 1936, and as such reprinted in J. Maritain and R. Maritain, *Oeuvres complètes, 1: Oeuvres de Jacques Maritain, 1906–20*, Fribourg and Paris 1986, 716–23: 718, 722–3. For the significance of Maritain in the Netherlands see F. Ruiter and W. Smulders, *Literatuur en moderniteit in Nederland 1840–1990*, Amsterdam 1996, 227–43. For Maritain's philosophy and aesthetics cf. J. M. Dunaway, *Jacques Maritain*, Boston 1978; for his view of art see also P. Nickl, *Jacques Maritain: Eine Einführung in Leben und Werk*, Paderborn 1992, 51–71. It is indicative of his influence that Maritain's philosophy brought together three Dutch writers: the non-Catholic Hendrik Marsman, the traditional Catholic Gerard Bruning and the modern Catholic Jan Engelman, who devised the plan of setting up a literary journal on the basis of his philosophy. According to Ruiter amd Smulders, this was even going to be called *Maritain*: here they refer to J. Goedegebuure, *Op zoek naar een bezield verband: De literaire en maatschappelijke opvattingen van H. Marsman in de context van zijn tijd*, Amsterdam 1981, I, 216, but this does not mention the name of the journal.

71 Maritain, *True Humanism* (n. 69), esp. 64–7.

72 Ibid., 66–7.

73 Schillebeeckx, 'Considérations' (n. 64), 47.

74 Maritain, *True Humanism* (n. 69), xii. For the content and significance of this book cf. H. Opdebeeck, '1936 – "Humanisme Intégral" van Jacques Maritain: Pleidooi voor een profaan-christelijke cultuur', in *Ex Libris van de filosofie van de 20ste eeuw*, 265–77.

75 For Maritain's social and political philosophy see H. Bars, *La politique selon Jacques Maritain*, Paris 1961; Nickl, *Jacques Maritain* (n. 70), 81–110.

76 Schillebeeckx, 'Situatie', 608.

77 Id., 'Humble Humanism' (n. 65), 30.

78 Schillebeeckx, 'Pogingen tot een concrete uitwerking' (n. 51), 655–6.

79 Schillebeeckx calls the position which he advocates in 1949 emphatically 'not supernatural exclusivism but supernatural absolutism', because 'exclusivism' suggests that the natural is excluded, and the point is that it is viewed in the light of the supernatural. According to his theology it is essential to 'take account of both supernatural and natural factors, nevertheless, in such a way that the supernatural appreciation bears and directs everything'. See the article published under his designation 'Pater Meester' [= Spiritual director of the students], 'Vos qui vocati estis sancti', *Biekorf* 32, 1949, autumn, 2–13: 12.

80 Thus, in E. Schillebeeckx, 'Cultuur, godsdienst en geweld: "Theologie als onderdeel an een cultuur"', *TvT* 36, 1996, 387–404: 394 n. 6.

81 'Situatie', 232 n. 1.

82 Arch. 198 and 760 contain three notebooks with notes, entitled 'Foundations for a Theology of Culture'. The cover of the first notebook also has the words 'doctoral thesis', and other variants of the title are given: 'Christian View of Life', 'Foundations of a Theology of Culture', 'Theological Contributions to a Christian Humanism', and 'Earthly Elements of our Supernatural View of Life'. Arch. 718 comprises two notebooks with notes entitled 'The Integration of Earthly and Temporal Values in the Kingdom of God' (in French) with the inscriptions 'Notes for doctoral thesis' or 'Bibliography doctoral

thesis'. Looking back later, he himself was to give as the subject of his doctorate 'nature and supernature', 'religion and world' (see Puchinger, *Toekomst*, 139).

83 'Situatie', 602–3; for a development of the model of Abraham's sacrifice see Schillebeeckx, 'Considérations' (n. 64).
84 Schillebeeckx, 'Situatie', 607.
85 Ibid., 596.
86 Hoogeveen and Maas, 'Ik hoop op nieuwe dingen' (n. 52); on the initial period of *TGL* see especially 183–4.
87 See S. Axters, 'Inleiding', in *Mystiek brevier*, ed. S. Axters, I. *Het Nederlandse mystieke proza*, Antwerp 1944, XV–XVIII: XXVII. For Axters see Struycker Boudier, *Wijsgerig leven* II, 194.
88 'Na twee jaar "Tijdschrift voor geestelijk leven"', *TGL* 3, 1947, 3–7: 5.
89 H. Schillebeeckx, 'In memoriam pater Van Hulse', *TGL* 6, 1950, 433–4.
90 'Na twee jaar' (n. 88), 6.
91 Hoogeveen and Maas, 'Ik hoop op nieuwe dingen' (n. 52), 184.
92 'Aan onze lezers', *TGL* 1/1, 1945, 3–6: 3.
93 'Na twee jaar' (n. 88).
94 H. Schillebeeckx, 'Schepselbesef als grondslag van ons geestelijk leven', *TGL* 1, 1945, 1, 15–43.
95 Constitution *Dei Filius* (1870), c.1, cf. Denzinger 3002. According to P. Thibault, *Savoir et pouvoir. Philosophie thomiste et politique cléricale au XIXe siècle*, Quebec 1972, precisely this is the significance of neoscholastic thought for the church's politics. The thesis that creation points to God expresses the conviction that the knowledge of God is necessary for understanding human beings and the world; the thesis that what and how God is can be derived only from the revelation which is under the control of the (hierarchy of the) Catholic Church expresses the conviction that one is dependent on the church for a proper understanding of human beings and the world. Thus, the figure of thought is necessary, but in content inaccessible to human thought, and therefore dependent on the revelation controlled by the church. Schillebeeckx's attempts to break through this division between the natural and the supernatural order are therefore of great significance and affect the whole self-understanding of church and theology.
96 Schillebeeckx, 'Schepselbesef' (n. 94), 28–30.
97 Ibid., 23.
98 Ibid., 41.
99 Ibid., 33. For the topics mentioned, see for example H. Schillebeeckx, 'De Heilige Communie als menselijk-godsdienstige daad', *Ons Geloof* 28, 1946, 283–8; id., 'Spanning tussen Misoffer en Kruisoffer', *De Bazuin* 35, 1951–52, no. 38, 2; 'Het offer der Eucharistie', ibid., no. 36, 6–7; id. 'Het sacrament van de biecht', *TGL* 8, 1952, 219–42; id., 'Is de biecht nog up to date?', *Thomas* 6, 1952–3, no. 3, 5ff.; no. 5, pp. 3ff,; id., 'Rozenkrans, bidden in nuchtere werkelijkheid', *De Bazuin* 33, 1949/50, no. 1, 4–6; id., 'De gezinsrozenkrans', *TGL* 6, 1950, 523–32; id., 'Providentieel redmiddel', *De Rozenkrans* 82, 1955/6, 18–21; id., 'De leer van het rozenkransgebed', ibid., 53–5; id., 'Rozenkransgebed verantwoord gebed', ibid., 84, 1957/8, 7–6; id., 'De eigen techniek van de rozenkrans', ibid., 85, 1958/9, 208–11; id., 'De ascetische toeleg van de klosterling', *TGL* 3, 1947, I, 302–20; id., 'Kloosterlijke gehoorzaamheid', ibid., 12, 1956, 352–6; id., 'De dood, schoonste mogelijkheid van de christen', *De Bazuin* 35, 1951/52, no. 9, 4–5; id., 'De dood lichtende horizont van de oude dag', ibid., 39, 1955/56, nos 11–12, 4–5; id., 'De dood van een christen', *Kultuurleven* 22, 1955, 421–30, 508–19. Schillebeeckx's theology of Mary will be discussed at length in the next chapter.
100 E. Schillebeeckx, 'In memoriam Yves Congar, 1904–1995', *TvT* 35, 1995, 271–3.
101 Ibid., 271, cf. E. Schillebeeckx, 'In memoriam M.-D. Chenu (1895–1990)', *TvT* 30, 1990, 184–5.

102 'La théologie et la vie. Un entretien avec le père Chenu', in *Inform. cath. internat.* no. 233, 1965, 28–30: 30, quoted in Schoof, *Breakthrough*, 104.

103 Chenu's 1937 article from *Vie intell.* is reprinted in his *Parole de Dieu*, II, 87–108.

104 See especially M.-D. Chenu, *La théologie comme science au XIIIième siècle*, Paris 1943 (earlier version 1927); for Chenu's interpretation of Thomas cf. van den Hoogen, *Chenu*, 105–12, 263–7.

105 For an extended description of Chenu's 'theologizing from the dynamic of faith' cf. van den Hoogen, *Chenu*, 195–214; for the connection between his theology and the 'development of culture', cf. ibid., 113–61; for the connection with the 'development of the church', see ibid. 163–94; Chenu himself speaks at length about his view of theology in *Duquesne*.

106 For the following picture of the history of French Catholicism see the attempt to synthesize the extensive historical investigation by Fouilloux, 'Bewahrende Kräfte und Neuerfahrungen im Christentum Frankreichs', in *Die Geschichte des Christentums*, ed. J.-M. Mayeur et al., *XII: Erster und zweiter Weltkrieg, Demokratien und totalitäre Systeme (1914–1958)*, Freiburg, Basel and Vienna 1994, 552–631, esp. 598. Some concrete facts are easier to find in P. Blet, 'The Catholic Church of France', in *The History of the Church*, ed. H. Jedin, K. Repgen and J. Dolan, VII: *The Church in the Modern Age*, 583–99. Cf. also van den Hoogen, *Chenu*, 2–90.

107 For the picture of Lacordaire among the Dominicans involved here cf. Y. Congar, 'Le père Lacordaire, ministre de la Parole de Dieu' (1948), in id., *Les voies du Dieu vivant: Théologie et vie spirituelle*, Paris 1962, 323–34.

108 Cf. Y. Tranvouez, 'La fondation et le début de *La vie intellectuelle* (1928–1929)', *Arch. de sociol. des religions* 32, 1976, 57–96.

109 The order of origin, though, was exactly the opposite in France: *La vie spirituelle* had already existed since 1919 and *La vie intellectuelle* emerged from it.

110 Chenu speaks about this case in *Duquesne*, 88. For the history of *Sept*, cf. A. Coutrot, *Un courant de la pensée catholique: L'hebdomadaire 'Sept' (mars 1934 – août 1937)*, Paris 1961; id., *Sept, un journal, un combat (mars 1934 – août 1937)*, Paris 1982.

111 Leprieur, *Rome*, 23; cf. M.-D. Chenu, 'La J. O. C. au Saulchoir' (1936), in id., *La Parole de Dieu*, II, 271–4.

112 P. Lhande, *Le Christ dans le banlieu: Enquête sur la vie religieuse dans les milieux ouvriers de la banlieu de Paris*, Paris 1927.

113 For Suhard and his development see *Cardinal Suhard: Vers une Église en état de mission*, ed. O. de la Brosse, Paris 1964; J. Vinatier, *Le cardinal Suhard (1874–1949): L'evêque du renouveau missionaire*, Paris 1983, 221–3.

114 H. Godin and Y. Daniel, *La France, pays de mission?*, Paris 1943.

115 Cf. Vinatier, *Le cardinal Suhard* (n. 113); for the intensive involvement of Dominicans in the worker-priest movement see Leprieur, *Rome*.

116 Y. Congar, 'Une conclusion théologique à l'enquête sur les raisons actuelles de l'incroyance', *La vie intell.* 7, 1935, 37, 214–49.

117 Cf. *Duquesne*, 132–61.

118 Schillebeeckx, *Testament*, 27–8; cf. Puchinger, *Toekomst*, 138.

119 *Duquesne*, 119–22.

120 Leprieur, *Rome*, 295–397; cf. M.-D. Chenu, 'Note sur le sacerdoce des prêtres-ouvriers' (1954), in id., *Parole de Dieu* II, 275–81.

121 Cf. A. Gardeil, *Le donné révélé et la théologie* (1909), Paris 1932. For Gardeil see J. Bunnenberg, *Lebendige Treu zum Ursprung: Das Traditionsverständnis Yves Congars*, Mainz 1989, 337, who bases himself above all on R. Aubert, *Le problème de l'acte de foi: Données traditionelles et résultat des controverses récentes* (1945), Louvain ³1958, 396–410; for Chenu's attachment to Gardeil cf. ibid., 37–45, and see also M.-D. Chenu, 'Préface

pour la deuxième edition', in Gardeil, *Le donné révéle*, VII–XIX, reprinted in id., *La Parole de Dieu* I, 277–82; cf. also id., 'Foi et théologie d'après Père Ambroise Gardeil', ibid., 269–75.

122 Cf. M.-D. Chenu, *Une école de théologie: Le Saulchoir*, Paris 1985, 130–50: it deals specifically with 'relativism' and 'relativity' of theology and theological expressions on 125–6, 140 and 173, and 'relativity' of Thomistic philosophy on 163.

123 Chenu, ibid., 148–9.

124 Ibid., 136.

125 For the history around the condemnation of *Une école* and its significance for church politics see G. Alberigo, 'Christianisme en tant qu'histoire et "théologie confessante"', ibid. (n. 122), 11–34, esp. 22–6; E. Fouilloux, 'Le Saulchoir en process (1937–42)', ibid., 41–59.

126 H. Schillebeeckx, 'Het niet-begrippelijk kenmoment in onze Godskennis volgens St Thomas' (1952), in *Revelation* II, 'Appendix', 157–206. That during the period of the Council Schillebeeckx twice returns at length to the interpretation of Thomas and the view of theology that he defends here – once in the framework of the theological training for the Council fathers around the relationship between truth and tolerance –, that here he evidently sees himself compelled to oppose the neoscholastic, 'conceptualistic' interpretation of Thomas and theology which in his view is too focused on concepts, and that in 1966 he brought these three articles together into a long section on the value of our talk of God and our concepts of faith, in *Revelation* II, 5–29, makes it clear how important he felt this point to be for his view of faith and theology. Cf. 'Het waarheidsbegrip en aanverwante problemen', in *Kath arch*.17, 1962, 1169–86 (for the most part reprinted in *Revelation* II, 5–29; the shorter part on tolerance is reprinted in *World and Church*, 194–203), and 'Het niet-begrippelijk kenmoment in de geloofsdaad volgens Thomas: kritische studie' (1963), in *Openbaring en Theologie*, 233–81 (reprinted in *Revelation* II, 30–75). Cf. also the articles he wrote on the mystery of faith ('Geloofsgeheim') and the truth of faith ('Geloofswaarheid') in *Theolog. woordenboek* (2, 1957, 1730–2 and 1755–8). Here – with a reference to M. Matthijs – he emphasizes that the insight into the truths of faith as truths of faith is dependent on the light of faith, which in his view is embodied in 'our religious, supernatural experience of God'.

127 E. C. F. A. Schillebeeckx, *Op zoek naar de levende God*, Nijmegen 1959; reprinted as 'The Search for the Living God', in *God and Man*, 18–40: 25; the affinity of these expressions to the quotation that stands at the head of this chapter ('Situatie', 589) is striking.

128 Schillebeeckx, *Testament*, 28; cf. also Puchinger, *Toekomst*, 138–9; Oosterhuis and Hoogeveen, *God New*, 15.

129 Cf. 'Technische heilstheologie' (1945), reprinted as 'Truth or relevance for the Christian life in scholastic theology,' in *Revelation and Theology*, 266–84, etc. In fact this is a revision of his *lectio inauguralis*, 'Naar een levenstheologie', which was discussed at length in the previous chapter.

130 M.-J. Congar, 'Theologie', *Dict. de théol. cath.* 15, 1946, 341–502, especially from 447 on (there is a not very satisfactory translation: *A History of Theology*, Garden City, New York 1960).

131 Chenu, 'Foi et théologie d'après le Père Ambroise Gardeil' (n. 121), 275 n. 1.

132 Cf. E. Schillebeeckx, 'Ter school bij prof. A. Dondeyne', *TvT* 2, 1962, 78–83: 78–9. In fact this article is an extended review of Dondeyne's *Geloof en wereld*, Baarn 1961, but it is also about his *Foi chrétienne et pensée contemporaine: les problèmes philosophiques soulevés dans l'encyclique 'Humani generis'*, Paris 1952.

133 E. Suhard, *Essor ou déclin de l'église*, see *Cardinal Suhard* (n. 113), 186–221.

134 Y. Congar, *Une passion: l'unité. Réflexions et souvenirs 1929–1973*, Paris 1974, 60; *Duquesne*, 140.

135 Puchinger, *Toekomst*, 139.
136 'Cultuur en godsdienst in het huidige Frankrijk' (1936), in *Wereld en Kerk*, 11–26; unless otherwise indicated the reference is to this latest version, with the page numbers in brackets in the text (the article was not included in the English translation).
137 In 1945 J. Daniélou wrote an article entitled 'La vie intellectuelle en France. Communisme, existentialisme, christianisme', *Études* 78, 1945, 240–54; for his encounter with Daniélou at lectures cf. Schillebeeckx, *Testament*, 197 n. 11.
138 Schillebeeckx indicated in Puchinger, *Toekomst*, 138; Schillebeeckx, *Testament*, 27, that he studied with Lavelle and Le Senne. For Lavalle's philosophy see *Christliche Philosophie* (n. 67), III, 465–78; for that of Le Senne, ibid., 456–64; for that of the book series 'Esprit' which they produced together, ibid., 449–55.
139 For Chenu's view of the social and economic conditions under capitalism and their importance for theology see van den Hoogen, *Chenu*, 114–28.
140 Schillebeeckx marks the sentence between quotation marks in French, as a quotation: '*le vertige d'une grande époque à venir*'. It accurately expresses the atmosphere in the French church in the post-war period: the dominant unrest (his own) was seen as a sign of a new spring: see the Lenten letter by E. Suhard, *Essor ou declin de l'eglise?*, Paris 1947.
141 See *AAS* 41, 1949, 31 and 334.
142 See *Docum. cath.* 46, 1948–9, 327–9. For background information about the history surrounding the UCP see Y. Tranvouez, *Catholiques d'abord: Approches du mouvement catholique en France (XIXe-XXe siècle)*, Paris 1988, 132–71.
143 H. Schillebeeckx, 'Vormen van morgen: Bedenkingen rond het christelijk progressisme in Frankrijk' (1949), in *Wereld en kerk*, 26–38 (not in the English translation). Page numbers are given in brackets in the text.
144 Suhard, *Essor ou declin?* (n. 140), 1094.
145 Puchinger, *Toekomst*, 140.
146 Schillebeeckx, *Testament*, 30. Cf. also the text which according to his own account he wrote when he was master of students – he does not give a more precise indication of time – and later reworked as a lecture for the 'national congress of Flemish masters from the different religious institutions, which was held at Louvain from 28 to 30 April 1957'. The text can be found under the title 'De menselijke en godsdienstige situatie van de jongeren in het huidige kloosterleven', in *Zending*, 205–34 (not in the English translation).
147 Hoogeveen and Maas, 'Ik hoop op nieuwe dingen' (n. 52), 184.
148 Oosterhuis and Hoogeveen, *God New*, 17–18; U. Engel, 'Zur Zukunft des Ordenslebns in Europa: Ein Gespräch mit Edward Schillebeeckx OP', *Wort und Antwort* 34, 1993, 157–63: 162f.
149 Cf. H. Schillebeeckx, 'Hebben wij het beste deel gekozen?', *Dominikaans Leven* 9, 1952–3, no. 2, 8–10; 'Het dominikaanse evenwicht', ibid., no. 5, 5–7; id., 'Contemplata aliis tradere', ibid., no. 6, 7–9; id., 'Dominikaanse durf, nooit op schorvrije voeten', ibid., 10, 1953–4, nos 3,7–10; id., 'Dominikaanse geest. De blijde geest der dominikanen', ibid., 11, 1954–5, nos 6,7–9; id., 'Dominicaanse spiritualiteit' (= special issue of *Biekorf*), Christmas 1954. There are handwritten notes on the copy in Arch. 635, clearly with a view to printing or publication. In the copy there are colour drawings on black card of a stylized Dominic, under which is the text '*Dominican Spirituality* by Pater Doctor Henricus-Maria Schillebeeckx', apparently a sketch for a cover. The page numbers are again in brackets in the text.
150 Cf. Thomas Aquinas, *Summa theol.* I, q. 7, art. 1. Moreover it is striking that here too Schillebeeckx still strongly distinguishes Dominican spirituality from that of the Jesuits; cf. ibid., 21: the reference to Ignatius' *Spiritual Exercises* as an example of a spirituality which above all emphasizes human effort instead of God's grace.

151 Moreover, here Schillebeeckx makes extensive use of the newest insights into the mediaeval history of theology and the religious orders as these are described among others by Chenu.

152 On ibid., 13, Schillebeeckx says that 'throughout the history of the order ... St Thomas ... is rightly regarded as the teacher in Dominican spirituality. It is not that he is said to be the founder of this spirituality, quite the reverse. The spirit of the order made a St Thomas possible in its bosom, so that we have to say that in his *Ascetica et mystica* St Thomas ultimately gave a theological expression to the spirituality from which the order was already living.' *Ascetica et mystica* is not a writing by Thomas; the term is customary in neoscholasticism to denote texts about spirituality and the life of the order. Apart from occasional works, Thomas deals with this above all in *Summa theol.* II-II, q. 1. 79–89. Although in this context it makes no sense to investigate the historical accuracy of Schillebeeckx's assertions, it is striking that he has little eye for the impulses from the broad poverty movement which are said to have influenced Dominic. Dominic is depicted only as the one who corrected particular tendencies in other mendicant movements. This seems to be connected with Schillebeeckx's concentration on the theological idea of the order as it is developed by Thomas and his desire in his duplicated text to sketch an organically coherent, all-pervasive spirit of the order. In his later publications he was to have more of an eye for the social and ecclesiastical context of Dominic in a broad movement concerned with poverty and reform, also on the basis of new research, and in his own 1954 copy of *Dominicaanse spiritualiteit* he put a note right at the beginning: 'Introduce *lay movement* in the twelfth century' (ibid., 6).

153 The designation 'notional' for conceptual knowledge comes from John Henry Newman and there stands over against 'real', knowledge woven into life and comprised in it.

154 In a recollection which remains somewhat unclear, Schillebeeckx explains that the great freedom of movement which he allowed his students caused him 'quite a lot of difficulties with superiors ... An attempt to depose me as *magister spiritualis* failed thanks to an intervention by the General of the Order, Pater Suarez, who wanted to "postpone" things a few years so as to be able to discover precisely where the "wrong" lay (Puchinger, *Toekomst*, 140). Later he said more specifically that 'in 1955–6 (I do not know precisely when)' he had 'a kind of reprimand from the provincial chapter of the Flemish Dominican province, a serious censure of my conduct', a rebuke which was subsequently to be deleted from the record through a later intervention by the Superior General. This makes it impossible in retrospect to check precisely what happened. Schillebeeckx himself connects this only with personal provocations, but he does speak of a 'degree of manipulation' in this decision by the chapter (*Testament*, 30, 197 n. 13).

CHAPTER 3

1 For this picture of existentialism see H. van Stralen, *Beschreven Keuzes: Een inleiding in het literaire existentialisme*, Louvain and Apeldoorn 1996, esp. 11–86.

2 M. Merleau-Ponty, *Phenomenology of Perception* (1945), London 1962. Along the line of De Petter's own view of his philosophy, S. van Erp puts the emphasis on De Petter's criticism of Husserl (*Intentionaliteit en Intuitie: De Petters formulierung van de realistische metafysica tegen de achtergrond van de 'traditionele' metafysica en de husserliaanse feno-menologie*, theological faculty thesis, Tilburg 1995), but it would be worth making a more precise investigation of the connection between this critique of Husserl and that of Merleau-Ponty.

3 Cf. De Petter, *Begrip*, 159–63. Moreover in the later work of Merleau-Ponty there is indeed an opening to being as the supportive ground of existence, and thus indirectly to

God; cf. R. C. Kwant, *From Phenomenology to Metaphysics: An Enquiry into the Last Period of Merleau-Ponty's Philosophical Life*, Pittsburgh and Lucerne 1966, 241–3.

4   A. Camus, *The Plague*, Harmondsworth 1960, 207, 208, 209, 213. For the interpretation see van Stralen, *Beschreven Keuzes* (n. 1), 165–93; C. Gadourek, *Les innocents et les coupables: Essai d'exégèse de l'oeuvre d'Albert Camus*, The Hague 1963, 116–31.

5   Id., *The Rebel*, London 1953; for the links between the writing of *The Rebel* and *The Plague* at the time of and with reference to the problems, cf. the notes to Albert Camus, *Théâtre, récits, nouvelles*, ed. R. Quilliot, Paris 1962, 1609–50. For the content of the book see Gadourek, *Les innocents et les coupables* (n. 4), 154–66.

6   Puchinger, *Toekomst*, 139.

7   Thus in an interview quoted in Gadourek, *Les innocents et les coupables* (n. 4), 117.

8   For Paneloux's first sermon see Camus, *The Plague* (n. 4), 78–84: 83.

9   For the second sermon cf. ibid., 180–7: 183, 187.

10   For the general pattern and for Schillebeeckx's position within it see Schoof, *Breakthrough*, 157–227.

11   H. Schillebeeckx, *Heilseconomie*. The examiner was A. Dondaine, a specialist in the history of mediaeval theology, especially on Thomas; probably because Chenu was not available after his condemnation.

12   Pius XII, encyclical *Humani generis* (12 August 1950), no. 11.

13   Id., Apostolic Exhortation *Menti nostrae* (23 September 1950), no. 105.

14   Id., *Humani generis* (n. 12), nos 1, 11 and 12.

15   Ibid., 17, 6, 12. From the beginning '*nouvelle théologie*' seems to be a pejorative expression, comparable to 'modernism', and to have been used for the first time in 1946 by Pius XII himself. For the fate of the concept cf. C. Frey, *Mysterium der Kirche, Öffnung zur Welt*, Göttingen 1969, 55–61; for the questions which were on the agenda, ibid., 55–104: for a detailed analysis of *Humani generis*, including an attempt to discover to whom the charge is addressed, cf. ibid., 88–104.

16   Pius XII, address *Quamvis inquieti* to the twenty-ninth general congregation of the Society of Jesus (17 September 1946), no. 12. Some days later, in the same spirit he was to address the chapter of the Dominicans on the abiding significance of the doctrine of Thomas Aquinas as a starting point in philosophy and theology (address *Par est laeto* to the delegates to the general chapter of the Dominicans [22 September 1946], nos 7–10).

17   Id., *Humani generis* (n. 12), nos 15–16.

18   Y. M-J. Congar, 'Bulletin de théologie dogmatique: I. Introduction et methodologie', *Rev. sc. philos théol.* 35, 1951, 591–603: 597.

19   A. H. Maltha, *De nieuwe theologie: informatie en oriëntatie*, Bruges 1958, 13–29, German translation *Die neue Theologie*, Munich 1960. However, Frey regards Maltha's book as a sign that the campaign against the so-called 'new theology' ended in ridicule, *Mysterium der Kirche* (n. 15), 61f.

20   E. Schillebeeckx, '"Nieuwe theologie"', *Kultuurleven* 26, 1959, 122–5. Earlier, with more restraint but no less clearly, he had described Maltha's way of doing theology as 'too much theory, too little reflection'; see his review of Maltha and Thuys, *Dogmatiek*, in H. Schillebeeckx, 'Recente eucharistieliteratuur', *TGL* 7, 1951, 381–4: 383–4. It seems that the lecturers of the Nijmegen theological faculty agreed with this judgement and therefore did not want Maltha as professor of dogmatics. With some effort, especially by the dean, Willem Grossouw, they were able to get Schillebeeckx from Louvain in his place (see W. Grossouw, *Alles is van u: Gewijde en profane herinneringen*, Baarn 1981, 282–6). Perhaps this event explains why Schillebeeckx seems to regard Maltha's *Nieuwe theologie* as an example of the Dutch theological climate. 'Perhaps people in the Netherlands would do well to talk rather less for or against the "*nouvelle théologie*" and rather more to practise genuine Catholic theology.' This is unjust, in so far as quite sophisticated literature was

available (cf. especially A. van Rijen, 'Een nieuwe stroming in de theologie', *Ned. kath. stemmen* 44, 1948, 177–88), but there was no genuine theological engagement. As T. Schoof rightly remarks, 'The theology of renewal was first passed on by the journals which were orientated on the pastorate or were more generally cultural' ('Contouren van veertig jaar theologie. Het "Werkgenootschap" binnen de katholieke kerk van Nederland', *TvT* 27, 1987, 139–54: 141). The *'nouvelle théologie'* was felt to be something that fell outside the usual practice of theology, something to which one had to react. Here Schillebeeckx emphasizes that: 'Theology is already a *living* theology, if it wants to be true to its name: a contemporary reflection on the reality of revelation which produces the continuity through living growth.'

21 H. Schillebeeckx, *'Humani generis'*, *Theol. woordenboek* 2, 1957, 2300–2. The *Theologisch woordenbook* (which was edited by A. Maltha, among others) contained a specific discussion of several encyclicals, evidently in the conviction endorsed in *Humani generis* that what is expounded in encyclicals is not infallible doctrine, but what is stated in them is taught by virtue of the ordinary magisterium, to which the saying 'Whoever hears you, hears me' (Luke 10.16) applies. And that does not just relate to fundamental documents with a great influence like *Aeterni patris* (1879), in which Leo XIII made Thomism the doctrine of the Catholic Church, and *Rerum novarum* (1891), in which the same pope gave the first formulation of official Catholic social teaching. Usually, however, the content of the document in question is indicated only very briefly.

22 Schillebeeckx, *'Humani generis'*.

23 Thus Schillebeeckx in a lecture to the Flemish Association for Theology in 1954, entitled 'Around the papal encyclical *Humani generis'* (Arch. 968), reprinted as part of 'Het begrip waarheid', in *Kath. arch.* 17, 1962, 1169–80, ET in *Revelation* II, 5–29.

24 Ibid., 190, 192.

25 Ibid., 194–5; cf. also 'What is Theology?' (1958), in *Revelation* I, 93–183, esp. 131–8.

26 'Het niet-begrippelijk kenmoment in onze Godskennis volgens St Thomas' (1954), in *Openbaring*, 201–32: 212 (ET in *Revelation* II, 30–75). De Petter himself also tried some years later to root his philosophical view of human knowledge in Thomas's work, probably also for church-political reasons. Cf. 'De oorsprong van de zijnskennis volgens de H. Thomas van Aquino' (1955), in De Petter, *Begrip*, 94–135.

27 A. Willems, *Terug naar de ervaring: Geloof tussen vrijheid en bevrijding*, Baarn 1980, 17.

28 H. Schillebeeckx, 'Herbronning van het priesterlijk apostolaat en activiering van het laïcaat', *Biekorf* 34, 1952–3, 159–204; there is a somewhat abbreviated reprint, 'Priest and Layman in a Secular World', in *World*, 32–76. Incidentally, the fact that Schillebeeckx included this quite informal article in the collection is an indication of the importance that he attached to it for his development.

29 Quotations, ibid., 32, 37, 40, 38, 42; Chenu had developed his standpoint publicly in his 'Note sur le sacerdoce des prêtres-ouvriers' (1954), in id., *Parole,* II, 275–81, but it is already formulated in his 'Notes sur la lettre de Mgr Ancerl aux prêtres-ouvriers' of October 1951; cf. Leprieur, *Rome*, 324–9.

30 Ibid., 44: 'Op zoek naar Gods afwezigheid' (1957), in *Wereld,* 38–58: 48 (not included in the English edition); a review of the first volume of I. Rosier, *Ik zocht Gods afwezigheid: Psychologische peilingen inzake religieus sociale toestanden in Europa, I: Frankrijk – Spanje*, The Hague n.d. (1955), *II: Italie-Oostenrijk*, ibid., n.d. (1957). This account of an investigation involving workers in different European countries, in which the author indicates finding more authentic and Christian religion among them than one might expect on the basis of alarmist accounts of the de-Christianized working-class world, attracted great interest, cf. *Soc. kompas* 3, 1955, 2 and 3.

31 Cf. ibid., 46–66; for the above 62, 64.

32 Leprieur, *Rome*, 303–23. In the course of this development the first Dominican worker-

priest, Jacques Loew, who in 1941 went to work in Marseilles as a dock worker, argued for a structure in which the pastorate for workers was associated with a parish. He replaced the term *'prêtres ouvriers'* by *'prêtres travailleurs'*; cf. his *Journal d'une mission ouvrière 1941–1959*, Paris 1959, 247–54: 'Réponse à un projet d'organisation de la mission ouvrière' (1951).

33   Schillebeeckx, *Heilseconomie*; he summarized the book in *Sacramentaire structuur*, cf. also id., 'The Sacraments: An Encounter with God', in D. Callahan et al. (eds), *Christianity Divided*, London and New York 1961; id., 'Sacrament', in *Theologisch woordenboek* 3, 1958, 4185–231: *Christusontmoeting* (1958), reprinted in an enlarged and revised version as *Christ the Sacrament*.

34   H. Schillebeeckx, 'Sacramenteel leven', *Thomas* 3, 1949–50, nos 3, 5–6; ibid., no. 4, 2–4: nos 3, 5. The quotation which stands at the head of this chapter also comes from here.

35   H. Schillebeeckx, 'Zien en getuigen zoals Christus', *TGL* 5, 1949, II, 145–54: 147, 148, 153. In the way in which he uses the psychology of Jesus Christ to connect his life with that of Christians, who are then urged to incorporate themselves into his mystery of life, Schillebeeckx is influenced by his reading of R. Guardini, *The Lord*, Washington, DC 1996 (original *Der Herr: Betrachtungen über das Leben Jesu Christi*, Würzburg 1937); see his review 'Guardini's *De Heer*', *TGL* 4, 1948, II, 54–7, esp. 56.

36   'Sacramenteel leven' (n. 34), nos 3, 4; cf. also already H. Schillebeeckx, 'De heilige kommunie als menschelijk-godsdienstige daad', *Ons geloof* 28, 1946, 283–8.

37   H. Schillebeeckx, 'Ik geloof in de levende God', *TGL* 6, 1950, 523–32: 457.

38   H. Schillebeeckx, 'Het sacrament van de biecht', *TGL* 8, 1952, 219–42: 237. He also expounds in this direction the classical idea that the sacraments work from the power of ritual itself, *'ex opere operato'*; cf. H. Schillebeeckx, 'Het *"opus operantis"* in het sacramentalisme', in *Theologica: Voordrachten en discussies 1951–1952*, Vlaams werkgenootschap van theologen, I, Ghent 1953, 59–68.

39   Cf. U. Valeske, *Votum ecclesiae, I: Das Ringen um die Kirche in der neueren römisch-katholischen Theologie, dargestellt auf dem Hintergrund der evangelischen und oekumenischen Parallel-Entwicklung*, Munich 1962, 217–36; it is generally thought that S. Tromp, *Corpus Christi quod est ecclesia*, I, Rome 1937, underlies this document.

40   Pius XII, encyclical *Mystici corporis* (1943), no. 17, cf. 66.

41   Ibid., no.18.

42   M.-J. Congar, *The Mystery of the Church* (1941), 1960, 75.

43   Quotations from a lecture given by Schillebeeckx on 21 October 1953 to the 'Centre for Religious Reflection' in Louvain, which was concerned with the advanced theological education of priests and laity (Arch. 593, with the title 'De actualiteit van de sacramenten'). Cf. also the article 'Godsdienst en sacrament', *Stud. Cath.* 65, 1959, 267–83, which was likewise based on a lecture for a broad public.

44   Y. Congar, 'Une conclusion théologique à l'enquête sur les raisons actuelles de l'incroyance', *La vie intell.* 37, 1955, 214–49, esp. 220–1. For what follows see Frey, *Mysterium der Kirche* (n.15), 118–50.

45   For the history of the idea of 'incarnation' cf. B. Besret, *Incarnation ou eschatologie? Contribution à l'histoire du vocabulaire religieux contemporain 1935–1955*, Paris 1964, esp. 23–104.

46   L. Bouyer, 'Ou en est la théologie du Corps Mystique', *Rev. sc. Rel.* 22, 1948, 313–33: 315.

47   Congar, *Mystery* (n. 42), 68–9.

48   Ibid., 80–2.

49   Ibid., 85–6.

50   Ibid., 90–1.

51   Dogmatic Constitution on the Church *Pastor aeternus*, 1870, no. 1.

52   Cf. Congar, *Mystery* (n. 42), 70, where he sees the relationship between being inspired by

the Spirit and building up the body as the dialectic of the '*donné*' and the '*agi*'.

53 *Mystici corporis*, 55 and 82. The tendency to regard the Christian as a second Christ is to be noted particularly in Germany, especially in the book by O. Pelt, *Der Christ als Christus: Der Weg meines Forschens*, Berlin 1938, 145, which appeared exclusively as a manuscript: 'To sum up, then, we may say that as true members of the true and only body of Christ we belong to the second person of God' (quoted in C. T. M. van Vliet, *Communio sacramentalis: Das Kirchenverständnis von Yves Congar – genetisch und systematisch betrachtet*, Mainz 1995, 78 n. 237).

54 For the background to the doctrine of the three offices of Christ in the history of theology cf. L. Ullrich, 'Ämter Christi: Theologiegeschichtlich', in *Lex. Theol. Kirche* 1, [3]1993, 562.

55 *Mystici corporis*, nos 16–19.

56 Cf. *Mystici corporis*, nos 16–19: 17.

57 'Sacramentaire structuur', 785: for a reflection on the sacraments – and on the church as 'primordial sacrament' ('*Ursakrament*': O. Semmelroth) – as a possible way of bridging the gulf between the emphasis on the external structure of the church in *Mystici corporis* and the traditional insight that the church is a body ensouled by Christ, cf. K. Rahner, 'Membership of the Church according to the Teaching of Pius XII's Encyclical *Mystici Corporis Christi*', *Theological Investigations* II, London and New York 1963, 1–88. This article originally dates from 1947, but in the reprint on p. 1 n. 1 Rahner refers to *De sacramentele heilseconomie*.

58 'Het sacrament van de biecht' (n. 38), 237.

59 'Sacramentaire structuur', 797.

60 H. Schillebeeckx, 'Beschouwingen rond de misliturgie', *TGL* 7, 1951, 306–23: 309, 314, 321. For the background literature see id., 'Recente eucharistieliteratuur' (n. 20), 381–4.

61 E. Schillebeeckx, 'Priesterlijke narcissus of mislukt theoloog?', *Kultuurleven* 27, 1960, 24–9, a review of J. L. M. Descalzo, *Ik ben een mens . . . : Bekentenissen van een jonge priester*, Tielt and The Hague 1959 (original Spanish 1955), quotation 205, the passage which reflects on absolution: 268. Literally, it says: 'I prayed for all the dead in the train disaster – according to the newspapers there were 37 of them – as if they were my own brothers and sisters. I felt so close to people . . . I looked at my hands . . . They are already in heaven. Perhaps there is already someone in heaven thanks to these hands.'

62 'Priest and Layman' (n. 28), 42f.; cf. also 'Bezinning en apostolaat in het leven der seculiere en religieuze priesters', *TGL* 19, 1963, 307–29, esp. 311–26: 'Collaboration of religious with the episcopate, with the secular clergy and with each other' (lecture 1964), *Mission*, 188–204, in 'Theologische bezinning op de geestelijke begeleiding', *TGL* 20, 1964, 513–27, Schillebeeckx drew from this the conclusion that the priest was in a special way responsible for the spiritual well-being of Christians during their life in the world and had to be confronted with this responsibility.

63 For Schillebeeckx, see ibid. In concrete, Schillebeeckx's view of the status and future of the worker-priest project seems to correspond closely to that of his fellow-Dominican Humbert Bousse, an ex-pupil of Suhard who taught theology at Saint-Alban-Leysse, the house of studies of the Dominican province of Lyons. In the midst of the conflicts around the worker-priests, on 10 February 1952 in a report entitled 'Sacerdoce et mission ouvrière' (cf. Leprieur, *Rome*, 329–40), he had explained that the worker-priests performed tasks which really should be done by the Catholic laity, but for which they were not as yet sufficiently equipped. Whether Schillebeeckx knew about this report, which existed only in duplicated form, is unclear. Moreover similar views led the Dominican Jacques Loew, one of the original worker-priests, to establish the so-called secular institute 'Mission ouvrière Saint-Pierre-et-Paul', a community of priests and laity who led a life of action and contemplation, prayer, study and missionary activity in the world, with the aim of 'evangelizing the world of work', cf. his *Journal* (n. 32), 394–469. Schillebeeckx does not see much

in secular institutions, cf. H. Schillebeeckx, 'Priesterschap en episcopaat: Beschouwingen bij een recent boek', *TGL* 11, 1955, 357–67, esp. 357–9; the book in question is J. Beyer, *Les instituts séculier*, Bruges 1954. He evidently regarded Loew's institute as a way of giving the form of authentic Dominican 'life in the world' to 'really "secular Dominicans"'; in 1960 he argued for a reform of the Dominican 'Third order', consisting of laity associated with the order, along these lines: 'Derde Orde "nieuwe stijl"', *Zwart op wit* 30, 1960, 113–27. On p. 123 he discusses Loew, and relates that Loew had originally addressed his proposal to establish a secular institute to the Dominican order. In the apostolic constitution *Provida mater ecclesia* (1947), Pius XII recognized the secular institutes officially as 'associations of priests or laity whose members bear witness to the counsels of the gospel with the aim of attaining Christian perfection and exercising the apostolate in the full sense' for the background, theology and documents cf. Optatus, 'De seculiere of wereldlijke instituten', in *Arch. v.d kerken* 9, 1954; 169–24; Beyer, *Les instituts*.

64   Dogmatic Constitution *Lumen gentium*, no. 31: 'Their secular character is proper and peculiar to the laity ... By reason of their special vocation it belongs to the laity to seek the kingdom of God by engaging in temporal affairs and directing them according to God's will ... It pertains to them in a special way so to illuminate and order all temporal things with which they are so closely associated that these may be effected and grow according to Christ and may be to the glory of the Creator and Redeemer'; cf. also the decree on the lay apostolate *Apostolicam actuositatem* (1965). Of course the beginning of the pastoral constitution *Gaudium et spes* (1965) is in fact about a much more far-reaching, as it were 'laicized', perspective on the church as a whole: 'The joy and hope, the grief and anguish of the men of our time, especially of those who are poor or afflicted in any way, are the joy and hope, the grief and anguish of the followers of Christ as well' (no. 1).

65   Cf. Pope John Paul II, Post-synodal Apostolic Exhortation on the Call and Mission of the Laity in the Church and the World, *Christifideles laici* (1988): here once again the image of the church with different members, each of whom have their special character, along the line of *Mystici corporis*, plays a prominent role. For the hidden continuity between this encyclical and *Lumen gentium* cf. S. Alberto, *'Corpus Suum mystice constituit' (LG 7): La Chiesa Corpo Mistico di Cristo nel Primo Capitolo della 'Lumen Gentium'. Storia del Testo dalla 'Mystici Corporis' al Vaticano II con riferimenti alle attività conciliare del P. Sebastian Tromp, SJ*, Regensburg 1996. For a critical evaluation of the theology of the laity which arose from the 1950s on, including that of Vatican II, see P. Neuner, *Der Laie und das Gottesvolk*, Frankfurt 1988 (for Congar, 162–70; for – the later – Schillebeeckx, 186–90); cf. also the much more militant H. Haag, *Worauf es ankommt: Wollte Jesus eine Zwei-Stände Kirche?*, Freiburg, Basel and Vienna 1997, esp. 11–34.

66   For the standpoint of the Council of Trent see Denzinger 1767, for the position of Pius XII in *Mediator Dei*, ibid., 3849–51.

67   Y. M.-J. Congar, *Jalons pour une théologie du laïcat* (Markers for a Theology of the Laity), 1953; ET *Lay People in the Church*, 1961. Of the articles which preceded it the most important are 'Sacerdoce et laïcat dans l'Eglise', *La vie intell.* 14, 1946, 6–39; 'Pour une théologie du laïcat', *Études* 256, 1948, 42–54, 194–218. As a direct sequel he published further articles which were collected in *Sacerdoce et laïcat devant leur tâches d'évangelisation et de civilisation*, Paris 1962.

68   Y. Congar, 'Mon cheminement dans la théologie du laïcat et de ministères', id., *Ministères et communion ecclésiale*, Paris 1971, 9–30: 22.

69   Haag, *Worauf es ankommt* (n. 65), 17.

70   'Priest and Layman' (n. 28), 68–76.

71   Thus Schillebeeckx himself in 1968, in an introductory piece to a collection of articles about the place of priest and laity which he wrote between 1949 and 1966; see *Zending*, 73 (not in the English translation).

72 H. Schillebeeckx, 'Theologische grondslagen van de lekenspiritualiteit' (1949), in *Zending*, 73–86 (not in the English translation).

73 According to the editorial board, *Carmel* (which in 1969 was to change its name to *Speling*) was in the Carmelite tradition, 'in a practical way and taking account of current problems', orientated on 'teaching the people of this time to pray and disclosing for them the riches of intimate life with God': 'Ten Geleide', *Carmel* 6, 1953–4, 3. For an account of the study conference which took place from 18 to 20 September 1953 and was repeated on 10–11 October with a meeting specially intended for young people, cf. M. Arts, 'De evangelische mens: Onze studiedagen op Drakenburgh', ibid, 171–3.

74 H. Schillebeeckx, 'Evangelie en Kerk', *TGL* 10, 1954, 93–121: 93–4: page references are given in brackets in the text.

75 The passage in which this argument is to be found was added to the text later; cf. the text with that of 'Evangelie en kerk', *Carmel* 6, 1953–4, 129–57, where this passage is missing. According to 93 n. 1, the text was revised for *TGL* 'in the light of the debate, from which it proved that some remarks were understood wrongly by the listeners', but the text about compulsory measures seems in any case also to refer to the course of events around the measures against Chenu and Congar.

76 The quotation from Thomas comes from *Summa theol.* III, q. 64, art. 2. In writing 'Evangelie en kerk' Schillebeeckx seems to have allowed himself to be strongly guided by Thomas's answer to the third argument for his statement that sacraments must necessarily be instituted by God himself, and also by a statement that he does not quote from it: 'The apostles and their followers are God's representatives with respect of the leadership of the church built up by faith and by the sacraments of faith. Therefore just as they are not free to found another church, so they are not allowed to proclaim another faith or to institute other sacraments.'

77 Cf. id., '*Variae species apostolatus earumque mutua relatio*', in *Le forme fondamentali dell'apostolato, de apostolatu moderno*, Acta Congr. Internat. O.C.D., Rome 1953/4, 7–15.

78 This is the fourth conclusion of the World Congress for the Lay Apostolate which was held in Rome from 7 to 14 October 1951. See *Kath. arch.* 6, 1951, 889.

79 Cf Pius XII's address to the participants in the World Congress for the Lay Apostolate, ibid. 6, 1951, 881–7.

80 On this point there is a clear difference between their approach and that of Karl Rahner in his article 'Notes on the Lay Apostolate', *Theological Investigations* II (n. 57), 319–52, which tried to increase the scope for lay people by broadening the conception of office and showing that, theologically speaking, many so-called laity belong to the clergy, cf. Neuner, *Der Laie und das Gottesvolk* (n. 65), 190.

81 Cf. the address of Pope Pius XII to the Second World Congress on the Lay Apostolate, 6–13 October 1957 in Rome, in *Kath. arch.* 12, 1957, 1189–1202.

82 'Editoriaal', *De Maand* 1, 1958, 1–5: 3–4; for the congress cf. *De leek in der moderne wereldcrisis: Verantwoordelijkheid en vorming, Nationaal congres van het lekenapostolaat*, no place, 1957.

83 For the development of *Te Elfder Ure*, its orientation and the tensions which this produced, also on the editorial board, and the history which led to a kind of second founding in 1954, cf. G. Dierick, 'De Christofoorgroep en het tijdschrift *Te Elfder Ure* in de jaren 1945–1953', *Jaarb. Kath. Docum. Centrum* 13, 1983, 35–94.

84 Editorial, 'Hoogspanning', *Te Elfder Ure* 1, 1950, no. 1, 1.

85 'Van de redactie', ibid., 1, 1954, 1.

86 For this history cf. H. M. Ruitenbeek, *Het ontstaan van de Partij van de Arbeid*, Amsterdam 1955.

87 'Bisschoppelijk mandement *De katholiek in het openbare leven van deze tijd*', in *Kath. arch.* 9, 1954, 489–520.

88 'Radiotoespraak van de voorzitter van de Katholieke Werk-Gemeenschap in de PvdA, d.d. 2–6–'54', ibid., 9, 1954, 621–3.

89 B. Delfgaauw, 'Persoonlijke waarheid en georganiseerde macht', *Te Elfder Ure* 1, 1954, 279–85.

90 D. de Lange, *Vijf jaar Katholiek Nationaal Bureau voor de Geestelijke Gezondheidszorg*, Utrecht 1957, 24.

91 Thus rightly T. Akkerman, 'Inleiding: Ontzuiling, gezinspolitiek en feminisme in Nederland', in *De zondige Rivièra van het katholicisme: Een locale studie over feminisme en ontzuiling 1950–1975*, ed. T. Akkerman and S. Stuurman, Amsterdam 1985, 11–37: esp. 16–17. For the affair cf. A. A. A. Terruwe, *Opening van zaken*, Nijmegen 1964; H. Suèr, *Niet te geloven: De geschiedenis van een pastorale kommissie*, Bussum 1969; R. Abma, 'De katholieken en het psy-complex', *Grafiet* 1, 1981, 165–97.

92 A. A. A. Terruwe, *De neurose in het licht van de rationele psychologie*, Roermond 1949.

93 This expression comes from Suèr, *Niet te geloven* (n. 91), 18.

94 For the opposition in Nijmegen see Grossouw, *Alles is van u* (n. 20), 252–5.

95 '*Quaedam admonitiones ad theoriam et praxim curationis spectantes psychoneurotisi laborantium*', in *Anal. v.h. aartsbisdom* 29, 1956, 166–7. For an illuminating commentary on the content see H. Ruygers, 'Zielzorg en psychotherapie: Kritische beschouwing van een document', *TvT* 5, 1965, 60–88, an almost unaltered publication of a piece which had been written for internal use directly after the appearance of the *admonitiones*.

96 Cf. H. Westhoff, *Geesteljke bevrijders: Nederlandse katholieken en hun beweging voor geestelijke volksgezondheid in de twintigste eeuw*, Nijmegen 1996; for the period 1945–60, 175–394; for the Terruwe-Duynstee case, 296–305.

97 W. K. Grossouw, 'Theologische week 1957', *Stud. Cath.* 32, 1957, 167–8, here 168. For the facts about the participants see 'Eerste theologische week van Nijmegen over de kerk', in *Kath. arch.* 12, 1957, 1213–18.

98 Grossouw speaks of the organization of the 'theological week' and the promotion of Schillebeeckx's nomination in Nijmegen in *Alles is van u* (n. 20), 281–6.

99 For the history cf. *Hoger instituut voor Godsdienstwetenschappen (Faculteit der Godgeleerdheid K. U. Louvain) 1942–1992: rondom catechese en onderricht*, ed. M. Lambergts et al., Louvain 1992.

100 *Christusontmoeting*, later reprinted several times in a revised and expanded version under the title *Christus sacrament van de Godsontmoeting* (ET *Christ the Sacrament*). Schillebeeckx presents the book as preceding at a more popular level the second volume of *De sacramentele heilseconomie* that he had announced at the end of the first volume, in which he was to give further 'positive theological' support to what he asserted in *Christusontmoeting* 'by way of synthesis'. However, the second volume of *De sacramentele heilseconomie* never appeared.

101 B. Delfgaauw, 'De leek in de kerk', *Stud. Cath.* 32, 1957, 291–303: 303.

102 Congar, *Lay People in the Church* (n. 67), xxviii.

103 H. Schillebeeckx, 'Het apostolisch ambt van de kerklijke hiërarchie', *Stud. Cath.* 32, 1957, 258–90: 282.

104 'Eerste theologische week' (n. 97), 1216.

105 H. Schillebeeckx, 'Diocesane spiritualiteit', *Kultuurleven* 19, 1952, 144–53, an extended disussion of G. Thils, *Wezen en spiritualiteit van de diocesane geestelijkheid*, Brussels and Amsterdam 1950 (original: *Nature et spiritualité du clergé diocésain*, Bruges 1948). The tone of the review is rather polemical, but in fact Schillebeeckx adopts Thils' inclination to seek the distinctive character of the priesthood in its responsibility for the well-being of the church. The polemic is directed above all against the tendency which he perceived in Thils' book to attribute this pastoral task exclusively to the diocesan clergy. Here Thils in fact makes use of what Thomas Aquinas writes about the '*vita mixta*' of love of God and

dedication to preaching, which should be characteristic of the mendicant orders, in fact Dominicans and Franciscans.

106 The historical facts are given at length in Schillebeeckx's article 'Priesterschap', in *Theol. woordenboek* 3, 1958, 3959–4003: 3959–80. In a number of places this article corresponds word for word with 'Het apostolisch ambt van de kerkelijke hiërarchie'.

107 Id., 'Het apostolisch ambt' (n. 103), 274.

108 Dogmatic Constitution *Lumen gentium*, ch. 3 (nos 18–29).

109 Pius XII, allocution *Quest'ora* on the beatification of Pius X, in *AAS* 46, 1954, 307–13.

110 Allocution *Si diligis* on the beatification of Pius X, ibid., 313–21.

111 In 'Priesterschap en episcopaat' he gives the following argument; it is somewhat technical, but it clearly deviates from the dominant view: 'For theological reasons ... I would insert ... the power of order into the power of jurisdiction. As a universal human social custom, appointing someone to a specific function is essentially a jurisdictional reality: a man- dating action by authority through which a subject gets a mandate or a mission, in this case the priestly mission. However, because of the distinctive nature of a particular domain of the priestly function of salvation, viz. the sacramental cult as the cult of Christ himself in and through his church, in this cultural sphere a purely jurisdictional mandate is not sufficient: the subject indicated or named must be equipped so to speak ontologically for it, and the tradition then calls this special equipping to perform the sacrament act in the cult the priestly "character" ... ' ('Priesterschap en episcopaat' [n. 63], 364).

112 H. Schillebeeckx, 'Het apostolisch ambt' (n. 10), 277–8.

113 'Bezinning en apostolaat' (n. 62), 317–29, where Schillebeeckx goes at length into the so- called exemption of the religious orders; cf. also 'Collaboration of religious with the episcopate, with the secular clergy and with each other', *Mission*, 188–204; 'Apostolat des réligieux et épiscopat', *Vie consacré* 38, 1966, 75–90. In content, the view in these articles from the 1960s corresponds completely to what can be found implicitly in Schillebeeckx's articles from the 1950s.

114 'Diocesane spiritualiteit' (n. 105), 151.

115 Viz. D. M. De Petter, 'Kloosterlijke geest', *TGL* 4, 1948, I, 300–320: 316–17; H. Schille- beeckx, 'Theologische grondslagen' (1949) (n. 72); cf. also 'De evangelische raden', *TGL* 9, 1953, 437–50. For Schillebeeckx's adoption of the standpoint formulated by De Petter and probably supported by his work as 'master of students' see also H. Schillebeeckx, 'Kloosterleven en heiligheid', *Ons geloof* 27, 1945, 483–6; id., 'De ascetische toeleg van de kloosterling', *TGL* 3, 1947, I, 302–30, esp. 314–15; id., 'Kloosterlijke gehoorzaamheid en geestelijke vorming', ibid. 4, 1948, I, 321–42.

116 'Theologische grondslagen' (n. 72), 78–9; cf. already 'De evangelische raden' (n. 115), 444, in which the religious state is seen as 'an extension of what the church experiences inwardly as a community of grace and thus as an entity which is not of this world'. In 1967, however, he was to contradict this in so many words: ' ... in the first instance Christian celibacy [is] not the abandonment ... of a natural value (marriage) for the sake of and with a view to a supernatural value. In the first instance celibacy is not a "supernatural value" but a human possibility of life which aims at a special dedication to a particular value'; see 'Het nieuwe mens- en Godsbeeld in conflict met het religieuze leven' (1967), in *Zending*, 235–62: 247 (ET in *Mission*, 132–70).

117 In the revision of the constitutions of the Dominican order after Vatican II, at the general chapter of River Forest it was resolved to write a 'fundamental constitution', which functions as a kind of preamble. Along the lines of the train of thought followed here by Schillebeeckx it is said there – about the significance of the priesthood of religious – that the members of the Dominican order 'have become fellow workers with the bishops through priestly ordination', that on being recognized by Pope Honorius III the order received the task of the prophetic preaching of the gospel, and that it is 'exempt' precisely

so as to be able to fulfil this task in the best way possible, in other words so that its members and goods do not fall under the local bishop.

118 H. Schillebeeckx, 'Dominikaanse spiritualiteit' (= special issue of *Biekorf*), Christmas 1954 (Arch. 635), 48, 45, 49, 50.

119 Ibid., 79: Schillebeeckx worked out the biblical – in fact the New Testament – basis for his "Christian humanism" in 'Religion and the World: Renewing the Face of the Earth' (1951), in *World*, 1–18. In his view, the foundation of the preaching task of the laity lies especially in the sacrament of confirmation: cf. 'Investituur tot meerderjarigheid. De gevormden zijn het verweer en de veroverende kracht van het christendom', *De Bazuin* 36, 1952–3, nos 32, 4–5; but above all the very long article 'Vormsel', in *Theolog. woordenboek* 3, 1958, 4840–70.

120 E. Schillebeeckx, 'God en de mens' (1958), reprinted as 'Dialogue with God and Christian Secularity', in *God and Man*, 210–33; id., 'De betekenis van het niet-godsdienstig humanisme voor het hedendaagse katholicisme' (1961), reprinted as 'Non-religious humanism and belief in God' (1961), ibid., 41–84.

121 'Theologische grondslagen' (n. 72), 74–5.

122 Ibid., 82; id., 'De leek in de kerk' (1959), in *Zending*, 87–103: 96–7 (not in the English translation).

123 H. Schillebeeckx, 'Pogingen tot concrete uitwerking van het lekenspiritualiteit', *TGL* 8, 1952, 644–56: 648 and 655–6. In the first case in the review of a book by M. Smits of Waesberghe (*Gods wil, uw heiliging: De volmaaktheid van den christen in de wereld*, Haarlem and Antwerp 1951), he opposes the author's notion that he himself is putting the 'whole *carrying capacity* of Christian lay experience in earthly commitment'; this controversy is a good indication of what is striking in his thoughts on a lay spirituality. In the second case Schillebeeckx discusses very positively the collection of articles which J. H. Walgrave wrote for *Kultuurleven* under the pseudonym 'Humanus'; this appeared as *Op menselijke grondslag: Christelijke verantwoording van de cultuur*, Antwerp 1951.

124 E. Schillebeeckx, 'Dogmatiek van ambt en lekestaat', *TvT* 2, 1962, 285–94: reprinted in a somehat abbreviated form in *Zending*, 104–33: 116 (not in the English translation). Nevertheless he signals a shift in the literature in the direction of his own standpoint, cf. E. Schillebeeckx, 'The typological definition of the Christian layman according to Vatican II' (1966), in *Mission*, 90–116: 107–13.

125 'Pogingen' (n. 125), 654: Schillebeeckx is here opposing a sentence which he meets in A. Verheul, 'De leek in de liturgische beweging', in *Het religieuze leven van de leek*, Antwerp 1951, 62–9: 62.

126 'De leek in de kerk' (n. 122), 93.

127 Cf. the striking article 'Een uniforme terminologie van het theologische begrip "leek"', *Zending*, 130–3; for the quotations in the text, 130–1 (not in the English translation). What is presented in the title as an attempt to achieve terminological clarification is in fact a description of this movement and at the same time a defence of it with a reference to 'the philosophy of language'. According to Schillebeeckx, this should have shown 'that an accentuated use of a word which establishes itself is not just a chance event, but has a place in a whole intellectual attitude, indeed is even connected with the whole tenor and orientation of an almost ideological relationship of human beings to the world' (131). For his view of lay as a term which indicates *both* membership of the people of God *and* a position over against the hierarchy, Schillebeeckx bases himself especially on I. de la Potterie, 'L'origine et le sens primitif du mot "Laïc"', *Nouv. rev. théol.* 80, 1958, 840–53. In this connection cf. also Schillebeeckx's article 'De leken in het volk van God', in *Godsvolk en leek en ambt*, DO-C dossier 7, Hilversum and Antwerp 1966, 49–58: 55–8, a text which comes from the discussions at the Council about the relationship betwween the church as the people of God and the hierarchy.

128 Cf. E. Schillebeeckx, 'The Ecclesial Life of Religious Man' (1959), in *World and Church*, 140–62, esp. 157–61.

129 'Theologische grondslagen' (n. 72), 85.

130 Schillebeeckx also makes this connection explicitly in 'The Ecclesial Life' (n. 128), 160f., where for the first time he also makes some explicit criticism of the Roman condemnation of the worker-priests (ibid., 154f.).

131 'Het apostolisch ambt' (n. 103), 267.

132 Ibid., 258–61. According to Thomas Aquinas (*Summa theol.* III, q. 7, art. 3), it was impossible to speak of 'faith' in the case of Jesus Christ. 'Faith' is spoken of because the divine reality is withdrawn from human sight and therefore is an object not of knowledge, but of faith. However, according to Thomas, Jesus as the incarnate Son of God has complete insight into the nature of God from his conception and therefore in him there can be no question of faith. This view was declared by the Holy Offfice to be official Catholic doctrine in 1918 (cf. Denzinger 3645–7). In an article in 1961 Schillebeeckx goes at length into the question of the earthly man Jesus Christ's knowledge of God, which was being intensively discussed among Catholics in the 1940s and 1950s. He tries to give as much room as possible to the humanity and the limited degree of Jesus's knowledge of God and at the same time to remain within the classic system of thought: 'Het bewustzijnsleven van Christus', *TvT* 1, 1961, 227–51. Moreover, in 1949 he already writes that for Jesus Christ the driving force is not 'God in the abstract' but 'God as *experienced*': 'Zien en getuigen zoals Christus', *TGL* 5, 1949, II, 145–54: 149.

133 'Het apostolisch ambt' (nn. 1–3), 264. The text has *haqal* instead of *qahal*, an obvious mistake.

134 Ibid., 264–7; for this view of the place and function of the hierarchy see also *Christusontmoeting*, 34–38; id., *Christ the Sacrament*, 57–9.

135 Augustine, *In evangelium Johannis tractatus*, XXI, 8.

136 Pius XII, *Mystici corporis*, no. 71.

137 H. M. Schillebeeckx, *Mary*, 169–71.

138 *Mary*, 53. Moreover, he maintains the classical notion that there is no more holiness in Christ and the church together than in Christ alone and that what is of exclusive importance is the personal appropriation of the redemption which has already taken place objectively; at the same time he calls this appropriation 'an element of the whole that God intends as the system of salvation'.

139 Pius XII, *Mystici corporis*, 74.

140 'Ik geloof in de levende God' (n. 37), 455, 459.

141 H. Schillebeeckx, 'The Place of the Church Fathers in Theology' (1957), reprinted in *Revelation* I, 215–22; for the picture of the church fathers in the renewal of Catholic theology see H. Crouzel, 'Die Patrologie', *Bilanz*, III, 504–29, esp. 525–9.

142 'Ik geloof' (n. 37), 457–8.

143 Cf. A. Darlap, 'Fundamentale Theologie der Heilsgeschichte', in *Mysterium Salutis: Grundriss heilsgeschichtlicher Dogmatik*, ed. J. Feiner and M. Löhrer, I. *Die Grundlagen heilsgeschichtlicher Dogmatik*, Einsiedeln, Zurich and Cologne 1965, 3–156, esp. 3–17.

144 Cf. R. Gibellini, *Handbuch der Theologie im 20. Jahrhundert*, Regensburg 1995, 245–60. For the significance of Rahner see H. Mühlen, 'Gnadenlehre', in *Bilanz* III, 148–92, esp. 161–3; as is well known, Rahner is not concerned with historicity as involvement in the vicissitudes of history but, following the thought of M. Heidegger, with 'historicity' in the sense of being bound to space and time. For the Protestant tradition of 'salvation-historical theology' see W. Pannenberg, 'Geschichte/Geschichtsschreibung/Geschichtsphilosophie, VIII. Systematisch-theologisch', *Theol. Realenz.* 12, 1984, 658–74, esp. 160–6. For the revival of Catholic exegesis cf. R. Marlé et al., 'Die Exegese und die biblische Theologie', in *Bilanz* II, 245–53 (on Cullmann, 359–622); L. Scheffzyck, 'Main Line of the

Development of Theology between World War I and Vatican II', in H. Jedin, K. Repgen and J. Dolan (eds), *The History of the Church* VII, 260–98: 285–8. For the favourable reception of Cullmann's salvation-historical thought among Catholic theologians cf. L. Bini, *L'intervento di Oscar Cullmann nella discussione bultmanniana*, Rome 1961, 114; Cullmann himself speaks of his connection with the project of Catholic theologians concerned for renewal in his *Peter: Disciple – Apostle – Martyr. The Historical and the Theological Problem of Peter* (1952), London 1953, 11–12; id., *Salvation in History: Salvation Historical Existence in the New Testament*, London 1967, 63–4; cf. also id., *Christ and Time*, Philadelphia and London 1951.

145 The lecture, under the title 'Groeicrisis in de theologie', given in Brussels in 1953 to the 'Flemish Association for Theology' (Arch. 968), is included in *Revelation* II, 79–105. The tendency indicated there is strongest in the introduction (265–70) and in section 2 (277–81).

146 Ibid., 274.

147 H. Schillebeeckx, 'Geschiedenis', in *Theol. woordenboek* 2, 1957, 1838–40: 1838. At this time a common criticism of Cullmann from the Catholic side was that his concept of salvation history paid too little attention to the presence of Christ's revelation of God in the church and to the redemption which is thus present for believers here and now.

148 'Sacramentaire structuur', 787.

149 'Geschiedenis' (n. 147), 1839.

150 Ibid., 1838.

151 'Sacramentaire structuur', 797.

152 Cf. G. Denzler et al., 'Die historische Theologie im 20. Jahrhundert', in *Bilanz* III, 435–529; Scheffzyk, 'Main Line of the Development of Theology' (n. 144), 282–5.

153 'Geschiedenis' (n. 147), 1839; id., 'Theology'; on 'positive theology' 117–25. M-J. Congar, 'Theologie', in *Dict. théol. cath.* 15, 1946, I, 3411–502, esp. from 3447 on.

154 'Theologie', 87; cf. Oosterhuis and Hoogeveen, *God New*, 14, where Schillebeeckx gives a positive answer to the question whether 'back to experience' primarily means back to the historical experience.

155 E. Schillebeeckx, *Op zoek naar de levende God*, Nijmegen 1959, reprinted in a somewhat abbreviated form in *God and Man*, 18–40: 26.

156 Cf. the eight-volume *Mysterium Salutis: Grundriss heilsgeschichtlicher Dogmatik*, ed. J. Feiner and M. Löhrer, Einsiedeln, Zurich and Cologne 1965–81, and the six-volume *Handbuch der Pastoraltheologie. Praktische Theologie der Kirche in ihrer Gegenwart*, ed. F. X. Arnold et al., Freiburg, etc. 1964–72.

157 K. Rahner, *Geist in Welt: Zur Metaphysik der menschlichen Erkenntnis bei Thomas von Aquin*, Innsbruck 1939.

158 Id., *Hearers of the Word: The Basis of a Philosophy of Religion*, New York 1969; for Rahner's anthropology cf. P. Eicher, *Die anthropologische Wende: Karl Rahners philosophischer Weg vom Wesen des Menschen zur personalen Existenz*, Freiburg 1970.

159 'Ik geloof' (n. 37), 458.

160 H. Schillebeeckx, 'Het hoopvole Christusmysterie', *TGL* 7, 1951, 5–33: 21; page references are in brackets in the text.

161 Cf. also 'Reikhalzend uitzien naar de komst van Gods dag', *De Bazuin* 36, 1952–3, no. 12, 6–7. 'Het hoopvolle Christusmysterie' works out an article which appeared under the title '*Vos qui vocati estis sancti*', in *Biekorf* 32, 1949, autumn 2–13; Arch. 3212. However, in 1949 the emphasis was on the still hidden presence of redemption and the psychological effects that this has for the believer, whereas in 1951 Schillebeeckx says that it is not just a matter of the internal psychology of hope but that hope points to 'the not-yet-being-completely-perfected of the mystery of Christ itself' (4–5). He must therefore have had this insight around 1950.

162 H. Schillebeeckx, 'De hoop kernprobleem der christelijke confessies', *Kultuurleven* 23, 1956, 110–25: 10.

163 Cf. Cullmann, *Christ* (n. 144).

164 Ibid., 22, with reference to *Summa theol.* II–II, q. 129, arts 6. and 8.

165 Cf. also his article 'Ascension and Pentecost', *Worship* 35, 1961, 336–6.

166 The quotations are from Eph. 4.15 and 1 Cor. 6.15 respectively.

167 See Maltha and Thuys, *Dogmatiek*, 579–80.

168 Schillebeeckx, *Mary*, 49–53. At this point, moreover, the text differs considerably from the first version, *Maria I*; cf. my 'Op zoek naar Maria ... en verder: Schillebeeckx' mariologie en haar actuele betekenis', *TvT* 33, 1993, 242–66, esp. 255–6, and also the conclusion of the chapter. 'Co-redemptrix' is a title for Mary which was being vigorously discussed in this period and which Schillebeeckx is thus here extending to all believers. At this time the relationship between objective and subjective redemption was being vigorously discussed in connection with the role of Mary in the redemption, cf. C. A. de Ridder, *Maria medeverlosseres: De discussie in de huidige rooms-katholieke theologie over de medewerking van de moeder Gods in het verlossingwerk*, Utrecht 1960, passim.

169 *Mary*, 151.

170 H. Schillebeeckx, 'Het mysterie van onze Godsliefde', *TGL* 7, 1951, 609–26: 609–10; references to the text are given in brackets. There is an English translation, 'Love comes from God', *Cross and Crown* 16, 1964, 190–204.

171 H. Schillebeeckx, 'De broederlijke liefde als heilswerkelijkheid', *TGL* 8, 1952, 600–19: 604; page references are given in brackets in the text.

172 This was the (one-sided) neoscholastic interpretation of Thomas Aquinas' statement (*Summa theol.* II–II, q. 25, art. 1) that God is the formal reason for love of neighbour.

173 Cf. the title of the French translation of this article, 'L'amour vient de Dieu: La charité fraternelle, mystère du salut', *Vie spirituelle* 88, 1953, 563–79.

174 H. Schillebeeckx, 'De heiligmakende genade als heiliging van ons bestaan', *TGL* 10, 1954, 7–27: 7; again page references are given in brackets in the text.

175 The process of beatification was set in motion very soon after Thérèse's death, and Pius X called her the most important saint of modern times; cf. *Sainte Thérèse de l'Enfant Jesus glorifiée par la Sainte Eglise: Actes officiels et discours pontificaux*, Lisieux 1931. In 1947, 50 years after her death, a special issue of *Tijdschrift voor Geestelijk Leven* appeared on Thérèse and her special significance as 'living word of God' and 'master in the spiritual life' with a 'new message of holiness'; for the other literature which appeared on this occasion and its tendency cf. D. M. De Petter, 'Peilingen naar de kern van Theresia's leven en leer', *TGL* 3, 1947, II, 207–18; id., 'Theresiana', *TGL* 5, 1949, 56–64.

176 For the significance of Thérèse of Lisieux for Suhard and the 'mission de France', cf. J. Vinatier, *Le cardinal Suhard (1874–1919): L'évêque de renouveau missionaire*, Paris 1983, 67–81: 221–52.

177 Cf. also H. Schillebeeckx, 'God in menselijkheid', *TGL* 13, 1957, 697–712: 708. Since the incarnation of God in Christ 'we know ... that we no longer need to seek the redemption for the problems of our life, for our weal and woe, and also for our unmerited happiness, in a beyond which is vague for us, beyond the limits of suffering and death and happiness. Redemption descended into suffering, life and death. We now rise above it in the pain itself.'

178 'De dood van een christen', *Kultuurleven* 22, 1955, 421–30, 508–19: 424; cf. also id., 'De dood. Schoonste mogelijkheid van de christen', *De Bazuin* 35, 1951–52, no. 9, 4–5; id., 'De dood, lichtende horizont van de oude dag', ibid., 39, 1955–56, nos 11–12, 4–5. In his reflections on death Schillebeeckx is clearly influenced by D. M. De Petter ('Pretiosa mors', *TGL* 6, 1950, 585–91).

179 'De dood van een christen' (n. 178), 425; moreover the Council of Trent declared the punitive character of death part of church doctrine, cf. Denzinger 1511–12.

180 'De dood van een christen' (n. 178), 429.

181 Ibid., 513–14.

182 *Maria I.* For an evaluation of Schillebeeckx's mariology and its theological future see my 'Op zoek naar Maria' (n. 168).

183 That Schillebeeckx's work met a need is evident from the frequency within which extracts and summaries of it and recapitulations of ideas from it appeared, often in journals addressed to a wider audience. Cf. H. Schillebeeckx, 'Het wonder dat Maria heet', *Thomas* 7, 1953–4, no. 7, 5–7; H. Schillebeeckx, 'Maria onze hoop', ibid., 8, 1954–5, no. 1, 4–6; H. Schillebeeckx, 'De zware strijd van Maria's geloof', ibid., no. 2, 6–7; id., 'De bruid van de H.Geest', ibid., no. 3, 3–5; H. Schillebeeckx, 'Betekenis en waarde van de Mariaverschijningen', *Standaard van Maria* 31, 1955, 154–62; id., 'De Schrift zwijgt over Maria', *De Bazuin* 38, 1955, no. 16, 2; id., 'De Mariaverschijningen in het leven van de kerk', *De Rosenkrans* 84, 1957–8, 131–3; id., 'Maria "meeste-verloste Moeder"', *De Linie* 13, 1958, no. 641; id., 'Die Maria-gestalte in het christelijk belijden', *Stud. Cath.* 3, 1958, 241–55; id., 'Verschillend standpunt van exegese en dogmatiek', in *Maria in het boodschapsverhaal (Verslagboek der 16e mariale dagen 1959)*, Tongerloo 1960, 53–74; id., 'Het mensdom is reeds verheerlijkt in Christus en Maria', *De Rosenkrans* 88, 1961–62, 136–7; cf. also id., 'Rond het geval "Konnersreuth"', *TGL* 11, 1955, 52–63. The translations of the second version into French, English, Italian, Catalan, Portugese and Spanish also say something about the reception of Schillebeeckx's mariology, but they all date only from the 1960s.

184 The article 'Maria' in *Theol. woordenboek* 2, 1957, 3078–151, consists of three sections: one on biblical theology by J. van Dodewaard (3078–86), one on the history of dogma by E. Hendrikx (3086–124), and the section by Schillebeeckx, meant as a 'theological synthesis' (3126–51). This is a brief summary and survey of Mary. Cf. also his contribution 'Maria' in *Catholica: Geillustreerd encyclopedisch vademecum voor het katholieke leven*, The Hague [2]1961, 1040–4.

185 See *AAS* 45, 1953, 757.

186 Pius XI, *Quas primas*, no. 36.

187 See especially the encyclical *Supremi apostolatus* (1883); cf. B. C. Pope, 'Immaculate and Powerful: The Marian Revival in the Nineteenth Century', in *Immaculate and Powerful*, ed. C. W. Atkinson et al., Boston 1985, 173–200: 183.

188 Pius XII, address *La testimonianze* of 1 November 1954 (*AAS* 46, 1954, 662–6), no. 9. The phrase *acies ordinata* comes from the breviary prayer for the Festival of the Assumption of Mary.

189 Pius XII, encyclical *Ad caeli reginam* (1954), no. 45.

190 Pius IX, encyclical, *Ineffabilis Deus* (1854), no. 24.

191 Pius X, encyclical, *Ad diem illum* (1904), nos 19, 24–6; cf. E. Maeckelberghe, *Desperately Seeking Mary. A Feminist Appropriation of a Traditional Religious Symbol*, Kampen 1991, 98–9. M. Warner (*Alone of All Her Sex. The Myth and the Cult of the Virgin Mary*, London 1976, 237) and B. C. Pope ('Immaculate and Powerful' [n. 187]) wrongly emphasize only this last.

192 Pius XII, bull *Munificentissimus Deus* (1950), no. 42.

193 Cf. S. de Fiores, 'Maria in der Geschichte von Theologie und Frömmigkeit', *Handbuch der Marienkunde* I, ed. W. Beinert and H. Petri, Regensburg [2]1996, 99–266, esp. 208–12. G. Söll indicates four novelties in the most recent Marian dogmas: they are not the repudiation of a heresy but the product of the dynamic of faith; they were not proclaimed by a council but by the pope; they cannot be based on the Bible; they appeal to the sense of faith in the living church ('Mariologie', *Handbuch der Dogmengeschichte* III/4, Freiburg, Basel and Vienna 1978).

194 Without explicitly saying so, here Schillebeeckx is taking up the structure of Thomas's

Summa theologiae, which puts the questions relating to Mary (III, q. 27–30) in the middle of the questions about Jesus Christ (III, 1.1–59).

195 *Maria I*, 12 and 16.

196 Schillebeeckx himself indicates this in the retrospect on his early mariological publications. See his 'Mariology: Yesterday, Today, Tomorrow', in id. and Catharina Halkes, *Mary, Yesterday, Today and Tomorrow*, London and New York 1993, 12–42: 18–19.

197 Again this is also a Thomistic motif. Thomas opposes the idea that Mary is redeemed by anything other than 'through the sacrifice of Christ' and emphasizes that she is not redeemed in the womb from the guilt to which all of nature is subject (*Summa theol.* III, q. 27). As a consequence of this there was an extensive discussion about the relationship of Thomas – after all the Catholic thinker *par excellence* – to the dogma of the immaculate conception. Schillebeeckx goes into this question in *Mary*, 62–3, and interprets 'St Thomas's denial of the immaculate conception' as emphasis on the fact that Mary is really redeemed by Christ. Duns Scotus, he says, will 'only have' to add 'by exemption' for the full and real significance of the absence of original sin in Mary to emerge in its precise dimensions: '*sublimiore modo redempta*, truly redeemed, but in an exceptional and unique manner' (69–70).

198 *Maria I*, 22.

199 Ibid., 32.

200 Ibid., 23–25. The idea that virginity stands for receptivity is especially worked out by the Dominican mystic Eckhart. The image of Mary as 'daughter of Zion', in other words as a Jewish woman, is a central point in the mariological discussion after the war: cf. H.-M. Köster, 'Die Mariologie im 20. Jahrhundert', *Bilanz* III, 126–47, 136, and the literature mentioned there.

201 *Maria I*, 27, 28–9, 31–2.

202 Schillebeeckx even sees a 'break' between the views in the two editions (see his 'Mariology: Yesterday, Today, Tomorrow' [n. 196], 17–18); however, this seems an exaggeration.

203 *Mary*, 9.

204 'God in menselijkheid' (n. 177), 707–8: cf. also 'Jesus Christus, II: theologisch', *Catholica* (n. 184), 675–80.

205 *Mary*, 11, 42, 45. In the first chapter Schillebeeckx largely takes up his article 'Het geloofsleven van de "Dienstmaagd des Heren"', *TGL* 10, 1954. For the developed argument he is strongly dependent on R. Laurentin, *Court traité de théologie mariale* (²1953), 19–29, and for his treatment of the Magnificat on A. Gelin, *Les pauvres de Yahvé*, Paris 1953, ch. 6.

206 Ibid., 11–12.

207 Ibid., 13–14.

208 Ibid., 36–8.

209 Cf. De Ridder, *Maria medeverlosseres* (n. 168). For the relationship between subjective and objective redemption see *Mary*, 48–53; Schillebeeckx develops his thought on this in '*Mutua correlatio inter redemptionem obiectivam eamque subiectivam B. M. Virginis*', in *Virgo Immaculata, Acta congr. Mariologici-Mariani 1954*, IX, Rome 1957, 305–21.

210 *Mary*, 158, cf. 99–101. Strangely enough, in *Maria I* Schillebeeckx had paid no attention to Mary's assumption.

211 *Mary*, 159: '*Maria portio est Ecclesia, sanctum membrum, excellens membrum, supereminens membrum, sed tamen totius corporis membrum*' (Augustine, *Sermo 25 de verbis evang. Matt. XII*, 41–50; PL 46, 938).

212 *Maria I*, 35–42; cf. *Mary*, 105–16, 157–9. During the Second Vatican Council, along these lines Schillebeeckx was to oppose the title 'Mary, Mother of the Church', proposed in the first drafts of the council documents and announced in 1964 by Pope Paul VI; cf. his 'Mariology: Yesterday, Today, Tomorrow' (n. 196), 212, and the notes on what was

planned as a separate council document on Mary, to be found in the Schillebeeckx archives.

213 *Mary*, 100.

214 Ibid., 159.

215 *Maria*, 58–9; *Maria*, 141–2. This thought is along the lines of Jung's view that the Marian dogmas of 1854 and 1950 could be regarded as an elevation of the feminine principle and as a metaphysical rooting of the equality of the woman and man ('Answer to Job', in *Psychology and Religion* II, Collected Works, London 1958, 355–474). Only much later does an interpretation of mariology along these lines become more common: cf. R. R. Ruether, *Mary: The Feminine Face of the Church*, Philadelphia 1977; A. M. Greeley, *The Mary Myth. On the Femininity of God*, New York 1977; L. Boff, *The Maternal Face of God. The Feminine and Its Religious Expressions*, New York 1987; C. Mulack, *Maria; Die Geheime Göttin im Christentum*, Stuttgart 1985.

216 *Mary*, 184–8.

217 Ibid., 234.

218 Ibid., 217. Cf. H. Schillebeeckx, 'Het gebed, centrale daad van het menselijk leven', *TGL* 10, 1954, 469–70: 473: 'Religion now is none other than the experience of the depth-dimension of our life, but at the same time as a relief of our existence-in-the-world. Religion is thus a depth meaning, a fine sense of the deepest and most silent in all things, in ourselves and others: God's intimate presence which is a giving and getting, attractive, ever-active presence. Prayer is none other than the meaningful experience of this situation.'

219 Ibid., 217, 219.

220 The propagation of the prayer of the rosary had long been entrusted to the Dominicans, and in Dominican circles also led to the notion that the rosary came from Dominic. Schillebeeckx, however, resolutely rejects this view. *Mary*, 210–19, contains a section on the rosary, in fact a somewhat revised version of Schillebeeckx's article 'De gezinsro-zenkrans', *TGL* 6, 1950, 523–32. Cf. already his 'Rozenkrans, bidden in nuchtere werke-lijkheid', *De Bazuin*, 1949–50, nos 1, 4–6. Parts of the article on the rosary in *Mary* were later used in the journal of the Flemish apostolate for the rosary, cf. 'Providentieel red-mittel', *De Rozenkrans* 82, 1955–6, 18–21: 'De leer van het rozenkransgebed', ibid., 53–5; 'Rozenkransgebed: verantwoord gebed', ibid., 8, 1957–8, 6–7; 'De eigen techniek van de rozenkrans', ibid., 85, 1958–9, 208–11.

221 'De hoop kernprobleem' (n. 162): for the documents see *The Evanston Report: The Second Assembly of the World Council of Churches 1954*, London 1955. Unlike Congar, who wrote a major ecumenical study before the war (Y. M.-J. Congar, *Divided Christendom* (1937), London 1939), Schillebeeckx had occupied himself with ecumenism only incidentally.

222 Cf. J. Moltmann, *Theology of Hope,* London 1967.

223 'De hoop kernprobleem' (n. 162), 115, 119, 123.

224 'Supernaturalism, Unchristian and Christian Expectations of the Future' (1959), in *World*, 163–76.

225 Cf. especially 'Enkele katholieke notities over de intrede Gods in die geschiedenis', reprinted in a publication by the Nederlands Gespreks Centrum which aimed at encouraging ecumenical contact, *Het wonder*, Kampen, etc. 1963, 52–5, but written earlier as a contribution to the discussion.

CHAPTER 4

1 H. Häring, 'Met mensen op weg, voor mensen op weg: Over het theologisch denken van Edward Schillebeeckx', in *Mensen maken de kerk*, ed. H. ter Haar, Baarn and Nijmegen 1989, 27–46: 35.

2   According to the editors, the *Theologisch woordenboek* came into being in the conviction that 'theology as the science of God's revelation ... [is] so important that it is very desirable to open up the possibility for more advanced Catholics in the [Dutch-language] area to have a rapid and easy orientation on the theological questions which must attract their attention in one way or another'. It was meant 'for priests in pastoral work, for theological students, and for laity with an academic training'. The view of theology was in the first place rather traditional: 'By theology is understood the communication and scientific study of the truths which are taught to us by revelation.' The dogmatic and doctrinal contributions in the first part, which appeared in 1952, were almost all written by A. H. Maltha. Schillebeeckx wrote 7 in the first volume, 16 in the second, from 1957, and 23 in the third and last volume, from 1958. On some occasions material from his lectures can be found in these contributions. That the growing number of contributions also indicated a growing openness to his theological views is especially clear from the fact that in the third part he takes a considerable amount of space – 58 columns – to expound his dynamic view of theology.

3   P. Tillich, *Systematic Theology* I, Chicago 1951, 12 and 14. For Tillich's theology of culture see especially his 'Über die Idee einer Theologie der Kultur', in id., *Die religiöse Substanz der Kultur: Schriften zur Theologie der Kultur*, Gesammelte Werke IX, Stuttgart 1967, 13–31; id., 'Religion und Kultur', ibid., 82–93; id., 'Über die Grenzen von Religion und Kultur', ibid., 94–9; id., 'Aspekte einer religiösen Analyse der Kultur', ibid., 100–9 (from 1919, 1938, 1954 and 1959 respectively). For Tillich's place in the discussion of culture and in German Protestant theology since the nineteenth century see F. W. Graf and K. Tanner, 'Kultuur II. Theologiegeschichtlich, I', *Theol. Realenz.* 20, 1990, 187–209.

4   See esp. 'Correlation between human question and Christian answer' (1970), in Schillebeeckx, *Understanding*, 78–101.

5   For the 'method of correlation' cf. Tillich, *Systematic Theology* I (n. 3), 59–66; Schillebeeckx, 'Correlation' (n. 4), 78–101. For Tillich's relation to existentialism cf. A. Horn, *Verantwortung heute: Eine philosophisch-theologische Auseinandersetzung mit dem Denken Martin Heideggers, Jean-Paul Sartres und Paul Tillichs zur Frage nach Verantwortung und Verantwortlichkeit des Menschen*, Würzburg 1980; for his relation to socialism, including the thought of the Frankfurt School, cf. T. Brattinga, *Theologie van het socialisme. Een studie over het religieus socialisme, met name de theorie over het religieus socialisme zoals die is ontwikkeld door Paul Tillich*, Bolsward 1980.

6   Tillich 'Über die Idee einer Theologie der Kultur' (n. 3), 28.

7   *Systematic Theology* I (n. 3), ix.

8   See especially his books *Heilseconomie, Christusontmoeting/Christ the Sacrament*, and *Marriage*. The first and last books are both the first parts of diptychs which were never completed.

9   Schillebeeckx, *Inleiding*, 263.

10   *Systematic Theology* 1 (n. 3), 3–8; here he has especially the followers of Karl Barth in view; in his eyes they tended towards a position which he calls 'neo-orthodox'.

11   For this view of the history of Catholic theology see Schoof, *Aggiornamento*, 105–63; for the position of Schillebeeckx in it, ibid., 148–55.

12   Cf. his reflections on this along the lines of what Thomas himself says about the so-called '*auctoritates*' in the articles 'Gezagsargument' and 'Loci theologici' in *Theol. woordenboek* 2, 1957, 1908–20, 3004–6, brought together in one article in *Revelation* I, 245–65. Later, when he was newly arrived in Nijmegen, Schillebeeckx was to give lectures on the theology of Thomas in its historical context, very much in line with the work of M.-D. Chenu. Cf. Arch. 355 from 1958–59, in which Chenu is followed very closely, and Arch. 3099.

13   F. de Grijs, 'Wat kan er eigenlijk op de punt van een naald? Over de anagogische zin van

de geschiedenis', in *Meedenken met Edward Schillebeeckx*, ed. H. Häring et al., Baarn 1983, 69–79: 69.

14 E. C. F. A. Schillebeeckx, *Op zoek naar de levende God*, Utrecht and Nijmegen 1959, 21–2.

15 H. Schillebeeckx, lecture 'Naar een levenstheologie?' (Arch. 358), 0; cf. Ch. 1, pp.61–7 above.

16 Schillebeeckx, *Inleiding*, 263.

17 Cf. esp. M.-D. Chenu, *Introduction à l'étude de Saint Thomas d'Aquin*, Montreal and Paris 1950.

18 On this point it is worth examining the approach of Schillebeeckx's lectures alongside that of Karl Rahner, with whom Schillebeeckx is often compared, and all of whose works, according to reliable witnesses, he read in this period. Rahner's lectures on creation, grace and sin, which date from the same period as Schillebeeckx's Louvain lectures, have been edited (K. Rahner, *Sämtliche Werke VIII: Der Mensch in der Schöpfung*, Zurich and Freiburg im Breisgau 1998, 41–511: '*Tractatus de Deo creante et elevante et de peccato originali*'). Whereas Schillebeeckx tries to show that Thomas's thought is tailored to current problems and subordinates the aim of his lecture to that, in Rahner the neoscholastic approach is largely maintained and the renewal comes about through a substantially new interpretation of the data of the church's magisterium, the Bible and tradition, brought together in the classical way. In the systematic treatment of these data Rahner reinterprets them in the direction of a theological anthropology on an existential basis (for a brief presentation see K.-H. Neufeld, 'Editionsbericht', ibid., XI–XXVI: XIII–XV).

19 To this degree there is an important agreement between Schillebeeckx's approach to Thomas and that of his younger colleague and later friend Johann Baptist Metz in Metz's *Theologische Anthropozentrik: Über die Denkform des Thomas van Aquin*, Munich 1962. Neither concentrates on Thomas's external system but on the 'basic view' or 'thought form' which inspires the system, and both locate Thomas's interest in the way in which he connects human life as 'nature' with God and takes it up through 'grace' into supernature. However, Schillebeeckx does not share Metz's standpoint that Thomas's thought in this way, prompted by biblical anthropocentrism, represents the 'historical inauguration' of modernity (ibid., 125). For a comparison of both views of Thomas see A.-M. Korte, *Een passie voor transcendentie: Feminisme, theologie en moderniteit in het denken van Mary Daly*, Kampen 1992, 12–20, 48–59.

20 Thus Schillebeeckx in *Jesus*, 618f.

21 For a good assessment of the continuity and discontinuity on this point cf. P. Kennedy, *Deus Humanissimus: The Knowability of God in the Theology of Edward Schillebeeckx*, Fribourg 1993, esp. 200–16.

22 E. Schillebeeckx, 'Voorwoord', in *Theologisch perspectief. I. Fundamentele problemen*, ed. E. Schillebeeckx, Bussum 1958, 7–8; this is the translation of the whole of a German collection edited by others, in which he had written an article: *Fragen der Theologie heute*, ed. J. Feiner et al., Einsiedeln 1957.

23 Schillebeeckx, *Heilseconomie* V. Given the success of this book he was at least partly right here. But one must also say that it is evident from this how much he sees the contemporary problems from the perspective of the professional theologian, cf. Borgman, 'Universiteit'.

24 *Op zoek naar de levende God* (1959), ET 'The Search for the Living God', in *God and Man*, 18–40.

25 'Voorwoord', 7; cf. also id., 'Geloofswaarheid', in *Theol. woordenboek* 2, 1957, 1755–8.

26 *Heilseconomie* V. Cf. Schillebeeckx's striking exposition of the 'mystery of faith' as something that is not incomprehensible to human understanding, but 'on the contrary is a light that puts life in a quite different perspective and helps us to understand sufficiently how to live from it within the mystery of the mystery of faith', *Theol. woordenboek* 2, 1957, 1750–2: 1751.

27   Cf. H. Schillebeeckx,' Geschiedenis', in ibid., 1838–40; id., 'Theology', 110–16.
28   Schoof, 'Aandrang', 13–14: 14.
29   See especially A. R. Van de Walle, 'Theologie over de werkelijkheid: Een betekenis van het werk van Edward Schillebeeckx', *TvT* 14, 1974, 463–90.
30   Oosterhuis and Hoogeveen, *God New*, 2–3.
31   Quoted by A. L. Mayer, 'Liturgie und Laientum', in *Wiederbegegnung von Kirche und Kultur in Deutschland*, Munich 1927, 225–41: 241; see T. Ruster, *Die verlorene Nützlichkeit der Religion: Katholizismus und Moderne in der Weimarer Republik*, Paderborn, etc. 1994, 264. For Mayer's views cf. A. Schilson, *Theologie als Sakramententheologie: Die Mysterientheologie Odo Casels*, Mainz 1982, 91–7: for the history of the liturgical movement, of which there is as yet no consecutive history, cf. H. C. Schmidt-Lauber, 'Liturgische Bewegungen', in *Theol. Realenz.* 21, 1991, 401–6: 404–6, and the literature mentioned there, also Schilson, *Theologie*, 51–97.
32   Cf. A. Haquin, *Dom Lambert Beauduin et le renouveau liturgique*, Gembloux 1970; for the text of Beauduin's report see 238–41.
33   That is done by V. Warnach, 'Mysterientheologie', in *Lex f. Theol. u. Kirche,* ^{2}1961, 724–7.
34   Cf. Schilson, *Theologie als Sakramententheologie* (n. 31), 50–7; Ruster, *Die verlorene Nützlichkeit* (n. 31), esp. 113–79.
35   O. Casel, 'Die Wende zum Mysterium' in id., *Das christliche Kultmysterium* (1932), Regensburg ^{4}1960, 17–25: 19 and 21.
36   Cf. id., 'Situierung der katholischen Liturgischen Bewegung' (1929), reprinted in id., *Mysterientheologie: Ansatz und Gestalt*, ed. A. Schilson, Regensburg 1986, 29–32.
37   For Casel's theology cf. V. Warnach, 'Odo Casel', in *Tendenzen der Theologie im 20. Jahrhundert: Eine Geschichte in Porträts*, ed. J. Schulz, Stuttgart and Freiburg 1966, 277–82; B. Neunheuser, 'Casel, Odo', in *Theol. Realenz.* 7, 1981, 643–7; Schilson, *Theologie als Sakramententheologie* (n. 31); id., 'Odo Casel und seine Mysterientheologie: Aspekte eine produktiven Erinnerung', in *Mysterientheologie* (n. 36); Ruster, *Verlorene Nützlichkeit* (n. 31), 247–68.
38   Thus in a 1927 address: reprinted in O. Casel, *Mysterium der Ekklesia: Von der Gemeinschaft aller Erlösten in Christus Jesus*, Mainz 1961, 349–55: 349, 355.
39   'Liturgische Handlung und katholische Aktion' (1930), reprinted in id., *Mysterium der Ekklesia* (n. 38), 266–72: 270.
40   Through his kindred spirit, Ildefons Herwegen (1874–1946), the promoter of the liturgical movement from Maria Laach, who as his abbot was at the same time the one who from 1927 to 1941 gave him the influential post of editor of the *Jahrbuch für Liturgiewissenschaft*, Casel was associated with the political Catholicism of this time. In 1933 Herwegen remarked: 'what the liturgical movement is in the religious sphere, Fascism is in the political sphere'. Casel himself seems to concentrate all his attention on the liturgy: his archaic, ecclesiocentric and hierarchical picture of society nowhere becomes a political programme. Cf. R. Faber, *Roma aeterna: Zur Kritik der 'Konservativen Revolution'*, Würzburg 1982, 136–58; Ruster, *Verlorene Nützlichkeit* (n. 31), 253–6, For the relationship between Casel and Herwegen cf. Schilson, *Theologie als Sakramententheologie* (n. 31), 60–81.
41   O. Casel, 'Die Stellung des Kultusmysteriums im Christentum' (1930–31), in id., *Das christliche Kultmysterium* (n. 35), 25–74: 25.
42   This is the beginning of the French summary at the end of the book, which Schillebeeckx emphatically describes as 'not so much a resumé of this part of the book as a succinct rendering of the basic ideas' of the study; see *Heilseconomie*, 665–72: 665.
43   This led to fierce polemic over Casel's 'Mysterientheologie' (cf. T. Filhaut, *Die Kontroverse über die Mysterienlehre*, Warendorf 1947), which was further accentuated by the remark in the encyclical *Mediator Dei* (1947), no. 163, that Christ's mysteries remain 'ever present

and active', not, however, 'in a vague and uncertain way as some modern writers hold, but in the way that Catholic doctrine teaches'.

44 O. Casel, *Glaube, Gnosis, Mysterium*, Münster 1941, 19–20 n. 19; for Casel's theological teaching see Schilson, *Theologie als Sakramententheologie* (n. 31), 109–17.

45 Ibid., 111, 113.

46 Here Schillebeeckx takes up an analysis of Casel's theology by the Dutch Jesuit L. Monden (*Het misoffer als mysterie. Een studie over de heilige Mis als sacramenteel offer in het licht van de mysterieleer van dom Odo Casel*, Roermond and Maaseik 1948, 85–6), who thinks that Casel has a tacit philosophical presupposition. On the basis of his study of the Bible and the church fathers Casel thinks that the liturgy is presented as symbols which make believers of like form to Christ by participation in his act of redemption. According to Monden, his conclusion that therefore Christ's act of redemption must really be present under the external symbols is based on the presupposition that 'making like in form and participation [are] not possible without the actual presence of that to which one is made of like form'. Cf. *Heilseconomie*, 217; for a more detailed discussion of Monden's work see ibid., 223–7.

47 For Casel's view of the pagan mystery religions cf. Schilson, *Theologie als Sakramententheologie* (n. 31), 254–64.

48 O. Casel, 'Antike und christliche Mysterien' (1927), in id., *Das christliche Kultmysterium* (n. 35), 75–89:79; here he quotes a paper of his own from 1926.

49 Contrary to what has been suggested (J. Ambaum, *Glaubenszeichen: Schillebeeckx' Auffassung von den Sakramenten*, Regensburg 1980, 234–5), there is a clear affinity between Schillebeeckx's approach to the early Christian vocabulary and the approach of the so-called 'Nijmegen school' of J. Schrijnen and C. Mohrmann, which started from the notion that language was above all a social fact and tried primarily to discover the meaning of the word behind its usage within the Christian group language., See J. Schrijnen, *Characteristik des Altchristlichen Latein*, Nijmegen 1932; C. Mohrmann, 'L'etude de la latinité chrétienne', in *Conférences de l'Institut de Linguistique de l'Université de Paris* 10, 1950–51, 125–41: for the background see M. Derks and S. Verheesen-Stegeman, *Wetenschap als roeping: Prof. Dr Christine Mohrmann (1903–1988), classica*, Nijmegen 1998. Mohrmann formulated her view of the development of the meaning of '*musterion/sacramentum*' (which differs from that of Schillebeeckx) in her article 'Sacramentum dans les plus anciens textes chrétiens', *Harv. Theol. Rev.* 47, 1954, 141–52. Schillebeeckx took account of this view in his articles 'Mysterie' and 'Sacrament' in *Theol. woordenboek* 3, 1958, 3387–92 and 4185–231.

50 *Heilseconomie*, 21–106: 23. For a summary of this part see Ambaum, *Glaubenszeichen* (n. 48), 23–8. Schillebeeckx sums up his view of the relationship between the Christian cult and that of the mystery religions in 'Mysteriecultus', *Theol. woordenboek* 3, 1958, 3392–5; in his view one can 'at most speak of an "influence in form"'. The term 'primordial sacrament' was later to be made familiar by O. Semmelroth, *Die Kirche als Ursakrament*, Frankfurt am Main 1953, but Schillebeeckx here seems to be using the term independently of him. The approaches of the two authors are related, and later (in *Christ the Sacrament*, 57f.), Schillebeeckx also speaks emphatically of the '*primordial sacrament* that the church is here on earth after the ascension of Christ' (cf. also *Christusontmoeting*, 34ff.: 'The church: primordial sacrament of the glorified Christ within the world'). But there is a difference of emphasis between the two: in Schillebeeckx, the sacraments as pointers to Jesus Christ as primordial sacrament are in fact the basis of the church; in Semmelroth – and in his footsteps in K. Rahner – the church as the sacramental presence of Jesus Christ is, rather, the basis of the sacraments. Semmelroth's view directly influenced the talk of the church as a sacrament in the Vatican II dogmatic constitution *Lumen gentium*, esp. nos 1 and 9. For the connection between Schillebeeckx's views and those of Semmelroth and

Rahner cf. P. P. M. Guglielminetti, *L'estensione e l'approfondimento della nozione di sacramento in K. Rahner, E. Schillebeeckx, O. Semmelroth*, Rome 1971; B. Prezwozny, *Church as the Sacrament of the Unity of All Mankind in* Lumen gentium *and* Gaudium et spes *and in Semmelroth, Schillebeeckx and Rahner*, Rome 1979.

51 For the quotation see Schilson, *Theologie als Sakramententheologie* (n. 35), 258; cf. also Casel, 'Die Stellung' (n. 41), 53–5.

52 Schillebeeckx's attitude is also connected with his view of the church fathers as authoritative but in principle nevertheless 'ordinary' representatives of the post-biblical tradition: see his contribution 'The Place of the Church Fathers in Theology' (1957), in *Revelation* I, 215–22. For a fundamental discussion of the question of the 'non-Christian influence on the patristic reflection on faith' and Schillebeeckx's markedly philosophical and theological–anthropological answer cf. *Heilseconomie*, 21–61: 51. Ambaum, *Glaubenszeichen* (n. 49), 235 n. 7, rightly calls this influence a premise of Schillebeeckx's. He traces his view of the relationship between nature and supernature back to the approach to the early church by the 'history-of-religions school'.

53 It is beyond the scope of this study to answer the question whether Schillebeeckx's view of the history of the term *musterion/sacramentum* is adequate. It is clear that in *Heilseconomie* he reads the facts within the Thomistic framework which he develops later in the book. In a later article ('Sacrament' [n. 49], 4185–9) he adjusts his view of the specific history of the term on the basis of more recent studies, cf. Ambaum, *Glaubenszeichen* (n. 49), 24–5, 236–7, nn. 9–12.

54 C. E. O'Neill, 'Die Sakramententheologie', *Bilanz* III, 244–94: 256. Cf. also A. Haquin, 'Naar een fundamentele theologie van de sacramenten: Van H. Schillebeeckx tot L.-M. Chauvet', in *Hedendaagse accenten in de sacramentologie*, ed. J. Lamberts, Louvain and Amersfoort 1994, 65–85, esp. 70–3.

55 *Summa theol.* III, q. 62, art. 6; see A. Vonier, 'A Key to the Doctrine of the Eucharist', reprinted in the *Collected Works of Abbot Vonier, II: The Church and the Sacraments*, London 1952, 228–360. For the significance of this book see O. Neill, *Die Sakramententheologie* (n. 54), 249–50; Sudhir Kumar Kujur, *The Eucharistic Theology of Dom Anscar Vonier, OSB*, Rome 1992. Along the same lines see M. de la Taille, *Mysterium fidei*, Paris 1921.

56 *Heilseconomie* VI: the rest of this section is cited in the text with page numbers in brackets.

57 Cf. the whole section ibid., 2–17. This view of the *Summa theologiae* clearly makes Thomas a theologian and dismisses the notion that he was really a speculative metaphysician of a Christian kind. In fact to the present day this notion dominates the picture of Thomas in broad circles, though meanwhile it has often rightly been disputed.

58 Ibid., 125–31. The theology of the sacraments is especially to be found in the fourth book of Thomas, *Scriptum super Sententiis*.

59 Ibid., 131–8. Schillebeeckx's use of 'cultual' seems to have derived from the French *cultuelle*: relating to worship.

60 For this view Schillebeeckx bases himself on Thomas's statement: 'the things of the senses *by nature* have a certain aptness for indicating spiritual effects, but this aptness is applied through divine instruction with a view to a special designation': see *Summa theol.* III, q. 4, art. 2, quoted in *Heilseconomie*, 140: Schillebeeckx's italics.

61 H. Schillebeeckx, 'Sacramenteel leven, I' , *Thomas* 3, 1949–50, nos 3, 5–6: 5.

62 Here Schillebeeckx bases himself on D. M. De Petter, 'Het persoon-zijn onder thomistisch-metaphysiche belichting' (1948), reprinted in *Begrip*, 186–208. For the significance of De Petter's philosophy in Schillebeeckx's theology of the sacraments cf. Ambaum, *Glaubenszeichen* (n. 49), 72–89.

63 Cf. the decree *Ad consummationem salutaris* (1547), can. 8 (Denzinger 1608). For Schillebeeckx's interpretation of the teaching laid down at Trent, cf. *Heilseconomie*, 185–98.

64 Schillebeeckx is here referring to P. Ellerbeck ('Schets van een anthropologie der sacramenten', *Bijd. Ned. jez.* 7, 1943–45, 1–47), who develops an anthropology of the sacraments on the basis of the philosophy of J. Maréchal. Schillebeeckx corrects his position especially on the point of the relationship of the sacraments to reality.

65 Cf. Schillebeeckx's interpretation of the so-called 'sacramental hylemorphism' of scholasticism which especially forms the background to the doctrine of 'transubstantiation', according to which the eucharist changes the essence – the substance, form – of bread and wine into the body of Christ, but the external form – the accidents, the matter – of bread remains (*Heilseconomie*, 355–91). After a detailed analysis he ultimately explains this hylemorphism as giving meaning to the material world by means of words of faith. In the 1960s, during and after the Second Vatican Council, a discussion developed over the question how Christ's real presence in the eucharist was to be understood and whether the doctrine of transubstantiation was still adequate: for this, and for Schillebeeckx's role in it, see the next chapter.

66 'Sacrament' (n. 49), here 4195: quoted from L. Monden, 'Symbooloorzakelijkheid als eigen causaliteit van het sacrament', *Bijdr* 13, 1952, 277–85: 278. This article, which defends a position closely related to that of Schillebeeckx, is the text of a lecture which had been given in Louvain as early as 1949.

67 For Schillebeeckx that is the theological importance of the liturgy, cf. his article '*Lex orandi, lex credendi*' (1957), reprinted in *Revelation* I under the title 'The Liturgy and Theology', 240–4.

68 Quoted literally in 'Sacrament' (n. 49), 4204; rather differently in *Heilseconomie*, 172.

69 Schillebeeckx refers (ibid., 162) to Thomas's treatment of the different elements from the history of Jesus Christ as '*mysteria*' (*Summa theol.* III, q. 31–57) and argues that 'no modern treatise on the incarnation ... [is] constructed so much in terms of *salvation history*' as Thomas's discussion of this topic. That it is about the way in which the New Testament tells the story and how the stories about it are understood in the church tradition was evidently as yet no problem to Schillebeeckx in 1952.

70 *Heilseconomie*, 164–81: 177. Schillebeeckx indeed spoke of a 'distortion' of salvation by the sacraments, but in fact meant 'signification'; it is not a matter of 'mis-representation'. Schillebeeckx once said to Ted Schoof that he used the word because he needed an active term. '*Betekening*' in Dutch is currently used in precisely this sense as the translation of the French '*signification*'.

71 'Sacrament' (n. 49), 4211–13: *Christusontmoeting*, 87–93; here Schillebeeckx bases himself especially on what K. Rahner says about the sacrament of marriage: 'Kirche und Sakramente: Zur theologischen Grundlegung einer Kirchen- und Sakramentenfrömmigkeit', *Geist und Leben* 28, 1955, 434–53: 448–51. This argument fits better into Rahner's theology and his concentration on the church as the primordial sacrament than into that of Schillebeeckx.

72 *Christusontmoeting*, 156.

73 Ibid., 134. For the history of the idea of the character up to Thomas see *Heilseconomie*, 487–99; for Thomas's view of this see ibid., 501–27. For the historical background to the idea of the character he based himself especially on L. Grollenberg, 'Bij Thomas' leer over het *character sacramentalis*', *Stud. cath.* 19, 1943, 215–18. For the central importance of the idea of the character in Schillebeeckx cf. Ambaum, *Glaubenszeichen* (n. 49), 55–63. Schillebeeckx's view of baptism, confirmation and ordination is directly connected with his view of the place of the laity in the church, which shifted considerably in the 1950s (see the previous chapter). His view of the way in which these sacraments give believers a share in the high priesthood of Christ also changes accordingly. Cf. *Heilseconomie*, 528–52; *Christusontmoeting*, 136–50; H. Schillebeeckx, 'Merkteken', *Theol. woordenboek* 2, 1957, 3231–7; id., 'Priesterschap', ibid 3., 1958, 3959–4003; id., 'Vormsel', ibid., 4840–70; 'Wijding', ibid,., 4967–82.

74   Cf. *Christusontmoeting*, 36.

75   For this last cf. *Heilseconomie*, 417–84; *Christusontmoeting*, 75–86.

76   *Christusontmoeting*, 105–28; cf. *Heilseconomie*, 557–63.

77   This also implies a degree of relativization of the sacraments as concrete actions and rites: they are not the only access to God and Jesus Christ and shed their light above all also on those who cannot fully take part in them, cf. H. E. Schillebeeckx, 'Begierdetaufe', in *Lex. für Theol. u. Kirche* 2, [2]1958, 112–15.

78   *Christusontmoeting*, 18–23.

79   *Christ the Sacrament*, 244–76, quotations 265, 268.

80   Ibid., 268. Here what was said earlier about the difference between Schillebeeckx's approach and that of Semmelroth and Rahner applies. Whereas for the two latter, sacramental action is above all action of the church, for Schillebeeckx it is action which makes visible God's involvement in the world and thus as it were time and again gives rise to the church. This is reflected in the fact that according to Schillebeeckx, unlike Rahner, the incarnation alone is not sufficient basis for the redemptive significance of Jesus Christ (cf. J. M. Powers, *Symbolic Instrumentality in the Sacramental Theology of E. H. Schillebeeckx OP*, excerpta diss. Ad Lauream Gregoriana, Rome 1972). This significance must emerge in its history, but ultimately also time and again in the history of those who believe in him.

81   Schoof, 'Aandrang', 38.

82   Schillebeeckx, *Testament*, 29.

83   Cf. Schoof, 'Aandrang', 13. That does not mean that Schillebeeckx did not give more lectures on other topics in his Louvain period. Lectures 'on the one God' – *De deo uno*' can be found in Arch. 498 and 3117 respectively, and under no. 522 a lecture on 'the threefold God' – '*De Deo trino*'. Moreover in Arch. 554 there is a course on the eucharist evidently given repeatedly in Louvain and one more time in Nijmegen, cf. also Arch. 3119. It is one of the peculiarities of the Schillebeeckx tradition that originally not all the lecture notes were put in the Schillebeeckx archive in the version in which they circulated.

84   Parts of the notes for this course can be found under Arch. 284, 488, 492, 493, 747, 751, 3123. The text of the course which is followed here, with *Inleiding tot de theologie 1951–52: Pro Manuscripto* on the title page, is paginated as follows: I–III (table of contents for the first part); 1–51, 14–100, 100A–100K, 101–166, 167A–167M, 167–209; I–III (table of contents for the second part), 211–72, 311–26, 326 bis, 327–406. Pages 273–310 were reserved for a survey of 'the different centres of theological work in the world with their special orientations' and also 'the existing tools of work (the big reference works, the theological journals, congresses, etc.)' (272). For this, however, reference is made to V. Morel, *Inleiding tot de theologie*, Antwerp 1955, 305–21, on 'the contemporary organization of theological work'. According to the table of contents this whole set of notes is a second book: '*tomus secundus de Doctrina*'. Perhaps the course on the faith which Schillebeeckx gave as early as 1944–5, the year before he went to Le Saulchoir, on 'the structure of the faith orientated on God' – '*de structura actus fidei theologalis*' – was the first part; for the lecture notes, still wholly in Latin, see Arch. 284. In the text reference is made to the lecture notes *Inleiding tot de theologie* with page numbers in brackets; the 'duplicate' pages are prefaced with a [2] (e.g. [2]14).

85   Here Schillebeeckx clearly bases himself on articles by Chenu which were famous at this time, collected in his *Parole* I, 115–40 ('position de la théologie') and 243–68 ('La théologie au Saulchoir').

86   *Summa theol.* II–II, q. 1, art. 2, ad 2.

87   Here Schillebeeckx himself refers to his 1945 article 'Technische heilstheologie' (included in *Openbaring*, 171–81 [not in the English edition]), which is discussed in Chapter 1. In this

connection he speaks emphatically about God's being as Trinity and comes strikingly close to the formulation which Karl Rahner would later make very well known among theologians: 'the immanent Trinity is the Trinity of the economy of salvation and vice versa', in *Mysterium Salutis* 2, 1967, 317–401),

88 Cf. the part on 'the general division of religion' – though it proves rather sweeping – in *Inleiding* (265–72), where Schillebeeckx compares the independence of the various theological disciplines which have grown up in history with the unity of theology emphasized by Thomas, and on the basis of Thomas's view sketches the systematic connection of theology as he sees it.

89 Among other things Schillebeeckx derived from this the conclusion (ibid., 248–51) that there is an intrinsic connection between the spiritual life and theology, although at the same time he emphasizes the independence of theology as an intellectual activity: in his eyes the spiritual life offers 'the optimal and even connatural condition of life for theology, which nevertheless remains formally an *opus rationis* bound up with faith'.

90 On pp. 45–48 he investigates J. A. Möhler (1796–1838), J. H. Newman (1801–90), J. B. Franzelin (1816–86), L. Billot (1846–1931) and J. V. Bainvel (1858–1937) and after that discusses recent work by A. Deneffe (*Der Traditionsbegriff: Studie zur Theologie*, Münster 1931), J. Ranft (*Der Ursprung des katholischen Traditionsprinzips*, Würzburg 1931), L. Charlier (*Essai sur le problème théologique*, Thuillies 1937) and rather more obliquely R. Draguet (*Histoire du dogme catholique*, Paris 1941). Draguet was a pupil of Chenu and Charlier again one of his pupils, and in 1942 both were affected by church measures at the same time as Chenu. Charlier's book was put on the index. Both Draguet and Charlier strongly emphasized that the living tradition of the church is its own measure. Schillebeeckx takes their line, but looks within it for an independent place for the Bible as a criterion; he sums up his position on this point in the article 'Overlevering', in *Theol. woordenb.* 3, 1958, 3683–93.

91 For Trent cf. the decree *De libris sacris et de traditionibus recipiendis* (1546: Denzinger 1501), for Vatican I the dogmatic constitution *Dei Filius* (1870, Denziger 3011). Schillebeeckx goes into the Tridentine view at length in *Inleiding* [2]37–43, and very briefly into Vatican I, ibid., 444–5.

92 W. H. van de Pol, 'Openbaring en traditie', *Vox theol.* 18, 1947, 39–44: 43, quoted in *Inleiding* 100A.

93 Dogmatic Constitution *Dei verbum*, 1965, nos 9 and 10.

94 L. S. Thornton, *Revelation and the Modern World: Being the First Part of a Treatise on the Form of the Servant*, London 1950, 205; quoted *Inleiding*, 54. Cf. also Schillebeeckx's article 'Schrift, H.', in *Theol. woordenboek* 3, 1958, 4294–9.

95 Y. Congar, *Vraie et fausse réforme dans l'église*, Paris 1950, 490–2; see *Inleiding*, [2]49–50. In 1956 Rahner developed a view which was in some respects comparable. In a book about the divine inspiration of the Bible he located this in the constitutive significance of the biblical writings for faith and the formation of the primitive church (*Über die Schriftprinzip* [1956], Freiburg 1958).

96 For the patristic view of tradition cf. *Inleiding*, [2]28–31; for that of Thomas, ibid., [2]32–7.

97 Congar, *Vraie et fausse réforme* (n. 95), 525; *Inleiding*, I, [2]49.

98 For the later more detailed working out of Schillebeeckx's view on this point, in discussion with M. Seckler (*Instinkt und Glaubenswille nach Thomas von Aquin*, Mainz 1962), see his article 'Het niet-begrippelijke kenmoment' (1965), in *Openbaring*, 233–61 (not in the English translation).

99 It is striking that here Schillebeeckx bases himself on K. Bühler, *Sprachtheorie: Der Darstellungsfunktion der Sprache*, Jena 1934, according to F. Kainz in the 'Geleitwort' to the second impression (Stuttgart 1965, V-XIX) a 'truly classical work on its subject', namely the sociology and philosophy of language. Schillebeeckx thus occupied himself in

the early 1950s with linguistic theory: linguistic discussions were to play an important role in his later theology.

100 Schillebeeckx discusses J. H. Newman (*Essay on the Development of Christian Doctrine*, 1845) and here, in passing, also ideas of J. S. Drey and J. A. Möhler, especially through the analyses by J. H. Walgrave, M. Blondel (*Histoire et dogme*, 1904), H. de Lubac ('Le problème du développement du dogme', *Rev. sc. relig.* 35, 1938, 240–60), L. Charlier, *Essai sur le problème théologique* [n. 90]) and N. Sanders ('Openbaring, traditie, dogma-ontwikkeling', *Stud. cath.*15, 1939, 1–12); see *Inleiding*, 83–96.

101 For Schillebeeckx's view of the experience of faith, wholly based on De Petter's philosophy, cf. *Inleiding*, 100–46.

102 On the magisterium as the *de facto* determinative centre of judgement – '*regula proxima*' and 'index' for the development of tradition, cf. ibid., 145–8.

103 For Schillebeeckx's view and his attitude to other views, see his 'Dogma-ontwikkeling', in *Theol. woordenboek* 1, 1952, 1087–106.

104 The reading of what Thomas says about faith was to a large degree based on M.-D. Chenu, 'La psychologie de la foi dans la théologie au XIIIe siècle' (1932), in *Parole* I, 77–10;, cf. also id., 'La raison psychologique de développement du dogme d'après saint Thomas' (1924), ibid., 51–8.

105 G. Tyrrell, *Through Scylla and Charybdis*, London 1907, 116ff.

106 Pius XII, encyclical *Humani generis* (1950), nos 15, 18.

107 For the modernists cf. *Inleiding*, 157–63; Schillebeeckx here discusses above all the work of G. Tyrrell. For the '*nouvelle théologie*' cf. ibid., 161–6: here Schillebeeckx discusses the work of H. Bouillard and the polemic which arose over his book *Conversion et grâce chez Saint Thomas d'Aquin*, Paris 1944, 211–24. This polemic was especially between the Jesuits of the faculty of Lyon-Fourvière and the journal *Recherches de Science religieuse* on the one hand and the Dominicans of the *Revue Thomiste* on the other, later supported by R. Garrigou-Lagrange, who in a malicious and suggestive way associated the '*nouvelle théologie*' of Lyon-Fourvière with modernism ('La nouvelle théologie où va-t-elle?', *Angelicum*, 23, 1946, nos 2–4, 126–45). The polemic is collected in *Dialogue théologique*, ed. N. Labourdette et al., St Maximin/Var 1947. For this polemic and the background to it cf. Schoof, *Aggiornamento*, 210–21; R. Gibellini, *Handbuch der Theologie im 20. Jahrhundert*, Regensburg 1995, 156–65.

108 Bultmann was to become influential in Catholic theology – and in Dutch theology generally – only after the Second Vatican Council, when the question of the relationship between secularized culture and theology became unavoidable. Schillebeeckx was then again to enter this discussion with his work.

109 D. M. De Petter, 'Zin en grond van het oordeel', in id., *Begrip*, 89; quoted in *Inleiding*, 176.

110 Cf. J. Ramírez, '*De analogia secundum doctrinam aristotelico-thomisticam*', *Ciencia Tomísta* 11, 1921, 20–40: 12, 1922, 17–38; A. de Witte, *Analogie*, Roermond 1946. The declaration from the dogmatic constitution *Dei Filius* (1870) of Vatican I is included in Denzinger 3008.

111 Cf. N. Balthasar, 'Intition humaine et experience métaphysique', *Rev. néoschol. de philos.* 41, 1938. 262–6; D. M. De Petter, 'Impliciete intuitie', in id., *Begrip*, 25–43: 25.

112 For the discussion of analogy, see *Inleiding*, 359–78. Schillebeeckx's standpoint is based on an extensive analysis of *Summa theol.* I, q. 13, art. 1–12, on talking about God; see ibid., 334–54. He brings together his findings more systematically in H. Schillebeeckx, 'Het niet-begrippelijk kenmoment in onze godskennis volgens Thomas van Aquino' (1952), in *Openbaring*, 201–32 (not in the English translation).

113 Thus Schillebeeckx in 1954 in a lecture – 'conference' – for the Flemish Werkgenootschap voor Theologie on 'De waarde van onze begrippen', reprinted in *Openbaring*, 187–96 (not in the English translation).

114 Seen against the church-political background and the consequences which church pronouncements had for theologians, the way in which Schillebeeckx dissociates his own and De Petter's approach from that of Blondel, Maréchal and also the Jesuits of Lyon-Fourvière, and the way in which he courts the church's suspicion of them by connecting them with modernism does not always make a sympathetic impression; cf. here by contrast Schoof, *Aggiornamento*, passim, who rightly emphasizes the affinity between all attempts to break through the impasse of the fixation of concepts by ecclesiastical Thomism. However, this remark stands apart from a verdict on the theological importance of Schillebeeckx's insistence on the value of concepts of faith. In my view this importance is great, not only for his specific theological approach, but also for a proper understanding of theological and intellectual activity and their relationship to faith as it is lived out.

115 E. Schillebeeckx, 'Het niet-begrippelijk kenmoment' (n. 98), 233; to some degree the boldness of the formulation seems to be the consequence of the freedom from neoscholasticism which developed at the time of Vatican II.

116 Again (cf. n. 99), it is striking that here Schillebeeckx refers to the studies in the philosophy of language by the Jesuit J. Reichling, *Het woord: Een studie omtrent de grondslag van taal en taalgebruik*, Nijmegen 1935; also to M. J. Langeveld, *Taal en denken: Een theoretiese en didaktiese bijdrage tot het onderwijs in de moedertaal op de middelbare school, inzonderheid dat der grammatika*, Groningen 1934; he will have been particularly interested in ch. III, on the significance of the development of language for psychological development, 81–108. Moreover, Schillebeeckx says elsewhere (*Inleiding*, 403), evidently with the hot breath of the condemnations in *Humani generis* on his neck, and in order to emphasize the real epistemological value of the concept of faith, that they are 'in no sense metaphors or parables; they are more than that. The conceptuality of faith really discerns as it were a conceptuality, but this stands open to the mystery.' He also connects the question of the expressive value of the statements of faith with what later was to be called the contextuality of theology, and here enters into conversation with missiological studies which touch on the question of the relationship between Catholicism and culture. He thinks that because any formulation of faith is a conceptual expression of the intuition implicit in faith as it is lived, it is possible to express what the formulations aim at – he speaks of the *significatum* – in 'non-Western concepts' in Chinese, Congolese or Japanese conceptuality. However, because any culture and any concept expresses a partial perspective on this *significatum* and thus adds something to concepts used earlier, in his view the plurality of expressions which then comes into being will be one of the factors which favourably influence the development of the explicit consciousness of faith – the 'development of dogma'.

117 'In the defining of dogma ... the descending agape of God coincides with the response in love to it of the "*Sponsa Christi*, i.e. *ecclesia*": the definition of dogma is the good news of Christ's redemptive love confirmed by the "*fides ecclesiae*".'

118 This becomes clear in 1968 in the troubles surrounding the encyclical *Humanae vitae*; cf. H. Küng, *Infallible? An Inquiry* (1971), London and New York ²1994.

119 Id., 'De natuurwet in verband met de katholieke huwelijksopvatting', in *Jaarboek 1961 v.h. Werkgenootschap v. Kath. Theologen in Nederland*, Hilversum 1963, 5–51: 56.

120 Cf. the subtle discussion of the question, which steers round all the rocks of the church's doctrinal statements, by A. H. Maltha, 'Evolutie', in *Theol. woordenboek* 1, 1952, 1465–80; he eventually came to the conclusion that the theory of evolution in relation to the human body is not in conflict with Catholic faith; in *Humani generis* (no. 36), Pius XII had emphatically defined as doctrine the special creation of the human soul – as opposed to its origin through evolution – and the descent of the human race from the first human being, Adam (no. 37). At this time Karl Rahner, too, wrote an extremely subtle article to reconcile so-called 'monogenism' with the facts of evolution: 'Theological Reflexions on

Monogenism', *Theological Investigations* I, London and New York 1961, 229–96.

121 Pius XII, speech to the tenth international congress of historians on 7 September 1955, in *AAS* 47, 1955, 672–82, esp. 677–8. Boniface formulated the doctrine of two swords in the bull *Unam sanctam* (1302).

122 In the 1940s and 1950s theologians quite generally pointed out that there is no mention of fire in the doctrine of purgatory as laid down at the Council of Trent and in other official documents. However, to say, as Schillebeeckx does, that the doctrine of purgatory has nothing to do with the idea of fire goes a step further and in fact represents a standpoint in the theological discussion of the meaning of purgatory; cf. further his lecture notes on eschatology and the treatment of it below: 'Today one can note a stricter theology of purgatory (a kind of 'temporal' hell) alongside a milder trend, which puts more emphasis on the purifying mystical stage of love and seeks to see purgatory more as a prelude to heaven' (I. W. Driessen, 'Uitersten', in *Theol. woordenboek* 3, 1958, 4627–58: 4645); Schillebeeckx doubtless belonged to this latter trend. Moreover, here he meets up with the tendency in Thomas Aquinas's treatment of purgatory; for this see J. Le Goff, *La naissance du purgatoire*, Paris 1981, 357–72.

123 Cf. also id., 'Dogma', in *Theol. woordenboek* 1, 1952, 1078–81: 1078–79.

124 Cf. also id., 'Ketterij', in *Theol. woordenboek* 2, 1957, 2784–5.

125 He bases himself in particular on *Summa theol.* II–II, q. 1, artt. 7 and 8, cf. A. R. Motte, 'Théodicée et théologie chez S. Thomas d'Aquin', *Rev. sc. philos. theol.* 26, 1937, 5–26.

126 Thomas speaks of the *occultum divinitatis* and the *mysterium humanitatis Christi* as principles of synthesis in the Apostles' Creed in *Summa theol.* II–II, q. 1, art. 8.

127 Schillebeeckx denotes these two elements with the traditional terms 'positive theology', the usual designation for the study of facts from the history of theology and dogma, and 'speculative theology'; however, he emphatically says that these are not separate activities but two phases of the one theological activity. Almost 25 years later his former fellow Dominican W. Vander Marck was to claim on the basis of an analysis of Thomas's work that this already broke with the idea of a collection of statements as the basis of faith ('Faith, What It Is And What It Relates To. A Study on the Object of Faith in the Theology of Thomas Aquinas', *Rech. théol. anc. mediév.* 43, 1976, 121–66).

128 It is interesting that he quotes Karl Barth to support this view (*Church Dogmatics* I/1, *The Doctrine of the Word of God*, Edinburgh ²1975, 3–11) and does so affirmatively. This is exceptional: he usually refers to Barth to distance himself from Barth's anti-metaphysical tendency and emphasis on revelation in contrast to his own emphasis on creation.

129 'The Search for the Living God' (n. 24), 46.

130 Cf. *Inleiding*, 231–42, among other things in discussion with Barth and Cullmann: 'The subject of theology is *Deus sub ratione deitatis*, and therefore *Deus salutaris* but its basis is salvation-historical and thus christological' (239). There are fragments of lectures on christology in Arch. 503–8, 749 and 3118. In the copy used, with 'Christologie, Louvain 1953–54' added later, the pages are numbered I-V; 1–2; I, 51–I, 109; II, 1– II, 301. A synthesis – 'Synthetic treatise of the redemptive mystery of Christ' – which should be numbered III is only announced; reference is made to the second volume of *De sacramentele heilseconomie*, which never appeared. On I, 1–I, 50 there should have been an analysis of Old Testament messianic ideas, New Testament images of Christ and the view of Christ in patristics. In what follows, this too is referred to in the text by page numbers in brackets.

131 For an analysis of Schillebeeckx's christology lectures see G. Vergauwen, 'Edward Schillebeeckx – Lecteur de saint Thomas', in *Ordo Sapientiae et Amoris: Image et message de Saint Thomas d'Aquin à travers les récentes études historiques, herméneutiques et doctrinales*, Fribourg 1993, 655–73; translated as 'Edward Schillebeeckx – Leser des Thomas von Aquin', in *Wahrheit: Recherchen zwischen Hochscholastik und Postmoderne*, ed. T.

Eggensperger and U. Engel, Mainz 1995, 70–91.

132 In his standpoint on the question Schillebeeckx partially bases himself on *Summa theol.* III, q. 12: *'de scientia animae Christia acquisita vel experimentali'*, in which according to him Thomas, 'contrary to all contemporary theology', states that in Christ there is normal human knowledge of the world which develops (*Christologie* II, 254).

133 For a rudimentary survey of the discussion of the questions see H. Riedlinger, 'Wissen und Bewusstsein Christi', in *Lex. für Theol. u. Kirche* 10, [2]1965, 1193–4; at length in id., *Geschichtlichkeit und Vollendung des Wissens Christi*, Freiburg, Basel and Vienna 1966.

134 See Denzinger, 3432–5 (Decree *Lamentabili* of the Holy Office, 1907); 3645–7 (= Decree of the Holy Office, 1918); cf. ibid., 3812 (= Pius XII, enc. *Mystici corporis* 1943, no. 77).

135 For the whole question see ibid., II, 204–74; for Schillebeeckx's own synthesis, ibid., II, 256–74. The discussion here is of the views of A. Günther (1783–1871) – who according to him put the question of Jesus's self-awareness on the theological agenda but whose works were condemned in 1858 – and above all of P. Haltier (*L'unité du Christ: Être, personne, conscience*, Paris 1939). He thought that this last got stuck in abstract distinctions and wanted an approach which did justice to Jesus as one concrete person.

136 For the theological analysis of the *mysteria carnis* in Thomas Aquinas see *Summa theol.* III, q. 27–59.

137 For the whole passage cf. II, 115–20; Schillebeeckx bases himself here above all on K. Adam, *Jesus Christus*, Augsburg 1933, from which the last quotation is directly taken (ibid., 154f.). As is well known, according to Thomas, in Jesus there could be no question of faith, because the object of faith is a hidden divine reality and from his conception Christ saw God completely in his essence (*Summa theol.* III, q. 7, art. 3). Indeed Schillebeeckx does not speak of 'faith' in connection with Jesus but calls him a 'religious' man who experiences God in 'an I-Thou relationship'.

138 *Inleiding*, 401.

139 See also II, 124, where he says of the second divine person who becomes incarnate, 'the Verbum', that it is a *Deus humanissimus*; see again *Jesus*, 669: 'Through his historical self-giving, accepted by the Father, Jesus has shown us who God is: a *Deus humanissimus.*' Cf. Kennedy, *Deus Humanissimus* (n. 21), esp. 23–5. The term 'human heart of God' is almost a reversal of 'the Sacred Heart of (the man) Jesus', veneration of which was widespread among Catholics in the 1950s. 'The Sacred Heart' was regarded as a kind of divine basis of Jesus's redemptive speaking, acting and suffering which conversely are its manifestations. Schillebeeckx emphasizes that they are manifestations of Christ's humanity and that his very humanity is the revelation of his divinity: thus his humanity does not disappear into his divinity, but his divinity transforms his humanity. Moreover, alongside the Sacred Heart tradition, which was propagated especially by the Jesuits, in the twentieth century there was also a distinctively Dominican tradition of the Veneration of the Sacred Heart of Jesus which was also propagated by the popes and became particularly popular; here all the emphasis is put on Jesus's heart as a place where the divine human love dwells. Cf. A. Walz, *De veneratione divini Cordi Iesu in ordine praedicatorum*, Rome 1937.

140 Here Schillebeeckx quotes Luther following A. von Harnack, *Lehrbuch der Dogmengeschichte, III: Die Entwicklung des kirchlichen Dogmas*, Tübingen [4]1910, 662.

141 Here he quotes his own *Heilseconomie* V, and moreover refers to his lectures, *Inleiding*, 245–8, where he resumes his old opposition to an exclusively kerygmatic theology.

142 Here Schillebeeckx is commenting on Thomas, *Summa theol.* III, q. 1.

143 Here Schillebeeckx refers to Chenu (*Introduction* [n. 17]), 160–2), who makes a distinction between a deductive reasoning and a *resolutio* which brings to light the inner conceptuality of a thing by reducing its complexity: according to Schillebeeckx this argument of Thomas's is a *resolutio*. He himself still points out that the incarnation cannot be a necessity, but must have the character of a free action of God: 'God who is good becomes

428

human purely because he willed it lovingly so freely' (II, 9).

144 *Summa theol.* I, q. 2, prol.: *'Christus, secundum quod homo, est via nobis tendendi in Deum'.* For the exposition of art. 2 see *Christologie* II, 9–13.

145 For the Bible and the church fathers see *Christologie* II, 14–19: it is striking that here Schillebeeckx makes no distinction between the Greek and Latin church fathers, who according to the current interpretation differ from one another essentially on this point: in the Greek church fathers the emphasis was on the divinization, and in the Latin church fathers on redemption from sin.

146 For Thomas's development see ibid., II, 20–3; for Duns Scotus' view, 23–6.

147 In further working out the meaning of the incarnation Schillebeeckx goes into all kinds of subtle distinctions with reference to its purpose, motive and intended benefits, cf. ibid., 30–47.

148 Schillebeeckx discusses the history of christology in the Middle Ages up to Thomas (*Christologie* II, 63–71) and the tendencies after Thomas and interpretations of him (73–6) more sweepingly than is customary for him. He finds all the christologies that he sketches out unsatisfactory, evidently apart from that of Thomas, which he goes on to analyse at length.

149 In this last part Schillebeeckx developed a more systematic view of the person of Jesus Christ, not directly on the basis of an analysis of Thomas but arguing along the lines of the article by D. M. De Petter, 'Het persoon-zijn onder thomistische-metafysiche belichting', reprinted as 'Persoon in personalisiering', in id., *Begrip en werkelijkheid*, 186–208.

150 E. Schillebeeckx, 'Persoonlijke openbaringsgestalte van de Vader', *TvT* 6, 1966, 274–88: 276. This article is to be regarded as a transition between the approach in Schillebeeckx's Louvain course – to which this also refers and the results of which he sums up extremely briefly – and the approach that was to lead to *Jesus*. He writes – and those who read it can hardly see this as other than an announcement – that we can 'only speak of the man Jesus in the light of his human expressions, in which this person reveals himself to his fellow human beings. We shall have to retrace the way, we shall have to start from the man Jesus as he appeared in Palestine ... [We shall again have to experience and perceive the uniqueness that the first Christians experienced in him] in order, on the basis of that, to come to a renewed reflection and again make it possible to experience the Christian view in the present-day world' (ibid., 279).

151 In *Christologie* II, 298, Schillebeeckx begins with a new chapter: 'The theandric activity of Christ: Jesus Christ as primordial sacrament of redemptive grace'. After some pages (II, 301), the text then breaks off; as I have remarked, the 'Synthetic treatise of the receptive mystery of Christ' is also missing.

152 Here Schillebeeckx bases himself especially on *Summa theol.* III, q. 7, art. 912.

153 Here Schilebeeckx formally bases himself on *Summa theol.* III, q. 8, but in fact he tried to argue that one first of all has to see Jesus Christ as redeemer of humankind and only in the second instance as head of his mystical body, the church. He engaged in discussion with L. Malevez, 'L'église dans le Christ: Étude de théologie historique et théoretique', *Rev. sc. relig.* 25, 1935, 257–91; M. J. Congar, 'Sur l'inclusion de l'humanité dans le Christ', *Rev. sc. philos. théol.* 25, 1936, 489–95 and F. Malmberg, 'Onze eenheid met de Godmens in de kerk', *Bijdr.* 4, 1942, 172–204. In fact this meant distancing himself from the notion that Jesus Christ had redeemed human beings *by* founding the church, which was ultimately the position of the traditional doctrine of redemption, in favour of the thought that the church was *at the service of* redemption and itself has to be the sacrament of God in the world.

154 See his analysis of the so-called *analogia fidei* in *Inleiding*, 399.

155 This is therefore participation in Christ's ongoing incarnation, not living in the spirit of the *'mystique d'incarnation'*, a Christian life that is completely incarnated in the world.

156 Schillebeeckx, *Christusontmoeting*, 13–25: 'Christ the primordial sacrament'; I assume that

this is a summary of what Schillebeeckx wanted to work out as a synthetic view of Jesus Christ and the redemption brought by him. Cf. id., 'Verrijzenis', in *Theol. woordenboek* 3, 1958, 4741–8; see also his article 'Jesus Christus', in *Catholica: Geillustreerd encyclopedisch vademecum voor het katholieke leven*, ed. A. M. Heidt, The Hague [2]1961, 675–80: 679–80.

157 E. Schillebeeckx, 'Kerk en wereld: de betekenis van "Schema 13"' (1964), reprinted in *World* as 'Church and World', 96–114: 99, 101. 'Schema 13' was the designation for the preliminary drafts of *Gaudium et spes*.

158 For this terminology see Riedlinger, 'Wissen und Bewusstsein Christi' (n. 133), 21.

159 Parts of lectures on eschatology can be found in Arch. 540, 542, 748, 750, 3117. In the lecture notes *De eschatologie* which are followed here – with no separate title page and undated – the pages are numbered: I–V, 1–7, 85–168, 251–80, 4–13, 291A–291B, 14–26, 305–24, 28–57, 355–536. For clarity I shall act as if the pagination is normal from 25, with the insertion of 291A and 291B. That fits precisely and thus is clearly the intention; this numbering has been put on the archive copy by hand. It will be referred to from now on in the text, with just the page numbers in brackets.

160 Driessen, 'Uitersten' (n. 122), 4627.

161 Following Y. B. Tremel ('L'homme entre la mort et la résurrection d'après le Nouveau Testament', *Lumière et vie* 24, 1955, 33–58), on whom he seems especially to base himself, Schillebeeckx speaks of 'the rabbinic literature': technically speaking, however, rabbinic Judaism came into being only in the second century of our era.

162 Here Schillebeeckx mentions Cullmann's notion that Jesus Christ is 'the centre of time' (see ibid., 278; cf. esp. O. Cullmann, *Christ and Time* [1948], Philadelphia and London 1964). However, he does so 1. as a Catholic theologian by taking a positive view of the doctrine that the souls of the saints have a vision of God immediately after their death (cf. the *ex cathedra* declaration by Benedict XII in the constitution *Benedictus Deus* [1334], see Denzinger 1000); 2. as a Thomist by connecting this notion with the distinction between nature and grace and seeing Jesus Christ as the full realization and source of the divine grace; 3. as a personalist and pupil of De Petter, by approaching the dialectic of nature and grace, and thus also of Christ as the centre of time, more emphatically than Cullmann through anthropology.

163 See the whole framework of the part on heaven, *Eschatologie*, 251–410.

164 For an impression of the usual textbook treatment of this question see the contributions by A. H. Maltha in *Theol. woordenboek*, 'Genade' (2, 1957, 1772–815), 'Rechtvaardig-making' (3, 1958, 4096–108), and 'Verdienste' (ibid., 4689–705). See also Maltha and Thuys, *Dogmatiek*, 383–458.

165 See the whole passage 120–9; as a background cf. F. Edwards, 'Molina/Molinismus', in *Theol. Realenz.* 23, 1994, 199–203; F. Dominguez, 'Bânez, Domingo', in *Lex. f. Theol. u. Kirche* 1, [2]1993, 1384–6; J. Martin-Palma, *Gnadenlehre. Von der Reformation bis zur Gegenwart* (= Handbuch der Dogmengeschichte, III/5b), Freiburg, Basel and Vienna 1980, 103–8.

166 In his lectures on eschatology Schillebeeckx borrowed from M. Schmaus, *Von den letzten Dingen*, Regensburg and Münster 1948, much of the general line and many of the details, and especially Schmaus's existential interpretation of heaven and hell.

167 For a view comparable with that of Schillebeeckx on the involvement of the body in the glorification of human beings see R. Guardini, *Die letzten Dinge: Die christliche Lehre vom Tode, der Läuterung nach dem Tode, Auferstehung, Gericht und Ewigkeit* (1940), Würzburg 1952, 49–64.

168 Cf. the whole part on heaven, ibid., 251–410, especially the chapter on 'the heavenly beginning stage', 251–79. Here Schillebeeckx on the one hand maintains the Catholic dogma that before the universal judgement at the end of time souls have a share in the blessed vision of God (cf. the Constitution *Benedictus Deus* of Pope Benedict XII [n. 162])

and on the other hand tries to bring this into harmony with the biblical view of a history which runs in the direction of an end-time. Here, probably being cautious about the traditional view, he remains markedly ambivalent: 'We claim ... that the saints in heaven now already possess complete spiritual communion with God, but that this spiritual communion is not yet communicated to the integral human subject [in other words, having a body, being involved in relationships, living in the world]. No more needs to be added than in a participative, and thus non-additive, sense' (274).

169 In IV *Sent.* d. 45, q. 1, a.1, qla. 2 (quotation from Gregory the Great) and d. 43, a.1, qla.1 (reference to Aristotle's statement that soul and body belong together as form and matter). Part of this early work, Thomas's commentary on the *Sentences* of Peer Lombard (1253–7), was later added by others to the *Summa theologiae* which had been left incomplete; for the present references see *Summa theol.* Suppl. q. 60, art. 2 and q. 75, art. 1.

170 Quotation from De Petter, 'Persoon' (n. 149), 206. De Petter's text continues as follows: 'If for human beings the earth is an indispensable basis, then on the other hand it is human beings who give the earth its final significance, and here, in a sense, a title to co-incorruptibility.' Schillebeeckx uses the expression 'title to co-incorruptibility' further down the same page, in quotation marks but without a reference: in fact he develops this notion further.

171 In his interpretation of the biblical data Schillebeeckx bases himself largely on K. Heim, *Der evangelische Glaube und das Denken der Gegenwart, 6: Weltschöpfung als Weltende*, Hamburg 1952, and also takes over much from R. Guardini, *Das Harren der Schöpfung. Eine Auslegung von der Römerbrief, 8. Kapitel, 12–39*, Würzburg 1940.

172 After first collecting the biblical (413–22) and the traditional material (422–30) about hell and investigating 'the dogmatic definitions and church doctrine concerning the punishment of hell' (43–7), Schillebeeckx develops his theological reflection on the dogma of the punishment of hell, 437–48.

173 Schillebeeckx discusses the *apokatatasis panton* in Origen and his pupils and the church's condemnations of this doctrine (Denzinger 409, 411), ibid., 425–7.

174 The dogma is formulated in the bull *Laetentur caeli* (1439, Denzinger 1304–6); the summary of the stipulations comes from the second council of Lyons (1274, Denzinger 856). Schillebeeckx's discussion of purgatory in terms of the history of theology and dogma is on pp. 453–93. He goes extensively, and in discussion with specialist studies, into the difference of opinion between East and West (469–75, 479–86), and much more briefly into the controversy with the Reformation (486–9). For the current state of knowledge of this history cf. E. Koch, 'Fegfeuer', in *Theologische Realenz.* 11, 1983, 69–78; for the views of the Reformers see E. Kunz, *Protestantische Eschatologie: Von der Reformation bis zur Aufklärung* (= Handb. d. Dogmengesch. IV/7/c/1), Freiburg, Basel and Vienna 1980, 3–41; for the reaction of Trent to this see P. Schäfer, *Eschatologie: Trient und Gegenreformation* (ibid. IV/7/c/2), Freiburg, Basel and Vienna 1984, 3–40; for purgatory, 35–40.

175 In the course of his discussion Schillebeeckx repeats this regularly in different words. In this connection it is striking that Schillebeeckx pays only very brief attention to so-called limbo (*limbus puerorum*) to which according to church doctrine those go who die in original sin but without having committed mortal sin. They are in hell, in other words cut off from God, but not subject to the pains of hell. On the one hand he thinks that this argument is logical: 'if it has died without grace, life is definitely not in grace', but there is no personal guilt, so there cannot be personal consequences of it. It is a 'limbo of children' because it is impossible for anyone who has come to the years of understanding 'to live only in original sin', and a deliberate human action is always implicitly or explicitly a 'statement for or against God'. On the other hand he emphatically states, though without further argument, that 'this dogma ... does not mean that a child who dies unbaptized *per se* dies in original sin'; cf. also his article 'Voorgeborchte', in *Theol. woordenboek* 3, 1958,

4830–4. His standpoint is directed against a conclusion that was very common as a result of Catholic views of the time, and was the cause of much fear and sorrow among Catholics, and also of the practice of baptizing children as quickly as possible after birth. For an impression of the development of theological opinion about this see J. Hill, *The Existence of a Children's Limbo According to Post-Tridentine Theologians*, Shelby 1962. After the Second Vatican Council the 1966 *New Catechism* (ET London 1967), published on behalf of the Dutch bishops, was to adopt the common-sense judgement, widespread among Catholics, that God does not allow anyone to be lost 'except for sin personally committed' (295–6). The 1992 Roman *Catechism of the Catholic Church* here takes a step forward by saying that God's mercy and Jesus's affection for children certainly allow us 'to hope that there is a way of salvation for children who have died without Baptism', but at the same time calls 'all the more urgently' 'not to prevent little children coming to Christ through the gift of holy Baptism' (no. 1261).

176 For a comparable view of purification after death see Guardini, *Die letzten Dinge* (n. 167), 34–40.

177 For the connection with mysticism he refers to R. Garrigou-Lagrange, *Perfection chrétienne et contemplation selon S. Thomas d'Aquin et S. Jean de la Croix*, Saint-Maximin 1923, 182–3, who again bases himself on some passages in John of the Cross.

178 Taken up with somewhat more restraint in 'Schat der kerk', *Theol. woordeenboek* 3, 1958, 4247–8; for the historical facts and their interpretation Schillebeeckx bases himself especially on B. Poschmann, *Der Ablass im Licht der Bussgeschichte*, Bonn 1948; for the theological assimilation of these facts he refers to K. Rahner, 'Forgotten Truths Concerning the Sacrament of Penance', *Theological Investigations* II, London and New York 1963, 135–74. Much later Schillebeeckx used the material from his lectures in the article 'The Spiritual Intent of Indulgences', *Lutheran World* 14, 1967, 3, 11–32.

179 Fragments of the lecture notes on creation are to be found in Arch. 161, 3117, 3120, 3121. The text followed here, dated at the end of the introduction 'September 1956', and thus evidently made for lectures in the academic year 1956–7, is almost a collage. It is a sign that Schillebeeckx worked most intensively on this text and that in a certain sense it was closest to his heart. The numbering is as follows: I–III, 1–203, 1–22, 20–42, 79A–79J, addenda 1–4, 141A–141H, 153A–153E, 153–64, 86–99, 99A–99B, 100–18, 193–205, 39–61, I-IV, 256–6, II, 201–II, 206 ,72–75, 75A-75V, II, 233–II, 418, 267–356, 329–40. I follow the numbering by hand added later, I, 1–367 and II, 201–520; this is given in brackets in the text. The scheme from which the quotation is made here is on II, 419.

180 See Maltha and Thuys, *Dogmatiek*, 257–61. This too is stated by Vatican I, see Denzinger 3025; the former statement is in Denzinger 3004 and 3026.

181 In this lecture Schillebeeckx does go at length into the doctrine of equal creation in Thomas; following De Petter, he regards this as human 'participation' in being, which comes from God (I, 251–64). Along the line of his earliest articles he then concludes: 'We depend totally on God, but God does not depend on us: his active indwelling holds us in existence. and we shall only be completely human if we "enter into" this indwelling' (I, 259).

182 The picture that Schillebeeckx gives here of the moment of Israel's election, which thus in his view is at the same time the revelation of God, leans strongly on a theory of the Protestant exegete M. Noth (*Das System der zwölf Stämme Israels*, Stuttgart 1930) about the origin of belief in Yahweh which was influential at the time but which has meanwhile come to be regarded by exegetes as outdated. Previously independent tribes are said to have gathered to form a cultic community around a Yahweh sanctuary and thus at the same time to have arrived at a covenant with this God and with one another. Gerhard von Rad, another Protestant exegete, gave Noth's theory a place within his 'salvation-historical' view of the biblical traditions, in which he took account of the fact that the biblical faith was

faith in a salvation history as the revelation of God and combined this with the conviction that any expression of faith was itself historical and situated in a concrete situation. In his view of the relationship between creation faith and the salvation-historical revelation, to an important degree Schillebeeckx seems to base himself on von Rad's 'The Theological Problem of the Old Testament Doctrine of Creation' (1936), in *The Problem of the Hexateuch and Other Essays*, Edinburgh 1966, 131–43. For a summary of von Rad's position see R. Smend, 'Rad, Gerhard von (1901–1971)', in *Theol. Realenz.* 28, 1997, 89–91; for the theological relevance see W. Pannenberg, 'Glaube und Wirklichkeit im Denken Gerhard von Rads', in *Gerhard von Rad. Seine Bedeutung für die Theologie*, ed. H. W. Wolff et al., Munich 1975, 37–54. Schillebeeckx's openness to the Protestant exegesis which set the tone in the 1950s was not uncontroversial. In his summary sketch of the origin of the first five books of the Bible and of the creation story in Genesis in particular, Schillebeeckx therefore seems to refer quite deliberately to the Dominican R. de Vaux, Director of the École Biblique in Jerusalem, under whose leadership work was being done at this time on a Catholic translation of the Bible on the basis of modern exegetical insights, the so-called 'Jerusalem Bible'. In introductions to the provisional version of the Genesis translation, de Vaux gave a synthetic picture of the origin of the Pentateuch, of which Schillebeeckx said in his lecture that this 'excels in its sense of tradition and at the same time its progressiveness, so that both the restraining excesses of many Catholics and the disruptive excesses of rationalists ... are avoided' (I, 34); cf. 'Introduction générale au Pentateuque' and 'Introduction à la Genèse', in *La Genèse, La Sainte Bible* 1, Paris 1951, 7–24, 25–37.

183 Quite in passing, Schillebeeckx points out that a synthesis is to be found in the Old Testament of 'the fresh creation faith that is bound up with nature of the primitive peoples and the salvation-historical creation faith that ends in Christianity (and as a result is purified and ennobled, exalted to a higher level)' (I, 127).

184 In this connection Schillebeeckx also demonstrates that what in the Bible are called 'God's wondrous acts' are events which bring God's system of salvation to light (I, 86–96). So this is a different idea of miracle from the Christian notion of the breaking of natural laws. Elsewhere in his course Schillebeeckx goes at length into the significance of miracles, stigmatizations and visions (II, 284–349). Here he in fact reflects the scholastic definition of miracle as something that cannot be explained from natural causes. He maintains that a miracle is an anomaly, but at the same time emphasizes that it is not a new creation from nothing, but God's use of causes within the world. So first of all he looks for a 'natural explanation', not out of rationalism but out of 'a true sense of the authentically religious' and in the conviction that to attribute something to natural causes does not mean that it is removed from God (II, 311). It is not the sensationally miraculous but the 'religious context' of an event which makes it recognizable as a miracle, in other words as an effect of 'the divine sign activity' (II, 289). Cf. also his article, 'Rond het "geval Konnersreuth"', *TGL* 11, 1955, 52–63, and his article 'Reliquienverering', in *Theol. woordenboek* 3, 1958, 4118–23.

185 Alongside creation in the church's creeds (I, 174–84), Schillebeeckx also discusses 'the dogma of creation in the definitions of the councils' (I, 184–200); here the declarations of the First Vatican Council (Denzinger 3020–5, cf. ch. 1 of the dogmatic constitution *Dei Filius*, Denzinger 3001–3) form a highpoint in his presentation (I, 193–9). In his summary of the 'fact defined as dogma' he leans heavily on the Vatican I text: 'The one true living God, Father, Son and Holy Spirit, is the one principle in the creation of all that exists outside God (material beings, angels and human beings). He created all these things as they are out of nothing; he did this wisely and omnipotently, in a sovereignly free way and out of sheer goodness and love, without winning or enriching himself in so doing, but loading the creatures with goodness, yet in such a way that these exist in their own worth to his glory.

The initiative of creation gave an absolute beginning to the world of creation, which abidingly stands under the caring providence of God. This initiative is the first beginning of salvation history: the saviour and redeemer is the creator God' (I, 199–200).

186 Schillebeeckx makes this statement in a discussion of the biblical view of God's wondrous acts as the elements in which God's system of salvation particularly comes to light, and presents this as an alternative to the notion that God comes to light in miracles which contradict the laws of nature (I, 87–96).

187 In this emphasis on the moral character of the Old Testament revelation of God and its universal character, Schillebeeckx seems to have been influenced by the sketch of the abiding importance of the Old Testament by H. H. Rowley, *The Rediscovery of the Old Testament*, London 1946, 187–207, which was written for a wide audience.

188 Schillebeeckx's view of the origin of Israel's conviction that universal history is in God's hand, extended between the primordial event and the end of time, seems to be influenced by O. Procksch, *Theologie des Alten Testaments*, Gütersloh 1950, esp. 582–600. G. von Rad wrote a preface to the book. But the remarkable statement that this emerges from a historicizing and eschatologizing of creation faith – and thus for example evidently not from a universalizing of the Old Testament historical consciousness – seems to come from Schillebeeckx himself.

189 Schillebeeckx also sees the logic of the New Testament notion that Satan is the 'prince of the world' along these lines (II, 362–6). Here he also tries to explain how the sin of Adam could influence the human situation so much: 'It was [God's] principle (as also in Christ) to give grace to all human beings in and through one man's representative act of grace.' And: 'Precisely this failed, as a result of which it has become impossible for humanity as a whole to realize the "vocation to supernatural life" through its head' (II, 368f.). In the end Schillebeeckx's concern in these reflections, too, was to bring out more sharply the redemption in Christ as the firstborn of a new creation: 'God himself takes the provocation of original sin on himself, in his humanity ... And with this sin all its consequences', and thus also human suffering and death (II, 400). But Schillebeeckx seems to feel that this explanation of the dogma of original sin is unsatisfactory, since at the same time he dissociates himself from the usual pattern of thought with its concentration on Adam and the handing on of his original sin. He points out that *Humani generis* does not say that original sin came into the world through Adam as the father of all humankind, but only that it is impossible to see how the dogma of the existence of original sin can be reconciled with the view that humanity did not come from one ancestor (II, 370). He seems to envisage a view in which both of these can be reconciled. In his discussion of original sin Schillebeeckx refers especially in a positive way to K. Rahner, 'Über den theologischen Begriff der Konkupiszenz', in id., *Sämtliche Werke* VIII, 3–37, and P. Schoonenberg, *Het geloof van ons doodpsel: I. God, Vader en Schepper: Het eerste geloofsartikel*, 's-Hertogenbosch 1955, 166–95. Schoonenberg was later to develop his view of original sin as 'human situation' in *Het geloof van ons doopsel, IV: De macht der zonde: Inleiding op de verlossingsleer*, 's-Hertogenbosch 1962.

190 Given the central place that the idea assumed in scholastic theology as the occasion for redemption by Christ, the boldness with which Schillebeeckx deals with the notion of an 'original sin' is striking. He noted that it is a constant conviction in the biblical writings that 'the history set in motion by creation [is] an actual history of disaster, which is reinterpreted because of Yahweh's faithfulness to a salvation event' (I, 110), but that this sinful situation is expressed in different ways. He does not deny that there was an original sin which the first human couple committed and which by being 'handed on' has marked all human history since then, since this interpretation of the story of Adam's fall was laid down bindingly by the Council of Trent and emphatically affirmed once again in *Humani generis* (cf. Denzinger 1513, 3897). He does, though, point out that 'Adam' in Hebrew

means 'the human being' and that the creation story of Genesis 2 and 3 tried to explain the actual situation of sin by relating that the first human being already sinned: 'Adam, the ancestor of humankind, thus gives in his life as it were the typical experience of what happens throughout humanity' (I, 112). In that context, at relative length (I, 112–14), he puts the speculative interpretation of the story of the Fall by G. Lambert ('Le drame du Jardin Eden', *Nouv. Rev. Théol.* 76, 1954, 917–48), which interprets Genesis 2–3 wholly as a rejection of idolatry and as an incitement for modern men and women to turn away from the false gods.

191 The notion that the so-called 'delay of the parousia' is the cause of a presupposed de-eschatologizing of early Christian theology was expressed in an influential way by H. Conzelmann, *The Theology of St Luke* (1954), London and New York 1960, schematically summed up in id., 'Parusie', in *Die Religion in Geschichte und Gegenwart* 5, 1961, 130–2. Schillebeeckx in fact keeps to the position of Cullmann, *Christ* (n. 162), according to whom the 'revolutionary Christ event' qualifies past, present and future from within.

192 Schillebeeckx remarks: 'the influence of the wisdom literature on St Paul and St John has become one of the main slogans of contemporary exegesis, a statement which is confirmed by all kinds of facts, and is more than just plausible' (I, 149); here he refers explicitly to M. E. Boismard (*Le Prologue de Saint Jean*, Paris 1951) and A. Feuillet ('L'Eglise, plérôme du Christ d'après Ephés. I, 23', *Nouv. Rev. Théol.* 88, 1956, 449–72: 593–610).

193 Denzinger 3004, cf.3026 (see also n. 185). Schillebeeckx's interpretation of Vatican I is contained in I, 4–20; in the second instance he tried sweepingly to derive the same notions from scholastic theology, and then of course especially from the theology of Thomas (I, 20–6).

194 M. Merleau-Ponty, *Sens et non-sens*, Paris 1948, esp. 351–70: 'Foi et bonne foi'. Schillebeeckx quotes with great freedom from the work of existentialists, whom he has also studied at length: in the course see 214–30, clearly an older level. In this formal refutation of Merleau-Ponty he clearly recalls a philosophical analysis by L. Lavelle, *De l'acte*, Paris 1946, 331–4, which he cites at length (II, 271–3).

195 Cf. De Petter, 'Persoon' (n. 149); in addition to this, Schillebeeckx still refers emphatically to A. Dondeyne, 'Approches du mystère de la liberté', *Rev. internat. de Philos.* 2, no. 6, 1948, 23–44, which gives a survey of contemporary views of freedom, and G. Gusdorf, *La découverte de soi*, Paris 1948, which was strongly inspired by Merleau-Ponty.

196 On the basis of Gusdorf (*Découverte* [n. 195], 500–10: 'Conclusions') and J. Mouroux (*Le sens chrétien de l'homme*, Paris 1947, 145: 'La liberté spirituelle'), Schillebeeckx emphasized the growing awareness of man as time and again 'defining himself in constantly changing situations which can alienate him from himself. Man does not define himself in one act but in a historical course, so that before death his self-determination is never "finished" and constantly remains open.' In this connection he interprets the classical Catholic distinction between mortal sin and daily sins as a distinction between actions which fundamentally break off the Christian project of life and actions which represent only practical, subordinate deviations from it. 'We have a closer definition in our "good deeds", the everyday goods and the important good deeds (typically, theology has no appropriate terminology for this)' (II, 246–50).

197 In fact this view of human responsibility for the creation is very anthropocentric. Schillebeeckx sees creation faith very markedly as giving meaning to reality, which in itself asks for meaning rather than 'being already rich in meaning itself' (II, 246). In his view this also applies to animals (II, 357); in 1960 this last conviction leads him in 'De zin van het dier voor de mens' (reprinted as 'The Animal in Man's world', *World*, 257–68) to the far-reaching statement that things, plants and animals 'have no distinctive value of their own in the strict sense of the word' but are a subordinate part of 'a continuous cosmic development'. From this he draws the conclusion that 'from an ideological standpoint

there is no objection against laboratory experiments in which human beings must deliberately inflict pain on animals in order to test all kinds of reactions to pain for the benefit of human healing'. When in 1977, in *Christ* (515–29), he emphatically dissociates himself from an exclusively salvation-historical approach to creation faith and states that 'creation faith ... [has] ... a relative independence alongside the distinctive faith in Yahweh's saving action with Israel', he seems especially to be turning against this anthropocentric narrowing of creation faith and wanting to take more seriously the idea that the same God who speaks in salvation history also comes to light in creation.

198 For the first time in 'Het nieuwe Godsbeeld, secularisatie en politiek' (1968), *TvT* 8, 1968, 44–65: 57–8. For the experience of contrast in Schillebeeckx and further references see my 'Universiteit', 51–2: 'Sporen', 11–12; P. Kennedy, *Deus Humanissimus: The Knowability of God in the Theology of Edward Schillebeeckx*, Fribourg 1993, 238–49.

199 Here (II, 253), Schillebeeckx quotes Mouroux, *Le sens chrétien* (n.196), 138: 'spiritual freedom is the commitment by which a person possesses himself, develops and fulfils himself, by giving himself to God', but in fact he reverses the focus of this sentence: 'In concrete man ... comes to possess himself by giving himself to God in performing his task of giving meaning in the world'; for him the emphasis is that the giving of meaning is a matter of giving away. In the same context, strikingly he also quotes *I and Thou* by the German Jewish theologian Martin Buber (1923, Edinburgh 1937) – but in a French translation and obviously supposing that Buber is a Protestant – which shows God to be the meaning of life in human action on behalf of another. Later he was to refer to the Jewish philosopher Emmanuel Lévinas in the same sense. See already, 'Evangelical purity and human authenticity' (1963), in *God and Man*, 160–209: 176 n. 14, in which two years after its appearance he refers to Lévinas' *magnum opus Totality and Infinity* (1961), Pittsburgh 1969; cf. further *Jesus*, 638; *Christ*, 48; *Jesus in Our Western Culture*, London and New York 1987, 56–8; *Church: The Human Story of God*, London and New York 1990, 92–4.

200 Here Schillebeeckx makes use of the distinction between 'external' grace and its 'internal' consequences in human beings which Thomas uses to distinguish the divine initiative from the internal human change which is its result and its aim, and to connect it with this, cf. *Summa theol.* I–II, esp. art. 1 and 2.

201 *Interim Report on the Books* Jesus *and* Christ, London and New York 1980, 105–24: 116. In the framework of his new interpretation of the saving significance of Jesus's history he indeed departs radically from the notion that suffering could have a meaning in itself and that the reason for it must be sought in whatever way in God: cf. *Jesus*, 272–317; 'Mysterie van ongerechtigheid en mysterie van erbarmen', *TvT* 15, 1975, 3–24; *Christ*, 724–31. For a discussion of this question in connection with the interpretation of Jesus cf. H. Häring, 'Verlossing – ondanks Jezus lijden en dood?', in *Meedenken met Edward Schillebeeckx*, ed. H. Häring et al., Baarn 1983, 171–87.

202 This gives Schillebeeckx's position a high degree of distinctiveness in the midst of other attempts within Catholic theology to find a middle way between on the one hand the 'extrinsecism' of neoscholasticism which as it were adds grace to a human existence that is already closed to it, and an 'intrinsecism' which sees grace as an implication of human existence as spirit. For him, all attempts to find a point of contact in human nature for a 'supernatural existential', an idea developed especially by Karl Rahner, are 'just incomprehensible' (II, 481), ultimately because they continue to start from a *natural pura* which abstracts from grace, precisely in order to make grace comprehensible as a free gift. He refers to Karl Rahner, 'Concerning the Relationship between Nature and Grace', in *Theological Investigations* I, London and New York 1961, 277–318; H. U. von Balthasar, *The Theology of Karl Barth*, New York 1972, 202–27; id. and E. Gutwenger, 'Der Begriff der Natur in der Theologie', *Zts. für kat. Theol.* 75, 1953, 452–64: 452–61, and an article

published under the pseudonym 'D', 'Ein Weg zur Bestimmung des Verhältnisses von Natur und Gnade', *Orientierung* 14, 1950, 138–41; cf. also K. Rahner, 'Eine Antwort', ibid., 141–5, in which Rahner introduces the 'supernatural existential'. Moreover, Rahner, too, does not seem to be concerned with a specific characteristic of abstract human nature, but with the discovery in the light of the actual reception of grace that the whole of human subjectivity is in fact orientated on this grace.

203 *Summa theol.* I, q. 48, art. 2: *utrum malum inveniatur in rebus?*

204 This is a surprising interpretation, although the notion that God's toleration of evil is not indolence but 'long-suffering' because 'he does not want some of you to be lost but all to be converted' has New Testament roots (2 Peter 3.9). In theology the idea of God's *permissio peccati* usually functions as an attempt to resolve the incompatibility between God's goodness and omnipotence on the one hand and the existence of evil and suffering on the other.

205 But according to Schillebeeckx not all suffering is meaningless. Precisely in order to prevent people from too quickly evading a supernaturalistic interpretation of suffering, he also shows that a certain degree of suffering can quite well be given a meaningful place in human development (II, 392–5). He also maintains the traditional notion that suffering can have a 'pedagogic function in salvation'; it can break through the illusion of human prosperity in the world and thus open people to God (II, 396–8).

206 Here, strikingly enough, Schillebeeckx bases himself on the argument developed by the English mediaevalist and convert to Anglicanism, C. S. Lewis (1898–1963), in his book *The Problem of Pain*, London 1940, esp. 77–97, which is more religious than technical and theological; Schillebeeckx quotes it in a French translation.

207 Schillebeeckx combines this with the classical question why redemption had to be achieved specifically through suffering; he said that the answer of Anselm of Canterbury (1033/4–1109), which had become very authoritative in the history of theology, the penalty for the insult to God's glory could be paid only by an infinite sacrifice, the so-called satisfaction theory, was 'not incorrect but inadequate' (II, 401).

208 *Marriage*, I, xvii–xvi; from this point page references to the quotations in the text are in brackets. For a survey of the flood of Catholic literature on marriage of every kind and level which appeared in this period, within the Netherlands and outside, cf. S. G. M. Trooster, 'Capita selecta', *Kath. arch.* 11, 1956. 1201–64; 13, 1958, 353–84; 14, 1959, 537–72; 15, 1960, 765–808; 17, 1962, 453–506.

209 Pius XI, encyclical *Casti connubii* (1930), no. 14; decree of the Holy Office of 1 April 1944, in *AAS* 36, 1944, 103. Canon 1055 of the post-conciliar canon law book of 1983 explicitly states that the marriage bond is by nature orientated on the well-being of the couple and the procreation and upbringing of children.

210 A. C. Kinsey, *Sexual Behavior in the Human Male*, Philadelphia 1948; id., *Sexual Behavior in the Human Female*, Philadelphia 1953.

211 In 1955, Michel's book appeared in a Dutch translation under the title *Het huwelijk: Een antropologie van het geslechtelijk samenzijn*, strikingly enough from the Protestant publisher Callenbach in Nijkerk. In the foreword J. H. van der Berg refers to the history surrounding the condemnation of the book, refutes the reasons given for it and praises the author as someone who as a Catholic, 'that speaks for itself, holds to the official statements of his church as far as he can but who also so much wants to put them in the special state of present-day marriage that his reflections are important for everyone' (9).

212 Moreover, the movement for the spiritual health of the people led to a distinctive Dutch contribution to the discussion of the relationship between psychology and morality, between spiritual health and religious salvation. In 1955, in a speech to celebrate the twenty-fifth anniversary of the Catholic Central Association for the Spiritual Health of the People, the question of this relationship was emphatically raised by the priest-psychologist

H. M. M. [Han] Fortmann (*Een nieuwe opdracht: Poging tot historische plaatsbepaling van de geestelijke gezondheidszorg in het bijzonder voor het katholieke volksidee*, Utrecht 1955) and emphasized its importance. Fortmann answers this question himself at length in his major study, *Als ziende de onzienlijke: Een cultuurpsychologische studie over de religieuze waarneming en de zogenaamde religieuze projectie*, Hilversum and Antwerp 1964–8.

213 Cf. E. Simons and L. Winkeler, *Het verraad der clercken: Intellectuelen en hun rol in de ontwikkelingen van het Nederlandse katholicisme na 1945*, Baarn 1987, 63–70; for a very extensive history of the Catholic movement for the spiritual health of the people see H. Westhoff, *Geestelijke bevrijders: Nederlandse katholieken en hun beweging voor geestelijke volksgezondheid in de twintigste eeuw*, Nijmegen 1996.

214 In fact it was an initiative taken by the president of Catholic Action, Ludolf Baas, and the 'adviser in pastoral psychology to the Catholic National Bureau', Hein Ruytgers, lecturer at the major seminary of the diocese of Den Bosch at Hoeven before in 1958 he was appointed adviser to the National Centre of Catholic Action as a special collaborator for the section on marriage and family. Cf. Westhoff, *Geestelijke bevrijders* (n. 213), 381f.; P. de Haan, *Van volgzame elite-strijder tot kritische gelovige: Geschiedenis van de Katholieke actie in Nederland (1934–1966)*, Nijmegen 1994, 275–6.

215 De Haan, *Van volgzame elite-strijder* (n. 214), 275–9; Westhoff, *Geestelijke bevrijders* (n. 213), 285–8; for Hein Ruygers cf. ibid., 175–394 passim, esp. 361–5. There is a copy of the provisional 'report to the Dutch bishops on the situation in marriage and family' in e.g., Schillebeeckx, Arch. 303.

216 Westhoff, *Geestelijke bevrijders* (n. 213), 388–90; the 'Proposal for a meeting of theologians' is in Schillebeeckx, Arch. 304.

217 B. J. Alfrink, 'Toespraak bij gelegenheid van het 40–jarig bestaan van de r.k.artsen-vereniging op. 7, nov. 1959', in *Kath. arch.* 1, 1959, 1029–34: 32.

218 E. Schillebeeckx, 'De natuurwet' (n. 119), 5–51: 25; he gave this lecture in September 1960, shortly before the provisional report of the Investigation into Marriage and Family was sent to the bishops.

219 Ibid., 15–20. He bases himself on S. Pinckaers, 'La structure de l'acte humain suivant saint Thomas', *Rev. Thom.* 63, 1955, 393–412; C. Anderson, 'De natuurwet', *Jaarboek 1960* of the Working Group of Catholic Theologians in the Netherlands, Hilversum 1961, 125–37.

220 For the first, ibid., 23; for the last, 34f.

221 For Schillebeeckx's reaction to the report and especially to the account of the meeting of theologians cf. Westhoff, *Geestelijke bevrijders* (n. 213), 390–1; see Schillebeeckx's own 'Reflections on the "account of the meeting of theologians"', appendix to the Report to the Dutch bishops on the situation of marriage and family' (Arch. 302).

222 Schilebeeckx, 'De natuurwet' (n. 119), 28–31; the lecture is dated 'September 1960', but among other things at this point by his own account Schillebeeckx tried to make the published text clearer; cf., however, also 'Gedachtenwisseling', ibid., 51–61, esp. 55f., indicating a change of mind. He worked out this dynamic view of being human as a 'task' more closely on pp. 36–40 of the published text – a quotation from 'Roeping, levens-ontwerp en levensstaat' (1961), reprinted in *Zending* (not in the English translation) – and drew from it the consequences of the view of morality on pp. 40–51.

223 Schillebeeckx, 'De natuurwet' (n. 119), 30. It appears that he was convinced of the complete legitimacy of his own view in his work for the section on marriage in the Vatican II constitution *Gaudium et spes*, cf. the way in which he in fact set out the same view in E. Schillebeeckx, 'De wisselende visies der christenen op het huwelijk', in *Kerk en wereld*, DO-C dossiers 10, Hilversum and Antwerp 1996, 91–114, esp. 105–14.

224 Reprinted as 'Huwelijksliefde en verantwoordelijkheid', included e.g., in *Bisschop Bekkers: Negen jaar met Gods volk onderweg*, Utrecht 1966, 127–30: 128.

225 De Haan, *Van volgzame elite-strijder* (n. 214), 281: Westhoff, *Geestelijke bevrijders* (n. 213), 391–3.

226 'Aangenomen aanbevelingen inzake het rapport "Huwelijk en gezin"', in *Pastoraal Concilie van de Nederlands kerkprovincie, IV. Derde plenaire vergadering. Zedelijke levenshouding, huwelijk en gezin, jeugd*, ed. W. Goddijn et al., Amersfoort 1969, 269–71: 269; cf. 'Rapport "Huwelijk en gezin"', ibid., 60–85: 79. For the discussion carried on see 'Discussie Maandag 6 januari 1969', ibid., 176–213.

227 Cf. K. Steur, *Dogmatisch tractaat over het sacrament van het huwelijk*, Bussum 1947, where there is a reference in the foreword to the importance of a break with Catholic tradition in order to treat marriage rightly in the framework of canon law and sexuality in the framework of morality. That Steur was condemned as a 'modernist' and that this was probably also connected with his publications on marriage and sexuality (id., *Liefde 1: Liefdestreven: Conferenties voor verloofden, II. Liefdesleven. Conferenties voor jonggehuwden*, Bussum 1947), once again makes clear how sensitive these questions were.

228 O'Neill, 'Die Sakramententheologie' (n. 54), 278; Ambaum, *Glaubenszeichen* (n. 49), 127–40, seems far more restrained.

229 *Gaudium et spes*, nos 47–52, discuss marriage. In the article 'Het huwelijk volgens Vaticanum II' (*TGL* 22, 1966, 81–107), Schillebeeckx comments on this passage wholly in line with his views developed earlier.

230 In the period between 1962 and 1966 Schillebeeckx lectured extensively on marriage, cf. Schoof, 'Aandrang', 11–39: 21f. Moreover, in 1970 he was still announcing the appearance of the second volume of *Het huwelijk*; cf. his article 'Het christelijk huwelijk en de menselijke realiteit van Solomon huwelijksontwrichting', in *(On)ontbindbaarheid van het huwelijk*, Bussum 1970, 184–214: 213 n. 6.

231 For the lectures see *Jaarboek 1960, WKTN* (n. 219); in addition to Schillebeeckx the speakers were W. Grossouw, H. Boelaars, B. Speekenbrink and P. Schoonenberg; the last two were involved as theologians in the discussion of the investigation. For the two books see *Huwelijk en sexualiteit*, Bussum 1961; H. Spee, *Huwelijk in Kristus: Een teologisch onderzoek over het kristelijk huwelijk*, Tilburg 1960; R. Kuiters, 'Kleine dogmatiek van het huwelijk', *Stud. cath.* 35, 1960, 73–233.

232 'De zegeningen van het sacramentele huwelijk' (= *De Bazuin* 43, 1959–60, no. 18, 7 Feb. 1960).

233 'De natuurwet' (n. 119), 5.

234 See Schillebeeckx, *Marriage* I, 1–20: 'General Introduction: The Modern Pattern of Marriage as an Opportunity for Grace'.

235 'De natuurwet' (n. 119), 5.

236 Denzinger 2990–3. For Trent see *Marriage* II, 165–82; for the church's reaction to tendencies towards secularization, ibid., 186–91. Schillebeeckx is extremely summary and restrained over the developments after Trent.

237 Here Schillebeeckx's approach breaks through the limits which he in fact still observed in *Heilseconomie*. There he limited himself to handing on explicit views, as these were expressed in liturgical texts, church doctrinal statements and the writings of theologians. Here he opens up the possibility of reflection in faith on reality as actually lived, in conversation with other scholarly approaches. The background to this is formed by the developments in his theological views sketched out in the previous chapter. Moreover, in *Marriage* he himself does not use this possibility, and even in 1983, in his last publication on marriage and sexuality ('Kerkelijk spreken over seksualiteit en huwelijk', in *Het kerkelijk spreken over seksualiteit en huwelijk: Een bundel filosofische gedragswetenschappelijke en theologische studies*, Baarn 1983, 215–38), he does not get beyond summing up factors of which talk in faith must take account in this connection. The starting point is the experience that there is no area 'in which the discrepancy between the official statements of the church and the convictions of many believers as put into practice is as great as in the

sphere of sexuality in marriage', and he argues especially for a more listening attitude.

238 For the facts of the history of theology in connection with marriage he seems to base himself largely on G. Le Bras, 'Mariage, III: Le mariage d'après des théologiens', *Dict. théol. cath.* 9/II, 1927, 2123–317.

239 For 'Marriage as a means of revealing the community existing between Yahweh and Israel' see *Marriage* I, 60–101; for 'Marriage and Christ's covenant of grace with the church' in Paul, ibid., 164–73.

240 In Thomas's incomplete *Summa theologiae* there is no section on marriage. For his view Schillebeeckx bases himself especially on the fourth book of Thomas's *Scriptum super sententiis*, dist. 26–42.

241 Cf. 'De natuurwet' (n. 119), esp. 31, where Schillebeeckx explains that to regard the sexual act as a *human* act means that account must be taken of its focus on procreation, of the fact that it is the expression of 'the personal loving fellowship of man and wife' and the relationship that this has to the rest of 'the world and society'. It is striking in this connection that he criticizes Thomas where Thomas's starting point is that outside pro-creation and everything that goes with mutual agreement (the so-called *officium naturae*) the man has no further reason for association with the woman (*Marriage* I, 144). He also regards the way in which Paul bases the inequality between man and woman on the bond with Christ as time-conditioned and a perverse 'theologizing' of human structures.

242 'De zegeningen' (n. 232), 7–8.

243 'De zegeningen' (n. 232), 9. The argument that marital openness was for children as a gift of God is ultimately derived from the work of Gabriel Marcel, the philosopher who was influential among Catholics in this period (cf. *Homo viator: Prolégomènes à une méta-physique de l'espérance*, Paris 1944, 95–132). Schillebeeckx refers to the popularizing use of this by Fons Jansen, at this time editorial secretary for the military *G-3: Goede Geest Gemeenschap in leger en luchtmacht* (the Good Spirit Fellowship in the army and air force), a Catholic journal which was an important and pioneering voice in the sphere of sexual experience and the author of a number of enlightening books on intercourse, marriage and sexuality: 'All we can do is to allow or hinder. If we allow it, the child is literally and figuratively put into our laps and entrusted to us' (*Het huwelijk in kerk en wereld: Ver-kenning voor het geweten*, Hilversum 1959, 19).

244 'De zegeningen' (n. 232), 9.

245 It was evidently the intention that material from the lectures which Schillebeeckx gave in 1964–5 and 1965–6 and which he later annotated in order to have it typed out should be part of the second volume of *Marriage*. The papers in Arch. 821, 'Metabletica van de christlijke sexualiteit', are mainly historical: on the basis of lecture notes by pupils, Schoof made a further reconstruction ('Aandrang', 22 n. 19). Here too Schillebeeckx does not in principle break the link between sexuality and procreation. His conclusion on the sig-nificance of sexuality is primarily negative: there is no distinctively Christian view of sexuality; people always begin from what at that moment is regarded as 'the humane'. Moreover, seen from the hostility of the Christian tradition to the body that he himself indicated, this conclusion was liberating, since it offered the possibility in his own time, too, to investigate what was regarded as 'the humanum'. For a Catholic theology of human sexual experience which does start from the idea that it can make a positive contribution to 'the restoration of all things in Christ', cf. G. Moore, *The Body in Context: Sex and Catholicism*, London 1992.

246 'De zegeningen' (n. 232), 10, 7.

247 From autumn 1959 to 1966 he gave lectures in Nijmegen on the 'theology of earthly values'; from 1963 the 'invasion' of the problem of secularization can be traced in his lectures, via discussion with J. A. T. Robinson and the 'Death of God' theology. Cf. Schoof, 'Aandrang', 18, 22–3.

CHAPTER 5

1   This feeling is expressed in these words in S. Donders, 'Geloven in meervoud: Bazuin-lezing', *De Bazuin* 80, 1997, nos 9, 15–21: 16–17.

2   Especially in the 'Pastoral Constitution on the Modern World', *Gaudium et spes* (7 December 1965), which began with the sentence which is quoted from in the text and which in the translation made by Schillebeeckx in collaboration with L. van Belder runs: 'Joy and hope, sorrow and fear of people today, above all of the poor and of those who have to suffer in whatever way, are equally the joy and hope, the sorrow and fear of the disciples of Christ: really nothing can be found among human beings which does not find an echo in their heart.' For the place of the Second Vatican Council in the developments in Catholicism before and after, cf. G. Alberigo, 'Das II. Vatikanum und der kulturelle Wandel in Europa', in *Das II. Vatikanum: Christlicher Glaube im Horizont globaler Modernisierung, Einleitungsfragen*, ed. P. Hünermann, Paderborn, etc. 1998, 139–57. For the Council as still having a determinative influence on the present-day situation of church and theology see this collection and also *Die Rezeption des Zweiten Vatikanischen Konzils*, ed. G. Alberigo, Düsseldorf 1987; O. H. Pesch, *Das Zweite Vatikanische Konzil (1962–1966), Vorgeschichte – Verlauf – Ergebnisse – Nachgeschichte*, Würzburg 1993.

3   Opponents of conciliar renewal have always argued this; from a sociological perspective it is claimed by B. McSweeney, *Roman Catholicism: The Search for Relevance*, Oxford 1980. For the statement that Vatican II was in fact a (belated) modernization of the church but that this does not necessarily imply ideological assimilation and that the effect of this modernization must be investigated further cf. especially. F.-X. Kaufmann, 'Zur Einführung. Probleme und Wege einer historischen Einschätzung des II. Vatikanischen Konzils', in *Vatikanum II und Modernisierung: Historische, theologische und soziologische Perspektiven*, Paderborn 1996, 9–34; K. Gabriel, 'Die Interpretation des II. Vatikanums als interdisziplinäre Forschungsaufgabe', in *Das II. Vatikanum* (n. 2), 35–47.

4   E. Schillebeeckx, 'John is his name: Twenty-five years after the death of John XXIII', in id., *For the Sake of the Gospel*, London and New York 1989, 130–40; cf. id., 'Terugblik vanuit de tijd na Vaticanum II: De gebroken ideologieën van de moderniteit', in *Tussen openheid en isolement: Het voorbeeld van de katholieke theologie in de negentiende eeuw*, ed. E. Borgman and A. van Harskamp, Kampen 1992, 153–72: 153–6.

5   Cf. H. Häring, 'De opkomst van de aandacht voor bevrijding in de Westerse theologie', in *Bevrijdingstheologie in West-Europa*, ed. B. Klein Goldewijk et al., Kampen 1989, 13–25; H. Holping, 'Die Kirche im Dialog mit der Welt und der sapientale Charakter christlicher Lehre: Pragmatik und Programmatik des II. Vatikanums im Kontext der Globalisierung', in *Das II. Vatikanum* (n. 2), 83–99; J. Noemi Callejas, 'Das II. Vatikanum im Kontext globaler Modernisierung aus einer lateinamerikanischen Perspektive', ibid., 101–6.

6   Quoted in W. Grossouw, *Alles is van u: Gewijde en profane herinneringen*, Baarn 1981, 284; for the story about the skirmishing to get Schillebeeckx to Nijmegen, see ibid., 280–6; R. Auwerda, *Dossier Schillebeeckx. Theoloog in de kerk der conflicten*, Bilthoven 1969, 22–3.

7   'Kreling was "*homo unius libri*", a man of one book – Thomas': 'Kreling en de theologische situatie van zijn tijd', in *Het goddelijk geheim: Theologisch werk van G. P. Krelnig OP*, ed. F. A. de Grijs et al., Kampen 1979, 47–68: 66–7; for an assessment of Kreling's significance of a clearly different kind see F. A. de Grijs, 'De beschouwende theologie van G. P. Kreling', ibid., 69–121; id., 'Doctor discipulus. Terugblik op het werk van G. P. Kreling', *TvT* 19, 1979, 4392–410. For the biography of Kreling see F. Haarsma, 'Gerardus Kreling (1888–1973): Een biografische schets', in *Het goddelijk geheim*, 15–46: for a bibliography, ibid., 476–502. For the central significance of the divine mystery in Kreling see his address 'Het goddelijk geheim in de theologie' (1939, reprinted ibid., 258–71) and the article 'Het heilig geheim' (1964, reprinted ibid., 463–78).

441

8   E. Schillebeeckx, '"Nieuwe theologie"', *Kultuurleven* 26, 1959, 122–5, a review of A. H. Maltha, *De nieuwe theologie: Informatie en orientatie*, Bruges 1958, but in fact the qualification applied to all Maltha's work. He was later to become the spokesman for a conservative Catholicism in the Netherlands. For a survey of his work see Struycker Boudier, *Wijsgerig leven* II, 214–16.

9   E. Schillebeeckx, *Testament*, 38.

10   Cf. ibid., 33–4. See Grossouw, *Alles is van u* (n. 6), 284–5.

11   *Testament*, 34.

12   Ibid., 34–5; Puchinger, *Toekomst*, 143.

13   For the ecumenical movement among Dutch Catholics see J. Roes, 'Een hele beweging . . .: Nederlandse katholieken van hereniging naar oekumene', *Heel de kerk: Een oekumenisch werkboek*, ed. A. Houtepen et al., Hilversum 1977, 10–64, and especially J. Jacobs, *Nieuwe visies op een oud visioen. Een potret van de Sint Willibrord Vereniging 1948–1998*, Nijmegen 1998; for the developments at the level of the world church see J. J. MacDonnell, *The World Council of Churches and the Catholic Church*, New York and Toronto 1981, esp. 107–221; for the ecumenical movement in the Catholic Church see E. Fouilloux, *Les catholiques et l'unité chrétienne du XIXe au XXe siècle*, Paris 1982. Dutch developments are discussed in this context on pp. 711–17.

14   Summed up as tasks by Grossouw in his address to the readers of the lay journal *Te Elfder Ure* in 1952, printed as 'Katholieke reveil en spiritualiteit' in *Cahiers Te Elfder Ure* no. 2, Laren n.d. 7–28, here esp. 24–8.

15   *Geloofsinhoud en geloofsbeleving. Een peiling binnen reformatie en katholieke kerk in Nederland*, ed. H. van der Linde and F. Thijssen, Utrecht and Antwerp 1951.

16   For the theological climate in the Netherlands in this period see J. Grootaers, 'Une restauration de la théologie de l'épiscopat: Contribution de Cardinal Alfrink à la preparation de Vatican II', in *Glaube in Prozess: Christsein nach dem II. Vatikanum*, Freiburg, Basel and Vienna 1984, 778–825, esp. 791–8; T. Schoof, 'Contouren van veertig jaar theologie. Het "Werkgenootschap" binnen de katholiek kerk van Nederland', *TvT* 27, 1987, 139–54, esp. 140–6. Immediately after the war, in his unpublished 1948 doctoral thesis, Schoonenberg had already brought out a clear affinity to *'nouvelle théologie'*, and spoken of theology as the 'language of faith' (see L. Bakker, 'Schoonenberg's theologie: Spiegel van onze eigen ontwikkeling?', *TvT* 11, 1971, 355–81, esp. 355–63) and had again taken up this notion in 1956 ('De verhouding tussen theologie en wijsbegeerte: I. Theologie in zelfbezinning', in *Annalen van het Thijmgenootschap* 44, 1956, 225–36); on the basis of this dynamic view, in the 1950s he was working on a kind of dogmatics for Catholic laity under the title *Het geloof van ons doopsel* (I: *God, Vader en Schepper*, Den Bosch 1955; II. *Jesus, de Christus, de Zoon Gods*, ibid. 1957; III. *De mensgeworden Zoon van God*, ibid. 1958; IV. *De macht der zonde*, ibid. 1962).

17   Puchinger, *Toekomst*, 242.

18   Schoof, 'Aandrang', 19–20; id., 'The Later Theology of Edward Schillebeeckx', *The Clergy Review* 55, 1970, 943–60.

19   Schoof, 'Aandrang', 16–17.

20   'The Search for the Living God', in *God and Man*, 18–40; quotations 26 and 39.

21   The more or less personal messages to a number of groups of people which traditionally end an inaugural address are not reprinted in *God and Man*; for them see E. C. F. A. Schillebeeckx, *Op zoek naar de levende God*, Utrecht and Nijmegen 1959, 20–2.

22   Ibid., 18. Cf. also the much later 'The Sorrow of the Experience of God's Concealment', in *World*, 77–95.

23   Ibid., 32. A year later he worked this out further in 'God in Dry Dock', reprinted in *God and Man*, 3–17, where he also takes up the suggestion which was becoming usual at this

time that believers are to blame for the reactions against faith and that therefore modern atheism is an opportunity for grace.

24 For what follows see Schoof, 'Aandrang', 19–20; Schillebeeckx, *Testament*, 35.

25 Editorial board, 'Ter Orientering', *TvT* 1, 1961, 1–2. Cf. Schoof, 'Contouren' (n. 16), 145. Except for the literature quoted, my description of the early history is based on information from Ted Schoof and minutes of meetings of the editorial board of *Tijdschrift voor Theologie* which I was able to inspect.

26 In the strict sense the first thematic number of *TvT* is no. 2 of 1962, entitled *Theologisch congres over het Concilie/Nimegen, 11–13 April 1962*. However, this issue contains only a number of reports by the congress on two topics which were to be central at the coming council, 'primacy and episcopacy' and 'laity and office'.

27 Reprinted in *Openbaring*, 282–312 (not included in the English translation). He devoted the most extensive and detailed attention to the influence of existential thought, which is clearly present in his Louvain work (291–303).

28 J. H. Walgrave, 'Standpunten en stromingen in de huidige moraaltheologie', *TvT* 1, 1961, 48–70.

29 Cf. G. Alberigo, 'The Announcement of the Council: From the Security of the Fortress to the Lure of the Quest', in *History of Vatican II, 1: Announcing and Preparing Vatican Council II: Toward a New Era of Catholicism*, ed. G. Alberigo, Maryknoll and Louvain 1995, 1–54: 18–33; for the Netherlands, Jacobs, *Andere kerk*, 18–22.

30 See W. A. Visser 't Hooft, *Memoirs*, London 1973, 327; see the whole chapter on the mobilization of the Roman Catholic Church, ibid., 319–39.

31 E. Schillebeeckx, 'Het komend concilie van de R.-K. Kerk' (1960), in *Concilie* I, 19–26: 19–20.

32 In *Nieuwe visies* (n. 13), Jacobs only once connects Schillebeeckx directly with a formal ecumenical initiative (103): as a brand new professor at Nijmegen, on his installation in 1959 he became a member of the Theology and Praxis commission of the St Willibrord Association, the Dutch Catholic organization for ecumenical matters. Around the same time he was asked to take part in a working party of the Nederlands Gespreks Centrum which was preparing a report on 'miracle': because of health problems he had to stop making contributions to this at the beginning of the 1960s; cf. *Het wonder*, Kampen, etc. 1963.

33 Cf. *Kath. arch.* 14, 1959, 268–9.

34 Homily *Venerabiles fratres*, in *AAS* 50, 1958, 884–8: 885.

35 John XXIII, *Questa festiva ricorrenza* (15 January 1959), in *Acta et documenta concilio oecumenico Vaticano II, Series prima (antepreparatoria) I: Acta summi pontificis Iohannis XXIII*, Typis Polygl. Vatic. 1960, 3–6. For a survey of the results of the diocesan synod for the city of Rome, which in fact proved a fiasco, cf. I. Dekkers, 'De synode van Rome', in *Ned. kath. Stemmen* 57, 1961, 225–30.

36 For Roncalli's consistent emphasis on the pastoral aspect of episcopacy and papacy and for the pastoral background to his proposal for a council cf. the summary in Alberigo, 'The Announcement' (n. 29), 7–12; in n. 85 he mentions an unpublished study by A. Melloni, who has counted the word 'pastoral' 2000 times in Roncalli's writings. Cf. also B. R. Bonnot, *Pope John XXIII, an Astute Pastoral Leader,* New York 1979; for the emphasis on the pope as an authoritarian father in Pacelli's view cf. R. Christian, *The Understanding Pope Pius XII had of the Paternity of the Holy Father*, Rome 1984.

37 John XXIII, *Ad Petri cathedram*, no. 33.

38 Address *Il mondo interno* (9 August 1959), in *Acta et documenta* I (n. 35), 45–7: 46.

39 John XXIII, *Il convenire* (25 January 1959), *AAS* 51, 1959, 70 4: 72. For all this see Alberigo, 'The Announcement' (n. 29), 33–44.

40 C. de Gaulle, *Mémoires d'espoir. Le renouveau 1958–1962*, Paris 1970, 205.

41 Address to the presidents of Catholic Action for Italian youth on 31 January 1959, see *Acta et documenta* I (n. 35), 10.

42 For the statement that the pontificate is characterized by an 'institutional isolation' of the pope in the midst of the Vatican apparatus of government cf. G. Lercaro, *Per la sforza dello Spirito: Discorsi conciliari*, Bologna 1984, 287–310.

43 John XXIII, *Journal of a Soul*, London and New York 1965, 303.

44 Ibid., 326.

45 Cf. exhortation *A quarantacinque anni* to the clergy of Venice (1959), in *Acta et documenta* I (n. 35), 19, the *motu proprio Superno Dei nutu* to the preparatory commission of the Council (1960), ibid. 93–6: 93, and many mentions in the meantime and later, cf. *Il Concilio Vaticano II: Cronache de Concilio Vaticano II edite da 'La Civiltà Cattolica'*, ed. G. Caprile, I: *L'annunzio e la preparazione 1959–62, I: 1959–1960*, Rome 1966, 44–5.

46 L. Capovilla, 'Il concilio ecumenico Vaticano II: la decisione di Giovanni XXIII. Precedenti storici e motivazioni personali', in *Come se é giunti al concilio Vaticano II*, ed. G. Galeazzi, Milan 1988, 15–60, quoted in Alberigo 'The Announcement' (n. 29), 13; cf. also *Il Concilio Vaticano II, I/1* (n. 45), 39–44. G. Zizola, *L'utopie du pape Jean XXIII*, Paris 1978, 227–9; cf. also in P. Hebblethwaite, *Pope John XXIII: The Pope of the Council*, New York 1984, 312–18.

47 Quoted in Zizola, *L'utopie* (n. 46), 229; cf. also Hebblethwaite, *Pope John XXIII* (n. 46), 314–15. Both refer to Tardini's note on the same conversation, made that same evening, which is strikingly matter-of-fact.

48 Cf. C. Caprile, 'Pio XI e al ripresa del Concilio Vaticano', in *Il Concilio Vaticano II, I/1* (n. 45), 3–14; id., 'Pius XII. und das Zweite Vatikanische Konzil', in *Pius XII. zum Gedächtnis*, ed. H. Schambeck, Berlin 1977, 649–91; F.-C. Uginet, 'Les projets de concile général sous Pie XI et Pie XII', in *Le deuxième concile du Vatican (1959–1965)*, Rome 1989, 65–78.

49 Address *Volge il settimo mese* (1959), included in *Acta et documenta* I (n. 35), 24–5: 25: the composition of the pre-preparatory commission – '*commissio antepreparatoria*' – is in ibid., 22–3.

50 Thus the description by the French newspaper *La Croix* on 30 Jan. 1959; see *Il Concilio Vaticano II*, I/1 (n. 45), 64.

51 Thus É. Fouilloux, 'The Antepreparatory Phase: The Slow Emergence for Inertia (January, 1959 – October, 1962)', in *History of Vatican II* (n. 29), 55–166: 90. The term 'the Roncalli mystery' as an indication of the contrast between his activity as a church diplomat and as pope, and the question of the relationship between the two, comes from a famous article by Robert Rouquette, which appeared immediately after John XXIII's death under the title 'Le mystère Roncalli' in the journal *Études* of the French Jesuits; it is included in R. Rouquette, *La fin d'une chrétiente: Chroniques I*, Paris 1968, 307–22.

52 For the favourable press for John XXIII in Italy during the first months of his pontificate see M. Marazziti, *I Papi di carta: Nascita e svolta dell'informazione religiosa da Pio XII a Giovanni XXIII*, Genoa 1990, 47–126.

53 For the significance of this pontificate for various facets of church life cf. *Pius XII. zum Gedächtnis* (n. 48), and especially G. Schwaiger, 'Pius XII in der Kirchengeschichte', ibid., 693–766. For his views on the 'ordinary' papal magisterium cf. G. Rheinbay, *Das ordentliche Lehramt in der Kirche: Die Konzeption Papst Pius XII. Und das Modell Karl Rahners im Vergleich*, Trier 1988, 26–64.

54 In the memorial speech which Suenens gave on 28 October in the council hall based on John 1.6–7: 'There came a man sent by God, his name was John. He came to bear witness to the light, that all might believe', focused wholly on Roncalli. Suenens' text is printed in the Dutch edition of John XXIII's journal: *Geestelijk dagboek en andere geestelijke Geschriften*, Tielt and The Hague 1965, 521–8.

55 E. Schillebeeckx, 'Paus Johannes en het tweede Vaticanum' (1963), in id., *Concilie* I, 66–78.

56 Ibid., 66; cf. K. Rahner, 'Eine neue Epoche in der Kirche eingeleitet: Der "Übergangs-
papst" Johannes XXIII. vollzog den Übergang der Kirche in die Zukunft', *Der Volksbote*
64, 1964, no. 23 (8 June), 2.

57 Ibid., 67 and 71–2.

58 The metaphor of head, heart and hands comes from a 1949 article written by Roncalli
himself; cf. A. G. Roncalli, *Mission to France 1943–1953*, ed. L. Capovilla, New York
1966, 105–6: the metaphor of the eye and the ears and the remark about planning to
obscure nothing comes from a note from 1947 in *Journal of a Soul* (n. 43), 269. For
Roncalli's activity in Paris see Hebblethwaite, *Pope John XXIII* (n. 46), 199–235; É.
Fouilloux, 'Roncalli: Aussenordentlicher Botschafter? Paris 1944–1953', in *Ein Blick
zurück – nach vorn: Johannes XXIII, Spiritualität – Theologie – Wirken*, ed. G. Alberigo
and K. Wittstadt, Würzburg 1992, 73–110. For the feeling from the French side that as
nuncio Roncalli had clearly been misjudged see Rouquette, 'Mystère' (n. 51).

59 'Paus Johannes', in *Concilie* I, 71–3.

60 Ibid., 75 and 71; Schillebeeckx seems to have taken the emphasis on Roncalli's modesty
from Rouquette, 'Mystère' (n. 51), esp. 319.

61 'Paus Johannes', in *Concilie* I, 71.

62 Alberigo, 'The Announcement' (n. 29), 22; for a discussion of the reactions see ibid., 18–
33.

63 Reprinted as 'Les conciles dans la vie de l'Église', in Y. M.-J. Congar, *Sainte Église: Études
et approaches ecclésiologiques*, Paris 1963, 302–5. The article opens with the sentence
quoted.

64 My hypothesis is that this is the background to the dissatisfaction of Archbishop
Alfrink of Utrecht with the reports about the Council in the press immediately after the
announcement. On the occasion of the first reports on 25 February 1959, at the inauguration of a new building of the *Twentse Courant*, he spoke sternly to the Catholic
journalists and urged them to keep to the official reports in their reporting of the
Council (see *Kath. arch.* 14, 1959, 307–10; cf. Van Schaik, *Alfrink*, 276; Jacobs, *Andere
kerk*, 23–4). Alfrink wanted to keep his powder dry on this sensitive point and not be
pushed.

65 For a survey of the first press reactions see *Il Concilio Vaticano II*, I/1 (n. 45), 57–67.

66 He had reacted in this way to an investigation of the accession of the new pope, according
to a note on 25 November 1958 in his Council diary, unpublished but quoted by É.
Fouilloux, 'Comment devient-on expert à Vatican II? Le cas du père Congar', in *Le
deuxieme concile du Vatican* (n. 48), 307–31: 310.

67 Thus Congar himself in a later note added to his unpublished *Journal du concile*, in
Alberigo, 'The Announcement' (n. 29), 36.

68 *De Bazuin*, 42, 1958–9, no. 18, 4–6 (7 February), reprinted in *Concilie* I, 10–18. By a
fortunate coincidence, in 1957 Schillebeeckx had written the article 'Kerkvergadering' for
the *Theol. woordenboek* (2, 1957, 1773–6) and thus had already steeped himself in the
significance of a council for church and theology.

69 Ibid., 17.

70 Ibid., 12. For the background to these thoughts expressed by Congar see his article
'Concilie', *Catholicisme* 2, 1949, 1439–43 and his argument for renewed reflection on this
topic. Schillebeeckx certainly read this article and that probably explains the agreement
with Congar's contribution. For Congar's first difficulty with episcopal collegiality see
especially his 'Faits, Problèmes et Réflexions à propos du pouvoir d'ordre et des rapports
entre le presbytérat et l'épiscopat' (1948), in id., *Sainte Église* (n. 63), 275–98: for a
summary of his view see C. T. M. van Vliet, *Communio sacramentalis. Das Kirchenverständnis von Yves Congar*, Mainz 1995, 178–87.

71 Congar quotes E. Carton de Wiart, former Bishop of Tournai ('Les conciles' [n. 63], 309),

from 1932. This notion of things was later to be taken over by Pope Paul VI and thus to gain semi-official status: cf. his address at the conclusion of the second session of the Council on 4 December 1962, in *AAS* 56, 1964, 31–40.

72 For the quotations see Schillebeeckx, *Concilie* I, 10–12.

73 Ibid., I, 15.

74 Ibid.

75 'Het komend concilie van de R.-K. Kerk' (1960), reprinted in *Concilie* I, 19–26: 23: in the next issue of *Elseviers Weekblad* the Reformed theologian G. C. Berkouwer was to illuminate the Protestant view of the coming Council. A variant of Schillebeeckx's *Elsevier* article was published as 'Het concilie en de geest van Christus', *Om De Heraut van het Heilig Hart* 91, 1960, 74–6; a longer version with footnotes appeared shortly afterwards under the title 'Het komende concilie als opdracht voor de gelovigen', *TGL* 16, 1960, 365–76.

76 'Het komend concilie van de R.-K. Kerk' (n. 75), 23; 'Het komende concilie als opdracht' (n. 75), 373.

77 Cf. especially the dogmatic constitution *Lumen gentium*, nos 18–27.

78 'Préface', in J. Colson, *L'épiscopat catholique: Collégialité et primauté dans les toios premiers siècles de l'Eglise*, Paris 1963, 7–13: 7.

79 *Acta et documenta concilio Vaticano II apparando. Series prima (ante-preparatoria), II: Consilia et vota episcoporum ac prelatorum, 1: Europa*, Typis polygl. Vatic. 1960, x–xi; cf. Fouilloux, 'The Antepreparatory Phase' (n. 51), 92–4.

80 Given the great difference in the attitudes of the two Dominicans to church politics after the Council, the great conflicts which this caused and the role which van der Ploeg seems to have played in Schillebeeckx's later difficulties with Rome, the collaboration is striking.

81 For the history of the Nijmegen proposals see Jacobs, *Andere kerk*, 62–8. For the commission's letter to the Catholic universities dated 18 July 1959, see *Acta et documenta concilio oecumenico Vaticanum II apparando, Series prima (ante-preparatoria), IV: Studia et vota universitatum et facultatum ecclesiasticarum et catholicorum I: Universitates et facultates in Urbe, facultates extra Urbem*, Typis polygl. Vatic. 1961, 475–80.

82 After Vatican II, and as a result of discussions about it at the Council, the Roman Catholic Church again recognized the diaconate as a 'proper and permanent rank of the hierarchy' (Dogmatic Constitution *Lumen gentium*, no. 29). As we know, discussion of the position of women in the hierarchy was to begin in the course of the 1970s and has still not fallen silent despite the solemn declarations, by the Congregation for the Doctrine of Faith (*Inter insigniores*, 1976) and by Pope John Paul II (*Ordinatio sacerdotalis*, 1994), that it is theologically impossible for women to be admitted to the priesthood, that the decision is definitive and that the discussion about it needs to be ended.

83 Jacobs, *Andere kerk*, 68.

84 For the composition and the content of the vota of the Dutch bishops see Jacobs, *Andere kerk*, 41–60; cf. id., 'Les "vota" des évêques néerlandais pour le concile', in *À la veille du Concile Vatican II: Vota et réactions en Europe et dans le catholicisme orientale*, ed. M. Lamberigts and C. Soetens, Louvain 1992, 98–110.

85 For the address see *Kath. arch.* 15, 1960, 429–31: 430.

86 Indicated by M. van der Plas, *Brieven aan paus Johannes*, Weesp 1984, 41. For an impression of the content of the enormous number of vota which were sent in see Fouilloux, 'The Antepreparatory Phase' (n. 51), 97–132.

87 For the composition of Alfrink's vota see Jacobs, *Andere kerk*, 41–60; cf. also J. van Laarhoven, '*In medio ecclesiae ... :* Alfrink op het Tweede Vatikaanse Concilie', in *Alfrink en de Kerk 1951–1976: Historische en theologische essays*, Baarn 1976, 12–33, 19; Van Schaik, *Alfrink*, 298.

88 As early as 1954, the episcopal charge on 'The Catholic in the public life of this time'

indicated the need for a 'broad Catholic social programme'; an 'honest search to give each his own will ... certainly, despite difficulties, bring forth the fair fruit of a communal social programme' (*Kath. arch.* 9, 1954, 489–520: 510). Between 1960 and 1953 *Welvaar, welzijn en geluk: Een katholiek uitzicht op de Nederlands samenleving* (5 vols), Hilversum 1960–1963, appeared in answer to the gap indicated.

89 For Alfrink's proposal see *Acta et documenta* II/1 (n. 79), 509–16.

90 See the detailed survey of Dutch literature between 1953 and 1959 in J. Grootaers, 'Une restauration' (n. 16), 791–8. In his view the content is clearly influenced by Jan Groot, the professor of dogmatics at the major seminary of the diocese of Haarlem, who was later to become theological adviser to the Dutch bishops alongside Schillebeeckx; cf. esp. J. C. Groot, 'Diocesane bisschop en wereldkerk', in *Jaarboek 1954 Werkgenootschap van Katholieke Theologie in Nederland*, Hilversum 1954, 58–73 (text of 11 September 1953); also id., 'De bisschop en zijn ambt', *Het schild* 30, 1963, 184–94; id., 'Bezinning op de collegialiteit', in *Jaarboek 1963/64 Werkgenootschap van Kath. theol. in Nederland*, Hilversum 1965 (text of Feb. 1964). With reference to the more direct dependence, Jacobs (*Andere kerk*, 60) indicates almost word-for-word agreements with sentences from articles by H. Fortmann ('Primaat en episcopaat', *Ned. Kath. Stemmen* 55, 1995, 190–2) and H. Boelaars ('Over het oecumenisch concilie', ibid., 193–8).

91 B. Alfrink, 'Herderlijk schriven', in *Kath. arch.* 10, 1955, 1233–6: 1233. This striking sentence is quoted by E. Schillebeeckx in his article '"Wie geloof heeft, beeft niet": Het kerkbeeld van kardinaal Alfrink', in *Alfrink en de Kerk* (n. 87), 144–76: 149. He adds to the quotation: 'Here the principle of collegiality already appears clearly. It struck me so much that – out of curiosity – I began to read around twenty pastoral letters of recently consecrated bishops abroad in the years 1950–1959. They certainly speak of concern for their own diocese and of the bond with the Holy See, but nowhere did I find any mention of the "bond with brothers in the episcopate throughout the world".' Schillebeeckx once again brings out how important collegiality was for Alfrink at the time of Alfrink's death: 'Where are the Eleven?', in *For the Sake of the Gospel* (n. 4), 145–7.

92 Alfrink clearly arrives at this formulation from the experiences of his conflict with Rome after the Council; cf. his address to the university of Villanova on 18 June 1973, 'De toekomst van der kerk', in *Arch. van de kerken* 28, 1973, 825–34: 829.

93 See Y. Congar and B.-D. Dupuy (eds), *L'episcopat et l'Église universelle*, Paris 1962; *La collégialité épiscopale: Histoire et theologie*, with an introduction by Y. Congar, Paris 1965.

94 E. Schillebeeckx, *Bernard Jan Cardinal Alfrink*, Men who make the Council 24, Notre Dame 1965 (abbreviated Dutch version, id., 'Bernard kardinaal Alfrink', in Alfrink, *Vragen*, 5–28). Cf. also Schillebeeckx, '"Wie geloof heeft, beeft niet"' (n. 91).

95 'Bernard kardinaal Alfrink' (n. 94), 27.

96 For the text of the address see Alfrink, *Vragen*, 63–84; for the background and further developments cf. Van Schaik, *Alfrink*, 314–16.

97 *Bernard Jan Cardinal Alfrink* (n. 94), 14–15; 'Bernard kardinaal Alfrink' (n. 94), 11–12.

98 For the work of the 'Central Commission' see J. A. Komonchak, 'The Struggle for the Council during the Preparation of Vatican II (1960–1962)', in *History* (n. 29), 167–356, esp. 300–18; for Alfrink's contribution to the work of the 'Central Commission' see van Laarhozen, '*In medio ecclesiae* ... ' (n. 87), 20–5; Jacobs, *Andere kerk*, 125–40; Van Schaik, *Alfrink*, 309–16.

99 Jacobs, *Andere kerk*, 149–54.

100 Cf. E. Schillebeeckx, 'De liefde boven de letter', in *Bishop Bekkers: Negen jaar met Gods volk onderweg*, Utrecht 1966, 54–64: 58–9; J. A. Brouwers, *Vreugde en hoopvolle verwachting: Vaticanum II – terugblik van een oggetuige*, Baarn 1989, 24, 46–7; J. Bluyssen, *Gebroken wit: Vrijmoedige herinneringen*, Baarn 1995, 110–11.

101 *Bernard Jan Cardinal Alfrink* (n. 94), 15; 'Bernard kardinaal Alfrink' (n. 94), 12: the words

in double quotation marks are an indirect quotation from a statement by Alfrink on the work in the 'Central Commission' made in his address on the occasion of the tenth anniversary of the Catholic Training Centre for the Military, 'De Waalheuvel', on 30 November 1961; cf. Alfrink, *Vragen*, 48–53.

102 '"Wie geloof heeft, beeft niet"' (n. 91), 151–62, quotations 160 and 156. For Alfrink's view of his responsibility for his own diocese and episcopal collegiality, he bases himself especially on Alfrink's speech at Trier on 3 May 1973, 'Taak en positie van de nationale kerken en de eenheid binnen de rooms-katholieke kerk', in *Arch. v.d. kerken* 28, 1973, 780–8. For his view on the relationship between hierarchy and democracy he bases himself on the speech which Alfrink gave at Nijmegen on 22 October 1966 on democracy in the church; see Alfrink, *Vragen*, 532–44.

103 Cf. '"Wie geloof heeft, beeft niet"' (n. 91), 162–72.

104 The quotation refers to Bishop Willem Bekkers and comes from the speech which Schillebeeckx gave at the academic memorial service at the Catholic University of Nijmegen on his death in 1966, see 'Die liefde' (n. 100), 64.

105 Address printed in *Kath. arch.* 23, 1968, 1078–83: 1081–2.

106 At this time – up to 1964 – in Nijmegen only advanced study in theology was possible, i.e. specialization in a theological discipline after one had been to the seminary of a diocese or an order or congregation. De facto this excluded women and lay people from theological study, though some registered and were admitted on the basis of a degree in another discipline. In Nijmegen Alfrink was professor of Old Testament and Hebrew, from 1945 until his nomination to the episcopate by Cardinal De Jong in 1951; see Van Schaik, *Alfrink*, 162–84.

107 *Bernard Jan Cardinal Alfrink* (n. 94), 43; 'Bernard kardinaal Alfrink' (n. 94), 25. One finds more attention to the psychological aspect of Alfrink's appearance in Rome in Schillebeeckx, '"Ik zou hetzelde hebben gedaan"', in *Herinneringen aan kardinaal Alfrink*, ed. H. Mourits, Amsterdam 1997, 96–103.

108 L. Tegenbosch, 'Lekepraat over het oekumenisch concilie', *Plein* 7, 1960, nos 3/4, 31–5.

109 See J. C. Groot, 'Wij en het Concilie', *St Adelbert*, 1960, nos 1, 3–4: M. Bruna, 'Een leek beraad zich over het Concilie', ibid., nos 2, 21–3; H. Bouchette, 'Verontruste gedachten rond het Concilie', ibid., 4, 53–7. This last article was to stir up a lot of dust because of its tone, but it also found assent. Alfrink told the governing body of the St Adelbert Association that the article should never have been published, but the governing body indicated to him that it did not agree and explained its standpoint through the President, F. J. G. Baron van Voorst tot Voorst, at the fifth anniversary congress on 24 September 1960 in Amsterdam. Quotations in Jacobs, *Andere kerk*, 77–8; for the course of events see ibid., 75–9; Van Schaik, *Alfrink*, 299–300.

110 Address in his honour during an academic session for his elevation to cardinal, in Alfrink, *Vragen*, 33–41: 39–41.

111 J. C. J. van Kilsdonk, 'Vrijheid – Geweten – Leergezag: De noodzaak van een loyale oppositie', in *Geest van de tijd: De redevoeringen van de Adelbert-landdagen*, Utrecht 1964, 213–32: 216–17 and 223.

112 Address, 6 October 1962, in Alfrink, *Vragen*, 90–3: quotations 90, 91, 93. For the congress, Alfrink's reaction and the subsequent skirmishes see Jacobs, *Andere kerk*, 201–6; Van Schaik, *Alfrink*, 320–3. Van Kilsdonk himself reports this in 'Interview met Ton Regtien' (1980), reprinted in *Brieven aan pater van Kilsdonk*, ed. L. Quant and B. Rootmensen, Delft 1982, 127–39: 131.

113 E. Schillebeeckx, 'Communication between priests and lay people', in *Mission*, 171–87: 87. The printed text was used as a lecture three times in the month of September 1962.

114 Address on 11 September 1965, in Alfrink, *Vragen*, 429–36: 433, 435–6.

115 The text of *De bisschoppen van Nederland over het concilie* can be found in *Kath. arch.* 16,

1961, 369–84. The brochure was officially dated Christmas Eve 1960, but appeared around two weeks later, together with a pastoral letter which was read out in all Catholic churches on 8 January 1961 (ibid., 55–8); it emphasized the need for prayer and living together in faith.

116 For the content of the letter cf. Jacobs, *Andere kerk*, 88–92: Grootaers, 'Une restauration' (n. 16), 804–6.

117 Quotation from J. M. M. de Valk, 'Leek en concilie', *Te Elfder Ure* 8, 1961, 129–30; cf. also T. Govaert-Halkes, 'Kritiek der gelovigen', ibid., 65–6. For the influence of J. M. Groot on this passage cf. Jacobs, *Andere kerk*, 85–6.

118 The first and last quotations by P. Reckman are from *Plein* 8, 1961, nos 1, 21; the others come for Govaert-Halkes, 'Kritiek der gelovigen' (n. 117). The description 'a new mandate' comes from 'De kerk vergadert: Het komend concilie meer dan een gesprek der herders', *De Bazuin*, 1960–1, no. 16, 1.

119 For the mandate and the reactions to it see Chapter 3. Moreover the mandate was never formally withdrawn, but in 1965 the prohibition against membership of the NVV was revoked (see *Kath. arch.* 20, 1965, 989–90). On this occasion bishop Bekkers said that the episcopal advice against membership of the PvdA was also revoked.

120 J. C. Groot, 'Binnenkerkelijke gesprekken', in *Het komende concilie*, Hilversum 1961, 63–8. This series of radio broadcasts by prominent Catholics on conciliar themes, given in autumn 1968 under the title 'Introduction to Sunday', was part of the publicity offensive launched in this period for which *De bisschoppen van Nederland over het concilie* formulated the theological basis.

121 *De bisschoppen van Nederland* (n. 115), 376; cf. virtually the same thing in Schillebeeckx, 'Het komende concilie' (n. 75); id., 'Het concilie en de geest van Christus', ibid., 75; 'Het komende concilie als opdracht', ibid., 372. In the last article Schillebeeckx expounds this further in a note and attempts to get round all the difficulties. The consequence is that the problem of the personal infallibility of the pope comes to light more clearly: 'It is not that the official statements of the pope simply take on their infallibility by virtue of the approval of the bishops. But on the other hand it is also not the case that the bishops are simply consulted by the pope, as theologians can be consulted. An infallible statement by the pope always means that there is at least an implicit unanimity of faith among the world episcopate. This unanimity of faith is again itself reflected in the infallible papal declaration: these two can never be isolated from each other' (ibid., n. 5).

122 *De bisschoppen van Nederland* (n. 115), 376–8.

123 Ibid., 373.

124 As well as the decree on the lay apostolate, *Apostolicam actuositatem* (1965), see especially the Dogmatic Constitution on the Church, *Lumen gentium* (1964), ch. 4, nos 30–8.

125 The background to the notions developed in the episcopal brochure and the link with the theological position which Schillebeeckx adopts in *Heilseconomie* comes to light in E. Schillebeeckx, 'De kyriale waardigheid van Christus in de verkondiging' (1958), published in *Openbaring*, 27–35, and 'Parole et sacrement dans l'Eglise', *Lumière et vie* 46, 1960, 25–45 (reprinted ibid., 33–49), not in the English translation.

126 Ibid., 371; cf. Schillebeeckx's *Jesus* and *Christ*.

127 *De bisschoppen van Nederland* (n. 115), 381.

128 See Alfrink, *Vragen*, 63–84: 82; the characterization of Alfrink's view as 'conservatively reformist' comes from Van Schaik, *Alfrink*, 317.

129 Cf. ibid., 316.

130 'A new type of layman' (1967), reprinted in *Mission*, 117–31: 128. Cf. also 'De leken in het volk van God', in *Godsvolk en leek en ambt*, DO-C dossier 7, Hilversum and Antwerp 1966, 49–58: esp. 53–5: 'The typological definition of the Christian layman according to Vatican II', in *Mission*, 90–116.

131 *De bisschoppen van Nederland* (n. 115), 372.

132 For the developments surrounding the letter cf. R. Auwerda, *Dossier Schillebeeckx* (n. 6), 30; Jacobs, *Andere kerk*, 183–5; Van Schaik, *Alfrink*, 316–17. Under no. 3204 the Schillebeeckx archive contains the secret papers of an investigation of the orthodoxy of the letter by the Holy Office to which he evidently referred. On the basis of a difference between the views which are expressed in the letter and those of the first *draft* texts for the constitutions on revelation and the church, we are to conclude that a new letter with clarifications was needed. Almost immediately after the Council, what in the meanwhile had come to be called the Congregation of the Doctrine of Faith was to begin an investigation into 'doctrinal errors' in the Dutch church province. From its appearance in 1966 the Dutch *New Catechism* became a target (cf. *Het dossier van de Nederlandse Katechismus*, ed. A. Chiaruttini, Utrecht and Antwerp 1969); a first process against Schillebeeckx began in 1968.

133 Brouwers, *Vreugde en hoopvolle verwachting* (n. 100), 255–6.

134 Schillebeeckx, *Testament*, 49.

135 No titles by Schillebeeckx appeared in English before 1961; between 1961 and 1970 there were 67, 20 of them books; in French, 5 titles appeared before 1961 and 50 between 1961 and 1970, including 13 books; in German 2 titles appeared before 1961 and 43 between 1961 and 1970, 10 of them books; nothing appeared in Italian before 1961, and 29 titles between 1961 and 1970, all of them 29 books; in Spanish or Catalan before 1961 1 title appeared and between 1961 and 1970 34, including 15 books; in Portuguese nothing appeared before 1961 and between 1961 and 1970 13 titles appeared, 3 of them books. See *Bibliography*, 177–92.

136 Y. Congar, 'La théologie au Concile: Le "théologiser du Concile"', in *Situation et tâches présentes de la théologie*, Paris 1967, 41–56: 47.

137 For the Council as the emancipation of the intellectual in the Catholic Church with all the responsibilities and dangers that that involved, cf. *Conc.* 11, 1975, no. 1, especially the articles by G. Baum and A. Greeley (this issue did not appear in English).

138 *God New,* 121.

139 Cf. A. van den Bogaard, 'Letter from the President of Concilium', *Conc.* 1990/1, 3–10, esp. 3–4; P. Brand and H. Häring, 'Aggiornamento als wissenschaftliches Projekt: Über Anfänge und Programmatik der Internationalen Zeitschrift für Theologie "CONCILIUM"', in Hans Küng, *Neue Horizonte des Glaubens und Denkens*, ed. H. Häring and K.-J. Kuschel, Munich and Zurich 1993, 779–94 (this article is not in the abbreviated English translation). For a time, on the occasion of the twenty-fifth anniversary, there was a suggestion that the history of the journal should be investigated and written. Regrettably, that has not happened. However, the filling of this gap goes far beyond the scope of this study.

140 K. Rahner and E. Schillebeeckx, 'General Introduction', *Conc.* 1/1, 1965, 3–4. *Concilium* was to become the organ *par excellence* of progressive Catholic theology in the period after the Council. Reflection on the place of theology within the church and culture was central, and for example the challenges to classical theology from liberation theology – and in a broader sense the rise of distinctive forms of theology in the different regions of the Third World – and feminist theology – were seen at an early stage.

141 See J. A. Komonchak, 'The Struggle' (n. 98), 167–356; for a survey of the dispute over the preparatory texts see esp. 227–318; cf. also Hebblethwaite, *Pope John XXIII* (n. 46), 425–34.

142 'Hoop en bezorgdheid: Aan de vooravond van een concilie' (1962), reprinted in *Concilie* I, 28–33: 31. It is striking that already in the first phase of the Council Schillebeeckx engaged in a discussion which erupted vigorously only at a later stage. In the English journal *The Spectator* (no. 7031, 23 November 1962, 786–8) Evelyn Waugh, the author and convert to

Catholicism, had written an article *opposing* in the name of the laity the majority of reforms that were being asked for in the pre-preparatory stage. His objection was above all that especially the liturgical reforms that were being aimed at would disturb the character of faith as a mystery and deprive the laity of the possibility of participating in this mystery in their own modest and moderate way, through devotional forms which had arisen in time as an expression of and in answer to their needs. Waugh was against lay theologians, for 'sharp minds may explore the subtlest verbal problems, but in the long routine of the seminary and the life spent with the Offices of the Church [as priests cultivate them] the truth is most likely to emerge ... Anything in costume or manner or social habit that tends to disguise that mystery [of the unique vocation of the priest] is something leading us away from the sources of devotion. The failure of the French "worker-priests" is fresh in our memories' (787). Schillebeeckx took seriously Waugh's claim to be speaking in the name of the silent Catholic majority and in 'The Voice of Everyman on the Council' he opposed what he perceived as the inexorable attitude of many progressive priests and intellectuals to ordinary believers. He does see that Waugh is 'only a conservative spirit who is fighting for established positions and the recognition of deliberate moderation and leaves no room for the really distressed consciences of the "progressives" who want things to be "different" in order to be able to live. But by means of the distorted picture of "Everyman Waugh" he evokes for us the figure of the little Everyman, the many who have no say in this world, in either religious or secular matters, but whose song of praise in heaven will audibly drown our voices, which are tuned to the theological diapason. At least, God, the great and Merciful One, has not forgotten them: the *"anawim"* of the Gospel' (1962, reprinted in *Concilie* I, 57–65: 64–5). In reaction, Willem Grossouw above all emphasized the importance of style in liturgical renewal, and thought that Schillebeeckx overlooked the fact that Waugh as 'a lover and an extraordinary skilful user of the most attractive English that is being written' – rightly – opposed a 'cowardly flight into a woolly and unstylish modernity' which in his view was emerging in all kinds of liturgical experiments ('Evelyn Waugh en de anawim', *De Bazuin* 46, 1962–53, no. 25, 4–5). In his 'Wederwoord', Schillebeeckx (ibid., 5) expresses agreement with this objection but says that he is above all convinced that 'some reactions of ordinary church people are an expression of authentically Christian values which are often suppressed in the life of intellectuals, both conservatives and progressives'; in his view this fact above all needed 'closer analysis'.

143 See his 'Indrukken over een strijd der geesten: Vaticanum II' (1962), in *Concilie* I, 34–41; 'Misverstanden op het concilie' (1962), ibid., 42–56. For the conciliar discussions Schillebeeckx summed up the theological view on truth and historicity which he developed in this period: 'Het waarheidsbegrip en aanverwante problemen' (1962), in *Openbaring*, 185–200 (not in the English translation. He also steeped himself again in the truth of faith according to Thomas Aquinas, on the occasion of a recent book by M. Seckler, *Instinkt und Glaubenswille nach Thomas von Aquin*, Mainz 1962; cf. his 'Het niet-begrippelijke moment in de geloofsdaad volgens Thomas: kritische studie' (1963), in *Openbaring*, 233–61 (not in the English translation).

144 Schillebeeckx, *Testament*, 46.

145 With a reference to the famous book on the Russian revolution by the American journalist John Reed, *Ten Days that Shook the World*, Hebblethwaite (*Pope John XXIII* [n. 46], 435) speaks of 'sixty days to change the Church'; in reality, of course, it was fifty-nine. For a description of the dispute and for Schillebeeckx's role in it see Schoof, *Aggiornamento*, 245–55.

146 Respectively 'Hoop en bezorgdheid' (n. 142) and 'Indrukken' (n. 143).

147 Respectively 'Indrukken' (n. 143), 40; 'Misverstanden' (n. 143), 42; 'Indrukken' 36; 'Misverstanden', 56.

148 Address *Gaudet mater ecclesia*, in *AAS* 54, 1962, 786–95: 789, 793–4.

149 Ibid., 791–2.
150 The first quotation is from J. L. Suenens, *Terugblik en verwachting: Herinneringen van een kardinaal*, Tielt 1991, the second from Brouwers, *Vreugde en hoopvolle verwachting* (n. 100), 41; cf. also Bluyssen, *Gebrokene wit* (n. 100), 115.
151 For Alfrink's intervention see *Vragen*, 122–4; for the general atmosphere and the standpoint of other council fathers see Brouwers, *Vreugde en hoopvolle verwachting* (n. 100), 47–51; for the theological commitment see Schoof, *Aggiornamento*, 237–57. For Schillebeeckx's views on revelation and tradition see the previous chapter. He had summed up this view once again in his commentary on the draft texts of the council for the bishops (cf. Schoof, *Aggiornamento*, 248–9).
152 Dogmatic Constitution *Dei verbum* (1965), nos 8 and 9.
153 'Indrukken' (n. 143), 38; in this article, on the basis of the outcome of the vote on the draft text on revelation, Schillebeeckx speaks of bishops, 63% of whom thought in existential and 37% in essentialist terms.
154 See Schillebeeckx, *Testament*, 46, and Schoof, 'Contouren' (n. 16), 146.
155 Alfrink's intervention in *Vragen*, 125–8: 125.
156 Brouwers, *Vreugde en hoopvolle verwachting* (n. 100), 54–7; Suenens, *Terugblik* (n. 150), 71–86.
157 Address *Prima sessio* (1962), in *AAS* 66, 1963, 35–41, 38 and 39.
158 Christmas message to the faithful and all the world *Natale di quest'anno* (1962), in *AAS* 55, 1963, 13–19: 15; cf. earlier the radio broadcast to the people and governments on keeping the peace, *Seigneur, écoute* (25 October 1962), 861–2.
159 Encyclical *Pacem in terris* (11 April 1963), quotation from Suenens' speech in *Kath. arch.* 18, 1964, 724. For the background and significance of the journey to New York and the message to the United Nations cf. Suenens, *Terugblik* (n. 150), 87–9, 102–110.
160 'Paus Johannes en het tweede Vaticanum' (n. 55), 78.
161 In the Pastoral Constitution *Gaudium et spes* (1965), no. 1; the chapter on peace in this constitution (nos 77–90) leans very heavily on *Pacem in terris* and develops its thoughts further.
162 Pastoral letter of the Dutch bishops on the death of Pope John XXIII and as preparation for the conclave (14 June 1964). 841–59: 845–7.
163 Address *Salvete*, in *AAS* 55, 1963, 841–59: 845–7.
164 Address on the occasion of the election of Montini as pope, Alfrink, *Vragen*, 164–6: 165.
165 Suenens, 'Gedenkrede' (n. 54), 521 and 522–3. Like Alfrink, Suenens was part of the group of prominent 'Montiniani'; at a later phase both were to come into major conflict with him; cf. P. Hebblethwaite, *Paul VI: The First Modern Pope*, New York and Mahwah, NJ 1993, 324, 328, 331.
166 Address to the members of the Roman Curia, *Quali siano* (21 September 1964), in *AAS* 55, 1963, 793–800: 796, 798–9.
167 'Verwachte grote lijnen van het concilie' (1963), reprinted in *Concilie* I, 80–3: 80.
168 For *Humanae vitae* see Hebblethwaite, *Paul VI* (n. 165), 514–21. For the reactions see *The Bitter Pill: Worldwide Reactions to the Encyclical* Humanae vitae, ed. F. V. Joannes, Philadelphia and Boston 1970; Humanae vitae *and the Bishops: The Encyclical and the Statements of the National Hierarchies*, ed. J. Hogan, Shannon 1972. The booklet by the Catholic philosopher Bernard Delfgaau, *Sexualiteit, pauselijk gezag, geweten*, Baarn 1968, which emphatically defended the right to decide on the basis of one's own conscience, is representative of the Dutch reactions.
169 Cf. W. Goddijn, *De moed niet verliezen: Kroniek van een priester-socioloog 1921–1972*, Kampen 1993; id., *Rode oktober: Honderd dagen Alfrink. Een bijdrage tot de empirische ecclesiologie (1968–1970)*, Baarn 1983; R. Auwerda, *De kromstaf als wapen; Bisschopsbenoemingen in Nederland*, Baarn 1988; Van Schaik, *Alfrink*, 433–86.

170 For the fluctuating image of Paul VI, cf. Hebblethwaite, *Paul VI* (n. 165), esp. 1–16: 'Introduction: The Fluctuating Image'. For the reactions to the activity of Paul VI during the Council in the international press cf. the descriptions in 'Appendice I: Gli attegiamenti dell'opinione publica sugle interventi di Paolo VI durante il secondo e il terzo periodo del concilio', in *Paolo VI e i problemi ecclesiologici al concilio, Colloquio internazionale di studio, Brescia 19–20–21 settembre 1986*, 429–559. The international success of the sensational book on the first period of his pontificate by an author who called himself Michael Serafian, *The Pilgrim*, New York 1964, based on an exaggerated conspiracy theory, was significant of the rapidly deteriorating image of Paul VI.

171 'De tweede sessie van Vaticanum II' (1964), reprinted in *Concilie* I, 84–105: 97.

172 Ibid., 101.

173 Ibid., 102.

174 For the course of events and the substance of the pope's difficulties on this point cf. C. Troisfontaines, 'A propos de quelques interventions de Paul VI dans l'élaboration de "Lumen Gentium"', in *Paolo VI e i problemi* (n. 170), 97–143.

175 Quoted in *Kath. arch.* 20, 1965, 188–90: 189.

176 In the printed version of this lecture, which was to appear in January 1965, after Schillebeeckx had first taken fright, the text was sensitively nuanced. On the one hand there is much greater emphasis that the *nota praevia* gives a possible interpretation of the text of the document: the pope was not attacking the Council. At the same time, however, he thinks that the only question is how in their vote the Council fathers really took account of the *nota praevia*: he decided from this that the note does not lay down the authentic Catholic view of collegiality for ever – 'the Council fathers themselves did not want to exclude further development' – which leads to the comforting conclusion: 'on the matter of collegiality the Council is only a link in an ongoing dogmatic development ... even after the conclusion of a Council the life of the church continues to grow': 'Vaticanum II: 3e sessie' (1965), reprinted in *Concilie* II, 13–31: 23–6.

177 Address *Post duos menses* (21 November 1964), in *AAS* 56, 1964, 1007–18: 1015. For Montini's mariology see P. Hebblethwaite, 'The Mariology of Three Popes', in *The Way Supplement* 51, Autumn 1984, 56–68: 59–63; for the history of the bestowing of this honorific title see R. Laurentin, 'La proclamation de Marie "Mater ecclesiae" par Paul VI: *Extra Concilium* mais *in Concilio* (21 November 1964). Histoire, motifs et sens', in *Paolo VI e i problemi* (n. 170), 31–75.

178 Dogmatic constitution *Lumen gentium* (1964), 55–59: 61.

179 In Schillebeeckx's commentary on the first drafts of the Council texts for the Dutch bishops in connection with the first version of the independent document on Mary which was then envisaged, it is indicated that a mariological pronouncement in the sense customary since the nineteenth century would cause great offence ecumenically. Schillebeeckx argues that Mary should not be set above the church and that her special place in salvation history should be strictly connected with the fact that she is the mother of Jesus Christ – in other words precisely what was to happen. On 18 September 1964 Alfrink in fact expressed this view in an intervention in the name of 124 other bishops, see *Vragen*, 237–40. For Schillebeeckx's own estimate of his influence on developments at the Council, directly and indirectly, cf. E. Schillebeeckx, 'Mariology: Yesterday, Today, Tomorrow', in id. and Catharina Halkes (ed.), *Mary: Yesterday, Today, Tomorrow*, London 1993, 12–46,: 12–17. For the mariology of the Council cf. R. Laurentin, *La Vierge au Concile*, Paris 1965; for Mary's place in the history of theology cf. S. De Fiores, 'Maria in der Geschichte von Theologie und Frömmigkeit', in *Handbuch der Marienkunde* I, ed. W. Beinert and H. Petri, Regensburg 1996, 99–266: 240–4.

180 'Vaticanum II: 3e sessie' (n. 176), 15.

181 'De tweede sessie', *Concilie* I, 89.

182 'Vaticanum II. 3e sessie' (n. 176), 16–23, here esp. nn. 21, 23. Page 21 also contains the quotation stands at the head of this chapter.

183 J. A. T. Robinson, *Honest to God*, London 1963, quoted in 'Ten geleide', *TvT* 3, 1963, 229. For the reactions see D. L. Edwards (ed.), *The Honest to God Debate*, London 1963; for an attempt to show that *Honest to God* was the starting point for fundamental theological debates which are still going on today see H. Häring, 'Eerlijk voor God? Over de resultaten van een voortgaande discussie', *TvT* 31, 1991, 285–314; cf. also the second part of *Thirty Years of Honesty: Honest to God Then and Now*, ed. J. Bowden, London 1993, 53–100.

184 'Vaticanum II. 3e sessie' (n. 176), 27.

185 E. Schillebeeckx, 'Kerk en wereld: de betekenis van "Schema 13"' (1964), reprinted in *Wereld*, 96–114: quotations 128 and 141–2 (not in the English translation). This text is based on a lecture in Rome on 16 September 1964. The last quotation is taken virtually word for word from 'Vaticanum II. 3e sessie' (n. 176), 30.

186 For these reactions cf. J. Grootaers, 'L'opinion publique en Belgique et aux Pays-Bas face aux événements conciliaires des 1963 et 1964', in *Paolo VI e i problemi* (n. 170), 431–9, esp. 440–8.

187 'De waarheid over de laatste concilieweek', *De Bazuin* 48, 1964–7, no. 12, 4–6: 6.

188 Four long readers' letters were printed in *De Bazuin* 48, 1964–5, no. 16 (23 January 1965), a selection from what according to the report of the editors was 'a very large number of reactions from readers' to Schillebeeckx's article: the letter referred to, by J. van Kortland from Rosendaal, is on p. 3. In content Schillebeeckx's reaction largely corresponds to that of Congar in *Inform. Cath. Internat.* of 11 January 1965 (reprinted in *Le concilie au jour de jour: Troisième session*, Paris 1965, 115–29). On 4 February 1965 Alfrink arrived at a closely related analysis of the event in an address to the Catholic student conference in Delft ('Vooruitzichten na de zwarte week', in *Vragen*, 241–51, esp. 244–9).

189 'Wij denken gepassioneerd en in clichés', *De Bazuin* 48, 1964–5, no. 16, 4–6: 4, 5.

190 'De waarheid' (n. 187), 4–5, 6.

191 Cf. especially the long and perceptive letter by 'Prof. dr. J. A. A. van Leent' from Wageningen, *De Bazuin* 48, 1964–5, no. 16, 1–2.

192 'Kerk en Wereld' (n. 185), 133–4; 'The Church and Mankind', reprinted in *World*, 115–39. Schillebeeckx here expresses his interpretation of the dynamic of *Gaudium et spes*.

193 Cf. Borgman, 'Cultuurtheologie', esp. 357–60.

194 Bluyssen, *Gebroken wit* (n. 100), 456–8; Van Schaik, *Alfrink*, 361–2: the pope's letter and that of the Dutch bishops have not been published. In 1965 the bishops in fact issued pastoral letters 'on penitence and forgiveness' (*Kath. arch.* 30, 1965, 472–6) and on the eucharist (ibid., 597–600); they were expressly complimented by the pope on the latter (ibid., 948–9).

195 There were also to be a number of skirmishes around the sacrament of confession and the forgiveness of sins. A commission was set up after the Council which was to give advice on the sacramental character of the practice of communal penitential ceremonies without private confession, which had also grown up in the Netherlands. For the Dutch developments and commentaries on them cf. J. Meyer Schene, *Die häufige Beichte: Studie zur Literatur der letzter Jahrzehnte*, Vienna 1968, 64–73. According to a later, markedly unnuanced commentary by Schillebeeckx, the intention of the original commission was to give sacramental status to the practice which had grown up and to allow communal celebration without private confession of sins to apply as the normal form of sacramental forgiveness. However, as a result of intervention from above, a new commission was formed which gave sacramental status to communal penitential ceremonies only in very exceptional cases and emphatically left private confession as the norm. Cf. E. Schillebeeckx, 'Over vergeving en verzoening: De kerk als "verhaal van toekomst"', *TvT* 37,

1997, 368–83: 382 n. 11. For a summary of the theological discussion around this question see H.-P. Ahrendt, *Busssakrament und Einzelbeichte: Die tridentinischen Lehraussagen über das Sündenbekenntnis und ihr Verbindlichkeit für die Reformen des Busssakramentes*, Freiburg, Basel and Vienna 1981, 3–34: for the work of the two commissions and its outcome cf. T. L. Fleming, *The Second Vatican Council's Teaching of the Sacrament of Penance and the Communal Nature of the Sacrament*, Rome 1981, 161–88.

196 There was a sensationalizing article – 'Is the bread flesh or meaning?' – in *Time Magazine* under the title 'Beyond Transubstantiation' (2 July 1965, 52–5); cf. attempts to provide more factual information in *Inform. Cath. Internat.* 243 (1 July 1954), by A. Kreykamp, the chief editor of *De Bazuin*, and in *Herder Korresponden*. 19, 1965, 517–20.

197 Encyclical *Mysterium fidei* (3 September 1965). According to Hebblethwaite (*Paul VI* [n. 165], 430), the pope had no immediate involvement in the text, which was written by the Augustinian theologian Agostino Trapè; he even mentions an 'unverifiable rumour' that the encyclical was a direct attack on Schillebeeckx (ibid., n. 2).

198 Address at the opening of the Dutch Documentatie Centrum Concilie (15 September 1965), Alfrink, *Vragen*, 428–36: 431. An article by the Jesuit E. Schoenmaeckers, 'Die katholische Kirche der Niederlande in der Krise der Gegenwart', *Orientierung* 28, 1964, 19–22, reprinted in an updated version as 'Catholicism in the Netherlands', in *The Month* 219, 1965, 335–46, particularly influenced the image of the Dutch church. It claimed that Dutch Catholicism was undergoing the worst crisis since the Reformation, that the mood was strongly anti-Roman and that there was the threat of a schism. He made the remark that 'church life in the Netherlands … at present [gives] the same impression as modern art: formless and chaotic' (21).

199 Encyclical *Mysterium fidei*, no. 11. For a summary of the content of Schillebeeckx's reaction cf. *Kath. arch.* 20, 1965, 1018–19; the Dutch text of his account has not been published, but translations of it have: see 'Transsubstantiation, Transfinalization, Trans-signification' (unfortunately the last word is rendered 'Transfiguration'), *Worship* 40, 1966, 324–8: 322. In the period after the council Schillebeeckx was often to appear as the defender of views and publications of others suspect in Roman eyes, most prominently in the notorious affair surrounding the *New Catechism*, written and published under the auspices of the Dutch bishops; cf. *Het dossier van de Nederlandse Katechismus* (n. 132), 95–199; for his anger over the whole affair surrounding this book cf. 73–5: 'Nieuwe bloei van integralisme' (originally in *De Volkskrant*, 23 November 1966).

200 *Mysterium fidei*, no. 24.

201 Cf. Denzinger nos 1651–2.

202 'Transsubstantiation, Transfinalization, Transsignification' (n. 199), 325.

203 L. Smits, 'Nieuw zicht op de werkelijke aanwezigheid van Christus in de eucharistie', *De Bazuin* 48, 1964–5, no. 9, 4–5, and also id., 'Van oude naar nieuwe transsubstantiatieleer', *De Heraut v.h. H. Hart* 95, 1964, 340–5. Smits makes some statements more precise in id., 'Brood en wijn zijn niet louter signal, want Christus is zelf tegenwoordig, méér dan ik vroeger durfde vermoeden', *De Bazuin* 48, 1964–5, no. 23, 4–6, and in id., *Actuele vragen rondom de Transsubtantiatie en de Tegenwoordigheid des Heren in de Eucharistie*, Roermond and Maaseik 1965, esp. 48–80.

204 J. Möller, 'De transsubstantiatie', *Ned. Kath. Stemmen* 56, 1960, 1–14; id., 'Existentiaal en categoriaal denken', ibid., 166–71; P. Schoonenberg, 'De tegenwoordigheid van Christus', *Verbum* 26, 1959, 148–57; id., 'Eucharistische tegenwoordigheid', ibid., 194–205; id., 'Een terugblik: Ruimtelijke, persoonlijke en eucharistisch tegenwoordigheid', ibid., 314–27; id., 'Tegenwoordigheid', ibid., 31, 1964, 395–415; id., 'Eucharistische tegenwoordigheid', *De Heraut v.h. H. Hart* 95, 1964, 333–6; id., 'Nogmaals: eucharistische tegenwoordigheid', ibid., 96, 1965, 48–50; also in the newspapers *De Tijd* of 21 December 1964 and *De Volkskrant* of Maundy Thursday 1965. Here, moreover, after 1963 Schoonenberg could in

a certain sense refer to the Constitution *Sacrosanctum Concilium*, which in no. 7 states that Christ is present in 'the sacrifice of the mass', both in the person of the minister and under the eucharistic action, in the power of the other sacraments, in the word of the scriptures and in the praying and singing of the church. But it is significant that the constitution starts from the eucharist and Schoonenberg from the presence of Christ among the believers; for an attempt at further clarification in terms of the phenomenology of religion see C. J. M. Dupont, 'De Eucharistie is Gods zichtbare liefde', *De Bazuin* 48, 1964–5, no. 22, 47. 'De discussies rond de eucharistie', *Kath. arch.* 20, 1965, 626–45 offers a summary presentation of the different standpoints.

205 'Transsubstantiation, Transfinalization, Transsignification' (n. 199), 330.

206 Möller, 'De transsubstantiatie' (n. 204), 2. Cf. also A. Vanenste, 'Bedenkingen tegen de scholastike transsubstantiatieleer', *Coll. Gandav. Brug.* 2, 1956, 322–5; id., 'Nog steeds bedenkingen tegen scholastieketranssubstantieleer', ibid., 6, 1960, 321–48.

207 E. Schillebeeckx, 'Christus tegenwoordigheid in de eucharistie' (1965), together with the later article 'De eucharistische wijze van Christus' werkelijke tegenwoordigheid' (1966), reprinted in *The Eucharist*, to which reference will be made from now on: here 20. In the Louvain period Schillebeeckx regularly gave lectures on the eucharist, and on the basis of the same material he did so again in 1958–9, his first complete year in Nijmegen, in the lectures on Wednesday at noon which were open to all students of Nijmegen University; for stencilled notes, see Arch. 554 and 3119. The material from this lecture clearly forms the background to these texts in *The Eucharist*.

208 For a detailed theological, historical and at the same time to some degree hermeneutical investigation into the doctrine of the eucharist at Trent, cf. J. Wohlmuth, *Realpräsenz und Transsubstantiation im Konzil von Trient: Eine historisch-kritische Analyse der Canones 1–4 der Sessio XIII*, Bern and Frankfurt am Main 1975; the Dutch discussion is analysed on pp. 30–47 as the background to the question.

209 *Eucharist*, 44–51. Schillebeeckx's interpretation is in line with that of Karl Rahner in 'The Presence of Christ in the Sacrament of the Lord's Supper', in *Theological Investigations* 4, London and New York 1966, 287–311. According to Schillebeeckx, his interpretation shows that the controversy between G. Ghysens, who thought that Trent had distanced itself from the Aristotelian concept of substance ('Présence réelle eucharistique et transubstantiation dans les définitions de l'Eglise Catholique', *Irénikon* 32, 1959, 420–35), and E. Gutwenger, who thought that the Council had deliberately opted for the Aristotelian framework of thought and had to some degree hallowed this ('Substanz und Akzidenz in der Eucharistielehre', *Zts. f. kath. Theol.* 83, 1961, 257–306), rests on an incorrect hermeneutic. Cf. *Eucharist*, 101f.

210 Quotations are from *Eucharist*, 159f. and 82.

211 Cf. respectively *Eucharist*, 83f., 89–92 and 143.

212 'Transubstantiation' (n. 109), 324, 333. Here he refers especially to articles by Bishop Carlo Colombo, who, challenged by modern science, when he was still a seminary professor had argued that transubstantiation was not a physical but an ontological change; by contrast, F. Selvaggi of the Gregorian University stated that the dogma was in fact about a physical change. Cf. also *Eucharist*, 94–5.

213 The article was 'De eucharistische wijze' (n. 207), here 84, 72.

214 Ibid., 84–94; p. 85 n. 19 refers for the first approaches to J. de Baciocchi, 'Les sacrments, actes libres du Seigneur', *Nouv. rev. théol.* 83, 1951, 681–706; id., 'Le mystère eucharistique dans les perspectives de la Bible', ibid., 87, 1955, 561–70; id., 'Présence eucharistique et transubstantiation', *Irénikon* 32, 1959, 139–61.

215 *Eucharist*, 155f, 150: Schillebeeckx's italics.

216 For this criticism see already the article which appeared immediately after the German translation of *The Eucharist*, by G. B. Sala, 'Transsubstantiation oder Transsignifikation.

Gedanken zu einem Dilemma', in *Zts. f. kath. Theol.* 92, 1970, 1–34, esp. 27–33. N. Slenczka, *Realpresenz und Ontologie: Untersuchung der ontologische Grundlagen der Transsignifikationslehre*, Göttingen 1994, consistently goes further along this line.

217 For this see P. J. FitzPatrick, *In Breaking of Bread: The Eucharist and Ritual*, Cambridge 1993, esp. 49–107, who speaks of the 'fallacy of replacement'.

218 *Heilseconomie*, 140. Such an interpretation was in fact only in a certain sense along the lines of this study, given that in it Schillebeeckx based himself on Thomas Aquinas. His theology of the eucharist puts all the emphasis on the change and the offering of the earthly reality in favour of a spiritual significance.

219 *Eucharist*, 126–37, quotation 136.

220 Slenczka, *Realpräsenz und Ontologie* (n. 216), rightly draws this conclusion; cf. my 'De gedaanteverandering van de theologie: Meegeslept door het scheppend geloof van Franz Kellendonk', in *Breuklijnen: Grenservaringen en zoektochten*, ed. E. Schillebeeckx et al., Baarn 1994, 199–212.

221 *Eucharist*, 92–3. To this degree the evaluation by J. Ambaum (*Glaubenszeichen. Schillebeeckx' Auffassung von der Sakramenten*, Regensburg 1980, 111) that Schillebeeckx 'puts the eucharist without concessions in the context of sacramentality' is inaccurate.

222 So I disagree with Hebblethwaite that *Mysterium fidei* 'made little impact and sank without trace' (*Paul VI* [n. 165], 430). The encyclical prevented fundamental discussion on the meaning of the eucharist from really breaking through. And at that moment for a large number of people – especially priests and theologians – that was a discussion on which the credibility of the renewal at the grass roots of the notion that the church was the sacrament of God's grace in history, which had begun with the Council, stood or fell; cf. C. Davis, *A Question of Conscience*, London 1967, 230–5; for Davis's own contribution to the discussion on the eucharist see his 'Understanding the Real Presence', in *Word in History: The St Xavier Symposium*, ed. T. P. Burke, New York 1966, 154–78.

223 I am referring to the new approaches by L.-M. Chauvet, *Symbole et sacrement: Une relecture sacramentelle de l'existence chrétienne*, Paris 1987; see also id., *Les sacraments: Parole de Dieu au risque du corps*, Paris 1993; cf. A. Haquin, 'Naar een fundamentele theologie van de sacramenten: Van E. Schillebeeckx tot L. M. Chauvet', in *Hedendaagse accenten in de sacramentologie*, ed. J. Lamberts, Louvain and Amersfoort 1994, 65–85. The Protestant theologians Slenczka (*Realpresenz und Ontologie* [n. 216]) and Fitzpatrick (*In Breaking of Bread* [n. 217]) also develop innovative notions. Meanwhile, at any rate in the Netherlands, practical experimentation with the eucharist outside the official framework has continued, cf. my 'Liturgie en ritueel: Een pleidooi voor zwakke sacramenten', *TGL* 52, 1996, 527–41.

224 'Herdelijk schrijven', in *Kath. arch.* 20, 1965, 969–73: 929, 970; with this last sentence they are quoting from the pope's opening speech at the third session.

225 The closing evaluation appeared in 1966 almost simultaneously in the journal *Oecumene* and at somewhat greater length under the title 'Eindresultat Vaticanum II' in *Kultuurleven*; the last version is reprinted in *Concilie* II, 57–84. For his view of the Constitution on Revelation *Dei verbum* cf. 'De Godsopenbaring en de heilige boeken volgens het tweede Vaticaans concilie', *TGL* 21, 1965, 461–77; on the Constitution on the Church *Lumen gentium* cf. 'The Reformation of the Church' (1965), reprinted in *Mission*, 1–19; and on *Gaudium et spes* cf. '*Ecclesia in mundo huius temporis*', *Angelicum* 43, 1966, 340–52.

226 Address *In hoc laetamur*, in *AAS* 57, 1965, 794–805: 801.

227 Address *Au moment*, in *AAS* 57, 1965, 877–85: 878–9; cf. Hebblethwaite, *Paul VI* (n. 165), 435–43.

228 Address *In hoc laetamur*, in *AAS* 57, 1965, 804. For the regulation see the *motu proprio Apostolica sollicitudo*, ibid., 773–80; for Alfrink's attitude to the synod of bishops see *Leven in de kerk: Michel van der Plas im gesprek met kardinaal Alfrink*, Baarn 1984, 100–4.

229 Cf. Hebblethwaite, *Paul VI* (n. 165), 441–2.
230 E. Schillebeeckx, 'Het celibaat van de priester', *TvT* 5, 1965, 296–329: 296; for the connection between (the discussion on) compulsory celibacy for priests and the (changing) image of the priest see also id., *Het ambts-celibaat in de branding. Een kritische bezinning*, Bilthoven 1966, 7–11, on the question of a new image for the priest. The remarkable prehistory of these texts has been disclosed to me by Ted Schoof. When the copy of the thematic number of *Tijdschrift voor Theologie* on 'The Present-day Situation of the Priest' needed to be delivered, Schillebeeckx in fact proved to have written a book and thought that he could not say what he had to say more briefly. Schoof did not agree and with Schillebeeckx's approval shortened the text. The abbreviated version was published as an article in *TvT*, the original version later appeared as a book.
231 *Het ambts-celibaat* (n. 230), 88–101; 'Het celibaat' (n. 230), 321–5.
232 *De presbyterorum caelibatu libellus patribus in sacrosanctu et universali synodo Vaticana secunda congregatis, humiliter oblatus*, Rome n.d.; Dutch translation in *Kath. arch.* 21, 1965, 43–7: 44.
233 In a discussion of *Ambtscelibaat in de branding* P. Schoonenberg rightly points out (in *Streven* 19, 1966, 836–40) that there is still a remnant of dualism in Schillebeeckx's argument. Whereas he says 'In my view one does not renounce marriage "for God's sake", nor even simply "for the sake of the kingdom of God" ... God and his kingdom transcend all values but are therefore just as much in all values and immanent in each, including marriage,' for Schoonenberg the intensive fellowship and personal relationship with 'the God-man Jesus Christ' are from a Christian perspective the ultimate motive of celibacy; those who hold office can encounter him within the church in 'the fellow human being' or 'the church fellowship'. *To this degree*, according to Schoonenberg, there is an affinity between office and celibacy, but that is a special charisma (cf. also his 'Theologie der maagdelijkheid', *Ned. Kath. St.* 51, 1955, 308–20). In his reaction to Schoonenberg's criticism Schillebeeckx does not adopt Schoonenberg's concentration on the relationship with Jesus Christ, but he does start from celibate existence as 'the positive choice of a way of life which is, in itself, naturally and humanly meaningful'. He interpreted celibacy as 'an extremely radical attitude towards God and man and the world', as being 'so fascinated by a particular value that [one] wishes to make the whole of [one's] life subject to its invitation and its service'; in Christian celibacy this is the kingdom of God proclaimed and embodied by Jesus ('Religious Life in a Secularized World' [1967], in *Mission*, 132–70: 149).
234 Grossouw, *Alles is van u* (n. 6), 256–77; for the details see Goddijn, *Rode oktober* (n. 169).
235 For the first see his 'Basis en ambt. Ambt in dienst van nieuwe gemeentevorming', in *Basis en ambt*, Bloemendaal 1979, 43–90. Subsequently cf. *Ministry. A Case for Change*, London and New York 1981, esp. 85–99; *The Church with a Human Face. A New and Expanded Theology of Ministry*, London and New York 1985, esp. 209–53.
236 Letter, composed by an initiative group of nine priests and sent to all the priests in the Netherlands working directly in pastoral care, who at that time numbered around 5000, with the intention of getting the question of celibacy on the agenda of the Pastoral Council; for the text see *Kath. arch.* 21, 1966, 1243–5. The Pastoral Council's report *Naar een vruchtbare vernieuwing van het ambt* was not itself to argue theologically either, but in pressing for the abolition of compulsory celibacy based itself on questionnaires among priests and other believers which showed that a large majority was in favour of abolition, and on the fact that the picture of the church which had emerged after Vatican II among the majority of Catholics made it impossible to establish a compelling connection between priesthood and celibacy. However, it was still emphasized that celibate life remained a meaningful possibility. For the text see *Pastoraal Concilie van de Nederlandse Kerkprovincie, VI: Vijfde plenaire vergadering: De religieuzen en de ambtsbediening*, ed. W. Goddijn et al.,1970, 68–150, esp. 132–3.

237 For Schillebeeckx's remarks see Oosterhuis and Hoegeveen, *God New*, 122f.; in his sketch of the pre-history of the chapter on marriage in *Gaudium et spes* B. Häring, *Lex. Theol. Kirche* 14, ²1968, 423–5, makes emphatic mention of Heylen and Schillebeeckx as evidently important voices in the sub-commission. For Schillebeeckx's identification with the text see his commentary in 'Het huwelijk volgens Vaticanum II', *TGL* 22, 1966, 81–107.

238 B. Häring, *Krise um 'Humanae vitae'*, Bergen-Enkheim 1968, 7.

239 See Hebblethwaite, *Paul VI* (n. 165), 442–5.

240 Thus X. Rynne, *The Fourth Session: The Debates and Decrees of Vatican Council II*, London 1966, 323.

241 For literature on *Humanae vitae* and its reception see n. 167 above.

242 Apostolic adhortation *Postremo sessio* (4 November 1965), in *AAS* 57, 1965, 865–71: 867.

243 See 'Eindresultaat', in *Concilie* II, 79–84.

244 For the texts at the conclusion of the Council see *AAS* 58, 1966, 5–18: 9.

245 Apostolic Constitution *Mirificus eventus* (7 December 1965), in ibid., 945–51.

246 Text published in *Kath. arch.* 21, 1966, 488–91.

247 For the framework and organization cf. the 'note on the history of preparation' (*Kath. arch.* 21, 1966, 221–32: 1221), composed by the secretariat on the basis of official documents and reports and decisions of the Central Commission of the Pastoral Council. For an evaluation of the whole process as a discussion by the whole Catholic community of faith in the Netherlands see *Pastoraal Concilie (1965–1970): Een experiment in kerkelijk leiderschap*, ed. W. Goddijn et al., Baarn 1986.

248 E. Schillebeeckx, 'You and I have a right to be there', reprinted in *For the Sake of the Gospel* (n. 4), 151–9. In terms of content here, twenty years after the conclusion of the Council, he explained once again what a breakthrough Vatican II represented and what a task it was for the church really to take it seriously. Cf. also E. Schillebeeckx and J. B. Metz, 'The Legacy of the Council', *Conc.* 180, 1985, ix–xi. For the prehistory and significance of the Eighth of May Movement cf. 'Van Pastoraal Concilie tot Acht Mei Beweging', in E. Borgman et al. (eds), *De vernieuwingen in katholiek Nederland: Van Vaticanum II tot Acht Mei Beweging*, Amersfoort 1988, 13–30; E. Borgman, 'Over de Geest die de Act Mei Bewegung bezielt', *Speling* 50, 1998, no. 1, 33–9.

249 'Pastoraal concilie: óók theologisch beluisteren van Nederlandse situatie; Op zoek naar een "fundamenteel document"', *Kosmos en Oecumene* 1, 1967, 181–92: 182. The theologians with whom Schillebeeckx had carried on a dialogue are mentioned on p. 192: J. C. Groot, P. Smulders, C. de Jong, B. van Leeuwen, A. van Rijen.

250 Address at the proclamation of the Dogmatic Constitution on Revelation and the Decree on the Lay Apostolate *Publica haec sessio*, in *AAS* 57, 1965, 978–84: 983.

251 Quoted in 'Eindresultaat', in *Concilie* II, 57.

252 Cf. Schoof, *Aggiornamento*, 245–57.

253 'Eindresultaat', in *Concilie* II, 57.

254 Ibid., 59. For this shift in Schillebeeckx's view see Schoof, 'Aandrang', 20–4. According to Schillebeeckx the 'structures of dialogue' on which the Council insisted are of fundamental importance particularly in a church which is really a 'sacrament of the world'; see 'Het concilie en de dialogale strukturen', in *Die concilieboodschap voor de kerk in Vlaanderen*, Louvain 1966, 43–62.

255 'Eindresultaat', in *Concilie* II, 59–63.

256 Ibid., 63–6: for the later arguments for a democratic church see especially E. Schillebeeckx, *Een democratische kerk* (Bazuin lecture 1989), Nijmegen 1989, and *Church: The Human Story of God*, London and New York 1990, 214–28.

257 'Eindresultaat', in *Concilie* II, 66–8.

258 Ibid., 69, 75.

259 Robinson, *Honest to God* (n. 183).

260 For Schillebeeckx's reaction to Robinson see 'Evangelische zuiverheid en menselijke waarachtigheid', *TvT* 3, 1963, 283–326, and 'Herinterpretatie van het geloof in het licht van de seculariteit: Honest to Robinson', ibid., 4, 1964, 109–50; both articles are reprinted, in reverse order and worked into one chapter, as 'Life in God and Life in the World' in *God and Man*, 85–149. The analysis of Schillebeeckx's reactions and their significance for his development and of the articles which he wrote in this period 'with almost feverish haste' follow in Volume II of this study. Meanwhile cf. Borgman, 'Cultuurtheologie', 346–52.

261 Schillebeeckx gave several lectures on these questions; the texts of some of them can be found in the archives. However, I shall limit myself to texts which have been published. The tendency which becomes evident here is also characteristic of the other texts.

262 'De zin van het dier voor de mens' (1960), reprinted as 'The Animal in Man's World', *World*, 257–68: quotations 259, 278, 259, 261. Recently, in the wake of the criticism of the anthropocentrism of modern culture which is a consequence of the environmental crisis, there has been renewed attention to a theology of animals, but with a radically different direction from that of Schillebeeckx here, cf. e.g. A. Linzey, *Animal Theology*, London and Illinois 1994.

263 'Wijsgerig-theologische beschouwingen over man en vrouw', *Katholiek artsenblad* 40, 1961, 85–92, esp. 89–92.

264 'De theologische zienswijze nopens het probleem van de menselijke verantwoordelijkheid', *R.-K. Artsenblad* 37, 1958, 361–3.

265 'The Intellectual's Responsibility for the Future', in *World*, 269–81: here 274–6.

266 'De verantwoordelijkheid van de theologie voor de toekomst', in *Onsere verantwoordelijkheid voor de toekomst: Nijmeegsch Studenten Corps Carolus Magnus, 7e lustrum 1050, katern III: Theologie*, 5–9: 6–7.

267 For a development and expression of this view see 'Van Pastoral Concilie tot Acht Mei Beweging' (n. 248).

268 'The Catholic Hospital and Health Service', (1958), reprinted in *World*, 21–2: 26.

269 'Social Structures, Social Work and Charity', a duplicated proposal dated 1962 for the Landelijk Sociaal-Charitatief Centrum voor Katholike Maatschappelijk Werk (Arch. 172), included in a revised version in *Wereld*, 199–212: 203.

270 'The Catholic hospital' (n. 268), 220–4; 'Social Structures' (n. 269), 207–12. The so-called personalist view of society in which the state is responsible for the 'bodily', in other words the economy and the just distribution of its fruits, and the world-view organizations and especially the churches are responsible for the 'spiritual', in other words for mutual bonds and human well-being, was popular among Dutch Catholics at the end of the 1950s and the beginning of the 1960s. This view is systematically expounded by J. H. Walgrave in the programmatic opening chapter of the report *Welvaart, welzijn en geluk: Een katholiek uitzicht op de Nederlands samenleving I*, Hilversum 1960, 9–128, on 'Responsibility and structure of a Catholic personalistic doctrine of community', which was produced with the encouragement of the Dutch bishops and Catholic social organizations which collaborated. Schillebeeckx adopts elements of this view but maintains that the bodily and spiritual spheres form a synthesis and need to be illuminated theologically together and in a linked way.

271 'The Church and Mankind', in *World*, 115–39: 115 and 139.

272 'Het nieuwe Godsbeeld, secularisatie en politiek', *TvT* 8, 1968, 44–66: 44–5.

273 Reprinted in *Nijmeegs Universiteitsblad* 14, 1964–5, no. 20, 3–4, under the title 'Kritisch geloofsdenken als eredienst en apostolat'. Schillebeeckx would still use a version of this text, adapted to the different vocabulary of radio broadcasting, in 1987; for the text see E. Schillebeeckx, *For the Sake of the Gospel*, London and New York 1989, 125–9.

274 This is a striking interpretation of Thomas's last words, quoted by Schillebeeckx from the

French translation of the acts of the process of his beatification in 1319 (*Saint Thomas d'Aquin: Sa Vie, par Guillaume de Tocco/Les témoins au process de canonisation*, Toulouse and Paris 1924, 289). According to the evidence given, Thomas spoke these words on seeing the host, and the tendency is to emphasize Thomas's firm belief in the real presence of Christ in the eucharist. That Schillebeeckx sees it as a description of his theological work suggests how much he recognizes himself in this qualification.

275   The title of an article in *TvT* 7, 1967, 288–302.

276   'The intellectual's responsibility' (n. 265), 279.

277   'The significance of a catholic university for the world and the church', reprinted in *World*, 282–298, esp. 290–4. For Schillebeeckx's further trouble over the discussion of the (Catholic) university cf. 'Deconfessionalisering der universiteit?', *Universiteit en Hogeschool* 13, 1966/67, 428–34; *Katholieke Universiteit? Kritische reflectie over eigen karakter en functie van de Katholieke Universiteit te Nijmegen*, ed. E. Schillebeeckx et al., Bussum 1971; 'Toelichting bij het rapport "Katholieke Universiteit?', in *Katholieke Universiteit?, II. Reacties en meningen*, Bussum 1972, 8–15; 'Het "project Katholie Universiteit?": Geen stok om te slaan maar een staf om te gaan', in *Democratisering en identiteit: Beschouwingen over de Katholieke Universiteit Nijmegen 1968–1983*, Nijmegen and Baarn 1983, 11–23. For his further reflections on theology in the midst of the other disciplines see 'Het kritisch statuut van de theologie', in *De toekomst van de kerk: Verslag van het wereldcongres 'Concilium' te Brussel 12–17 September 1970*, Amersfoort and Bussum 1960, 56–62; 'Kritische bezinning op interdisciplinariteit in de theologie', *Vox theologica* 45, 1975, 111–25. An attempt to reflect along these lines on the place of theology in the university in present circumstances can be found in my article 'Tot leven wekken van stervende woorden: Pleidooi voor een instituut voor cultuurtheologie aan de KUN', in *De theologie uitgedagt: Spreken over God binnen het wetenschapsbedrijf*, ed. R. van den Brandt and R. Plum, Zoetermeer 1999, 129–65.

POSTSCRIPT

1   T. Merton, *The Other Side of the Mountain: The End of the Journey* (= The Journals of Thomas Merton 7), San Francisco 1998, 297 (25 November 1968).

2   Cf. B. A. Willems, 'Edward Schillebeeckx', in *Tendenzen der Theologie im 20. Jahrhundert: Eine Geschichte in Porträts*, ed. H. J. Schulz, Stuttgart, etc. 1966, 602–7; M. J. Houdijk, 'E. Schillebeeckx', in *Modern Theologians, Christians and Jews*, Notre Dame 1967, 84–107; P. Bourgy, 'Edward Schillebeeckx', in *Bilan de la théologie du XXme siécle*, II, Tournai and Paris 1970, 875–90 (remarkably enough not included in the German edition which appeared at the same time).

3   Cf. the introduction to *Revelation*, where a systematic plan is given in eight volumes: 1. Revelation and theology; 2. God and man; 3 Priest and layman; 4. Church and world; 5. Jesus the Christ; 6. Church and sacraments; 7. The 'spiritual life' of Christians; and 8. The religious life and Dominican spirituality. The volumes on Jesus, church and sacraments. and 'spiritual life' did not appear. The relationship between priest and layman and the religious life were discussed in *Mission*, though not quite at the length originally planned.

4   Thus the introduction to *Zending*, 9, dated 1968 (not in the English edition).

5   'Preface', in *God and Man* [dated June 1964], v–vii: v.

6   In 1971 a fifth volume of theological soundings appeared under the title *The Understanding of Faith*, but the aim was fundamentally different from the first four. For Schillebeeckx the problem of the interpretation of and criticism of the Christian tradition which is central here became pressing only after the Council, and the articles collected in *The Under-*

standing of Faith were all written after the Council.

7   For an explanation of why the articles on the Christian situation were not included cf. 'Ten geleide' in *Wereld*, 9–10, dated July 1965 (not in the English translation).

8   Cf. T. M. Schoof, 'Jezus, God werking voor ons heil: Peiling naar de theologische procedure van Thomas van Aquino', *TvT* 14, 1974, 217–43.

9   For the significance of the problems surrounding the historicity of faith and theology see Schoof, *Aggiornamento*, 164–236.

10 'Ten Geleide', in *Zending*.

11 This in fact happens in the theology of J. Ratzinger and K. Wojtyla, or Pope John Paul II; cf. H. Häring, '"Kerk, wat zeg je van jezelf?"': De theologie van Johannes Paulus II', *TvT* 25, 1985, 229–49; id., 'Eine katholische Theologie? J. Ratzinger, das Trauma von Hans im Glück', in *Katholische Kirche – wohin? Wider den Verrat am Konzil*, ed. N. Greinacher and H. Küng, Munich and Zurich 1986, 241–58; L. Boeve, 'Kerk, theologie en heilswaarheid. De klare visie van Joseph Ratzinger', *TvT* 33, 1993, 139–65; cf. also E. Schillebeeckx, 'Terugblik vanuit de tijd na Vaticanum II: De gebroken ideologieën van de moderniteit', in *Tussen openheid en isolement: Het voorbeeld van de katholike theologie in de negentiende eeuw*, ed. A. von Harskamp and E. Borgman, Kampen 1992, 153–72.

12 He did this at a number of places and moments, including the initial period of the Dutch Eighth of May Movement, the platform – later forum – of Catholic organizations for the renewal of the church and society which came into being in protest against the censorship which the bishops imposed on the presentation of the church situation on the visit of Pope John Paul II to the Netherlands. For Schillebeeckx's own reflections on developments after the Council see 'John is his name: Twenty-five years after the death of John XXIII', reprinted in *For the Sake of the Gospel*, London and New York 1989, 130–40; 'Terugblik' (n. 11), 153–72.

13 ' "Wider die Entmündigung": Die Kölner Erklärung deutsprachiger Theologen', *Herder Korr.* 43, 1989, 126–9: 129.

14 Cf. – the examples are necessarily quite arbitrary – J. Borella, *Le sens du surnaturel*, Geneva 1996; H. De Dijn, *Hoe overleven wij de vrijheid? Modernisme, postmodernisme en mystiek lichaam*, Kapellen and Kampen 1993; K. Flanagan, *Sociology and Liturgy: Representation of the Holy*, London 1991; id., *The Enchantment of Sociology: A Study of Theology and Culture*, London 1996; J.-L. Marion, *Dieu sans l'être*, Paris 1982; J. Milbank, *Theology and Social Theory: Beyond Secular Reason*, Oxford 1990; id., *The Word Made Strange: Theology, Language, Culture*, Oxford 1997; C. Pickstock, *After Writing: On the Liturgical Consummation of Philosophy*, Oxford 1998.

15 For a consistent series of attempts to choose a theological position within postmodernity and the questions that this culture poses see the so-called cahiers of the Dutch Dominican Centre for Theology and Society: *Herfsttij van de moderne tijd: Theologische visies op de postmoderne*, Nijmegen and Zoetermeer 1995; *Scherven brengen geluk: Identiteit en geloven in een wereld van verschillen*, ibid., 1996; *Bouwen met los zand: Theologische reflecties over verschil en verbondenheid*, ibid., 1997; *Bedacht zijn op het onbedachte: Over het alledaagse en het goddelijke in theologisch perspectief*, ibid., 1998.

16 Encyclical *Fides et ratio* (1998), no. 91.

17 For the position that society cannot be known from within and thus cannot be improved, and that qualitative progress therefore requires submission to a comprehensive theory of this society which is accepted as true, see G. Lukács, *History and Class Consciousness: Studies in Marxist Dialectics* (1923), Woodbridge 1975. Such a progressive longing for redemptive authority can also assume a religious form and see faith in God as necessary for the commitment to a better world, cf. R. Garaudy, *Avons-nous besoin de Dieu?*, Paris 1993. This conviction seems to live on in a weakened form among politically somewhat 'left-wing' Christians.

18 M. Foucault, *Les mots et les choses: Une archéologie des sciences humaines*, Paris 1966, 339–46; for this interpretation see A. van Harskamp, 'Kerkelijk gezag: vluchtoord voor moderniteit? Een interpretatie van Johann Adam Möhler's denken over de kerk', *TvT* 28, 1977, 135–54: esp. 150–3. For an approach along these lines to religious fundamentalism – and religious authoritarianism against that background – see id., 'Boze droom van het christendom? Verkenningen rond het fundamentalisme als idee en verschijnsel', *TvT* 33, 1993, 5–26.

19 For the picture sketched out of the modern scientific idea of a 'culture of critical discourse' (A. W. Gouldner) and the importance of this for a theology which credibly wants to express the God of salvation see Borgman, *Sporen*, 5–7, 290–3. The reasons given here rightly made J. B. Metz emphasize, above all in the early phase of his political theology, that theology must make a positive choice in the so-called 'dialectic of the Enlightenment' (M. Horkheimer and T. W. Adorno); in other words, modern critical thought must accept also religion and the church, precisely where this criticism relates to itself, but on the basis of a recollection of suffering – of Jesus Christ and in thus of all sufferers – at the same time it must ensure that its critical force is also directed against the oppressive sides of modern life and thought; cf. above all *Kirche im Prozess der Aufklärung: Aspekte einer neuen 'politischen Theologie'*, J. B. Metz et al., Munich and Mainz 1970, and id., 'Erlösung und Emanzipation' (1973), in id., *Glaube in Geschichte und Gesellschaft, Studien zu einer praktischen Fundamentaltheologie*, Frankfurt am Main 1977, 104: 119. Schillebeeckx would take over this conviction in a global sense in the 1970s.

20 See my interpretation of Schillebeeckx's development in Borgman, 'Cultuurtheologie'.

21 For this formulation see P. Moyaert, *De mateloosheid van het Christendom: Over naastenliefde, betekenisincarnatie en mystieke liefde*, Nijmegen 1998, esp. 15–92: 'Naastenliefde: de opschorting van de ethiek in de ethiek'.

22 In 'Het niet-begrippelijk kenmoment in onze Godskennis volgens Thomas van Aquino' (1952), in *Openbaring*, 201–332: 204 (not in the English translation). Here Schillebeeckx bases himself on *Summa theol.* I, q. 12, art. 12. Cf. also in this connection already his interpretation of the vision of God in 'Als de ziele luistert ... ', *Biekorf* (1936–7) no. 3, which was discussed in Chapter 1 above.

23 Ibid., 201. Here Schillebeeckx quotes M. T.-L. Pénido, *Le rôle de l'analogie en théologie dogmatique*, Paris 1931, 123.

24 *Summa theol.* I–II, q. 3, art. 5.

25 M. Heidegger, *Metaphysical Foundations of Logic*, Bloomington 1984, criticizes precisely the idea of God as a highest entity accessible to speculative vision, from which in his view Thomas starts (in *Summa theol.* I–II, q. 3, art. 5). On the basis of this, J. D. Caputo argues that at this point one should go further with Thomas the mystic than Thomas the metaphysician, who is said to be speaking here, and see God as the one who constantly becomes present in connection with being and as pastor of it (*Heidegger and Aquinas: An Essay on Overcoming Metaphysics*, New York 1982, 271–9). My point here is that Schillebeeckx does this to a certain degree, and already in his Flemish period begins to transcend the metaphysic of presence and participation which he was later to criticize so emphatically, especially in De Petter.

26 *Inleiding*, 228, 196–7.

27 Ibid., 203.

28 'The Search for the Living God' (1959), in *God and Man*, 18–40: 39.

29 E. Schillebeeckx, 'Paus Johannes en het tweede Vaticanum' (1964), in id., *Concilie* I, 66–78: 73.

30 'Vaticanum II: 3c sessie' (1965), in *Concilie* II, 13–31: 21, 23.

31 E. Schillebeeckx, 'Church and World', in *World*, 96–114: 113; cf. id., 'Vaticanum II: 3e sessie' (n. 30), 30.

32   Cf. K. Barth, *Evangelical Theology: An Introduction* (1960), London 1965, 154: 'Theological work is distinguished from other kinds of work by the fact that anyone who desires to do this work cannot proceed by building with complete confidence on the foundation of questions that are already settled and results that are already achieved ... His only possible procedure every day, in fact every hour, is to begin anew at the beginning ... Yesterday's memories can be comforting and encouraging for such work only if they are identical with the recollection that this work, even yesterday, had to begin at the beginning and, it is to be hoped, actually began there. In theological science, continuation always means "beginning once again at the beginning".' For an attempt to describe theology consistently as a science which constantly founds itself anew but is never founded, see F. Schüssler Fiorenza, *Foundational Theology: Jesus and the Church*, New York 1984.

33   The title of a 1966 article, 'The sorrow of the experience of God's concealment', is symptomatic (reprinted in *World*, 77–95): the title is a quotation from the Dutch Protestant theologian K. H. Miskotte (*When the Gods are Silent*, London 1967). I have worked out how Miskotte's thought about God's presence as the 'presence of an absence' can be an adequate theological starting point in the present situation along Schillebeeckx's in 'Negative Theology as Postmodern Talk of God', *Conc.* 1995/2, 102–11.

34   For this criticism by a group of young, primarily Dominican, theologians who studied with J. B. Metz and between 1969 and 1972 published their own journal under the title *Tegenspraak* see F. van den Oudenrijn, *Opstandig geloven*, Utrecht 1968, 32–5. For a critique of present-day tendencies to 'theologize' phenomenology cf. D. Janicaud, *Le tournant théologique de la phénoménologie française*, Combas 1991; for a critique of this critique and a plea for a nuanced investigation of the mutual connections and differences see J. Greisch, 'The Same and the Other: Philosophy and Theology in the Twentieth Century', in *The Return of God: Theological Perspectives in Contemporary Philosophy*, ed. N. Gronkjaer, 49–73.

35   Thus Schillebeeckx on 4 December 1968 in an account of the state of his theological development at that moment to the students at the Dominican house of studies in Nijmegen which still existed at that time; he lived there but did not teach there. There is a transcription of the tape-recording of this, seven pages long, in the Schillebeeckx archive under no. 472: the quotation is on p. 1.

36   'Kritisch geloofsdenken als eredienst en apostolaat', *Nijmeegs Universiteitsblad* 14, 1964–5, no. 20, 3–4.

37   Cf. *The Understanding of Faith*, and above all the lectures on hermeneutics which he gave in Nijmegen for about fifteen years. For the far-reaching consequence of the fundamental hermeneutical insight that knowledge arises only through interpretation see G. Vattimo, *Beyond Interpretation. The Meaning of Hermeneutics for Philosophy*, Oxford 1997. Lecture notes and student's notes of Schillebeeckx's Nijmegen lectures are in a separate archive at the theological faculty in Nijmegen and may also be consulted there. For the lectures on hermeneutics see Schoof, 'Aandrang', 24–7.

38   *Inleiding*, 253: the text at the head of this Postscript is taken from this passage.

39   Metz, *Glaube in Geschichte* (n. 18), 195–203.

40   I take this thought about writing as autobiography in the global sense from the philosopher Jacques Derrida, cf. R. Smith, *Derrida and Autobiography*, Cambridge 1995.

41   For this see my articles 'Gefundeerd, naar niet te funderen: Theologie als bevrijdende hermeneutiek', *TvT* 28, 1988, 113–34; 'De kerk als schijnbaar fundament. Over het zwijgen van de theologie, en het doorbreken daarvan', ibid., 35, 1995, 358–72; 'A Possible Heresy, when Cynicism is God: An Essay on Being Religious in Postmodernity', in *Die widerspenstige Religion: Orientierung für eine Kultur der Autonomie?*, ed. T. van de Hoogen et al., Kampen 1997, 104–25. For the criticism that Schillebeeckx does not completely do precisely this in his work and for reflection on what it would mean to do it see my

'Kultuurtheologie', esp. 357–60: cf. also 'God Geest over de wateren: Sporen van God temidden van de bedreigende moderniteit', *TvT* 32, 1992, 143–64. For an attempt to do this, moreover with the explicit recognition of being inspired by Schillebeeckx, cf. my *Alexamenos aanbidt zijn God: Theologische essays voor sceptische lezers*, Zoetermeer 1994.

Index

Adam, Karl 53–61, 62, 72, 74, 87, 90, 91, 95, 201, 235
Alfrink, Bernard 273–4, 309–16, 317, 319, 320, 326, 338
Aquinas, Thomas 38, 39, 40, 45, 49, 52, 53–4, 63–4, 66, 84, 89, 96, 104, 110, 146, 170, 173, 175, 194, 196, 207, 212–13, 218, 221, 222, 224, 226, 230, 231, 236–7, 238–9, 269, 274, 280, 342, 364, 368, 374–5, 378
Aristotle 40, 43–4, 45, 92, 102, 120, 245
Augustine 120, 164, 172, 186, 267
Axters, Stefan 99–100

Bánez, Domingo 243
Beauduin, Lambert 200
Beemer, Theo 274, 275
Bekkers, Willem 275, 276, 311, 312
Benedict of Nursia 33
Beranos, Georges 75, 155
Berkhof, Hendrik 295
Berdyaev, Nikolai 95
Bergson, Henri 112
Bernadot, Marie-Vincent 105–6
Blondel, Maurice 227
Blum, Leo 106
Bluyssen, Jan 228
Boniface VIII (pope) 229
Boudewijn (king of Belgium) 78, 87–8
Brand, Paul 322
Browne, Michael 287
Bultmann, Rudolf 225
Buytendijk, F. J. J. 272

Camerlynck, L. 287
Camus, Albert 123–4, 127, 267
Canetti, Elias 68
Cardijn, Joseph 82–3, 107

Casel, Odo 201–7
Catherine of Siena 330
Chenu, Marie-Dominique 52, 67, 103–5, 108–10, 111, 112, 113, 127, 133, 146, 198, 221, 284
Clérissac, Humbert 33, 34, 45, 121
Cocteau, Jean 95
Congar, Yves 12, 86, 103–4, 107–8, 110–11, 112, 127, 128–9, 136–9, 142, 154, 221, 303–4, 310, 321
Cullmann, Oscar 167

Daniel, Yvan 107
Daniélou, Jean 112
Delfgaauw, Bernard 150, 153–4
Dondeyne, Albert 74, 111
Driessen, L. W. 242
Duynstee, Willem 151, 152, 291

Engels, Friedrich 19–20

Féret, Henri-Marie 127
Fortmann, Herman 309
Foucault, Michel 372

Garrigou-Lagrange, Réginald 36
Gardeil, Ambroise 108–9
Gaulle, Charles De 297
Gezelle, Guido 43, 44, 45
Gijssen, Johannes 330
Godin, Henri 107, 120
Grollenberg, Lucas 291
Groot, Jan 316, 317
Grossouw, Willem 152–3, 285–6, 287, 288, 291
Guardini, Romano 201

Haarsma, Frans 291
Hammaskjöld, Dag 283
Heylen, Victor 250
Hooft, Willem 294
Huijbers, Johannes 309
Hulsbosch, Ansfried 291
Hulse, Bavo Van 100
Husserl, Edmund 41, 48

Ignatius of Loyola 32, 33
Irenaeus of Lyons 269

John XXIII (pope) 2, 75, 189, 283–4, 295, 296–302, 303, 306–7, 310, 319, 325, 327, 328, 329, 330, 354, 355, 376
John Paul II (pope) 371
Jungmann, Joseph Andreas 61–2

Kennedy, John Fitzgerald 283
Kilsdon, Jan Van
Kinsey, Alfred 271
Koepgen, Georg 62–4, 204
Kreling, G. P. 286
Kuitert, Harry 295
Küng, Hans 2, 322

Lacordaire, Henri-Dominique 33–4, 105, 106
Lavelle, Louis 112, 196
Leibniz, G. W. Von 84
Leo XIII (pope) 27, 27, 38, 39, 40, 49, 81, 85, 181, 195, 201, 229, 371
Leopold II (king of Belgium) 77–8
Lhande, Pierre 106
Luther, Martin 235–6

Maes, Johannes Dominici 53
Magnus, Albertus 119–20
Maltha, Andreas 129–30, 286
Maréchal, Joseph 227
Maritain, Jacques 74, 95, 96–7, 105
Martin, Raymond-Marie 52
Martin, Thérèse (St Thérèse of Lisieux) 178, 248
Marx, Karl 19–20, 54
Matthijs, Mannes 35, 39, 247
Mauriac, François 74
Mehring, Walter 68–9
Mercier, Désiré 24, 40, 200
Merleau-Ponty, Maurice 48, 112, 123, 261
Merton, Thomas 366
Metz, Johann-Baptist 177
Meynard, André-Marie 36
Michel, Ernst 272
Mindszenty, József 114
Möhler, Johann Adam 63
Moltmann, Jürgen 189

Newman, John 84
Noël, Léon 41

Oraison, Marc 272
Ottaviani, Alfredo 311, 321

Paul VI (pope) 82, 321, 328, 329–30, 333, 336, 337, 338, 339, 341, 344, 346–9, 350, 351, 352, 354
Perquy, Jules 51–2
Pétain, Marshal 111
Petter, Dominicus De 37, 40–3, 46, 49, 52–3, 89, 108, 109–10, 122–3, 131–2, 157–8, 210, 222, 224, 225, 226, 274, 287, 289, 376, 378
Pius IX (pope) 27, 181
Pius X (pope) 27, 80, 82, 128, 148, 156, 181, 182, 194
Pius XI (pope) 80, 81, 82, 105, 148, 182, 271, 300, 350
Pius XII (pope) 126, 127–8, 129, 136, 142, 148, 155, 156, 167, 180, 181, 182, 224, 229, 283–4, 296, 300, 301, 302–3, 350
Ploeg, Jan Van Der 308
Pol, Willem Van De 220
Post, Reinier 291
Przywara, Erich 201

Rahner, Karl 2, 3, 86, 167, 170, 171, 322, 323
Ratzingerm Joseph 63
Robinson, John 334–5, 358–9
Rodano, Franco 114
Roey, Joseph Van 78, 81
Rousselot, Pierre 53–4
Rutten, Ceslaus 52
Ruygers, Hein 273

Sartre, Jean-Paul 69, 112, 113, 248
Schillebeeckx, Constant 19, 24, 25, 26, 29, 33, 36
Schillebeeckx, Greta 19
Schillebeeckx, Louis 29, 31, 366
Schillebeeckx, Petronella Calis 19, 25, 29, 36
Schoof, Ted 291
Schoonenberg, Piet 288, 291
Schuman, Robert 283
Scotus, John Duns 237
Semprun, Jorge 88
Senne, René Le 112, 196
Sertillanges, Antonin-Gilbert 53
Simonis, Adrianus 330
Smits, Luchesius 340
Steur, Klaas 151
Stravinsky, Ivor 95
Suenens, Leo 327–8, 329
Suhard, Emmanuel 107, 111–12, 114–15, 116, 178
Suso, Henricus 35

INDEX

Tardini, Domenico 299
Teresa of Avila 330
Terruwe, Anna 151, 152
Thils, Gustave 74
Thornton, Lionel 221
Tillich, Paul 192–5, 198
Tromp, Sebastiaan 151, 152, 311
Tyrrell, George 224

Vanhengel, Marcel 322
Vonier, Anscar 206

Walgrave, Jan-Hendrik 83–4, 86, 113, 160, 287, 289, 291
Wallace, William 31
Walschap, Gerard 70–1
Wijers, Fons 273
Willems, J. N. 150
Wit, Fr De 26, 30
Wust, Peter 74

Zwingli, Huldrich 344–5